ARSENAL OF
WORLD WAR II

ARSENAL OF WORLD WAR II
THE POLITICAL ECONOMY OF AMERICAN WARFARE, 1940–1945

PAUL A. C. KOISTINEN

UNIVERSITY PRESS OF KANSAS

To the memory of
Joshua S. Epstein
and
to welcome
Tomoko Furukawa,
Andrew Harris,
and
Elizabeth Koistinen Harris

Published by the University Press of Kansas (Lawrence, Kansas 66049), which was organized by the Kansas Board of Regents and is operated and funded by Emporia State University, Fort Hays State University, Kansas State University, Pittsburg State University, the University of Kansas, and Wichita State University

Library of Congress Cataloging-in-Publication Data

Koistinen, Paul A. C.
    Arsenal of World War II: the political economy of American warfare, 1940–1945 / Paul A. C. Koistinen.
        p.   cm. — (Modern war studies)
    Includes bibliographical references and index.
    ISBN 0-7006-1308-0 (alk. paper)
    1. World War, 1939–1945—Economic aspects—United States.   2. United States—Defenses—Economic aspects—History—20th century.   3. United States. National Defense Advisory Commission.   4. United States. Office of Production Management.   5. United States. War Production Board.   6. Industrial mobilization—United States—History—20th century.   I. Title: Arsenal of World War 2.   II. Title: Arsenal of World War Two.   III. Title: Political economy of American warfare, 1940–1945.   IV. Title.   V. Series.
    HC110.D4K636   2004
    940.53'1—dc22   2003020126

British Library Cataloguing in Publication Data is available.

Printed in the United States of America

10 9 8 7 6 5 4 3 2 1

The paper used in this publication meets the minimum requirements of the American National Standard for Permanence of Paper for Printed Library Materials Z39.48-1984.

CONTENTS

ILLUSTRATIONS

Charts

Tables

ACKNOWLEDGMENTS

I have benefited greatly from the assistance of others in putting this fourth volume of my study into its final form. At California State University, Northridge, John J. Broesamle and Ronald Schaffer read the entire manuscript and provided me with excellent insights and advice. Theodore A. Wilson used his vast experience and keen analytic skills in advising me on how to shorten, tighten, and make more accessible a long and challenging volume. Finally, a host of student research assistants served me over the years in an always diligent and often selfless way. I could not ask for more from a publisher than the services provided by the University Press of Kansas. Michael Briggs, editor-in-chief, oversees the project with a sure but gentle hand, and his capable and dedicated staff—including Susan Schott, marketing manager, and Melinda Wirkus, senior production editor—go about the wonders of converting manuscripts into published volumes with a high level of professionalism.

My debt to all these people is matched only by my gratitude for their labors and contributions. Needless to say, I, not they, am responsible for all that is and is not said in this book.

Much precedes the review and publication of a manuscript. Archivists and staff of the numerous record collections and papers cited in the notes and bibliographic essay have provided me over many years with invaluable and unfailing guidance and assistance. Without the Oviatt Library at California State University, Northridge (CSUN), especially its interlibrary loan services, I would have been hard-pressed to complete this work. Charlotte Oyer, Donald L. Read, Michael Barrett, and Felicia Cousin worked endlessly on my behalf. Finally, the continued support, encouragement, and love of my wife, Carolyn Epstein Koistinen, is crucial to what I do.

For financial support, I have had many benefactors, including research fellowships from Harvard's Charles Warren Center for Studies in American History, the American Council of Learned Societies, and the National Endowment for the Humanities. Furthermore, CSUN's History Department and College of

Social and Behavioral Sciences and the university as a whole have assisted me in numerous ways for many years.

The volume is dedicated to family. Josh Epstein, my father-in-law, was a remarkable person, particularly in his nearly unmatched dedication to improving the human condition. Still missed, he will always be remembered. But gain replaces loss. David, our son, looked to Asia for his loved one and spouse, Tomoko, our daughter Janice to Europe for Andrew. Together in England, Janice and Andrew enormously enriched the lives of my wife and me with the birth of our first grandchild, Beth. In life or in memory, we love and treasure them all.

ABBREVIATIONS

AAF   Army Air Forces
ACWA   Amalgamated Clothing Workers of America
AFL   American Federation of Labor
AMPC   Area Manpower Priorities Committee
ANMB   Army-Navy Munitions Board
APUC   Area Production Urgency Committee
ASF   Army Service Forces
ATC   Army Transportation Corps

BEW   Board of Economic Warfare
BLS   Bureau of Labor Statistics
BOB   Bureau of the Budget

CCS   Combined Chiefs of Staff
CFB   Combined Food Board
CIO   Congress of Industrial Organizations
CMP   Controlled Materials Plan
CNO   Office of the Chief of Naval Operations
CPA   Civilian Production Administration
CPRB   Combined Production and Resources Board
CRMB   Combined Raw Materials Board
CRWA   Committee on Records of War Administration
CSAB   Combined Shipping Adjustment Board

DCD   Division of Contract Distribution
DCS   Defense Contract Service
DPC   Defense Plant Corporation

EDB	Economic Defense Board
EPF	Emergency Plant Facilities
FEA	Foreign Economic Administration
GOPO	government owned, privately operated
ICC	Interstate Commerce Commission
IMP	Industrial Mobilization Plan
JCS	Joint Chiefs of Staff
JPSC	Joint Production Survey Committee
MAB	Munitions Assignment Board
MLPC	Management-Labor Policy Committee of the WMC
MTCA	Military Training Camps Association
NDAC	National Defense Advisory Commission
NDMB	National Defense Mediation Board
NHA	National Housing Agency
NLRB	National Labor Relations Board
NRA	National Recovery Administration
NWLB	National War Labor Board (same as War Labor Board)
OASW	Office of the Assistant Secretary of War
OCR	Office of Civilian Requirements
OCS	Office of Civilian Supply
OCS	Office of Contract Settlement
ODT	Office of Defense Transportation
OEM	Office for Emergency Management
OES	Office of Economic Stabilization
OLLA	Office of Lend-Lease Administration
OPA	Office of Price Administration
OPACS	Office of Price Administration and Civilian Supply
OP&M	Office of Procurement and Material
OPM	Office of Production Management
OUSW	Office of the Under Secretary of War
OWM	Office of War Mobilization
OWMR	Office of War Mobilization and Reconversion

PARB	Policy Analysis and Records Branch
PAW	Petroleum Administration for War
PEC	Production Executive Committee
PECS	Production Executive Committee Staff
PPB	Production Planning Board
PRP	Production Requirements Plan

RFC	Reconstruction Finance Corporation
RRC	Rubber Reserve Company

SA&Ss	supply arms and services
SFAW	Solid Fuels Administration for War
SPAB	Supply Priorities and Allocations Board
SSRC	Social Science Research Council
SSS	Selective Service System
SWPA	Surplus War Property Administration
SWPC	Smaller War Plants Corporation
SWPD	Smaller War Plants Division

UAW	United Automobile Workers of America
UMW	United Mine Workers of America
USCS	United States Conciliation Service
USES	United States Employment Service

WAA	War Assets Administration
WDLB	War Department Labor Branch
WFA	War Food Administration
WIB	War Industries Board
WLB	War Labor Board (same as National War Labor Board)
WMC	War Manpower Commission
WPB	War Production Board
WRB	War Resources Board
WRS	War Records Section
WSA	War Shipping Administration

INTRODUCTION

Arsenal of World War II is the fourth in a five-volume study of the political economy of American warfare—the means that the nation has employed to mobilize its economic resources for defense and hostilities. The volume covers the period 1940–1945, the years of economic mobilization for World War II. Volume 1—*Beating Plowshares into Swords: The Political Economy of American Warfare, 1606–1865* (1996)—covers the colonial period through the Civil War. Volume 2—*Mobilizing for Modern War: The Political Economy of American Warfare, 1865–1919* (focuses on the Gilded Age, the Progressive Era, and World War I. Volume 3—*Planning War, Pursuing Peace: The Political Economy of Modern Warfare* (1998)—deals with the interwar years, 1920–1939. Volume 5 will conclude the study with the Cold War period.

My goal in this multivolume study is to provide scholars and other readers with what is now unavailable: a comprehensive, analytic, and interdisciplinary study of the economics of America's wars from the colonial period to today. In doing so, I hope to demonstrate the impact of the political economy of warfare on domestic life and what economic mobilization for defense and war reveals about the nature and operations of power within society. I also seek to expand on the study of military history by examining in depth and breadth an aspect of warfare that is often ignored or treated in a perfunctory manner. This different perspective leads to different insights and conclusions about civilians, soldiers and sailors, and warfare. If I raise as many questions as I answer, I will have more than accomplished my purpose.

Analyzing how America has mobilized its economic resources for war and defense is important for a number of reasons. Logistics are basic to warfare and depend on the nation's ability to marshal its economic might effectively. Over the centuries, economic mobilization has followed a discernible evolutionary pattern that illuminates the study of warfare and the military. Furthermore, how the United States has mobilized its economy reveals a great deal about institutional and power structures. Indeed, the stress and demands of warfare make manifest social patterns that are less evident or are obscured during years of peace.

The political economy of warfare involves the interrelations of political, economic, and military institutions in devising the means to mobilize resources for defense and to conduct war. In each war, the magnitude and the duration of the fighting have dictated *what* the nation had to do to harness its economic power, but prewar trends have largely determined *how* this mobilization took place. Four factors are essential in determining the method of mobilization. The first is economic—the level of maturity of the economy. The second is political—the size, strength, and scope of the federal governments. The third is military—the character and structure of the military services and the relation between them and civilian society and authority. And the fourth is technological—the state of military technology.

Patterns of economic mobilization for war have passed through three major stages over the course of American history. The Revolutionary War, the Civil War, and twentieth-century warfare, respectively, best characterize these stages, which I have labeled *preindustrial, transitional,* and *industrial.* Altering the four factors—economic, political, military, and technological— modifies each stage of mobilization. The factors have seldom changed at the same time or at the same pace, but, over time, each has had to keep up with the others so that viable patterns of economic mobilization could be maintained.

The preindustrial stage of economic mobilization for war extended from the colonial period to approximately 1815 and included the Revolutionary War and the War of 1812. During the American Revolution, economic, government, and military institutions were in an embryonic state and were not clearly distinguished from one another. Military technology was relatively primitive and varied little from production in the peacetime economy. Hence, economic mobilization involved increasing civilian output and diverting products from civilian to military use in order to supply the armed forces without converting the economy. Nonetheless, to maximize output, comprehensive regulation of the emerging nation's economic life became essential. Yet the undeveloped nature of economic, political, and military institutions, not only prevented such regulation from ever working well, but also resulted in private and public, civil and military activities becoming inextricably intertwined. Merchants simultaneously served as public officials and military officers while they continued to conduct their private affairs.

The effects of harnessing the economy for war carried over into the years of peace. By highlighting the weaknesses of the Articles of Confederation, economic mobilization helped create the momentum for the ideas underlying the Constitution. And, during the early national period, intense conflict grew between the factions that became the Federalist and the Republican Parties over the strength and policies of the national government under the new charter. This strife weakened the federal government and stunted the growth of the armed services, a major source of dispute. Consequently, although the economy was much stronger in 1812 than in 1776 and military technology had changed little since the Revolution, economic mobilization for the War of 1812 was not measurably improved over that for the Revolutionary War.

The second, or transitional, economic mobilization stage extended from 1816 to 1865. During this period, the economy developed enormous productive capacity; it became diversified and quite industrialized, and specialized functions emerged in manufacturing, marketing, banking, and the like, although the size of firms remained comparatively small. The federal government was limited in size, scope, and activity, but it was capable of expanding in order to handle economic mobilization effectively and efficiently. Both the army and the navy, for their part, had professionalized to the point where they had definable structures and missions. But military technology still had not experienced any dramatic change. Since weaponry remained basic, economic mobilization required only expanding and diverting civilian production, not economic conversion.

Harnessing the economy for war was more readily accomplished in the transitional stage than in those stages that preceded and followed it. The pattern was evident in the Mexican War but was best demonstrated by the Union during the Civil War. Operating under the direction of the president, the War, Navy, and Treasury Departments acted as the principal mobilization agencies. They relied on market forces in a strong competitive economy, not on the elaborate regulation of the preindustrial and industrial stages, to maintain economic stability while meeting the enormous demands of war. Moreover, institutional barriers were not breached. In the economic realm, little mixing of activities or personnel occurred among private and public, civilian and military affairs. The only major exception involved the railroads, which had begun to organize as modern corporations before hostilities. The telegraph system followed a similar trend.

Union success contrasted sharply with Confederate failure. The South was closer to the preindustrial than to the transitional stage. Like the colonies/ states during the revolutionary years, the Confederacy experimented with comprehensive economic regulation, without much success. Weak economic and political systems consistently undermined the Confederacy's economic mobilization effort and played an important role in the South's defeat.

Modern warfare in the twentieth century represents the third, or industrial, economic mobilization stage. By 1900, the United States had become a mature industrialized nation with a modified capitalist system. Although market forces remained significant in the production and distribution of goods, the administered decisions of several hundred modern corporations exercised strong, at times dominant, influence over the economy's direction. In order to make concentrated and consolidated economic power more responsible to the public and to stabilize an enormously complex economy, the federal government started to act as economic regulator. The growth of huge bureaucracies in the corporate and government spheres began to blur the institutional lines between both. Businessmen often staffed the government's regulatory agencies, and, as during the preindustrial stage, the affairs of government and business touched or merged at many points. A government-business regulatory alliance began to emerge during the Progressive Era.

For a time during the late nineteenth century, the military services entered a period of relative isolation in America as the nation became absorbed in industrialization, the threat of war receded, and the army and navy became intensely involved in professionalizing their functions. A technological revolution in weaponry in the later years of the nineteenth century, however, drew the civilian and military worlds back together. The consequences of this revolution were first manifest with the navy. In order to build a new fleet of steel, armor, steam, and modern ordnance, a production team consisting of political leaders, naval officers, and businessmen was formed. Although its composition, responsibilities, and operation have varied over the years, that team has continued to exist. The army was slower to feel the impact of technology, but it eventually experienced the same needs, and a relation with industry and civil authorities similar to the navy's developed.

By the eve of World War I, therefore, the federal government, the industrial community, and the military services had developed complex, modern, and professionalized structures, each dependent on the others in terms of national defense. Economic mobilization for World War I (unlike that for the brief and limited Spanish-American War) forcefully demonstrated this institutional interdependence. The quantity and sophistication of military demand meant that increasing and diverting civilian production was no longer adequate; market forces could not be relied on. Production had to be maximized and industries converted in order to manufacture the often-specialized military hardware that war required. Priority, allocation, price, and other controls had to be introduced. Existing government departments and agencies were unequal to the task. New mobilization bodies had to be created, the most important being the War Industries Board (WIB). Through the board, centralized control over a planned economy was established and carried out by representatives of the government, the business community, and the military. The process obscured institutional lines.

Civilian and military, private and public activities combined. For very different reasons, and with quite different results, the first and the third mobilization stages are strikingly similar.

World War I mobilization left an indelible imprint on national life. During the interwar years, direct and indirect economic planning patterned after the WIB was tried. Congress and other government bodies repeatedly investigated the methods and consequences of harnessing the World War I economy in order to understand better what had taken place, to prevent future mobilization abuses, and to head off the perceived threats of modern warfare. Moreover, close ties between the civil and military sectors of the government, the industrial community, and other new and old interest groups were maintained in order to design, produce, and procure specialized munitions and to plan for industrial mobilization. During World War II, a modified form of the World War I model was used to mobilize the economy for meeting the astronomical and often highly specialized demands of the armed forces and America's allies. With the Cold War following World War II, the nation for the first time in years of peace supported a massive military establishment, one that became inordinately expensive because of its size and because of a continuing transformation of weaponry through scientific and technological advancement. As a result, a defense and war "complex" included and affected most private and public institutions in American life.

Economic mobilization has been carried out largely by political, economic, and, ultimately, military elites. Economic and political elites are closely related and constitute the nation's upper classes. In the late eighteenth century and the early nineteenth, they included merchants, planters and large landowners, and the professional elements. As the economy matured, people involved with banks, railroads, and manufacturing gained in importance, and the twentieth-century economic elite is primarily based in the vast corporate and financial communities.

Military elites as a distinct group did not work in close association with economic and political elites until the industrial stage. In the preindustrial period, no clear line separated the military from the civilian world. During the transitional stage, both the army and the navy distanced themselves from civilians as they began to professionalize and acquire separate identities. But, in the industrial stage, military leaders had to join their political and economic counterparts in order successfully to mobilize the economy for war.

Elites shaped economic mobilization in a number of ways. The federal executive—or what approximated it during the Revolution—devised and implemented the methods for harnessing the economy for war. Throughout American history, the highest appointed officials in the executive branch have been drawn predominantly from among the wealthy or those associated with them. Moreover, the federal government has turned to the nation's business leaders to assist in economic mobilization. These people have acted as temporary or permanent advisers to government mobilizers, served in established or newly created federal agencies with or without pay, or engaged in some combination of these activities.

Harnessing the economy for war has generated a great deal of political controversy in America.. Much of the conflict grows from the fact that economic mobilization highlights the nation's most basic contradiction: an elitist reality in the context of a democratic ideology. During years of peace, that dynamic contradiction tends to be obscured; during years of war, it is magnified by elitist economic mobilization patterns. Excluded interest groups and classes inevitably challenge the legitimacy of mobilization systems run by the few as unrepresentative and as failing to protect larger public interests. Their resentment is exaggerated by widespread aversion to and fear of government at the national level. Moreover, economic mobilization for war elevates the armed services to positions of central importance, intensifying the strong antimilitary strains in American thought. Opposition to war among nonelites also often leads to adverse critiques of economic mobilization policies. There is a close correlation between antiwar and antielite attitudes.

Controversy over the political economy of warfare was greatest in the preindustrial and industrial stages. By requiring a form of planning, underdeveloped and highly developed economies have made elites quite visible. Market economies do not have as exaggerated an effect because mobilization agencies combining political and economic elites are unnecessary. Consequently, economic mobilization caused less political turmoil in the transitional stage.

Throughout the course of American history, the role of political, economic, and military elites in economic mobilization for defense and war can be understood fully only within the four-factor, three-stage paradigm. If, instead of including the entire colonial era, the preindustrial stage is dated from 1765 to 1815, it lasted only about fifty years, approximately the same duration as the transitional stage. Accelerated physical and economic growth quickly modified institutions and power operations, altering in the process the stages of economic mobilization. Rapid industrialization after the Civil War ushered in the last mobilization stage, one that has had a permanence of sorts to it. Since the late nineteenth century, political, economic, and military elites have been absorbed in creating and refining planning structures to cope with the ongoing weapons revolution, a revolution that has comprehensively affected how America prepares for and conducts warfare.

Arsenal of World War II is the first comprehensive analysis of economic mobilization for World War II published since the official histories of the

Bureau of the Budget, *The United States at War: Development and Administration of the War Program by the Federal Government* (Washington, DC: Bureau of the Budget, 1946), and the Civilian Production Administration, *Industrial Mobilization for War: History of the War Production Board and Predecessor Agencies, 1940–1945* (Washington, DC: Civilian Production Administration, 1947). In a very general way, the Bureau of the Budget volume deals with all or most agencies engaged in harnessing the economy for defense and hostilities; that of the Civilian Production Administration concentrates on the War Production Board and its bureaucratic antecedents and treats with other administrations principally as they affected the board's operations. Together these volumes have provided the foundation on which the study of the World War II economy has taken place for the past fifty years and more. Yet why, how, and by whom the books were written has never been closely examined or explained. I undertake that task in the bibliographic essay, not only because the story is a fascinating one, but also because it highlights the strengths and weaknesses of these enormously influential works.

Arsenal of World War II is also the first full-scale study of mobilizing the World War II economy researched and written by one person. Others have begun such a project but, for various reasons, never completed it. Understanding why is not difficult. The complexity of the subject is matched by the nearly overwhelming documentation concerning it. In one way or another, I have been grappling with World War II economics since 1961, when I began research for my Ph.D. dissertation, completed in 1963 and published by Arno in 1979 as *The Hammer and the Sword: Labor, the Military, and Economic Mobilization, 1920–1945*. I summarized that study's contents in the article "Mobilizing the World War II Economy: Labor and the Industrial-Military Alliance" (*Pacific Historical Review* 62 [November 1973]: 443–78) and then revisited World War II mobilization in a long essay written a number of years later, "Warfare and Power Relations in America: Mobilizing the World War II Economy" (in *The Home Front and War in the Twentieth Century: The American Experience in Comparative Perspective*, ed. James Titus [Colorado Springs, CO: United States Air Force Academy, 1984], pp. 91–110, 231–43). Only after tracing the political economy of American warfare from its colonial origins through 1939 in the first three volumes of the present work did I feel prepared to take on once more, and in a total and final way, mobilizing the World War II economy.

Although such a project has not been attempted since 1947, the scholarship on the World War II homefront is hardly lacking. Indeed, the quantity of work on the subject is enormous and the quality often outstanding. Moreover, as history and related disciplines have gone in new directions, the war years have been analyzed and reexamined from different and innovative perspectives. Without the publications of numerous other authors, I could not have finished this work. The notes and bibliographic comments amply attest to my great and enduring debt to scholars, old and new, traditional and revisionist, whose work has assisted me in understanding the broad themes and intricate details of America's last major economic mobilization for hostilities.

This volume logically is centered around the principal mobilization agencies of the defense and war years: the National Defense Advisory Commission (NDAC); the Office of Production Management (OPM); the Supply Priorities and Allocations Board (SPAB); and the War Production Board (WPB). Unlike practically all other publications on the World War II economy (including that of the Bureau of the Budget, that of the Civilian Production Administration, and my own previous work), which skim over the NDAC, OPM, and SPAB to concentrate on the WPB, this volume spends a considerable amount of time on the WPB's predecessor agencies. It does so because, by the time the WPB was organized in January 1942, the basic policies and patterns for its operations had already been well set by the NDAC, OPM, and SPAB (even though many of the mechanics for managing a command economy had yet to be perfected). The major theme running throughout the years from 1940 through 1945 is the growing mobilization alliance between the corporate community, whose members predominated in the WPB and its forerunners, and the armed services, which were responsible for most wartime demand. That being the case, this volume also devotes a great deal of space and effort to the military's supply and procurement systems.

No significant temporary or permanent administration involved in economic mobilization, however, is neglected. For differing reasons, some agencies receive more attention than others, and various organizations are treated only in passing. Since I analyzed at great length and in great depth labor relations and supply in my dissertation, for example, I spend less time with these subjects in this volume. While offices responsible for housing, social welfare, and community facilities are of interest and significance, I must restrict my purview to their immediate impact on the war effort and, specifically, the workforce. Because of their enormous importance, some administrations must be carefully analyzed. These include the Office of Price Administration and Civilian Supply and their successors, the Office of Economic Stabilization, and the Office of War Mobilization and Reconversion and its predecessor. But an extended examination of the Solid Fuels Administration for War is unnecessary. I do little with the Board of Economic Warfare, the Office of Lend-Lease Administration, and related agencies because they were peripheral to mobilizing the economy per se. The Office of Scientific Research and Development and other administrations will more appropriately be analyzed in volume 5.

That a modified form of the World War I mobilization model was used in harnessing the World War II economy does not mean that the latter was simply a replay of the former. Significant change occurred between the wars and during World War II. My four-factor paradigm for analyzing the political economy of warfare set forth earlier is useful for examining the difference. Despite the Great Depression, the potential in 1940 of the economy—as the first factor—was considerably greater than it was in 1915, and, through increased consolidation of economic power, the growth of trade associations and other business organizations, and government efforts, the corporate community was much more open to and familiar with economic planning than was the case earlier in the century. For its part, the federal government—the second factor—had grown rapidly during the New Deal in size, sophistication, quality of staffing, and range of activities, and it was more attuned to an aroused public, organized labor, and other interest groups. Through interwar procurement and economic planning, the armed services—the third factor—were ready and eager, as they were not during World War I, to participate in a mobilized economy. Finally, the technology of warfare—the fourth factor—which was just beginning to manifest accelerated change during World War II with motorized vehicles, aircraft, and submarines, experienced during World War I the full force of involvement by the industrialist, the engineer, and the scientist. The length of World War II and its nearly global reach, of course, made World War I for the United States seem almost limited by comparison.

The third factor, civil-military relations, and to a lesser degree the fourth, the quality and quantity of weaponry, were the most important in shaping the political economy of World War II. Nonetheless, the economic and political factors—the first and second—were still consequential. After a loss of prestige and power during the Great Depression, corporate America was determined to use the wartime economy to refurbish its image and tighten its hold on American society. To a degree, the Franklin D. Roosevelt administration was able to resist those drives because the New Deal strengthened the nation's liberal and progressive forces, particularly a revived and vastly enlarged labor movement. The reform movement also brought into government service a host of economists, statisticians, and other professionals and academics who provided the federal government with nonbusiness personnel for staffing agencies both before and during the war.

As a result, beginning with NDAC, and continuing throughout the years of WPB, the principal mobilization agencies were torn with dissension as New

Deal and corporate elements battled for control over harnessing the economy. Ultimately, corporate America succeeded in bending the reformers and professionals to its will. It did so only with the crucial support and clout of the armed services, which emerged quite suddenly as the principal customers of a command economy. Modified civil-military relations of World War II, therefore, helped neutralize reform to the benefit of both the corporate and the military worlds.

The intense and ongoing tumult of World War II mobilization was not about how to harness the economy for war. On the basis of World War I and interwar developments, the nation in 1940, unlike the nation in 1915, knew what it had to do. Instead, the unending strife of World War II mobilization involved struggles for power and position among interest groups and classes.

I am fully aware that my analysis of World War II mobilization is long, detailed, and demanding. A shorter version would be more easily grasped, but at the cost of exploring in depth important subjects and substantiating adequately controversial interpretations. I have adopted various strategies to assist readers in dealing with the subject's complexity. The volume is divided into three parts, each of which opens with short explanatory statements about the overall themes of the chapters that follow. Most chapters include introductions and conclusions, summarizing the analysis and relating their contents to what preceded and follows them. And the final chapter sets forth the principal points of the book as a whole. Looking over chapter 18 first and consulting it from time to time will assist readers in keeping track of the larger issues that the detailed analysis elucidates. Also, organizational charts are provided for the NDAC, OPM, and WPB. Moreover, chapters 1, 4, and 8—the first chapters of the three parts—in effect explain and analyze those charts in a way that summarizes the major trends of the three principal mobilization agencies and those related to them. The charts and chapters should prove helpful in understanding the nature and importance of the mobilization bureaucracies that grew over the years. Finally, a glossary of wartime agencies and their acronyms is included in the front matter.

To avoid lengthening the volume even more, I have made only summary statements about my four-factor analysis where I have dealt with subjects in previous volumes or others have adequately covered the topic. The nature and structure of the corporate economy on the eve of World War II and the growth of the federal government during the New Deal have been analyzed in *Mobilizing for Modern War and Planning War, Pursing Peace* and have been studied at length by numerous other scholars. Those topics require no elaborate treatment on my part here. The same is true with World War II weaponry. I deal with the tools of war when they are crucial to mobilization, but not beyond that point. Hence, for example, the growth and output of the aircraft industry and the role of Detroit in its accomplishments are covered, but not the types of planes that rolled off the lines. A similar approach is taken with ships for the navy and merchant marine. Some attention is given to the electronics industry, without considering the invention and production of radar, proximity fuses, and the like. I also note when emergencies developed or disputes broke out over the priority of weapons output. Despite advancement in weaponry, massive output was the critical World War II development, and that depended on successful economic mobilization policies, the principal focus of this volume.

PART ONE
NATIONAL DEFENSE
ADVISORY COMMISSION

With war breaking out in Europe in September 1939, the Franklin D. Roosevelt administration initiated action to prepare the economy for possible American entry into hostilities. It did so by reactivating the World War I National Defense Advisory Commission (NDAC) in mid-1940. With the nation deeply divided over the European war, the president proceeded cautiously. He turned to NDAC as least likely to raise strong protests among isolationists and noninterventionists.

Although the commission was a weak and awkward agency that lasted only six months, it made manifest two critical trends. First, reform elements, including New Dealers, labor, and consumer advocates, were out front in the drive to increase military requirements and expand munitions output. Beginning in 1940, and continuing into 1943, New Deal professionals also led in devising the regulatory devices essential for maximizing war output while maintaining economic stability. For a number of reasons, the armed services hesitated about expanding their size, and industry remained focused on growing civilian markets.

These dynamics revealed the second major trend: with preparedness growing, industry and the military drew together as the principal sources of supply and demand. Together, they constituted a conservative mobilization alliance.

The two trends created odd patterns in the operations of NDAC and its successors. Liberal reformers tried to use the commission for maintaining civilian control over economic mobilization, while corporations worked with the armed services' procurement structures practically independently of NDAC. Two half-baked mobilization systems began emerging in 1940 that were not effectively coordinated with one another. This curious development resulted partially from New Deal and corporate-military elements competing to dominate the harnessing of the economy.

1
ORIGINS, STRUCTURE, AND STAFFING OF THE NDAC

ORIGINS

Economic mobilization for the Second World War began in earnest with the Reorganization Act of April 1939. After years of effort and often intense controversy, Franklin D. Roosevelt and the President's Committee on Administrative Management, which he appointed in 1936, succeeded in gaining legislative sanction to reorganize the executive branch for purposes of efficiency. Working primarily with the committee and with Harold D. Smith, director of the Bureau of the Budget, the president between April and September 1939 restructured the executive branch. Most important, he created an Executive Office of the President, made up principally of a White House Office (which included the president's existing staff and several new administrative assistants) the Bureau of the Budget (transferred from the Treasury Department and expanded to assist the president in fulfilling his responsibilities through research, planning, and coordination), and the National Resources Planning Board.[1]

The executive order of September 1939 defining the various divisions of the Executive Office of the President also provided for an Office for Emergency Management (OEM).[2] In an actual or threatened emergency, the president could create and use such an office to assist him in handling the crisis. Roosevelt originally intended to have all or most emergency mobilization agencies placed in OEM and, hence, under his direct authority, perhaps even supervision.

OEM was of the greatest significance to economic mobilization for war in several ways. The president was the OEM'S principal author. Moreover, OEM highlighted a bitter struggle within the Roosevelt administration over economic mobilization for war, a struggle that began in 1939 and continued through 1945. Executive Order 8248 of September 8, 1939, initially had spelled out

15

in detail the functions of the OEM, but, when published, it said only that the president could create such an office. By then, the War Department–led War Resources Board (WRB) was attempting to commit the administration to the military's Industrial Mobilization Plan (IMP), patterned after World War I mobilization methods.[3] Within the Roosevelt administration, New Dealers vehemently opposed the WRB as an attempt on the part of big business and the military to seize control of a wartime economy. The president shared some of these concerns and informed the WRB that, at best, it would be part of a mobilization system of balanced interest groups that would operate under him. The WRB and the military never fully accepted Roosevelt's position and pressured him sufficiently that he excised all details about the OEM from the executive order and provided only for its possible creation. That left the military and its supporters with more room in which to maneuver.

A running battle had begun within the administration over mobilizing the economy for war. The advocates of the IMP basically set the terms of the debate. They favored a clearly defined, centralized system proven during World War I and refined in the interwar years. The opposition was against the IMP and usually for more pluralistic and less centralized mobilization schemes, but the alternatives that it offered were often vague, unproven, unwieldy, or unrealistic.

Finally, OEM signaled that Roosevelt intended to keep control over the controversial economic mobilization process in his own hands. This was thoroughly consistent with his views, those of the President's Committee on Administrative Management, and key assistants such as Bureau of the Budget Director Smith. The Executive Office of the President created the structure for the president to preserve his authority over an expanding government and to carry out more effectively his duties as Washington's top, overall manager. OEM was intended to help achieve those ends under the enormous demands and strains of war. Roosevelt and the Committee on Administrative Management insisted that the president could not delegate responsibility for major policy decisions without seriously compromising his authority. In reviewing the recommendations of the WRB, Smith noted that an irritated Roosevelt snorted: "What do they think they are doing, setting up a second Government?"[4] While the president was intent on preventing such incursions on his prerogatives, he was fully aware of the constant challenges that he would face.

The deliberations of the WRB and the authorization of the OEM produced no concrete results in 1939. With the war in Europe in its "phony" phase and the debate at home over foreign policy and preparedness growing more heated, Roosevelt deferred decisions on economic mobilization. Germany's invasion of Denmark and Norway, the Low Countries, and France beginning in April 1940 forced the president's hand. He began to prepare the nation for war. To initiate economic mobilization, Roosevelt created the OEM and defined its function by administrative order on May 25, 1940. OEM was to assist the president in creating, directing, and coordinating temporary defense and wartime administrations. William H. McReynolds, a presidential assistant, headed the office. Although many defense agencies established between 1940 and 1941 originated within OEM, that office remained relatively unimportant to economic mobilization before the nation entered hostilities, and it gradually became inactive after Pearl Harbor. The ineffectiveness of OEM stemmed in part from McReynolds. Although a knowledgeable administrator who was thoroughly familiar with the ways of Washington, he was not a leader, disliked the job, shunned publicity, could be petty and devious, stressed procedure and detail, and viewed himself more as the president's eyes and ears than as an executive.[5]

A few days after OEM was set up, Roosevelt reestablished the World War I Advisory Commission to the Council of National Defense, also known as the National Defense Advisory Commission (NDAC). He had been considering this option since at least 1937 and appeared to be close to adopting it late in 1939. NDAC offered several advantages. Since the enabling statute was still in effect, economic mobilization could be started without the lacerating legislative process. Also, the commission allowed the president to appoint a pluralistic agency, representing differing interest groups and varying ideologies. Furthermore, with only advisory powers, NDAC was limited in what it could do and easily kept under presidential control. That was particularly the case since Roosevelt decided against activating the Council of National Defense, which had given cabinet officers, and especially the secretary of war, considerable authority over harnessing the World War I economy. Roosevelt worked out the details of how NDAC would function and made the final selection of personnel through consultations with Bureau of the Budget Director Smith, members of the now-defunct President's Committee on Administrative Management, McReynolds, Harry L. Hopkins, and Secretary of the Treasury Henry J. Morgenthau, Jr.[6]

The president's decision to reactivate the NDAC met opposition. Leading Republicans, including Alfred M. Landon, Thomas E. Dewey, and Frank E. Gannet, the newspaper magnate, preferred acting on the recommendations of the WRB. The War Department believed that along with the Army-Navy Munitions Board (ANMB), it could handle initial mobilization.[7] Moreover, when in June 1940 Roosevelt selected Henry L. Stimson and Frank Knox as secretaries of war and the navy, respectively, he brought into the cabinet powerful, business-oriented Republicans who supported a WRB-approach to economic mobilization for war. All this meant that the NDAC's pluralism faced formidable challenges from the advocates of a centralized mobilization structure under industry-military direction as proposed in the IMP.

STRUCTURE AND STAFFING

Seven "advisers" made up the NDAC and were assigned various specialties: William S. Knudsen, president of General Motors Corporation, industrial production; Edward R. Stettinius, Jr., board chairman of the United States Steel Corporation, industrial materials; Sidney Hillman, president of the Amalgamated Clothing Workers of America, employment; Leon Henderson, a New Deal economist from the Securities and Exchange Commission (SEC) who had served in the National Recovery Administration and on the Temporary National Economic Committee, prices; Chester C. Davis, former administrator of the Agricultural Adjustment Administration and governor of the Federal Reserve Board, farm products; Ralph Budd, president of both the Chicago, Burlington and Quincy Railroad and the Association of American Railroads, transportation; and Harriet Elliott, a University of North Carolina political scientist identified with the underprivileged, consumer interests (see chart 1). McReynolds was designated secretary of the NDAC, but the commission would operate without a chairman.

Roosevelt and Bureau of the Budget Director Smith, who acted as the president's chief adviser on emergency management at this point, expected NDAC members to initiate economic mobilization by acting as facilitators to coordinate procurement and expand industrial production. While the advisers needed to cooperate, they basically acted separately. At the outset, only Knudsen, Stettinius, and Hillman would serve full-time, with the others working only part-time. To the degree possible, the NDAC advisers would utilize existing government agencies in carrying out their duties. In his first meeting with the commission, the president made it clear that he remained in charge and would oversee their activities through weekly sessions and personal conferences or through McReynolds's office.[8]

Smith, McReynolds, and others believed that this makeshift arrangement would work. Whether the president shared their views is unclear. Political expediency dictated that he proceed cautiously, and he appeared determined to keep the reins of economic mobilization in his own hands for the time being. Most likely, Roosevelt was experimenting, as was typical with him, this time with the loosely structured, ill-defined, and largely powerless NDAC as a convenient means for initiating economic preparedness. Mobilization methods could be tested, leadership potential examined, and the agency modified or replaced depending on circumstances and need.

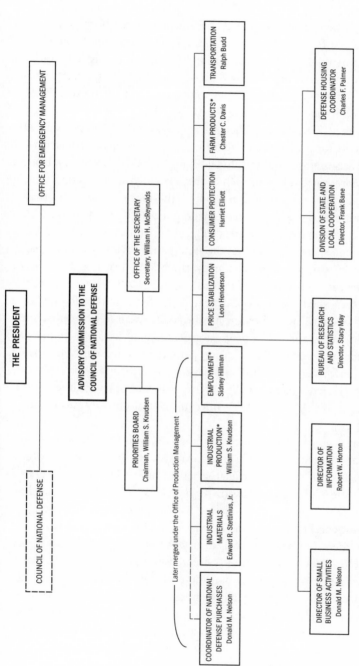

Chart 1.   Organization of NDAC, October 30, 1940. *Source:* Civilian Production Administration, *Industrial Mobilization for War: History of the War Production Board and Predecessor Agencies, 1940–1945* (Washington, DC: Civilian Production Administration, 1947), p. 37.

*By September 1940, Knudsen adopted the simpler title Production Division, and Hillman and Davis changed the titles of their organizations to Labor Division and Agriculture Division, respectively. The titles given in the chart are those assigned by the president and the Council of National Defense.

19

Almost from the outset, the NDAC became a collegial body of full-time executives instead of a collection of individuals. And, through its own initiative and assignments from the president and Congress, the agency took on operational, not just advisory, duties. This occurred despite the fact that the commission was without a leader. McReynolds would not act as executive secretary, and he opposed much of what NDAC was doing.

To coordinate activities among themselves and with the War and Navy Departments, the major procurement agencies, each of the seven advisers over time created a liaison staff, and, in July 1940, the NDAC established a Liaison Committee, representatives from each of the seven divisions meeting weekly to exchange information. The commission, furthermore, set up an elaborate series of committees to study and recommend policy (e.g., the Committee on Contract Policy), to explore new areas (e.g., the Committee on Small Business), and to fulfill specific tasks (e.g., the Emergency Facilities Committee).[9]

But even more was necessary. Gradually, the NDAC organized a series of subdivisions to carry on critical functions. In June 1940, for example, the commission established a Bureau of Research and Statistics headed by Stacy May, who had been assistant director for the social sciences in the Rockefellar Foundation, and staffed with professionals, many of whom were on loan from other federal agencies. The division gathered needed data from other agencies and performed statistical analyses for the various advisers. Various commissioners preferred one centralized bureau instead of seven different statistical centers in NDAC, but May's bureau was not entirely successful in achieving that end.[10]

By far the most important addition to the NDAC was the Office for Coordination of National Defense Purchases. Donald M. Nelson headed the office, and he emerged as the overall coordinator between the NDAC and the armed services and as the advisory commission's general executive. This was as close as the body came to having a chair. Nelson had been executive vice-president of Sears, Roebuck and Company, and he had served for a short period as chief of the Procurement Division of the Treasury Department before moving to the NDAC. His office was technically created by the Council of National Defense in June 1940, and he was considered to be the equal of the other seven advisory commissioners. Initially charged with coordinating all defense purchasing and related policies, Nelson also handled policies on and programs relating to emergency plant sites, contract negotiations, and certification for rapid amortization, and he was appointed director of small business activities and administrator of priorities.[11]

Despite the various additions and other devices intended to facilitate mobilization, the seven advisers and their offices remained basic to the operations of the NDAC. Knudsen and Stettinius had the most important assignments, with Hillman following behind. Henderson and, to a lesser degree, Davis emerged as major forces in formulating economic mobilization policies. Budd was not especially active, and Elliott did not have much impact. Nelson in effect became an eighth member of the commission and played a vital role as a diligent, hardworking conciliator.

Kundsen's Production Division had the task of facilitating the manufacture of munitions not normally produced by the economy.[12] That meant gathering or estimating military requirements, establishing the productive capacity of the economy for specific goods, and determining whether new plant and equipment were necessary. In order to maintain the nation's industrial balance, the division had to play a role in locating and building or expanding productive capacity. It also had to have some voice in negotiating contracts with manufacturers and ensuring that they delivered quality goods on time. All these activities involved the legal responsibilities of the procurement agencies. Consequently, the Production Division worked much more closely with the armed services, and particularly the War Department, than its counterparts did.

Knudsen drew his staff principally from engineers and production experts in the automobile and related industries. He organized the division into eight commodity sections, including Aircraft, headed by George J. Mead, former vice-president of the United Aircraft Corporation; Ammunition and Light Ordnance, directed by E. F. Johnson, a former vice-president of General Motors who had managed the Du Pont Company's Old Hickory powder plant during World War I; and Tanks, Trucks, and Tractors, led by John D. Biggers, president of Libby-Owens-Ford Glass Company.

Obviously, the large corporate community played a vital role in the operations of Knudsen's division. Almost all the section heads served for a dollar-a-year, and the same was true of other major executives in the division. To carry out its duties, the division also made extensive use of industrial advisers and consultants and industry advisory committees, especially trade associations and their officials. For example, Pyke Johnson, executive vice-president of the Automobile Manufacturers Association (AMA) and chairman of the American Trade Association Executives, offered his services to Knudsen early, and the AMA played an essential role in organizing the Automotive Committee for Air Defense, which helped work out an airplane parts production plan. The National Machine Tool Builders Association joined the NDAC from the outset in mobilizing an industry indispensable to all munitions production. This pattern was followed with practically every other industry with which the Production Division dealt, and, if a trade association did not exist, the division called manufacturers together when assistance was needed.

The Production Division, however, did not manifest blatant conflicts of interest. Perhaps this reflected Knudsen's personality. He was a low-key individual who attempted to avoid conflict. Indeed, Knudsen does not stand out in the records of the NDAC. But he selected for his deputy director John D. Biggers and gave him wide latitude. The latter was an ambitious, driven, and highly ideological spokesperson for corporate America who had a big impact on NDAC operations. Biggers made the Production Division a center of controversy in the operations of the commission.

Stettinius's Materials Division performed the same functions for industrial materials that the Production Division did for finished products.[13] The dividing line between the two was fabrication. Hence, the Materials Division covered steel and armor plate but not ships and tanks, which belonged to Knudsen. Facing actual or potential shortages of critical materials, the Materials Division, usually working with other government agencies, also assumed a leading role in stockpiling rubber, antimony, and tungsten, limiting the exports of products like scrap steel, and diverting copper from civilian to defense usages.

Stettinius divided his division into three major subdivisions: first was Mining and Minerals Products, under the direction of William L. Batt, president of SKF Industries, and further divided into sections for iron and steel, copper, aluminum, tin, etc.; second was Agricultural and Forest Products, directed by Clarence Francis, president of General Foods Corporation, with sections for textiles, leather, paper, rubber, and so forth; third was Chemical and Allied Products, headed by Dr. Edward R. Weidlein, director of the Mellon Research Institute, and having sections on petroleum, nitrogen, and the like. The division was also assigned heat, light, and power, and Stettinius created a unit to cover these services.

The Materials Division led all other NDAC divisions in the use of organized industry and its leaders. In part, this reflected Stettinius's background and orientation. He was viewed as an enlightened business leader interested in advancing and improving relations between industry and the government. To further that end, he had served as a liaison officer between the National Recovery Administration (NRA) and its Industrial Advisory Board and as a member of the Commerce Department's Business Advisory Council. Shortly after his appointment to the NDAC, Stettinius recruited a group of fifteen prominent executives to act as the leadership nucleus of his division. Seven of the group were from the Business Advisory Council, and most of the others had previous government experience.

This group relied heavily on trade associations and their officials to carry out their duties, often with conflicts of interest rife. Trade association officials and their assistants were placed in charge of sections involving the industries that they represented. For example, Walter S. Tower, president of the American Iron and Steel Institute, headed the section on iron and steel products. The same relation developed with electricity, cotton textiles, and rubber and rubber products. These leaders naturally turned to their associations for assistance in carrying out their responsibilities. Other sections of the Materials Division also called on trade associations. The U.S. Copper Association and the American Zinc Institute played vital roles in surveying their industries and helping their respective sections deal with production potential. The Chemical and Allied Products Section and other subdivisions of the Materials Division also made extensive use of the industry advisory committees organized by the ANMB to facilitate its work. Those committees were usually composed of representatives of trade associations and leading companies in an industry.[14]

The Materials Division's mode of operations made it difficult to determine where the NDAC and private industry and its organizations started and stopped. Industry cooperation was indispensable to the operations of the division. However, the way Stettinius and his associates utilized industry caused problems. Some charged that conflicts of interest within the Materials Division retarded critically important industrial expansion. New Dealer Leon Henderson bluntly claimed that some members of Stettinius's division "do not know who their client is."[15] Others felt this way as the Materials Division led in the drive to suspend or modify the use of antitrust laws and adopt lenient policies on plant amortization in order to further industry's cooperation with the defense program.

Hillman's Labor Division was vaguely defined at the outset, but it took on critically important functions.[16] Basically, the division faced the need to focus the efforts of numerous federal agencies dealing with the working population on matters of national defense. To fulfill that goal, Hillman organized his division into three functional sections. The first was Labor Relations, headed by Joseph D. Keenan, secretary of the Chicago Federation of Labor. The section was intended to head off and settle labor disputes that could adversely affect national defense, and Hillman took a very active interest in its operations himself. The second was Labor Requirements and Employment Standards, under Isador Lubin, chief of the Bureau of Labor Statistics (BLS) in the Department of Labor. Its job was to estimate the need for labor in numbers and type, work for standardized wages and hours within geographic and functional areas, and review defense contracts for the purpose of protecting labor standards. The third was Labor Supply and Training, led by Floyd W. Reeves, director of the National Youth Commission. Working largely through other government agencies, it was to increase the supply of skilled workers for defense contractors. The section emphasized a "training-within-industry" program and vocational training in state schools.

Dollar-a-year personnel did not figure prominently in the Labor Division, and, although the division used some advisory committees, their influence was never great. Hillman set up a sixteen-person Labor Policy Advisory Committee composed of labor-federation members. The reach of this committee never extended beyond that of the Labor Division, which was quite limited. More specialized labor groups worked with manufacturer committees to stabilize the workforce in the shipbuilding and aircraft industries. Also, the coordinator of national defense purchases and the Consumer Division turned to labor advisory committees at times in dealing with specific problems. In general, however, organized labor, unlike organized industry, was not called on in any systematic way by the NDAC to assist economic mobilization. Nonetheless, the Labor Division still managed to do a reasonably good job in the areas it covered.

Hillman tried to extend the influence of his division over plant sites, contracts, housing, and the like because all these activities had a great impact on labor supply and labor relations. He was consistently rebuffed by industry and its representatives in the NDAC and the procurement agencies and largely confined to traditional trade union activities. Labor's restricted role in economic mobilization became a matter of increasing acrimony within the NDAC and successor agencies.

Henderson's Price Stabilization Division was designed to monitor prices and recommend policies and procedures to prevent inflation.[17] Henderson focused almost exclusively on wholesale prices of basic commodities. Although the division was organized into various sections, he relied more on various advisers to carry out his job, such as David Ginsburg, his attorney from the SEC, John E. Hamm, from the Russell Sage Foundation, and Milton Katz, of Harvard Law School. Prices remained relatively stable during the NDAC period because the nation's industrial capacity was sufficient to absorb the defense load without overheating. Nonetheless, Henderson's division policed prices diligently.

Henderson's impact extended far beyond pricing. Henderson emerged in the NDAC as the principal spokesperson for centralized mobilization programs in which the influence of industry and the military would be tempered. He acted as more than an advocate. He led or actively participated in having the NDAC operate as a body, not a collection of individuals, and in devising policies for antitrust, rapid amortization, priorities, and the initial phases of economic warfare. All this, he argued, was directly or indirectly related to his charge of controlling prices. Moreover, he was focusing on the larger, longer-run issues because others in and outside the NDAC were not doing so. While a hard-nosed New Dealer, Henderson was attuned to the operations of power, was action oriented, and was usually pragmatic in approach.

As in the Labor Division, in the Division of Price Stabilization dollar-a-year men were unimportant to operations. To carry out its responsibilities, the division relied heavily on the Department of Labor's BLS and the NDAC's Bureau of Research and Statistics, which in time came under Henderson's direction. Additionally, the National Association of Cost Accountants and the Controllers Institute volunteered their services and facilities to the division. Henderson was also the primary exponent of "spot" meetings of industry. Since he lacked authority over prices short of the president commandeering plants, Henderson had to rely on persuasion and threats against unwarranted price increases. If such pricing was taking place, the commissioner of price stabilization called a meeting of industry, consisting usually of representative firms and trade associations, to arrive at solutions to reverse or limit the practice. In doing so, he often worked with the Materials Division. Generally speaking, this approach proved to be successful.

Chester Davis had a greater impact in the NDAC as an advocate of liberal economic mobilization policies than as the head of the Division of Farm Products.[18] That was the case because, in 1940, the nation's farm problems still involved excess production, which the Department of Agriculture and other agencies could handle. Davis appeared to be on the commission more to give farmers a voice than to advance the course of economic mobilization. With a regular staff of sixteen organized into eight sections, Davis's division studied matters such as locating defense plants in rural areas to absorb surplus labor, production under emergency conditions, trading excess agricultural products abroad for strategic goods such as rubber, and ensuring that farmers had adequate supplies of phosphates and nitrates in an emergency and that enough steel was available to manufacture critical farm machinery and implements. Study was seldom followed by action. Those conditions perhaps drove the activist Davis to insist that the NDAC function as a collegial body and to join Henderson, Hillman, and others in working for locating defense plants in rural areas, denying contracts to labor law violators, enacting excess profits taxes, and in general making the economic mobilization program one that protected the public interest and served the many, not the few. Davis's role in the NDAC was such that he had little need for either dollar-a-year men or advisory committees.

The presence of Budd's Transportation Division was hardly felt within the NDAC.[19] Two reasons account for this situation. First, the nation had a surplus of transportation facilities that many believed to be adequate for meeting most emergency situations. Consequently, no sense of urgency was associated with Budd's assignment, which involved facilitating coordination of transportation during an emergency and anticipating any problems in the area through consultation and study. Second, Budd abhorred the notion of greater government meddling in the nation's transportation system. The commission had been appointed only to advise the president, he argued, and it should not go beyond that role.

Those realities led Budd to keep his office small and relatively inactive. It consisted of little more than himself, two other executives, and some clerical help. Budd was often in Chicago attending to his duties as president of the Association of American Railroads (AAR), leaving his deputy in charge. The best way to keep the government out of the transportation field, he reasoned, was to increase the level of industry cooperation. To further that purpose, he organized sections for the principal modes of domestic transportation, including railroad, bus, truck, automobile, pipeline, inland water, and air. Budd looked after the railroads himself through the AAR, which he also called on to provide statistical and other services for his division. For the other sections, he appointed eleven dollar-a-year consultants to handle matters. These were individuals from the relevant industry itself and usually trade association officials who turned to their organizations for assistance as Budd did with the AAR. Budd refused to deal with transportation rates and routes because these were the domain of the Interstate Commerce Commission and other government agencies. He also showed little interest in ocean shipping, which belonged to the United States Maritime Commission.

Overall, the Transportation Division did little in the way of study or action. Budd and his associates took some steps to prepare the railroads and their users for heavier traffic and made some inquiries and recommendations involving inland waterways, highways, airplanes and airports, and plant sites and the warehousing of strategic and critical materials, but the efforts were usually preliminary or perfunctory. Even the division's interaction with its NDAC counterparts was limited. Protecting the transportation sector from the regulatory hand of the government remained Budd's first priority.

Elliott's Consumer Protection Division was charged with looking after the interests of the consumer under the pressures of national defense and coordinating federal health and welfare activities related to defense.[20] Her assignment was the broadest and vaguest of the seven NDAC commissioners'. Theoretically, it included responsibility for the nation's entire population, and Elliott interpreted her assignment broadly. She organized divisions for economics, civic organizations, business and consumer groups, health and welfare, and housing, and turned principally to government officials and academics for staff and advisers. To assist its work and build public support for its efforts, the division worked closely with the League of Women Voters and other civic groups and also had the support of many members of Congress and Eleanor Roosevelt. Such backing helped the division in its endeavors to educate the public on matters of prices, retail products, and government services. Elliott also turned to business organizations. Fifty national retailer organizations and trade associations for the wholesale distributors of consumer goods appointed advisory committees to assist the division in trying to hold down prices. The division also initiated many studies of the effects of national defense on the consumer.

Despite valiant efforts and good intentions, the Division of Consumer Protection never made its mark within the NDAC. It was not taken seriously by the other divisions and was often ignored when important policy decisions were made. In part, this stemmed from Elliott's limitations. She was out of her league and neither a good administrator nor a bureaucratic infighter. Even more important was the fact that her assignment was nearly impossible. She was a high-minded, gentle woman called on to protect unorganized civilian consumers in an agency of hard-nosed, interest-oriented men focused on munitions production. Moreover, what she was protecting was unclear since the notion of consumer affairs was hard to define and involved most facets of defense and numerous government agencies. This led to Elliott engaging in constant battles for administrative turf with other agencies, struggles that she invariably lost. As her ineffectiveness became obvious, Elliott lost control over health and welfare and her voice in housing, and, in time, the remnants of her division were absorbed by another agency.

Donald Nelson carried out his numerous duties as coordinator of national defense purchases by organizing his office into a number of functional and commodity sections.[21] The former involved procurement and related activities, specifications and standardization, contract clearance, priorities, and the like, while the latter included equipment and supplies, subsistence, clothing, and equipage. For staffing, Nelson relied primarily on dollar-a-year men who filled seventeen of the twenty top slots in his office. He also used industry advisory committees in which trade associations were prominent. To assist both his office and the Quartermaster Corps, with which he worked closely, Nelson arranged to have the wholesale food industry organize an advisory committee with a series of subcommittees. To deal with lumber, he turned to industrial committees set up by Stettinius's division. When appointed administrator of priorities in October 1940, Nelson helped institute policies that established committees for various industries headed by an administrative officer from outside the trade and four other members: one each from the army and the navy and two from industry, representing both the producers and the consumers of the regulated product or material. The industry representatives usually came from existing advisory committees or trade associations. Unlike other NDAC advisory committees, those of the Priorities Board had an official status. They recommended policies to the board, and, if their advice was accepted, the committee's administrative officer implemented it. Under these procedures, the NDAC began instituting a priorities system based on industry's cooperation instead of compulsion or its threatened use.

Nelson's role in the NDAC highlights the dynamics and tensions of that extraordinarily complex agency. For a number of reasons, his duties expanded from coordinating procurement to include plant amortization, priorities, small business, and other areas. First, procurement cut across all mobilization functions. That made Nelson's office the logical one for handling matters such as priorities as they became necessary. Second, the NDAC commissioners were extremely sensitive about power and position and agreed to increase Nelson's range of responsibility where they were reluctant to do so for a competing colleague. Nelson's place in the NDAC was unique in that he was considered an equal, but not a rival, of the commissioners who had, in effect, created his office. Third, Nelson occupied the middle ground in the numerous disputes that erupted in the NDAC among liberals and conservatives, management and labor, and advocates of government and those of business. As an enlightened businessperson who identified with the New Deal, he was accepted by differing interest groups and those of varying ideology as open-minded and fair. At a minimum, the contending parties within the NDAC preferred to increase his power rather than that of their opponents.

The logic and circumstances that made Nelson the "focal point" of economic mobilization in 1940, however, did not provide him with the authority necessary to do his job. Throughout the NDAC period, the War and Navy Departments maintained their procurement rights undiminished. The commission and Nelson had only advisory powers, except for priorities. Those conditions allowed the armed services to set the tempo for and shape the nature of the mobilization program and severely limited what the NDAC could accomplish. Leon Henderson, John Biggers, and Nelson, representing left, right, and center in the divided commission, all agreed that the military should continue to procure, but only under the centralized direction of the coordinator of national defense purchases. Otherwise, civilians could not control mobilization, and the economy would be seriously distorted.[22]

THE SIGNIFICANCE OF STRUCTURE AND STAFFING

Several qualities of the NDAC structure and staffing stand out and provide insight into the economic mobilization process. First, planning by civilians and the military in the interwar years provided continuity between mobilizing the economy for World War I and mobilizing it for World War II. Very few NDAC executives had participated in World War I economic mobilization, but almost a fifth of those from business and industry had served in the NRA, on the Business Advisory Council of the Department of Commerce, or in similar assignments. Nelson, Stettinius, and the latter's influential legal counsel, Blackwell Smith, had all served in the NRA. Moreover, trade associations played as important a role in the NDAC, as they had in the NRA.[23] There were also significant links between the WRB and the NDAC.

Second, industrialists emerged as dominant in the NDAC. This is hardly surprising in the light of the overwhelming importance of industry to economic mobilization. The commission's use of dollar-a-year men and industry advisory committees well illustrates business's power.

Most dollar-a-year men were from industry or associated with it and served in the Production, Materials, and Transportation Divisions and the Office for Coordination of National Defense Purchases. These were the units most important to the commission's mobilization activities. No alternate policies for staffing these divisions at the highest levels were either considered or feasible, and World War I mobilization and the NRA provided ample precedent for using business volunteers in government. Policies and practices involving dollar-a-year men were lax in the NDAC. At first, review procedures were at best casual, with some individuals serving without any scrutiny. By late 1940, reasonable standards and procedures were in place and direct and flagrant conflicts of interest avoided. Nonetheless, a person could serve in the NDAC while on full salary from another source and under conditions in which indirect conflicts of interest were obvious, especially where trade association officials, private consultants, and practicing attorneys were involved. Stettinius's division stood out in its use of questionable personnel practices.[24]

Industry advisory committees were as critical to the operations of the NDAC as were dollar-a-year men. Indeed, most of the commission's progress resulted from these committees at a time when goals were uncertain and NDAC authority slight. At a minimum, the NDAC relied on such committees for providing reliable data on production and capacity, disseminating information on defense requirements, instituting plans for expansion, standardization, and conservation, and facilitating procurement. Yet such committees operated throughout the NDAC period without established rules or uniform procedures. In June 1940, the Justice Department vetoed an NDAC proposal for a statute to legalize such committees, and the department's own proposal for overseeing a certification process never worked out. Without NDAC guidelines, the various divisions proceeded on their own. A threatening legal cloud always hung over what was done because of the Justice Department's very active antitrust activity and particularly that growing out of industry's collusive practices associated with the NRA. Blackwell Smith, Stettinius's legal counsel, who had been assistant general counsel in the NRA, tried to introduce procedures to guard against illegal activities by industry advisory committees in both the Materials and the Production Divisions, with little success. In those divisions, the Transportation Division, and the Office for Coordination of National Defense Purchases, the use of industry advisory committees was widespread, was based primarily on trade associations, and included voluntary priority and allocation activity, which was probably illegal. The use of advisory committees by the Labor, Price Stabilization, Agricultural, and Consumer Divisions was much less common and comparatively innocuous.[25]

The use of dollar-a-year men and advisory committees, therefore, gave industry a substantial hold on the NDAC. Significantly, Donald Nelson, viewed as a moderate conciliator, relied heavily on both practices to carry out his duties, highlighting their acceptable, probably inevitable, character. The nation's dependence on industry and its leaders to prepare the economy for war generated an aggressiveness in some business circles. Here was the opportunity to reclaim national dominance after a decade of depression with declining prestige, growing government, and rising, and, in the eyes of many industrialists, abusive, interest groups such as organized labor. Looking back on economic mobilization in 1956, Herbert Emmerich maintained: "When big business realized it had lost the elections of 1932 and 1936, it tried to come in through the back door, first through the NRA and then through the NDAC and OPM and WPB." To achieve that goal during the defense and war years, Emmerich further implied, required corporate America working in close harmony with the military in harnessing the economy as set forth in the IMP, a strategy in which Stettinius played a key role.[26]

A third significant attribute affecting NDAC was that a much stronger national government existed on the eve of World War II as a result of New Deal expansion than was the case before the First World War. Washington was also more responsive to public welfare and nonbusiness interest groups after the onset of the Great Depression. These realities presented significant obstacles to industry's control of economic mobilization. Heading the Price Stabilization Division in the NDAC, Leon Henderson was a prominent New Dealer dedicated to an enlarged, activist state that would regulate the economy, tame corporate behavior, and protect the consumer, and he aggressively pursued those goals in the commission. Henderson had no counterpart in the NDAC of World War I; the earlier commission had no representative for agriculture or the consumer; and labor's spokesperson, Samuel Gompers, had been accommodating compared to Sidney Hillman.[27]

While withholding support for most of Henderson's statist views, Roosevelt favored representation for various interest groups and closely guarded his own prerogatives. This had led him to reestablish the NDAC in order to begin preparing the economy for war. The president turned to the Bureau of the Budget to work out the administrative details for his thinking. Harold D. Smith, the director, members of his staff, and others were public administration specialists who had participated in or were associated with executive reorganization in the 1930s and who generally shared the outlook of the President's Committee on Administrative Management (labeled "the Budget boys" by an angry Leon Henderson). They tended to think in terms of administrative organization more than power operations. By comparison, Roosevelt was a shrewd calculator of power who seldom let organizational details hinder achieving the goals he sought. Since economic mobilization actually involved power more than organization, Smith and his associates over time lost influence and were reduced to the role of technicians working out the administrative details for implementing the president's decisions. In November 1940, Henderson lamented the "tragedy" of the defense effort getting "completely away" from OEM.[28] McReynolds as head of OEM and secretary of NDAC thought in terms of bureaucracy and public administration.

Under Roosevelt's direction, the methods for mobilizing the economy gradually reflected more accurately the contours of power within the American political economy. Government would have a larger role than it had had during World War I, other interest groups, such as organized labor, would have a greater voice, but industry would remain in a dominant position.

Fourth, and finally, a divided NDAC was less influential in shaping economic mobilization than were the military services that controlled procurement. Henderson, Davis, Hillman, and Elliott wanted the commission's power defined broadly so that economic mobilization could be carried out with proper attention paid to liberal social and economic policies. Stettinius and Knudsen favored a restrictive interpretation so that the large corporations and the procurement agencies would be least disturbed in concentrating on maximizing defense production in the shortest possible time. Budd generally favored an NDAC with restricted, not expanded, powers, but, as a Midwesterner, he wanted to see Washington direct defense industries away from the Northeast and toward his region and the South. While these divisions began to appear regularly in NDAC deliberations and operations, they became the most intense and consequential over plant site locations, contract clearance, and the enforcement of federal labor laws.[29] Although a minority, Stettinius and Knudsen in effect won most of the disputes because the armed services favored their position and used their procurement authority to work with the corporate structure in implementing it.

This outcome contained a larger and enormously important truth: the conservative military was much more significant in determining how the economy was mobilized for World War II than were the civilians of the liberal, New Deal state.

2

THE MILITARY AND ECONOMIC MOBILIZATION

THE WAR DEPARTMENT

The military was better prepared than were the civilians for World War II economic mobilization. This was particularly true for the army, which made up for the deficiencies of the navy and led the military in industrial mobilization during the years 1939–1945. Basic to procurement in both services were the supply bureaus. In order for the War and Navy Departments adequately to meet the growing demands of defense expansion, the Franklin D. Roosevelt administration replaced the secretaries and under secretaries in both departments in mid-1940. The new leaders began centralizing control over the bureaus and taking other measures to prepare the army and navy for war.

The armed services clearly demonstrated their preparedness in the years 1940–1941, which contrasted so sharply with the chaotic defense period preceding World War I. Several reasons account for the difference. Most of the officer corps had participated in World War I. More important, the army had been planning for procurement and economic mobilization for nearly twenty years under the direction of the Office of the Assistant Secretary of War (OASW).[1] Procurement planning gave the army a reasonably good idea of what was needed in an emergency and how to go about obtaining it. Economic mobilization planning made the service fully aware of its dependence on civilian institutions and of what those agencies should be like and how they should function. The planning was based on the concept of M-Day, in which war or a national emergency would mark a sharp break between planning and actual mobilization. No such clear demarcation ever emerged as the nation slowly and uncertainly began preparing for hostilities. That development threw off the War Department mobilization to some extent, but in no major way.

The transition from planning to large-scale procurement varied among the supply arms and services (SA&Ss). Nonetheless, to different degrees, all the bureaus fell back on the decentralized procurement districts to handle their load and turned primarily to allocated facilities in the awarding of contracts. This took place even though the OASW never officially ordered the prewar allocation system into effect, the mobilization program having begun gradually and abundant facilities being often available as a result of the depression. On their own, the SA&Ss implemented a system that had been devised over a twenty-year period. They logically turned to facilities that had been surveyed and that in many cases had schedules of production and factory plans. For their part, industrial managers were usually willing and able to deal with the military since they knew the army and its procedures and were not frightened by the often large and complex orders. The allocation system was intended to speed up the mobilization process, avoid competition within and among procurement agencies, and distribute the wartime load more evenly throughout the nation so as to avoid overloading some regions and starving others.

During the defense period, the first two objectives were met well. Within eighteen months, the foundations for wartime procurement were laid, and the OASW and the Army-Navy Munitions Board (ANMB) acted to settle any conflict involving facilities among the various bureaus and the two services. However, most of the contracts were still crowded into the major production centers of the Northeast. This grew out of the SA&Ss dealing primarily with the nation's giant firms and existing production facilities in the interwar years.

Wartime procurement was centered in the Ordnance Department and the Quartermaster Corps. Between March 1942 and December 1945, the Army Service Forces expended over $69 billion. Of that amount, Ordnance accounted for 49 percent, and Quartermaster 31 percent. The other bureaus spent modestly by comparison, with the Corps of Engineers accounting for 7 percent, the Signal Corps 6 percent, the Transportation Corps and the Chemical Warfare Service (CWS) each 3 percent, and the Medical Department 1 percent.[2]

The Ordnance Department made the smoothest and quickest transition from peace to war. This is hardly surprising since the bureau was the most active in and benefited most from the procurement planning of the interwar years. Able leadership also served Ordnance well. Chief of Ordnance General Charles M. Wesson led the bureau steadily from the beginnings of expansion in 1938 to total mobilization in 1942. His successor, General Levin H. Campbell, directed the department boldly and imaginatively throughout the remainder of the war. From May 1940 to June 1942, personnel at the Washington headquarters expanded from four hundred to five thousand. Despite this growth, decentralization remained the department's hallmark. As much authority and responsibility as possible was delegated to arsenals, procurement districts, and new subdivisions for handling plants built by the government, but operated by private contractors and centers, to build tanks and other motor vehicles.

In August 1940, Ordnance activated its procurement districts, which had in their files the technical data for most articles, including drawings, specifications, and descriptions. Nearly all of Ordnance contracts went to allocated firms. In April 1941, the department took a major step to strengthen further what Campbell called "the industry-ordnance team." It created twenty-five engineering advisory committees, made up of engineers, industrialists, and an Ordnance officer, to review all aspects of Ordnance demand, including design, specifications, production, and materials. Once he took over, Campbell moved even further in tapping industry's expertise. Interwar planning failed to prepare Ordnance for its enormous wartime expansion in only one way: the building of or contracting to build forty-nine plants to make powder, ammunition, and arms and accoutrements, virtually a new industry. Some critics have subsequently contended that the department grossly overbuilt in this area. Overall, however, the department performed exceptionally well during the defense and war years.[3]

Although the Signal Corps resembled Ordnance in many ways, its overall wartime performance was wanting until the last years of hostilities. Like Ordnance, the Signal Corps had planned well in the interwar years, decentralized its operations as procurement expanded, and built—probably overbuilt—numerous government plants to manufacture the specialized items it needed. Signal Corps supply operations before and during the war were practically an extension of the so-called Big Five in the communications industry (which accounted for around 80 percent of Signal Corps contracts): General Electric Company; Western Electric Company; Radio Corporation of America (RCA); Westinghouse Electric Manufacturing Company; and Bendix Radio Corporation. The industry worked closely and, for the most part, harmoniously with the Signal Corps and went from basic assembly to mass production techniques in 1942–1943 to meet the military's massive, high-quality wartime demand. Yet Signal Corps supply chronically fell well below its own and army goals throughout a good part of the war.

The basic problem was that the corps lacked production and distribution experts and refused to separate mass supply operations from those of research and development. The latter function interfered with and distracted attention from the former. General Joseph O. Mauborgne had been relieved of duty as chief signal officer in August 1941 in favor of General Dawson Olmstead because of the faltering supply effort. However, despite numerous reorganizations and the study and recommendations of a blue ribbon advisory council from the communications industry that included David Sarnoff (president of

RCA), Olmstead never resolved the corps's supply problems. As a result, the Signal Corps lost to the Army Air Forces all development and procurement of electronic equipment and to G-2 of the General Staff signal intelligence involving intercept and cryptanalysis. Only when Olmstead was replaced by General Harry C. Ingles in June 1943 did the Signal Corps begin to solve its problems. As part of a major reorganization, Ingles finally separated supply from research and development and put it under William H. Harrison, former vice-president of American Telegraph and Telephone Company, who had been serving in the economic mobilization effort since 1940. Within a short period of time, Harrison consummated a "Signal Corps–Communications Industry Team" that put the corps's supply operations on a sound basis.[4]

The Corps of Engineers and the CWS participated in interwar procurement planning on a limited level. Their efforts in the 1920s and 1930s focused on bureau operations rather than including the broader perspective of the OASW, as was the case with Ordnance and the Signal Corps. Nonetheless, that planning helped make their transition to defense and warfare successful. Two other circumstances eased the course of the Corps of Engineers from war to peace. First, most of its equipment involved standard or modified commercial products, which made procurement relatively uncomplicated. Second, in peacetime, the corps's Civil Works Division was usually very active on rivers and harbors and other public works, and such projects increased substantially in numbers during the Great Depression. This acted to keep the corps current with advances in the construction industry and in contact with engineers and other specialists whom it could recruit for wartime expansion. It also provided it with a field service that could be merged with the procurement districts to handle the emergency load. Beginning in the defense period, and continuing in the war years, the corps gradually decentralized its procurement operations, turned to allocated facilities, and generally met its new demands without major difficulties.[5]

As a new SA&S created by developments in the modern chemical industry, the CWS was open to planning and sought civilian assistance. Throughout the interwar years and World War II, it worked closely with the American Chemical Society and the Manufacturing Chemists Association and called on private and university laboratories to help fulfill its responsibilities. From CWS activities, a Chemical Advisory Committee with an elaborate set of subcommittees was created in 1939 to advise the ANMB. These committees and subcommittees remained active throughout the war years. The corps also considered allocated facilities and educational orders to be vital to meeting its mission, and the regular and reserve officers who headed its procurement districts were well trained in industrial, financial, and commercial functions. Procurement plans, including specifications and blueprints for arsenals and factories, prepared the service well for wartime expansion. During the defense and war years, the CWS decentralized its procurement operations and generally met its supply goals in an efficient manner.[6]

The Medical Department did not cause exceptional problems in terms of wartime supply operations. Its requirements were limited in number and did not vary much from civilian use. Vast wartime expansion in supply was met through advertised bidding and the use of allocated facilities. Consequently, the department's interwar planning, restricted though it was, still proved helpful.[7]

The Transportation Corps fell into a category all its own since it was created in stages between March and July 1942. The Quartermaster Corps historically handled transportation for the army. Its interwar planning was inadequate, and, during the defense period, G-4 of the General Staff and the OASW became increasingly involved with transportation matters in a way that created considerable confusion. In an attempt to bring greater order to the critical transportation area, the Army Service Forces in March 1942 placed transportation functions under what ultimately became the Transportation Corps. The corps was responsible for all transportation at home and abroad, with the exception of air transportation, which was handled by the Army Air Forces. From the outset, the Transportation Corps had to contend with inadequate preparation, training, and personnel in handling its vast responsibilities. It was not until 1944 that the corps was fully on top of its job and had resolved numerous obstacles, of which supply was just one. By the end of hostilities, however, the corps was functioning in an effective way.[8]

The Quartermaster Corps was among the SA&Ss least prepared for World War II. That was the case because its interwar planning was among the weakest. At no time between 1939 and 1942 did the corps's operating and planning units merge; instead, they proceeded as if on unrelated planes until almost the end of 1942. The confusion resulting from those conditions was compounded by three different sets of requirement figures. Additionally, the corps was organized along centralized, commodity lines. That meant that major policies originated in Washington and that depots and other subdivisions specialized in one product, for example, subsistence, which they managed from procurement to issue. This structure was contrary to the whole thrust of interwar planning based on decentralization in order better to balance a vastly expanded emergency load.

The Quartermaster Corps managed to meet its responsibilities in the defense period despite its inadequate organization. The allocated facilities program proved to be helpful. Like all the other SA&Ss, the corps usually turned to those firms in awarding contracts. With Pearl Harbor, however, Quartermaster was forced to reorganize. Before that occurred, the War Department began to remove from the corps important functions, some of which the corps had handled since the Revolution. In December 1941, construction was placed under the Corps of Engineers; in March 1942, transportation was taken over by the Transportation Corps; and, finally, in August 1942, motor transportation was transferred to and consolidated in the Ordnance Department. Under the pressure of the Army Service Forces, the Quartermaster Corps was in a state of nearly constant reorganization throughout most of 1942. It adopted a functional organization—for example, procurement, storage, distribution, and the like—in place of the commodity structure. The corps also experimented unsuccessfully with decentralization. In the end, the Quartermaster Corps had a hybrid structure. It was mostly functional, with some commodity units, and principally centralized, although decentralization existed. That this system worked and was devised in the midst of crushing wartime demand stemmed in part from the quartermaster general, General Edmund B. Gregory, who served from 1940 into 1946. Gregory was an exceptionally flexible and able leader who was able to satisfy and win the support of both those above and those below him.[9]

Although Air Corps mobilization planning in the interwar years was also lacking, the corps's close working relations with the aircraft industry compensated for the weakness. Consequently, when wartime expansion got under way early in 1939, the Air Corps, more than other SA&Ss, drew on its practical knowledge to handle mobilization. Moreover, a flood of foreign orders soon acted to stretch the industry to its limits and increase industrial capacity. Until around mid-1940, the Air Corps's Materiel Division continued peacetime buying practices, which were based principally on the procurement districts. However, in December 1939, the planning and procurement functions were integrated, and, in 1940, the Air Corps seriously began using educational orders, small contracts negotiated with few restraints that were intended to prepare firms for mass production.

Roosevelt's fifty-thousand-plane program announced in May 1940 acted to free the Air Corps from the restrictions of peacetime procurement. Through a complex set of national and international agencies, and in combination with industry, the navy, civilian mobilization agencies, and spokesmen for foreign demand, the Air Corps (the Army Air Forces as of June 1941) became a major participant in a procurement process that made the United States the world's leading producer of military aircraft by December 1941. Before hostilities ended, the nation built nearly 300,000 military planes at a cost of around $45 billion, almost 25 percent of the nation's total munitions spending for World

War II. To achieve that record, the aircraft industry had to be vastly expanded at the government's expense, converted from hand to mass production, and greatly assisted through subcontracting to the converted automobile industry along with numerous other firms. War production made aircraft among the nation's giant industries. Buying aircraft and procurement planning in the inter-war years, along with developments during the defense period, prepared the military and the aircraft industry for the remarkable wartime achievements.[10]

The various SA&Ss remained the basic units for War Department procurement throughout the defense and war years. As defense spending began to increase from 1939 on, the bureaus' different structures, approaches, and levels of competence caused problems and concern. As long as Harry H. Woodring and Louis A. Johnson remained secretary and assistant secretary of war, respectively, and carried on their running battles with one another, department supply operations did not get the attention they needed. All that changed, however, when Henry L. Stimson and Robert P. Patterson took over as civilian heads of the War Department in July 1940.

Stimson's selection for the War Department office was largely the work of Grenville Clark, with Felix Frankfurter, then a Supreme Court justice, acting as intermediary with the White House. Clark was part of the upper-class, elite group in the Theodore Roosevelt–Elihu Root neo-Hamiltonian circle that was active in the pre–World War I preparedness movement and closely identified with the Plattsburg Movement.[11]

Once appointed secretary of war, Stimson created the most powerful executive department in Washington. The army's role as the largest of the armed services and the most important procurement agency in a major war automatically made the department a center of power. Stimson's prestige and the nature of his staff acted to multiply the War Department's influence several fold. Seventy-two years of age, Stimson was quintessentially elite in terms of education, wealth, social standing, and public service. He had been secretary of war and secretary of state in addition to holding other government posts. Both inside and outside government, when Stimson spoke and acted, others listened and moved. To carry out his duties as secretary of war, Stimson recruited a talented and influential staff, one that included Harvey H. Bundy, Robert A. Lovett, and John J. McCloy. More often than not, these men were New York attorneys and investment bankers trained at Yale or Harvard Law School and identifying with the international wing of the Republican Party. The war years prepared them for even more lofty roles. In the postwar years, they and those of similar backgrounds and persuasions conceived and implemented the nation's containment policies. Stimson, the figurative heir of the

Rough Rider and his coterie, was the mentor and model of America's "national security managers" during the Cold War years.[12]

As assistant secretary of war, Patterson was part of the deal that made Stimson secretary of war and added to the latter's political clout. He was also Harvard Law, had clerked in Clark's prestigious New York law firm (Root, Clark, Bucker, and Ballantine), and, at the time of his appointment, was a United States Circuit Court judge.

Heading the OASW, Patterson directed War Department procurement during the critical period July 1940–March 1942, when the Army Service Forces was created. In December 1940, Stimson persuaded Congress to amend the National Defense Act of 1920 in such a way that the assistant secretary of war was made an under secretary and performed his procurement and planning duties under the direction of the secretary instead having the statutory authority to do so on his own. By eliminating a legislative quirk of the 1920 law, this change gave the War Department a unified civilian command system and avoided a repetition of the paralyzing and unseemly conflict fought out by Woodring and Johnson.

In July 1940, Patterson reorganized his office so that the Current Procurement Branch, which had been relatively unimportant before 1939, could better handle its burgeoning load. It was divided into two branches. One, Purchases and Contracts, established and oversaw procurement policy, including legal and legislative affairs, and coordinated the activities of the SA&Ss. The other, Production, expedited the production and delivery of munitions and other products after contracts were let. Included in its duties were assembling requirements information, surveying industrial facilities, and administering priorities. Both branches operated through a number of subdivisions.

Patterson's reorganization was a step forward, but it caused problems for the Planning Branch, which had been instrumental to most of the procurement and economic mobilization planning in the interwar years. Without an M-Day and the creation of a single, authoritative civilian mobilization agency, as envisaged in the Industrial Mobilization Plan, the Planning Branch was thrown off balance. Had those developments taken place and army preparations been activated, all the numerous War Department supply subdivisions would have implemented mobilization plans, allowing the OASW and the ANMB to integrate army procurement into the operations of the civilian mobilization agency. Without an M-Day, and with the appointment of the amorphous National Defense Advisory Commission (NDAC), the Planning Branch and Patterson resisted merging the Planning Branch with the operating branches (the Purchases and Contracts Branch and the Production Branch) out of the hope that the Industrial Mobilization Plan would still be implemented and the Planning Branch accorded its proper place. Hence, the Planning Branch and the operating branches continued to function even though many of their duties overlapped. This created confusion in the War Department and among the SA&Ss.

In time, the Planning Branch and the operating branches worked out a compromise in which the former largely confined its activities to those handled by the ANMB and involving the larger aspects of economic mobilization, such as priorities, raw materials requirements, and relations with the NDAC and its successor agencies. Since, throughout most of 1940–1941 as before, the Planning Branch continued to do most of the work of the ANMB, this arrangement had positive aspects to it in the short run. In the long run, however, the Planning Branch inevitably slipped into insignificance along with the ANMB as various War Department reorganizations occurred. These developments were unfortunate since they gave an unintegrated quality to the mobilization effort of the Office of the Under Secretary of War (OUSW).[13]

Even merging the activities of the Planning Branch and the operating branches would not have ensured smooth operations in the OUSW. Patterson found the undistinguished quality and comparatively low rank of the officers in his office to be a hindrance to handling the vastly expanded and growing procurement program. Those limiting characteristics had plagued the OUSW before 1939, and they grew more serious after the outbreak of war in Europe as the responsibilities and size of the office grew exponentially. In July 1939, the office had a total strength of 78 officers and civilians. By November 1941, the number had grown to 1,136, 257 officers and 879 civilians. Facing a crushing load themselves, the SA&Ss continued to withhold their best men from the under secretary's office. Officers in general shunned supply assignments for command and combat roles, reserve officers tended to be of questionable ability, and talented civilians were difficult to recruit and harder to free from the supervision of mediocre officers.

Patterson quickly built up a personal staff of high-quality civilians and a few reserve officers to offset the personnel problems of his office. Although small in number, this staff played a major role in shaping policy for and determining the direction of the OUSW. Among its members was Julius H. Amberg, who acted as legal adviser to Patterson, as the under secretary's deputy at meetings of the civilian mobilization agencies, and as a principal spokesman for the War Department before Congress and in other capacities. Edward S. Greenbaum was another valued addition; he became Patterson's personal adviser and special representative and later served as general counsel to the Ordnance Department. Howard C. Petersen, a protégé of Grenville Clark, became Patterson's executive assistant and specialized in manpower policies and public relations. A young, bright, and energetic group of law school graduates, such as John H. Ohly and William Marbury, took on a variety of assignments. These men shared several characteristics. They were all attorneys who either graduated from Harvard Law or practiced in New York—usually both. A few varied from this pattern: Michael J. Madigan was a New York builder who first advised the under secretary of war on cantonment construction and later took on broader assignments; and Edward F. McGrady was a former assistant secretary of labor with extensive experience in labor relations who guided the office's contacts with unions and at times acted as a general troubleshooter. Patterson's staff members worked well together and were exceptionally loyal to him. Although at first resented by the regular army officers in the office, the newcomers were in time accepted by most because of their obvious talent and the invaluable assistance that they provided in handling the nearly overwhelming demands of the burgeoning munitions program.[14]

The composition of Patterson's staff was predictable, and it had both positive and negative qualities. The under secretary naturally turned to his profession, region, and class in recruiting the talent that he needed to fulfill his enormous responsibilities. Moreover, since expanding the munitions program was principally contractual, attorneys were probably best for getting procurement under way rapidly, a matter of the very highest priority for Stimson and Patterson. Along those lines, Patterson's staff proved to be especially bold and imaginative in circumventing the numerous peacetime obstacles to efficient procurement before Congress provided the exemptions necessary to handle the emergency. Additionally, for a number of reasons, the OUSW found it easier to attract first-rate legal talent than first-rate industrialists. This may have been a disadvantage in the long run. Industrialists might have brought greater perspective to the OUSW and convinced it that careful planning to maintain economic balance over a number of years was more important than speed in converting and expanding the economy for war production. Throughout the defense and war years, the War Department consistently stressed production without restraint and, too often, without adequate thought. That approach could and did act to the detriment of the department and the larger mobilization effort.

More immediately, Patterson and his aides could not correct the fundamentally flawed nature of the OUSW. They provided the leadership and improvisation essential for getting the office through the transition to war without securing its future. The office had not established effective control over the SA&Ss' procurement operations in the interwar years, and that goal could not be achieved under the intense pressures existing during the 1940–1941 defense period. Consequently, the SA&Ss remained a collection of independent fiefdoms largely answerable only to themselves. That was a reality that the chief of staff–General Staff found annoying in peacetime and totally unacceptable during hostilities. Even before Pearl Harbor, the chief of staff and his deputies had begun preparing to bring supply operations under their direction, and they quickly did so after war was declared.

Still, the OASW's interwar accomplishments far outweighed its failings. Twenty years of economic planning had converted the army as a whole to the imperatives of modern, industrialized warfare and prepared it to participate in the mobilization of the economy. Since that was the case, the chief of staff–General Staff's wartime takeover of supply operations had no ill effects. Even before the takeover occurred, Patterson recognized the importance of the interwar procurement planning to the progress that he and his staff made.[15] In a meaningful way, the military was better prepared for economic mobilization on the eve of World War II than were civilians, particularly when such weak and awkward agencies as the NDAC were involved. This situation created enormous problems between the military and civilians over harnessing the economy for war and made the conflict fundamentally different from that of World War I. During that war, the military resisted civilian authority because it did not know what to do and feared losing vital functions to civilian agencies; during World War II, a knowledgeable military viewed civilian agencies as standing in the way of the aggressive economic mobilization that the armed services favored.

THE NAVY DEPARTMENT

The Navy Department was less prepared than the War Department for the Second World War in terms of industrial mobilization.[16] During the interwar years, the department felt no urgency about supply and did not emphasize it. That was the case because the navy's efficient supply system built up during the late nineteenth century and the early twentieth had, unlike that of the army, met the procurement demands of World War I without difficulty. Confidence led to neglect. Moreover, with the National Defense Act of 1920, the War Department, not the Navy Department, received the statutory authority to carry out procurement and economic mobilization planning. The OASW attempted to draw the Navy Department into the planning through the ANMB, with only indifferent success. In the interwar years, the secretary of the navy, the supply, or material, bureaus, and the chief of naval operations all had some part in procurement and economic mobilization planning, but their roles and responsibilities—*cognizance* in navy parlance—were never clearly defined or even understood. Not recognizing the importance of such planning, the department's civilian and naval leadership did not move to improve it. As a result, the planning was carried out in a halfhearted way by officers without distinction or clout. Furthermore, the Bureau of Supplies and Accounts, which had emerged in the late nineteenth century and the early twentieth as the general purchasing agent for the navy and was a key source of the service's excellent performance during World War I, ossified in the 1920s and 1930s to the point that, when the defense expansion began in mid-1940, it saw no need even to modify peacetime practices.

In mid-1940, five bureaus procured and handled supply for the navy. The Bureau of Ships was responsible for the design, building, and maintenance of vessels; the Bureau of Supplies and Accounts took care of feeding and clothing the navy, general purchasing, the processing of orders by other bureaus, and maintaining money accounts and property inventory for the navy; the Bureau of Aeronautics purchased aircraft and other goods; the Bureau of Ordnance manufactured and bought guns, ammunition, bombs, torpedoes, armor, and the like; and the Bureau of Yards and Docks was responsible for the shore facilities at home and away from the continental borders. (The Bureau of Navigation—which became the Bureau of Naval Personnel in 1942—and the Bureau of Medicine and Surgery also did some buying, but the amounts were comparatively insignificant.) While the various bureaus varied in the quality of their operations, individually they were fiercely independent, often antiquated in operations, and largely uncoordinated. The navy's bureau system, unlike that of the army, was simply unprepared for the vast expansion during the defense period and after.

The basis for updating the navy's supply system emerged in July 1940 when Roosevelt selected Frank Knox, a prominent Republican and publisher of the *Chicago Daily News,* as his secretary of the navy. In August 1940, Knox turned to James V. Forrestal to fill the post of under secretary. President of the prestigious investment house Dillon, Read, and Company before coming to Washington, Forrestal ultimately struck a close alliance with Patterson, his counterpart and friend in the War Department, and recruited important elite representatives to help him fulfill his enormous responsibilities. First as under secretary of the navy, and later as secretary of the navy and the nation's first secretary of defense, Forrestal would join Stimson and Patterson in playing an important role in shaping the nation's Cold War defense establishment.

Knox assigned Forrestal the nearly overwhelming task of directing the material side of the Navy Department. That required bringing order, efficiency, and direction to the supply bureaus. Forrestal's first major step in that direction involved streamlining the navy's contracting system, which was divided among various bureaus, based largely on competitive bidding, and inadequately reviewed by the antiquated Judge Advocate General's office or the tiny Office of the Secretary of the Navy. After having the department's contracting methods reviewed by H. Struve Hensel, a prominent New York attorney, Forrestal moved as quickly as possible during the summer of 1941 to create in his office the civilian-staffed Procurement Legal Division. Through this division and its representatives serving in each of the bureaus, the under secretary of the navy, battling mightily the Judge Advocate General, the Bureau of Supplies and Accounts, and their supporters in the service and Congress, was able to begin modernizing the department's contracting process and establishing centralized control over it.

The legal and contractual reforms were only a beginning. Until the bureaus in general were brought under centralized control, the navy simply could not handle a wartime load. In January 1942, after receiving the recommendations of civilian assistants and some high-ranking naval officers, studying the situation for months, and considering various alternatives, Forrestal took advantage of the Pearl Harbor emergency to have created under his jurisdiction the Office of Procurement and Material (OP&M). The OP&M was the Navy Department's counterpart of the OUSW. On the basis of requirements from the chief of naval operations, it was to direct the bureaus' procurement, represent the navy in and before the civilian mobilization agencies, and take all other steps to ensure that the service's material needs were met. To head this office, Forrestal selected the chief of the Bureau of Ships, Admiral Samuel M. Robinson. The OP&M itself was staffed principally with civilians or recently commissioned reserve officers.

With these two major reforms, Forrestal and his assistants had gone far in changing the navy's business operations to meet the demands of a total war. Throughout hostilities, however, the secretary and under secretary, assisted by the personal intervention of the president, constantly had to guard against and beat back the efforts of Admiral Ernest J. King, commander-in-chief of the United States Fleet and chief of naval operations, to place the supply bureaus directly under his authority so as to eliminate any meaningful civilian control within the Navy Department. Such an outcome could have been disastrous for the navy since, unlike the army, its officer corps had not been educated about the procedures and necessities of mobilizing a mature industrial economy for war.

THE ARMY-NAVY MUNITIONS BOARD

Patterson and Forrestal, who took office at approximately the same time, began using the ANMB to coordinate the mobilization activities of the War and Navy Departments and to deal with the NDAC.[17] Patterson had headed the board as the army's representative, first as the assistant secretary, then, after December 1940, as under secretary. Forrestal did not sit on the board as joint chairman until June 1941. With two under secretaries in charge, the board now had greater prestige and power. Shortly after the under secretary of the navy joined the board, he and Patterson called on Ferdinand Eberstadt, a mutual friend and former partner in Dillon, Read, to review the ANMB's operations and propose changes to make it a more effective agency. On the basis of Eberstadt's thorough evaluation and proposed reforms, the ANMB was fundamentally reorganized in February 1942 and Eberstadt appointed its civilian chair. Actually, Eberstadt began to implement his recommendations in December 1941, before the reorganization became official. The board's greatest contribution to economic mobilization for war, therefore, came after the nation entered the Second World War. Nonetheless, it still had an effect on the effort to harness the economy during the defense period.

Under Secretary of War Patterson and Under Secretary of the Navy Forrestal both made significant progress in preparing their departments for the vast supply operations of World War II. Both relied heavily on an infusion of civilian elites for carrying out their duties. Through improvisation, Patterson succeeded in making the army's supply structure, which had been revamped after World War I, meet the growing defense requirements. Forrestal, however, immediately had to begin reforming his department since the navy had allowed its efficient supply system of World War I to stagnate. Beginning in the defense years, and continuing during World War II, the army led military procurement operations. It did so because its requirements were much greater than the navy's and its supply system more advanced.

3
THE NDAC IN OPERATION

Military requirements determined the nature and pace of the economic mobilization effort during the years of national defense and war. Since the armed services set their own requirements and procured their own goods, they played a critical role in shaping the operations of the prewar and wartime economy. Indeed, the military requirements and their feasibility were at the heart of the repeated controversies that racked the process of harnessing the economy for war between 1940 and 1945.

By July 1940, the Franklin D. Roosevelt administration had worked out a defense program through an elaborate negotiating process that involved the armed services, the National Defense Advisory Commission (NDAC), Congress, and, most important, the president. It included peacetime equipment for a 1.2-million-man army; reserves of critical items for another 800,000 men; industrial facilities essential to produce this equipment; a nearly 1.5-million-ton increase in the navy, which would expand its size by 70 percent and provide for a two-ocean force; and around 25,000 aircraft, with the navy receiving about 7,000 and the remainder going to the army. With modifications for aircraft and cantonment construction, this program defined the nation's defense effort through June 1941.[1]

In order to have meaning, this very general defense program had to be broken down into specific munitions, equipment, and supplies, components, and raw materials. Only in that way could the NDAC assist the armed services in scheduling production, ensuring that adequate facilities existed, and determining that overall demands on the economy were feasible.

Throughout 1940, the NDAC found the armed services to be deficient in providing it with the required information in a usable form. Partly this resulted from attitude. The navy was more cooperative than the army. With twenty years of economic planning on which to rely, the latter felt less dependent on civilian agencies than did the former, which had neglected the area. Probably of greater significance was the fact that neither of the services had adequate statistical capabilities. That and their decentralized procurement systems made it exceptionally difficult for them to provide reliable requirement figures. As a result, the NDAC often received statistics that changed radically within a short period of time, waited months for information on critical items such as high-octane aviation fuel, or had to make do with its own estimates. Actually, the army had better requirement figures than the navy, and the Army-Navy Munitions Board (ANMB), which the former dominated, provided the NDAC with quite good requirements for exclusively military products, projected on a month-to-month basis for two years and broken down according to raw materials and facilities. The ANMB, however, could not do the same with standard commercial products used by the Quartermaster Corps and the Bureau of Supplies and Accounts.[2]

Despite the limitations involving requirements, the NDAC cooperated with the armed services in getting the economic mobilization program under way between May and December 1940. Its most significant activity related to military procurement and included clearing contracts, passing on plant sites, arranging to build new or expand existing facilities, devising methods to finance the building/expansion effort, and formulating and administering priorities.

CONTRACT CLEARANCE

Contract clearance involved reviewing contracts to avoid conflicts among competing agencies, to maintain economic balance, and to protect the public interest.[3] Since contracts were the lifeblood of economic mobilization, this function could have placed in NDAC's hands centralized economic control. That did not turn out to be the case. The military managed procurement and largely negotiated or awarded its contracts subject only to nominal review by the NDAC. At all times the commission's authority in this area was nebulous. Two weeks after assigning, on May 24, 1940, the secretary of the treasury the task of reviewing all contracts for airplanes and their engines, the president transferred this responsibility to William S. Knudsen, the commissioner of production, and expanded it to include all "important" War and Navy Department contracts, important contracts ultimately coming to be defined as those totaling $500,000 or more. When Donald M. Nelson was appointed coordinator of national defense purchases, he was also directed to oversee government purchasing. The presidential assignments were strengthened by various provisions in congressional appropriations acts between June and October 1940, the Selective Service and Training Act of 1940, and other statutes. Nonetheless, the statutory authority to procure remained with the military, and the executive and legislative authorizations to the NDAC were always vague and subject to interpretation and challenge.

The NDAC ultimately divided the clearance functions between Knudsen and Nelson. The former handled ordnance and other "hard goods," while the latter concentrated on quartermaster supplies and "soft goods." Nelson had a greater impact on military procurement practices, but Knudsen's assignment affected the mobilization program more consequentially.

Knudsen's influence over procurement was never substantial because of his own attitude and the actions of the armed services. He worked closely with and deferred to the military, viewed the commission basically as an agency to facilitate expansion of the the army and the navy, and believed that the services should have the final say in ordnance and other products of a strictly military nature. On their part, the military services did not welcome the NDAC into the contracting process. While they submitted contracts to the commission for clearance, they usually did so when negotiations were all but completed. That left Knudsen and his associates with only a veto power, which they were hesitant to use out of fear of delaying the defense program. Moreover, once the NDAC had cleared a contract, the military felt free to modify the reviewed agreement.

To try to make the clearance function more effective, the NDAC between June and September 1940 worked out, in consultation with the War Department, an elaborate nine-point guide for military contracting. Besides speed, price, the reliability and experience of contractors, and the use of negotiated contracts where possible, the guide provided for relieving unemployment, avoiding congestion, and abiding by existing labor laws and other statutes and practices designed to protect the health and welfare of the worker and the general population. These guidelines were intended to include more NDAC members in the contract clearance process. In general, they changed little. More commissioners involved in clearance did not improve the NDAC's impact on contracting, and the army and navy continued to rely principally on speed of delivery and contractor reliability in awarding contracts. This resulted in most contracts going to congested or potentially congested areas and led to the neglect of social considerations. For example, the attempt of Sidney Hillman, Leon Henderson, and others to deny defense contracts to firms like the Ford Motor Company that violated the National Labor Relations Act led to a major showdown between management and labor and their private and public allies. In such encounters, labor invariably lost.[4] At the end of 1940, Knudsen was still struggling to improve the clearance function, without much success.

Donald M. Nelson had a greater impact on procurement because he worked with general, commercial products for which, unlike munitions, ample production facilities usually existed. Hence, by way of contrast with Knudsen, Nelson dealt principally with procurement, not production. Additionally, since the military claimed no expertise or pride of development and production in these areas, it was easier to work with. Moreover, while the coordinator of national defense purchases cleared contracts, more of his time was spent educating the military supply bureaus, and particularly the army's Quartermaster Corps, about the intricacies of purchasing standard commercial items in quantity. In general, the Quartermaster Corps and other military supply units cooperated well with Nelson and appreciated the assistance of his office.

Nelson recruited a group of talented executives to work with the military supply bureaus. These included Frank M. Folsom, executive vice-president of a Chicago department store, Robert A. Roos, president of a retail clothing firm in San Francisco, Douglas C. MacKeachie, New England purchasing director of the Great Atlantic and Pacific Tea Company, and Albert J. Browning, president of the United Wall Paper Factories of Chicago. They persuaded the armed services to rely on negotiated contracts over competitive bidding whenever possible in order to enhance control; to standardize, simplify, and broaden specifications so as to maximize the use of existing production facilities; and to time purchases so as best to exploit market conditions. Under prodding from Nelson's office, and with excellent results, the Quartermaster Corps scrapped decentralized buying of produce and meat for centralized procurement with middlemen excluded. In its most important reform, the Office of the Coordinator of Purchases instructed the military on "distributive buying": that is, distributing contracts according to the availability of facilities, workforce, materials, and infrastructure and the promise of continued production and stable prices. To facilitate such contracting, Nelson's office cleared contracts on the basis of information provided by the Departments of Labor, Commerce, and Agriculture and other government agencies such as the Federal Reserve System. Under all the above practices, it was much easier for the Quartermaster Corps and other supply bureaus to pay attention to the NDAC guidelines on contracting than was the case with munitions, and they did so. Nonetheless, the Office of the Coordinator of Purchases was efficient and effective, and Nelson was less beholden than Knudsen to the military, broader in outlook, and more liberal in his persuasions.

But Knudsen dealt principally with the nation's giant corporations, which received the bulk of contracts (measured in value), while Nelson, as reflected in his advisers and assistants, worked mainly with more modest-size businesses. From June to December 1940, the armed services awarded over $11 billion in contracts, with 60 percent going to twenty firms and 86.4 percent to one hundred companies. Consequently, what Knudsen did was always much more important than was the case with Nelson. That meant that the NDAC's clearance function was not particularly significant in shaping the program of economic mobilization in 1940.

PLANT SITES

Contract clearance was closely related to the NDAC approving sites for new or expanded munitions facilities financed by the government. These were usually plants manufacturing ordnance and other specialty products for the armed services. In appropriating funds to the War and Navy Department for such plants between June and October 1940, Congress required that the location and general plans for facilities be approved by the NDAC.

This congressional authorization set off a running dispute in the commission involving the agency's control over contracting. At the poles of this high-stakes quarrel were Chester C. Davis, commissioner of farm products, and Edward R. Stettinius, Jr., commissioner of industrial materials. Davis pushed for a broad interpretation of the congressional authorization: to fulfill its responsibilities, the NDAC needed to participate in and approve all armed services activities preliminary to and following plant site selection, including negotiating and overseeing the contract. Stettinius echoed the services' strict construction: the commission could suggest projects to the army and navy and veto their proposals; otherwise, their contracting powers, including plant site selection, remained inviolate. Davis could count on Henderson, Hillman, and Ralph Budd (who was interested in placing new plants in the Midwest and the South) to back him up. Nelson generally supported Davis, as did Harriet Elliott when she became involved in the process. Stettinius could depend on the support of Knudsen. At the request of the NDAC, the attorney general in February 1941 wrote an opinion in which he sought middle ground by arguing that, while the NDAC's powers were not simply passive and it could take an active role in plant expansion, the commission could not encroach on the military's statutory contracting authority. The decision was moot by that time since the moneys had already been spent and the commission had all but expired.[5]

Before that occurred, the NDAC attempted, without much success, to make its role in plant location meaningful.[6] Most of the problems stemmed from the War Department. The department created a Plant Site Board chaired by General Harry K. Rutherford, director of the Planning Branch, to coordinate facilities expansion by the various supply bureaus. This board dealt with the NDAC. On its part, the commission appointed Nelson, the coordinator of purchases, to act as liaison with the procurement agencies. The services were to submit proposals for new or expanded facilities to Nelson with information on what was to be built and the suitability of the site. Nelson would check with each commissioner; if there were no objections, the proposal would be approved. In practice, this procedure quickly broke down. War Department proposals usually included little information, dealt with one site only, and called for almost immediate approval. Furthermore, negotiations with contractors were already well advanced. The NDAC could do little but approve.

In an attempt to remedy this situation, new procedures were adopted in July and August at the instigation of Davis and Nelson. The War Department Plant Site Board and the NDAC would receive notice of a proposed site simultaneously and have five days to pass on it. Furthermore, the NDAC's Bureau of Research and Statistics would provide both the commission and the board with information on industrial profile, labor supply, housing, transportation, and the like for plant sites in order to facilitate intelligent decisionmaking. These reforms changed nothing. Some proposals never reached various commissioners, the army still insisted on almost instantaneous approval, and, if the NDAC rejected sites, the War Department simply resubmitted them. The last attempt at reform came in October 1940 when the NDAC and the War Department agreed that John Kenneth Galbraith—a member of Davis's staff who would be assisted by representatives from each commissioner and the Bureau of Research and Statistics—was to work directly with the Plant Site Board and have eight days to pass on all proposals, which would have alternate sites included. Again, there were no positive results. The War Department now strong-armed Galbraith, getting its way, and the NDAC legitimized decisions after the fact. A showdown of sorts occurred in November 1941 when Davis and Henderson tried to block a TNT plant in Sandusky, Ohio, because the area was already industrially impacted and alternate sites were available. Under sustained pressure from the War Department, the two commissioners ultimately backed off. In January 1941, the NDAC went so far as to approve a new Curtiss-Wright Corporation plant even though Davis and Hillman refused to go along.

The NDAC had little impact on plant site selection because the armed services refused to relinquish any of their statutory authority over contracting. And, within the commission, both Knudsen and Stettinius usually supported their position. For both the army and the navy, but especially the former, speed and reliability remained the principal criteria for selecting contractors. This meant turning to the nation's largest corporations. These firms either expanded their existing plants or built new ones, tending to prefer having additional facilities close to the existing ones east of the Mississippi. Indeed, when

in July 1940 the War Department submitted a map for locating new munitions firms to the NDAC, Budd and others were shocked to see that the western half of the United States was excluded. This orientation grew out of the
twenty years of planning by the Office of the Assistant Secretary of War
(OASW) involving existing industry concentrated mostly in the Northeast.
That reality, however, violated a basis tenet of the president, who declared in
May 1940 that, for strategic reasons, the nation would locate new production
facilities between the two main mountain ranges. It also violated the president's declaration that economic mobilization would result in neither the
neglect nor the reversal of the social gains made by the New Deal. As it turned
out, labor supply, labor policy, community facilities, and existing infrastructure had little or nothing to do with the location of expanding industrial facilities. The demands of the Midwest and the South for industrial plants to aid in
diversifying their regions and generally improve economic conditions also went
unheeded.

With both contracting and plant sites, an informal economic mobilization
structure, shaped by the ideals of the Industrial Mobilization Plan (IMP), was
emerging from the outset of the NDAC. It was one in which the armed services, the large corporate structure, and the commissioners of industrial production and industrial materials began working as a team representing demand
and supply and adopting and implementing policies that were mutually beneficial. This team regularly turned back the advocacy of the commissioners of
labor and agriculture, spokespersons for less developed regions, and representatives of consumers along with those such as Henderson who viewed themselves as guardians of larger public concerns.

FACILITIES EXPANSION

The dynamics of contracting and plant sites was also evident when it came to
the decisionmaking process for expanding basic industries. However, that
process was open to different influences because of the methods used to
finance industrial growth. NDAC as a whole was able to make its voice heard
for a time. And, with the government financing most plant expansion, Congress and other federal agencies helped set policy.

The NDAC played a significant role in getting over $9 billion in facilities
expansion under way. This was the commission's most significant accomplishment.[7] The commission also contributed meaningfully to the Roosevelt
administration's economic mobilization goals. Given limited military and naval
appropriations in 1940, the administration, on the basis of anticipated strate-

gic conditions, emphasized building plant and equipment. According to this thinking, the expanded manufacturing capacity would be completed in 1941, and the mass flow of weapons and supplies would commence in 1942.

Plant expansion met great resistance. Industry was not anxious to take up munitions production in 1940, for a number of reasons. Expanding capacity after a decade of depression was hazardous; civilian markets at home and abroad were growing; the outcome of the war in Europe was uncertain; and government contracts meant red tape and dealing with the New Deal enemy. For their part, the armed services estimated requirements that were generally low, unreliable, and shifting, which complicated planning for industrial expansion enormously and often resulted in the military siding with industry in resisting growth, particularly where basic industries such as steel, aluminum, rubber, and copper were involved. Finally, prior to the major German offensive launched in the spring of 1940, Congress dragged its heels on increasing military appropriations, never provided enough money for facilities, and was slow in passing legislation to encourage plant growth.

Attitudes toward facilities expansion outside NDAC were reflected within the agency. Stettinius was most strongly influenced by industry's opposition to expansion, and he was usually supported by Knudsen where basic industries were involved. (However, the latter played a critical role in expanding the output of aircraft and other munitions.) The principal advocates of maximizing the nation's general and munitions production capacity were Nelson, handling purchasing, Henderson, covering prices, and Hillman, speaking for labor. Budd, Davis, and Elliott, representing transportation, agriculture, and consumers, respectively, were more interested in where facilities were located and how they affected communities and interest groups than in expansion per se.

Even general agreement on the need to expand the nation's plant for war would not have produced the desired results in the NDAC period. Congress appropriated only around $750 million to the armed services for building additional facilities in the last half of 1940. To advance the munitions program, the Roosevelt administration had either to induce private financing or to devise new approaches. It met the challenge through accelerating the amortization of defense plants, the Emergency Plant Facilities (EPF) contract, and, most important, the Defense Plant Corporation (DPC).

Given the World War I experience, most assumed that private financing would cover the majority of defense and war plants. That was not the case. From 1940 to 1945, the nation increased its inventory of manufacturing plant and equipment for defense and war by nearly $26 billion, roughly two-thirds of the unadjusted dollar value of what existed at the beginning of 1940. Only $8.6 billion, or about one-third of the growth, was covered by private sources.

The rest came from direct government financing (principally by the army and navy), which totaled approximately $8.9 billion, indirect government financing through the Reconstruction Finance Corporation (RFC) and its defense subsidiaries, which made loans totaling over $7 billion, and miscellaneous sources, which provided a lesser amount.

Public policies to facilitate these results were not easy to come by. Between July and October 1940, the Roosevelt administration and Congress struggled long and hard to fashion legislation to encourage private expansion of defense plants yet protect the public against the real and alleged abuses of World War I. Industry was anxious to have additional defense plants in private hands, and bankers were eager to participate in the new opportunities. Both desired to keep government construction and financing to a minimum and feared any additional New Deal experiments. New Dealers were just as concerned that the Roosevelt administration not become the captive of industrial and financial interests.

Within NDAC, John D. Biggers, Nelson, and Henderson—representing the commission's right, center, and left, respectively—led in devising policies of compromise to further private plant expansion. In October 1940, Congress largely enacted their handiwork in the Second Revenue Act. The legislators suspended provisions of the Vinson-Trammel Act of 1934, which had been amended by June 1940 to limit profits on army and navy contracts and subcontracts for aircraft and vessels to 8 percent of costs, and substituted a new excess profits taxation law. They additionally adopted a program for accelerating depreciation of plant and equipment from the usual twenty and ten years, respectively, to five years or the duration of the emergency for facilities completed after June 10, 1940 (later moved back to December 31, 1939). To qualify for the faster amortization, the NDAC and either the secretary of war or the secretary of the navy had to issue a certificate of necessity confirming that the facility was essential to national defense. A second validation by the same sources was also required: either a certificate of nonreimbursement, to ensure that the contractor was not including in the price of his product more than normal depreciation of the facility; or, if the contractor was doing so, a certificate of government protection, guaranteeing that the government's interest in future use or disposition of the facility was protected.

Accelerated depreciation worked only where the facility had unquestioned commercial value. Where that was not the case, Washington turned to the EPF contract and the DPC. The NDAC devised the EPF contract between June and October 1940. It worked in this way. The armed services or other procurement agencies negotiated with a firm a supply contract that included the construction or conversion of buildings and, optionally, equipment. The contractor financed the expansion on his own. On completion, and when production of the end item was under way, the procurement agency reimbursed the contractor for all costs through sixty equal payments and, at the end, took title to the property. This arrangement precluded the contractor from including any compensation for the facility in the supply price. When the contract was completed, the contractor could buy the facility for cost less depreciation or a negotiated price. The government agreed not to operate the plant for commercial purposes and to allow the contractor to buy the plant before selling it to a third party. To ease the way for these contracts, Congress, at the behest of the NDAC, passed the Assignment of Claims Act of October 1940, which allowed the sixty government payments to the contractor to go directly to a financial institution. In that way, the contractor could more readily obtain financing to build and equip the facility.

The DPC as a source for financing plant expansion originated with liberal and imaginative staff members of the conservatively run, cautious RFC who were anxious to increase output for defense. Backing from the White House also helped. In June 1940, Congress passed legislation allowing the RFC to further national defense through financial assistance and the creation of subsidiary organizations. Under these new powers, the RFC made a limited number of loans for plant construction, equipment, and working capital, but its most significant contribution came from the operation of four defense subsidiaries: the Rubber Reserve Company and the Metals Reserve Company, created in June 1940, and the Defense Supplies Corporation and the DPC, established in August. Of the four, the DPC was the most important.

The DPC financing of plant and equipment was basically worked out in the last half of 1940. It was based on supply contracts awarded by the War Department and other procurement agencies during an emergency of five years or less. Several approaches were used. For noncompetitive plants manufacturing specialized products for the military, the DPC financed approved facilities, took title to the property, leased it to the contractor for only a nominal rent, and prohibited him from including any cost of the plant in calculations of prices or tax liabilities. The War or Navy Department, in turn, paid the DPC around two-fifths of all costs within a few years and committed itself to cover the rest through future appropriations. When all costs were paid, title would be transferred to the War or Navy Department. At the end of the emergency, the contractor had the option of buying the plant under complicated formulas intended to cover costs to the government. Variations on this formula existed for competitive facilities producing exclusively for the government, those dividing output between defense and commerce, those supplying defense contractors, and those manufacturing basic commodities such as aluminum. In these instances, actual rents were paid, pricing and depreciation practices differed, and the procurement agencies' financial obligations to the DPC varied.

Rapid amortization, the EPF contract, and DPC financing had mixed results in 1940. The encouragement of private financing of defense facilities through accelerated depreciation got off to a slow start. Once the statute was on the books, the NDAC and the War and Navy Departments had to set up organizations and write regulations to administer the law. Particularly challenging were the certificates of necessity, nonreimbursement, and government protection. The military could not proceed without NDAC approval, as was the case with contracts and plant sites, and the commission would not rubber-stamp armed services decisions. Some industrialists within the NDAC worried about overexpanding the productive base, and others in Henderson's orbit wanted to ensure that business did not reap undue gain and that the public was protected. As a result, and to the growing anger and frustration of the military, which stressed speed over close scrutiny, the NDAC at times proceeded deliberately in passing on the various certificates. Ultimately, the military also got its way in this area. The commission began bowing to army and navy pressure by granting certificates with less than conscientious review. Finally, in October 1941, Congress ended the NDAC's existence by removing it as a certifying agency, in effect leaving the matter solely to the procurement agencies.

Despite numerous delays, accelerated amortization still accounted for 57 percent of defense facilities completed before Pearl Harbor. The figure dropped to about 33 percent for the defense and war years as a whole. The War Department was the largest certifying agency, with the aircraft, aviation gasoline, light metals, machinery and electrical equipment, and machine-tool industries, along with the railroads, the main beneficiaries of the practice. Although most certificates were for plant and equipment under $300,000, eighty-nine of the nation's largest firms, such as the United States Steel Corporation, received somewhat over half the certificates of necessity.

The EPF contract, by comparison, was a flop. Throughout the defense and war years, only $350 million in such contracts was negotiated. This attempt to encourage private financing turned out to be a bureaucratic nightmare for all involved. It made nearly impossible demands on industry, threatened the interests of manufacturers and bankers alike, and needlessly tied up scarce government funds earmarked for new facilities. Although never enthusiastic about the EPF contract, the War Department finally gave up on this fundamentally flawed instrument.

The DPC was to defense financing everything that the EPF contract was not. It was flexible and simple and provided the security that industry needed. The DPC staff had excellent relations with the procurement agencies and would initiate financing on a call from them. Since the procurement agencies paid only a portion of DPC-financed facilities, their appropriations for plant were stretched manyfold—over three times, according to one estimate for the War Department. Without publicity, and facing much opposition, DPC financing reached $250 million by the end of 1940 and then grew rapidly. The War Department was the biggest user of the DPC, accounting for around 40 percent of its loans, with the Army Air Forces responsible for nearly 83 percent of that figure. The average DPC loan was $3 million, and most loans went to commercial-type facilities, especially the aircraft, basic metals, synthetic rubber, shipbuilding, and machine-tool industries. At least half of DPC investment was for plants operated by giant corporations, with the Aluminum Company of America (Alcoa), the General Motors Corporation, U.S. Steel, and the Curtiss-Wright Corporation topping the list.

Before financing arrangements had been completed for defense plants, other steps were taken to speed munitions production. Starting in June 1940, Congress passed legislation to allow the military to let contracts by negotiation instead of advertised bid, to use the cost-plus-fixed-fee contract, to ease financing by making substantial advances of working capital to contractors, and to waive or limit the use of various cumbersome bonds in the contracting process.

The NDAC participated in almost all the facilities expansion during the last half of 1940, with Knudsen's Production Division leading the way. For military construction, the division's Construction Section, headed by William H. Harrison, vice-president and chief engineer of the American Telephone and Telegraph Company, joined the Quartermaster Corps and the Bureau of Yards and Docks to assist in huge building programs. The section's greatest contribution involved recruiting architects and engineers to plan the army's cantonments and camps and then assisting in almost every stage of construction. Defense housing presented greater difficulty for the commission. Knudsen wanted control in the area, but so did Hillman's Labor Division and Elliott's Consumer Protection Division. In an attempt to get around the jurisdictional dispute, the commission created the position of defense housing coordinator in July, but the contending forces in the NDAC refused to give the coordinator the latitude needed to do his job. As a result, Roosevelt moved the coordinator's office from the NDAC to the Office for Emergency Management in January 1941. Nonetheless, other federal agencies moved to commit $227 million for defense housing in the last half of 1940, and private investment went as high as $1,237 billion. Overall, the NDAC contributed in ways big and small to having the defense building program on schedule by the end of 1940.

The NDAC's role in expanding industrial plant was crucial. Again, Knudsen's division was the key one. Growth was greatest in the aircraft industry.

In 1938, the industry had begun to expand under the stimulus of domestic and foreign demand and, particularly, orders from Great Britain and France, which became heavy in 1939–1940. By mid-1940, the aircraft industry had spent over $52 million in new plant and equipment, and investment by Great Britain and France went over $72 million. As a result, floor space for airframes more than doubled and for engines tripled. When Roosevelt called for an annual aircraft capacity of fifty thousand planes in May 1940, the industry could produce only fifteen thousand a year maximum. In 1944, the nation turned out more than ninety-six-thousand military planes. To accomplish that remarkable record, the industry had to be vastly expanded, converted from a handwork to a mass production basis, and assisted by subcontractors from the automobile and other industries. Between 1940 and 1945, nearly $4 billion was invested in the aircraft industry, 90 percent of which was direct government investment, primarily through the DPC, and most of the rest was covered by accelerated depreciation.

Knudsen and his high-powered Aeronautical Section joined Under Secretary of War Patterson and Air Corps officers in Washington and Wright Field to get the expansion under way. Practically an extension of the National Advisory Committee for Aeronautics, the Aeronautical Section was led at the outset by George J. Mead, a former vice-president of United Aircraft Corporation, and Theodore P. Wright, vice-president of Curtiss-Wright Corporation.[8] While the Navy Department also procured planes, the Air Corps had the navy's agreement to take responsibility for most plants as the major buyer.

In the first phase of expansion, summer and fall 1940, the major airframe firms, such as North American Aviation, Incorporated, Consolidated Aircraft Corporation, and Douglas Aircraft Company, Incorporated, preferred to expand their existing plant, and that was the principal mode of growth, although some new facilities were also built and equipped. Engines were the bottleneck of production and presented greater problems. Wright Aeronautical Corporation and Pratt and Whitney Aircraft dominated the industry and could not increase their output enough to meet demand. The automobile industry had to be brought in. In June 1940, Knudsen arranged for the Packard Motor Car Company to take up production of the British Rolls-Royce Merlin engine, and, in September, he persuaded the Ford Motor Company to build a new plant to manufacture engines as a licensee of Pratt and Whitney. This was the start of a much larger role for Detroit in the airplane field. The government's aircraft production team also had to coordinate the simultaneous expansion of propellers, landing gear, and other parts and accessories.

This initial expansion had barely started in the fall of 1940 when demand for bombers skyrocketed, setting off a second wave of growth. The old pattern of building on the basis of the existing airframe firms had to be scrapped for another approach, one involving new locations and again including automobile companies. In order for that new approach to be implemented, several conditions had to be met. First, the government had to take responsibility for building plants to overcome industry's fear of owning excessive and useless capacity in an uncertain postwar world. It did this with the EPF contract, accelerated amortization, and, most important, DPC financing. Second, aircraft firms had to have a guarantee from the automobile companies that the latter would not enter the former's postwar markets, and such an assurance was given. Third, leadership and coordination were essential for organizing what turned out to be production pools. These came largely from Knudsen and his Aeronautical Section, the Air Corps's Materiel Division, backed up by the under secretary of war, and, to a lesser degree, the Navy Department's Bureau of Aeronautics. Critical assistance was also supplied by industrial organizations such as the Automobile Manufacturers Association and the Automotive Committee for Air Defense.

Ultimately, four new bomber plants were located in Omaha, Nebraska, Kansas City, Kansas, Tulsa, Oklahoma, and Fort Worth, Texas. These were locations that were uncongested, had good flying weather, and had or could easily be provided with the necessary housing, transportation, labor supply, and the like. The major airframe firms operated these plants, at which they manufactured the fuselages and assembled the planes. Parts and accessories (e.g., instrument panels, tires, gun turrets, and oleo struts) and subassemblies (e.g., wings and tail sections) were supplied by the automobile companies and other firms. At the Omaha plant, for example, the Glenn L. Martin Company was the contractor and the Chrysler, Hudson Motor Car, and Goodyear Aircraft Corporations the subcontractors. The automobile companies used their existing plants or privately financed expansion. Ford's new Willow Run facility for "knockdown" and "flyaway" planes was an exception. At the urging of Knudsen and others, automobile firms followed the example of Packard and Ford to take up aircraft engine production, usually as licensees and in new government-built plants.

Contracts for the new airplane production pools were not signed until February and March 1941. Nonetheless, they were an outstanding accomplishment of the NDAC. In the last six months of 1940, $81 million was spent on new plant and equipment for airplane production, $50 million of which was private. An overall total of $516 million in facility expansion had been initiated.

After aircraft, the military built and financed directly most defense facilities in the last half of 1940. For the army, these were so-called government-owned, contractor-operated plants for the output of arms, ammunition, and other munitions. They had virtually no commercial value, and the military preferred to own them in order to maintain reserve production capacity during years of peace. By early 1941, the War Department had let contracts for over $1 billion in this category, with most facilities built for the Ordnance Department and the rest divided among the Chemical Warfare Service, the Air Corps, and other bureaus.

Facilities for shipbuilding and ship repair also expanded. Less urgency existed in these areas since the 70 percent growth in the navy's fleet was scheduled to take place over a six-year period from 1940 through 1946. Nonetheless, substantially more plant was needed. Demand for smaller vessels, such as landing and patrol craft and motor torpedo boats, went up along with requirements for cargo ships. Additionally, the United States Coast Guard and the army also began to procure. To oversee and coordinate naval and private shipbuilding, Knudsen received the president's approval for Admiral Emory S. Land, chairman of the United States Maritime Commission, to serve simultaneously as head of the Production Division's Shipbuilding Section.

In mid-1940, the nation had a substantial plant on the Atlantic, Pacific, and Gulf Coasts for building deep-water ships. It consisted of twenty private yards with eighty-two shipways and eight navy yards with eighteen shipways. Most of those yards could be expanded. Additionally, 174 yards existed for constructing smaller vessels, and a number of idle facilities could be activated. With these facilities, the navy was able to begin the vast expansion authorized in June and July 1940 without difficulty, and both the navy and the private yards began to increase their capacity to handle a growing load. It was mid-1941 before the navy undertook extended expansion of shipbuilding capacity to meet its needs. Cargo ships did not become a problem until Britain requested that sixty Liberty ships be built in the United States and the United States's own projected requirements began to be considered. This led to a proposal in December 1940 for building seven new yards with fifty-one shipways. Contracts were signed and the program initiated in February 1941. Much greater and faster growth in yards and ways followed.

Bottlenecks for naval and maritime shipbuilding stemmed more from shortages of equipment, materials, machinery, and parts than from yards. As early as fall 1940, the limited supply of machine tools constituted a threat to shipbuilding, and, by spring 1941, turbines, gears, and steel valves joined the list. Labor, and particularly skilled labor, was a chronic problem. One of the greatest threats was the shortage of steel, anticipated as early as fall 1940, and a reality as early as spring 1941.

All in all, the NDAC, the armed services, and the Maritime Commission did remarkably well in beginning the vast expansion of facilities for munitions during the last half of 1940. The Production Division and Knudsen himself played a vital role in most of what was done.

A similar record was not achieved by Stettinius's Industrial Materials Division. Indeed, the reluctance to expand the nation's plant in terms of basic metals, synthetic rubber, and other products remains controversial even today. Actually, much of what the Industrial Materials Division did grew out of the interwar commodity committee planning of the OASW. The OASW's work after 1939 was done in the name of the ANMB. The relation between Stettinius's division and the ANMB was that proposed in the IMP. Such an outcome is hardly surprising since, in 1939, Stettinius chaired the War Resources Board (WRB), which endorsed the IMP, and key industrialists, their spokesmen, and the War Department never surrendered their commitment to the ANMB's handiwork. In a sense, then, the WRB continued after its formal demise late in 1939 in the form of Stettinius's division.

The ANMB had calculated anticipated requirements and supply for most of the nation's industrial materials, classifying them as *strategic* (e.g., ferrograde manganese), *critical* (e.g., wool), or *essential* (e.g., lumber). It usually worked closely with industry during the 1920s and 1930s in arriving at its figures, and the Industrial Materials Division endorsed these calculations. For chemicals, Stettinius's division simply took over the ANMB's Chemical Advisory Committee, using the requirements and supply figures of its subcommittees to guide its work for aviation gasoline, explosives, and synthetic rubber. In general, the ANMB estimated that, for metals, minerals, chemicals, and agricultural and forest product, supplies either were adequate or could quickly be made so and that little basic expansion of capacity was necessary. Stettinius's division accepted and worked on this premise.

The Industrial Materials Division and ANMB responsibilities carried over into export controls and the stockpiling of strategic and critical materials. The combined statistical and industrial information of the division and the board was used to set policy for limiting the export of materials and goods essential to the national defense. It also gave them a key role in stockpiling strategic and critical materials. Between June 1939 and June 1940, Congress appropriated $70 million for that purpose, and a host of government agencies strove to implement goals set by the NDAC and ANMB. Stettinius's division was given to extremely optimistic assessments of the success of the stockpile, which were misleading and not justified by the facts. Those within the Industrial Materials Division and the ANMB who were in the know forced a reassessment.

What occurred with stockpiling was symptomatic of the Industrial Materials Division's approach to production capacity for basic metals. The division was sanguine about the ability of existing plant to meet defense and wartime demand and very hesitant to push for expansion. It was reflecting the industry's concern about excess capacity, market shares, government regulation, and the like. Moreover, ANMB figures on supply and demand supported the Industrial Materials Division's complacency. Consequently, the division accepted the steel industry's assurance that it could handle military needs; it refused to move on high-octane gasoline without requirement figures from the armed services. It also assumed that Alcoa's expansion and the new entry of the Reynolds Metal Company ensured ample aluminum production despite burgeoning airplane requirements, and it allowed the RFC to take responsibility for synthetic rubber and cut projected production first by 60 and then by 90 percent. Some expansion occurred voluntarily in various industries, the division increased output for heavy steel forging and armor plate, and capacity was expanded to some degree for manganese, zinc, and copper. However, such progress was in response to immediate demand, not projected need for future emergencies. The Bureau of Research and Statistics, along with various statistical offices in the Industrial Materials Division, did persuade the division to raise its requirement figures substantially. Additionally, numerous agencies and individuals involved with the defense program insisted that the productive plant for high-octane gasoline, steel, and other materials was inadequate. Either they had no impact, or the action taken was inadequate.

A common problem plagued the Production and the Industrial Materials Divisions in their approach to facilities expansion: no long-term munitions program existed to guide their work. Hence, the NDAC was forced to make decisions on the basis of immediate demand and vague proposals about future requirements. To correct this condition, both Knudsen and Stettinius favored creating a high-level executive council to formulate national defense strategy.

Leon Henderson, however, was the most consistent and persistent advocate of such a council during the NDAC period. He proposed that the president set up a planning agency to work out a wartime national economic strategy that would cover a three- to four-year period and would include the requirements of Great Britain as well as the United States. Representatives from the State, War, and Navy Departments and the NDAC would make up this panel. It would guide the commission or a like body in working out and implementing general and specific policies for economic mobilization in which all procurement would be scheduled, plant sites and contracts properly reviewed, and decisions on prices and priorities made free of industry and military control. Donald M. Nelson seconded Henderson's proposals, and nearly all members of the NDAC at a minimum supported strengthening and centralizing the commission's functions.

Agreement about the need for a new or restructured economic mobilization system broke down over how the economy should be prepared for war.

This was made clear by the differing views on plant expansion. Stettinius argued that the nation's basic industries, such as steel and oil, could handle all antici- pated demand, obviating the need for a larger plant. Knudsen was less sanguine but maintained that, where additional capacity was necessary, it be created by the building of new plants. Henderson and Nelson insisted that the demands of war required expanding the industrial base. In addition, they argued, indus- trial conversion for war purposes had to be initiated and the defense and war load distributed among small businesses, not concentrated solely in the hands of the industrial giants. Budd stood somewhere between Knudsen and Hen- derson, while Hillman, Davis, and Elliott sided with Henderson.

The NDAC never arrived at any set policy on plant expansion, which left matters to the day-to-day decisionmaking of the Production and Industrial Materials Divisions, working with the armed services. The outcome was in- creased production capacity, but through the building of new or expanded facilities principally by big corporations, not the conversion of existing facili- ties or the use of the nation's entire industrial plant.

The NDAC made some effort to include small business in the expanding defense program, without much success. Nelson had focused on the matter from the outset, and, at his initiative, he was appointed director of small busi- ness activities in October 1940. He used the Federal Reserve System as his field staff and to facilitate finances. Sidney Hillman's Labor Division also assisted Nelson's activities. Despite imaginative programs for pooling small business plants and resources for handling larger contracts or subcontracts, little headway was made. The procurement agencies preferred to deal with the reliable large firms that they had surveyed in the past, and they had no poli- cies involving subcontracting. Some small and medium-size firms benefited from subcontracts, but most subcontracts went to large companies.

PRIORITIES

Priorities was the one mobilization function in which the NDAC gained some meaningful authority.[9] This was of great importance since, in theory, priori- ties could be used to shape the entire economic mobilization program. Rank- ing contracts according to importance determines the use of facilities and the flow of materials and labor. From June to October 1940, when industrial capacity was adequate to meet all demand, priorities were intended to prevent the army and navy from distorting the economy by competing for output, overloading contractors, hoarding goods, and the like. In the last months of the year, demand in some areas was beginning to exceed what the existing plant could produce. The priorities function then had to begin expanding to handle private and foreign as well as public requirements.

By December 1940, the War and Navy Departments had successfully out-maneuvered the NDAC in a protracted struggle over priorities. The services always had an advantage over the commission because of their procurement rights, planning and contracting experience, and field staff. However, the NDAC was not without strength. Most recognized that a general mobilization agency, not claimants, needed to control priorities in order to maintain economic balance. Roosevelt endorsed that position by delegating to the NDAC his statutory authority over priorities.

Congress created the legal basis for a priority system in an act of June 28, 1940, that authorized the president to grant priority to orders for the army and navy over those for private use or export. Anticipating the statute, on June 17, 1940, the ANMB set up a Priorities Committee, and Nelson, when appointed coordinator of national defense purchases on June 27, was charged with studying and making recommendations to the president on priority matters. The ANMB and Nelson worked together in devising a voluntary system of *preferences*—a euphemism for *priorities,* used to avoid alarming the public—in which the ANMB would assign ratings to military orders according to their urgency. Since Roosevelt had yet to delegate his priority authority and the economy could handle all known demand, this informal approach was considered to be adequate. Procurement officers assigned the preference ratings under the direction of the ANMB's Priorities Committee, and the committee settled conflicts between the army and the navy. Difficulties that could not be worked out at this level were referred to Nelson for resolution. When the armed services tried to gain independent priority powers through provisions of the Selective Service and Training Act of September 1940, the NDAC moved quickly to block their way. At the outset, therefore, the NDAC and the military shared responsibility over the operations of a voluntary priority scheme.

A production crisis in October resulted in a restructuring of the priorities system. By that time, the combined American and British aircraft program had become so great that firms could no longer meet their schedules for producing commercial planes. The War Department proposed solving the problem by halting most commercial output, a solution that the NDAC believed to be detrimental to defense production and the nation's foreign commitments. This dispute raised the issue of priorities as they applied to civilian output. To protect the economy, the NDAC had to take a more direct and active role in determining priority policy.

Two months of bureaucratic jockeying produced a more formal priority system. Acting on the initiative of the NDAC, the president in October issued an executive order creating within the commission a Priorities Board and delegating to it his statutory powers over priorities. The NDAC and the War and Navy Departments then engaged in extended negotiations over how the modified system would work. Under an agreement finalized in mid-December 1940, the voluntary preference approach for military orders was continued, such controls could be extended to the civilian sector, and mandatory ratings could be introduced when necessary and possible.

The NDAC's Priorities Board exercised supervisory control over priorities, settled any conflict between the armed services and other government agencies or foreign sources, and handled nonmilitary ratings. Operating under the Priorities Board, the ANMB's Priorities Committee continued to oversee preference ratings for the army and navy, including the mediation of disputes. To assist industries critical to national defense and facing production problems, the NDAC Priorities Board set up special priority committees. These committees were made up of representatives from the armed services and the industries involved. The Priorities Board appointed such subordinate bodies for commercial aircraft, machine tools, iron and steel, aluminum, and synthetic rubber. Most priority activity still took place under the ANMB, but the NDAC's Priorities Board and its subdivisions also began to issue preference ratings. Throughout the NDAC's active life, however, all priority ratings remained voluntary.

The importance of priorities was demonstrated by the fact that, in the last months of 1940, various NDAC divisions began shifting sections, such as that dealing with machine tools, and personnel to the Priorities Board. Activity within the commission naturally gravitated to the genuine source of power.

Nonetheless, the armed services ended up dominating the new priorities system. Donald M. Nelson, the administrator of priorities, inexplicably, and over the protests of the Industrial Materials and Production Divisions, granted the ANMB Priorities Committee the authority to write its own rules and determine which items would be subject to preference ratings. The Priorities Board reserved the right to concur and approve changes involving priorities, but this negative control proved to be all but meaningless. The ANMB's Priorities Committee, therefore, began operating autonomously and even extended its reach over civilian production. However, the ANMB never established meaningful control over the army and navy supply bureaus. That left procurement officers to operate largely without supervision. As a result, by December 1940, the armed services had already issued so many preference orders that the priorities system was threatened.

That outcome was predictable. In the NDAC period, the armed services under War Department leadership proved to be very adept at holding off NDAC control (as took place in contracting, plant sites, and facilities expansion) and taking over functions (such as priorities) that only a general mobilization agency could meaningfully perform. The military was much less effective in conducting its procurement in a way that maintained economic balance. The large corporate structure with which the army and navy principally dealt offset the services' parochialism to some degree. Nevertheless, the corporate giants realized that the army and navy could not safely be allowed to operate on their own. Stettinius's Industrial Materials Division, which big business dominated, was the most persistent voice insisting that the NDAC forcefully supervise priority operations. Moreover, Knudsen and his assistant Biggers, along with Nelson and Henderson, argued that, if procurement had been carried out in a more rational way, the need for using priority controls would have been much less. Later in 1940, an angry Biggers protested that the armed services cooperated with the commission at the outset because they depended on its prestige to accelerate economic mobilization. Once large-scale procurement was under way and the military had ample congressional appropriations, the army and navy went off on their own since they felt less beholden to the commissioners. This undermined the NDAC's efforts to harness the economy effectively for defense and war production.[10]

Priorities involving domestic production were closely related to foreign trade and output and to aid for the Allies. The Roosevelt administration created in July 1940 an administrator of export control to regulate the flow abroad of strategic and critical materials and to initiate elements of economic warfare. The NDAC and ANMB played a significant role in guiding the activities of this administration. Economic warfare also involved aiding the Allies. Roosevelt depended on an informal structure to facilitate this process in 1939–1940 and then in mid-1940 set up the Interdepartmental Committee for Coordination of Foreign and Domestic Military Purchases (or the President's Liaison Committee), under Treasury Department direction, to oversee Allied purchases and American assistance to Great Britain. Allied buying here accelerated the growth of the domestic munitions plants, and American assistance to Great Britain grew increasingly large and important throughout 1940, especially where aircraft were involved.[11]

CONCLUSION: FROM NDAC TO OPM

The NDAC's usefulness was largely over by the end of 1940. A more effective mobilization body had become imperative. Military demand was growing rapidly, what would become Lend-Lease was in the works, and the nation was inching closer to war.

Actually, the commission had accomplished quite a bit despite its awkward, makeshift nature. Under steady pressure from the commissioners, the armed services had upped their requirements. More generally, the NDAC had introduced, if not implemented, most controls basic to economic mobilization, including coordinating procurement, assessing and expanding facilities, considering the feasibility of defense demand, regulating prices, and determining priorities. The most outstanding achievement was the commission's role in initiating a multimillion-dollar facilities construction program that provided the basis for vastly expanded munitions production in subsequent years.

Nonetheless, the commission's liabilities outweighed its strengths. NDAC was intended only to advise the president on economic mobilization policies. By necessity, seven independent commissioners began operating collectively in order to carry out mobilization functions that no other agency existed to perform. Despite assignments from the president and Congress, however, the NDAC never had sufficient authority to fulfill its responsibilities.

The commission's weakness was most consequential in dealing with the armed services and their procurement functions. In six months of operations, the commission could not make its decisions stick for contract clearance, plant site location, the building and financing of facilities, or priorities. With the War Department leading the way, the military ignored the commissioners or manipulated and bullied them to get its way. Since throughout most of 1940 the nation was still flush in terms of plant, materials, labor, utilities, and transportation, the NDAC could assist the armed services on their terms without harming the economy. By late 1940, however, those conditions were changing. Huge procurement programs were creating general or regional shortages of plant, material, labor, housing, community facilities, and the like. Maintaining economic balance depended on the civilian mobilization agencies having enough authority to bend the military services to their will in key areas such as procurement practices and priorities.

Roosevelt had neither the time nor the inclination to restructure the mobilization system until after the presidential election.[12] Once the election campaign was behind him, the president faced intense pressure from all sides to institute change. Corporate America rallied behind the IMP, which the WRB had reviewed and endorsed late in 1939. Wendell L. Wilkie supported such an approach while campaigning for the presidency, Robert Taft (R-OH) introduced a bill in the Senate to accomplish the same end, and William Knudsen spelled out in detail for the president how such a system would work. Since the IMP originated with the War Department, it had the full support of the military.

But the IMP was no more acceptable to the president late in 1940 than it had been in 1939. Turning the economy over to one-man rule under industry-military domination was out of the question. America was still too divided about foreign policy, class passions from the depression remained strong, and interest groups like organized labor were opposed to the way even the NDAC worked. Instead, these interest groups favored Leon Henderson's proposal for centralizing mobilization functions and freeing them from industry and military control. Additionally, the president was still determined to keep the economic mobilization reins in his own hands.

Prospects for reorganizing the mobilization system intensified the struggle between business and New Dealers that had racked the NDAC from the outset. Significantly, the military stepped in to bolster industry, while the White House acted on behalf of New Dealers. With Roosevelt unwilling to accept the IMP, Secretary of War Henry L. Stimson in December led in working out an alternate approach. He combined his efforts with those of Secretary of the Navy Frank Knox, Assistant Secretary of the Navy James V. Forrestal, and William S. Knudsen to come up with a proposal for a three-man board to direct industrial mobilization, made up of Knudsen as chair and the secretaries of war and the navy. Such a board, ideally, would ensure sound mobilization policies and win the support of both industry and the military. In that way, two related problems would be solved: the troublesome pluralism of the NDAC would be ended, and the new board, in contrast with the commission, stood a good chance of having its decisions enforced.

Roosevelt accepted Stimson's recommendation, with one major modification. He dictated that the three-man board be expanded to include Sidney Hillman as Knudsen's equal. The president appeared to be acting on the advice of Harry L. Hopkins. Knudsen was taken aback by this change, but the War and Navy Departments went along because they felt that Hillman could be handled.

Pressured by the military, and disturbed by the growing mobilization power struggle, Roosevelt late in December rushed to announce the creation of the four-man board that ultimately was named the Office of Production Management (OPM). He did so before the proposal had been fully worked out or an executive order to implement it written. The details were left to the Bureau of the Budget and several presidential assistants. That created another round of intrigue as industry, with at least the backing of the military, sought to have Hillman demoted to Knudsen's assistant in the executive order setting up the OPM. Roosevelt and Hopkins again stepped in to protect Hillman.

Throughout the period from November through January, the Bureau of the Budget constantly fretted about the right system for harnessing the economy. It proposed that Roosevelt scatter responsibility among various agencies that would be under a small, elite staff in the Office for Emergency Management. This staff would oversee all mobilization functions and also plan for the future. Bureau of the Budget Director Harold D. Smith, public administration specialist Louis Brownlow, and others favored this approach in order to maintain executive control over the homefront and to initiate long-term, comprehensive planning that neither the NDAC nor any other government agency was performing. Also involved was Smith's ambition to act as assistant president for domestic affairs, a position eventually filled by James F. Byrnes during the war years. Roosevelt was initially favorable to the Bureau of the Budget approach, but Stimson's group swayed him to its position. The closest that the Bureau of the Budget came to having its views adopted was in blocking Knudsen from appointing Frederick M. Eaton—his legal counsel in the NDAC—as secretary of the OPM. At the suggestion of Smith, Roosevelt selected Herbert Emmerich for the post (which was later elevated to executive secretary) to help straighten out the twisted mobilization system and bring professional credentials to it.

Emmerich was a Louis Brownlow protégé and civil servant who had been involved in the reorganization of the executive branch in the late 1930s. In a sense, Emmerich was taking over the position in OPM that William H. McReynolds held in NDAC. If the former, unlike the latter, could make his office a center of power in the OPM, Smith and his associates as civil servants would play a major role in economic mobilization.

Both the Bureau of the Budget and New Dealers considered the OPM a victory for business. And they were right. The institutionalized pluralism of the NDAC was being narrowed. Gone from the policymaking board for economic mobilization were representatives of agriculture and the consumer. Agencies in their behalf, as was the case with price controls, would be set up outside the office. OPM narrowed the economic mobilization focus to munitions and what was essential to produce them. A labor/New Deal representative was a member of OPM, but Stimson was right in assessing Hillman as no more than a manageable irritant. On any critical issue, the spokesmen for industry and the military could easily push through their goals.

The key to OPM was bringing industry and the military institutionally closer together. That would serve more effectively than NDAC to link the procurement operations of the latter with the mobilization functions of the former for the purpose of maximizing production while maintaining economic balance. For those goals to be achieved, however, industry had to be much more willing to lean on the military than had been the case in the NDAC. But that did not take place. Consequently, with OPM, as with NDAC, two only partially related mobilization systems in effect continued to operate, which limited what could be done.

Roosevelt was aware of what was taking place. He used the initiative and ideas of others to shape OPM as he wanted. The president favored the desire of Smith, Brownlow, and others to have economic mobilization directed by civil servants from the Office of the President. He also shared some of the statist views of Henderson, although without the latter's aggressiveness. But he was more interested in getting the job done than in pursuing administrative theories about the executive or righting the scales of power in a corporate capitalist system. In that regard, he supported Henderson, Hillman, and Nelson, at least in part because they were the most astute and zealous in advancing economic preparedness. Moreover, the president was genuinely sympathetic to interest groups other than industry, and he was fully aware of the need to cover his political flank as he maneuvered the nation along a path that currently meant extending unlimited aid to the Allies and would most likely lead to war.

With the OPM, the president kept economic mobilization decisions in his own hands and gave labor and reformers a voice in the new agency. That allowed him to take another major step in cementing the alliance between industry and the military. The president was not ideologically wedded to that alliance, nor did he appear particularly concerned about its long-run consequences.[13] However, his decisionmaking clearly indicated that he saw such an alliance as the safest and surest way of ensuring that the economy was effectively mobilized. Always the pragmatic reformer, the president understood that the vast corporate community had to be the foundation for any mobilization system. Since the armed services had the responsibility and the authority for procuring most defense and war demand, they would have to work closely with business. Exactly how industry and the military were coordinated within mobilization structures depended on the opportunities and the needs that arose as America inched closer to hostilities.

PART TWO
THE OFFICE OF PRODUCTION MANAGEMENT AND THE SUPPLY PRIORITIES AND ALLOCATIONS BOARD

The Office of Production Management (OPM) supervised economic mobilization throughout 1941. Focusing principally on munitions, benefiting from better organization, and gaining a greater measure of authority, the office was an improvement over the National Defense Advisory Commission (NDAC). OPM managed escalating weapons demand more effectively as the United States continued to prepare for war in Europe and Asia and increased assistance to its future allies.

Despite greater strength, OPM faltered in mastering multiple challenges. External and internal sources disrupted its operations. From the outside, the armed services caused the most grief. Consistent with past practices, they were deficient in providing the office with adequate requirement figures, and they continued to resist the office's role in contract clearance, plant site location, facilities programs, and priorities. Economic mobilization still emanated from two poorly coordinated centers.

Conflict inside the civilian mobilization system compounded OPM difficulties. The Franklin D. Roosevelt administration in April 1941 created the Office of Price Administration and Civilian Supply (OPACS) to control prices and to protect the civilian sector as defense production caused shortages in basic materials. Leon Henderson headed the new agency, one staffed principally with economists, academics, and civil servants. For civilian supply, Henderson's organization operated through the OPM, an arrangement bound to generate trouble since OPACS favored converting civilian industries to maximize defense output. The industry-dominated OPM opposed most OPACS initiatives, leading to growing disputes between the two agencies and within OPM because some of its executives favored the OPACS approach.

73

OPM's troubles with the military and OPACS were related in curious ways. Despite numerous differences, OPM business executives and armed forces officials shared mobilization outlooks. As a carryover from NDAC, William S. Knudsen and his lieutenants considered OPM to be a service agency for the army and navy. In the face of conflict over fundamental issues, industry and the military tended to stand together. Opposition to this informal alliance came from "all-outers," such as Donald M. Nelson in the OPM and Henderson in OPACS.

By mid-1941, mobilization disputes reached the point of threatening current and future defense production. To resolve the strife, Roosevelt in August 1941 separated price control from OPACS and moved civilian supply to OPM. Simultaneously, the president placed OPM under the Supply Priorities and Allocations Board (SPAB), a policymaking body weighted in favor of all-outers. While organizationally awkward, SPAB succeeded in estimating requirements for global war, protecting aid to the Allies, hastening the expansion and conversion of industry, and refining priority and allocation functions. By the time of Pearl Harbor, the nation had been made ready for a centralized agency to direct the wartime economy.

4
STRUCTURE AND STAFFING
OF OPM, OPACS, AND SPAB

The Office of Production Management (OPM) improved the mobilization structure considerably. Although awkward, a dual directorship was better than no executive head, as was the case with the National Defense Advisory Commission (NDAC). Centered around divisions for production, priorities, and purchasing, OPM also concentrated more directly on munitions output than had its predecessor. By drawing industry and the military closer together, OPM was a more conservative agency than was NDAC. This trend was made obvious in a number of ways. Labor, for example, began declining in power. Along the same lines, nonbusiness professionals in the Bureau of Research and Statistics came under sharper attack and faced organizational challenges from newly created subdivisions like the Production Planning Board (PPB). The rightward trend of OPM was most clearly manifest in reorganizations that structured the office so that it more closely resembled the World War I War Industries Board (WIB) as proposed by the military's Industrial Mobilization Plan (IMP). Accordingly, dollar-a-year men from industry, business, and finance, assisted by industry advisory committees, increased their hold on OPM even though they operated under greater restrictions than they did during World War I.

Under the conservatively directed OPM, however, harnessing the economy for war stalled. Industry opposed rapidly accelerating the mobilization program, and an uncertain military held back from pressuring corporations to do more. To stimulate munitions output and bring greater balance to the mobilization effort, President Franklin D. Roosevelt in April 1941 created the Office of Price Administration and Civilian Supply (OPACS). The new office was headed and largely staffed by hard-hitting New Dealers who were also "all-outers" in terms of preparing the economy for war. OPACS succeeded in invigorating the mobilization program, but at the cost of instigating bureaucratic warfare with OPM. Roosevelt resolved the conflict in August 1941 by dispersing OPACS's operations and placing OPM under the direction of the

Supply Priorities and Allocations Board (SPAB). Dominated by New Deal all-outers, the board helped restore order and give momentum to the mobilization effort in the months before Pearl Harbor. In a masterful performance, the president maneuvered among reform and nonreform groups to get mobilization under way in 1940 and 1941.

OPM

An executive order of January 7, 1941, charged the OPM with taking all possible measures to expedite defense production, including activity in the areas of requirements, procurement, facilities and equipment, and raw materials.[1] In pursuing these responsibilities, the office was restricted to surveying, planning, advising, stimulating, and coordinating. Only with priority functions was it granted some real authority. Nonetheless, OPM was a significant step in the direction of centralizing control over a mobilized economy, particularly when it is compared with the formless NDAC. This was evident in policymaking and executive direction. A four-person council composed of the secretaries of war and the navy and William S. Knudsen and Sidney Hillman formulated policy for OPM. The office was supervised by a dual executive, with Knudsen serving as director general and Hillman as associate director general.

The OPM's charges were much more specific than were the NDAC's. However, its latitude was narrower since it was restricted to defense production. The secretaries of war and the navy were included in the OPM's policy council to gain military support for OPM activity and to relate more closely production and procurement functions. In that way, the armed services as the major defense claimants on the economy could act to strengthen the civilian mobilization agency instead of undermining it, as had occurred with NDAC.

The OPM was also strengthened by the selection of Herbert Emmerich as secretary (elevated to executive secretary in September 1941) and the creation of the Legal Division, headed by John Lord O'Brian as general counsel. Emmerich was a public administration specialist in the Louis Brownlow circle who had served as deputy governor of the Farm Credit Administration and as a consultant to the President's Committee on Administrative Management. The Bureau of the Budget hoped that Emmerich would succeed in bringing active, professional, and nonpartisan direction to the OPM instead of repeating William H. McReynolds's dismal performance in a similar position with the NDAC. Actually, Emmerich owed his appointment to Hillman's staff. Frederick M. Eaton, who had served as Knudsen's counsel in NDAC, took over as acting secretary of OPM. When the executive order for the office was being written, Eaton joined John D. Biggers and others in attempting to subordinate Hillman to Knudsen. Hillman was willing to overlook Eaton's maneuvering, but Hillman's staff and various New Dealers were not, and they took their case to the president. Agreeing that a neutral professional should fill the position, Roosevelt adroitly forced Emmerich on a surprised and displeased Knudsen. In the light of the extraordinarily complex dynamics and politics of OPM, Emmerich did reasonably well in the job.[2]

The impact of John Lord O'Brian was even greater. O'Brian had had a long and distinguished government career as director of the Justice Department's War Emergency Division during World War I and the Antitrust Division under the Herbert Hoover administration. His appointment stemmed from the OPM council's decision to end the exceptionally divisive NDAC practice of each division appointing its own counsel. O'Brian moved quickly to centralize and professionalize legal operations in the OPM. All divisions were assigned an assistant legal counsel operating out of the Legal Division. O'Brian would allow no member of the Legal Division to be hired on a dollar-a-year status or to continue a private practice. He also insisted that no person with legal training could serve OPM in any capacity without his approval.

Working with the attorney general, O'Brian began to write and institute explicit rules for the use of those serving in OPM without salary or for nominal pay. He also introduced new policies on the use of industry advisory committees designed to end WIB and National Recovery Administration (NRA) practices in which businessmen directly and indirectly made public policy. O'Brian sought to strengthen both the Legal Division and the OPM as government agencies clearly distinguished from industry and its representatives. He was only partially successful in attaining the goals.[3]

THE DIVISIONS OF PRODUCTION, PRIORITIES, AND PURCHASING

Although OPM differed from NDAC in a number of important ways, the office still evolved from the commission instead of being a significantly new agency. OPM was built around three NDAC divisions or subdivisions that were transferred to it because they dealt most directly with output for defense: Production; Priorities; and Purchasing—see chart 2. (Offices for prices, labor, agriculture, consumers, and transportation were brought into the OPM only later, were set up as separate entities, or were handled by other agencies.) OPM was also largely staffed by those who had served in NDAC, although there were some new faces and various officers moved to different positions.

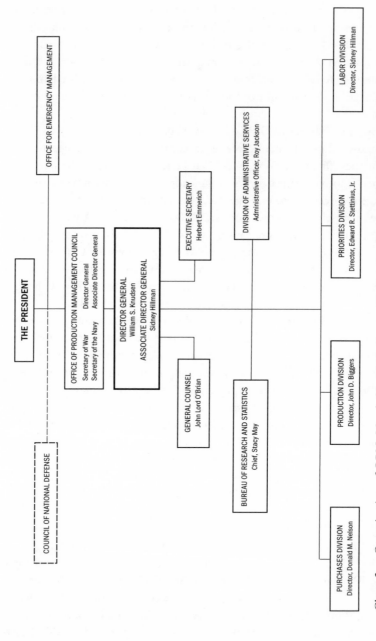

Chart 2. Organization of OPM, March 31, 1941. *Source:* Civilian Production Administration, *Industrial Mobilization for War: History of the War Production Board and Predecessor Agencies, 1940–1945* (Washington, DC: Civilian Production Administration, 1947), p. 99.

As with the NDAC, key executive positions were filled with dollar-a-year men, who were growing in numbers. The Production Division accounted for half of such personnel, with nearly one-quarter of its people in that category. Over one-fifth of the Priorities Division served for a nominal salary, and, in the Purchases Division, the figure was in excess of one-third. Additionally, the informal and varied industrial advisory committees of the commission carried over to serve various divisions of OPM for a few months, with the Priorities Division leading in their use.[4]

All in all, then, OPM was a pared-down version of NDAC, one that was focused on defense output and that ultimately gained a greater measure of authority than the NDAC had had. It was an important, interim step in the direction of creating the War Production Board (WPB) as the principal agency for mobilizing the World War II economy.

Of the three principal OPM subdivisions, the Production Division was the most important. John D. Biggers, who had served as Knudsen's assistant for production in the NDAC, now directed production activity, and William L. Batt took over as deputy director. The Industrial Materials Division, which Edward R. Stettinius, Jr., had headed in the NDAC, was downgraded to a branch of the Production Division. Two other branches filled out this division—one for aircraft, ordnance, and tools, the other for ships, construction, and supplies.

With its responsibilities overlapping those of other OPM subunits, the Production Division acted to ensure that sources of supply were adequate to meet existing and anticipated defense demand. Continuing NDAC activity, that meant expanding plant where necessary for critical materials, equipment, and manufactured items, and importing and stockpiling goods. New approaches became necessary, however, as defense output grew, shortages of materials and plant multiplied, and economic dislocations mounted. Building or expanding facilities and continuing unlimited production for civilian uses had to be curtailed. The massive consumer durable goods industries, like automobiles, simultaneously had to be converted to defense output both to halt their consumption of vital commodities and to increase munitions production, as with airplanes. Curtailment inevitably led to unemployment, which conversion could solve. If labor was adversely affected by the defense program, so too was small business. Military contracts went principally to big business at a time when growing shortages of critical materials threatened the existence of small producers. Special effort was required to channel defense contracts to small manufacturers.[5]

With defense production increasing in 1941 and shortages of plants, equipment, and materials becoming more common, the Production Division relied increasingly on the Priorities Division to fulfill its duties. Stettinius, who had directed Industrial Materials in the NDAC, took charge of Priorities. At the outset, his division, like NDAC, had only the president's delegated and limited statutory authority. By May 1941, however, the Priorities Division was positioned to wield real, instead of circumscribed, power when Congress extended significantly the president's priority authority. Intense mobilization conflict delayed Roosevelt's action until the end of August 1941.[6]

Donald M. Nelson's purchasing staff from NDAC moved over practically as a unit to constitute the OPM's Purchasing Division. The division was to direct all purchasing, instead of having that function divided between the Production Division and the coordinator of national defense purchases, as was done in the commission.

Nelson had to fight hard between January and March 1941 to gain for his division meaningful authority over military purchasing, including specifications, contract clearance, plant sites, subcontracting, and facilities expansion. Moreover, if disagreements arose between his division and the armed services, Nelson insisted, he had to have the final word as director of purchases. Otherwise, he maintained, OPM would be as ineffective in this vital area as the NDAC had been. Nelson's interpretation apparently had been agreed to in advance because Roosevelt in general terms endorsed it when announcing the OPM's creation. However, Secretary of War Henry L. Stimson and Secretary of the Navy Frank Knox rejected granting Nelson such unlimited authority, insisting that his division should have no more than advisory powers. The two secretaries were supported by Knudsen, who seemed rather unsure and confused about the issues involved and was being pushed by John D. Biggers (still playing the unofficial role as Knudsen's deputy) and Frederick M. Eaton (serving as acting secretary of the office). The latter two were out to enhance their own power, reduce that of Nelson, and protect industry-military relations as they had operated in NDAC. Nelson's threat to resign, and the intervention of the Bureau of the Budget and the president on his behalf, resolved the dispute in the favor of the director of purchases. He was granted most of the powers that he desired, but not that of settling disputes between his office and the armed services.[7] Despite this substantial victory, the army and navy continued to procure largely free of OPM supervision.

THE LABOR DIVISION

Transferring the Labor Division from NDAC to OPM was also complicated and took place under circumstances that created present and future problems.[8]

The Bureau of the Budget considered moving NDAC's Labor Division to the Office for Emergency Management so that it would have direct access to the president. Such a solution was impractical for a number of reasons. Most immediately in the eyes of Roosevelt and others, Hillman could not head an agency outside OPM and still be OPM's associate director. Yet no one else could effectively lead the Labor Division. Hillman stood practically alone in the promise of bridging the bitter divisions between the American Federation of Labor (AFL) and the Congress of Industrial Organizations (CIO) while attempting to convince management of the crucial role of unions in mobilizing the economy. Hillman wanted to direct the Labor Division within OPM but without answering to Knudsen, a solution that was unfeasible. Hillman's illness and uncertainty about where the Labor Division should be delayed its transfer to OPM until mid-March 1941. Labor was the only subunit of the OPM in which one or both of the dual executives wore two hats, although Knudsen virtually acted as head of the Production Division.

The Labor Division never became a meaningful participant in the production functions of OPM. This resulted partly from Hillman's view of his office. Basing his position on NDAC operations, he considered labor to be an "equal and coordinate," rather than an integral, part of the mobilization agency. Had the head of the Labor Division thought otherwise, however, the outcome would probably have been the same. The business, industry, and finance executives staffing OPM and their advisers generally frowned on labor serving in the agency, and they were determined to keep unions out of production matters and limited to labor relations and labor supply matters.

Various labor spokesmen in and outside OPM sought to extend labor's role in the office to include all aspects of defense production. At best, they received only tepid support from a cautious Hillman. Their ambitious goal for unions in OPM operations was always an uphill fight, one made much more difficult by the fact that the Labor Division was deeply divided on many levels.

Matters were made worse by the fact that Hillman's division was never in full charge of defense labor policy. The Labor Department resented it as a competitor for power, the National Labor Relations Board was free of its control, the National Defense Mediation Board was created in March 1941 outside its structure, and the army and navy's labor offices paralleled in part its structure.

Facing numerous challenges with divided ranks, the Labor Division was not well positioned to extend its reach from labor to production functions. Nonetheless, before Pearl Harbor, it made some progress in broadening its field of operations.

THE BUREAU OF RESEARCH AND STATISTICS AND
THE PRODUCTION PLANNING BOARD

The Bureau of Research and Statistics faced almost as much hostility from industry as did the Labor Division.[9] Consequently, transferring the bureau from the NDAC to the OPM was not easy. The Bureau of the Budget favored placing Research and Statistics in the Office for Emergency Management so that it could serve as a centralized statistical office for the entire mobilization effort. This idea was rejected early since OPM insisted on independence in the area. A struggle then ensued as to the place and role of the bureau in OPM.

Absorbed in immediate production problems, industrialists tended not to be convinced of the need for statistical services, they suspected the Bureau of Research and Statistics to be a stronghold of New Dealers and academics intent on increasing the pace of defense production (a group now labeled *all-outers*), and they were concerned about the influence of statisticians and economists on policymakers. To protect their interests, businessmen wanted to subordinate statistical functions and planning to operations. Industry's hostility toward Research and Statistics began in the NDAC. Henderson had the bureau placed under his jurisdiction in the commission to preserve its existence and to prevent its duties from being divided among various divisions.

The wrangle over the bureau's status was not a petty bureaucratic matter; it was central to power and control in the mobilization agencies. Statistical functions and economic analysis and planning could be used to shape the nature and tempo of the mobilization program. Of particular importance were military requirements, the drive wheel of any mobilization program. If statistical services were in production units, armed services demand would be handled at that level; if those functions were centralized, the army and navy would deal with offices above the commodity sections.

The OPM was essentially offered three proposals for dealing with the Bureau of Research and Statistics. Stacy May, chief of the NDAC bureau, favored a centralized, divisional office that would calculate military and civilian requirements, measure them against productive capacity, and determine the impact of defense output on the economy. The operating divisions could carry out research in specialized areas. Biggers, the most aggressive spokesman for corporate America in NDAC and OPM, insisted on decentralizing research and statistical analysis to the operating units. A centralized management committee would then set appropriate statistical standards and perform duties common to all divisions. Isador Lubin, who was commissioner of labor statistics in the Department of Labor and who had served in Hillman's NDAC and OPM divisions, offered a compromise in his plan for Research and Statistics to remain a bureau (instead of becoming a division), reporting to Knudsen and Hillman. It would perform OPM's statistical, research, and economic planning functions and arrange for the operating units to carry out research particular to their needs.

Once reconciled to Research and Statistics being located in OPM, the Bureau of the Budget supported Lubin's ideas. In working to implement this approach, the bureau had to block a move to place Research and Statistics under a management or sponsoring committee, as was proposed by the bureau's critics and adamantly opposed by Stacy May. With Knudsen's backing and the help of William L. Batt (a patrician industrialist wedded to New Deal flexibility), the Bureau of the Budget by early March implemented Lubin's system by making Research and Statistics's charges general and avoiding whenever possible the most controversial areas. Nonetheless, the bureau ultimately operated largely as May had intended. Although a committee made up of representatives of OPM divisions, procurement agencies, and others was set up to advise May, it disbanded after one meeting.

The dispute over Research and Statistics had grown so acrimonious that Stacy May felt obliged to offer his resignation to Knudsen, a gesture the latter politely turned aside. Nonetheless, the future success of May's bureau depended on its ability to convince industrialists of the importance of statistical services to policymaking. Conservative forces within the mobilization structure also had to be assured that an agency controlled by economists, statisticians, and academics did not threaten their interests.

In February 1941, before the Bureau of Research and Statistics was transferred to OPM, conservative forces created the PPB as a counterweight to it.[10] John D. Biggers led the way. The PPB was the lineal descendant of the War Resources Board (WRB), which had achieved continuity of sorts through Stettinius's Industrial Materials Division in the NDAC.

Biggers argued that the operating executives of OPM would be so absorbed in everyday production problems that short- and long-term planning would be neglected, leaving OPM as rudderless as the NDAC had been. He wanted the PPB to serve under OPM, but Knudsen, who never fully appreciated or supported planning and perhaps sensed that PPB would compete with the Bureau of Research and Statistics, insisted that the board serve in Biggers's Production Division. Biggers wanted PPB to plan for immediate and long-run needs in harnessing the economy by studying World War I mobilization, the IMP, and the NDAC experience.

The board's personnel established its close link with the War and Navy Departments' industrial mobilization planning: John Lee Pratt, formerly a General Motors Corporation executive vice-president, had served on the WRB;

William E. Levis, chairman of the board of Owen-Illinois Glass Company, had worked with the Production Planning Division of the Surgeon General's Office; General Harry K. Rutherford, who replaced the original army appointee shortly after the board got under way, headed the Office of the Under Secretary of War's Planning Branch and had been secretary of the WRB; retired Admiral William H. Standley had been chief of naval operations from 1933 to 1937; and the chair, Samuel R. Fuller, Jr., president of both the North American Rayon Corporation and the American Bemberg Corporation, had headed up steel and machine-tool purchasing for the navy during World War I. On the board also sat Robert E. Doherty, president of the Carnegie Institute of Technology, George W. Meany, an AFL officer, and James B. Carey, spokesman for the CIO. Harry L. Hopkins was also appointed to the board in the hope of establishing a direct line to the White House, but he dropped out after the first meeting, apparently sensing that the board would go nowhere. Like the WRB, the PPB tapped the Brookings Institution—presided over by WRB member Harold G. Moulton—for research purposes.

During its short life of around five months, the PPB was unable clearly to define its planning role or even how its economic analysis should be carried out. Rutherford attempted to convince the board that any long-range planning depended on concentrating on current mobilization problems such as the economy's productive capacity and the availability of industrial facilities and materials to meet estimated defense requirements. He pointed to aircraft and ordnance production goals as examples. Knudsen similarly urged PPB to zero in on shortages of aluminum, magnesium, and other critical materials as a way to assist the operating units of OPM. To accomplish such goals, Rutherford maintained that the PPB required an economic analysis subdivision similar to the Bureau of Statistics and Research. The board never followed this advice in any systematic way. Instead, individual members cursorily studied military requirements, critical raw materials, priority and allocation systems, labor supply, and like subjects. Specific recommendations resulting from these studies were by necessity superficial; they were supplemented by PPB generalizations about its functions and the board's overall assessments of OPM progress and failures. At least touching on nearly every major issue of consequence to economic mobilization, PPB's piecemeal, scattershot approach minimized its impact on OPM.

Despite its limitations, the PPB still made a positive contribution. The board's legacy resulted from its tenacious, even rigid, championing of two principal causes: restructuring the principal economic mobilization agency along the lines set forth in the IMP and establishing set strategic goals to facilitate calculating short- and long-run requirements. The board led in initiat-

ing the first reorganization of the OPM in June 1941 along commodity section–industrial advisory committee lines reminiscent of the World War I WIB.
Moreover, the PPB had a part in getting under way during the summer of
1941 what came to be called the Victory Program (still being refined at the
time of Pearl Harbor): an assessment of munitions output necessary for defeating potential enemies if the United States were to assist the Allies either as a
belligerent or as a nonbelligerent.

Before its major achievements were realized, the PPB sought to elevate its
status by being placed under the OPM's director and associate director. This
objective was attained in June, but it did not improve the board's performance. PPB could not demonstrate its usefulness to OPM or the various operating divisions, and it began to divide over basic recommendations to Knudsen
and Hillman. Doherty, who became chair in April, tried to regain momentum
for the board by strengthening its research arm. As the board's end neared in
July, he rather desperately proposed, along with other options, reorganizing
PPB and providing it with a small professional staff assisted by the Brookings
Institution and the Bureau of Research and Statistics. In that way, the board
could coordinate divisional activity. But by then it was too late. Roosevelt
called for what became the Victory Program at about the same time that
Doherty was casting about for ways to make the PPB meaningful. The statistical analysis for the president's project had to be done by the Bureau of
Research and Statistics because the PPB could not handle the job. The board,
in effect, was left with nothing to do. Doherty resigned, and the PPB met for
the last time on July 23, 1941.

The PPB was paradoxical from beginning to end. Conservative forces in
the OPM neither wanted nor trusted planning bodies outside their control.
Hence, they set up PPB to check the Bureau of Research and Statistics without hiring the statisticians and economists necessary to do so. (The then moderately conservative Brookings Institution was no substitute in that regard.)
Had Biggers and others worked either to provide PPB with an adequate staff
or to incorporate the Bureau of Research and Statistics in the board, they
would then have ended up with another suspected, perhaps feared, institution. Corporate executives attempted to mobilize the economy without proper
statistical and economic analysis. That approach worked with the NDAC after
a fashion because facilities and materials were in ample supply. Widespread
and growing shortages during the OPM era necessitated a more rigorous, systematic method, one of which an ineffective PPB was not capable.

By placing OPM under the high-powered SPAB late in August, Roosevelt
opened the way for the needed change. Operating through OPM, the SPAB
had the Bureau of Research and Statistics direct the calculation of long-term

American requirements so as intelligently to guide curtailment and conversion of industry and the proper use of priority and allocation systems. The armed services were only a small measure better than corporate executives where planning agencies for economic mobilization were involved. General Rutherford, the army's representative on the PPB, spelled out quite early what the board had to do to meet its responsibilities. Secretary of the Navy Knox also favored elevating the PPB's status in OPM. But the army and navy used neither their policymaking positions on OPM nor their procurement power to improve the operations of the PPB or to support the Bureau of Research and Statistics. Statistical analysis was not a strong suit for the military, and the services avoided action that could adversely affect their relations with industry or limit their options. In both NDAC and OPM, industry and the military would have preferred mobilizing the economy through contractual relations between themselves.

OPM REORGANIZATIONS

The PPB aimed most of its criticism at the OPM's functional organization, which was based on divisions for production, purchases, and priorities. As had been the case with the NDAC, that structure proved to be extremely limiting. With overlapping responsibilities, the divisions began to set up duplicate commodity groups, resulting in confused and wasted effort. These conditions became more exaggerated and consequential as economic mobilization grew. Expanding controls affected increasing numbers of industries and spurred the formation of additional industry committees. Efficiency suffered, and industry had difficulty obtaining clear and consistent information on what it faced.[11]

Restructuring OPM along more logical lines was delayed for a number of months until the agency completed the transition from the NDAC and settled various controversies. The leading advocates for change came from the Production Division, particularly the Materials Branch, and the PPB. In April 1941, the PPB led in a drive to institute the IMP with a vertical, as opposed to a functional, organization similar to that of the WIB and the NRA. Mobilization would be directed basically by groupings of commodity sections working in tandem with war service committees. Early in May, OPM created an interdivisional committee chaired by Emmerich to review the PPB's proposal. On May 28, the committee reported on a compromise that rejected a wholesale adoption of the IMP but recommended a quasi-vertical restructuring of OPM.[12]

The Emmerich committee's recommendations were implemented between June and July 1941. Existing commodity sections—soon to be renamed commodity or industry *branches*—were divided among the Production, Purchases, and Priorities Divisions depending on whether the primary problem was manufacturing, buying, or shortages. No duplication would take place, and the three divisions would coordinate activity on the products or materials in their sphere among OPM, industry, and government departments. Industry branches would be made up of an OPM official and consultants from OPM divisions, along with representatives from other agencies. They would be advised by an industry advisory committee. Under these guidelines, the Production Division directed all military output (including aircraft, ordnance, and shipbuilding), machine tools, and various materials (including steel, aluminum, and chemicals). The Purchases Division covered areas like clothing, food, drugs, textiles, and leather, while the Priorities Division had responsibility for tin, rubber, tungsten, mica, lead, zinc, and copper, all actually or potentially in short supply. The Priorities Division, however, retained jurisdiction over all priorities.

Of critical significance to the June reorganization was the role of industry advisory committees.[13] Under NDAC, big business and trade association officials had dominated these committees, which operated in a legally dubious manner and largely without established rules or much scrutiny. The same practices continued during the early months of OPM. However, the OPM industry advisory committees were more consequential than were those of the NDAC. In 1940, the principal thrust of the NDAC had been expanding the industrial plant, which, when essential, usually required only occasional meetings with industry. With growing scarcity of materials and products, OPM began stressing priority, allocation, curtailment, substitution, and other regulatory devices. These controls necessitated ongoing consultation between OPM and the industrial community. Indeed, such contact was nearly indispensable for OPM since, with responsibilities far exceeding its powers, the agency depended on industry's voluntary cooperation.

Most of industry cooperated with OPM through advisory committees because it wanted to prevent the further extension of priorities or to temper the effect of such mandatory regulations, goals shared by the majority of OPM officials. By March 1941, the office was working with nearly all raw material industries and machine-tool manufacturers. At the outset, the mobilization agency obtained from industry spokesmen basic data about production and consumption to facilitate its planning. It then devised with industry groups voluntary programs for increasing supply through plant expansion, planned distribution, and reduction in types and varieties of products made. When shortages became so extreme that priority action was essential, OPM joined forces with industry committees to institute action that would keep priorities voluntary or limited in their application. Accordingly, industry agreed to preferences in distribution, allocation of orders and deliveries, changes in specifications, and substitutions in the production process. If even these measures did not suffice and priorities became necessary, industry committees often helped write and even administer the preference system.

With variations, the scenario described above took place with steel, pulp and paper, rubber, chemicals, and zinc. In the case of zinc, committees selected by the American Zinc Institute between late 1940 and June 1941 actively participated in devising and implementing voluntary and then mandatory priorities for the industry. Under OPM, zinc committees and leaders worked with both the Production and the Priorities Divisions. To make the action legal, and contrary to what was done, OPM claimed that all decisions originated with the office. OPM operations in the first half of 1941, therefore, approximated what was done under the WIB of World War I.

OPM was not WIB, however. From the outset, industry advisory committees came under attack from nonbusiness elements. The dispute fed industry's intense resentment of economists, statisticians, and academics such as Leon Henderson and those in the Office of Price Administration and Civilian Supply (OPACS), the Bureau of Research and Statistics, the Labor Division, and other OPM subdivisions. In the minds of businessmen, such individuals approached industry from theory rather than from practical experience, failed to appreciate industry culture and needs, and harbored antibusiness, if not anticapitalist, values. Since industry owned and operated the plant, corporate executives insisted, it should carry out economic mobilization under the general direction of agencies like the OPM. This was the most expedient approach and also one consistent with the nation's ideology. The War Department's IMP—founded on WIB's commodity section–war service committee system—was the ideal mobilization blueprint.

For their part, nonbusiness representatives believed that industrialists tended to be too narrowly focused on profits instead of on public interests, thereby neglecting long-run considerations of defense and possible war. While industry had to play a vital role in economic mobilization, New Dealers were convinced that its shortsighted, if not greedy, outlook had to be balanced in the mobilization agencies by neutral experts like themselves who better understood the imperatives of harnessing the economy and of protecting the public interest.

Working with Attorney General Robert H. Jackson, General Counsel John Lord O'Brian rejected outright industry advisory committees as they had functioned during World War I, in the NRA, and under NDAC. Indeed, the attorney general had turned aside efforts to gain legal sanction for NDAC's industry committees. Neither O'Brian nor Jackson was a crusading New Dealer. Instead, reflecting changed views of the state that the New Deal had brought about, and recognizing that the magnitude and duration of war mobilization could have an enormous impact on society, both were determined to do all that was possible to keep control of the war economy in government hands.

O'Brian and Jackson insisted that industry should and could assist OPM without suspending the antitrust laws or delegating to private business the public's regulatory authority. Industry advisory committees could only advise the OPM; they could neither make nor enforce decisions. Between February and April 1941, O'Brian and Jackson wrote the rules for achieving those ends. First, these committees could be formed only to advance national defense, they should be restricted to major industries that had to be consulted regularly over a substantial time period, and they had to be representative, meaning elected or selected by an industry conference in Washington. Second, the Justice Department, the OPM's general counsel, or other OPM sources had to approve the subjects and actions that the advisory committees would address. And, third, meetings of industry advisory committees should be called by OPM officials or the armed services. Their representatives would attend conferences, minutes would be kept, and any recommendations would be reduced to writing. Furthermore, all discussion had to be kept general so as to avoid details that could result in or be construed as formulating policy.

Late in June 1941, OPM officially put the new system into effect and created the Bureau of Clearance of Defense Advisory Committees to implement it. Sidney J. Weinberg headed the bureau. A Goldman, Sachs and Company partner who was close to Donald M. Nelson, he had formerly been assistant director of the Purchases Division. Weinberg reported directly to the director general and the associate director general. The bureau's staff was kept small, numbering in January 1942 only eleven executives who, like Weinberg, served for a dollar a year and came primarily from industry and finance. Cumbersome procedures acted to limit the organization of formal committees, as opposed to meetings of industry called to deal with specific problems. In January 1942, only thirty-three formal committees had been set up under the new procedures. The slow pace was favored by the Legal Division because it curbed industry's desire to create committees more for purposes of prestige and prominence than of national defense.

Although O'Brian's approach to industry advisory committees halted the fast drift to World War I practices under NDAC and the early months of the OPM, the new rules were violated as much as observed during the last half of 1941, for reasons that were both obvious and subtle. Industrialists who had worked together as mobilization agency executives and on industry advisory committees for over a year advertently or inadvertently resisted changing procedures that were familiar, that worked, and that were, they felt, right. Resistance took many forms. Trying to elect representative committees was impossible, and attempting to select them by industry conference opened the door to gross manipulation by a branch chief determined to have the committee he wanted. If a committee had existed in June 1941, the likelihood was strong that the same individuals, including paid trade association officials, would continue on the newly formed committee. In the case of steel, for example, Walter S. Tower, president of the American Iron and Steel Institute, Benjamin F. Fairless of the United States Steel Corporation, Tom M. Girdler of the Republic Steel Corporation, Eugene G. Grace of the Bethlehem Steel Corporation, Edward L. Ryerson of the Inland Steel Company, and Ernest T. Weir of the National Steel Corporation held dominant positions in committees organized before and after June. Similar patterns were repeated in copper, zinc, and pulp and paper. And the industry committee picked members for subcommittees. With the same people serving on advisory committees, past practices tended to continue, rules notwithstanding.

Furthermore, O'Brian's regulations applied only to formally selected committees. Many branch chiefs met with industry's representatives informally, at times away from Washington, outside the presence of unwanted government officials and without minutes or other written records kept. This practice became so prevalent that O'Brian attempted to bring it under control, without much effect. Industry and OPM officials argued that the new methods could be counterproductive because efficiency and candor were reduced by the presence of too many government officers. In November 1941, at a formal meeting of a Rubber Industry Advisory Committee, thirty-three government officials outnumbered twenty-six industrialists. A branch chief also had the legally dubious option of using the industry committees of the Army-Navy Munitions Board (ANMB), which resembled the war service committees of World War I. The Chemical Section of the Production Division turned to the ANMB's Chemical Advisory Committee for assistance as if it were an OPM creation.

In short, new rules did not disturb working relations that OPM officials and industry found to be satisfactory. Even when industry advisory committees were organized for the first time after June 1941, O'Brian's preferred approach could be ignored if industrialists were so inclined. Such action could take place either without the Legal Division's knowledge or in violation of the rules. When that occurred, smaller business units in an industry constantly complained that they were unrepresented or underrepresented.

OPM, however, was divided about the formation and use of industry advisory committees after O'Brian changed procedures. The Production Division, which included major, heavy industries, continued to be sympathetic to business. The Priorities Division became less committed to industry, and agencies outside OPM, such as OPACS, could be unsympathetic to business. These differences could lead to intense strain inside the mobilization agency and often underlined the basic economic mobilization conflict between industry and New Dealers. In June 1941, for example, the Priorities Division, working with OPACS, took over the allocation of cork supplies without consulting industry or the appropriate branch of the Production Division. James S. Adams, chief of the Agricultural and Forest Products Section of the Materials Branch, exploded in anger, charging that he was being undermined, that the industry was being betrayed, and that the action was ill-advised.

The most prominent conflict over industry advisory committees took place, not within OPM, but between it and OPACS over converting the automobile industry to munitions production. OPM wanted to proceed with caution, while OPACS was intent on quick action to cut Detroit's voracious consumption of a whole host of vital materials.

The underlying tension between OPM and OPACS was resolved late in August 1941 with a reshuffling of agencies that changed substantially the dynamics of economic mobilization. On August 28, the president placed civilian supply within OPM, delegated to that agency his vastly expanded powers over priorities, and set up the SPAB to oversee priorities and the allocation of goods on the basis of the estimated overall requirements for total war. All industry advisory committees would now be under OPM. More important, the board was less dependent on industry's cooperation for advancing mobilization because its mandatory priority and allocation authority now covered practically the entire economy. OPM having the power to compel also made the industry advisory committees less legally vulnerable when they worked with the board. The August 1941 reorganization theoretically shifted control over mobilization away from industry and more toward government.

Actually, OPM's relations with industry advisory committees changed in no dramatic way after the August reorganization. The office, for example, began working with the pulp and paper industry in June 1941 on voluntary programs to reduce the use of chlorine and other materials critical to defense production. As military demand increased until Pearl Harbor, OPM and industry advisory committees extended optional conservation measures and agreed on various mandatory controls to protect both output for defense and the industry as a whole. In natural rubber, the industry opted for mandatory regulations because they were easier to administer than voluntary efforts. After August 1941, OPM had obligatory powers in most areas except standardization and simplification of goods and substitution of materials for production. Yet it was in these areas that scarce materials could be conserved, avoiding mandatory controls wherever possible, an approach that OPM and industry preferred.

Not all industries were as cooperative as pulp and paper and natural rubber. As the defense program grew and more materials became scarce in the later months of 1941, increasing numbers of industries faced shutdown or changing lines of production. Such drastic action, compared with what was required in 1940 and the earlier months of 1941, led to industry in general growing more resistive. Corporations opposed priority, allocation, price, conversion, curtailment, and expansion programs. Turning a deaf ear even to their trusted friends, manufacturers were often unwilling to move on mobilization controls until OPM threatened obligatory regulations—and then only far enough to prevent or curb mandatory action. The outstanding example was the automobile industry, which used its enormous power to keep producing at peacetime rates until after Pearl Harbor. Automobiles were hardly alone. In September 1941, the steel advisory committee argued long and hard against expanding annual capacity despite a favorable recommendation by a consultant acting at the request of the president. Arthur D. Whiteside, chief of the Iron and Steel Branch, finally warned steel spokesmen that their obduracy could have unfortunate consequences for their industry. The leather and shoes industries went further in September and October 1941, refusing to alter peacetime practices to head off compulsory curtailment and allocations. They preferred freedom of action in a circumscribed environment over having more latitude with the government telling them what to do.

As resistance increased, some branch chiefs avoided organizing industry advisory committees or using them if they existed. Working with uncooperative industrialists seemed to be a waste of time. For various reasons, other branch chiefs chose to make decisions without industry's participation. This occurred in November and December 1941 when the Farm Machinery Industry Advisory Committee was totally ignored in the writing of a curtailment order for the industry it represented. Even when mandatory orders were involved and no rules required consulting industry, OPM officials in general, and Weinberg's Bureau of Clearance of Defense Advisory Committees in particular, were anxious that industry be included. Almost inevitably, businessmen participating in writing orders and programs for their industries were more content than when they were ignored. Moreover, and more important, both the producers and the consumers of goods could provide information and insight about an industry, thus avoiding problems within it and improving methods for regulating it.

After Pearl Harbor, OPM moved quickly to streamline its procedures for industry advisory committees along lines that had been under consideration for some time. Before entry into war, Weinberg's agency had its name shortened to the Bureau of Industry Advisory Committees. After hostilities were joined, OPM and the Justice Department agreed on changes in policy. First, any future committee would be selected by the branch or section chief under proper review by his superiors. Second, notices and reports about the creation, meetings, operations, and action of the industry advisory committees were decentralized and simplified. And, third, all meetings with industry, formal or informal, representative or unrepresentative, were subject to the same set of rules. In rewriting the regulations, OPM also stated firmly that industry was to be consulted in the policies that affected it. These new approaches helped OPM deal with the flood of new industry advisory committees that came into being once the nation was at war.

The OPM's general counsel also brought greater order and restrictions to the use of dollar-a-year men.[14] NDAC practices had been rather lax. O'Brian quickly established proper procedures for the appointment of dollar-a-year men, all of whom still had to be cleared by the White House. As OPM's operations grew, so did the use of dollar-a-year men, who increased in numbers by over 40 percent between March and December 1941. Expanded use of such personnel and the growing impact of mobilization on more industries resulted in rising discontent with the use of noncompensated personnel. Bills were introduced into Congress to ban and/or more closely regulate the use of dollar-a-year men, and both houses of Congress—particularly the Senate Special Committee to Investigate the National Defense Program (known as the Truman Committee, after its chair, Senator Harry S. Truman [D-MO])—scrutinized the appointment of such personnel. Close examination hastened O'Brian's tighter control over dollar-a-year men, including banning the appointment of trade association officials or OPM executives from representing their industries at trade association functions, requiring their full-time employment, and prohibiting them from serving on industry advisory committees. Ending such controversial practices did not quell congressional dissent. Late in 1941, and early in 1942, the Truman Committee became harsher in its assessment of noncompensated personnel and more demanding in the data that it wanted on such executives. Before the attack peaked, the WPB replaced OPM in January 1942, leaving Nelson to answer to Congress on the touchy subject.[15]

OPM did, however, persuade the president in October 1941 to delegate his authority for appointing dollar-a-year men to the using agencies. At that time, White House clearance was taking three to five weeks, an intolerable delay for OPM and other agencies as their responsibilities multiplied. Facing a rising tide of opposition to industrialists serving in the mobilization structure, the OPM adopted careful rules to ensure that those whom it appointed to dollar-a-year service were necessary, qualified, and of good character. Despite various changes in dollar-a-year-man service under OPM, the office's practices for staffing its various subdivisions were not significantly different from those of the NDAC.

A WPB official historian studying industry advisory committees claims that O'Brian's rules and their determined enforcement created for OPM a "system designed to provide necessary interest representation without interest domination."[16] The assertion is open to question. The OPM's industry advisory committees were not the war service committees of the WIB in form. Yet meetings with industry were so varied and so subjective in nature that generalizing about them is difficult, if not impossible. O'Brian's rules certainly built no fire walls between industry's representatives and the OPM. Indeed, if such walls had existed, the committees would have been useless. With OPM staffed primarily with corporate executives who served for a dollar a year (albeit under tougher regulations than existed or were enforced during World War I) and who turned to other corporate executives for assistance in fulfilling their duties, industry's collective influence in the board was more than present; it approached being dominant.

Indeed, reorganizations of OPM in September and December 1941 brought the office closer to the IMP favored by industry, the military, and conservative forces in general. In September, OPM was restructured so as to serve better as the operating body for the SPAB (see chart 3). Materials and Civilian Supply Divisions were added, under the direction of William L. Batt and Leon Henderson, respectively. The Materials Division took over industry or commodity branches in its area previously assigned to the Production and Priorities Divisions. This left the Priorities Division without industry branches but still with authority for issuing all priority orders. Civilian Supply had responsibility for all industries producing 50 percent or less for the defense program, including most of the consumer durable goods industries like automobiles, which faced curtailment and conversion to munitions output. In general, the September reorganization further rationalized OPM and was another step away from a functional to a more centralized mobilization system.

The September restructuring also included important changes in executive staffing. William H. Harrison replaced John D. Biggers as head of the Production Division. The latter had emerged as the principal defender of corporate America and its resistance to converting the economy for war. Nelson took over the critical Priorities Division from the ineffective Edward R. Stettinius, Jr. In this position, in addition to his appointment as executive director of SPAB, Nelson became a, even the, primary leader in harnessing the economy.

The final reorganization of OPM took place in December 1941 after the

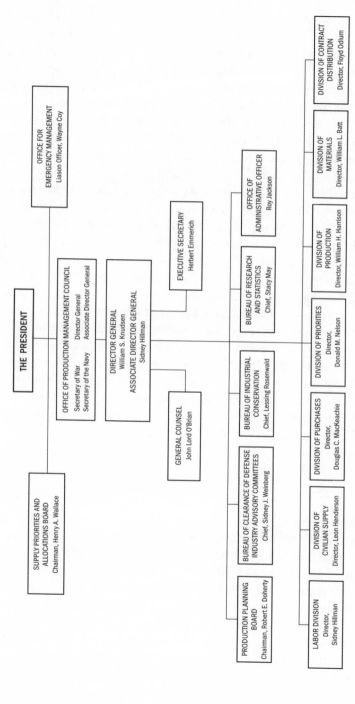

Chart 3.   Organization of OPM, October 1, 1941. *Source:* Civilian Production Administration, *Industrial Mobilization for War: History of the War Production Board and Predecessor Agencies, 1940–1945* (Washington, DC: Civilian Production Administration, 1947), p. 112.

nation entered hostilities and total mobilization became necessary. OPM finally elected to centralize control over most industry branches under the Materials Division, which was most active in that area. The consolidation took place indirectly by placing the industry branches of Purchases and Civilian Supply under the authority of the director and the associate director and then appointing the deputy director of the Materials Division to supervise their activities. Before this new scheme could be implemented fully, WPB took over from OPM in January 1942. Nonetheless, the OPM reshuffle was continued, and the centralization was made more direct through the creation of the Bureau of Industry Branches.

In general, WPB continued the operations of OPM and the SPAB in a refined form and under the leadership of a single chief executive. That made the WPB close to the model of the World War I WIB and what was proposed in the IMP. The major difference was more restrictions on the use of dollar-a-year men and on industry advisory committees. These controls resulted from a strengthened New Deal government, a more liberal Congress, and the dissent of competing interest groups such as organized labor, small business units, and others that the New Deal had energized. Whether the diligence of government and the countervailing power of other interest groups could make a significant difference in industry's domination of economic mobilization was problematic. Despite all the changes wrought by the New Deal, big business had a formidable new partner for economic mobilization in the armed services as the principal procuring agents. The IMP indicated that the military services were fully dedicated to working with, not against, industrial America, as had repeatedly been demonstrated during the years under the NDAC and the OPM.

OPACS

As a competing mobilization agency, the OPACS played a key role in forcing the restructuring of OPM and the creation of the SPAB.[17] It did so through insisting that civilian supply could be protected only by making the mobilization program more efficient and effective.

OPACS was created in April 1941 by combining the Price Stabilization and Consumer Protection Divisions of the NDAC. Leon Henderson was director and Joseph L. Weiner deputy director. The latter was an attorney who also had a public service background as assistant corporate counsel for New York City and director of the Public Utilities Division of the Securities and Exchange Commission. The new agency was staffed (like the two NDAC divisions that it replaced) with economists, academics, and civil servants, and it had the hard-hitting, New Deal characteristics of its leader. Next to OPM, OPACS was the most important civilian mobilization agency at that time. The office was charged with stabilizing prices, holding down the cost of living, and guarding against profiteering, hoarding, and similar abuses. On the production side, and after "military defense needs" were met, it was to maximize output of materials and commodities for civilian use and to work to ensure their equitable division among competing parties.

OPACS was set up as an agency separate from OPM for a number of reasons. Price controls had been handled by a distinct administration during World War I, and there was some justification for continuing that practice. Of more immediate importance, with OPM concentrating on munitions, civilian supply was being neglected. Output for defense was already beginning to affect civilian production adversely. By April 1941, aluminum, magnesium, zinc, and other metals were in short supply, and steel looked like it would soon join them. Such shortages, combined with the fact that big business held most defense contracts and did little subcontracting, threatened to cut back or shut down smaller industries. Of even greater significance was the fact that heedlessly reducing civilian supply could distort the economy and adversely affect its production potential, including military output.

OPM and OPACS clashed from the outset because their responsibilities overlapped.[18] Pricing was not the problem. OPM welcomed anti-inflationary efforts, which remained essentially voluntary throughout 1941 and did not impinge on the office's operations. Production for civilians was another matter. Curtailing the consumer durable good industries, such as automobiles, and converting them to munitions output became the major source of contention between the two agencies. Ironically, OPACS (set up to protect civilian supply) advocated aggressively cutting back these industries, while OPM (charged with furthering munitions output) favored only slowly reducing their manufacture.

According to OPACS, consumer durables, and particularly the automobile industry, were absorbing a large percentage of critical materials that were already in short supply and, therefore, because of a fundamentally flawed priority system, adversely affecting munitions output. Radically curtailing the industries would simultaneously ease material shortages and provide ample industrial capacity for additional munitions manufacture. According to what he called his seed-corn plan, Henderson argued, freed-up steel could then be used to expand steel capacity to provide for both military and civilian requirements during a protracted war.

OPM rejected wholesale shutdowns of consumer durables. Knudsen and his industrial lieutenants insisted that curtailment had to be gradual and synchronized with increasing munitions demand. Otherwise, the result would be idle factories and unemployed workers. Besides, much of the plant and equipment of the automobile and other industries was unsuited for defense. New or reequipped facilities would be necessary. Furthermore, curtailment and conversion could not intelligently take place until current and more long-term requirement figures for the armed services and other claimants were made available.

Theoretically, OPM had the upper hand in the dispute over basic mobilization policy with OPACS. At the instigation of John Lord O'Brian, the two agencies in April had agreed on procedures for avoiding conflict in their operations. OPACS could work out voluntary "programs" with industry involving civilian supply, but these could be made mandatory only through the OPM's priority powers. Time and circumstances, however, operated in favor of OPACS. By mid-1941, munitions orders expanded as the United States inched closer to war and aid to the Allies, soon to include the Soviet Union, grew. Highlighting these developments, the president on May 27, 1941, declared a state of unlimited national emergency. Roosevelt and the secretary and under secretary of war also went on record in favor of cutting back unessential civilian industries to ensure the availability of materials and facilities for defense.

A major break in mobilization patterns occurred on May 31, 1941, when Congress extended priority controls to include essential civilian production and authorized the president to allocate materials. Tension between OPM and OPACS shot up as the two agencies competed to administer the new grant of power. Because the stakes were so high, Roosevelt held back in delegating his enhanced authority to OPM, which acted to strengthen OPACS. Late in July, the latter agency moved to break its stalemate with OPM by putting forward a plan for reducing production by 50 percent in automobiles, domestic refrigerators, and household laundry equipment over a twelve-month period. Before OPACS's aggressive thrust could be acted on, the president restructured the economic mobilization system.

SPAB

By executive orders late in August and early in September 1941, Roosevelt instituted a scheme for the better handling of civilian requirements within the context of the general economic mobilization program. Civilian supply was separated from the Office of Price Administration and placed in OPM as a division, with Henderson still heading both units. OPM was reorganized to include, besides civilian supply, a new division for materials, which William L. Batt led. Donald M. Nelson replaced Stettinius as director of priorities, and Biggers was also forced out of OPM. Additionally, commodity sections were further rationalized. Most important, the SPAB was set up as a top-level policymaking body to act for the president. It was to determine overall requirements for defense, civilians, and all other needs, and to establish how priority and allocation systems would operate in fulfilling those demands. In carrying out its duties, SPAB relied principally on OPM since it had no operating structure.[19]

Although bureaucratically awkward, SPAB was ingenious in its own way. Liberal all-outers dominated the new board, while OPM remained in conservative hands. Roosevelt obviously was out to accelerate and rationalize economic mobilization without disrupting power operations unnecessarily.

Industry was holding back mobilization by its desire to exploit growing civilian markets and to avoid excess capacity in uncertain times. The military contributed to sluggish mobilization by its inability to produce reliable requirement figures, its belief that these were not that important since the economy was a bottomless well, and its willingness to follow industry's lead in OPM. Yet the peculiarities of America's political economy led industry to dominate economic mobilization agencies and the armed services to control their own procurement. World War I had established those realities. Without a higher civil service system, dollar-a-year men and industry advisory committees became central to economic mobilization. By necessity, then, procurement had to remain in the military's hands. Any attempt to alter those realities would set off a political storm threatening all current and future efforts at harnessing the economy. Roosevelt got around those restraints by placing over the existing mobilization system a prestigious policymaking body controlled by New Deal planners who wanted to maximize defense output.

The SPAB served its purposes well. Turning to the Bureau of Research and Statistics, it put together the Victory Program for guiding mobilization. Through the use of its priority and allocation powers, it began the essential task of curtailing civilian industries and preparing them for massive munitions output. By the time of Pearl Harbor, the economy was ready for full-blown mobilization, a condition that did not exist when the SPAB was created in August 1941.

CONCLUSION

The OPM represents a curious phase in the transition to a fully mobilized economy. Neither industry nor the military would lean on the other to achieve a better, faster mobilization system. Consequently, the Roosevelt administration turned increasingly to members of the New Deal coalition to move along economic preparation for defense and war.

Industry's resistance to economic mobilization is more easily understood in the light of its hostility to the New Deal, absorption in growing civilian demand, and concerns about the future. By comparison, the army and navy are studies in contradiction. Their logical allies for accelerating economic mobilization were all-outers. Nevertheless, they tended to look on Henderson, Hillman, and even Nelson unfavorably because these officials' liberal values threatened or challenged business which the army and navy depended on to carry the burden of economic mobilization. This trend was evident in 1939 with the WRB's endorsement of the IMP; it was strengthened when aggressive conservatives like Henry L. Stimson and to a lesser degree, Frank Knox took over in the War and Navy Departments. Roosevelt adroitly finessed the armed services' mobilization contradictions until the United States entered World War II. The president then allowed the natural alliance of the military and industry gradually, albeit tumultuously, to take control of mobilizing the economy. In a meaningful sense, Roosevelt had no alternative. The contours of power in America made industry central to any effort to harness the economy, and the military's interwar industrial mobilization planning adjusted the services to that basic reality.

Liberal reformers acted as catalysts and analysts for economic mobilization in 1940–1941. They worked to speed up the pace of munitions output while simultaneously devising the statistical and economic methods for rationalizing mobilization. Theirs was an essential but thankless task, one that they would continue to play when full economic mobilization began after Pearl Harbor, but under circumstances in which reformers continued to lose power and influence to industry and the military.

5

THE MILITARY AND OPM

The army and navy services worked more closely with the Office of Production Management (OPM) than they had with the National Defense Advisory Commission (NDAC). Nonetheless, they still maintained a level of independence from the OPM that adversely affected economic mobilization. The armed services' behavior resulted from both strength and weakness. Their statutory authority to procure allowed them to go their own way in many areas. This tendency was strengthened by the multiple defects of the military's supply systems. Until fully and firmly in control of massive economic operations, the armed services kept the OPM at arm's length whenever possible so as to safeguard their prerogatives.

WAR DEPARTMENT

From the time he took office in July 1940 until the creation of the Army Service Forces in March 1942, Under Secretary of War Robert P. Patterson struggled to have his office carry out its crushing mobilization load effectively. War Department expenditures for munitions and government-financed war construction jumped from $1.3 billion in 1940 to $7.5 billion in 1941. To handle these demands, the personnel in the under secretary's office multiplied over sixfold between mid-1940 and the end of 1941, growing from 181 to 1,136. Management and organization, however, did not come easily to Patterson, making his job of directing the army's massive procurement and supply operations all the more difficult. The under secretary, for example, tended to operate informally, without proper records being kept, which could deny staff and subdivisions information on decisions and developments essential to their duties.[1]

The Office of the Under Secretary of War (OUSW) had grown in a reckless fashion from 1939 through 1941. As in the past, low-quality officers abounded, now supplemented by often ill-trained civilians and reserve officers who were not of the highest caliber. The OUSW operated principally through four branches: Purchase and Contract; Production; Statistics; and Planning.

The Purchase and Contract Branch oversaw all aspects of supply arms and services (SA&Ss) procurement. Its large size was matched by its hidebound qualities. As responsibilities proliferated, so too did the list of officers required to concur in what was done. The growing red tape in part reflected the personality of the branch's director, Colonel John W. N. Schulz, who attempted to oversee personally all the detailed transactions of his office. His staff, which, unlike that of other OUSW subdivisions, consisted primarily of regular army officers, did not offset Schulz's perfectionism, and the branch resisted and resented assistance from civilians. Since the Purchase and Contract Branch supervised the supply bureaus, its plodding ways set the pace for OUSW operations, a situation that agitated Patterson's numerous civilian aides and assistants.[2]

The Production Branch, charged with expediting production once contracts were let, contrasted sharply in personnel and approach with the Purchase and Contract Branch. As the newest and smallest of the OUSW subdivisions, it was unhindered by tradition or size. Headed by Ordnance Department officers trained at the Army Industrial College, the branch was staffed more with civilian than with military personnel, including five civilian production consultants and expediters attached to the director's office. Energetic, resourceful, and imaginative, this branch served the under secretary well as it pursued ways to shrink the time between signing contracts and delivering goods.[3]

The Statistics Branch, which traced its origins to August 1939, was a sprawling and diffuse bureaucracy of nineteen sections staffed with 248 people, most of whom were civilians. It was the weakest of the OUSW subunits and never functioned properly. Its first director was Leonard P. Ayres, an army officer who had headed statistical services for World War I mobilization agencies. Ayres was called from civilian life to take over leadership of the branch in October 1940. Despite expertise and reputation, he failed to improve the branch's performance because he focused more on public relations than on restructuring and reforming the agency. Inordinate amounts of time and effort went into preparing the frequent presentations (and answers to anticipated questions) that the director made to congressional committees and subcommittees on the army's production record. This material was drawn from a series of reports on army procurement and contracting that went to the secretary and under secretary of war, the chief of staff, the SA&Ss, high administration officials, and, ultimately, the president.

The Statistics Branch did little that was right. In order to operate effectively, it had to have personnel who were properly trained in statistical methods, familiar with the bureaus' procurement procedures and the technical aspects of the weapons and supplies that they acquired, and knowledgeable about industrial productivity. Singly or together, these qualities were scarce among the staff, resulting in uncertainty about the branch's mission. As a result, the branch duplicated work already done in the statistical units of the SA&Ss, sought information readily available in the Statistics Branch or other subdivisions of the OUSW, could not interpret reports sent to it, made repeated requests of the bureaus for unessential, irrelevant, or inappropriate data, collected useless statistics, and failed to collate information in a meaningful way. Reports of the Statistical Branch appeared to be excessive in numbers and, more seriously, were too often of dubious merit or incomplete, unreliable, or contradictory in nature. Most egregiously, some sections of the Statistics Branch attempted to use their responsibility for gathering data about procurement to determine and direct procurement policy. Alarmed by this state of affairs, Booz, Fry, Allen and Hamilton—a consulting firm surveying the OUSW for Patterson—advised the under secretary of war: "Statistics is not an operating function. Management *uses* statistics."[4]

The Planning Branch acted as the army's half of the Army-Navy Munitions Board (ANMB). The board coordinated the two services' supply activities and collaborated with the civilian mobilization agencies in implementing controls such as priorities. By concentrating on facilities, materials, and labor, the branch dedicated itself to maximizing output for the armed services. Once having negotiated the transition from planning to operating, the branch functioned with moderate success, even though its staff was inadequate in numbers and talent. The ANMB itself performed in a rather desultory manner.[5]

Missing from the OUSW was a legal center. Consequently, the various branches had their own legal staffs. Handling legal affairs in a decentralized manner led to duplication and lack of uniformity, an outcome particularly damaging for an office dealing with contracts, financing, and other functions requiring extensive legal services. The quality of attorneys available to the OUSW was also a problem. Those coming from the Judge Advocate General's Office—which provided for the War Department's legal needs—were regular army or reserve officers who were usually either too narrowly trained or not of the caliber necessary for the immense challenges that the OUSW faced. To cope with these adverse conditions, the under secretary of war turned increasingly to high-quality civilian attorneys acting as special assistants and occasionally serving in uniform.[6]

Under Secretary of War Patterson never succeeded in making the office that he inherited run efficiently. Despite patchwork reforms, the OUSW remained a disparate collection of parts, not a centralized whole. Largely uncoordinated, and without clearly defined missions and roles, the Purchase and Contract, Production, Statistics, and Planning Branches often duplicated and competed with one another in key areas such as priorities, statistics, facilities, and materials. These conditions created a sense of uncertainty and confusion in the office. They also weakened the OUSW in its relations with both the SA&Ss and the G-4 (supply division) of the General Staff. The supply bureaus felt free to act independently whenever possible. On its part, G-4 did not reliably provide the OUSW and the SA&Ss complete requirement figures simultaneously. Setting and adjusting the amount, kind, and timing of army demand required that G-4, OUSW, and the SA&Ss work together with reasonable harmony. Otherwise, the entire program of economic mobilization could suffer.[7]

By June 1941, Patterson concluded that thorough, not piecemeal, reform of his office had become essential. He turned to Booz, Fry, Allen and Hamilton for assistance. After months of meticulously analyzing the structure and function of the OUSW, the firm presented the under secretary with a carefully considered plan for restructuring his office in late December.[8] But, by then, it was too late. After Pearl Harbor, the General Staff moved quickly to take over supply and procurement operations, a goal instituted in March 1942.

Despite its flawed organization and operation, the OUSW still succeeded in directing the War Department's huge procurement programs and the vast expansion of plant and equipment for future output. It did so through determination and improvisation. Although not a skilled manager, Under Secretary of War Patterson was a strong leader. Intensely patriotic and committed to military values, he was single-mindedly determined to carry out his duties. Patterson's stubborn resolve about ends was matched by a flexibility concerning means. He was constantly accessible to and supported and protected those he led, was open to ideas and criticism, and was remarkably casual about guarding his bureaucratic turf as long as larger War Department interests were being served. These qualities won him the loyalty and dedication of highly talented assistants like Julius H. Amberg, Howard C. Petersen, Edward F. McGrady, and John H. Ohly.[9]

Patterson relied on his office as it existed whenever possible and improvised if problems arose. When appointed under secretary of war (actually assistant secretary at the time) in July 1940, Patterson had the services of Colonel James H. Burns as executive officer, or general manager, of the OUSW. The latter was an exceptionally able officer who approached industrial mobilization with long experience, deep understanding, and broad perspective. Not only did Burns educate the under secretary of war about his responsibilities, but he also made Patterson's job easier by maximizing the performance of the awkwardly structured OUSW, on the basis of his skills and the respect that he commanded from those he directed, the SA&Ss, and the General Staff. In May 1941, Burns was tapped by Harry L. Hopkins for lend-lease duties. General Harry K. Rutherford, who had been serving as director of the Planning Branch, replaced him as the OUSW's executive director. Booz, Fry, Allen and Hamilton concluded that Rutherford was unqualified for his job and that he hindered OUSW operations because of the low esteem in which he was held inside and outside the War Department. During the last half of 1941, therefore, the under secretary of war lost the assistance of a first-rate executive officer and acquired a mediocrity in directing his office.[10]

Patterson increasingly used new or irregular channels to bolster the efficiency of his office, among the most important of which was direct and frequent contacts with the supply bureaus. Louis A. Johnson, Patterson's predecessor, had initiated weekly meetings with the chiefs of the SA&Ss to expedite the defense program. Patterson expanded the practice to twice-a-week events, which eventually also included the leading officials of his office and usually a representative from G-4. In the words of a leading historian of the OUSW, these conferences constituted an informal "Industrial Staff of the War Department." The purview was both broad and detailed, including an overview of the department's and the nation's mobilization effort as well as technical aspects of procurement and production. At these meetings, the under secretary prodded the SA&Ss when necessary, and the supply bureaus articulated their complaints and recommendations. Since the meetings were so frequent, they provided an ongoing forum in which top War Department officials could advance army procurement.[11]

Patterson additionally turned to personal assistants for help in running his office. Amberg became his legal counsel; attorneys, like Edward S. Greenbaum, advised or were assigned to various branches, SA&Ss, and other OUSW subdivisions to solve problems; Michael J. Madigan, a construction engineer, focused on cantonments; and McGrady oversaw labor affairs. Through this group, Patterson was able to reach out to direct the numerous parts of the large and cumbersome office that he headed. Most advisers were attorneys who proved adept at accelerating procurement. Missing were industrial production experts. Patterson was aware that he needed their services, but he had difficulty recruiting top-notch talent.

Patterson's use of untraditional methods created resentment and resistance among the subdivisions of his office and the SA&Ss. Civilian advisers were especially disliked. Nonetheless, the under secretary of war's leadership was gradually accepted, even embraced, because any alternative was worse. He was making a jerry-built system work in meeting unprecedented demand under relentless pressure. Without him, there was a genuine threat of OUSW being overwhelmed, opening the door to the General Staff taking over supply operations, as had happened during World War I, or civilians doing so under a munitions ministry.[12] Unlike in World War I, in World War II the War Department knew what to do in terms of economic mobilization for war even if its system for accomplishing the purpose left much to be desired.

NAVY DEPARTMENT

The Navy Department, unlike the War Department, had nothing comparable to the OUSW for handling the vastly expanded defense program. With navy spending for munitions and government-financed construction shooting up from $0.6 to $3.1 billion between 1940 and 1941, the service faced crisis conditions.[13] Procurement was decentralized to five bureaus, with the Bureau of Supplies and Accounts covering general buying and related duties and the Bureaus of Ships, Aeronautics, Ordnance, and Yards and Docks handling more specialized supply operations. In theory, the secretary of the navy supervised the bureaus. With an office consisting of himself, the assistant secretary, several naval aides, and a few clerks, that was not possible even during the tranquil years of peace. While the chief of naval operations could also oversee supply bureau activities, his grant of authority was vague, his staff inadequate, and his initiative weak. Hence, the bureaus functioned virtually free of direction, and they tenaciously guarded their turf. They asserted that Congress made appropriations to them, precluding the secretary from transferring funds within the department. Furthermore, the secretary of the navy could create no new offices in the department without congressional authorization. With backing from the Judge Advocate General and close ties with Congress, the bureaus could usually checkmate any secretary challenging their entrenched power. Willing to cooperate with the chief of naval operations in furthering logistics, the bureaus insisted that his office could issue no orders to them.[14]

The supply bureaus, therefore, in effect ran what was called *the shore establishment* and even had some influence in the operations of the fleet. Antagonisms naturally existed among the bureaus, the Office of the Chief of Naval Operations (CNO), and the line. Nonetheless, the naval establishment tended to pull together when facing threats to its authority from civilian sources, including the secretary of the navy. In general, and particularly among the bureaus, the view was widespread that the navy had an efficient and proven system of procurement and supply that could be expanded to handle an emergency of any magnitude. Organizational change was unnecessary.

During the interwar years, a small group of line and staff officers thought otherwise. Study at the Naval War College and, more important, the Army Industrial College convinced them that the logistics of modern warfare required institutional innovation. Similar views prevailed in the Office of the Secretary of the Navy and Congress. A dispute involving the authority of the chief of naval operations over the supply bureaus led to reform. Representative Carl Vinson (D-GA), chairman of the House Committee on Naval Affairs, in 1933 introduced a bill creating an Office of Naval Material that would be equal in power to a strengthened CNO. Such a reorganization would have given the navy a structure similar to that of the army. Objections from the General Board blocked the reform. In 1939–1940, first Vinson and then Secretary of the Navy Charles Edison proposed a variation on Vinson's earlier plan that now ran into general opposition from the naval establishment. To salvage some gain from the push for reform, Congress and the Navy Department fashioned a compromise enacted in June 1940 in which the secretary of the navy would delegate to a newly created Office of Under Secretary of the Navy the task of coordinating the navy's industrial activities. Even this modest change required the intervention of President Franklin D. Roosevelt.[15]

Secretaries of the navy played a crucial role in the service's mobilization for World War II. Charles Edison, who served as assistant secretary from November 1936 to July 1939 and then took over first as acting and then as secretary of the navy from July 1939 to June 1940, was instrumental in creating the Office of the Under Secretary of the Navy, consolidating bureaus to facilitate ship construction, and making navy procurement procedures more flexible. Frank Knox, his successor, served from July 1940 until his death in April 1944. Knox is often portrayed as a lightweight, little more than Republican window dressing for the Democratic Roosevelt. This assessment is far from the mark. In an unspectacular but steady, astute, and wise fashion, he first led and then supported James V. Forrestal and others in fundamentally reorganizing the Navy Department so that it could handle the gigantic wartime procurement load. Additionally, Knox was extremely sensitive to the need for maintaining civilian control of the military, and he frequently called on the president to help ensure that goal during the turbulence of war.

Knox has been viewed in a negative light partly because he had little or no role in operations. Roosevelt, acting as his own secretary of the navy, and Admiral Ernest J. King, who between December 1941 and March 1942 became both commander-in-chief of the fleet and chief of naval operations, played key roles in determining naval strategy during World War II. Persistently attempting to subordinate or eliminate civilian influence in naval affairs, King went out of his way to humiliate and denigrate Knox, in the process tarnishing his own image. The fact remains, however, that Knox contributed significantly to producing the material might indispensable for the navy's outstanding wartime record.[16]

Almost immediately on taking over as secretary of the navy, Knox realized that he would have to restructure his office to meet his vast responsibilities. For assistance, he turned to the management consulting corporation of Booz, Fry, Allen and Hamilton, which had offices in Chicago and New York and which he had previously used for business purposes. This was the same firm that Patterson later turned to for assistance, probably at the urging or example of the Navy Department. The Booz group proved so successful in helping reorganize the secretary's office for better management that its services continued to be used throughout the war years. In the spring of 1942, an Office of Management Engineer was set up in the Executive Office of the Secretary to modernize the navy's administration. It was headed by a member of Booz's firm, who was given a naval reserve commission. This office and Booz, Fry, Allen and Hamilton surveyed and reorganized all the bureaus, along with the CNO and other units. Members of the Booz group additionally worked out the administrative structure for what became in January 1942 the Office of Procurement and Material (OP&M), the principal agency that Under Secretary of the Navy Forrestal used to direct the navy's wartime contracting and supply operations. Knox and Forrestal, in short, relied heavily on Booz's firm in restructuring the naval establishment to meet the astronomical material demands of modern warfare.[17]

The OP&M resulted from Forrestal's drive to create an organization through which he could effectively coordinate the supply bureaus' contracting and purchasing activities.[18] Forrestal entered public life in June 1940 as one of Roosevelt's administrative assistants and then in August moved to the Navy Department as under secretary, a position more suited to his talents. William O. Douglas and Thomas G. Corcoran appear to have played a key role in his appointment to both posts. Forrestal was a Democrat, and Roosevelt was interested in tapping his broad knowledge of the industrial personnel who would be needed for mobilizing the economy.

Forrestal was the first under secretary of the navy appointed under the June act. Knox immediately assigned to him the duty of directing the bureau's supply and procurement activities. Unlike his War Department counterpart, however, Forrestal had no staff to carry out his enormous responsibilities, although Commander John E. Gingrich, his naval aide, proved invaluable and remained in Forrestal's office until the war was nearly over. Forrestal began assembling a staff by recruiting a team of attorneys, including Charles F. Detmar, Jr., and others from the law firm that acted as counsel to Dillon, Read and Company,

Forrestal's investment banking company. Detmar remained as the under secretary's special assistant for legal affairs throughout most of hostilities.

Forrestal had to move quickly to bring order to the navy's contracting procedures. Over the decades, the service had allowed practices to evolve that were both archaic and irrational. Using standardized forms and competitive bidding, the supply bureaus negotiated most contracts without supervision and with only nominal review on the part of the Judge Advocate General's Office. While this approach could be made to work during the leisurely pace of peace, it began breaking down under the intense pressures of escalating demand during the defense period. So much confusion existed over the five-year amortization program for defense and war facilities, for example, that the Navy Department was virtually unable to process the required certificates on behalf of its contractors. As a result, plant expansion was delayed.

In December 1940, Forrestal called on H. Struve Hensel and W. John Kenney—well-regarded attorneys from New York and California—to recommend and implement a system for handling amortization applications, a process that was ultimately centralized in the under secretary's office. Once effective procedures were under way, Hensel and Kenney turned their attention to the larger problem of contracting in general.

Forrestal found existing practices to be unacceptable. He was called on to approve without review an unending flow of contracts from the supply bureaus. These contracts lacked uniformity, granted the bureaus power to purchase as they chose, and kept the under secretary in the dark about what was taking place. After assessing navy contracting methods, Hensel in March 1941 argued that Forrestal could fulfill his responsibilities only through a centralized system of negotiated contracts overseen at every stage by attorneys from the under secretary's office. In that way, skilled attorneys with commercial experience could combine their talents with the technical knowledge of the bureaus to handle the navy's burgeoning contractual duties. Various acts of Congress in 1939 and 1940 allowed the secretary of the navy to institute negotiations over competitive bidding, and, when the United States entered hostilities, negotiated contracts became mandatory. Negotiations, furthermore, allowed the navy to adapt its contracts to specialized conditions instead of relying on crude standardized forms that failed to protect the service and were unacceptable to many industrial firms.

To accomplish those ends, Hensel proposed that Forrestal create in his office a Procurement Legal Division that would be responsible for the drafting, reviewing, and approving of all navy contracts. The division would assign attorneys to the various bureaus to direct and assist contractual work. To carry out its duties, Hensel insisted that the division be staffed only with civilians and that special counsel be answerable to the Procurement Legal Division, not to the bureaus in which they served. Such a system would centralize procedures and place in the secretary of the navy's hands firm control over contracting.

After careful consideration and, at times, intense opposition from the Judge Advocate General, the bureaus, the chief of naval operations, and Congress, Forrestal in July 1941 ordered into effect the Procurement Legal Division. Hensel and Kenney were logically selected to act as director and assistant director, respectively, of the new unit, which operated along the recommended lines. Knox's support was critical in establishing the Procurement Legal Division. Even then, the new division faced ongoing hostility from numerous sources for well over a year. Nonetheless, the division gradually proved its worth. By the end of 1942, all bureaus with the exception of Supplies and Accounts accepted the civilian legal structure and appreciated its substantial contribution to the navy's material operations.

Despite the obvious need for it and the modest institutional adjustments that it required, the Procurement Legal Division initiated a profound shift of power within the Navy Department. It was for that reason that the division generated such strong resistance. On the basis of the authority of the secretary of the navy, Forrestal, through the Procurement Legal Division, placed in every supply bureau attorneys answerable to him who had the right to determine how contracting—basic to bureau domination of the navy—was carried out. For the first time in history, the secretary of the navy, through the Office of the Under Secretary of the Navy, reached down to dictate in detail how the bureaus operated. The Procurement Legal Division, therefore, began the process of creating an office that would allow the secretary of the navy actually, not just nominally, to direct and coordinate the navy's supply and procurement activities. Moreover, the division was a major step in the direction of maintaining civilian control of the military during the maelstrom of war, when such control is under the greatest threat. Because the secretary and under secretary of war were much less diligent about civilian authority than were their navy counterparts, civilian control of the army during World War II was much less secure than was civilian control of the navy.

Accurate statistics on present and projected demand were as important to the secretary of the navy's management of material resources as was centralized contracting. Shortly after taking office, Secretary Knox became aware that the service's statistical services were totally inadequate. The bureaus and subdivisions in the secretary's office and the CNO collected some figures, but they were at best piecemeal and unreliable. These circumstances left the secretary without the crucial data that he needed to do his job, and they prevented the navy from providing the NDAC, OPM, and other civilian agencies with accurate statistics, something indispensable for economic mobilization. Faced with increasing requests from OPM for data on overall requirements, the Navy Department could do little more than combine the estimates of the bureaus, try to translate appropriations into material goods, and use other devices that produced figures that were all but useless.

Attempting to cure the situation, Knox in August 1940 set up a statistical unit in the War Material Procurement Section of the CNO. This unit, however, did little more than pass along requests to the bureaus and collect and collate information coming from them, advancing statistical services not at all. In December 1940, therefore, the unit was moved to the Office of the Secretary of the Navy. However, progress was again thwarted when statistical functions were integrated into an Office of Budget and Reports, which emphasized fiscal, not material, considerations. Throughout 1941, therefore, the navy remained unable to mobilize reliable statistics on the defense program for use in and outside the Navy Department.

Forrestal became as concerned about statistical operations as Knox was. In October 1940, he called on C. Douglas Dillon and August Belmont (II) to survey the department's methods for collecting data and what could be done to improve this function. Reporting late in November, the two financiers found that statistics available to the civilian mobilization agencies and the secretary of the navy were at best incomplete, at worst misleading. At all levels, staffing, training, and experience were minimal or missing. Yet reliable statistics on munitions and supplies projected years in advance were becoming increasingly necessary for the NDAC, the secretary of the navy, and others to do their part in mobilizing the economy. To achieve that end, the navy required a centralized statistical office under the secretary of the navy's control, one that was adequately and competently staffed and directed. This recommended goal was not fully realized until the nation entered World War II.

Statistical functions as part of a larger effort to direct and coordinate the navy's entire supply program centrally reached a satisfactory level only with the creation of the OP&M in January 1942. This office was the culmination of the steady reforms that Knox and Forrestal began instituting in July 1940. These reforms included reorganizations and management techniques resulting from surveys by Booz, Fry, Allen and Hamilton, the office staff recruited by Forrestal, creation of the Procurement Legal Division, efforts to improve statistical services, and the numerous other changes that took place over a period of nearly eighteen months.

The inadequacies of the bureaus and the CNO in material operations were as important in creating OP&M as were the positive developments in the Office of the Secretary of the Navy. While at least competent and often excellent in their technical specialties, the bureaus were lacking in the legal, commercial, statistical, and related capabilities that had become basic to economic mobilization for modern warfare. Without assistance from and direction by a higher office, they could not handle what would become over $90 billion in expenditures for defense and war from July 1940 through June 1945. Repeatedly throughout 1940–1941, the CNO demonstrated that it was unqualified to provide the coordination that the bureaus required, as its neglect of the statistical unit illustrated. With rare exceptions, the typical line and staff officer remained ignorant about and uninterested in the material side of war. During the interwar years, a Material Division appeared and disappeared in the CNO structure without its presence or absence having much effect.

The Navy Department faced the dilemma of the bureaus and the CNO being unable to handle defense procurement either on their own or together yet resisting the secretary's efforts to prepare them for the task. Hence, the under secretary of the navy had a tougher challenge than did the under secretary of war. Not only did Forrestal have to improvise in making the navy's supply system work under an enormously increased load in 1940–1941, but he also had to put together a new system equal to the even greater demands of war. To accomplish both purposes simultaneously, the under secretary of the navy relied heavily on civilian assistants like Detmar, Hensel, and Booz, outstanding naval officers such as Gingrich and Admiral C. W. Fisher, and the Procurement Legal Division and other newly established offices. In addition, he met regularly with the supply bureaus to coordinate activities, formulate policies, solve problems, and exchange information.

By the time of Pearl Harbor, Forrestal fairly well knew the type of organization that he needed in order to direct the navy's full material mobilization for war. He turned to key civilian and naval aides—including Ferdinand Eberstadt, who was restructuring the ANMB for war purposes—to work out the details of what became the OP&M. The shock of sudden hostilities provided an opportunity for the under secretary of the navy to push through his far-reaching reforms before his numerous opponents could unite to block the way. Knox issued a general order setting up OP&M on January 30, 1942. Although Forrestal was the moving force behind this radical change, Knox's contribution was significant in terms of both the action that he took and the consistent support and protection that he provided the under secretary of the navy in 1940 and 1941.

Serving directly under Forrestal, OP&M initially had four branches: Planning and Statistics; Production; Procurement; and Resources. The Material Division and other units of the CNO and the secretary of navy's office were transferred to the OP&M. Samuel M. Robinson, chief of the Bureau of Ships, who played a role in founding the new office, was promoted from rear to vice admiral to head OP&M. A mix of naval officers and civilians, the office was clearly dominated by the latter.

With the Planning and Statistics Branch, the navy for the first time had the capability of providing accurate requirements data. It was almost totally a civilian organization, led by Donald R. Belcher, treasurer of the American Telephone and Telegraph Company. Compiling the navy's existing and future demand, the branch broke it down by materials and components. To facilitate logistic planning, the branch put out monthly and other reports on actual and projected munitions production. It also worked with the bureaus in perfecting the calculation of material requirements, general and specific record keeping, inventory control, and the scheduling of production. The branch's work was vital to economic mobilization within and outside the Navy Department.

Joseph W. Powell, an Annapolis graduate who left the service to become a shipbuilder and had served as a special assistant to Knox, became chief of the Production Branch. Branch members worked closely with and frequently served in the War Production Board (WPB). Their primary assignment was to expedite output and solve or avoid production delays involving materials, components, and facilities.

The Procurement Branch was under the direction of Frank M. Folsom, a longtime assistant of Donald M. Nelson, chairman of the WPB, who nominally continued to serve on the board while he also directed navy procurement. His branch set policy for and oversaw the bureau's negotiating and awarding of contracts, including form and terms, pricing, financing, and facilities. It also cleared bureau contracts, which allowed the branch to ensure that navy buying was consistent with the larger mobilization effort, that contracts went to smaller business whenever possible, and that subunits were not overordering or hoarding. The Procurement Branch logically worked closely with the Procurement Legal Division. At the outset, the latter was slated to be included in the former, but Hensel insisted that his division would lose its impact if placed in normal navy bureaucratic channels, and, thus, the division remained in the under secretary of the navy's office.

Captain Timothy Kelcher, USN, who served in the ANMB, took over the leadership of the Resources Branch. This branch was the navy half of the ANMB, and Kelcher reported both to Robinson, the OP&M head, and Eberstadt, chairman of the ANMB. The board coordinated the mobilization activities of the army and navy and related the services' operations with those of the WPB. By participating in these functions, the Resources Branch was indispensable to the navy and the larger mobilization program.

In May 1942, after nearly a year of effort, Forrestal succeeded in having created in the OP&M an Office of Inspection Administration. Its chief was Rear Admiral Bryson Bruce, USN, from the Bureau of Ships. He was to co-ordinate various inspectors of materials for navy use or production to ensure uniform standards and practices.

OP&M had a critical role in naval logistics, a role that included setting, procuring, and distributing requirements. The CNO remained responsible for determining what navy demand would be, the OP&M then took charge of procuring and producing the needed supplies and munitions, and the CNO once more was responsible for delivering goods and output to the des-ignated areas.

In fulfilling its duties, the OP&M faced constant tension from above and below. The bureaus resented losing a significant measure of their indepen-dence and a large share of their power. Skillful leadership on the part of Robin-son won the cooperation of the bureaus' top leadership, but resistance to OP&M continued unabated throughout the war years at the lower echelons, which never appreciated the significant role that the office played in making navy logistics so successful.

OP&M relations with the CNO were also tense but more consequential. Outside the secretary's office and the supply bureaus, line and staff officers rarely understood the need for the OP&M, let alone the WPB. As far as they were concerned, these organizations unnecessarily duplicated the work of the CNO. Indeed, OP&M was created while Admiral King was distracted in orga-nizing his new office as commander-in-chief of the fleet. Thereafter, he regu-larly sought to do away with OP&M or place it securely under CNO control. Only the tenacious resistance of Forrestal and Knox and the timely interven-tion of Roosevelt prevented that from happening. Nonetheless, King and the CNO fought back in their own way. To maximize OP&M effectiveness, Robin-son should have joined King when the Joint Chiefs of Staff determined strategy so that he would be appraised of current and future demand. Failing that, requirement figures could have gone from the CNO to the OP&M. Instead, the former sent them directly to the supply bureaus, forcing the latter to go to its subordinate units to learn what overall naval demand was and would be.

Whatever opposition and obstacles the OP&M endured, it turned out to be an excellent office, the best the navy had ever had in terms of material pro-curement and production. Through OP&M, the navy met the astronomical demands of World War II efficiently, an accomplishment that would have been impossible under the conditions that Knox and Forrestal faced when taking office in mid-1940.

ARMY-NAVY MUNITIONS BOARD

By assisting the War and Navy Departments in 1940–1941, the ANMB compensated to a degree for the deficiencies of their supply and procurement systems. It did this by coordinating and settling conflicts between the services
and representing their interests before the civilian mobilization agencies. For
most of the defense period, as during the interwar years, the War Department—more specifically the Planning Branch of the OUSW—acted for the
ANMB, with the Navy Department playing little more than a nominal role.
Only in mid-1941, when Under Secretary Forrestal joined Under Secretary
Patterson as cochair of the board, did the navy begin to carry its weight.

The ANMB made its principal mobilization contributions in five major
areas: regulating foreign purchasing; stockpiling; maximizing the availability
of machine tools; assigning priorities; and assisting army and navy procurement and supply. Discounting the War Resources Board's drive of mid- to late
1939 for implementing the Industrial Mobilization Plan, the ANMB in a sense
initiated economic mobilization for World War II with its insistence that, if
left unregulated, foreign purchasing could adversely affect American mobilization for defense and war. In 1938 and 1939, British and French purchases
of airplanes, airplane parts, and other munitions had become so great that the
ANMB in June 1939 urged Roosevelt to create an agency to regulate this
activity. The board suggested that it was prepared to undertake such an assignment. The request led to the president first placing ANMB under his direct
supervision—consistent with his determination to keep economic mobilization centered in the White House—and then designating the board to oversee
foreign munitions purchases.

To carry out its assignment, the board in July 1939 set up a Clearance
Committee to pass on buying from abroad. If orders required expanded or
new plant, the ANMB usually proposed that the procuring nation finance such
growth. It also acted to block sales or negotiated to substitute products or
manufacturers in instances where American national defense could be adversely
affected.

With the outbreak of the European war late in 1939, Roosevelt in December 1939 switched control over foreign munitions sales from the ANMB to a
new agency ultimately called the Interdepartmental Committee for Coordination of Foreign and Domestic Military Purchases, or the President's Liaison Committee. It was dominated by the Treasury Department. This action
was protested by the War and Navy Departments, protests ignored by the
president, who was more interested in assisting the Allies than in protecting

American munitions supplies. Secretary of the Treasury Henry J. Morgenthau, Jr., shared Roosevelt's outlook, while the military services looked to guarding their arsenals. After the passage of the Lend-Lease Act of March 11, 1941, the President's Liaison Committee was replaced first by the Division of Defense Aid Reports and then by the Lend-Lease Administration. Whatever the agency, Roosevelt kept aid to the Allies in his own hands. The military services directly or indirectly continued to influence decisions in this vital area, but never to the degree that they had under the ANMB from July to December 1939.[19]

ANMB involvement in export policies was not limited to munitions but included all resources necessary to conduct war. Interwar planning for vital raw materials kept ANMB and the OUSW constantly active in export policies that could affect national defense. Their role became more important when Roosevelt used an act of July 1940 to appoint an administrator of export control. The administrator relied on a licensing system for curtailing or halting foreign buying that could further war-making capacity. In carrying out his duties, the administrator turned to the NDAC for assistance, but the ANMB was most influential in regulating the export of strategic, critical, or essential materials such as manganese, vanadium, and steel because of its extensive commodity committee activity in the 1920s and 1930s. In time, the administrator of export control went from protective to offensive operations, such as preclusive buying to deny key materials to the Axis powers. In July 1941, the administrator's duties were taken over by the Economic Defense Board, which in April 1942 became the Board of Economic Warfare. As the civilian agencies gained in experience and knowledge of their responsibilities, the direct influence of the ANMB on their operations diminished.[20]

Stockpiling was another key activity of the ANMB. Throughout the 1920s and 1930s, the OUSW on its own and through the ANMB persistently but unsuccessfully pushed for stockpiling of materials essential to war production. In the 1938 Naval Appropriation Act, Congress finally earmarked $3.5 million for the navy to accumulate manganese and other strategic materials. Pushed by the ANMB and the State and Interior Departments, the national legislators went further with the passage in June 1939 of the Strategic War Materials Act, which authorized the ANMB, operating through the Treasury Department and assisted by several other executive departments, to acquire strategic stockpiles. The program never advanced well because of various obstacles. One of these was actual funding through March 1940 that was only about $13 million even though the ANMB felt that $200–$700 million was necessary to make a difference. Seeking another approach, the ANMB led in having Congress authorize the Reconstruction Finance Corporation (RFC) in June 1940 to set up subsidiaries for acquiring up to $300 million in materials. RFC organized the Rubber Reserve Company, the Metals Reserve Company, and the Defense Supplies Corporation for this purpose, all of which the ANMB had an initial hand in overseeing under the direction of the secretaries of war, the navy, and the interior. Once again, the ANMB encountered intense frustration as the RFC moved slowly and allowed stockpiles to dwindle before Pearl Harbor.[21]

Despite all that was not done in stockpiling, the progress made stemmed largely from ANMB's efforts. By mid-1940, the board's influence and activity in this area diminished significantly as the NDAC and successor agencies assumed responsibility for strategic materials.

Machine tools were less familiar to the ANMB than export controls and stockpiling. The board's interwar planning for machine tools had been erratic and inconclusive despite the fact that machine tools were basic to most industrial output and particularly so for munitions.[22] Although both the NDAC and the ANMB set up subunits to handle these tools, the subunits' spheres were not well established, and available data on machine tools were incomplete or contradictory. Additionally, while the NDAC and its successor unit in OPM had able and knowledgeable leaders, the ANMB had leaders who were unfamiliar with machine tools. By late 1940, a shortage of machine tools was threatening defense production. Alarmed by this situation, Under Secretary of the Navy Forrestal in December 1940 turned to Ferdinand Eberstadt, a friend and former business colleague, for assistance.

Eberstadt knew the industry well because his investment banking firm had been involved in financing, marketing securities for, and reorganizing numerous machine-tool firms in the 1930s. After spending a number of months surveying the industry starting in the spring of 1941, Eberstadt reported to Forrestal early in July. He made a number of recommendations for increasing production and improving supply that OPM concurred with and had itself already arrived at. Meaningful progress in solving the machine-tool bottleneck, however, waited until January 1942, when the United States was at war and Eberstadt had taken over as head of the ANMB. After Pearl Harbor, demand for machine tools was projected to triple in 1942, while actual supply had declined in the last months of 1941. Eberstadt joined forces with the Tools Branch of the WPB to address this menacing situation. Conferring with machine-tool manufacturers, and drawing on past practices, the ANMB and WPB ultimately hammered out a program that met the crisis.

Solutions involved increasing production and improving distribution. Output could be accelerated substantially with existing plant—and, where necessary, with new or augmented facilities—by expanding the workforce and the number of shifts per day and by subcontracting. For that to take place, man-

ufacturers had to have orders to absorb the added production. Forcing contractors to place orders immediately on signing contracts, instead of holding
off until they were ready to begin operations, led to a huge jump in demand.
So too did "pool" or unassigned buying. On the basis of projected demand,
government agencies like the armed services bought large blocks of commonly
used machine tools that they held in reserve for future contractors. Pool buying, however, could lead to delayed payments to machine-tool firms, reducing their working capital. To get around this obstacle and speed up plant
growth, the mobilization agencies turned to the Defense Plant Corporation
for advances on pool orders and assistance with financing facilities and equipment. Through these approaches, machine-tool output in 1942 exceeded by
sixfold its prewar annual record.

The full benefit of vastly expanded machine-tool production would not be
realized without a drastically altered system of distribution. Since 1940, the
NDAC and OPM, in combination with the ANMB, had struggled to refine
the priorities system in such a way that machine tools would be in the right
hands at the right time. Success always eluded them. Consequently, they
switched to an allocation approach when implementing the production reforms. Seventy-five percent of total monthly machine-tool output went to the
armed services and the United States Maritime Commission, with the remainder reserved for foreign and civilian demand. The ANMB subdivided the military portion among the two services, which in turn allotted their share to the
various supply services according to quantity and type needed. The supply
bureaus were responsible for ensuring that their contractors were supplied
with essential machine tools. Although not without flaws, the new allocation
system ended competition among the services, encouraged the most efficient
use of scarce machine tools, and halted hoarding and overordering, all of
which contributed to the crisis at the end of 1941. Machine tools remained
scarce until almost the end of the war, but that resulted from demand exceeding supply, not from the unsound mobilization practices of 1940–1941.

Priorities were the most important function performed by the ANMB since
they acted to shape the entire mobilization program. For this reason, ANMB
and the armed services always fought aggressively to maintain as much independence in the area as possible. Their persistence paid off and had weight
because of the military's size as a mobilization claimant, its statutory authority over procurement, and its extensive field staff. During the NDAC period,
the ANMB, under the general direction of the commission's Priority Board,
managed to maintain its control over military priorities and even extended its
reach into civilian affairs.[23] This same pattern continued with OPM in 1941
as material and other shortages grew and priority functions went through a

transition from voluntary to mandatory enforcement. Gradually, under the WPB, priorities gave way to allocations, in which the board granted the armed services and other claimants a percentage output of key materials, which they distributed to their contractors, as was done earlier with machine tools. This system gave the armed forces even greater control over determining the order of urgency for their production. Eberstadt and the ANMB played an influential role in refining the allocation system in late fall 1942. By then, the ANMB was losing power and beginning to slip into insignificance.

The ANMB dominance of the priority system caused serious problems. Without quantitative controls, the board and the army and navy supply bureaus rated so many contracts at the most urgent level that the designation lost meaning as demand far exceeded supply. The system was strained further by the needlessly cumbersome and inefficient operations of the OPM Priorities Division. Beginning late in 1940, and continuing throughout 1941, OPM and ANMB constantly struggled to make the system work, without much success. Before Pearl Harbor, OPM leaders were becoming convinced that priorities would have to be scrapped in favor of allocations.[24]

In addition to foreign purchasing, stockpiling, machine tools, and priorities, the ANMB worked with the army and navy and their supply bureaus in performing a host of services involving procurement. These duties included assigning to the armed services industrial facilities and settling any conflict between them over productive capacity, assisting the military in financing new or expanded facilities for munitions output, helping the army and navy in the calculation of requirements, and working with the services in reconciling their demands for available facilities, equipment, and materials.[25]

The greatest failure of the ANMB and the armed services during 1940–1941 was their inability to provide the NDAC and the OPM with reliable statistics on immediate and long-run demand broken down into finished products and their components, parts, and materials. Without such figures, no program of economic mobilization could be effectively planned. Gross figures on troops and weapons were helpful to the civilian mobilization agencies, but, standing alone, they were never enough.

In terms of general requirements, the War Department outperformed the Navy Department. Under pressure from the NDAC on the outside and the OUSW on the inside, the army calculated what came to be called the Munitions Program of June 30, 1940. It called for supplying a 4-million-man army and the capacity to produce thirty-six thousand planes by stages over an approximately two-year period or as soon as possible. Army planners set the costs of the expansion at approximately $6 billion, around half their original figure, which Roosevelt had insisted on revising downward. These goals were modified upward during 1940–1941 according to need and possibility.[26] Throughout most of 1941, however, the army was in the process of formulating a more accurate and flexible program. Roosevelt accelerated its effort in August 1941 when he announced what came to be called the Victory Program: estimates for total national war production required for achieving victory over the Axis powers. The army and navy in September came up with figures placing the cost ultimately at around $150 billion and projected maximum army strength at almost 9 million. When the Victory Program went through a transition to the War Munitions Program after Pearl Harbor, overall army spending alone was estimated at $63 billion in a two-and-one-half-year period. Hence, throughout the defense years, the army, prodded by supply planners in or from the OUSW (particularly Colonel [later General] James H. Burns, the office's executive officer), did attempt to prepare statistics on present and future requirements for the War Department's own operations and those of the civilian mobilization agencies.[27]

By comparison, the navy never came up with anything similar to the army's 1940 Munitions Program, and its goals put forward in the Victory Program were no more than guesses. When pressed in 1940–1941 within and outside its structure for requirement figures, the Navy Department could do little more than total the requests of the material bureaus or translate appropriations into items of supply and munitions.[28]

In converting munitions and supplies into the materials required for production, however, the army did little better than the navy.[29] If the NDAC and the OPM were to do their jobs, they needed to know how much steel, aluminum, copper, and other materials were necessary to meet military requirements. That necessitated the services having bills of materials on each item procured. From its interwar planning, the army had such lists on many munitions, but those lists were often obsolete. And, in some instances, the army was in the dark. It did not know, for example, how much aluminum went into the manufacture of airplanes. The navy had no bills of materials at all. When the Bureau of Research and Statistics requested estimates of materials and components, the service either failed to respond or offered bogus figures. Under Secretary of the Navy Forrestal protested in 1941 that civilian agencies should be told that the service had no data instead of presented with attempts at deceit. Repeated investigations by the OPM of army and navy input figures revealed that they were usually unreliable and that the services would often revise them radically upward or downward over short periods of time.

The Bureau of Research and Statistics worked with the supply services of both the army and the navy in a futile attempt to improve their statistical methods. In desperation, along with other reforms it negotiated a procedure in which all requirement figures would be funneled to the OPM through the ANMB. The board improved conditions only minimally since it too depended on supply bureaus that used dissimilar methods and displayed differing attitudes, levels of competence, and degrees of cooperation. That left OPM with few options except to keep pressing for reform. Research and Statistics insisted that it had neither the staff nor the authority to take on the nearly overwhelming task of converting military demand into materials and components. But it could profitably review and evaluate the military's calculations. In working out what became the Victory Program in late 1941 and early 1942, the Bureau of Research and Statistics had to devise methods for estimating what was required to produce prospective military requirements. However, in doing so, the Supply Priorities and Allocations Board insisted on the armed services cooperating with OPM at a level that was unusual.

The War and Navy Departments' requirement deficiencies stemmed from attitude and competence. In 1940, both services assumed that the civilian economy could meet any level of demand; in 1941, as scarcity became a reality, they tended to believe that industries should be converted or expanded to meet their needs. Either situation relieved them of the diligence that the NDAC and OPM demanded. Moreover, the supply departments of both services resented the intrusion of civilian agencies into their affairs, and they looked on their requirements as a matter of security that should be beyond civilian scrutiny. Even if the army and navy were fully willing to cooperate with the civilian mobilization agencies, however, they were usually unable to do so. The navy lacked a centralized office of statistics and competent staff for making the calculations that NDAC and OPM desired. While the army was better off in terms of statistical services, the continuing decentralization of its SA&Ss prevented the service from providing OPM the requirement figures that it needed.

Only after the nation entered World War II did the army and navy restructure their supply systems and acquire the trained staff necessary for providing the WPB the requirement figures that it needed. With the creation of the Army Service Forces in March 1942, Commanding General Brehon B. Somervell ordered into effect the Army Supply Program, which not only set forth army requirements in time but also enumerated the facilities, materials, components, and other essential resources necessary to ensure their production. Forrestal accomplished a similar goal with his organization of the OP&M in January 1942, although, consistent with the 1940–1941 period, the navy still lagged behind the army by almost a year. Both services, however, benefited from the guidance and assistance of the ANMB in their newly detailed calculation of requirements.

Indeed, after Pearl Harbor, the ANMB entered its most significant period of activity and influence. Shortly after Under Secretary of the Navy Forrestal joined Under Secretary of War Patterson as cochair of the board in June 1941, the two turned to Ferdinand Eberstadt—who was still working on machine tools for Forrestal—to evaluate and recommend improvements for ANMB operations. Late in November 1941, Eberstadt filed his report, in which he proposed that the board be restructured, headed by a civilian, and converted into a hard-hitting advocate of the military before and within the civilian mobilization agencies. To protect the armed services, Eberstadt went on, board members had to deal with the operating units of the mobilization agencies, not just the executives at the top, as had been the case in the past. A reorganized ANMB would then break down army and navy requirements into raw materials, equipment, and production capacity so that it could work with the OPM and successor agencies in meeting demand. It would also help locate and deal with bottlenecks to military production and distribution. Additionally, the ANMB would keep highly placed military representatives in government agencies appraised of army and navy requirements so that they could effectively protect the services' interests. Naturally, the board would continue to coordinate the armed services' supply and procurement activities.

Eberstadt went on to point out that, in 1941, America's greatest contribution to the war effort was in the area of industrial production. Yet the armed services failed to recognize this fact by continuing to withhold support for and recognition of ANMB. As a result, the quality of officers assigned to the board was at best adequate, and rank was not commensurate with duties. ANMB's executive committee, for example, should be headed by a highly respected lieutenant general and an admiral, not a brigadier general and a captain. Until recently, most officers served only part-time since they had other regular duties outside ANMB. The board was also without an independent budget, making it dependent on the army for funding, space, and staff. A reorganized board, Eberstadt argued, must be led and directed in a way that gained the unquestioned confidence, support, and participation of the navy. Because the ANMB had always been largely a War Department operation, the Navy Department viewed it with caution, joined in its activities halfheartedly, and acted at times to weaken its influence. The board had to have the unified support of both services to succeed in advancing military interests in civilian-directed mobilization.[30]

Patterson and Forrestal immediately agreed to implement Eberstadt's recommendations and offered him the chair, a position he resisted taking until Pearl Harbor. When finally and formally approving the reorganization of the

ANMB on February 21, 1942, Roosevelt specified that the board would operate under the direction of the chair of the newly created WPB.[31]

The ANMB's membership jumped from 150 to 500 within five months after Eberstadt took over as its head in December.[32] More important, under Eberstadt, backed by Patterson and, to a lesser degree, Forrestal, the ANMB became the WPB's competitor. Generally, the ANMB acted as a coordinate, not a subordinate, agency to the WPB, with its representatives on the board answering to military, not civilian, sources. Specifically, it demanded that the WPB speed industrial conversion, institute gasoline rationing, cut back building and production not directly tied to the war effort, restrict railroad usage to national security purposes, and limit foreign assistance that competed with American military requirements. The ANMB's most aggressive move was going through the president to seize control of priorities involving all production, civilian and military alike.

The ANMB's influence was greatest when the WPB was working out its organization and policies in a hurried and tumultuous fashion. By the fall of 1942, the WPB had reached a level of relative stability. Nelson, chair of the board, elected to bring Eberstadt into the organization to benefit from his talents instead of having him undermine the WPB from the outside. The transfer occurred in September. Even if Eberstadt had remained in place, the ANMB could not have continued on its truculent path without harming more than helping economic mobilization. And ANMB faced severe challenges from within the military establishment. General Somervell, head of the Army Service Forces, for example, took every opportunity to weaken the board since he wanted no intermediary between his organization and the civilian mobilization agencies. On its part, the navy continued to neglect ANMB. Facing enormous pressures from above and below at a time when its principal leader moved over to the WPB, the ANMB slowly began to wane, slipping to insignificance in 1943.

The ANMB aided the armed services mainly by trying to shape economic mobilization in a way that served and protected military interests. This goal was fully evident in export controls, stockpiling, machine tools, and, particularly, priorities. The board also served the army and navy by allocating industrial facilities between them and performing other activities designed to prevent the services from competing with one another. In terms of military operations, however, the ANMB could seldom go beyond the services' capabilities, as became clear in efforts to provide the civilian mobilization agencies with usable requirement figures. While, in 1942, the reorganized board under Eberstadt's direction was more active, accomplished, and assertive, it acted to advance military interests at the expense of more rational mobilization policies, which probably detracted from more than added to efforts for harnessing the economy for hostilities. Such was the case with priorities. At best, therefore, the overall record of the ANMB is a mixed and problematic one.

At all times, however, the ANMB was principally a War Department operation. Throughout 1940–1941, army officers conducted most of the board's business, with navy officers often going along or only nominally represented. In 1942, the navy's participation was greater, but still less than the army's in terms of numbers and activity. Several reasons account for this difference between the services. The ANMB resulted from the War Department's interwar procurement and economic mobilization planning, in which the navy barely participated. Hence, the navy, unlike the army, had little investment in the agency. Actually, the navy's supply bureaus looked down on the board as an unnecessary encroachment on their operations. Furthermore, Forrestal and his numerous civilian and military assistants devoted most of their time in 1940–1941 to restructuring the navy's supply and procurement system, concerning which the ANMB could do little. Once the OP&M was in place in 1942, the under secretary of the navy viewed and participated in the ANMB without the fervor of either Patterson or Eberstadt. When in September 1942 Eberstadt left the board for the WPB, Forrestal saw no need for ANMB's continued operation, a position that Patterson opposed. To accommodate Patterson, Forrestal went along with the board remaining active even though its responsibilities were negligible.

The army's response to the ANMB, on the other hand, reflected attitudes about civilian control of the military. Secretary Knox and Under Secretary Forrestal were more willing to subordinate navy supply operations to the civilian mobilization agencies. In January 1941, and in an attenuated way in November 1940, for example, Knox proposed that the OPM take over priority functions from the ANMB so as to eliminate duplication between the two agencies. Secretary Stimson and Under Secretary Patterson squelched the move.[33] Patterson, backed by Stimson, was interested in building up the ANMB as an agency that was at least coordinate, not subordinate, to the NDAC, the OPM, and the WPB. Actually, Stimson, Patterson, and Eberstadt, in attitude and action, appeared to view NDAC, OPM, and WPB, not even as coordinate agencies, but rather as subordinate ones created to assist the War and Navy Departments' procurement operations. Consequently, from mid-1940 through the end of hostilities in 1945, the War Department led the military in resisting and weakening the authority of the principal civilian mobilization agencies. The end result was a harnessed economy characterized by chronic strife and often questionable mobilization policies.[34]

Knox and Forrestal did not manifest the martial zeal of their War Department counterparts. The navy civilian heads ultimately went along with War Department leadership, but without enthusiasm, and often in a passive way. Facing constant challenges to their authority from Admiral King, the material bureaus, and other naval sources, Knox and Forrestal may have been more sensitive to the necessity for civilian control. Additionally, the Navy Department had played only a minor role in the twenty years of procurement and industrial mobilization planning—planning that had convinced the War Department of its ability to manage economic mobilization. Finally, Knox and Forrestal appeared to maintain their identity as the civilian heads of the Navy Department. By way of contrast, Stimson and Knox seemed excessively absorbed in and dedicated to military values.[35]

The multiple differences between the War and the Navy Departments prevented the ANMB from ever performing well. In a sense, the ANMB's decline was for the best. In order to assist the WPB and its predecessors, ANMB had to be a full-fledged joint agency genuinely dedicated to coordinating the procurement operations of the armed services. ANMB never even approached that level of function. Instead, the War Department began using the board in its escalating challenge to civilian mobilization agencies. That development undermined any positive contribution that the ANMB could make, hastening its end.

6
OPM, OPACS, AND THE STRUGGLE TO EXPAND PRODUCTION

Although the Office of Production Management (OPM) had a dual directorship, William S. Knudsen was always its undisputed head. Because Knudsen, along with Sidney Hillman, was not a strong leader and the secretaries of war and the navy did not carry their weight, the OPM council turned out to be ineffective. As a result, OPM operated as a series of divisions instead of as a centrally directed agency.

The Production Division was OPM's must important subunit. It was responsible for ensuring an adequate level of munitions output. At best, the division's record was mixed. In terms of war construction projects, its achievements were positive. But the division fell down badly in the larger and more important areas of converting civilian industries to war production and expanding capacity for the output of basic materials. Early in 1941, the Office of Price Administration and Civilian Supply (OPACS) forced OPM to begin treating conversion seriously. Thereafter, New Dealers and their varied allies in and outside OPACS were out front in preparing the economy for war. The complicated dynamics involved in conversion and expansion are well illustrated by what took place in the automobile industry and aluminum, steel, copper, and rubber.

Throughout 1941, OPM operations were largely shaped by conservative industrialists resisting and liberal reformers, some business elements, organized labor, and various small business advocates pushing for accelerated economic mobilization policies. The armed services verbally favored increasing the rate of mobilization. In fact, however, they acted to bolster the position of corporate America in several ways. The army and navy preferred working directly with industry in the negotiation of contracts, bypassing OPM. When OPM could not be avoided in functions such as priorities and allocations, the War Department, and to a lesser degree the Navy Department, attempted to keep the office as weak as possible so as to interfere least with military economic operations.

OPM

The OPM was a seriously flawed agency because it operated more by impro-visation than by planning. That was the case because the council—consisting of Director General William S. Knudsen, Associate Director General Sidney Hillman, Secretary of War Henry L. Stimson, and Secretary of the Navy Frank Knox—never systematically formulated policy for OPM to implement under the leadership of Knudsen and Hillman. This situation denied the office the centralized direction essential for effective operation. As a result, the Produc-tion, Purchases, and Priorities Divisions continued to act as independent units, as they had under the National Defense Advisory Commission (NDAC). Overall coordination was missing, and vital information did not flow properly from the council to the operating divisions, and vice versa.[1]

The OPM's limitations were largely the fault of Knudsen. Never appreci-ating the need for planning and system, and preferring to work directly with the procurement agencies on an informal basis, he allowed the council to wither rather than making it the center for directing industrial mobilization. Meeting weekly, the council spent inordinate amounts of time on the details of production, Knudsen's specialty, and in the early months bogged down in labor relations. The director general reserved for himself the right to make up the weekly agenda. Occasionally, he allowed other members to add items and then insisted on keeping the agenda confidential. Inexplicable secrecy en-veloped the entire operations of the OPM council. Knudsen's approach pre-cluded a review of the topics to be considered and denied council members the time and information to prepare for meetings. Outsiders were seldom in-vited to council deliberations despite the almost constant need for expert ad-vice, and, except for rare appearances in July and August 1941, OPM division heads were not in attendance even when their activities were being consid-ered. Voting was at best informal, with dissent never recorded since disputes were resolved informally as they arose.

Actually, many critical decisions were made outside the council structure, through consultations among Knudsen, Stimson, and Knox. The director gen-eral had private telephone lines between his office and those of Stimson and Knox. Through daily communication with the secretaries of war and the navy, supplemented by personal letters from Knudsen to the two department heads, numerous issues were settled. This procedure acted to continue the informal military-industry production team that had dominated the operations of the NDAC.[2] It also undermined the administrative efficiency of OPM since deci-sions made by Knudsen, Stimson, and Knox were not regularly shared with the office's operating divisions.

Effective staff work could have compensated to some degree for the council's malfunction. Knudsen, however, never met on any regular basis with the heads of the OPM's various divisions. Such meetings were a standard practice in Leon Henderson's OPACs, and Under Secretary of War Robert P. Patterson and Under Secretary of the Navy James V. Forrestal used them with good effect in their offices. Staff conferences would have given Knudsen the opportunity to share data with his principal subordinates, allowed the latter to inform Knudsen and Hillman of crucial developments in their areas, and, ideally, furthered the cause of collective decisionmaking. Without such meetings, the OPM divisions were encouraged to operate as separate units, and Knudsen was denied information crucial to his stewardship. The director general, for example, did not become aware that the priorities system was breaking down until it was too late to institute reform.

The failures of Knudsen's leadership placed great pressure on Herbert Emmerich as secretary of the OPM.[3] From the outset, he was forced to act as executive secretary, although he was not officially elevated to that position until September 1941. At first, Emmerich could send no communications or directives to OPM subdivisions without first clearing them with Knudsen. Later, he was permitted to act on his own initiative in this regard. With sources for coordination weak within the office, Emmerich tried to fill the void as best he could, but without clear direction or authority. Indeed, the secretary took on the sensitive task of keeping Knudsen and Hillman up-to-date. Knudsen did not tell Hillman about what was occurring with production, and the latter kept the former in the dark on labor matters. Keeping abreast of what took place in both areas, Emmerich filled each of his bosses in on what the other was doing. The more responsibilities Emmerich took on, the more he felt compelled to remain impartial in the strife-ridden OPM, conditions deterring his ability to respond and leaving him open to ribbing about his compulsive "objectivity." Without Emmerich seizing the initiative, numerous crucial matters before OPM were never acted on.

Knudsen, however, was not solely responsible for the weak leadership at the top of OPM. The director general reflected the attitudes of corporate America, which at this point preferred casual over focused economic mobilization efforts. Also, Hillman, a poor administrator himself who concentrated on labor issues, made no attempt to strengthen the functioning of the council. Even if he had moved in that direction, there were always severe limits on what Hillman could accomplish.

But that was not the case with the War and Navy Departments. Controlling billions of dollars of appropriations, and holding the statutory power for procurement, they automatically affected mobilization policy by whatever they did. The armed services had been incorporated into what became the OPM council to further coordination between supply and demand, a quality that had been lacking in NDAC. In actuality, the armed services added little to the quality of OPM operations. They treated their presence on the OPM council as advisory, not executive, using their influence to benefit military supply operations without taking responsibility for the office's overall performance. Approaching economic mobilization in a parochial way, the armed services assumed that strong civilian agencies reduced their prerogatives. Hence, they did not seek to improve OPM functions unless they realized direct and immediate gain. As related in chapter 5 above, the military's response to OPM resulted as much from weakness as from strength.

Nonetheless, the War and Navy Departments were usually the most well-represented participants at the weekly OPM council meetings. By February 1941, the under secretaries of war and the navy had begun to attend council meetings in place of or along with the secretaries, and, by May, the former began to replace the latter, which was appropriate since, in both departments, the under secretaries directed supply and procurement operations. Whether the secretaries, the under secretaries, or both sat in for the departments, they were accompanied by legal counsel, Julius H. Amberg for the War Department and usually William W. Dulles for the Navy Department. Amberg was a Harvard Law classmate of Under Secretary of War Patterson who emerged in effect as chief counsel for the War Department during World War II in terms of supply and procurement. In that capacity, he played an important role in shaping policy and legislation, and he acted as a principal spokesman for the department before other government agencies and Congress. Dulles, who served in the law firm representing Dillon, Read and Company, was not as high-powered as Amberg, but Charles F. Detmar, Jr., who like Dulles came from Wright, Gordon, Zachary, Parlin, and Cahill and who occasionally attended OPM council meetings, was, and he played a role in the Navy Department similar to Amberg's in the War Department.[4]

OPM'S PRODUCTION DIVISION

The Production Division had two principal functions: overseeing facilities construction, conversion, and use and acting to ensure the availability of materials essential to defense and war production. Actually, the two responsibilities overlapped. By helping eliminate from or reduce in construction the use of critical materials such as aluminum, nickel, copper, and brass, the division conserved them for higher-priority needs.

For facilities, the Production Division assisted, guided, and regulated programs of the armed services and initiated projects of its own. The overall results were impressive. While building for defense totaled nearly $6.2 billion in 1940, the figure jumped to $16.7 billion in 1941. Of that amount, around $2.7 billion went for military construction, $3.7 billion for housing, $2.7 billion for industrial services, and over $7.6 billion for manufacturing, mining, and oil extraction. Late in 1941, the Shipbuilding, Construction, and Supplies Branch of the Production Division reported that practically all construction programs were on time, under circumstances in which the price of building materials had risen 9 percent in 1941 and wages only 5 percent in 1940–1941, with cost-plus-fixed-fee contracts giving way to negotiated or competitive lump-sum ones. Priority and allocation orders for protecting defense construction, along with conservation efforts, had made this record possible.

Until the creation of the Supply Priorities and Allocations Board (SPAB) in late August 1941, no restrictions existed on civilian construction. The board moved quickly to reverse that condition. Between early September and the first week of October, it halted all private and public civilian building, which consumed substantial amounts of critical materials without furthering national defense or protecting public health and welfare. These policies ran into intense opposition, but they nonetheless reduced by 24 percent construction projects in the East during the last months of 1941.[5]

By April 1941, the OPM in general, and the Production Division in particular, faced its greatest challenge. The growing defense program could no longer be handled under a "guns and butter" approach. Curtailing the output of civilian industries and converting their plant to production for defense purposes were becoming necessities. Critical shortages were developing in basic materials (e.g., steel) and equipment (e.g., machine tools). America could no longer simultaneously fulfill expanding munitions programs at home and abroad and escalating demand for consumer durable goods fed by the spreading prosperity that defense spending spurred. Trying to meet growing defense and civilian requirements through a massive, all-out building of new plants was not an acceptable solution. Such an approach would take too long and exacerbate existing shortages by placing an even greater strain on materials and equipment. Cutting back on consumer durables production, however, would automatically increase the supply of practically all materials and equipment as well as making America's most advanced plants available for munitions output. The automobile industry, for example, included the nation's best and most extensive collection of engineering talent. In 1939, automobiles absorbed 18 percent of total national steel output, 80 percent of rubber, 34 percent of lead, nearly 10–14 percent of copper, tin, and aluminum, and 90 percent of gasoline. Throughout 1940 and 1941, automobile production went up, taking proportionately even more materials and products indispensable for defense preparation.

In April 1941, the Bureau of Research and Statistics concluded that the combined demand of the army, navy, Maritime Commission, and British requirements totaled around $49 billion. That level of production under existing circumstances, the bureau explained, was unachievable. Except for the navy's, all the munitions were scheduled to be completed by the end of 1942. To meet production commitments for 1941 alone, output capacity for rifles, machine guns, small arms ammunition, and tanks would have to be expanded two- to fivefold. Existing shortages of materials and tools stood in the way, and shortages would grow more desperate as time wore on. Only by cutting back on consumer durable goods, the bureau insisted, could defense requirements be met. The Bureau of Research and Statistics's analysis became even more alarming after Congress expanded the defense load even further by passing the Lend-Lease Act on March 11, 1941, and appropriating $7 billion on April 27, 1941, to initiate aid. Along those lines, the president in April 1941 ordered assistance to Latin America to be treated on a par with domestic demand and in July approved a $1.8 billion lend-lease package to Russia—including aircraft, ordnance, machine tools, and whole plants for the production of aviation gasoline and automobile tires—that could take precedence over the nation's own needs. Beginning in May, Roosevelt also became increasingly insistent that OPM begin curtailing and converting civilian industry for defense purposes, and he was sporadically backed by the War and Navy Departments.[6]

Led by Knudsen and John D. Biggers, director of the Production Division, OPM as a whole generally insisted that any attempt to curtail and convert consumer durable goods industries had to take place gradually and cautiously.[7] The Production Division's Production Planning Board had initially supported fast action on cutting back on civilian output but eventually switched to favoring a slower approach. OPM maintained that defense needs could and should be met with the least dislocation to the existing economy. In order for that to take place, curtailment had to be based on as full knowledge of the various industries as could be obtained, and manufacturing should be cut back only when defense orders could be simultaneously phased in to take up the slack. Otherwise, industries would be closed, production teams dispersed, and unemployment fostered. None of these steps, OPM officials argued, could take place until long-run requirements—military, essential civilian, and foreign—could be determined. Fearful of unemployment, organized labor in and outside OPM either tended to proceeded cautiously on curtailment or sided with management. Under the general guidelines of Congress of Industrial Organizations (CIO) president Philip Murray, Walter Reuther in December 1940 attempted to move labor from a passive/defensive position on curtailment to an active/offensive one. His initiative involved tripartite planning for automobiles, first to take up unused capacity by producing planes alongside cars, and then, as defense needs grew, slowly to convert the industry to munitions. While ingenious, Reuther's plan would have rearranged power positions in Detroit radically, which doomed it to failure. Automobile firms resisted intensely any curtailment and conversion that disturbed competitive positions in the industry, let alone those that invited unions to the corporate boardrooms.

OPACS

The battles over curtailment began in April and grew in intensity throughout the year. Consideration of curtailment began in earnest in April after the Bureau of Research and Statistics reported that consumer durables had to be cut back to fulfill defense needs. Biggers turned to major automobile producers and the OPM executives for advice on the issue of cutting back automobile output. Shortly thereafter, OPACS was created, and it quickly became the leading advocate of converting consumer durables in order to meet defense demand and protect essential civilian needs in the long run. Almost immediately, OPACS and OPM became bitter rivals over economic mobilization policy and procedure. At the heart of the dispute was OPM's dedication to gradual curtailment and OPACS's insistence on speedy results. This difference was magnified by jurisdictional conflict between the two agencies and the fact that OPM was identified as an industry-oriented agency while OPACS carried the New Deal label. Competition became especially keen when, on May 31, 1941, Congress extended the president's priority power to include the civilian area as well as the allocation of materials. Both agencies tried to claim the new authority, forcing Roosevelt to reorganize the mobilization structure late in August and early in September before he would delegate his new powers.

Before that occurred, Leon Henderson's OPACS moved forcefully in June to protect essential civilian industries and services in the face of growing shortages of materials and equipment. In doing so, OPACS had earlier worked out with the Priorities Division procedures for applying priorities to civilian areas where defense was directly or indirectly involved. Relying on criteria designed to protect public welfare and achieve equity, OPACS in June introduced a program for allocating to civilian industries pig iron, ferroalloys, steel ingots and castings, and carbon and alloy steel products. Later in June and July, OPACS extended preferential treatment for materials and equipment to maintain and/or repair a host of services and industries. These included public transportation and communication networks, food processing and storage, trucks, and fire, police, and education systems.

With inflationary pressures rising, OPACS also moved to hold down prices. The lack of official authority to control prices did not deter Leon Henderson. When the major automobile manufacturers announced a general price increase in June 1941, the OPACS director asked them to rescind the action. An uncooperative stance on the part of the Chrysler Corporation and others led to Henderson unleashing a blistering public attack, stressing that huge profits made higher prices totally unnecessary. With Henderson threatening to go to the president and Congress in search of mandatory controls, the automobile firms finally backed down. When furniture manufacturers failed to heed OPACS's call for stable pricing, Henderson called on the Federal Trade Commission to investigate their market conditions. By July 1, the OPACS director publicly insisted that he needed statutory authority to carry out his price control responsibilities.

OPACS's major effort was devoted to curtailing unessential civilian production, particularly automobiles. Such action, Henderson and his lieutenants insisted, was imperative in terms of both advancing the defense program and protecting essential civilian industries and services. Consumer durables were absorbing massive amounts of materials and equipment already in short supply. And such output was growing, not diminishing. For example, between April and May 1941—within months of Pearl Harbor—automobile output had grown by 27 percent over the same months in 1940, and that pattern was continuing. This situation was breaking down the entire priority system. Automobile companies engaged in preemptive buying, inventory stocking, and the hoarding of steel and other metals to ensure output. Steel firms supplied the automobile companies, their best customers, ahead of other industries. With steel in short supply, procurement officers rated all orders as high as possible, denying industry proper priority guidance and leading to preference directives being ignored. These circumstances simply could not continue.

In terms of peacetime production, automobiles as civilian goods were the responsibility of OPACS. Well before this agency came into existence, however, OPM's Production Division worked with the automobile industry as defense producers of airplane and maritime engines and future aircraft, tanks, ordnance, and other munitions, and the division intended to continue making policy for Detroit. This trend was strengthened by the fact that Knudsen came from General Motors Corporation and Biggers from Libby-Owens-Ford

Glass Company, a major supplier to the automobile industry. Biggers began discussing a cutback with the industry early in April; early in May Knudsen announced that the office had worked out with Detroit a plan to reduce car output 20.15 percent between August 1, 1941, and July 31, 1942, a figure based on the previous year's production. In June, the OPM established an automobile industry section in the Production Division. OPM then scheduled a meeting with industry representatives for July 2 to select an industry advisory committee and subcommittees and prepare for creating a labor advisory committee to assist curtailment. At that point OPACS balked.

Henderson insisted that, unless military production was involved, the automobile industry was in his domain. He would keep abreast of OPM activity, but he would not work with the office's advisory committees. On July 15, Henderson's assistant administrator, Joseph L. Weiner, met with representatives of the automobile industry, a meeting that would have been tense under any circumstances since Henderson had just forced the automobile makers to surrender their declared price increases. These circumstances were aggravated further by Weiner indicating that his office lacked the OPM's solicitude for Detroit. The automobile industry, Weiner announced, was consuming vital materials and tools at an unacceptable rate, and, because of size, wealth, previous output, and potential convertibility, it could and should carry a greater burden of curtailment than other industries. Immediate curtailment was called for since vital industries like canning could no longer compete with the automobile industry for steel and even military contractors were unable to receive the steel that they needed. On their part, automobile executives argued fervently that they should not be punished simply for being big, that only a small portion of the industry's plant and tools was convertible to defense production, and that to cut automobile output excessively would produce unacceptably high levels of unemployment for no purpose.

Henderson moved boldly on July 20, 1941, to break the stalemate over curtailment. He announced OPACS programs for cutting by 50 percent over the next twelve months scarce materials going to the automobile and household refrigerator and laundry equipment industries. With attention focusing on Detroit, Henderson's action created a furor in Michigan, the OPM, management, and labor. Although OPM would not use its priority powers to implement OPACS's program, Henderson's aggressive tactics forced OPM to work out with the Automotive Defense Industry Advisory Committee and its subcommittees a curtailment program far beyond Knudsen's 20+ percent proposal of May 1941. With all agencies agreeing, including the Automotive Labor Advisory Committee, a curtailment program for Detroit was finally agreed to on August 21, 1941. Between August 1, 1941, and July 31, 1942, automobile output would be curtailed by 43.3 percent. The cutbacks would start gradually for the first quarter at 6.5 percent and grow until they reached 62 percent of the targeted goal in the last quarter. Major firms would be hit the hardest, but all corporations would be allowed to continue production. The program began to be implemented through OPM limitation, blanket preference, and conservation orders. Automobile curtailment got under way in 1941, but just barely before Pearl Harbor.

With the automobile industry serving as precedent and model, OPACS was prepared late in August to issue curtailment programs for domestic refrigerators, washing and ironing machines, cooking stoves, vacuum cleaners, and metal office furniture. Before OPACS could act, however, Roosevelt created the SPAB on August 28, 1941, which in turn led to the reorganization of OPM and the end of OPACS. Decisionmaking on curtailment and all other aspects of economic mobilization, therefore, shifted to a higher level.

Through its Materials Branch the Production Division also formulated policies for materials that were key to economic mobilization. Curtailment in 1941 was principally aimed at ensuring that defense manufacturers had adequate amounts of scarce or potentially scarce materials. For the first few months, W. Averell Harriman, chairman of the board of the Union Pacific Railroad, headed the branch. Then Samuel R. Fuller, Jr., president of the North American Rayon Corporation and the American Bemberg Corporation, moved over from the chair of the Production Planning Board to take over materials.

With serious shortages evident in key metals and other materials, expanding output became essential in 1941. Any progress made along those lines came only after a great deal of turmoil. Without reliable military requirements, calculating current and future demand was enormously taxing and always subject to dispute. Industry, which dominated OPM, usually resisted expanding its plant out of fear of excess capacity and other concerns. To get around industry's objections, the federal government financed and assumed nearly all the risk for new or expanded facilities beginning in 1941. Even then, New Dealers, academicians, public servants, and other like-minded people had to lead in initiating massive industrial growth. At all times, however, they had the support of various industrialists and businessmen who agreed with their analysis and had the expertise and prestige to convince industry that expanding America's plant for strategic materials had become essential. Without industry's cooperation, no matter how grudging and skeptical it often was, increased output potential could not have been achieved. Aluminum, steel,

copper, and rubber illustrate these realities. They are among the most important industries in which production fell critically short during World War II,
and they were in 1941 already experiencing trouble.

ALUMINUM

Along with machine tools, aluminum in February 1941 became the first prod-
uct subject to mandatory priority action.[8] Actually, aircraft firms complained of
aluminum shortages as early as September 1940, and by December 1940 the
NDAC was fully aware of grave problems with the metallic element. Once the
OPM came into existence, William S. Knudsen almost immediately asked the
Priorities Division to act on the growing aluminum crisis. Other than for pri-
orities, aluminum was under the direction of the Aluminum and Magnesium
Unit in the Materials Branch.[9]

Two-thirds of the aluminum produced during the war years went into the
construction of aircraft, and the metal was also used widely in ships, tanks,
ordnance, and numerous other munitions. The Aluminum Company of America (Alcoa)—the sole American producer of primary aluminum at the time—
had a manufacturing capacity of around 325 million pounds in 1939. At the
peak of wartime output late in 1943, the nation's capacity had grown to 2.3
billion pounds, over a sevenfold increase. That remarkable record was accomplished only after intense conflict.

Two principal problems involving aluminum plagued the NDAC and the
OPM. The first difficulty involved requirements. Neither the military, aircraft
firms, nor Alcoa knew how much aluminum went into the construction of
any one of a number of airplanes. Hence, when Roosevelt called for the production of fifty thousand planes a year in May 1940, estimates varied widely
as to how much aluminum this goal required. Until the United States entered
World War II, the army and navy's record in requirements did not improve
much, and, of crucial significance, the services were never able to break down
gross figures into alloy or type of aluminum for sheet, extrusions, forgings,
and tubing. Alcoa and the mobilization agencies, however, became increasingly adept at calculating how much and what type and form of aluminum
went into the manufacture of various aircraft.

The second source of trouble stemmed from Alcoa's monopoly in the production of primary aluminum. Throughout 1940, and into 1941, the corporation was reluctant to expand its plant out of a fear of creating excess capacity
and/or losing its monopolistic control. Challenging Alcoa was not easy since
few experts outside its own ranks existed. The Mineral Advisory Committee

to the Army-Navy Munitions Board (ANMB), for example, included in its subcommittee on aluminum and bauxite important officials from Alcoa. Indeed, throughout the NDAC period, Alcoa was directly or indirectly involved in practically all calculations of supply and demand involving defense. Only in the area of civilian demand did the Bureau of Research and Statistics operate independently of the corporation.

Alcoa's practical monopoly on expertise as well as production resulted in grave paradoxes during the NDAC period. In the commission, aluminum policies were shaped largely by Marion B. Folsom and Grenville R. Holden, Eastman Kodak Company executives who followed Alcoa's lead. The corporation had expanded its output during 1940 from around 325 to 400 million pounds, and by July 1942 it would be able to produce nearly 700 million pounds—amounts, Alcoa insisted, adequate for satisfying domestic and foreign defense requirements as well as growing civilian markets. In attempts to make their analysis credible, NDAC and Alcoa had to juggle and modify statistics on both supply and demand and improvise to meet emergency situations.

Edward R. Stettinius, Jr., head of the Industrial Materials Division, repeatedly had to step in to assure the press, the president, and the nation that all was well with aluminum. Nonetheless, challenges grew within and outside the commission. In the last quarter of 1940, complaints of aluminum deficiencies from aircraft manufacturers became more frequent and sharp. Finally, at the end of December 1940, the Northrop Aircraft Corporation announced that it was cutting work shifts from ten to eight hours because it was running out of aluminum. Alcoa all but wrote NDAC's public denials that shortages existed. Northrop's chairman of the board scolded Stettinius: "If a delay in the receipt of raw materials of nearly half a year is not a shortage, I don't know what one is."[10]

Shortly after OPM replaced NDAC in January 1941, Frank B. Cliffe, from General Electric Company, took over leadership of the Aluminum and Magnesium Unit. NDAC's optimism about aluminum quickly changed. The metal was placed under mandatory and strict priority control, and the need for increased capacity was affirmed. By then, Reynolds Metal Company—principally devoted to manufacturing aluminum foil but also involved in aluminum fabrication—had entered the field. Richard S. Reynolds, the company's driving president, late in 1940 began building in Alabama, and completed ahead of schedule, a fully integrated 60-million-pound plant for producing primary aluminum. Despite Reynolds's achievement, OPM concluded that multiplying demand could no longer be met by private enterprise: new plants financed by the government (ultimately totaling around $700 million) and supplied with electricity from public facilities had become essential. Private industry either could not or would not build the plant or provide the power that was needed. Under such circumstances, the aluminum industry would be opened to all bidders, no longer reserved alone for Alcoa. Nonetheless, because of its overwhelming presence, Alcoa by necessity would be closely involved in all decisions about aluminum made by the mobilization agencies.

Between April and May 1941, circumstances forced OPM constantly to up its plans for expanding primary aluminum plant from 200 to 600 million pounds. With 800 million pounds of capacity already existing or being built plus an anticipated 200 million pounds annually imported from Canada, the new facilities would give the United States around a 1.6-billion-pound-supply of ingot aluminum by the end of 1942. All the new facilities, except for Reynolds's Alabama plant, would be financed by the Defense Plant Corporation (DPC). The Aluminum and Magnesium Unit tried to attract as many firms as possible to build and operate the new facilities, but, in the end, only Alcoa, Reynolds, and the Olin Corporation participated, with Alcoa in charge of over 80 percent of the additional plant.

To get the expansion seriously under way, the Materials Branch in June 1941 had to bring in Arthur H. Bunker, executive vice-president of the Lehman Corporation. Trained as an electrical engineer, Bunker had a background in metallurgy. Without hesitation, he pushed the aluminum program forward, including action to ensure adequate supplies of raw materials (especially bauxite and cryolite), electric power, and equipment. When the DPC dragged its feet on financing the projects, Bunker in August and September successfully carried his fight for movement to OPM leaders, the press, the SPAB, and, finally, the Senate Special Committee to Investigate the Defense Program (also known as the Truman Committee). With the reorganization of OPM late in August, both Biggers and Stettinius, and their subordinates, left the office as the last of the old guard as far as aluminum policy was involved. This strengthened further the leadership positions of Bunker and the Aluminum and Magnesium Unit. The Truman Committee became an invaluable platform through which critics of NDAC and OPM aluminum policies could voice their dissent and have their views widely publicized (through committee hearings and reports).

Under directions from the SPAB in September 1941 to calculate requirements for a two-year period of warfare, Bunker and his associates concluded that the projected output of 1.2 billion pounds of aluminum by 1942 (down from the earlier figure of 1.6 billion pounds) would be too low by half to meet estimated needs. The figure would have to be at least 2.1 billion pounds, just slightly below the peak production capacity reached late in 1943.

Despite the nearly endless turmoil surrounding aluminum in 1940–1941, the expansion begun during those years provided a firm foundation for further growth during the war years. In September 1943, aluminum was no longer a problem, with national production capacity standing at about 2.3 billion pounds. By then, mobilization agencies had the luxury of considering stockpiles for emergencies and cutting back output as circumstances permitted.

STEEL

The steel industry, like aluminum, also resisted expanding productive capacity in the defense period.[11] Compared with aluminum's sevenfold increase in wartime output, steel's growth was modest. Total steel ingot output went up from about 67 to around 89.5 million net tons between January 1940 and January 1945, in excess of 33 percent. (Capacity percentage growth was even less for the same period, jumping from 81.6 to 95.5 million tons, or nearly 17 percent.) Nonetheless, since steel was basic to the operations of the economy, it was more important than any other single product to economic mobilization.

Steel was an oligopolistic industry dominated in 1940 by about thirteen integrated firms—such as the United States Steel Corporation (U.S. Steel), the Bethlehem Steel Corporation, and the Jones and Laughlin Steel Company—that accounted for 87.7 percent of total ingot production. U.S. Steel alone controlled over one-third of capacity. The remaining firms were relatively small and independent or only partially integrated. Beginning early in the twentieth century, U.S. Steel—later supported by the American Iron and Steel Institute (AISI)—played a key role in stabilizing the industry through eliminating price competition and dividing markets.

The trauma of the Great Depression caused leaders in steel to bristle at the notion of substantially increasing ingot capacity for war. Throughout the 1930s, production as a percentage of capacity ranged from a low of 19.5 to a high of 72.5 percent, averaging just short of 48 percent. In 1939, it stood at 65 percent. A decade of surplus capacity, combined with losses or only token profits for most of the decade, created a nearly unshakable conviction among corporate heads that they could meet practically any increase in demand with existing capacity. Steel's outlook was reflected in the mobilization agencies. Stettinius, who headed the Industrial Materials Division of the NDAC, was from U.S. Steel, and the commission's steel policies were shaped largely by the iron and steel products section, which was headed by Walter S. Tower, president of the AISI. In the OPM, first the Materials Branch of the Production Division and then the Materials Division were subject to the same steel industry influences, although during the last quarter of 1941 the Iron and

Steel Branch of the Materials Division showed more independence than had its predecessors.

Intense disputes over expanding steel capacity began in earnest late in 1940. With military and civilian demand growing at home and exports also increasing, steel ingot production rose to new heights, excess capacity all but disappeared, and shortages were already beginning to show up in plates, castings, and forgings, all critical to munitions manufacture. In December, Secretary of the Treasury Henry J. Morgenthau, Jr., warned the president that the need for greater steelmaking capacity was obvious. His argument was bolstered by a December 10, 1940, report on the steel situation that Marvin G. deChazeau and Douglass V. Brown (economists serving first in the NDAC and then in the OPM) forwarded to Stettinius. The two economists elaborated on convictions that were prevalent in the Roosevelt administration for some time and that grew in importance from September on. Conservatively estimating total demand at home and abroad against anticipated steel output capacity, deChazeau and Brown projected possible steel shortages as early as fiscal year 1941 and more likely in fiscal year 1942. National security demanded that steel expand its capacity or that civilian consumption of steel be curtailed. The NDAC's Bureau of Research and Statistics, along with members of the Federal Reserve Board, the Commerce Department, and the Treasury Department, voiced agreement with the position of deChazeau and Brown.

According to a scholar of the NDAC period: "Opposition to the Brown-deChazeau report was little short of violent."[12] Spokesmen for steel in and outside NDAC challenged both the methodology and the conclusions of the two economists and insisted that ample steel capacity existed for any reasonably predictable emergency. AISI President Tower went on to argue that building new or expanded plants within the coming eighteen months would harm more than help preparedness by diverting critical parts and materials away from the defense program. Besides, Tower insisted, shortages of raw materials and labor made any new plant at best problematic. Even before the flare-up caused by the deChazeau-Brown report, steel spokesmen had indicated that, if a shortage of steel arose, it could best be met by cutting back civilian consumption, regulating exports, and instituting priority and allocation controls, not by expanding steel.

Roosevelt turned to Stettinius for resolution of the steel controversy. Stettinius was the logical person for this role since he headed the Industrial Materials Division in NDAC and the Priorities Division in OPM, was well connected in the steel industry, but had the reputation of a moderate who looked favorably on the New Deal. Stettinius, in turn, argued that resolving the dispute required reliable figures on existing and projected supply and demand. To provide expert assessment, Stettinius in December 1940 turned to Gano Dunn, who had excellent credentials. He was a consultant in the Industrial Materials Branch, was president of both the J. G. White Engineering Corporation and Cooper Union, and a member of the board of directors of J. P. Morgan and Company. Stettinius expected Dunn to come up with a compromise position of moderately expanding steel capacity and persuading the industry's executives that such a step was essential.

Dunn did not go down the middle. Instead, in February 1941, he reported to the president that steel capacity was more than adequate for emergency needs, with excess capacity in 1941 running somewhere between 10 and 14 million tons. Although Roosevelt was skeptical, he felt compelled to endorse Dunn's work to avoid panic buying of steel, which would make conditions worse. While the steel executives were elated by what Dunn reported, they stood practically alone. The Bureau of Research and Statistics, OPM economists, and other mobilization authorities predictably attacked Dunn's work. So too did *Time* and *Fortune* magazines. Shaken by the widespread criticism and a rapidly changing reality, Dunn in a follow-up report to the president in May 1941 changed his forecast to one of modest shortages of steel in 1941 and substantial ones in 1942.

Part of the difficulty in assessing the adequacy of steel capacity for defense and war was the perennial problem of inadequate requirement figures from the armed services, let alone ones that were broken down by bills of materials. Throughout most of 1940–1941, estimated military demand was low, which served to validate the steel industry's claim that it could handle the emergency. In July 1940, for example, the ANMB set the maximum armed forces demand for steel in a year of war at less than 17 percent of current capacity. When combining military demand with that of exports, steel executives came up with a total of under 23 percent. These figures were vastly off the mark. By March 1941, defense orders accounted for 30 percent of output, and, in 1943–1944, direct military demand took over 54 percent of all steel production. While the army stood with steel against expansion in late 1940, in early 1941 the navy increasingly supported a greater plant.

Harsh realities settled the debate over steel capacity in favor of those insisting on expansion. In mid-1941, demand for steel exceeded supply. That critical condition continued throughout the years of World War II, making steel a primary factor limiting economic mobilization. Between June 1940 and June 1941, defense production doubled. With military budgets continuing to go up and the Lend-Lease Act passed in March 1941, economic mobilization pressures would grow more intense. Spot shortages of steel became evident as early as January 1941, and they reached crisis proportions in May. By March, the output of structural steel was two months in arrears, and new orders could not be filled for five months or more. With munitions claiming all of steel plate, shipyards were behind schedule in July, and the manufacture of railroad cars had to cease. Similar conditions prevailed with heavy forgings, tool steel, and other steel alloys.

By mid-1941, more rigid control over steel distribution had become necessary. But that was not enough to solve existing and future problems. Steel's productive capacity had to be increased substantially. The Roosevelt administration simultaneously moved to implement both approaches.

The system of voluntary priorities instituted in October 1940 would no longer suffice. Steel firms at times ignored the military's priority ratings in order to oblige principal civilian customers like automobile firms. With munitions orders threatened, the armed services demanded mandatory priorities. Civilian industries complained about practices that cut them out, and panic buying and hoarding became evident. As a result, OPM began tightening the regulation of steel. On May 1, 1941, the office issued General Metals Order No. 1, setting limits on inventories for a number of critical metals. More significantly, late in May, OPM began instituting various priority-type controls in attempts to ensure that general defense and essential civilian production as well as that for the military received adequate steel supplies. In August, the office began allocating pig iron, and it was prepared to implement OPACS programs for curtailing automobiles and other consumer durables to conserve steel, among other goals. Shortly after its creation late in August 1941, the SPAB made all priority orders mandatory and extended OPM's efforts for allocating materials, ultimately leading to the Controlled Materials Plan (CMP), implemented at the end of 1942 with steel in a central position. After Pearl Harbor, the nonessential use of steel was prohibited, and numerous other conservation measures were taken to increase the availability of the metal for war purposes.[13]

To break the logjam on larger plant, Roosevelt in May 1941 instructed OPM to study a proposal for 15-million-ton expansion. With steel and OPM executives either uncertain or opposed to increased capacity, the administration used a carrot-and-a-stick approach. Through the DPC, the government would finance the growth. In April 1941, Henry J. Kaiser had proposed a new company on the West Coast, and other competitors would also probably come forward if the industry continued to resist. Under this lure and threat, steel had to give way in the face of the palpable need for greater productive capacity. Responding to increasing demand and accelerated amortization, steel had already gradually expanded its plant between 1940 and 1941, primarily through private financing. Through tough bargaining beginning in mid-1941, steel executives first reduced Roosevelt's figures from 15 to 10 million tons and by September reached agreement on 13 million tons. Nearly all expansion was to be financed by the government, under contractual conditions in which existing steel companies would operate the new plant with the opportunity to buy it from the government at a reduced price at the war's end. Most of the construction added to existing facilities, although some wholly new plants in different locations were built. Operating through OPM, steel firms also managed to freeze out all new entrants. Kaiser succeeded in becoming a West Coast producer only in February 1942, after the outbreak of war.

Roosevelt wanted the new steel facilities to be operating by early 1942. None were. One-third of the plant was built by the end of 1942, and the entire program—with various modifications dictated by wartime needs—was not in place until mid-1944. A number of conditions accounted for the delays. First, industry remained unenthusiastic. Hence, OPM continued to resist expansion, and the Steel Division of the War Production Board (WPB) always displayed reservations about most wartime controls. Indeed, the division manipulated the WPB Requirements Committee and the Appeals Board in a way exaggerating its accomplishments and increasing the flow of steel to peacetime customers. Second, the armed services insisted on downgrading priorities for construction. They were convinced that additional steel output was unnecessary because it would go to civilian usage. Finally, increasing ingot production had to be coordinated with the supply of iron ore, coke, pig iron, and the like, all of which took time and careful planning.

Other factors were also involved. Throughout the defense and war years, various existing steel facilities had to be converted from the usual civilian output to the production of alloy, plate, fine wire, and heavy forgings to meet munitions needs. Steel alloys were especially in great demand. With the exception of molybdenum and nickel, the United States depended on often-threatened foreign sources for ferroalloys such as manganese, tungsten, vanadium, and cobalt. Through such strategies as emergency operations to protect imports, maximizing domestic output, stockpiling, substitutes, and more efficient usage, the nation managed to solve nearly all its ferroalloy problems by early in 1943.

Although there was never enough steel for all needs from 1941 into 1945, careful regulation of the metal prevented steel shortages from harming defense and war production in any major way. Ensuring that proper amounts of specified steel were in the right place at the designated time required intricate timing and execution. The planning was ultimately successful and depended heavily on the steel industry and its executives. Hence, in mobilizing for World War II, steel manifested both its worst and its best features. A determined oligopoly was able to resist expansion in the face of obvious need, accept growth only when its own self-serving terms were met, and obstruct mobilization policies that it opposed. Yet successfully harnessing this indispensable industry for war was made possible in large part by the quality of steel's peacetime planning, which oligopoly made possible.

COPPER

Copper was another metal that became critically short during the defense and war years.[14] Comprehensive regulation became necessary to prevent copper from disrupting munitions output. Not a bulk metal like steel, copper was a strategic one for an industrial society, particularly important for electrical lighting, heating, and equipment, telegraph and telephone systems, automobiles, and construction. During war, no airplane, ship, tank, or truck could operate without copper, let alone increasingly sophisticated communications systems and advanced weaponry. Practically all ammunition and shells were manufactured from copper alloys, brass and bronze.

The American copper industry was an oligopoly, increasingly dominated by the so-called Big Four: Phelps Dodge Corporation; Anaconda Copper Corporation; American Smelting and Refining Company; and Kennecott Copper Corporation. On the eve of World War II, the Big Four accounted for around 80 percent of American copper output, and their subsidiaries processed 50 percent of the copper that they produced. Not only was the United States the world's leading producer of copper, but Anaconda and Kennecott also had large copper holdings in Latin America, particularly Chile, the globe's second major source of copper.

These realities created a false sense of security about copper in defense circles. The ANMB in April 1939 saw no possibility of a copper shortage during a national emergency, and it basically reaffirmed that conviction as late as November 1940. The board's position was seconded in June 1940 by Stettinius, the NDAC commissioner of industrial materials, who estimated total military and civilian requirements for a two-year war at around 1.3 million tons of copper, with U.S. capacity set at approximately 1 million tons annually. In actuality, copper consumption at peak levels in 1943 exceeded 3 million tons annually. By the end of 1942, 85 percent of available copper went directly to war production, with the remainder divided among indirect wartime uses and essential civilian needs. Vastly increased wartime consumption was met through expanded domestic output, use of scrap, and imports.

The sanguine assessments about copper began to be doubted late in 1940 and gave way to growing anxiety about shortages early in 1941. In December, the ANMB for the first time designated copper a critical war material. By March 1941, an inadequate supply of fabricated copper required a general cutback in civilian manufacturing. In April, OPM officials estimated that demand for copper was about twice that of supply, with no relief in sight. Indeed, from mid-1941 on, copper requirements escalated as the armed forces expanded, the civilian economy grew, and exports, including lend-lease assistance, increased. By the time of Pearl Harbor, a copper shortage was among the principal obstacles to the full mobilization of the economy.

When the nation entered hostilities, the basically unregulated copper industry of January 1941 was more fully controlled than any other. Anticipating shortages, NDAC recommended that the president license copper exports, an act that he took early in February 1941. On May 1, 1941, copper was among the sixteen metals included in General Metals Order No. 1, which set policy on inventories. At the end of May, copper was placed under preference, or priority, control, which was modified and extended in July. Since the priority system in general never worked well, copper was allocated starting early in August. Henceforth, all copper produced from domestic ores was assigned through the Priorities Division to users on the basis of priority ratings. Since scrap accounted for nearly half of American refined copper, in September it was subjected to OPM direction. Finally, between October 1941 and January 1942, copper was gradually cut off from civilian users not in the essential category. This action was an extension of the curtailment program aimed at automobiles and appliances inaugurated by OPACS late in August 1941. Additionally, the NDAC late in 1940 began stockpiling copper to protect munitions output. The program never got very far. Even with output and imports growing, the copper stockpile at the end of 1941 was under 70,000 tons, less than 15 percent of the government's goal of 500,000 tons.

Controlling distribution was only a first step in solving the copper crisis; output had to be increased. In that regard, smelting and refining capacity was not a major issue. No expansion of smelting plant was planned in 1941. In September 1941, refining capacity stood at about 1.7 million tons annually. Only three additional plants were built during the war, adding around ninety thousand tons per year, all financed by the DPC. Greater facilities were deemed unnecessary because around 40 percent of America's copper supply during the defense and war years was imported, principally from Latin America and Canada, large amounts of which were in refined form, not ore. In terms of fabrication, the largest growth occurred with brass mills, which increased their wartime output between 1940 and 1945 over fourfold, with 70 percent going to the production of ammunition. To achieve such a record, plant capacity was almost doubled—principally through War Department financing—and government, management, and labor combined their efforts to ensure that facilities were used to the maximum and in the most efficient manner.

Mining was the big roadblock to increased copper production. In September 1941, American mining capacity was set at around 956,000 tons annually, with a nearly 306,000-ton yearly increase to be available by early 1943. Expanded output resulted from addition to plant financed privately and by the DPC and improved operating conditions. Moreover, the Reconstruction Finance Corporation (RFC) financed mine expansions in Mexico and Chile that produced a total of fifty-two thousand tons annually.

To increase production further without raising prices in general, OPM's Labor Division, ultimately backed by the principal union in the industry—the CIO's International Union of Mine, Mill, and Smelter Workers—in August 1941 proposed a differential price solution. This approach was first introduced for three high-cost mines in Michigan: the Metals Reserve Company (MRC), later the Treasury Department acting for the lend-lease program, agreed to purchase all their copper at a price one cent above cost and in disregard of OPACS's pegged price for refined copper. After the declaration of war, a full-blown program was adopted by the OPM and implemented by the WPB under the title of the Premium Price Plan. It included copper, lead, and zinc and was administered by the WPB, the Office of Price Administration (OPA), and the MRC. A Quota Committee determined the maximum production potential of the three types of mines for 1941. According to a complicated formula, production above a set quota would receive subsidies, in the case of copper five cents a pound above the OPA-set price of twelve cents. Of domestic output in 1942, 39 percent of zinc benefited from a premium price, 22 percent of lead, and only 13 percent of copper.

A chronic labor shortage that began during the summer of 1941 constantly plagued copper mining and ultimately reached smelting and refining as well as brass mills. Workers left mining in droves throughout the war years, attracted by ample jobs in shipyards, aircraft plants, and other war industries offering better pay, working and living conditions, safety factors, and morale. Voluntary or compulsory military service also took its toll, as did seasonal agricultural employment or farm labor as a refuge from the Selective Service System. In March 1942, the WPB's Labor Division implemented a seven-day, multiple-shift mine policy whenever possible. Numerous other government agencies affected by mining attempted to relieve labor pressures, but their scattered and piecemeal efforts were ineffective.

With problems mounting, the WPB in August 1942 organized an Interdepartmental Committee on Nonferrous Metals to coordinate policies for stabilizing the workforce. The committee was headed by the board's industry and labor representatives and included members from the War Manpower Commission (WMC), the War and Navy Departments, the Selective Service System, the OPA, and the Interior Department. The committee acted to improve housing, transportation, and community services, implemented worker training programs, and took other steps to enhance basic amenities and morale. Employers were also instructed on the operations of the Selective Service System and the services of the WMC. In September 1942, WMC instituted a stabilization order covering manpower for mining and smelting industries and lumbering operations in the Western states. Supposedly "freezing" the copper-mining workforce, the order was loosely enforced, yet, combined with other programs, it helped reduce out-migration by as much as 50 percent. Perhaps more effective was the National War Labor Board's decision in October 1942 to exempt copper, zinc, and lead miners in Idaho and Utah from the Little Steel formula of July 1942, which basically froze wages, by raising wages by $1.00 a day and, in subsequent years, providing other wage adjustments. Also in October, the WPB ordered the closing of the gold mines, releasing at least two thousand miners suitable for work in nonferrous mines.

All efforts to stabilize copper-mine labor proved inadequate late in 1942 and again in the third quarter of 1943, necessitating the furloughing of soldiers. Always opposed to releasing troops for industrial purposes, the army did so only under intense pressure, as a last resort, and after various demands were met. Although labor in copper production and fabrication, including brass mills, was never ample in 1944 and 1945, it did not reach the critical stages experienced in 1942 and 1943. Indeed, in the last two years of the war, and despite spot problems, the availability of copper was no longer a major concern.

Organized labor played a pivotal part in mobilizing the copper industry for war. The left-wing Mine, Mill, and Smelter Workers Union favored, and may even in part have authored, the Premium Price Plan even though it adversely affected wages. The union also led in devising structures and approaches for cooperating with management and mobilization agencies to resolve multiple production and manpower problems. That no serious strikes or shutdowns occurred during the war years in spite of the numerous aggravations and hazards involved in mining, smelting, and fabricating copper testifies to the quality of union leadership. Moreover, throughout hostilities, labor productivity increased from thirty tons of copper per man annually in 1939 to thirty-eight tons in 1944. WPB labor offices also played a significant and positive role in resolving production problems in nonferrous metals, especially copper.

Congress's role in mobilizing copper was a mixed one. On the basis of hearings held in December 1941, the Truman Committee criticized OPM for being slow in responding to the copper shortage and generally supported organized labor's approach to increasing output. Unlike the aluminum, however, the Truman Committee's involvement with copper was slight. That was not the case with the Senate Special Committee to Study and Survey Problems of Small Business Enterprises (the Murray Committee, after its chair, Senator James E. Murray [D-MT]). The committee, backed and at times prodded by Secretary of the Interior Harold L. Ickes, emerged as the defender of small mines, copper and otherwise, often victimized, in the committee's eyes, by monopolistic and oligopolistic interests shaping WPB policies.

As was true with most materials, reliable requirement figures for copper were unavailable during the defense years and the first year of war, principally because the armed services were unable to calculate their demand effectively. Once copper supply was deemed inadequate in 1941, policymakers simply aimed to maximize availability. The requirements riddle for copper was resolved only with the CMP, worked out in the last months of 1942, and implemented by stages in 1943. With this plan, the entire mobilization program revolved around the allocation of the three most basic materials, copper, steel, and aluminum. Under the CMP and related production scheduling, the armed services had to improve their requirement calculations and keep them within a feasible range. Facing increasingly desperate conditions, the WPB's Copper Branch had on its own in 1942 instituted allocation devices for copper that in crude ways anticipated the CMP.

RUBBER

Rubber differed from all other strategic and critical materials in that a virtually new synthetic rubber industry had to be created during hostilities to meet the massive demand indispensable for conducting war.[15] Mechanized warfare made the United States dependent on rubber to a degree never before known. Moreover, the American transportation system had become so tied to motor vehicles that the economy could barely function during a time of peace, let alone war, without an adequate supply of rubber for tires. With demand growing rapidly at home, U.S. consumption was around 600 million tons of crude rubber annually in the years before war. At the time of Pearl Harbor, the nation had built up a reserve nearly equaling a year's peacetime usage. Replenished from various sources during the war years, the crude stockpile nonetheless fell to just over 100 million tons in 1944. By that time, however, synthetic rubber was coming on the market in massive amounts to meet heavy military needs. America produced somewhat over 28 million tons of synthetic rubber in 1942, nearly 264 million tons in 1943, almost 857 million tons in 1944, and just under 922 million tons in 1945.[16]

Before hostilities, the nation's dependence on Southeast Asian natural rubber was almost total. America was the world's largest importer of rubber, the overwhelming percentage of which went into the manufacture of tires for motor vehicles. Since imports could be denied the United States during an emergency, the Office of the Assistant Secretary of War and the ANMB planned and prepared throughout the interwar years for dealing with such a crisis. They searched for rubber-producing vegetation other than the hevea tree and encouraged hevea cultivation in Latin America, Africa, and other locations more accessible to the United States, all without much promise. The solution was found in synthetic rubber, which the military increasingly focused on in the 1930s.[17]

With the outbreak of war in the Pacific, and with Japan moving into Southeast Asia, the worst-case scenario came to pass: the United States was cut off from its principal source of natural rubber. These developments placed rubber near or at the top of the list of America's strategic materials. Some prewar preparation had been made in anticipation of this disaster, and other action followed Pearl Harbor. A stockpiling program had been initiated in 1940. New sources of natural rubber were maximized from regions open to the United States, and scrap rubber was reclaimed to the degree possible. Conservation measures also grew progressively restrictive during and after 1941, including export and import controls, priority and allocation measures, and rationing first of tires and tubes and then of gasoline for motor vehicles, along with speed limit restrictions. All these expedients were used to buy time for the mobilization agencies to produce sufficient amounts of synthetic rubber for supplying military, essential civilian, and Allied needs. Without synthetics in requisite amounts, America could not have continued fighting.

From beginning to end, the defense and war rubber programs were plagued by weak, ineffective, or irresponsible leadership. The trouble started at the very top. Failing to appreciate the potentially dire situation that the United States faced with rubber, Roosevelt discouraged bold, preparatory action during the NDAC and OPM period, and the pattern continued with the WPB after Pearl Harbor. While a host of government agencies became involved in rubber policy, basic decisions ultimately became centered in the Rubber Reserve Company (RRC), dominated by oil firms, particularly the Standard Oil Company of New Jersey, and major rubber corporations, such as the B. F. Goodrich Company. Driven by economic and commercial more than strategic purposes, the RRC was going in directions that could end in America being denied the rubber it needed to conclude the war successfully. Led by the

Farm Bloc, which had a vested interest in synthetic rubber, an outraged Congress moved aggressively during the summer of 1942 to take control of the floundering rubber program.

Roosevelt now had to move quickly to preserve executive power in the area. In August 1942, he appointed Bernard M. Baruch (the self-appointed war mobilization specialist) and James B. Conant and Karl T. Compton (presidents, respectively, of Harvard University and the Massachusetts Institute of Technology and closely associated with the Office of Scientific Research and Development) to constitute a Rubber Survey Committee that would recommend ways to mobilize the rubber industry. The committee's principal contribution was to have a rubber director appointed in September 1942 with centralized authority over the industry and the government agencies dealing with it.[18] The director used his position to force through the badly flawed rubber program authored largely by the RRC. The nation had enough rubber in the critically important years 1943–1944, but principally because the Farm Bloc had insisted on alternate approaches for manufacturing synthetic rubber that the RRC had been obstructing.

Practically all experts recognized that synthetic rubber was the solution to America's rubber shortage. Synthetic rubber had a long, tangled, and controversial history. With its creation in May 1940, the NDAC replaced the Office of the Assistant Secretary of War and the ANMP as the principal government agencies focusing on rubber. Edward Stettinius's Industrial Materials Division divided policy between a Rubber Products Section in the Agricultural and Forest Products subdivision for dealing with natural rubber and a Synthetic Rubber Committee in the Petroleum and Natural Gas Products Section of the Chemical and Allied Products subdivision for handling synthetic rubber. A similar type of division for rubber continued with the OPM and WPB. The Rubber Products Section quickly turned to the RRC for stockpiling purposes, but the RRC also emerged as the dominant agency determining policy for synthetic rubber, particularly Buna S.

Buna S was recognized by 1940 as the best general-purpose synthetic rubber for manufacturing tires, the market for most rubber. Indeed, Buna S accounted for over 85 percent of the huge output of synthetics in the United States during World War II. That reality placed Standard Oil of New Jersey at the center of mass producing synthetic rubber for defense and war.

Standard's dominant position resulted from its contractual relations with Germany's I. G. Farbenindustrie A.G. (I. G. Farben) dating back to 1925. At that time, I. G. Farben was experimenting with the production of synthetic gasoline from coal. Standard had an obvious interest in I. G. Farben's venture, and the latter desired technical and financial assistance from Standard.

The promise of mutual benefit led to a series of legal agreements between the two firms beginning in 1927 with international control of petrochemicals and leading in 1930 to the organization of the Joint American Study Company (JASCO) in the United States. Each firm held 50 percent ownership of JASCO, which was designed to test and license new processes developed by either company in the oil and chemical fields. I. G. Farben in 1933 and 1934 patented in America Buna S (which it had patented in Germany in 1929) and Buna N (another synthetic rubber). The patents were held by JASCO. Once in power in 1933, the Nazis increasingly dictated I. G. Farben's operations in crucial areas. Not wishing to strengthen potential adversaries, for example, Adolph Hitler's government prohibited I. G. Farben from honoring its contractual obligations to share with Standard details of the manufacture of Buna S and Buna N. Nonetheless, Standard, living up to its commitments to the German firm, provided I. G. Farben with technical information on making butyl, a synthetic rubber developed by the New Jersey firm. After the outbreak of war in Europe, representatives of I. G. Farben and Standard met at The Hague in September 1939 to assign all JASCO-held patent rights (including those for Buna S and Buna N) to Standard for use in the United States, the British and French Empires, and Iraq. I. G. Farben held exclusive rights for the rest of the world. Standard now had undisputed dominance in the American synthetic rubber field.

Convinced that Buna S would yield enormous benefits, Standard consistently and aggressively discouraged work in the United States on any other general-purpose synthetic rubber. Between 1934 and 1939, for example, Standard deceptively led major rubber companies to believe that it would share Buna know-how with them. After gaining full control of the Buna patents in 1939, Standard offered rubber firms Buna licenses in 1940 only at extremely onerous terms and under conditions maintaining its monopoly. (I. G. Farben had followed a similar strategy with American rubber firms seeking assistance with Buna S throughout the 1930s.) The U.S. Rubber and Firestone Tire and Rubber Companies went along with Standard's harsh terms, but Goodrich and the Goodyear Tire and Rubber Company, drawing on past work, defied Standard and in 1940 began marketing Buna-type synthetic rubber. Standard retaliated by filing a patent-infringement suit against the two companies in October 1941. Legal action was dropped, however, when in December 1941 the RRC negotiated an agreement among four major rubber companies, Standard, and itself for sharing patents and technical information on wartime synthetic rubber production.

By then Standard faced severe legal problems of its own. In April 1941, the Justice Department began antitrust action against the company for conspiring to suppress the development and marketing of synthetic rubber. The case was settled in March 1942 with Standard pleading nolo contendere, the company, officers, and subsidiary firms fined, and Standard accepting a consent decree offering its synthetic rubber patents royalty free for the duration of the war. According to Assistant Attorney General Thurman Arnold, Standard's action constituted "treason" since the company intentionally chose to delay America's production of synthetic rubber in order to honor its relations with an enemy firm, I. G. Farben, named as a coconspirator in the suit.[19] The Truman Committee's judgment was more ambiguous. While finding the company's conduct "most compromising" and a threat to national security, the committee pointed out that Standard was playing the "big business game" according to existing rules as it "construed" them.[20]

Legal action notwithstanding, mobilization agencies beginning in 1940 virtually turned synthetic rubber over to Standard and the major rubber firms. Shortly after NDAC was created, Stettinius's Industrial Materials Division began surveying synthetic rubber and set up the Synthetic Rubber Committee. Between July and August, the committee met singly and together with most firms producing synthetic rubber or its principal raw materials, including U.S. Rubber, Goodrich, Goodyear, Firestone, Standard of New Jersey, E. I. duPont de Nemours and Company, Carbide and Carbon Chemical Company (a subsidiary of Union Carbide and Carbon Corporation), Universal Oil Products Company, United Gas Improvement Company, Shell Oil Company, Phillips Petroleum Company, and Dow Chemical Company. The Synthetic Rubber Committee concluded that around five thousand tons of synthetic rubber could be produced in 1940, with the figure growing in subsequent years.

No firm had the experience in large-scale production that an emergency would require. While some companies involved with synthetic rubber preferred private, competitive development, government financing or market guarantees would be essential to get a crash program under way because of uncertainties and risks. Together with the various companies, the Synthetic Rubber Committee proposed a program for facilities yielding 100,000 tons of synthetic rubber annually at a cost of about $50 million and requiring twelve to eighteen months to build and equip. To launch the program, U.S. Rubber, Goodrich, Goodyear, and Firestone financed and delivered in October engineering plans for plants manufacturing Buna S, and Du Pont did the same for neoprene. After agreeing to join the project only late in the game, Standard of New Jersey withdrew because of difficulties in producing butyl. Nonetheless, the company allowed other firms to use Buna S patents for experimental purposes.

According to Robert A. Solo, a scholar thoroughly familiar with synthetic rubber during the period, Standard was intent on the joint development of

Buna S production by rubber, petroleum, and chemical companies under terms allowing Standard to maintain majority control. If an emergency required rushed growth, Washington would have to finance Buna S production and suspend antitrust limitation to allow joint industrial cooperation. In this sense, I. G. Farben and Standard had been following a consistent policy on Buna S since the former first patented Buna in 1929.

By October 1940, synthetic rubber policy had passed from the NDAC to the RRC and its parent body, the RFC, and, hence, to Jesse H. Jones. RFC agreed to participate in financing synthetic rubber plants as early as August; in October, it demanded control of the project for doing so. NDAC agreed, insisting that all responsibility now rested with the RRC and warning Jones that expert advice was essential on numerous and vital unresolved issues of what type of rubber to produce, how to produce it, the size and number of plants needed, and arrangements for patents and licensing; financing was only the beginning.

These complications, combined with his own conservative and cautious business approach, led Jones by March 1941 first to cut the project to four synthetic rubber plants producing 40,000 tons annually, then to reduce the total to only 10,000 tons. The lesser figure was a compromise arrived at when the RFC head insisted that government financing be only partial and in the form of loans. The RRC, however, agreed to buy the rubber produced. Alarmed that no progress was being made with synthetic rubber, OPM in April and May 1941 insisted that a 40,000-ton capacity, to be built and owned by the government and operated under its direction, was a minimum figure that might soon have to be increased to 100,000 or 200,000 tons. Responding to such pressure, RRC returned to the 40,000-ton goal. In May, Jones negotiated contracts for one 10,000-ton plant each with the so-called Big Four, U.S. Rubber, Goodrich, Goodyear, and Firestone. With the president and the SPAB giving their general approval, a limited synthetic rubber program was just getting started at the time of Pearl Harbor.

After the outbreak of war, Buna S goals shot up within a matter of months from 40,000 to 705,000 tons. The government financed, owned, and leased to selected companies practically all the plants for manufacturing rubber and the raw materials essential to do so at a total cost of around $700 million. Yet, while spending such vast sums and creating an industry indispensable to the conduct of the war, Washington acted without the advice and guidance of an independent, fully competent scientific and technological staff. Instead, it relied principally on Edward R. Weidlein, director of the Mellon Institute of Industrial Research. Weidlein first headed the Chemical and Allied Products subdivision of the NDAC's Industrial Materials Division; later he served as the only technical adviser on synthetic rubber to the RRC, the OPM, and its successor. The whole while he continued serving with the institute. Moreover, the institute had compromising ties with Union Carbide, whose subsidiary was a synthetic rubber contractor.[21] Otherwise, RRC, OPM, and WPB relied on experts of the potential or actual rubber, petroleum, and chemical firms with which the federal government contracted. Under such circumstances, mobilization agencies had no way of determining whether national and private interests were the same or differed, whether strategic and commercial aims matched or diverged.

The strain inherent in public and private motives became obvious once the Buna S program was massively expanded after Pearl Harbor. Before any sizable increase could take place, the vital issue of the Buna patents had to be settled. The RRC began negotiations over the matter with Standard as early as June 1941, with an agreement reached on December 19, 1941, among RRC, Standard, and the Big Four rubber firms for cross-licensing patents, exchanging technical information, and scheduling royalty payments to Standard. With the consent decree of March 1942, a final settlement on royalties was postponed until six months after hostilities. The Justice Department ultimately gave its legal blessing to this arrangement as not violating antitrust laws. Subsequent contracts were worked out by the RRC during the war years amending the December 19 agreement and covering other synthetic rubber and raw materials for synthetic manufacture. With the technical aspects of these contracts largely dictated by the corporations involved, private firms during the war determined how data were exchanged, which companies and other government mobilization agencies were privy to privileged information, and how wartime operations were conducted so that participating corporations were favored when the government-built plants were sold after hostilities. In reviewing this situation, Robert A. Solo observes:

> The record . . . does not indicate that the great companies took over the synthetic rubber program in a conspiracy to further their self-interests. They dominated the program because they had created it. No agency in Government had taken the initiative or had been capable of . . . truly evaluating that program or of truly reshaping it. To the companies should go credit, not blame; yet, there were great dangers inherent in this surrender of the essential war function of centralized social planning to the interplay of corporate pressures.[22]

Throughout most of 1942, the synthetic rubber project was racked with controversy. The most serious debate involved raw materials. Buna S is manufactured by combining butadiene and styrene at a ratio of three to one.

Styrene presented few problems, but butadiene became the source of intense dispute because it can be made from a number of substances, most important alcohol and petroleum. The alcohol approach was used for production of Buna S or its equivalent in Germany, Russia, and Poland. It was a simple, proven technique, requiring plant and equipment that could be quickly and inexpensively built with few demands on strategic or critical materials; or alcohol could be used from existing facilities.

For the petroleum approach, butadiene was made from oil fractions, with butylene being the most popular. Working from petroleum gases for large-scale production, however, was untried and required a sophisticated plant that was slow and difficult to build and equip and drew heavily on critical materials. Moreover, butylene was in great demand in the manufacture of high-octane gasoline for aircraft. Making butadiene from it would put two of the most high-priority wartime products on an inevitable collision course. Butadiene from alcohol was 60–100 percent higher in price than butadiene from petroleum. But, if plant cost was figured in and government-owned grain used in alcohol output, any saving from oil could disappear. Existing refinery capacity with few additions to plant and equipment could also be used for a "quick" method of making butadiene, but the refining industry would have to be treated as a whole, and the process would be very expensive.

Between March and June 1942, the RRC let contracts for 646,000 tons of butadiene. Of that amount, 526,200 tons, or over 81 percent, would be produced from petroleum, 80,000 tons from alcohol, and 40,000 tons from benzene. All the alcohol-based butadiene went to Carbide and Carbon Company, using synthetic alcohol made from petroleum. Overall, then, nearly 94 percent of all butadiene would be derived from oil.

The farm community was livid. For many years, Midwestern universities, along with the Department of Agriculture, had engaged in research programs for producing butadiene from grain alcohol. Yet grain-alcohol advocates had been repeatedly brushed off in Washington. To find out why, Senator Guy M. Gillette (D-IA) held hearings between March and June 1942 as chair of a subcommittee of the Committee on Agriculture and Forestry. Beyond cost factors and the unavailability of industrial alcohol, no one had an explanation. Higher prices for the alcohol-butadiene process did not stand up to scrutiny. The WPB's Chemicals Branch, which claimed an alcohol shortage in January, found ample amounts in May after plants manufacturing alcohol from molasses were converted to grain and alcoholic beverage firms produced for industrial purposes. Moreover, many obsolete, small, and idle alcohol plants could be brought into production with only modest investments. Gillette charged that Standard exercised its power in the industrial alcohol field to block the availability of alcohol for butadiene production. Subcommittee members argued that "monopolistic" corporate forces influenced the government to protect their interests. Edward R. Weidlein candidly admitted that the future played a role in rejecting alcohol: led by Standard, the oil, chemical, and rubber industries focused on postwar synthetic rubber markets, not just immediate wartime crises.[23]

Congressional intervention led to change. In May 1942, the RRC moved to increase alcohol-based butadiene from 80,000 to 220,000 tons, or nearly 35 percent of the total, at the expense of petroleum products. But the action was not enough to silence congressional critics. Several days after Gillette introduced Senate Bill 2600 on July 18, 1942, both houses of Congress passed it decisively. It created a new agency with nearly unlimited powers for organizing an industrial structure to manufacture synthetic rubber with butadiene derived largely from agricultural commodities.[24]

While vetoing the bill early in August, Roosevelt simultaneously set up the Baruch-Compton-Conant Rubber Survey Committee. After hearings and investigations, the committee quickly reported its findings and recommendations on September 10, 1942. It proposed that a rubber director take charge of the numerous agencies that had made a mess of the rubber program. The committee also pushed for immediate gas rationing and other measures to conserve rubber. It further criticized RRC for operating without a technical staff. Baruch and his colleagues additionally favored some minor adjustments in the existing rubber program, including increased output goals, a modest "quick" refinery experiment for butadiene output, perhaps a plant for making butadiene from alcohol, and expanding grain alcohol production. The Rubber Survey Committee, however, basically endorsed the existing synthetic rubber program, with the rubber director instructed in "bulling" it through.[25]

In September 1942, Roosevelt tapped William M. Jeffers, the controversial president of the Union Pacific Railroad, as rubber director. Although his office was part of WPB, Jeffers operated as if he headed an independent agency, and he did so without challenge. Declaring that the Rubber Survey Committee's report was his bible, Jeffers set about instituting its recommendations with only a few modifications. A good part of 1942 went into legitimizing the fundamentally flawed synthetic rubber program worked out by the RRC in 1941–1942.

While Jeffers helped bring order to the confused system that he inherited, it was alcohol-based butadiene that saved the day for America's synthetic rubber program. The RFC had projected Buna S output at 400,000 tons for 1943; the Rubber Survey Committee was pushing for 425,000 tons. Those figures were based on military demand growing out of the United States and

Britain launching a Second Front in Europe in 1943, later postponed until 1944. The Rubber Survey Committee estimated that, between July 1, 1942, and January 1, 1944, the United States would have available to it around 631,000 tons of natural rubber. Military and other essential demand (excluding tires for passenger automobiles, possibly coverable by reclaimed rubber) for the same period was set at 842,000 tons, leaving a deficit of 211,000 tons. Synthetic rubber had to make up the difference, or the American war effort would begin to fail. The larger figure of 425,000 tons was essential to maintain rock-bottom reserves of 100,000 tons.

Actual Buna S production in 1943 was only 204,130 tons. That might have been enough to meet invasion requirements, but at the cost of leaving the United States with absolutely nothing in reserve, an unthinkable alternative. Rescheduling the Second Front from 1943 to 1944 saved the nation from disaster. Even without a major Allied invasion of Western Europe, the United States would have faced dire conditions without substantial amounts of synthetic rubber. The Buna S that was made available depended overwhelmingly on alcohol-derived butadiene. Without alcohol, according to Standard's official historians, the results would have been "catastrophic."[26] Eighty-three percent of all butadiene manufactured in 1943 came from alcohol; through August 1944, when the alcohol process was intentionally cut back, 80 percent of butadiene was derived from facilities using alcohol and producing at nearly double their rated capacity. By comparison, petroleum-based butadiene plants at best operated at or just slightly above their intended production goals. Besides predictably competing with high-octane gasoline, the petroleum-butadiene method ran into endless difficulties involved in building, equipping, and operating facilities. That was to be expected from an untried, highly complex industrial process.

By the war's end, the United States was annually producing close to 1 million tons of synthetic rubber, around 87.5 percent of which was Buna S; between 1942 and 1945, Buna S accounted for over 85 percent of all synthetic rubber manufactured. An entirely new industry had been put together under unusual circumstances in under five years. The analysis offered above makes clear, however, that the frequent claims of "miracles of production" are hardly accurate in the case of synthetic rubber. Indeed, in reviewing the World War II synthetic rubber record, Robert A. Solo insists that, "stripped of its mythology, the planning of the synthetic rubber industry was a scandalous, a complete, a nearly catastrophic foul up."[27]

For the Production Division of the OPM, synthetic rubber was not an isolated case. The division generally failed to prepare the economy for war by expanding the productive capacity for basic materials. Besides rubber, aluminum, steel, and copper are illustrative. Most of these industries began expanding through private investment to meet growing demand as early as 1939. But none of them were ready for the massive output required by entry into World War II. Indeed, without the federal government accepting almost total responsibility for financing, even the foundations for immense expansion that existed at the time of Pearl Harbor would have been missing.

By way of contrast, the division performed best when facing clearly defined goals, as was the case with expanding facilities for military construction, housing, and various industrial needs. It also responded well to increasing output of materials like nitrogen compounds and toluol for meeting military contracts and foreign orders for explosives.

A number of reasons account for the Production Division not accomplishing more with materials. Dominated by industry and major corporations, the division resisted expanding capacity as long as American entry into war was uncertain and requirements unknown. The business community in general preferred to focus on the actual and growing civilian markets, not the proposed military ones, and/or on preserving the industrial status quo. A decade of depression acted to reinforce this cautious approach. Ideology also played a part. With expansion and conversion for war pushed principally by New Dealers, labor, and academicians, industry's resistance to these policies was strengthened out of its desire to maintain control of mobilization agencies, which were assuming ever-greater influence over the operations of the economy.

Industry's general opposition to substantially increasing the plant for basic materials was, curiously, supported by other government agencies. That was the case with the RFC and its subsidiaries the DPC and the RRC. Economically conservative and cautious, Jesse H. Jones acted to retard or obstruct expansion of aluminum capacity, development of synthetic rubber, and stockpiling of strategic materials in general. For their part, the armed services had a mixed and contradictory impact on greater production capacity. Expanding rapidly, and anticipating hostilities, the army and navy naturally favored a larger plant for meeting their multiple needs. Yet, by often underestimating their demand in the event of war, and by failing to come up with reliable, consistent, and usable requirement figures, they lent support to those opposing plant expansion. Moreover, by generally identifying with industry in the mobilization agencies, as opposed to New Dealers, labor, academics, and the like, the military services in effect strengthened the hand of the OPM's more conservative forces.

OPM'S LABOR, PURCHASES, AND PRIORITIES DIVISIONS AND SPAB

The operations of the Labor, Purchases, and Priorities Divisions of the Office of Production Management (OPM) help explain why industry and the military from the outset dominated economic mobilization for World War II. In an administration controlled by corporate executives, labor's representatives were simply pushed aside. The Purchases and Priorities Divisions, however, always lacked adequate staff in Washington and the field to carry out vast and critical responsibilities.

By comparison, the Production Division, later the Materials Division, had ample personnel provided by industry branches with the assistance of the industry advisory committees. Corporate America tapped its own national structures, financial and legal systems, trade associations, and other organizations to ensure that divisions dealing with industry had the necessary executives. On their part, the armed services had organizations that reached down to the regional, state, and local levels and could be expanded practically at will. Moreover, both industry and the military were existing institutional systems adapting to emergency conditions. Under such circumstances, separately and together corporations and the armed services had a definite advantage over subdivisions of temporary mobilization agencies, such as the Priorities Division, carrying out wartime planning functions.

During the years of the National Defense Advisory Commission (NDAC) and the OPM, industry and the military worked together contractually outside the mobilization agencies. When they were required to function inside those agencies, as was the case with the clearance of contracts, they preferred that such NDAC and OPM subdivisions remain weak. New Dealers and other all-outers constantly fought a losing battle in trying to strengthen the central mobilization agencies for purposes of both speeding up munitions output and instituting greater balance in harnessing the economy. To achieve those ends, President Franklin D. Roosevelt had to set up new agencies controlled by all-outers, as occurred with the Office of Price Administration and Civilian Supply (OPACS) in April 1941 and then the Supply Priorities and Allocations Board (SPAB) in August 1941.

The New Deal no doubt strengthened the state. Economic mobilization for war still depended heavily on corporate America. And any ground that industry had lost to the government during years of peace was more than made up by the enormously strengthened and conservative military joining corporations in a wartime munitions alliance.

OPM'S LABOR DIVISION

Sidney Hillman concentrated on labor relations and labor supply without making the Labor Division the principal policymaking center for either area. As associate director of the OPM, Hillman also spoke for labor in its highest councils. Yet he was unable to win for the division a meaningful role in mobilizing the nation's industries. Overall, then, the Labor Division's impact was not great. Hillman's limitations as an administrator were only partially responsible for this outcome. Hillman faced nearly impossible odds in trying successfully to direct a division rent with conflict between the two major labor federations and trade union members and professionals. Competition from numerous outside agencies also plagued the division, as did industry's resistance to labor encroaching on management's prerogatives.[1]

Throughout 1941, the Labor Relations Branch became increasingly involved in heading off or resolving labor conflict. The burgeoning shipbuilding industry demanded attention in 1940 as labor supply and relations grew more difficult and threatening. To handle the situation, Hillman led in creating a Shipbuilding Stabilization Committee during September 1940 in NDAC's Labor Division. The committee carried over to OPM. It was chaired by a member of the Labor Division, and representatives from labor, management, and the government served on it. Between January and August 1941, the committee worked out a series of zonal agreements regulating wages, working conditions, and training programs along with provisions for settling grievances without interruptions in production by either management or labor. Although strikes took place, they were usually settled expeditiously, and the Shipbuilding Stabilization Committee modified the agreements as need arose. All in all, the committee played an important part in helping stabilize labor conditions in an industry that had become as volatile as it was vital.

Although in July 1941 the Labor Division worked out a nationwide stabilization agreement for the aircraft industry similar to that for shipbuilding, a reasonable level of industrial harmony was not achieved until the beginning of 1943. A new industry facing a major transformation with intensely competitive unions vying to represent its workforce defied any quick remedies. The most successful stabilization agreement worked out under the Labor Division was that for the building trades. After a month of negotiations between government and labor representatives, an agreement was reached in July 1941 for regulating labor conditions on government and defense-related work sites. A Board of Review was set up in OPM and carried over to the War Production Board (WPB) for interpreting, implementing, and adjusting an accord that all but eliminated work stoppages involving nearly 3 million employees. On a much more general plane, Hillman fought steadily from mid-1940 to mid-1941 to prohibit procurement agencies from awarding contracts to labor law violators—particularly where the National Labor Relations Act was involved—but he suffered a string of bitter and humiliating defeats.

When work stoppages took place, the Labor Division usually moved expeditiously to end them. It was more successful as a mediator in 1940 under the slower pace of the NDAC than it was later under the greater demands of the OPM. As the mobilization tempo increased in 1941, strikes multiplied and included some major producers of defense materials or products, such as the Aluminum Company of America and Allis-Chalmers Manufacturing Company. Where there had been 241 potential strikes during the last half of 1940, 4,200 work stoppages took place in 1941. Hillman's division was never alone in its attempts to avoid or halt strikes. The Labor Department's United States Conciliation Service dealt specifically with disturbances in the workplace and resented the intrusion of Hillman's division. Moreover, starting in 1940, and becoming more active as strikes grew in 1941, the War and Navy Departments—especially the former—became involved in work stoppages involving their contractors, most dramatically in June 1941, when Roosevelt ordered the army to seize the strike-bound North American Aviation, Incorporated, in Los Angeles. Finally, under pressure from the War Department, Congress, and other sources, Roosevelt in March 1941 created by executive order the National Defense Mediation Board to handle labor disputes that the Labor Department and OPM's Labor Division could not resolve. Although Hillman's division remained active in mediation and conciliation, its importance in those areas diminished throughout 1941.

The Labor Division accomplished even less with labor supply than with labor relations. Continuing activity begun under NDAC, Hillman's division approached manpower policies through the Labor Supply, Labor Priorities, Defense Training, and Training-within-Industry Branches as well as others. By conducting inventories, seeking to establish manpower requirements, making referrals, setting up training programs, directing contracts to distressed areas, and numerous other programs, the division tried to ensure that adequate labor existed in numbers and specialties for the burgeoning defense industries. Despite considerable progress, the division's overall performance was lacking. It had to rely on some twenty government agencies—such as the United States Employment Service, the Labor Department, the Civil Service Commission, and the National Youth Administration—in carrying out its responsibilities. Attempts at coordination were always difficult, and they became less successful as the year wore on. That the Labor Division approached the defense workforce from many branches, not one, also weakened its impact. Additionally, those branches dealing with labor supply were staffed principally with professionals and public servants, who were often at odds with the trade unionists who controlled the Labor Relations Branch. Unresolved feuding within the Labor Division inevitably distracted and discredited it. Finally, with unemployment still relatively high, Hillman had trouble convincing other mobilization authorities that labor supply demanded immediate attention. After Pearl Harbor, Hillman desperately fought to have all labor supply responsibilities in the wartime economy assigned to him, but the Labor Division's performance during 1940–1941 did not inspire confidence. When Roosevelt turned the job over to the newly created War Manpower Commission early in 1942, a bitter Hillman left government service.

As the defense program grew, the Labor Division had to broaden its purview to include the entire mobilization program. It did this in a number of ways. In May 1941, for example, Hillman set up a Priorities Branch to assist the division in dealing with unemployment and labor dislocation resulting from the reduced flow of scarce materials to civilian industries. The branch's activities blended with other division programs for directing defense contracts to depressed communities or those adversely affected by mobilization policies. Working with small business offices, the Labor Division sought to include lesser firms in defense production both to increase defense output and to reduce unemployment. It also tried to influence plant site decisions to lessen economic disruption.

While these activities were consequential, unions wanted a more substantial role. Under pressure from organized labor and Sidney's Hillman's Labor Division, the OPM council early in July 1941 unenthusiastically sanctioned labor advisory committees. By mid-January 1942, eleven formal and four informal labor advisory committees had been organized. They were only minor achievements in the drive of the Congress of Industrial Organizations (CIO) and American Federation of Labor (AFL) to win for labor a major voice in mobilization.

The CIO led the way. In 1940, Philip Murray, the federation's president, formulated a National Industry Council Plan for tripartite direction of economic mobilization by government, industry, and labor agencies on levels ranging from the national to the local. Murray's proposal received most attention when in December 1940 Walter Reuther, vice-president of the United Auto Workers (UAW), adapted it to the automobile industry under a program for "500 Planes a Day."[2]

Murray's plan never stood a chance of being accepted, and the labor advisory committees ran into a wall of opposition from the industry-dominated OPM. Their overall effect was minimal. Nonetheless, a few labor advisory committees left their mark at least temporarily. An aggressive United Rubber Workers–CIO forced joint meetings with labor and industry advisory committees in the rubber industry to limit management's ability to shift production from high-paying, union plants to low-paying, nonunion ones when civilian production was curtailed. The labor committee additionally secured agreements on the orderly transfer of workers from nondefense to defense work and seniority protection when plants were converted.

A few committees went beyond labor issues to deal with industries as a whole. For mechanical refrigerators, the AFL and the CIO combined their efforts in writing an outstanding conversion program. Similar results occurred in the silk industry. The Farm Equipment Workers Organizing Committee–CIO supported a plan for concentrating defense production in the hands of large firms so that the smaller ones could handle nondefense output. This experiment was tried for a time, only to be halted by the WPB. The most concerted drive for joint industry-labor committees to direct conversion took place in the automobile industry. Although the UAW never got its tripartite planning, industry finally agreed to share some decisionmaking with labor. However, at the highest levels of OPM and then WPB, even the more limited approach was vetoed. Once the nation was at war, industry was less inclined to cooperate with labor since the all-out drive for maximum production strengthened its hand further.

Labor also weakened its own committees by making poor appointments to them. The advisory committees had their influence reduced further by being attached to the Labor Division instead of to one of the operating divisions, which included the industry or commodity branches. Fighting between the two federations additionally lessened the effectiveness of the committees, as did competition and animosity in the Labor Division between union-oriented personnel and civil servants, economists, and academics.[3] However, all evidence points to the fact that, even if the labor advisory committees had functioned flawlessly, they would still have made little progress among the principal mobilization agencies, particularly once America was at war.

By the time of Pearl Harbor, the Labor Division practically had no definable role. Labor relations and supply either were or would be handled by existing or new agencies, and management was not about to share its functions with unions. A withered division was transferred to the WPB in January 1942, but Hillman had little to do. He left the board in April after failing to achieve control of wartime labor supply, resulting in the Labor Division sinking even lower.

OPM'S PURCHASES DIVISION

Of the three major OPM divisions (five after September 1941) not including the Labor Division, the Purchases Division turned out to be the least consequential in terms of accomplishments.[4] That was the case because, unlike Production and Priorities (later Materials and Civilian Supply), Purchases attempted to extend its reach over the prerogatives of the procurement agencies, particularly the army and navy. The Purchases Division's goals were hardly insignificant. Military buying and contracting constituted the bulk of defense and war spending. If the division succeeded in establishing meaningful control over military buying and contracting, it would subordinate the armed services to OPM operations; if it did not, the army and navy would remain basically independent of civilian mobilization agency authority. Intent on maintaining as free a hand as possible in procurement, the military had both the will and the means to resist direction from the Purchases Division.

Selected as director of the Purchases Division, Donald M. Nelson fought mightily and successfully to have his division designed as the one central authority in the OPM for clearing all procuring activities. To achieve that goal, he had to face down both William S. Knudsen and his principal assistants and the secretaries of war and the navy. Nelson's struggle was actually a continuation of the battle that New Dealers and their allies in the NDAC had fought with the emerging industry-military production team to make the armed services' economic operations more consistent with national planning, social goals, and civilian control.

As defined by OPM Regulation 2 of March 7, 1941, Nelson's powers were broad and substantial. He was authorized to review, clear, and coordinate all War and Navy Department buying, contracting, and construction involving $500,000 or more; he could include in his purview requirements, specifications, schedules of delivery, and procurement procedures; and he had practically blanket authority to extend his powers further and to include in his operations all defense spending by any agency of the federal government. Nelson gave every impression of trying to fulfill his assigned duties. He expanded his subdivisions to match his responsibilities, and he brought under his review purchasing and related activities, not only of the army and navy, but also of the Maritime Commission, the Office of Lend-Lease Administration (OLLA), and foreign governments. Furthermore, in April–May 1941, he instituted a program for furthering his control over all federal government buying before contracts were signed through statements of intention to purchase. The army and navy would submit to the Purchases Division at least two weeks in advance specifics about their intention to procure any items worth $50,000 or more that were scarce or for which there were shortages of raw materials or production facilities. The Purchases Division would clear such statements within forty-eight hours, making the appropriate recommendations. For all nonmilitary departments, the amount was set first at $25,000 and later reduced to $10,000. This program supplemented contracts clearance, and it was aimed at making the Purchases Division's operations more comprehensive and effective.

In order for the Purchases Division to fulfill its nearly overwhelming responsibilities, it would have had to have an enormous, highly trained staff. Although records of Purchases Division activity are poor, one source has it clearing over seventeen thousand contracts and related documents totaling billions of dollars between February and November 1941.[5] The division simply lacked the personnel, time, and expertise to handle such a load, particularly when its own staff and that of the OPM experienced a high turnover rate. To carry out its functions, it relied heavily on commodity sections or industry branches, only some of which were under its jurisdiction, and all of which varied in quality and function.

Some commodity sections performed their duties conscientiously; others did not. Even if the commodity sections had been uniformly good and answerable to it, the Purchases Division would still have faced daunting odds. Shortly after its creation, the Purchases Division tried to get all the procuring agencies to accept a standard form for submitting information on contract clearance. The War and Navy Departments and some of their subdivisions refused to go along. Nelson's division received requests for clearance that varied from brief memoranda, which forced the division to spend inordinate amounts of time trying to acquire the missing data, to entire files, which were difficult to process. When it received the proper information, forty-eight hours often proved inadequate for the various branches to pass on clearance requests, resulting in reviews that were at best cursory. In a manner reminiscent of NDAC experiences, the impatient armed services at times bypassed the clearance process entirely, began going around the Purchases Division to deal directly with the commodity sections, or submitted contracts that were all but signed and, hence, only nominally open to review. Moreover, clearance proposals could be and were changed after review without the approval or even the knowledge of the Purchases Division, which had no follow-up procedures.

Although improving its operations and receiving better information as the months wore on, the Purchases Division never mastered the clearance system. Statements of intention to purchase were designed to give the division greater control over contracting, but existing evidence indicates that any headway made was slight. The division also began assigning personnel to buying agencies like the Quartermaster Corps and the Treasury Department's Procurement Division to monitor and to guide their contracting. In this instance, any positive outcome was offset by the division losing the loyalty of the assignees or the latter proceeding with great caution so as not to alienate the agencies that they advised. Under the WPB, Nelson ended the clearance muddle by in effect turning the function over to the procurement agencies.

The Purchases Division appeared to have the least effect on the military's specialty production (e.g., aircraft, tanks, and ships), as opposed to commercially purchased or manufactured items (e.g., food and clothing), thereby informally perpetuating NDAC's distinction between "hard" and "soft" goods. Hence, like its NDAC predecessor, the division continued to advance the Quartermaster Corps's large-scale purchasing techniques, flexibility on specifications, and the like. Its work with the Navy Department never matched that of the War Department. Even with the Quartermaster Corps, however, there were always limits to what the Purchases Division could do. Throughout the NDAC and OPM periods, Donald M. Nelson persistently pressed the corps to institute long-range planning for commercially provided products. The harsh reality was that the corps never had reliable requirement figures well enough in advance to allow for such projections.

The Purchases Division depended on the full cooperation of the War and Navy Departments as the principal procurement agencies in order to carry out its clearance duties effectively. From their point of view, the armed services saw little advantage in going along with the division. Any gain on the part of the Purchases Division diminished their statutory authority to procure. Growing increasingly distrustful of the civilian mobilization agencies' ability and resolve, the army and navy would not willingly surrender power, and there appeared to be neither the will nor the way to require their compliance. Actually, even if the Offices of the Under Secretaries of War and the Navy had been willing to work hand in hand with the Purchases Division, as was in part the case with the Office of the Under Secretary of War, they could not easily have forced the supply bureaus, which negotiated the contracts, to follow their lead. The supply bureaus could and did passively and actively resist direction from the Offices of the Secretaries of War and the Navy, just as those offices did with the OPM.

Donald M. Nelson's leadership of the Purchases Division was at best curious. He threatened to resign in order to ensure that the division was properly empowered to carry out clearance functions. Once the division was under way and encountering nearly endless obstructions from the armed services, Nelson no longer fought on its behalf. (As administrator of priorities in the NDAC, he behaved similarly.) He may have been overwhelmed by the magnitude of the task that his division faced. More likely, he came to appreciate that civilian mobilization agencies could not effectively clear contracts without taking over procurement responsibilities from the military services. Whatever the case, Nelson's inconsistencies involving the Purchases Division foreshadowed his flawed leadership of the WPB.

The Purchases Division's operations were further burdened by duties involving plant sites and small business. Although OPM was to have general oversight of defense production facilities and the Purchases Division was specifically directed to clear construction contracts, the responsibility was left unaddressed. Hence, informally, and by default, the Production Division handled this vital matter. Congress forced OPM to deal more directly with the issue. Under great pressure from regions, states, and localities that felt themselves overlooked by the armed services, the nation's legislators in March 1941 threatened to create an agency dealing with the location of new defense facilities. To head off such action, OPM agreed to set up what became in May 1941 the Plant Site Board (PSB), located in the Purchases Division, and chaired by Nelson. The board was to clear all proposals for additions to manufacturing facilities costing $500,000 or more ($1 million after Pearl Harbor). In doing so, it was to work with the procuring agencies to ensure that existing facilities were used before new ones were built and that, whenever possible, new plants were geographically decentralized to locations having adequate labor, housing, utilities, transportation, and the like. To carry out its duties, the PSB depended heavily on information provided by other government agencies or subdivisions of the OPM, such as the Federal Power Commission, the coordinator of defense housing, the Bureau of Labor Statistics, the Labor Division, and commodity sections. The board's clearing process was separated from that carried out by the Purchases Division.[6]

OPM had greater influence over new plant sites than NDAC had had. In part that stemmed from the fact that, with PSB, facilities review was centered in one place instead of being scattered among a number of commissioners and that OPM had better data to guide its operations than NDAC had had. Moreover, with the defense program much further advanced in 1941 than in 1940, facilities had to be dispersed to avoid excessive congestion. Facing that reality, both the PSB and the military services shared the conviction that all but the most important manufacturing facilities had to be kept out of the area north of the Mason-Dixon Line and east of the Mississippi River. On more than one occasion, PSB withheld its approval of proposed plant sites, forcing the procurement agencies and their contractors to reconsider their plans. In that regard, PSB probably played a part in shifting defense plants away from already heavily industrialized areas like southern California, Detroit, and New Jersey and locating aircraft assembly units in the Midwest and shipbuilding facilities in inland waters.

Gains notwithstanding, the PSB still struggled with many of the same problems that plagued the NDAC. Major defense contractors insisted on building new facilities in existing locations or expanding standing plants. With the armed services reluctant to say no and the prospect of war increasing, PSB feared holding up munitions programs by using its veto power. Also, the procurement agencies continued to present facilities agreements that were all but signed or on a very tight schedule, practically forcing PSB to approve proposals after only a cursory review. As a result, the defense production overload grew in the heavily industrialized regions. While OPM's Plant Site Board was a distinct improvement over the NDAC and its crude procedures, its overall achievements were not outstanding. The procurement agencies and their principal contractors were still largely free to make facilities decisions to suit their mutual interests. More important, defense construction in general was handled by numerous subdivisions of OPM free of proper oversight by the office or coordination with agencies outside it affecting building plans. Within OPM, the Production Division, not PSB, remained most influential in dealing with facilities.

OPM'S SMALL BUSINESS OFFICES

The subdivision dealing with small business was under Purchases in the NDAC, was initially moved to Production in the OPM, and later became a division in its own right. Nonetheless, the small business office was sufficiently close to the responsibilities of the Purchases Division to justify analyzing it at this point.[7]

Backed by Leon Henderson and others, Donald M. Nelson, coordinator of national defense purchases, moved in October 1940 to have the NDAC create under his direction what became the Office of Small Business Activities. Nelson was concerned about spreading defense work as widely as possible so as to reduce unemployment, to utilize idle facilities, and also to prepare for expanding defense production. The Production Division under William S. Knudsen and the Industrial Materials Division under Edward R. Stettinius, Jr., opposed creating such an agency. Dominated by large corporations, these divisions resisted expanding Washington's power further, and they appeared to fear that small business might take over civilian markets as big business increased defense output. However, the reality of most contracts going to large corporations with smaller firms all but excluded forced the NDAC to act as Nelson requested.

The Office of Small Business Activities was still working out its organization and operations in January 1941 when OPM took over from NDAC. In February 1941, the office was transferred to OPM, placed in the Production Division, and renamed the Defense Contract Service (DCS). Robert L. Mehornay directed the DCS. He was president of the North Mehornay Furniture Company of Kansas City, Missouri, and he had run the small business office in the NDAC as deputy director.

A basic issue raised by NDAC and continuing throughout the war years was whether the mobilization agencies' primary concern should be maximizing defense output or protecting small business in an economy harnessed for war. Actually, the two goals were interacting and related. However, the mobilization agencies preferred to stress production, while Congress emphasized preserving smaller business units. The nation's legislators were under heavy political pressure to act. There were over 2.75 million small businesses in the United States. Of approximately 184,000 manufacturing firms, 98.9 percent had fewer than five hundred employees. As the defense program grew, the overwhelming majority of these companies faced an uncertain future without government contracts or subcontracts. From 1941 on, small business's lot in a wartime economy was never far from congressional scrutiny and action.

Continuing and extending activities that he began in NDAC, Mehornay worked to facilitate contracting and subcontracting among smaller industrial units. The DCS conducted surveys and gathered and distributed data from the army, the navy, and the Maritime Commission, business federations, and trade associations on requirements, contractors, and committed and unused facilities and equipment. Operating through regional field services, DCS then advised industrialists on contracting procedures, technical and engineering data, financing, bonding, and a host of other details involved in government work.

While commendable, these activities did not produce much in the way of results. A sense of urgency grew in the summer as strategic materials began to be cut off to nondefense firms and industries and Washington published figures on the distribution of defense orders. Late in July 1941, OPM reported that, in dollar value, almost three-quarters of army and navy supply contracts totaling over $10 billion went to fifty-six corporations. Six of the largest contractors held in excess of $3 billion. Bethlehem Steel Corporation was in front with nearly $1 billion in orders, followed by New York Shipping Corporation, General Motors Corporation, Curtiss-Wright Corporation, Newport News Shipbuilding and Drydock Company, and E. I. duPont de Nemours and Company.

Such concentration pointed to growing problems for various communities. Twenty industrial centers with 22 percent of the population received 72.8 percent of all defense contracts between June and December 1940. Geographic concentration was reduced only somewhat in 1941. Inevitably, these contractual patterns would lead to heavy labor migration to and, therefore, nearly intolerable loads placed on community services, utilities, and housing in high-contract areas; in the meantime, unfavored regions languished, even withered. Through investigations and reports of the Senate Special Committee to Investigate the Defense Program, the Senate Special Committee to Study and Survey Problems of Small Business Enterprises (also known as the Murray Committee), and the House Select Committee Investigating National Defense Migration, Congress grew increasingly critical of economic mobilization and its domination by big business, the role of the procurement agencies, and the neglect of smaller industries.[8]

OPM was seeking to strengthen its small business office in mid-1941 when, stung by the rising discord, Roosevelt moved on his own. Without notifying the office, the president by an executive order of September 4 replaced DCS with a Division of Contract Distribution (DCD), headed by Floyd B. Odlum, president of the Atlas Corporation of Jersey City. As was its predecessor, DCD was charged with working to distribute defense contracts as widely as possible, maximize subcontracting, and assist small business, and it also had the new responsibility of developing programs for converting industries from civilian to defense production. Since it was created by an executive order, the DCD had greater clout than DCS had had.

Convinced that he could succeed where others had failed, Odlum became a whirlwind of activity on behalf of small business. He reorganized his division to make it more effective, expanded the field service, and set up advisory committees from small business and engineering groups. Drawing on but going beyond programs that had preceded his, he publicized small business activities as never before by sending brightly and patriotically painted trains and trucks throughout the United States to display parts and products for small business to manufacture. Exhibits and industry clinics in cities big and small aimed at the same purpose, as did a flood of bulletins, booklets, manuals, and other publications. With all this activity, Odlum sought to draw together OPM officials, procurement agencies, prime contractors, and subcontractors.

Through Odlum's and the army's efforts, the nation by February 1942 had a better inventory of its industrial plants and existing machine tools than ever before. Odlum also managed to have representatives from his division work directly with procurement agencies in Washington and in the field to advance subcontracting, including the use of premium prices for both subcontractors and prime contractors to encourage better distribution of defense orders. The director of DCD additionally highlighted and extended the practice of pooling, or "defense production associations." Exempted from antitrust and other limiting statutes, a number of small manufacturers could combine their facilities, equipment, and talent to produce what would be beyond their individual capabilities. Between August and October 1941, for example, the household washer and ironing industry, made up of over thirty small firms, turned to DCD for assistance in handling defense-induced restrictions on production. With certification from the Labor Division that this was a "distressed" industry, Odlum was able to request from the army special and expedited action, leading in October to a $12 million contract for manufacturing antiaircraft mounts. In February 1942, Odlum claimed that his division had worked with some two hundred pools, thirty of which ended up receiving contracts totaling more than $100 million, figures challenged by the Murray Committee.

Odlum also struck out in new directions. His most original proposal involved setting aside 2 percent of critical materials for plants employing fewer than twenty persons, or around eighteen thousand of the twenty-eight thousand metal-using factories. With such an allotment, these firms would receive in 1942 nearly 75 percent of the materials that they used in 1940–1941. Since these plants were the most difficult to convert to munitions output, Odlum argued that his 2 percent approach would provide for vitally needed civilian products while rescuing companies facing disaster. Even when he reduced his proposal to 1 percent, however, the SPAB refused to go along because of administrative complexity and threats to defense output.

By January 1942, Odlum's outlook had turned gloomy: in spite of his frantic activity, little progress had taken place. Odlum's leadership qualities did not make the job any easier. His was a high-profile, one-man act that put off many in OPM because he plunged ahead without consulting his colleagues or thinking of the office as a whole. Partly as a result, the WPB, when organized in January 1942, returned the DCD to the Production Division, where it had originally been in OPM. Odlum willingly stepped aside in favor of his deputy, Walter H. Wheeler, Jr. Wheeler only reluctantly took over what he considered "an impotent appendage."[9]

Odlum, like his predecessors, encountered two harsh realities: prime contractors tenaciously resisted subcontracting with smaller units; and procurement agencies were largely uninterested in contracting with small business or insisting that their prime contractors subcontract. Since OPM was largely shaped by big corporations and the military, there was not much that Odlum or anyone else responsible for lesser business units could have done.

Within OPM, small business offices faced attitudes ranging from indifference to hostility, except from the Labor Division, the Bureau of Research and Statistics, and what became the Division of Civilian Supply. Moreover, with OPM's principal leaders arguing against the curtailment and conversion of consumer durables and the expansion of strategic and critical materials, the office helped create conditions favoring the largest corporations. Those corporations willingly took defense contracts and insisted that the government finance their expansion of plant and equipment when necessary. In that way, they could keep full control of the production process while benefiting from new facilities and maximized profits. Outside shipbuilding and aircraft, industry was not yet running at capacity in defense output. As long as those conditions existed, huge defense contractors were generally unwilling to subcontract or would do so only for the most troublesome, least profitable parts and assemblies and under unfavorable terms. Military procurement officers either backed or were unwilling to buck big corporation demands for new or expanded plant and full freedom in subcontracting.

Throughout most of 1940, and contrary to the military's interwar industrial mobilization planning, the armed services had no clearly defined policies for dealing with smaller producers.[10] Consequently, unless otherwise directed, the army and navy were bound to contract principally with the largest corporations. The economy's production potential was highly concentrated among several hundred corporations. They had the plant, the equipment, the labor, the experience, and the financial strength to manufacture munitions and supplies for defense and war on a massive scale. Whether contracts were let by bidding or by negotiation, small corporations could rarely compete with larger companies. And the military favored that outcome. Dealing with a few large firms was easier than treating with many small ones, and big firms could usually deliver the desired weapons and supplies with the speed, reliability, and quality that the armed forces demanded.

These conditions were strengthened by the fact that procurement officers in the armed services' various supply bureaus basically let contracts. While the War and Navy Departments set policies, procurement officers usually had a great deal of freedom in what they did. With defense spending growing exponentially in 1940–1941, enormous pressure, a sense of responsibility, and legal accountability inexorably pushed them in the direction of the biggest firms. Ample facilities, materials, and labor in 1940 encouraged the procurement agencies to follow the path of least resistance. As defense output faced growing restraints in 1941, the military, and particularly the army, tenaciously and shortsightedly struggled to continue contracting as if nothing had changed.

Working with small businesses, however, was often difficult. Most avoided defense work until facing a crisis. More important, many small businesses had limited plant and equipment and were often financially marginal, making them poor candidates for contracts or subcontracts. In September 1941, for example, the navy's Bureau of Ships had great difficulty filling emergency need for a large number of fans from lists of firms supplied by Odlum's division.

Nonetheless, mounting pressure from the public, the business community, the White House, and Congress forced the army and navy to be more sensitive about small business. Finally, in December 1940, the War Department advised the supply arms and services that subcontracting should be encouraged whenever possible. In February 1941, Under Secretary of War Patterson went one step further, allowing the supply bureaus to share with the DCS information on surveyed and allocated facilities, requirements, and other pertinent data if the service was willing to do the legwork involved. A different tactic was open to the War Department, as the secretary of war demonstrated. On February 19, 1941, he ordered the Ordnance Department to rely on subcontracting to hasten production schedules and to reduce the demand for equipment.[11]

The Navy Department was always more responsive to arguments on behalf of small business. Between January and April 1941, the secretary and under secretary of the navy directed the supply bureaus to substitute commercial products for those manufactured in naval establishments whenever feasible. They also appointed liaison officers to the DCS from the Offices of the Secretary of the Navy and the Chief of Naval Operations to further the service's work. The Navy Department additionally pushed subcontracts by inviting DCS personnel to join supply officers in surveying navy operations and authorizing procurement officers to use negotiations over competitive bidding when possible and necessary. Production within the naval establishment was substantial and responsive to the secretary's directives on subcontracting. However, that constituted only around 10 percent of navy demand; the other 90 percent involved outside contractors, who were not as easily controlled.[12]

Under Secretary of the Navy James V. Forrestal insisted that, for their own economic benefit, the procurement agencies had to spread the defense workload more evenly. But he went even further: if the public and its leaders believed that the military was not doing enough for smaller industrial units, the military had to do more. Accordingly, in August 1941, the Office of the Under Secretary of War created an Army Contract Distribution Division, and the Office of the Under Secretary of the Navy created the Contract Distribution Division. These divisions slowly worked out with OPM policies for channeling contracts and subcontracts to small businesses and to areas harmed by defense programs. Greater use was to be made of cost-plus arrangements, flexibility on bond requirements exercised, new facilities and equipment restricted if existing ones were available, and similar approaches implemented. Small business offices had been advocating such expedients for months. All these efforts received greater emphasis when the DCD took over in September.

While the military's policies toward small business changed, its practices were not quick to follow, for a number of reasons. The control of both the under secretary of war and the under secretary of the navy over the supply bureaus that they directed was at best tenuous. Patterson doggedly improvised to try to make his office work, and Forrestal strove feverishly to put together a system for carrying out his duties. Left with a great deal of latitude, the bureaus stressed their own interests and preferred to follow familiar practices. Even if the armed services were prepared to fulfill all declared policies, they would have been hard-pressed to do so since the small business offices in OPM were isolated from most centers of power and information. Without the backing of OPM, full and current data, and follow-up procedures, small business offices could not do their job.

The enormous challenge of small business is evident in Odlum's often contradictory observations and recommendations about handling it after the nation entered hostilities. On the one hand, he seemed to feel that the small business office should be included as a "civilian adjunct" of the army and navy. On the other hand, he worried that, if left in the WPB, the small business office would simply be pushed aside as irrelevant to war needs. In the WPB, it would have a chance only with the Division of Civilian Supply. After fighting so long for lesser firms, Odlum finally came to realize that their place in the economy and their role in mobilization could not easily be separated. Trying to convert large sectors of small business to war production, he concluded, was not worthwhile. Many of these firms would be better off being assured of raw materials to produce essential goods for civilians. What Odlum did not anticipate was that the large corporations and the armed services, which held back programs for small businesses in the defense period, would oppose their having too large a role in civilian output during the war years.[13]

By failing to make much headway in clearing contracts or plant sites, the Purchases Division, like the small business offices, was unable to bend the armed services to the will of OPM, supposedly guided by greater knowledge and a broader purview. The military was able to resist the Purchases Division's controls, not only because it had the statutory authority to procure, but also, and paradoxically, because the large corporations and their leaders in and outside OPM supported the widest latitude possible for the contracting agencies. Big business took that position because it was one assuring that most contracts would continue flowing to the corporate giants. Such a disturbing trend did go on after the United States entered hostilities, indicating that economic mobilization for war could have very distorting effects on the nation's immediate and more distant political economy.

OPM'S PRIORITIES DIVISION

Practically from the outset, the OPM began surrendering control over priorities to the armed services. OPM's failure in this area was more consequential than its failures in the areas of clearing contracts, plant sites, labor, and small business because the priority function was among the most important economic mobilization tools. Actually, the NDAC had allowed the procurement agencies to encroach on its priority powers, but OPM was much more extreme in that regard. The office's poor performance stemmed from its own ineptitude and the aggressiveness of the armed services.[14]

Edward R. Stettinius, Jr., headed the Priorities Division. Blackwell Smith served as his principal assistant and led in shaping policies. A Priorities Board made up of leading mobilization executives advised Stettinius, who served as its chair. Stettinius set up branches in his division for minerals and metals, chemicals, commercial aircraft, tools and equipment, and general products.

The executive order creating OPM delegated to the office the president's statutory authority for priorities under both the June 28, 1940, legislation giving army and navy orders precedence over those for private or foreign use and the Selective Service and Training Act of September 16, 1940, which allowed for the placement of compulsory orders. In creating OPM, the president invalidated previous executive orders that had set up a priorities system in NDAC. Hence, the OPM and the army and navy had to renegotiate an agreement on how priorities would operate under the office. Because the stakes were so high, the negotiations were long, complicated, and tense.

The priority—or, euphemistically, preference—system under NDAC had been voluntary in nature and based on a "Critical List" of two hundred items that the military ranked as most important to its operations. Through agreements with the NDAC, the Army-Navy Munitions Board (ANMB) administered priorities for the armed services. Restricted at the outset to military products, NDAC's priority system directly and indirectly began to include civilian goods in short supply.

The War Department wanted NDAC's priority approach modified under OPM so as to make the armed services dominant: all priority orders would be made mandatory and the Critical List eliminated so that the army and navy could assign priorities to any product, component, or material that they deemed necessary. Reluctant to surrender even more power to the ANMB, the Priorities Division under Blackwell Smith hammered out an arrangement with the military in January and February 1941 that essentially continued the NDAC system with the ANMB's priority hand strengthened only to a degree. While OPM preferred to keep the priority system voluntary, it could be made mandatory on a selective basis. While ANMB continued to assign priorities on the basis of the Critical List, the board could automatically extend priority coverage from a prime contractor to the first subcontractor in instances in which parts or components had no commercial or civilian use. The Critical List would then be expanded to include the new item. Any priorities below the first subcontract, and including raw materials, would be handled by the Priorities Division, with provisions for special treatment if a contracting officer felt that to be necessary. All priority action was to be based on priority certificates signed by the director of priorities. Unlimited numbers of blank, signed certificates would be made available to the army and navy.

Continuing NDAC practices, the Priorities Division operated through committees that made most of OPM's priority decisions. Committees existed for problem areas such as machine tools, chemicals, iron and steel, aluminum and magnesium, and commercial aircraft. These committees served under one of the division's five branches, and they were composed of representatives of producers, industrial users, civilian and labor interests, and the army and navy, with Production and Purchases Divisions members acting as consultants.

Badly flawed organization and operation prevented OPM's Priorities Division from ever functioning well. The priority committees gathered information and debated policy responsibly, but they made decisions in a slow and clumsy fashion. Matters grew worse after the June 1941 reorganization of OPM. With commodity sections and industry advisory committees reshuffled among the Production, Purchases, and Priorities Divisions, the priority system became even more bureaucratically complex, even unwieldy. All the while, the division had failed to recruit an adequate staff and to work out proper methods for handling the multiplying priority applications in an expeditious manner. The Priorities Board, intended to assist Stettinius in formulating general policies, was of no help in improving divisional operations. Hence, it was phased out in August and replaced by the SPAB.

A crippled Priorities Division had dire consequences. It could not deal effectively with the workload of either assigning civilian priorities or recording those issued by the procurement agencies. By mid-1941, priority applications poured into the division at twice the rate at which they could be handled, overwhelming the system. During the week before Nelson replaced Stettinius as director of priorities in September 1941, of five thousand incoming applications, only eighteen hundred had been issued, and more than eighteen thousand were being processed. By instituting simplified procedures, Nelson quickly cleared up the backlog, and the methods used improved until the WPB replaced OPM.

By the time Nelson took over priorities, however, the military services had gained dominance over that key function. Steadily throughout 1941, the army and navy weakened the importance of the Critical List, which OPM used to limit their activity. With no field staff to oversee military subcontracts below the first tier, as had been agreed on in February, the Priorities Division turned over to the armed services in March the authority to assign priorities to all military subcontracts included on the Critical List. From then on, the army and navy constantly pressured a reluctant Priorities Division to expand the list to include increasing numbers of materials, parts, and equipment, rendering it all but useless. Recognizing that reality, the Priorities Division abolished the Critical List in January 1942.

The priority system was starting to break down by mid-1941. The ineptitude of the Priorities Division and the freewheeling operations of the armed services exacerbated, but did not cause, the system's fundamental flaw: it was without quantitative controls. Priorities were a claim against output made without considering product availability. The more priorities' demand exceeded supply, the more meaningless the preference approach became. If, for example, the armed services claimed all aluminum at the highest rating, none would be available for priorities at the second, third, fourth, and lower levels. This scenario started to occur. Between November 1940 and July 1941, the army and navy included only a few of the most critical goods in the top priority classification. By August 1941, however, the ANMB began raising the priority ratings on military items, elevating many to the highest levels. Priority inflation threatened some national defense orders at the expense of others and also began cutting off materials, equipment, and supplies for civilian purposes. With priorities becoming little more than "hunting licenses," the entire mobilization program was threatened.

At best, a priorities system was vulnerable. For it to work well, a centralized agency that had reliable figures on supply and demand over time would have to rate scheduled production in such a way that all priorities would be valid. None of these conditions existed under OPM. The most serious failure was the inability of the armed services to come up with reasonably accurate requirements while still insisting on assigning priorities as they chose. A firm stand against the military's mode of operations by OPM and the Priorities Division could have preserved some of the regulating effects of priorities.

Why the Priorities Division remained so weak is both intriguing and predictable. When OPM was created early in January 1941, Secretary of the Navy Frank Knox proposed to William S. Knudsen that the Priorities Division take over all priorities, with ANMB ceasing to operate in the area. In Knox's mind, such an outcome would eliminate unnecessary duplication between the two agencies and could act to the navy's benefit since the army dominated ANMB. Knox's remarkable recommendation never went far. The War Department delayed action until apparently convincing the secretary of the navy that his proposition would gravely harm military procurement. In mid-February, the Navy Department withdrew Knox's suggestion.

While voicing support for Knox's idea, the Priorities Division did so without enthusiasm. Yet Stettinius and Smith protested the loudest about Nelson allowing the ANMB to seize the initiative over NDAC priorities in 1940. They showed no interest in attempting to regain what Nelson had lost. Indeed, Blackwell Smith later observed that the Priorities Division was "never geared up" to handle civilian priorities, let alone those for the armed services. That the army and navy desired to operate free of the Priorities Division's direction he found to be "perfectly logical."[15] The Priorities Division seemed to conclude that the most that it could do was to assist, and where necessary restrain, procurement agency priority action.

Such an outlook was consistent with the attitude manifested in the Production Division under both NDAC and OPM. Corporate America was in no hurry to strengthen the regulatory powers of the civilian mobilization agencies, and it preferred working directly as partner with the military services in initiating the defense program. In that way, national needs could be met with the least disturbance to corporate prerogatives. Moreover, New Dealers and all-outers such as Henderson, pushing for maximum munitions output through strong, civilian, and liberal mobilization agencies, would be thwarted. If OPM was not prepared to rein in the armed services on contract clearance, plant sites, and small business operations, it was unlikely to move boldly in the priorities area. Gaining meaningful control of priorities would have required OPM fundamentally to alter power operations within the office and between it and the armed services. Stettinius, Blackwell Smith, Knudsen, and other top OPM figures resisted such extreme measures.

With the priorities system never working well, OPM turned to complementary and supplementary controls for protecting and furthering defense output. These included preference ratings (P orders), allocations (M [materials] and E [equipment] orders), conservation (also M orders), and limitation (L orders). P orders were a blanket form of priority rating that firms and their subcontractors could use to obtain materials and components essential to the output of goods only indirectly involved in defense production and, hence, ineligible for direct priority protection. The first of such orders—for components and materials necessary to the manufacture of electric traveling cranes—were issued by OPM in March 1941, and they later came to include products ultimately involved in the output of airframes, propellers, engines, and specialized ship hulls.

Allocation orders apportioned among all claimants the entire national output of materials or equipment already in short supply. Under this approach, defense production received the highest claims, while nondefense users were gradually reduced to smaller allotments, in some cases nothing. The first M and E orders of February 1941 dealt with aluminum and machine tools, and, by the end of 1941, they covered magnesium, ferrotungsten, nickel and nickel steel, synthetic rubber, copper, pig iron, and steel.

Conservation orders limited in whole or part the use of materials in nondefense production, with the intent of forcing industry to find substitutes. The first such order of June 1941 involved tungsten and led to the substitution of molybdenum. Copper, silk, and numerous other products became subject to M orders as the defense program grew.

L orders prohibited the output of designated end items. Such drastic controls came only late and were intended to curtail industries and force their conversion to defense production. OPM held off until the very end of August 1941 in using an L order to halt the production of various trucks and buses. Along with these orders, OPM in May 1941 instituted a system of inventory control, prohibiting delivery of critical materials to manufacturers beyond their production requirements, to check hoarding.

The various orders usually originated with commodity sections, were passed on by industry advisory groups, and were cleared by the Priorities Division. When the SPAB came into existence in September 1941, it became the center for directing all priority and related functions. Compulsion was introduced into the distribution system only gradually. The legislation of June and September 1940 allowed military orders to be made mandatory beginning in 1941. The OPM's general counsel, John Lord O'Brian, argued early in March 1941 that this power could be extended to cover essential civilian goods, but the issue was not settled until Congress passed the statute on May 31, 1941, extending the president's priority power to include the civilian area, foreign goods, and allocations. Even then, the enhanced authority was not implemented until SPAB began operating in September 1941.

While useful and improving over time, the system of P, M, E, and L orders and controls was neither fully effective nor well integrated. Those orders and controls overlapped at points, and they were often difficult to understand and implement. Nonetheless, they were essential for making the growing defense production program work as numerous materials, equipment, and other shortages mounted. Indeed, the severe limitations of priorities led to OPM turning increasingly toward allocation systems as a better means for distributing scarce goods.

In terms of regulating distribution, priorities worked from the top down. They started with prime contractors, descending to subcontractors and, ultimately, raw materials. Allocations began at the bottom and proceeded upward from raw materials to finished products. Generally, allocation systems are a less complicated and more effective means for handling shortages than are priorities systems. However, piecemeal allocations suffer from the same principal limitation as priorities. Both approaches, for example, might ensure that a manufacturer received on time the steel that it needed for producing tanks but not the copper since the two metals would be treated separately. A comprehensive allocation system could overcome this basic fault. On the basis of a firm's calculations of all materials and goods required to manufacture tanks, the mobilization agency would schedule deliveries according to the company's needs. Such an approach is much more sophisticated than priorities, and it requires precise information and well-developed regulatory techniques.

OPM began experimenting with a general allocation system in May 1941 called the Defense Supplies Rating Plan. On the basis of the preceding quarter's defense work, a company could apply for the delivery of standard products such as industrial motors, lathe tools, and civilian aircraft parts for the succeeding quarter and before any contracts were negotiated. Although voluntary, the plan was sufficiently attractive that thousands of companies participated. The major limitations were that goods under the plan had a low preference rating and that the plan covered too little of the production process. Nevertheless, by allowing OPM to allocate products in advance of contracting, the plan functioned in such a way that its advantages outweighed its disadvantages.

Hence, on December 3, 1941, OPM introduced a much more complete allocation program called the Production Requirements Plan (PRP), which was also voluntary. Drawing on the previous quarter's record, a firm could apply for blanket priorities, including materials and goods for all its military and essential civilian output, for the following three months. OPM would then grant the firm one or a series of preference ratings depending on its needs. Starting first with firms, the PRP would later be expanded to industries. The plan was also intended to become mandatory, a development that took place under the WPB.

The PRP had one other major attribute. It would provide OPM, and later WPB, with comprehensive statistical data on the defense program, which it had never had before, and which was essential for distributing scarce products intelligently. No priority system alone could accomplish that goal.

Before the WPB replaced the OPM in January 1942, then, the latter had worked out most of the distribution and related controls necessary for mobilizing the economy. The PRP was the most important of these regulatory mechanisms.

THE SUPPLY PRIORITIES AND ALLOCATION BOARD

In terms of distribution controls, the most important step for advancing national defense production took place late in August 1941 with the creation of the SPAB.[16] Most immediately, the SPAB was set up to resolve a running dispute between the OPM and OPACS. Conflict between the two agencies peaked over the act of May 31, 1941, that extended the president's priorities power to cover essential civilian production, foreign buying, and subcontracts, along with authorizing him to use allocations. Actually, the SPAB had become necessary for the much larger purpose of making coherent and energizing the economic mobilization program, which was bogging down in confusion and conflict as the international situation deteriorated. Roosevelt had declared a state of unlimited national emergency on May 27, 1941, as conditions in Asia and Europe threatened the United States with the growing possibility of a two-front war.

The ongoing feud between OPM and OPACS basically came down to corporate America's caution over harnessing the economy versus New Dealers in Leon Henderson's circle insisting on an all-out approach. Hence, the battle between the two agencies went beyond priorities to incorporate most of the strife rending the mobilization program.

The Bureau of the Budget recognized this reality as it mediated between the two agencies while seeking to improve the economics of defense. Even before the May 31 statute was out of Congress, OPM and OPACS began pressing the Bureau of the Budget and the president to favor it in an executive order delegating the expanded priority power. Over three months of wrangling and deliberation took place before the issue was settled, with New Dealer Samuel I. Rosenman—Roosevelt's favorite troubleshooter—called in at the end to confer with Harold D. Smith's bureau.

By early July, the Bureau of the Budget had arrived at three principal conclusions. First, while OPM and OPACS could reach a compromise over their differences, they could not settle the unresolvable conflict of two agencies administering priorities when only one could do so effectively. Hence, OPM should absorb civilian supply and be responsible for all priorities. (Price controls should remain in an independent office.) Second, since OPM continued to view itself as primarily serving the armed services, civilian supply could be shortchanged. To guard against that development, Leon Henderson should head civilian supply in the OPM, and his position should be strengthened in other ways. Third, settling the priority issue had to take place within the context of creating a new planning body under the president and superior to OPM. The new agency would make policy for the entire economic mobilization program, a solution that ultimately anticipated in most details the SPAB.

Almost all parties agreed on the need for superior planning as set forth in the last point, but they disagreed over how to achieve it. The two most important recommendations came from Under Secretary of War Patterson and Leon Henderson. Patterson wanted the OPM council expanded to seven members for determining policy; Henderson went on record backing an approach very similar to that favored by the Bureau of the Budget. Neither the bureau nor Henderson was pleased with such a makeshift arrangement, but both probably felt that it was as far as they could then go. Working with Rosenman, the bureau late in August offered the president a number of alternatives for settling OPM-OPACS differences while providing for greater centralized direction of economic mobilization. Roosevelt quickly settled on the Bureau of the Budget–Henderson recommendation, leading to the executive order of August 28, 1941, centering the administration of priorities in OPM's hands, creating the SPAB, and instituting other changes.

SPAB was a top-level policymaking body for coordinating economic mobilization. Specifically, the board was charged with determining all defense and civilian requirements, the materials and components necessary for producing them, and policies for meeting essential demand. The board was also to determine policies and regulations for administering priorities and allocations. Serving on the board besides the four members of the OPM council—Knudsen, Hillman, Stimson, and Knox—were Vice-President Henry A. Wallace, who also headed the recently created Economic Defense Board (EDB) and whom Roosevelt designed as the SPAB's chair; Harry L. Hopkins, Roosevelt's special assistant for defense aid; and Henderson, who was in charge of civilian supply inside OPM and price controls outside it. Nelson was tapped as executive director. Herbert Emmerich and John Lord O'Brian acted as secretary and general counsel, respectively, for both the OPM and the SPAB. The new board would operate largely through the OPM, but it was unquestionably superior to it.

About the same time that SPAB was set up, OPM was reorganized in various ways. Civilian supply was moved into OPM as a division. The domain of the Division of Civilian Supply included any industries producing less than 50 percent for defense purposes, positioning it to have a dominant voice in curtailment policies and practices. The Office of Price Administration now stood alone, but Henderson headed both that agency and the OPM's Division of Civilian Supply. Materials was also separated from production and set up as a separate division. The industry and commodity branches were reshuffled among the Materials, Purchases, and Civilian Supply Divisions, with the Priorities Division stripped of all branches and the Production Division handling only those dealing with weapons and defense construction. Nelson replaced Stettinius as director of priorities, and the Priorities Board was disestablished. The rigid John D. Biggers was pushed out of OPM, and the more flexible William L. Batt began rising in importance.

Although placing SPAB over OPM was an awkward arrangement, the results were positive. A point had been reached where, although strengthening economic mobilization was essential, the president was not yet ready to place one person in charge. SPAB proved to be the right interim step. It allowed the administration to test further the qualities of Nelson as the probable mobilization czar. Even more important, it strengthened with the least amount of disruption those favoring maximum defense output.

Wallace, Hopkins, Henderson, Hillman, and Nelson were all-outers. They could be depended on to counter the conservative influence of Knudsen, Stimson, and Knox. Knudsen reflected corporate America's resistance to defense conversion and expansion, which the military supported because of its own procurement and supply limitations and the desire not to antagonize firms critical to production. By making Wallace chair of SPAB, the president was signaling the importance that he attributed to the board, an act bolstered by the fact that, as the president's closest adviser, Hopkins was also on the board and could speak directly for the White House. Placing Henderson's civilian supply agency in OPM at the same time that the strong-willed New Dealer was put on SPAB was a vote of confidence in that enormously talented public servant and the president's endorsement of balanced mobilization policies. In creating SPAB and making changes in OPM, the president and his advisers sent other significant signals. Biggers and Stettinius were removed from

OPM as drags on mobilization, and Nelson and Batt were rewarded for their positive contributions in harnessing the economy.

Major SPAB activity covered curtailment, expansion of output, allocation, and requirements. The board accomplished a remarkable amount in a four-month period.

One other SPAB achievement is significant. The SPAB was the first mobilization agency to focus on essential civilian requirements. OPACS had been created in part for that purpose but devoted most of its time and energy to curtailment, conversion, and expansion for meeting defense needs in the face of OPM's hesitancy and inactivity. With OPACS's goals being realized under SPAB, Henderson and his deputies had the opportunity to insist that sound mobilization had to protect the vital needs of the civilian economy. In pursuing that end, the Division of Civilian Supply could depend on the board's support, even initiative, although this area was not a major concern of SPAB.

Curtailment, however, was a major concern. And that crucial function was handled largely by the Division of Civilian Supply. The division was assigned responsibility for those industries producing 50 percent or less for defense purposes, such as automobiles and other consumer durables, pulp and paper, lumber and building materials, and rubber and rubber products. Moreover, the Division of Civilian Supply participated in issuing the various preference, allocation, conservation, and limitation orders since they usually involved its areas of concern. To gain maximum information for carrying out its responsibilities, the division appointed civilian allocation specialists to all industry and commodity branches. This arrangement was at best an uneasy one because, like OPACS, the Division of Civilian Supply was committed to maximum curtailment in order to accelerate defense output while most of industry's OPM representatives still opposed cutting back civilian output.

Differing outlooks only complicated the difficulties that curtailment entailed. Before decisions could be made, great amounts of data had to be collected and extended negotiations with industry and other OPM divisions carried out. Finally, all curtailment orders had to receive the approval of the Priorities Division, the OPM council, and SPAB. By early December 1941, besides automobiles, only refrigerators, domestic laundry equipment, vacuum cleaners, and metal office furniture and equipment had been curtailed among non- and less essential industries. Massive reductions in civilian production took place only after Pearl Harbor. Additionally, SPAB ordered an end to all construction that was not for defense or essential civilian purposes, and it all but prohibited the use of copper in civilian goods. Working through OPM, SPAB in the month after the nation entered war (and before the WPB was set up) launched a major drive to initiate, extend, and broaden the curtailment of civilian industries.

Curtailment was at first implemented to save scarce materials for defense purposes. Later in 1941, as the mobilization program accelerated, cutting back industries was seen as a way to force conversion so as to make more facilities available for munitions output as well as to avoid or reduce priorities unemployment and to open up greater opportunities for small business. Consequently, the Division of Civilian Supply was backed by labor and more modest business elements.

Scarce materials, however, remained a serious matter and one that was growing in severity as the defense program expanded. To gauge the extent of the problem, SPAB initiated a systematic review of materials that were already a problem or could be so in the future. It then took corrective action whenever possible, including building up stockpiles and expanding capacity. In the case of steel, for example, SPAB early in October ordered facilities to be increased by 10 million tons annually. Implementing the decision was not easy. Industry still held back on greater plant until the need was certain. Roosevelt had to intervene personally, for example, before steel would agree to enlarged capacity. Immediately after Pearl Harbor, SPAB moved quickly to maximize the supply and minimize the use of rubber, tungsten, manganese, tin, and other strategic materials.

In terms of allocations, SPAB continued existing programs and went in new directions. With Donald M. Nelson serving both as the director of OPM's Division of Priorities and as the executive director of the SPAB, the potential for improving distribution controls increased. Nelson wanted to reassert civilian direction of priorities to the degree that that was possible. He decided that industries devoting less than 50 percent of their output to defense would remain with the existing priorities system despite all its pitfalls; those above 50 percent would be gradually switched to an allocation approach. Hence, the Defense Supplies Rating Plan would be expanded and preparations for the PRP would go forward. Any full-blown allocation system, however, required vast amounts of information and intricate coordination, capabilities that the SPAB was striving to expand.

SPAB had its biggest impact in the area of allocating scarce materials between America's fighting forces and those of its potential allies. Russia stood out in this regard. Late in September 1941, Great Britain and the United States agreed in the Moscow Protocol to provide massive material assistance to the Soviet Union. In October, the SPAB approved the specifics, and Nelson rated the goods ahead of all domestic demand. Beginning in November, before deliveries began, the secretary and under secretary of the navy launched concerted drives to block shipments of machine tools and aluminum because their need was suspect, they could be either undeliverable or susceptible to German capture, or they were urgently required at home. Knudsen had earlier objected to providing Russia with strategic goods. From November through January, Roosevelt repeatedly had to intercede in SPAB affairs to ensure that the Soviet Union received the promised equipment and material.

Defeated in the SPAB, the Navy Department joined forces with the War Department in mid-November to try to have the board restructured in a way giving conservative forces the control that they had lost with the OPM council. Hopkins, Henderson, Nelson, and Hillman would have been removed from the board and Stettinius added. With an SPAB made up of Stimson, Knox, Knudsen, Stettinius, and Wallace, the War and Navy Departments could fairly well dictate mobilization policy and certainly determine the nature of assistance to Russia. Roosevelt used Wallace to checkmate the Knox-Stimson proposal. The armed services may have been motivated as much by protecting their own bases as by anti-Communist ideology. Stimson indicated that such was the case after Pearl Harbor by declaring that the whole thrust of Lend-Lease had to be reconsidered: victory for America depended on making the nation invincible, not assisting others. The military services' response to aiding Russia highlights their parochial outlook, contrasted with the far-sighted strategic thinking of the president. The episode also demonstrates the critical role that Roosevelt was still playing in shaping and advancing economic mobilization.

Actually, with the SPAB leading the way, the Roosevelt administration moved to coordinate foreign economic defense policy in general more effectively and to place it more firmly in civilian hands. At the end of July 1941, the administration created the interdepartmental EDB, headed by Vice-President Wallace, to oversee exports, imports, preclusive buying, finance, foreign exchange, transportation, and other policies related to national defense. Up until that time, the military-directed Office of Export Control (created in July 1940) had a leading role in international economics and was seeking to extend its reach in this area. In September, SPAB, assisted by the Bureau of the Budget, arranged for the EDB to absorb the Office of Export Control and a State Department subdivision so as to centralize under civilian direction economic policies and programs abroad. Among other responsibilities, the expanded EDB was to provide SPAB with export estimates of materials and components related to national defense. Such figures would aid the board in its calculations of overall defense requirements. The EDB did not cover the operations of the OLLA, formally set up on October 28, 1941, but it did work closely with those of the coordinator of inter-

American affairs. Before entering hostilities, therefore, America had made major strides toward rationalizing its bureaucracy in order to handle international economics, which took on such importance during hostilities.[17]

The SPAB's most important accomplishment was providing reliable estimates of existing and long-term defense and probable wartime requirements. Without such figures, mobilization agencies operated in the dark when passing on such vital issues as curtailment, construction, facilities expansion, essential civilian requirements, and priorities and allocation.

Just before Pearl Harbor, SPAB completed an ambitious study for a Victory Program that outlined in broad terms the economic output essential for defeating the Axis powers. The Bureau of Research and Statistics, all-outers such as Henderson, and others had been calling for such a program for months. OPM's Production Planning Board had made that goal its most immediate concern. Throughout 1941, the board had insisted to Roosevelt that, without at least general strategic goals, economic planning for war would always suffer. After the board's demise, Roosevelt in July and August 1941 finally moved on its recommendation. He called on the War Department to estimate what production potential was required for the United States and other nations to conquer Germany and its allies.

As soon as SPAB was set up, Leon Henderson and Donald M. Nelson joined forces to have the board on September 9 instruct Nelson to compile scheduled, overall military, civilian, and foreign requirements for the next eighteen months. He would request requirement estimates from the armed forces and appropriate civilian agencies. With such figures, Nelson would then rely on the Bureau of Research and Statistics for completing his study. A consolidated statement would include, not only end items, but also the materials, components, facilities, equipment, and labor essential for producing them. SPAB's authority and Nelson and his backers' determination ensured that, for the first time, mobilization agencies would have basic data on military objectives to guide their work.

Nelson requested from the procurement agencies major finished products, components, and raw materials broken down by months according to military objectives from October 1, 1941, to March 31, 1943. The army was able to provide rough general data on scheduled end items, but it made little headway with materials and components. Lagging behind the army in statistical services, the navy could come up with only piecemeal requirements even when assisted by personnel on temporary assignment from OPM. The recently created OLLA was unable to do much in terms of foreign demand, while the Maritime Commission never submitted a report of any kind.

Working with the requirements it received, and making projections where necessary, the Bureau of Research and Statistics by December 4, 1941, arrived at a Victory Program that went beyond the eighteen-month period to encompass a prospective war. To initiate an all-out, successful offensive against the Axis in 1943 would require aggregate spending at home and abroad of $142–$150 billion by September 30, 1943, or half a national income reaching $130–$140 billion in 1943. To meet that target, the existing defense program would have to be doubled, probably an unrealistic goal. Hence, the bureau concluded that about three-quarters of the Victory Program, or $110–$115 billion, could be fulfilled by the end of September 1943, with the total program completed during the spring of 1944. Even to meet that schedule, the Bureau of Research and Statistics concluded, maximum conversion and utilization of existing plant had to commence quickly so as to avoid wasting time and scarce materials building new facilities and equipment. In gross amounts, ample labor would be available, although particular skills would present challenges.

The Victory Program set off a high-stakes struggle between Nelson, speaking for SPAB, and Knudsen, representing OPM, over leadership of economic mobilization. By the time the program reached the president a few days after Pearl Harbor, Knudsen insisted that the nation could devote no more than a total of $100 billion to warfare by September 30, 1943, not the $110–$115 billion that SPAB advocated. The OPM's director was reflecting the views of the numerous production executives within the office. The usually cautious Nelson was being pushed aggressively to hold out for the higher figure by economists, statisticians, and planners such as Robert R. Nathan and Edwin B. George operating in and about the Bureau of Research and Statistics and usually associated with New Dealer Leon Henderson. Seeking to bolster the case for greater war production, Nelson turned to the War Department. However, its requirements were still on the low side and at best vague.

The arrival in Washington late in December of British Prime Minister Winston Churchill and his minister of supply, Lord Beaverbrook, swung the debate in SPAB's favor. With force and passion, Beaverbrook argued that all hope of defeating Germany depended on the Allies pushing their combined munitions output to unheard-of levels. An inspired and emboldened Nelson set about setting forth exactly what a Victory Program of $110–$115 billion by September 1943 meant in terms of gross weapons output. Before sending the document on to the president, the executive director first secured the SPAB's endorsement for what was now called the New War Munitions Program. Without comment, Knudsen went along. By the time he received Nelson's document on January 1, 1942, Roosevelt's hesitancy in the face of divided counsels had changed to match Nelson's call for maximizing war output at all costs.

The American war production goal for late 1943 was now set at Nelson's high figure of $110–115 billion, not Knudsen's more cautious one of $100 billion. For the first time in over a year and a half of effort, the nation had a defined goal for guiding its mobilization effort. Nelson's timely victory, his last real and symbolic battle with Knudsen and the OPM, was important in his selection as chair of the WPB.

OPM AND SPAB IN PERSPECTIVE

In an exceptionally brief period of around four months, the SPAB in practically every major category had advanced the United States to the point of mobilization for total war. In doing so, the board benefited from the steady advocacy of the all-outers, which began with the NDAC and accelerated under OPM. By August 1941, the battle within OPM between industrialists favoring business as usual and economists, academicians, and public servants insisting on maximum defense output had reached the point of practically paralyzing efforts to harness the economy. In this running battle, the armed services neutralized their potentially massive influence by, in effect, supporting both sides at different times but, in a crunch, coming down in favor of industry. Only by creating the SPAB, weighted in favor of the all-outers, was Roosevelt able to break the stalemate in a way that prepared the nation for the full mobilization of World War II without excessively disturbing the awkward, delicate bureaucratic structure built up so cautiously since mid-1940.

Much of what the SPAB was able to do, however, depended on the OPM's progress, limited though it was. OPM advanced facilities expansion and began conversion in the automobile and other industries. Despite general resistance, the real and potential output of basic materials such as aluminum, steel, and copper was increased and brought under greater regulation. Although OPM did not improve much on the NDAC's priorities record, it did begin instituting other controls, such as limitation orders critical to mobilization. Additionally, and of the highest importance, the office initiated the crucial transition from a failing priorities system to a much more promising allocations approach. In its most significant areas of failure, OPM was unable to rise above NDAC's experience. That was evident with contract clearance and plant sites. Moreover, OPM highlighted what was already becoming manifest with its predecessor: protecting the interest of small business during mobilization was nearly beyond reach; and organized labor—growth, militancy, and imagination aside—would be restricted to the important but still limited and traditional areas of labor relations and labor supply.

Even with SPAB's impressive accomplishments, there was a disturbing and portentous quality about the board's operations. On the tough, important, and controversial issues, Roosevelt constantly had to intervene to ensure that majority decisions were implemented. That occurred with lend-lease aid for the Soviet Union, steel expansion, and long-term requirements. Industry and the military could combine their strength to thwart SPAB operations even as a minority and before the full emergency after Pearl Harbor. That did not bode well for wartime operations since the WPB would be only a refined version of the OPM and the SPAB combined and staffed with most of the same personnel.

With Pearl Harbor unequivocally resolving the mobilization debate in favor of all-outers, the Roosevelt administration could now finally set up a centralized agency for harnessing the economy. Without the numerous critical, but unspectacular, achievements of the SPAB, the WPB would have faced an even greater challenge than it did. In the final analysis, the admittedly angular SPAB, which defied practically all rules of public administration and did not exhibit the required strength, still turned out to be a successful experiment in getting the stalled mobilization program moving rapidly in the right direction.

PART THREE
THE WAR PRODUCTION BOARD, 1942–1945

Industry and the military dominated the War Production Board (WPB), the principal wartime civilian mobilization agency. This trend began with the National Defense Advisory Commission (NDAC) and continued under the Office of Production Management.

In the processs, economists, statisticians, academics, businessmen like James S. Knowlson, and others, often associated with the New Deal, combined their talents throughout 1942 and into 1943 to ensure that the economy was properly harnessed. Also an extension of the defense years, this development was institutionalized with the Supply Priorities and Allocations Board.

Donald M. Nelson's success and failure as WPB chair resulted largely from ongoing friction between industry-military elements and economist-reformers over basic mobilization policies. Most industrialists preferred harnessing the economy with the least modification of peacetime practices. Many armed forces leaders argued that civilian mobilization agencies existed to assist the military in meeting their unreviewed requirements. Guarding their power, both business and the armed services favored either a weak WPB or one answerable to them. On a theoretical and practical level, Nelson realized that, left to themselves, industry and the military could disrupt a command economy. Neither appreciated the concept of feasibility: demand could not significantly outdistance the economy's capacity without potentially disastrous consequences. Nelson forced the entire mobilization structure to accept feasibility, along with the allocation of materials, the scheduling of production, and other practices essential for implementing it. He did so by relying on the sophisticated analysis and recommendations of the Planning Committee, headed by Robert R. Nathan and reporting directly to him.

Intense, often brutal bureaucratic brawling took place throughout a good part of 1942 over adopting and implementing policies for feasibility, materials

191

allocations, and production scheduling. While winning the battles, Nelson and the Planning Committee lost the war. Early in 1943, the committee disbanded; Nelson remained as WPB chair, but at the cost of surrendering most of his authority. In August 1944, he was finally forced out of WPB when he insisted upon going forward with a reconversion program against nearly insuperable odds.

Industry and the military resisted feasibility and related controls because they threatened intricate ties binding them in an alliance reaching back to NDAC. In implementing the regulatory devices, the corporate community and the armed forces protected their separate and mutual interests by dominating WPB through a newly created Production Executive Committee. In so doing, they replaced two mobilization centers with one by integrating civilian and military functions in the board.

Maneuvering over mobilization from 1940 through 1945 was intensely ideological. New Dealers in the Leon Henderson circle aimed at state-centered civilian agencies holding in line both the corporate structure and the armed services. Industry and the military were determined to limit Washington's reach both to check reform and to maximize their own latitude. When the two combined their power as major sources of supply and demand, they shaped the means for mobilizing the economy. By pitting himself against the corporate and military communities and identifying himself with New Dealers in the Henderson mold, Nelson lost the support essential for leading WPB.

Even when the industry-military team had achieved dominance in WPB, tumult went on. Offices for civilian requirements, small business, and labor constantly challenged corporate community–armed forces rule, arguing that their voices were ignored by the board and their interests slighted. Moreover, the WPB often clashed with separate agencies, such as the War Manpower Commission, the National War Labor Board, the Office of Defense Transportation, the Office of Price Administration, and other offices for food, petroleum, shipping, foreign economic affairs, and the like.

To free himself of a troubled homefront, the president late in 1942 turned to James F. Byrnes, who headed first the Office of Economic Stabilization and later the Office of War Mobilization (OWM)/Office of War Mobilization and Reconversion (OWMR). OWM ultimately eclipsed WPB as the primary mobilization administration. Thoroughly familiar with the capital, the moderately conservative and competent South Carolinian oversaw the successful economic stabilization program, authored at the outset principally by New Dealers. He also settled repeated conflicts among the numerous offices participating in the disjointed and tangled structure for harnessing the economy. In the last years of hostilities, Byrnes faced tougher times and exercised more power. Nonetheless, the OWMR director's success depended on knowing what Roosevelt wanted and how far he could go. Until his death, the president had the last word on mobilization policy and remained the final source of appeal.

8

WPB: ORGANIZATION AND STAFFING

President Franklin D. Roosevelt created the War Production Board (WPB) on January 16, 1942, and selected Donald M. Nelson, who had played a central role in economic mobilization since 1940, as its chair.[1] On the basis of the initial executive order of mid-January and subsequent ones, Nelson was granted nearly unlimited authority for harnessing the economy. From the outset, however, Nelson realized that the WPB could not perform on its own all or even most mobilization functions, as had been the case with the National Defense Advisory Commission (NDAC) and the Office of Production Management (OPM). He also led by seeking consensus rather than exercising executive command. Those realities, combined with constant challenges to his authority, led to the WPB chair compromising his authority before the WPB was fully under way. Over a year passed before the board gradually devised a structure for meeting its nearly overwhelming duties.

WPB's first year was a tumultuous period in which intense conflict erupted within the board and between it and the procurement agencies, particularly the War and Navy Departments. By March 1943, when WPB had fairly well taken on its final form, Executive Vice Chair Charles E. Wilson had replaced Nelson as WPB's effective operating officer, and the armed services had acquired extraordinary power and influence within the board. Additionally, WPB increasingly found itself subject to direction from the "assistant president for the homefront," James F. Byrnes, appointed first as director of the Office of Economic Stabilization in October 1942 and then as director of the Office of War Mobilization in May 1943.

INITIAL ORGANIZATION

In addition to Nelson, the WPB was composed principally of those who had constituted the Supply Priorities and Allocations Board (SPAB): Henry A.

Wallace, chair of the Board of Economic Warfare; Harry L. Hopkins, special assistant to the president; Secretary of War Henry L. Stimson; Secretary of the Navy Frank Knox; Leon Henderson, administrator of the Office of Price Administration; Federal Loan Administrator Jesse H. Jones; William S. Knudsen, ultimately as the War Department's production expert; and Sidney Hillman, speaking for labor—see chart 4. (New members would later be added and others dropped as the mobilization structure changed.) Since the board was only advisory to Nelson as chair, it did not emerge as a significant center of power within WPB.

With some critical modifications, Nelson temporarily fell back on the approximate organization of the OPM until he could work out a more effective system. Most of the principal executives from OPM also carried over to WPB. At the outset, WPB operated through six divisions. The Labor and Purchases Divisions turned out to be inconsequential. Sidney Hillman's Labor Division was left without an assignment. When the War Manpower Commission was set up outside WPB in April 1942, Hillman resigned, and the reorganized division that he had headed became rudderless and ineffective. Once Nelson decided to let the military and other claimant agencies conduct their own procurement, the Purchases Division was left with little more than ceremonial functions. The Division of Civilian Supply, which Henderson continued to direct, also lost ground under WPB. Without industry branches to direct, its clout was gravely reduced, weakening its efforts to convert industry to war and protect the civilian economy during hostilities.

The divisions for production and materials were of greater importance in WPB operations. William H. Harrison carried over from the OPM in directing the Production Division. Working with the armed services, the division was to expand munitions production potential through new facilities and subcontracting, to ensure the availability of essential tools and equipment, and to coordinate components, accessories, and subassemblies for the purpose of maximizing end-product output. Directing fourteen commodity branches as he had in OPM, William L. Batt continued as head of the Materials Division. This division's role was to ensure the availability of raw and industrial materials essential for war production in any way possible, including new or expanded plant, imports, purchases, and stockpiling.

The Division of Industry Operations was far and away the most important of those set up by Nelson at the outset. It was based on, but went beyond, organizational patterns evolving in OPM, which placed the division at the very center of WPB. James S. Knowlson, president of Stewart-Warner Corporation, a manufacturing firm, who had served as deputy director of priorities under Nelson in OPM, headed this crucial division. It had three main func-

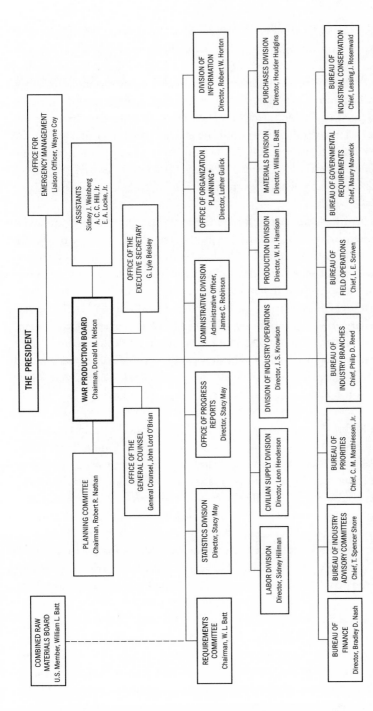

Chart 4. Organization of WPB, March 30, 1942. *Source:* Civilian Production Administration, *Industrial Mobilization for War: History of the War Production Board and Predecessor Agencies, 1940–1945* (Washington, DC: Civilian Production Administration, 1947), p. 238.

*Formerly established on May 14, 1942.

tions. On the basis of estimated demand, the division would direct the conversion of industry for war purposes but maintain adequate capacity for meeting essential civilian needs. Furthermore, working with the Requirements Committee, the division would direct, control, and maximize the flow of raw materials and equipment to manufacturing facilities. Finally, Knowlson's division had assigned to it all industry branches and their industry advisory committees. In that way, industries would have one point of contact with the WPB. To facilitate that approach, Knowlson also had under his jurisdiction the Bureaus of Priorities, Industrial Conservation, and Field Operations as well as others. The new division centralized control over industry to a degree never achieved before.

Also of enormous importance for WPB was the Requirements Committee, which was intended to continue the functions performed earlier by the SPAB. Serving as a staff agency under WPB, the committee was made up of representatives from all claimant agencies and was led by William L. Batt. It had an independent economic and research office headed by Edwin B. George, who had served under Stacy May and others in the OPM and SPAB. The committee was charged with determining for the WPB chair and appropriate board divisions basic information on total military, civilian, and other requirements for raw and industrial materials; establishing availability of such materials; and proposing and approving how they should be allocated. Centralized policy and statistics on materials would assist the work of the Division of Industry Operations.

Nelson additionally created several other staff agencies to assist him in carrying out his assignment. Of great significance was the Planning Committee, chaired by Robert R. Nathan, a statistician from the Commerce Department who had been performing economic analysis for war mobilization since the organization of the NDAC. While the committee performed numerous analytic and statistical functions, its greatest contribution involved long-range planning to ensure a feasible, balanced war production program. That placed the Planning Committee at the center of numerous battles fought within WPB and between it and claimants. The Planning Committee carried out—often brilliantly—the goals unsuccessfully pursued by the OPM's Production Planning Board.

Several other staff offices complemented the Planning Committee and were intended to strengthen Nelson's control of economic mobilization. The Office of Progress Reports was authorized to collect and analyze information from a broad range of sources on appropriations, requirements, facilities, production, deliveries, and the like. Regular reports would allow Nelson and WPB to assess progress, spot problems, and devise solutions. Stacy May directed both that office, with Nathan as assistant director, and the Statistics Division. In May 1942, Nelson added the Office of Organization Planning as a staff agency to help improve WPB structures. Luther Gulick chaired the office. Gulick had played a key role in restructuring the Executive Office of the President in the 1930s and, thereafter, remained active in government organization for war. From the WPB's outset, Nelson began strengthening what had been the Office of the Executive Secretary in the OPM to serve as a general secretariat for the entire board. This goal was largely reached by the end of 1942. The office not only provided the board with centralized office functions, but it also kept board subdivisions informed of major policy decisions and relevant developments among WPB's numerous and different parts. Such crucial coordination and integration had been missing in the operations of both the NDAC and the OPM.

Knowlson was intent on making the industry branches the principal operating units of the WPB. In that way, policymaking would be centralized, implementation decentralized. Philip D. Reed, formerly chairman of the board of the General Electric Company, acted as chief of the Bureau of Industry Branches. Conversion, financing of facilities, obtaining materials and equipment, and labor supply would all be carried out by the branches. Other divisions like production, statistics, and labor could assign representatives to industry branches for facilitating their work.

As with the NDAC and OPM, WPB's principal executives were dollar-a-year men, and that was particularly the case for the industry branches. Between January and December 1942, such personnel jumped from 310 and to a wartime high of 805, while WPB's total staff went from 13,626 to 22,591 between March and December 1942. The total numbers of without-compensation personnel (mostly part-time, temporary personnel in nonadministrative positions) combined with dollar-a-year personnel remained under 4.5 percent of WPB personnel for most of the war years. A survey in May 1944 established that about 66 percent of all dollar-a-year men came from manufacturing, most of the others were from the business world, and around 7 percent originated in universities, labor, or state and local governments. Over 40 percent of the industrialists were from the top two executive tiers of their firms.[2]

Dollar-a-year men were a source of constant concern throughout the war years. About the same time that the WPB was set up in January 1942, the Senate Special Committee to Investigate the National Defense Program (also known as the Truman Committee) issued a report sharply critical of such personnel and their potential abuses. Nelson appeared before the committee to defend their continued use as nearly indispensable, but he reassured the committee that he would enforce existing rules so that dollar-a-year men would be

used only when essential, that they would be of the highest character, as verified through investigation, and that they would not be allowed to engage in
conflicts of interest. Reluctantly and skeptically, the Truman Committee went
along with Nelson's decision.

In actuality, the use of dollar-a-year men in WPB varied little from their use
in OPM. John Lord O'Brian served as general counsel in both OPM and
WPB. He had led in introducing restricted use of dollar-a-year men and industry advisory committees in OPM, and those policies carried over to WPB, with
some modifications and changes in emphasis. What did change under the
WPB, as opposed to the OPM, was close scrutiny by WPB and Congress of
without-compensation personnel. Nelson appointed a special assistant to
define and enforce policies, and the chair's practices continued after he left
the board. The Truman and other congressional committees regularly called
for reports on dollar-a-year and without-compensation personnel. Such vigilance produced around fifty surveys and studies from early 1942 through early
1944, resulting at times in a number of individuals leaving the board or being
transferred to less compromising positions.

Nonetheless, policies and practices were still being refined and rewritten as
late as 1944, and violation of rules and questionable appointments went on.
Indeed, WPB prohibited executives only from heading their industries'
branches or divisions, not from serving in them. Over time, even those rules
were relaxed. Hence, industrialists ended up making decisions for their industries and even their own firms. The Iron and Steel and the Pulp and Paper
Branches (later divisions), for example, were dominated by individuals from
those industries and their trade associations. Moreover, executives from industry advisory committees continued to be appointed as WPB officials in violation of established policies.

Building on the foundations laid by OPM, WPB clearly ended the unpoliced, freewheeling dollar-a-year-men practices of NDAC—patterns reminiscent of the War Industries Board during World War I. Still, conflicts of interest
in various forms continued. More important, and despite extensive efforts to
protect against abuses of private businessmen exercising public power, the values and interests of industry, and usually large industry, shaped the operations
of the WPB, as had been the case before with NDAC and OPM. This theme
will be examined at length in the chapters that follow.

Industry's grip on WPB was strengthened by the vastly expanded use of
industry advisory committees. As with dollar-a-year men, O'Brian restricted
the use of such committees in OPM so that they would be legal and not encroach excessively on public decisionmaking. NDAC had used industry advi-

sory committees without established policies and in a way resembling the war service committees of World War I, in which private and public power became inextricably combined. Under WPB, industry advisory committees (not including subcommittees) grew from 33 to 465 between January and December 1942 and reached 750 by January 1944. These groups were under a Bureau of Industry Advisory Committee, which was later upgraded to an office.[3]

OPM policies carried over to WPB, with several significant modifications. First, the industry section, branch, or division chief could organize a committee when he believed that to be necessary. He could select members without calling a nominating conference or conducting an election. However, the committee should be representative in terms of firm size, geographic location, product segment, and trade association affiliation. With rare exceptions, all meetings of industry advisory committees were to be held in the capital. Second, the attorney general had little to do directly with committee organization and operation unless special conditions arose. The Office of the General Counsel and the Bureau of Industry Advisory Committees oversaw the advisory system.

The advisory committee system ran rather chaotically in 1942 as WPB went through the throes of converting the economy to full wartime production. Some industry representatives complained that they were informed or told what to do more than consulted about what should be done. In other instances, industry branches operated without committees or ignored them because of the chief's predilections or his concern about committee resistance. For the most part, however, industry branches tended to rely heavily on advisory committees for information and guidance on most mobilization decisions. That covered a long list of activities: conversion, allocation, and distribution of materials, components, and parts; production scheduling; conservation measures (including simplification, standardization, and substitution); expansion or contraction of production; facilities authorization; and a host of related functions.

Once WPB was through the most demanding phase of conversion in 1942, Nelson and other WPB executives insisted that all industry branches or divisions, and particularly those involving large industries, organize advisory committees and meet with them regularly. The committees were to be kept informed of major WPB policies and developments, and they were to review thoroughly all limitation, conservation, and other orders involving their industries, along with clearing plans for expanding facilities. Only in that way, WPB officials insisted, would the board benefit maximally from industry's expertise while minimizing complaints and winning the support of the business community. After he joined the WPB late in 1942, Ferdinand Eberstadt, echoing the ideas of Bernard M. Baruch, wanted to go further and formally include carefully selected industry advisory committees in the board's decisionmaking. Others persuaded him that such an approach would run afoul of the law. However, to ensure that industry branches used advisory committees, the WPB in 1942 allowed members of a committee to call meetings on their own.

Industry's voice in WPB operations was not restricted to advice. The Office of Industry Advisory Committees could not effectively police hundreds of committees holding thousands of meetings even with "industry advisers" assigned to the industry divisions to oversee committee use. Established rules, consequently, were violated with or without the knowledge of the office, and unofficial contacts took place regularly between industry and the branch or division directing it.

In March 1942, for example, officers of the Farm Machinery and Equipment Branch informed the general counsel of their intent to meet with the Farm Equipment Institute (whose membership accounted for up to 80 percent of the industry's output in dollar value) about conversion policies. Although O'Brian's office discouraged such exchanges, the division's leaders insisted that only through them could they do their job efficiently. In July 1942, an advisory committee to the Construction Machinery Branch called its own meeting to decide which types and sizes of equipment would be halted for conservation purposes. The branch chief was reduced to insisting that such initiatives be avoided in the future. Firms in the paper industry told the Pulp and Paper Branch in mid-1942 that they intended to organize a Paper Industry War Council to participate in most aspects of conversion and war production. Warnings against the illegality of such a move did not quickly persuade the corporations to back down, and, in 1942 and 1943, those firms participated in decisionmaking through advisory committees and branch/division executives who came from the industry and its trade associations.

When advisory committees met under established regulations, there was still no guarantee against irregularities. Other than branch and industry members, only representatives from WPB subdivisions and other mobilization agencies who had a direct stake in the proceedings were in attendance at meetings. No one among this group had any reason to report violations, and nonindustry members from labor and even the Division of Civilian Supply who might do so were blocked from participating in industry advisory committee meetings or could participate to only a limited extent.

Participation by various industries in WPB operations was also not always representative. WPB did away with OPM's distinction between formal and informal advisory committee meetings. Instead, the industry branches could convene conferences or meetings. Conferences, or task forces, were ad hoc arrangements called to address special problems or technical issues—such as acquiring maintenance, repair, and operating supplies in the steel industry—and need not be representative. Meetings meant organizing and convening a representative advisory committee for dealing with broad policies affecting an entire industry or a significant segment of it. Branches often favored conferences over meetings because they were free to work with preferred members of an industry. That was the case in March 1942 when the Office of the General Counsel had to explain away the Furniture Branch sending out invitations for a conference when a meeting was much more appropriate. This was hardly an isolated incident. Throughout 1943, General Counsel O'Brian constantly warned WPB officials that the Textile, Clothing, and Leather Goods Division as well as many others were exposing industries to antitrust prosecution by calling conferences of select industrialists instead of advisory committee meetings. Advisory committees, however, could also be unrepresentative, as indicated by complaints from industries about "inside information clubs," cliques, and other favored groups.

No matter how representative contacts between the industries and WPB were, members of advisory committees gained an advantage. That reality acted to favor large businesses over small to medium-sized ones because the bigger firms could more easily handle the finances of industrial gatherings. Data received or decisions or recommendations made at meetings could take weeks or even months to reach an industry, even when such information was critical for decisionmaking. And, for military or competitive reasons if material was confidential, it could not be disseminated. The WPB steadily worked to get around limitations to free the flow of information. Although some problems were intractable, obstacles diminished in 1944 and 1945 as the military situation improved for America and its allies.

All in all, then, WPB industry advisory committees were substantially different from the ones used during World War I. They were also a decided improvement over the committees of the NDAC period. However, they did not vary that much from those of OPM. The policing of WPB committees was more diligent and organized than it was of OPM committees. But, since WPB faced hundreds of committees where OPM dealt with only a few, the final outcome was probably the same. That meant that, through conferences and meetings, industry provided WPB with invaluable assistance in mobilizing and demobilizing the economy. It also meant that industry cemented further its dominant hand in the operations of WPB, a dominance that was already substantial through the use of dollar-a-year men.

JULY 1942 REORGANIZATION

By July 1942, strengthening the WPB's organization became necessary. Conversion was fairly well under way, the WPB was burgeoning in size, and Donald M. Nelson was clearer on what had to be done to meet his responsibilities. The restructured board freed Nelson from day-to-day direction of WPB activities so as better to focus on the larger issues of harnessing the economy. It also featured a greater degree of centralization and attempts to coordinate more effectively supply and demand.

William L. Batt was elevated to the newly created position of general vice chair, in effect Nelson's deputy. James S. Knowlson became vice chairman for program determination, making him also chair of the crucial Requirements Committee. His principal job was seeking to match output with claimant agencies' requirements in a way that would further the war effort while maintaining economic balance. By reducing the number of executives reporting to the chair, Batt and Knowlson would protect Nelson's ability to concentrate on policy issues. Nelson also sought to ease his load and increase his control over mobilization through appointing a deputy chair for program progress. This official was to keep the chair informed about the production program in general and about its actual and potential problems. For complicated reasons, the new position never worked out.

Of critical significance in the July reorganization was replacing the Division of Industry Operations with the director general for operations, who absorbed the Materials and Production Divisions, all commodity and industry branches, and various bureaus, such as those for priorities and industry advisory committees. Ernest Kanzler, chairman of the board of the Universal CIT Credit Corporation and formerly a Ford Motor Company executive, took over the operations slot in September 1942. For the first time, all operating units were now under central direction. But, since the director general for operations was independent of the vice chairman for program determination, the WPB had two, not one, centers of power that would have to be coordinated. Still, the restructured board was a major step forward in consolidating control within the WPB.

An important development of the July reorganization was strengthening the WPB's field staff. Knowlson, who had been working with the field structure since late 1941, largely directed the changes. The field staffs, which had grown under the NDAC and the OPM, were very ineffective, limiting severely the ability of the central civilian mobilization agency to carry out its responsibilities. Without adequate decentralization, for example, neither the NDAC, the OPM, nor the WPB was able to administer the priorities system. All ended up in effect turning the function over to the armed services, thereby surrendering vast power and control. Knowlson created under the director general for operations an Office of Field Operations. By slow stages, the office consolidated its power over the WPB's decentralized system, one based principally on twelve regional centers and seventy local or field offices. Although the field organization did not maximize its structure and operation until 1943, by late 1942 field operations had improved to the point that the WPB could perform critical tasks that had earlier been beyond its reach.

In July, the Division of Civilian Supply became the Office of Civilian Supply, answering directly to Nelson. Nevertheless, Leon Henderson's civilian supply unit lost even more power and prestige. The vice chairman for program determination now had the final word on requirements. On their part, the industry divisions increasingly and successfully asserted their right to define the needs of their industries, which accounted for around 80 percent of so-called civilian requirements. That left the Office of Civilian Supply to speak only for consumers absorbing the remaining 20 percent of civilian goods. The once-powerful office had been reduced to a weak claimant struggling to protect a general public that few felt at the time to be threatened. Production for war took precedence in the outlook of all major policymakers.

The success of the July reorganization depended heavily on Nelson's ability to correlate economic output with military demand, which was based on strategy. Only with that basic information would the vice chairman for program determination and the director general for operations be able individually and jointly to perform their assigned duties effectively. Nelson hoped to have the WPB carry out this vital function as the SPAB had done in the last months of 1941. The WPB was unable to do so because it lacked data on the armed services' long-range plans. Under Secretary of War Robert P. Patterson and Under Secretary of the Navy James V. Forrestal, who represented their departments on the board, were of little help. Their duties covered procurement and supply, not strategy.

The requirements that the WPB used to guide its operations were crude, unrefined, and unreliable estimates that were submitted by the army and navy without the review and approval of the Joint Chiefs of Staff, who were responsible for strategic decisions. Nelson unsuccessfully attempted to arrange through the president a system in which WPB would collaborate with the joint chiefs in working out balanced, feasible requirements rated in order of urgency for guiding the board. The most Nelson could achieve was having the Joint Chiefs of Staff in October 1942 arrange for military officers to advise WPB about requirements essential for meeting strategic needs. No set system for correlating production with strategy was ever implemented, an outcome that kept the board perpetually off balance and subject to demand over which it had no firm control.

AUTUMN 1942 REORGANIZATION

The independence of the military services in requirements, priorities, procurement, and production scheduling severely limited the WPB's ability to maintain economic balance despite improvements achieved with the July reorganization. Nelson had to reclaim for his agency the vast mobilization functions that he had delegated to the army and navy. By slow and acrimonious stages, the WPB reasserted its authority over economic mobilization between July and December 1942. It did so through an intricate negotiating process that involved switching from the Production Requirements Plan (PRP) to the Controlled Materials Plan (CMP) for allocating critical materials, instituting scheduling of all munitions production through the Production Executive Committee (PEC), and establishing the WPB's right to set feasible limits for military requirements. All these vital changes require extended analysis. Nonetheless, at this point, a general outline of what took place will be helpful.

Priorities and allocations had plagued the WPB from the outset. Following the example of the OPM, Nelson had delegated to the Army-Navy Munitions Board (ANMB) the authority to assign priority ratings to military production. Not only did ANMB use this grant of power to the full, but it also managed to extend its priority control over civilian goods. With the armed services issuing priorities in an indiscriminate manner while blocking preference for essential civilian goods, the priority system was overwhelmed and the overall needs of the economy threatened. To deal with a failing priority approach, the OPM had begun to emphasize allocation of critical materials, and the WPB continued this approach. Throughout 1942, the board had broadened the coverage of the PRP and was moving to make it mandatory for all output in the third quarter of 1942. The PRP was a horizontal form of control in which contractors reported to the WPB their multiple materials requirements. The board reviewed and approved their requests and allocated to each contractor various materials according to availability and need.

The PRP had the advantage of providing the WPB with detailed and general information on the entire war production program and a mechanism for directing it. It had the disadvantage of being extraordinarily complex and, hence, requiring a great deal of time and experience to implement. Because of these realities, there was considerable opposition to the PRP in WPB. Within the board, and among the military services, there was a preference for vertical, instead of horizontal, materials control. Under such a system, the WPB would, on the basis of requirements, allocate to the armed services and other claimants critical materials to meet their demand. The claimants would, in turn, distribute materials among their contractors, who would share them with subcontractors, and so forth. Materials, in other words, would follow and be distributed according to the pattern of contracting. Unlike the horizontal system, the vertical one was much easier to administer. It had the disadvantage, however, of diminishing WPB control over production by decentralizing materials distribution among the procurement agencies and their contractors.

Despite reservations among Nelson and his principal advisers, WPB late in 1942 elected to implement a vertical system of materials distribution that came to be known as the CMP. The board did so because the PRP was encountering exceptional difficulties that would take too long to resolve. Also, by switching to the CMP, the WPB could more easily reclaim priority powers and gain the cooperation of the armed services in the operation of both the preference and the allocations systems. To achieve the latter goals, however, Nelson felt compelled to bring Ferdinand Eberstadt, the civilian chair of the ANMB who was closely associated with both Patterson and Forrestal, into WPB as a leading vice chair. This was accomplished late in September 1942.

Preceding Eberstadt's transfer to the WPB in September, Nelson arranged for Charles E. Wilson, president of the General Electric Company (GE) and a production specialist, to join the board as chair of the newly created Production Executive Committee. Through the committee, Wilson would review and schedule all production programs of the armed services and other claimants. Production scheduling—a process that the military could not adequately accomplish on its own—was essential for making a materials allocation system operate effectively. Scheduling meant that materials, parts, and components would flow according to an established calendar so as to maximize output, prevent holdups, and discourage excessive inventories. Additionally, Wilson would act as a civilian counterbalance to the militarily oriented Eberstadt. The latter was brought into the board in part to reassure the army and navy that their interests would be protected as the WPB reasserted control over the war production program.

Eberstadt's success with materials and Wilson's progress with production scheduling depended on reliable and realistic requirements coming from the claimant agencies, particularly the armed services. In the midst of the struggles within the WPB and between it and the armed forces over priorities/allocations and production scheduling, the most bitter and consequential battle was fought out between July and November 1942 over the right of the WPB to set the parameters for requirements in what has come to be called the Feasibility Dispute.

In July 1942, the Planning Committee reported to Nelson that military requirements for 1943 were being set as high as $97 billion. Adding anticipated nonmunitions war expenditures of $18 billion totaled $115 billion, far beyond the economy's ability to produce. Direct war spending could not exceed $75 billion, which would grow to $93 billion when indirect war expenditures were calculated. Not only must military demand be reduced by around $35 billion, the Planning Committee insisted, but a supreme war production council made up of military, economic, and political leaders should be created to set and adjust requirements throughout the war period. The Planning Committee's analysis and prescription met resistance of the most extreme sort on the part of the military. Its proposal for a supreme war production council was never seriously considered, but its economic analysis could not be ignored. By November, the joint chiefs reduced munitions demand for 1943 to around $80 billion, which, while still high, the Planning Committee considered to be within the realm of the doable.

The Feasibility Dispute set a critically important precedent: the WPB had the right to determine whether claimants' demand was realistic in terms of the economy's potential. However, future review of military requirements was not handled by the Planning Committee, made up principally of economists, statisticians, and other professionals. Instead, that vital job was taken over by the PEC (usually building on the work of industry branches), which was headed by production experts but dominated in numbers by military officers. Nonetheless, with the PEC reviewing and authenticating overall wartime demand, materials could now be allocated and production scheduled so as to maximize output while maintaining economic balance.

Once differences over allocating materials, scheduling production, and determining feasible requirements were settled, WPB late in 1942 advanced another major step in centralizing control over a mobilized economy. Eberstadt, who joined the board in September, replacing James S. Knowlson as vice chair for program determination, became program vice chair in November 1942. His principal task was implementing the CMP through various subdivisions. However, in superseding the vice chair for program determination, the program vice chair expanded his authority to include that of the director general for operations. Eberstadt now directed, besides materials, all commodity and industry branches, field operations, and staff bureaus responsible for production, distribution, and facilities.

From his commanding position, Eberstadt restructured WPB activities around the industry branches, now elevated to divisions. Grouped according to product—minerals, commodities, consumer goods, equipment, and construction and utilities—the divisions were to act as small war production boards.

They were to reconcile supply and demand for the industry or industries they directed, distribute goods on the basis of higher policy and determination, and maximize supply through expanding capacity, curtailing less essential use, and conservation measures. With Eberstadt's restructuring and related changes, armed services representation in the industry divisions was both increased and systematized. Eberstadt's industry-division reforms bore the strong influence of Bernard M. Baruch and the War Industries Board of World War I.

Wilson's responsibilities as production vice chair required extended, intense negotiations with the anxious and aggressive armed services before they were finalized in December 1942. The president of GE was viewed suspiciously by the military as a civilian threat to its procurement turf. As head of the PEC, Wilson was to schedule all war production, resolve conflict among claimants, and ensure the feasibility of requirements. Moreover, Nelson consolidated airplane programs in and outside the WPB under Wilson's direction as chair of the newly created Aircraft Production Board. Besides Wilson, PEC members at the outset came almost exclusively from the top military ranks of the armed services' supply systems and the Maritime Commission.

Through the sweeping changes of late 1942, Nelson had succeeded in reestablishing WPB control in the critical areas of priorities and allocations, production scheduling, and review of requirements. The board was now better positioned to oversee economic mobilization than it had been before. However, Nelson had paid an extraordinarily high price for these gains. Eberstadt shared the view of the armed services, and the two key production subdivisions of the board were dominated by the army and navy. Moreover, the relationship and the distribution of jurisdiction between Eberstadt and Wilson, who had emerged as the two power centers in the board, were left ominously vague. Battles between the board's titans were soon to break out and in a way that had civilian versus military overtones. To settle what became all-out administrative warfare, Nelson ended up eroding even further his position and ability to lead.

FEBRUARY AND MARCH 1943 REORGANIZATION

By the early months of 1943, Ferdinand Eberstadt began to lose power and position to Charles E. Wilson. This trend in part reflected major mobilization developments. Through the CMP, Eberstadt began to bring order to the distribution of materials as the principal threat to the munitions program late in 1942 and early in 1943. Hence, the scheduling of production emerged as the more pressing function in WPB. Nelson and his advisers, moreover, favored

Wilson, an industrialist, over Eberstadt, a financier, because of his needed expertise and also because, unlike Eberstadt, he had not been involved in past conflict among civilian and military mobilization agencies. Even if there had been no tangible conflict between their roles, Eberstadt and Wilson were bound to clash as determined executives unwilling to take a subordinate position in WPB under Nelson.

The growing conflict between the program and the production vice chairs, as elaborated below, came to a head over direction of the industry and commodity divisions, the basic operating units of WPB. Through the reforms that he instituted late in 1942, Eberstadt controlled all the divisions. Yet Wilson insisted that he needed them to carry out production responsibilities. Consequently, early in February 1943, Nelson not only began transferring commodity and industry divisions from Eberstadt to Wilson but also indicated that he was preparing to make Wilson the WPB's senior vice chair. Eberstadt's ability to carry out his duties and his status within the board were threatened. To counter Nelson's moves, the War and Navy Departments combined their voices with that of Director of Economic Stabilization James F. Byrnes—closely associated with Bernard M. Baruch—to persuade Roosevelt to replace Nelson with Baruch. Since Baruch was seventy-two years of age and ailing, Eberstadt—now in Baruch's circle—would no doubt play a major role in running the board. Nelson outmaneuvered his detractors by moving with uncharacteristic speed and determination and forcing Eberstadt's resignation. Roosevelt, who was at best lukewarm about ousting Nelson, decided that he had to continue supporting Nelson for the time being.

In saving his job, Nelson accelerated his own decline. Wilson had gained the acceptance that Nelson lacked or had lost at the White House, in the WPB, and among the claimant agencies, especially the armed services. To shore up the board's authority, Nelson in effect turned control of WPB over to Wilson as executive vice chair. He was to direct all the board's programming and projects, control all the key staff and operating subdivisions, and make any changes in the board's organization and function that he considered to be necessary. Nelson was left supervising directly only the Offices of the General Counsel, the Executive Secretary, the Rubber Director, Civilian Supply, and War Utilities and the Smaller War Plants Division and Corporation.

Wilson continued to chair the PEC and the Aircraft Production Board. He oversaw the remainder of the WPB through four vice chairs. Two of them were of critical significance and continued a nearly insoluble tension inherent in the civilian mobilization agencies from the outset. The program vice chair set board policy on requirements, allocation of materials and components, order of urgency for military, foreign, and civilian requirements, and other programs necessary to achieve his goals. The operations vice chair implemented policies set by the program vice chair, and, in doing so, he directed most of the industry divisions, many of the staff bureaus dealing with production scheduling, industry advisory committees, and the like, and the field service.

Dividing duties between the two vice chairs made sense because the overall job was too much for one executive. Additionally, two coequal chairs balanced power in such a way as to protect the authority of the WPB's chair and executive vice chair. However, dynamics within the WPB almost inevitably made the two vice chairs rivals in a way that disturbed the smooth functioning of the board. The other two vice chairs included one to deal with international supply and another to serve as deputy to the executive vice chair.

Robert N. Nathan's Planning Committee became a victim of the intense battles fought over WPB policies and operations from mid-1942 through early 1943. The War Department came to view the committee with hostility. It was seen as the principal source of the WPB chair's drive and rationale for such proposals as feasibility, production scheduling, and coordinating production with strategy. The military interpreted these acts as threats to its procurement prerogatives. As Wilson sought to reestablish working relations with the armed services after the reorganization of February–March 1943, the army and navy made it clear that the Planning Committee had to go. Rather than accepting demotion and emasculation at Wilson's hands, the committee members resigned en masse as of April 1, 1943. The board, thereby, lost its main source of independent judgment on policy and programming. This had been a small but mighty institution tracing its antecedents back to the NDAC.

Several other changes were made in 1943 that fairly well stabilized WPB's organization through 1944 (see chart 5). In December 1943, divisions for industries and materials were further rationalized. Earlier, the Office of Civilian Supply was restructured as the Office of Civilian Requirements in order better to protect the homefront. After more than two years of agitation by organized labor and its supporters, two labor vice chairs were appointed in June 1943, one for manpower, the other for labor production. These positions turned out to be largely ceremonial. Membership on the WPB itself also changed, reflecting changes in organization and emphasis.

Nelson was weakened outside the WPB as well as within it. By an executive order of October 1942, Roosevelt appointed James F. Byrnes director of economic stabilization. While he concentrated on economic policy, Byrnes also began coordinating mobilization in general, superior in fact, if not in law, to Nelson and the WPB. That reality became even clearer in May 1943 when the president promoted Byrnes to head the Office of War Mobilization.

Byrnes was now performing the job that Nelson as chair of the WPB had

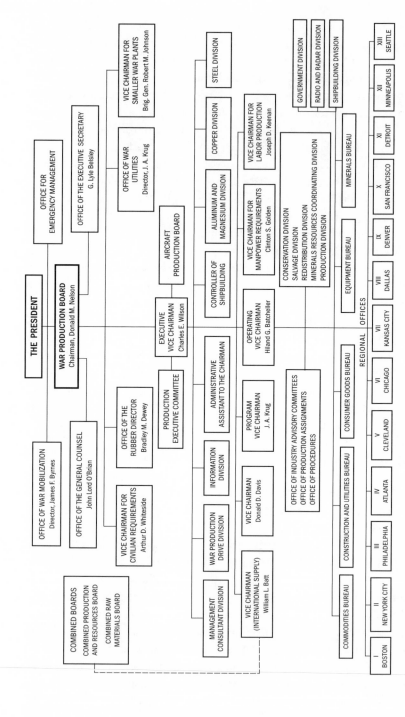

Chart 5. Organization of WPB, September 1, 1943. *Source:* Civilian Production Administration, *Industrial Mobilization for War: History of the War Production Board and Predecessor Agencies, 1940–1945* (Washington, DC: Civilian Production Administration, 1947), p. 593.

THE PRESIDENT

OFFICE FOR EMERGENCY MANAGEMENT

WAR PRODUCTION BOARD
Chairman, Donald M. Nelson

OFFICE OF WAR MOBILIZATION
Director, James F. Byrnes

OFFICE OF THE GENERAL COUNSEL
John Lord O'Brian

OFFICE OF THE EXECUTIVE SECRETARY
G. Lyle Belsley

OFFICE OF THE RUBBER DIRECTOR
Bradley M. Dewey

OFFICE OF WAR UTILITIES
Director, J. A. Krug

VICE CHAIRMAN FOR SMALLER WAR PLANTS
Brig. Gen. Robert M. Johnson

COMBINED BOARDS
COMBINED PRODUCTION AND RESOURCES BOARD
COMBINED RAW MATERIALS BOARD

VICE CHAIRMAN FOR CIVILIAN REQUIREMENTS
Arthur D. Whiteside

EXECUTIVE VICE CHAIRMAN
Charles E. Wilson

PRODUCTION EXECUTIVE COMMITTEE

ADMINISTRATIVE ASSISTANT TO THE CHAIRMAN

PROGRAM VICE CHAIRMAN
J. A. Krug

INFORMATION DIVISION

WAR PRODUCTION DRIVE DIVISION

MANAGEMENT CONSULTANT DIVISION

VICE CHAIRMAN (INTERNATIONAL SUPPLY)
William L. Batt

VICE CHAIRMAN
Donald D. Davis

OFFICE OF INDUSTRY ADVISORY COMMITTEES
OFFICE OF PRODUCTION ASSIGNMENTS
OFFICE OF PROCEDURES

AIRCRAFT PRODUCTION BOARD

CONTROLLER OF SHIPBUILDING

OPERATING VICE CHAIRMAN
Hiland G. Batcheller

ALUMINUM AND MAGNESIUM DIVISION

COPPER DIVISION

STEEL DIVISION

VICE CHAIRMAN FOR MANPOWER REQUIREMENTS
Clinton S. Golden

VICE CHAIRMAN FOR LABOR PRODUCTION
Joseph D. Keenan

CONSERVATION DIVISION
SALVAGE DIVISION
REDISTRIBUTION DIVISION
MINERALS RESOURCES COORDINATING DIVISION
PRODUCTION DIVISION

GOVERNMENT DIVISION

RADIO AND RADAR DIVISION

SHIPBUILDING DIVISION

COMMODITIES BUREAU

CONSTRUCTION AND UTILITIES BUREAU

CONSUMER GOODS BUREAU

EQUIPMENT BUREAU

MINERALS BUREAU

REGIONAL OFFICES

I BOSTON

II NEW YORK CITY

III PHILADELPHIA

IV ATLANTA

V CLEVELAND

VI CHICAGO

VII KANSAS CITY

VIII DALLAS

IX DENVER

X SAN FRANCISCO

XI DETROIT

XII MINNEAPOLIS

XIII SEATTLE

212

in January 1942 been charged with doing. Through delegation of authority and responsibility to other agencies and an unwillingness or an inability to assert and explore the full range of his powers, Nelson allowed the WPB to slip into the role of a coordinate mobilization body, now answerable to Byrnes.

WPB'S ORGANIZATION AND POWER, 1942–1943

Donald M. Nelson's leadership figures large in most studies of the WPB. His defenders argue that the WPB chair led by consent and consensus, avoided controversy and antagonizing others, made decisions only after full debate and examination of alternatives, and was careless about administrative turf. These guileless qualities left Nelson open to aggressive attacks from often ruthless bureaucratic infighters, diluting and fragmenting his authority. Nelson's detractors portray, not a victim, but a weak, indecisive, untrustworthy, and devious person unable to see or act on obvious imperatives. Various czars had to be appointed for handling crises that Nelson dodged or bungled, and frustrated, angered, and betrayed claimants like the military forced WPB's hand to protect their own and the nation's interests. These widely varying accounts, and even more balanced ones, generally imply or conclude that Nelson was unsuited for the critically important post that he held.[4]

Directing WPB was an enormous, nearly overwhelming challenge. Carrying over from NDAC, OPM, and SPAB were serious conflicts that approximated New Deal and anti–New Deal positions. In NDAC, OPM, and SPAB, members of the Roosevelt administration, academics, professionals, civil servants, and those associated with labor or small business led in preparing the economy for war. Through the Bureau of Research and Statistics and related agencies, they provided the statistical and economic analysis for guiding mobilization. The all-outers tended to support a liberal, activist state, favored planning, and suspected corporate values. The principal operating units of the mobilization agencies, however, were the industry and commodity branches grouped around production and materials divisions staffed chiefly with corporate officials serving for a dollar a year and assisted by industry advisory committees. For varying reasons, corporate America resisted expanding and converting for defense and war. Its attitudes were also conservative, and it distrusted and resented New Deal methods, values, and goals.

Throughout the period from mid-1940 through 1941, industry was on the defensive for dragging its heels on economic preparedness; momentum was with the all-outers, most dramatically illustrated by Roosevelt's creation of SPAB to accelerate actual and potential munitions output. Pearl Harbor dramatically changed the dynamics of mobilization. Fully converting the economy for war purposes was now a necessity, not a matter of debate, allowing corporate America to seize the mobilization initiative. The previous all-outers were now forced on the defensive. Calls for balanced mobilization, for protecting the civilian economy and reforms within it, for concern for labor and small business, and even for economic and statistical analysis from nonbusiness sources could be and were portrayed as interfering with the full mobilization of the economy.

Nelson rose to prominence during the all-outers' period, 1940–1941. He never successfully adjusted to the new corporate phase beginning with Pearl Harbor and leading to the creation of the WPB. In the prewar years, Nelson's talents as a flexible, imaginative conciliator able to work with New Dealers and industry, those pushing for economic mobilization and those hesitant about it, were essential. Under those circumstances, he could be tough when necessary, as demonstrated by his executive directorship of SPAB. Nelson's faltering performance as WPB chair stemmed as much or more from circumstances as from leadership abilities.

Nelson faced two massive tests in establishing WPB's authority in January 1942: he had to win the confidence and respect of corporate America; and he had to bend the armed services to his will. The two challenges were related in that industry and the military had begun working together under NDAC and OPM in a way that thwarted mobilization policies concerning the distribution of contracts and other practices. As the principal sources of supply and demand in a mobilized economy, corporations and the armed services could be expected to be drawn to one another. This tendency was strengthened by the conservative nature of both in opposing New Deal reforms both in general and as they affected economic mobilization in particular. The War and Navy Departments, for example, led in giving industry its way in terms of profits, financing of plants, and antitrust enforcement. An industry-military mobilization alliance, however, could serve the purposes of corporations and the armed services at the expense of larger public policies and to the detriment of such groups as labor, small business, and consumers.

Fearing the consequences of a continued and strengthened corporate community–military alignment, Nelson moved quickly to secure his relations with industry. The WPB chair defended dollar-a-year men and industry advisory committee practices against the criticism of the Truman Committee and others. He subordinated the Division of Civilian Supply within WPB, he proceeded cautiously on small business, and he practically excluded labor from a meaningful role in the board. In retrospect, Nelson could have done even more in terms of strengthening earlier the industry divisions and opting sooner for a vertical, as opposed to a horizontal, allocations system. Nonetheless, Nelson took early and major steps in winning industry's support and, hence, securing the supply side of the economic mobilization system.

Nelson's success, however, also depended on establishing WPB's control over and winning the cooperation of the armed services' procurement operations, which constituted a high percentage of the demand side. Not only did Nelson fail to achieve those goals, but they were also always beyond his reach. The WPB chair was right in not moving to take over procurement functions from the army and navy. (According to Luther Gulick, Nelson, the president, and the armed forces had informally agreed in advance that such a change would not take place.)[5] That was a massive task that the WPB was unprepared to handle. Trying to do so would have set off fierce resistance from the armed services, and many industry leaders in and outside WPB would have opposed such a drastic step. The War and Navy Departments had been gradually adjusting their supply systems to war since 1939; those systems were statutorily authorized; and, through command and hierarchy, the army and navy could impose and maintain united fronts. Moreover, in adjusting to war, the armed services had already established close and elaborate relations with corporate America. By comparison, NDAC and OPM were at best interim mobilization agencies. Within them, industry and New Dealers fought over policy and turf, and most tangible progress in harnessing the economy occurred through the armed forces and corporations working together.

Under those circumstances, the most that Nelson could reasonably achieve was forcing the military to accept the concept of feasibility, to surrender control of priorities and agree to an allocations system, and to accede to WPB scheduling its production. Even to implement these basic, indispensable regulatory mechanisms Nelson had to grant the War and Navy Departments vast powers within key sectors of WPB. The army and navy could threaten the effort to harness the economy until they got their way. But more was involved. Actively or tacitly, most industrialists within the WPB supported the military. They did so because, with war declared and total mobilization a necessity, they wanted to move from a partial defense-period alliance with the armed services to a full-scale one. Such an alliance ensured two critical goals: mobilization would be in the hands of trusted conservatives, not feared and resented reformers; and untold billions of contract dollars would flow during the war years along the same corporate channels as in the defense period.

As long as Nelson resisted the emerging industry-military connection and turned for advice to the Planning Committee and other New Deal sources, corporate America collectively would almost inevitably reject him. It did, but only after the WPB chair had succeeded in driving through WPB feasibility, allocations, and production scheduling. With those controls in place—regulatory devices the critical nature of which even industry understood when properly educated—Nelson lost much of his power, and the Planning Committee, labor, small business, and consumers were eliminated or pushed aside. Industry and the military had combined their power in an all-but-invincible alliance.

Even when the worst of WPB tumult was over early in 1943 (as discussed below), the board faced constant strife. Nelson's staff, consisting of professionals, civil servants, and progressive businessmen, never accepted the corporate community–military alignment dominating the board. They were joined by excluded or downgraded members from labor, consumers, and smaller business units, Congress, and the media. Furthermore, related or competing mobilization agencies such as the War Manpower Commission constantly challenged WPB operations. Consequently, the White House had to bring in James F. Byrnes as assistant president for the homefront to protect and, where necessary, temper the wartime partnership centered on WPB industrialists and the War and Navy Departments' procurement structures.

Could another WPB chair have performed better? Perhaps, but without accomplishing any basic change. The most he could have done was to make the mobilization process smoother and less controversial. To achieve even those limited gains would have required extraordinary talents. Charles E. Wilson was driven out of WPB at the same time as Nelson because he was too blatantly proindustry; William O. Douglas, often mentioned for the prospective WPB slot prior to Pearl Harbor, was totally unacceptable because of his strong New Deal identification.

What was called for was a soundly centered independent with broad experience in economic, political, and social affairs who had excellent administrative skills and a shrewd political sense. Lewis W. Douglas, Roosevelt's first director of the Bureau of the Budget and the extraordinarily able wartime head of the War Shipping Administration, comes to mind. Could he have been recruited for the WPB post—a questionable assumption— he would most likely have reined in both industry and the military, paid more attention to the civilian economy, done more to satisfy small business and labor, and so on. He would not have tried to alter (and he could not have succeeded in altering in any significant way) the operations of power in the mobilized economy. Nelson's 1944 experience with reconversion makes that point harshly. Despite often strong backing from the public, Congress, the media, labor, small business representatives, other mobilization agencies, and even, for a time, the White House, Nelson was politically crucified over the issue and sent into the political and economic wilderness from which he never really returned.

In assessing mobilization developments, keeping an eye on Bernard M. Baruch is instructive. He gained prominence through harnessing the World War I economy, and he devoted enormous energy to trying to shape the military's Industrial Mobilization Plans of the 1930s in a way that would result in balance and maintain civilian control. When as WPB chair Nelson continued to turn to Henderson, Nathan, May, and other liberal elements for guidance instead of Baruch, the latter figuratively and literally moved over to the War and Navy Departments, particularly the former, which led in ousting Nelson and ensuring industry-military dominance of the mobilized economy.

There was a possible downside of critical importance to an executive other than Nelson serving as WPB chair. Without a background in the NDAC, OPM, and SPAB, a new leader might not have learned the inestimable worth of Robert R. Nathan, Stacy May, and the offices that they headed and staffed. Such an outcome might have severely damaged any mobilization program operating without the imposed restraints of feasibility and related controls.

Donald M. Nelson was introduced to Washington as an imaginative and enlightened businessman in 1934 with the National Recovery Administration. That experience, combined with service in the mobilization agencies from 1940 through 1941, appears to have moved him further in the reform direction. Corporate America's unflattering prewar behavior compared with that of New Dealers in Leon Henderson's circle could not fail to impress the open-minded Sears, Roebuck and Company executive. Nelson not only carried his modified views into the WPB; he even began moving beyond them. That set him on a collision course with the industry-military production team taking control of the mobilization process. As the confrontation grew and expanded, Nelson held his ground on the principled issues. In the WPB, that quality became a major limitation to his leadership, but it spoke to his character as a person.

9
THE ARMED SERVICES' MATERIAL ORGANIZATION FOR WORLD WAR II

Shortly after Pearl Harbor, both the War and the Navy Departments established more centralized control over their procurement and supply operations. The services required reorganized systems to handle their astronomically escalating demand and to work more effectively with the civilian mobilization agencies in meeting their requirements. In a sense, the navy's structure was more centered on the supply bureaus in the nation's capital. However, ongoing Washington power struggles pitting the secretary and under secretaries against the commander-in-chief of the fleet/chief of naval operations and the supply bureaus led to greater fragmentation and conflict at the very top of the navy's system of command. While army operations were more decentralized among the supply bureaus' procurement districts, decisionmaking in Washington was less complicated. The chief of staff commanded the army on the basis of the support, and to some degree the participation, of the secretary and under secretaries of war.[1]

Although, when it came to military interests, the army and navy tended to present a united front before and within the civilian mobilization agencies, the navy was more flexible and less confrontational than the army. That outcome, paradoxically, stemmed in part from the navy's greater sensitivity about civilian authority since the secretary and under secretaries constantly fought to maintain their prerogatives in a service hostile to civilian influence. Also, the navy was less advanced than the army in economic mobilization activities, and the Navy Department procured considerably less than the War Department, the leading claimant on the wartime economy.

Differences aside, the military services gained a dominant role in the operations of the War Production Board (WPB), with the army leading the way. In achieving that goal, the services extended and broadened their alliance with corporate America that had begun to emerge during the operations of the National Defense Advisory Commission (NDAC) and Office of Production Management (OPM). That alliance was as natural as it was practically inevitable since big business and the military controlled wartime supply and demand. The large corporations owned the plant and had the expertise for war production, and the army and navy had the statutory authority to procure most wartime requirements. For this alliance to work from 1942 through 1945, the New Dealers, academics, civil servants, and others who had led in accelerating economic mobilization in 1940–1941 had to be subordinated in or eliminated from WPB and related agencies. That end was achieved, but never easily. Excluded groups, supported by congressional sources and the public, fought back, making economic mobilization for World War II exceptionally tumultuous.

Wartime divisions were never simply civilian versus military. President Franklin D. Roosevelt was as active and dominant a commander-in-chief as America has ever had. The armed services' supply systems were heavily staffed with civilians, beginning with the secretaries, under secretaries, and assistant secretaries. And, for complex reasons, most corporate executives in the WPB shared the outlook of the military on economic mobilization matters. At the heart of the conflict were interest group and class divisions. Also, more than a few civilians inside and outside the army and navy took on military outlooks.

ARMY SERVICE FORCES

The army's system of procurement and supply throughout World War II was directed by General Brehon B. Somervell commanding the Services of Supply, created in March 1942 and renamed the Army Service Forces (ASF) in March 1943. ASF was only part of a major reorganization of the army for fighting a world war.[2]

Various forces shaped the 1942 reorganization, the most important of which in 1941 was the necessity of freeing Chief of Staff General George C. Marshall from administrative duties so that he could focus on planning and policy. With over sixty officers and agencies reporting to him, Marshall threatened to be overwhelmed, often with trivia. A secret study of reorganization that Marshall initiated in November 1941 under the direction of General Joseph T. McNarney, an Army Air Forces (AAF) officer, was completed at the end of January 1942. Once agreeing to a radical restructuring of the army, Marshall moved with extreme speed in implementing it before opposition could block the way. His staff was given forty-eight hours to review the proposal. After Secretary of

War Henry L. Stimson and President Franklin D. Roosevelt had given their approval, the latter on February 28 ordered the reorganization into effect as of March 9, 1942.

The March reorganization created three new commands reporting directly to the chief of staff: the Army Ground Forces (AGF), under General Lesley J. McNair; the AAF, under General Henry H. Arnold; and the ASF, under Somervell, to oversee all supply and service functions and those activities not fitting properly under the other two commands. Assisted by a pared-down General Staff, the chief of staff could now effectively plan and direct a global war through three central commands. Marshall selected McNarney as the only deputy chief of staff to serve as his principal assistant in managing the army. Although limited to the years of war plus six months, this was the most far-reaching restructuring of the army since the reforms of Elihu Root at the turn of the century.

Somervell had as much influence as any one person in shaping the nature of the ASF. A West Point graduate assigned to the Corps of Engineers, Somervell had served with distinction in Europe during World War I. In an unorthodox military career, he made a number of important civilian allies who at critical points helped his advancement in the army. For example, he worked with Walker D. Hines, a prestigious New York corporate attorney and former head of the U.S. Railroad Administration, on regulating traffic on postwar European rivers. The two became lifelong friends. Throughout most of the interwar years, Somervell was engaged in engineering projects of one sort or another at home and abroad. From 1936 through 1940, he headed the Works Progress Administration (WPA) for New York City. Harry L. Hopkins selected him for the job, and the two remained on good terms thereafter. When leaving WPA, Somervell was tapped in December 1940 by Secretary of War Stimson to take over the floundering Construction Division of the Quartermaster Corps. The division was unable to handle vastly expanded building demands, particularly camps for hundreds of thousands of new troops. Within a year, Somervell brought army construction projects up-to-date and prepared the division for handling future demand. Yet Somervell's enormous talents, drive, and ability to get results were matched by great liabilities. Obsessed with advancement, and extremely protective of his own turf while regularly violating that of others, he was abrasive, ruthless, vindictive, and determined to succeed regardless of cost. Predictably, he made more enemies than friends.

Nonetheless, on the basis of his outstanding achievements with the Construction Division, Somervell was selected by Under Secretary of War Robert P. Patterson and Chief of Staff Marshall in November 1941 to head G-4 (supply) of the General Staff. Barely settled into his new assignment, he suddenly faced the nearly overwhelming logistics of a two-front war after Pearl Harbor. Concluding that the army's supply and procurement system could not cope with such a load, he called on Goldwaithe H. Dorr in early January 1942 to survey supply operations and recommend reforms. Somervell knew Dorr well as a law partner of the late Walker D. Hines. Dorr was also a personal friend and former professional colleague of Stimson. During the Great War, he had served as assistant director of munitions under Benedict Crowell.

Dorr assembled a study group made up mostly of civilians that included Robert R. West of the University of Virginia and Luther Gulick, who had been assisting the president with administration for a number of years. Military officers, such as Colonel Henry S. Aurand, also had a part. Working secretly, the Dorr group concluded that, as during World War I, supply and procurement would have to be centralized under one commander who reported to the chief of staff on military matters and to the under secretary of war on economic affairs. Early in February 1942, Somervell became aware of McNarney's reorganization proposals, which Marshall had adopted. Assisted by Dorr and his own staff, Somervell tailored Dorr's recommendations to the McNarney structure. Basically, he proposed combining the operations of the Office of the Under Secretary of War dealing with industrial mobilization and those of the General Staff's G-4 handling supply requirements. In that way, supply operations in the United States would be unified under one command with the under secretary of war and G-4 restricted to planning, policy, and supervision. Not understanding the intricacies of army supply operations, McNarney welcomed Somervell's help. While drafting a general outline for what became ASF, Somervell, in characteristic fashion, launched a campaign to head the new supply command. By February 18, Marshall and Stimson had agreed that he was the officer for the job.

Before the reorganization could go forward, Under Secretary of War Patterson had to approve. Marshall had ordered that even the under secretary be kept in the dark about reorganization. Late in February, when restructuring was all but an accomplished fact, Assistant Secretary of War John J. McCloy, who represented Stimson on reorganization, asked McNarney, Somervell, Dorr, and others to brief Patterson on the changes. Dorr assumed a major role in explaining to Patterson that the commander of ASF would be subject to his direction on procurement and related matters and under the chief of staff on military duties. However, Patterson would be left with only his personal advisers for carrying out his duties since his huge staff, along with most of G-4, would be transferred to ASF. These realities alarmed the under secretary's inner circle as well as the director of the Bureau of the Budget. Fearing that Patterson would be left with only a ceremonial role, they wanted key modifications of the scheme and written assurances preserving the under secretary's authority.

Always concerned more about the army's welfare than his own prerogatives, Patterson refused to block the reorganization, which he knew Marshall was intent on implementing at once. Despite misgivings, he approved it with only minor changes, convinced that any problems could be worked out in the future. Somervell's appointment as commander of the ASF, however, gave the under secretary pause. While admiring Somervell's gifts and accomplishments, he worried about the difficulties of working with him and whether Somervell could get on with others in such an important post. Patterson concluded that the army's need for aggressive leadership had to take precedence. On his part, Somervell was willing to defer to Patterson whenever necessary; he was just as aware that he owed his appointment to Marshall and that his tenure depended on maintaining the chief of staff's confidence.

The ASF was an awkward, sprawling command that included a maximum of 45,186 military and civilian personnel by July 1943 (not including the supply arms and services [SA&Ss]), over half of whom served outside the capital. By the end of hostilities the number had dropped to 34,138. (In July 1943, SA&Ss' military and civilian personnel at home totaled nearly 729,000; over 16,000 served in Washington, DC.) The command incorporated personnel, fiscal, legal, medical, and other major functions, along with lesser ones such as postal services and housekeeping operations for forts, camps, and stations. ASF's core, however, was the SA&Ss, which performed the procurement and supply operations constituting the command's principal duty.

In carrying out his vast responsibilities, Somervell demonstrated his exceptional talents as a manager of large systems. At the time, ASF far exceeded the size of the biggest corporate structures. Somervell devised an organizational system that allowed him effectively to supervise a bureaucratic empire. Although stable, the system was in the process of constant modification and improvement. Staff was as important as structure. Somervell expected his subordinates to take charge of their areas of responsibility. Once officers had his confidence, Somervell gave them the widest latitude and support in carrying out his orders and goals. Such an approach permitted Somervell to concentrate his efforts where they were needed or according to his priorities.

Staffing was most important for procurement and supply, which would determine the success or failure of ASF. Here is where Somervell chose his headquarters personnel with the greatest care. For his chief of staff, Somervell selected Colonel Wilhelm M. Styer, a colleague and friend who was as calm and congenial as his commander was high-strung and brusque. The two made an excellent, balanced team. Colonel Lucius D. Clay served as assistant chief of staff for materiel to direct procurement, and Colonel LeRoy Lutes became assistant chief of staff for operations to supervise overseas supply. A host of civilian talent was also tapped, including Howard Bruce, a Baltimore businessman and chairman of the board of the Worthington Pump Company, Fred C. Foy, from a large New York advertising agency, Joseph M. Dodge, president of a Detroit bank, and Maurice Hirsch, a prominent Houston attorney.

For the other administrative, service, and housekeeping duties falling into the ASF sphere, Somervell selected leaders who could be relied on to carry out these more mundane responsibilities efficiently with little attention and direction from the top. As many administrative and related responsibilities as possible were decentralized to the nine geographic corps areas, renamed service commands.

Among the most important units in the entire ASF structure was what eventually became the Purchases Division in Clay's Office of Materiel. Albert J. Browning, president of the United Wall Papers Factories, Incorporated, who had served in mobilization agencies with Donald M. Nelson since the NDAC, moved over from WPB to head ASF's division. Browning, along with Frank M. Folsom of the Navy Department, and representatives from the Maritime Commission, Treasury Department, and Office of Price Administration (OPA), served in the WPB's Procurement Policy Division, designed to set and coordinate policy among buying offices.

The Purchases Division determined policy for and oversaw the procurement activities of the technical services, including buying, geographic distribution of contracts, building facilities, scheduling, materials distribution, financing, pricing, renegotiation of contracts in terms of profits, contract termination, and all other related activities. The AAF was included in its purview. Throughout 1942 and the first half of 1943, the division concentrated on speeding the contracting process; from mid-1943, it had the luxury of increasingly refining army contracting methods.

At the outset, Purchases had to focus on making bureau operations as uniform as possible among and within their systems. With an essentially decentralized buying system carried out by technical services' procurement districts and exceptional authority and responsibility given to the contracting officer, similar, if not standard, methods were essential. To further its work, the Purchases Division established a War Department's Purchase Policy Advisory Committee, composed of contractors, industrialists, and trade association officials. By June 1942, the division had replaced fifteen hundred pages of often complex, contradictory, and arcane regulations with a hundred-page set of Procurement Regulations for all army buying. While the document grew in size during the war, it remained well organized, cross-referenced, and clearly written. This was followed in 1943 by a Procurement District Operating Manual to achieve standard operations among these numerous, varied, and key buying units. Later in 1943, the Purchases Division put out "Pricing in War Contracts." All these publications, and much of the activity of the Purchases Division, were aimed at making more effective the work of the Clearance Branch in the Purchases Division. In March 1942, the WPB had turned the clearing of contracts over to the procurement agencies. Through 1942 and into 1943, clearance on the part of the ASF was at best perfunctory. Once the heaviest peak was over, the Purchases Division became much more rigorous in monitoring contracting officers' work through the review process.

Increasingly, the Purchases Division concentrated its attention on pricing and profits among its contractors. Pricing was the key concern. When prices were too high, not only were government outlays too great, but also inflationary forces were increased and further strain placed on scarce materials and growing shortages of labor. Fair prices were key to the economic stability so vital to the success of procurement. By comparison, profits were much less important because they constituted such a small portion of the hundreds of billions of dollars spent on the war.

Congress and OPA forced the armed services to pay closer attention to the pricing and profits of war contracting. After revelations of gross contracting abuses involving profits, Congress in April passed the Renegotiation Act of 1942, requiring procurement agencies to renegotiate prime contracts over $100,000 where necessary to establish more realistic prices and recapture excess profits. The act was amended a number of times throughout the war years, easing its provisions in some regards and stiffening them in others. Additionally, in January 1942, OPA was granted the statutory authority to set maximum prices throughout the economy. From the beginning, the army and navy insisted on exempting all war contracting from OPA authority. OPA, backed by the president, resisted this move until November 1942. At that time, OPA's director, Leon Henderson, signed an agreement with the under secretaries of war and the navy that exempted at least two-thirds of military procurement from OPA pricing and, under various conditions, even more. In turn, OPA required the services to institute methods for ensuring reasonable prices and keep it informed of progress made.

Under the dual pressure of the Renegotiation Act and the OPA agreement, in addition to its own desire to lower prices to advance mobilization, the Purchases Division developed elaborate programs for what came to be called close pricing: prices at the origins of a contract that were as near to realistic as possible, with provisions for review as the contract progressed. Other programs were introduced and developed for pricing based on a company's total war

contracts, incentive pricing, converting cost-plus-fixed-fee to fixed-price contracts, and similar practices. While the army's chief aim was to lower prices,
profits were also lowered.

Through various programs, the Purchases Division and related agencies such
as the War Department Price Adjustment Board, directed by the under secretary of war, helped reduce War Department prices nearly 25 percent between
September 1942 and June 1945. A wartime congressional study placed overall
profits for war contracting and sales in 1943 based on net worth at around 15
percent for the largest firms and 30 percent for the smallest. All pricing and
profit-control programs were exceptionally complex, none more so than renegotiation. That was in part the case because the information necessary for
sound decisions was hard to come by, general rules were difficult to apply, and
decisionmaking often involved judgment as much as measurable data.

All War Department programs aimed at reducing prices and profits ran into
strong opposition from contractors. They wanted high prices to cover con-
tingencies and to maximize profits. Despite constant resistance, the ASF and
other units compiled a satisfactory record in their efforts to reduce prices and
profits. They largely failed in only one instance. Industry successfully kept the
conversion of cost-plus contracting to a bare minimum. It was price more than
profit reduction that gained support in War Department operations since those
goals stretched army buying power and aided the economy in general. The
War Department strove to lower profits because public relations and morale
were served, the law and the Roosevelt administration required such action,
and mobilization was made more efficient.

While most buying and contracting was carried out by the various bureaus
for their service, the army and navy voluntarily collaborated on a wide range
of procurement activities. The Army-Navy Munitions Board (ANMB), of
course, played an increasingly important role in military buying and mobilization from 1939 through 1942. But, outside ANMB's purview, much took
place among procurement agencies during and after its active period. The
army, for example, took over a good part of supply for the Marine Corps. On
its part, the navy bought all landing craft for the army. The AAF and the navy's
Bureau of Aeronautics cooperated more extensively than any other branches
of the services and participated in a complex set of agencies outside their own
systems. The two services in general shared facilities and research results in
the development of ordnance, armor, and other munitions, at times combining efforts with the Office of Scientific Research and Development; they
worked for the standardization of tools, equipment, and motor vehicles; and
they sought to achieve similar methods in cost reduction, pricing, profit controls, renegotiation of contracts, and termination policies. Whenever possible,

the Maritime Commission was included in the shared and joint ventures. The armed services also had their procurement activities coordinated to a degree by other mobilization agencies, such as War Food Administration, the Petroleum Administration for War, and the WPB's rubber director. Transportation was arranged through the War Shipping Administration and the Office of Defense Transportation.[3]

Although the Purchases Division of the ASF had the most contact with the technical services, the greatest sources of tension in bureau-ASF relations stemmed from the Control Division. This was Somervell's most significant and controversial innovation. Headed by Lieutenant Colonel Clinton F. Robinson, the division was intended to adapt army supply operations to business practices. It was also staffed principally with civilian management experts since few officers were trained or had experience in the field. Designed to assist Somervell in maintaining control of ASF, the division concentrated on improving organization, measuring efficiency, and standardizing and simplifying procedures and forms. Within a year, the division succeeded in eliminating around twenty-nine hundred reports and records of various sorts.

The division's most important contribution involved statistical analysis, which had been so wanting under the Office of the Under Secretary of War. On the basis of standardized figures and information compiled by the statistical units required in all technical services and staff and other agencies, the Control Division put together for Somervell a Monthly Progress Report. The report consolidated and analyzed statistics on all relevant and measurable ASF operations. From the document, the commanding general could determine the success of his organization and, more important, where problems existed. This was an invaluable tool, one that allowed Somervell to reach down and evaluate the smallest subdivision of his command while also still keeping an eye on the structure as a whole. Overall, the Control Division turned out to be an enormous plus in management technique. Through the division's diligence, ASF constantly improved its performance during the war years while reducing the number of its personnel. The ASF claimed that, between March 1942 and June 1945, it handled a workload that grew by threefold with a workforce that expanded by less than twofold.

The Control Division was not popular, particularly with the technical services. It spoke with Somervell's authority and was perceived as the commander's spy network. Few welcomed even the best management methods because they measured and pinpointed performance, particularly weaknesses and failures. Operating from a staff level, the Control Division was often seen as a detached and uninformed agency perpetually seeking to improve organization and procedure in a hurried and insensitive way. An essentially civilian agency devoted to furthering and gauging efficiency was bound to create hostility in an institution committed to routine and order. Actually, Somervell was the real target for most of the resentment falling on the division. The commanding general drove ASF relentlessly, was a severe critic, and rolled over opposition.

The SA&Ss (redesignated the *technical services* in 1943) were key to procuring for and supplying the troops at home and abroad. Here is where Somervell had to concentrate his attention. In 1942, there were six services: the Quartermaster Corps; the Ordnance Department (which took over procurement and supply for the Coast Artillery Corps); the Signal Corps; the Chemical Warfare Service; the Corps of Engineers; and the Medical Department. Additionally, between March and July 1942, ASF gradually created a seventh service, the Transportation Corps, for handling all army transportation except air services. As a separate command, the AAF carried out most of its own procurement and supply operations. War Department expenditures for munitions and supplies between 1942 and 1945 totaled around $102.2 billion. The Ordnance Department spent in excess of $33 billion, or 33 percent of total outlays; the AAF nearly $33 billion, or 32 percent; the Quartermaster Corps slightly under $22 billion, or 21 percent; and the other technical services from $5 billion to under $1 billion, or from under 5 to less than 1 percent.[4]

Somervell never worked out with the technical services a mode of organization with which he was satisfied. On their part, the Ordnance Department and other bureaus were always restless under ASF direction. Unlike other parts of his organization, the technical services could effectively resist direction from above. The bureaus had long and revered histories, they had their own budgets, which accounted for half the War Department appropriations, their chiefs were appointed by the president, and they had close congressional ties. Organizationally, however, they were a hodgepodge. Some, such as Ordnance, stressed commodities, others, like the Corps of Engineers, emphasized service, and the Quartermaster and Signal Corps combined both. All had procurement districts, but they varied in number, nature, function, and importance.

The ASF commander to a degree could and did bend the technical services to his will. When it was time for rotation, he skillfully maneuvered in 1942 to get the chief of ordnance he wanted. Somervell hounded the chief signal officer out of office in mid-1943, convinced that he was incompetent. He also participated or led in taking important functions away from the overloaded Quartermaster Corps. In December 1941, construction went to the Corps of Engineers; by July 1942, the Transportation Corps had assumed control of transportation under the direction of Colonel Charles P. Gross, Somervell's friend and the only technical service chief fully receptive to ASF direction;

and, in August 1942, the Ordnance Department took charge of designing, procuring, maintaining, storing, and distributing all general and specialized motor vehicles.

Somervell also insisted that the technical services report to the under secretary and General Staff through him. All bureaus additionally were required to set up a control division for improving operations, submitting major organizational changes for ASF approval, and providing the Control Division standardized statistics. Uniformity was sought in purchasing policies, contracts, and paperwork. And Somervell urged the technical services to pattern their structure to the degree possible after ASF so as to further similarity and facilitate headquarters working with them.

Piecemeal progress was never enough for Somervell, who insisted on tight organization and clear lines of authority. In mid-1943, he directed the Control Division to draw up plans for a fully integrated and rationalized ASF. The completed outline proposed to do away entirely with the technical services. Their commodity organizations would be replaced with nine functional staff units in ASF headquarters: for procurement, supply, transportation, communication, utilities, administration, personnel, finances, and medicine. Where necessary, as was the case with procurement and supply, commodity subunits would be created for weapons, clothing and equipage, communication equipment, construction supplies, and the like. All field services would be performed by service commands, reduced from nine to six, and restructured to match ASF headquarters.

Somervell presented a refined reorganization plan to Marshall and his deputy, McNarney, in August 1943. Both approved. With their backing, the ASF commander assumed the adoption of his sweeping proposal since he shortly departed for a series of foreign assignments that would keep him away from Washington for nearly four months. That left Chief of Staff Styer and the head of the Control Division to see the intensely controversial project through.

Trouble erupted almost immediately. Patterson opposed most of the plan as an unwarranted, drastic change that could disrupt the success of current procurement and supply functions, a reality that the Control Division admitted. With Marshall and Patterson dividing, Stimson's views became all-important. The secretary of war concluded that Somervell's goal was "ill advised," that a possible increase in efficiency was not worth the battle that would ensue and become public. During his first tour as secretary of war from 1911 to 1913, in working to strengthen the General Staff, Stimson learned well the ability of the bureaus to do battle against perceived threats. Neither the army nor the nation could tolerate a drawn-out controversy in the midst of war.[5] The president also had reservations about the overhaul.

The secretary of war did not succeed in heading off public furor. Once learning of Somervell's proposal, the technical services, led by Chief of Ordnance Levin H. Campbell, Jr., fought furiously against it. The fight broke out in Congress and the press in a very distorted way in September 1943. Somervell's plan for restructuring ASF became linked to Roosevelt's consideration of Marshall for the supreme command of the cross-Channel invasion. Republicans and a right-wing press imagined elaborate New Deal schemes concocted by Harry L. Hopkins and others to remove Marshall from Washington, install Somervell as chief of staff, and turn the army into a huge political machine for Democratic purposes and another Roosevelt reelection campaign in 1944. Those opposed to the war, suspicious of Britain, or resentful of Somervell joined the fray, as did Marshall's avid supporters. Quieting the uproar set off by Somervell's reorganization proposal was a major challenge. Stimson and Marshall had to reassure Congress that rumors involving the chief of staff were not true. Respected journalists like Walter Lippmann stepped in to counter various allegations. And even the president felt compelled to address the imbroglio at length at a press conference.

Marshall bowed to Stimson's judgment in September. Had the controversy remained in the War Department, Somervell might have benefited from a face-saving agreement allowing him to experiment with some initial reorganization steps. After matters became public, even that expedient became infeasible. In October 1943, Stimson officially turned down the entire enterprise.

The miscalculations of Somervell and his advisers on reorganization were legion. Missing in 1943 was the crisis that the army and navy had used early in 1942 to push through major reorganizations of their systems. Without a sense of fear, urgency, and confusion, basic structural change was much harder to achieve. Somervell also underestimated the clout of the technical services and the numerous enemies who gladly welcomed the opportunity to attack him. At the same time, the commander of the ASF overestimated Marshall's power. Finally, Somervell failed to appreciate that some laudable goals had to be negotiated, not imposed. He never consulted the technical services or even let them review his proposal. That denied him even a start in the direction of needed changes. Moreover, he grossly flouted military culture. The inspiration and plan for fundamental reordering came from the Control Division, almost entirely a civilian, industrial unit focused on efficiency without regard for sensitivity in a tradition-bound institution.

Somervell's problems with the AAF were more severe than and different from his problems with the technical services.[6] The bureaus were subordinate parts of the ASF; the AAF was in theory a coordinate command, but, in actuality, it was an independent one with Arnold operating practically on the same level as the chief of staff. Marshall's March 1942 reorganization was in part designed to keep the air arm within the army structure by granting it more autonomy. Determined to achieve full independence, the AAF was out to cut as many ties binding it to the army as possible. That drive put AAF on a collision course with ASF. The air forces, after all, accounted for about one-third of all War Department procurement expenditures. For purposes of efficiency, uniformity, and power, Somervell wanted ASF to act as the supply and services agency for AAF just as it did for the AGF. The latter welcomed ASF operating its bases, supplying its needs, and handling other functions so that it could concentrate on training troops. Moreover, AGF tended to side with ASF in its various clashes with AAF. Although conflicts did develop between ASF and AGF, they were relatively minor. In sharp contrast, the AAF incessantly sought to limit in every possible way ASF authority over its operations.

Even if ASF and AAF had not been antagonists, the Marshall reorganization would have created trouble between them. AAF itself procured all equipment "peculiar to the Army Air Forces"[7]—aircraft engines, frames, and specialized equipment. ASF procured food, clothing, general supplies, and most munitions and equipment. It also set policy for AAF buying. The air forces were willing to accept ASF policies on contracts, pricing, renegotiation, cancellation, and so forth as long as Somervell and his staff spoke as agents of the under secretary of war, who directed their supply under the March 1942 reorganization; they would not take orders from ASF as a coordinate command, as Somervell would have preferred. For aircraft, however, AAF determined its own requirements, dealt directly with the WPB, distributed materials to its contractors, and controlled production. The air forces would not even allow ASF to include airplanes in overall statements of army demand. AAF also balked at ASF serving as budget office for the army. Furthermore, anxious to control all AAF supply functions, the air arm consistently sought to limit the Ordnance Department's and the Chemical Warfare Service's role in manufacturing its weapons and bombs and the Quartermaster Corps's part in providing its food. In 1944–1945, over the vehement protest of ASF, the air forces largely succeeded in wrestling away from the Signal Corps the responsibility for supplying communication and radar equipment used in aircraft.

AAF bases and posts became an even greater source of contention. In the United States they were under the command of the air forces. However, ASF was in charge of services and activities ranging from legal affairs to laundry facilities. Such a division never worked and was under repeated attack from AAF, which insisted on undivided authority over its posts. Late in 1944, the AAF came close to achieving that goal when it was given control of air base appropriations. Still, ASF preserved a role in post operations, and the two commands were struggling over the matter when hostilities ceased.

Repeated gains for AAF at the expense of ASF acted to erode Somervell's authority. That was the case, not only with the air forces, but also with the technical services. The AAF's fight to free itself of ASF involvement fed the bureaus' resentment of Somervell. More than attitudes was at stake, however. Conflict between AAF and ASF often involved technical services like the Ordnance Department and the Signal Corps procuring for the air forces or the Medical Department and the Corps of Engineers providing various services. In settling disputes between two coordinate commands, the General Staff had to rely on the authority of the chief of staff or the secretary of war, not that of the ASF commander. Circumventing the ASF in dealing with the AAF over matters of supply and service theoretically strengthened the technical services' claims of legal independence vis-à-vis ASF.

Recognizing the mounting challenges to his command, Somervell in September 1944 asked Marshall to address and clarify relations between ASF and AAF. Beginning to focus on his goal of a single department of defense in the postwar world, the chief of staff wanted to present a united front in his own ranks, not divisions. Hence, he tried to deal with the growing disputes without fanfare and within existing structures. He called on the commanders of the AGF, AAF, and ASF to settle among themselves how responsibilities for supply and services and their relations to command should be handled. Such negotiations took place in November, but without success. The matter, therefore, returned to Marshall, who refused to make any major changes. Consequently, the battles within the War Department went on. By August 1945, Somervell again felt sufficiently threatened that he asked Marshall to reaffirm his authority. The war ended before the chief of staff could respond.

Somervell's attempt to hold on to AAF procurement was more than futile; it was quixotic. Marshall recognized that reality as he strove to finesse the essentially irresolvable tension between the AAF and the ASF. What ground had to be given was inevitably at ASF's expense.

Not only did the AAF spend around one-third of the total of War Department budget between July 1940 and August 1945, but they did so from practically an independent base. Beginning during the interwar years, the AAF and its predecessors had developed a supply system that differed significantly from that of the technical services such as Ordnance and Quartermaster. The AAF's Material Division (later Material Command and other designations) operated out of both Washington and Wright Field, Dayton, Ohio. The division grew along with and practically became a partner of the emerging aircraft industry. Once defense preparation was under way in 1939, the AAF's supply operations were coordinated with those of the navy, civilians, and foreign demand by various agencies, including the NDAC and the OPM. After Pearl Harbor, the WPB handled aircraft through a virtually separate organization, the Aircraft Production Division and its operating arm, the Aircraft Resources Control Office, which worked closely with the Aircraft Scheduling Unit, a subdivision of the Joint Aircraft Committee. The AAF also combined its efforts with those of the Munitions Assignment Board on international aircraft distribution. Aircraft were so important for the United States and its potential and actual allies and their production so technologically and industrially demanding that an extraordinarily intricate institutional web had to be created for output. Placed within that context, Somervell's running battles with the AAF over turf appear exceptionally petty and compulsive.

Throughout the war years, General Oliver P. Echols was, in effect, Somervell's AAF counterpart, and he acted as General Arnold's major adviser on supply. He did so as head of the Material Division/Material Command until March 1943 and then, after a thorough reorganization of the AAF, as assistant chief of the air staff, AAF headquarters in Washington. Dividing supply between the staff in Washington and operations at Wright Field made many tasks more difficult. Nonetheless, the Material Command met its staggering demands. The three, later six, procurement districts were helpful, but much less so than they were for the technical services since decentralization never worked well for the air forces. However, the navy used the Air Corps's procurement districts, rather than setting up its own, when the two services found it practical to combine buying operations.

Also, expanding at a rate exceeding all other arms or services, the Air Corps had to stretch its meager officer corps much further. As a result, many of its headquarters staff were civilians. This was less traumatic for the AAF, which was still free of tradition. Open to experimentation and new ideas, it welcomed civilian ideas, approaches, and solutions. Indeed, separating the Air Corps from industry was not really possible. To facilitate procurement, eight of the largest aircraft firms in April 1942 organized the West Coast Aircraft War Production Council, and Eastern firms followed suit in October. The two combined operations in April 1943 under the National Aircraft War Production Council, Incorporated. At Wright Field, and in the procurement districts, the Production Division dominated others, including Engineering, Procurement, and Inspection. That was the case because General Kenneth B. Wolfe was relentless in driving the Production Division to meet nearly impossible output goals.

Outside its unique qualities, AAF procurement followed most of the patterns of ASF and technical services procurement. The emphasis for the first year and a half of war was on expanding the production base and, thereafter, on refining methods and results. Procurement ultimately included the distribution of contracts, building and financing facilities, distributing materials, scheduling production, and inspecting end products. Moreover, the Material Command, under directions from the under secretary of war and on its own, strove to improve organization and methods, reduce costs, prices, and profits, and save materials and workforce.

For all its civilian antecedents and influences, the AAF ultimately concluded that it shared more with the military than with civilians. In August 1945, as the air forces prepared for the postwar world, they abolished the Management Control Office—the counterpart of ASF's Control Division—which had played such an active role in materiel organization during the war. The AAF, like the technical services and other parts of the army, realized that there were definite limits to applying civilian techniques to the structure and operation of an armed service.

Somervell also engaged in running battles with the Operations Division (OPD) of the General Staff throughout the war years.[8] Here, his struggle made sense, and his goals, in their more restricted sense, were unassailable. Where his conflicts with the technical services and the AAF aimed at maintaining his delegated powers, those with OPD grew out of Somervell's attempts to expand his authority. He tried to gain a role in strategic planning. Although the ASF commander made some headway, his efforts were largely blocked by the General Staff and its supporters.

OPD was the renamed War Plans Division, which predated Marshall's reorganization. It was the only division of the General Staff expanded in size and importance with the March 1942 reorganization. Charged with the "formulation of plans and strategic direction of the military forces in the theater of war," OPD became the chief of staff's Washington command post.[9] In carrying out its vast duties, the division represented the army in dealing with the navy, the Joint and Combined Chiefs of Staff, and the White House. OPD had a Logistics Group for handling supply at a policy level on the basis of information provided principally by ASF.

Emerging as Marshall's "principal advisor on supply and administration," Somervell became convinced that he should participate in strategic decisions.[10] Information about supply at the General Staff level, he argued, was at best superficial. Since strategy was largely driven by logistics, Marshall needed his expertise to direct the war. Furthermore, OPD attitudes about logistics were unsound. The division wanted ASF to build up as large a reservoir of munitions and supplies as it could to support any and all strategic possibilities. In Somervell's eyes, such an approach was wasteful, and it would be unacceptable to civilian mobilization agencies. Logistics should be guided by established, although not rigid, strategic plans. And, in logistic planning, ASF should not be relegated to a technical adviser's role, as OPD insisted, but should have a central part to play. Otherwise, the complications of supply, including the time required to fulfill military demand, would be ignored, with potentially disastrous consequences.

TORCH, the Allied invasion of French North Africa, initiated Somervell's drive to be included in strategic planning. The invasion was agreed to in July 1942. Yet, as late as September, OPD could not provide ASF with specifics on supply, creating a nightmare for Somervell and his staff. Convinced that he required all possible information on war fronts, Somervell in September 1942 recommended to Marshall that the Joint Chiefs of Staff (JCS) create a standing committee made up of himself and his navy counterpart for handling the logistics of strategic planning and that the Joint and Combined Chiefs of Staff have available to them ASF advisers on supply, procurement, transportation, and related activities. OPD thwarted Somervell by convincing Marshall that change was unnecessary. Conflict broke out again in the spring of 1943, however, when, in proposals for reorganizing the JCS planning system, OPD tried to insulate strategy even further from ASF influence. This time Somervell prevailed in his demand for representation. In a May compromise, an ASF representative sat on a JCS logistics committee, and ASF was also included on various other JCS committees dealing with matters of logistics.

These gains did not satisfy Somervell. ASF's voice was only advisory, and it was still kept away from the center of strategic planning and operations. Consequently, between April and June 1943, he launched a campaign to elevate the ASF to a command post at least equal to OPD. The General Staff would be stripped of all divisions except OPD and G-2, the Intelligence Division. What OPD did not absorb would go to ASF, and OPD would lose all logistics functions. That would leave ASF as the primary agency for logistics. Somervell would become the major adviser to the chief of staff on logistics and head of the operating logistics command. Marshall was not tempted by Somervell's aggressive, even outrageous, proposal. He agreed with OPD's argument that a system working reasonably well should not be changed. Marshall's Washington command post remained intact until the end of hostilities.

There were unintended consequences to Somervell's grab for power. First, it emphasized that, except for OPD, the General Staff had been allowed to atrophy. To protect the staff for the postwar period, it had to be strengthened during the war years. McNarney took up the challenge, starting in mid-1943 with G-4, the Supply Division. Although G-4 tried to reassert some control over ASF, it was not successful. But Somervell was creating more and more enemies in high places. Once hostilities ceased, the antagonists, led by OPD, combined to put an early end to ASF. With the war over, Marshall seemed to side with Somervell's enemies since he acted in a way that helped undermine ASF.

Despite Somervell's inability formally to advance his role as the army's expert on logistics, he in effect played that role. Throughout the war years, Marshall relied on him to guide supply. It was Somervell who authored the Army Supply Program (ASP), among ASF's major contributions to the war effort. Actually, Somervell got the program under way in December 1941 while heading G-4. He found the army requirements as stated in the Victory Program of September 1941 (which became the War Munitions Program in February 1942) to be too rudimentary, contradictory, and incomplete to guide decisionmaking. He therefore initiated what became the ASP: a comprehensive statement by quantity and dollar amount of total supplies, equipment, weapons, and materials that the army would be responsible for acquiring for itself, the navy, Lend-Lease, and any other purpose for a period of up to three years. Such a document would be used to plan army operations, direct the technical services, determine and defend appropriations, and work with civilian agencies.

Once ASF came into being, Somervell made ASP his highest priority. He set up the organization and arranged for the procedures to produce such calculations. The first ASP came out in installments between April and September 1942. Thereafter, the program went through a total of seven modified versions. Somervell had initially wanted ASP to be based on theaters of operation. However, with strategy vague, slow, and late in formulation, ASP initially had to be based on estimated troop basis and then adjusted to specific strategic plans as they became available. Although at first crude, ASP became increasingly refined and sophisticated. By 1944, it not only stated requirements but also included most of consumption. On the basis of that achievement, ASP was converted in January 1945 to the Supply Control System.

Despite all his abilities and accomplishments, Somervell—and ASF, which was always an extension of its commander—could operate effectively only under the conditions of war. In that regard, Marshall, Stimson, and Patterson all used Somervell to maximize army supply under vast and threatening conditions, just as Somervell used them to advance his career and prove his abilities. Once the war was over, Marshall no doubt recognized that a peacetime ASF might be a possibility, but not one led by or associated with Somervell. Hence, he passively allowed the organization to be killed. Somervell was simply too aggressive, too brutal for the operations of a peacetime army. During war, however, his harsh, relentless approach was deemed to be needed, although he had to be restrained from time to time. Reminiscing after hostilities, Marshall pointed out that "of course I had to fight Somervell down or he would have taken the whole damn staff" and that postwar reorganization was designed to avoid "any future development of a man like General Somervell." Nonetheless, Marshall concluded: "If I went into control in another war, I would start looking for another General Somervell the very first thing I did."[11]

Somervell was Marshall's, and in a sense Stimson and Patterson's, attack dog. The three controlled him to the degree that his enormous talents, energy, and drive could serve the army without needlessly disrupting it. They did not act similarly in terms of the army's relations with civilian institutions, especially the WPB and the War Manpower Commission. Here, they gave Somervell practically free rein—unless they were ordered or felt compelled to check him—because he served their purposes and probably expressed the raw, military side of their natures, which apparently they did not care fully to expose.

In that sense, their use of Somervell had an irresponsible quality to it. The army and economic mobilization would have been better served by an ASF commanding general who led by mastery of the subject and situation, strength of character, and cooperation, not confrontation. The army had an officer of that quality and caliber in General James H. Burns, executive officer to Patterson in 1940–1941 and the moving force behind what became the Victory Program of September 1942. He obviously was not a Marshall favorite and was so disliked by Somervell that the latter maneuvered elaborately to deny him the post of ordnance chief.[12]

OFFICE OF THE UNDER SECRETARY OF THE NAVY

The navy's wartime supply and procurement were supervised by Under Secretary James V. Forrestal.[13] Forrestal carried out his vast responsibilities principally through the Procurement Legal Division (PLD) and the Office of Procurement and Material (OP&M). As with the army, this system was put in place as part of a larger reorganization of the service early in 1942. The Navy Department, however, experienced more continuity in its supply structure between 1940 and 1941 and during the war years than did the War Department.

Between December 1941 and March 1942, the Navy Department radically reorganized its structure for handling the enormous demands of a two-front war. This was one of the most thorough reorganizations in the navy's history, exceeding in importance that of 1915, which had created the Office of the Chief of Naval Operations (CNO). The change was so significant that the specifics had to be constantly reworked and refined throughout the war years and, ultimately, consolidated by law in 1948.

The reform affected all parts of the navy. Shortly after Pearl Harbor, Admiral Ernest J. King, who had been commanding the Atlantic Fleet, was promoted to commander-in-chief of the United States Fleet and his headquarters relocated to the nation's capital. He was to direct all fleet operations. King's appointment immediately raised the question of his status and authority vis-à-vis that of Chief of Naval Operations Admiral Harold R. Stark. Since its creation in 1915, CNO had overseen the operations of the fleet and kept it prepared for war. There was no easy and logical division of duties between King and Stark. On the basis of the study and advice of the General Board, Secretary of the Navy Frank Knox recommended to President Franklin D. Roosevelt that the two offices be combined. That was done by an executive order of March 12, 1942.

These developments solved several chronic problems plaguing naval command while creating others. The chief of naval operations was given clear and direct authority over the supply bureaus, a critical matter in dispute since 1915. In determining strategy and directing the operations of the fleet, however, the commander-in-chief, U.S. Fleet, dealt directly with the president, bypassing the secretary of the navy. Contemptuous of civilian roles in the navy, and compulsively driven to control all that was in his reach, King wanted to go further by taking over the supply and procurement operations performed under Forrestal's direction. Throughout the war years, the secretary and under secretary of the navy had to remain vigilant in order to thwart King's ambitions and required the intervention of Roosevelt to do so.

The chief of naval operations had a definite part in naval logistics. His office set navy requirements in terms of quantity and kind and also handled distribution, what the navy called consumer logistics. Since King had little interest, knowledge, or talent in this area, he delegated the responsibility to the exceptionally well-qualified and -trained vice chief of naval operations, Admiral Frederick J. Horne. Basically, Horne acted as chief of naval operations and directed an office that had been revamped to handle logistics more effectively.

While the navy's system of command was being fundamentally reworked, Forrestal moved to extend and consolidate the reforms that he had been devising since he took over as under secretary of the navy in August 1940. Late in January 1942, Secretary of the Navy Knox by general order created the OP&M. Combined with the PLD, which Forrestal had earlier organized in July 1941, the OP&M now gave the under secretary the structure and authority to direct the procurement of the supply bureaus (or so-called producer logistics) and coordinate their operations with those of various civilian mobilization agencies. Since direction of bureau procurement remained under Forrestal's control during the war years, there was greater continuity in navy supply functions than in those of the army. The War Department set up a new system of command for supply in the reorganization of March 1942 with the ASF, which took over most of the responsibilities performed by the Office of the Under Secretary of War during 1940–1941.

Although OP&M experienced minor changes throughout the war years, it went through only one major restructuring, during the spring of 1943. In seeking to improve the navy's relations with the WPB, Admiral Samuel M. Robinson, OP&M's chief, in March 1943 called on G. A. Bower, a General Electric Company management engineer, to survey the office. Bower completed his study late in May. Finding OP&M to be fundamentally sound, he nevertheless recommended some changes. The Procurement Branch was fine in its supervision of bureau contracting. But the Planning and Statistics Branch and the Resources Branch, which had played dominant roles in OP&M operations during 1942, along with the Production Branch, required attention. Circumstances had changed since 1942, and adjustments had to be made accordingly. Planning and Statistics, Bower noted, had more than enough to do in collecting, collating, and analyzing data. Yet it had taken on functions, such as administrating the Controlled Materials Plan (CMP), that were beyond its proper realm. No rationale existed for continuing the Resources Branch. It had been created to coordinate navy supply activities with the ANMB. The board was practically defunct, but a new branch was needed for coordinating logistics and strategy. Bower was concerned that the Production Branch was the weakest of all OP&M subdivisions when it should have been the strongest. Most of what Resources did, and some of what Planning and Statistics did, should be transferred to Production and the branch in general beefed up.

Most of Bower's recommendations were implemented within a matter of weeks, although some were held off for more opportune times. Under the reorganization, the Production Branch emerged as the dominant unit in OP&M. It took charge of CMP functions, activities transferred to it from Planning and Statistics, and responsibilities of Resources as well as a broader range of duties. With the Resources Branch phased out, a new Program and Priorities Branch was set up. This branch was intended, among other duties, to improve war planning by coordinating more carefully the exchange of information on strategy and logistics between the JCS and the OP&M.

The approach never worked. The joint chiefs in general, and Commander-in-Chief King in particular, were opposed to supply planners having a role in or even proper information on strategic decisions. Through the backing of Chief of Staff George C. Marshall, General Brehon B. Somervell had managed to achieve some representation on the JCS. Admiral Robinson was denied even that minor role. In order to gain some information on strategy, Robinson secretly established contacts on King's staff, and Forrestal turned to Assistant Secretary of War John J. McCloy on Henry L. Stimson's staff (since Marshall conscientiously kept the secretary of war up-to-date on major developments).

Divesting the Planning and Statistics Branch of production duties was a wise move. Bower was right. The branch had plenty to do outside production, and nothing was more important in that regard than continuing to perfect the Monthly Status Report and documents related to it. This report became the navy's counterpart of the ASP. Once fully developed, the report presented a total statistical account of the navy's supply program, including finished products broken down into materials and components and their existing status. As with the ASP, the Monthly Status Report became an extremely useful tool for production control. It was used extensively within the navy and by nearly every agency involved with economic mobilization outside the department. Since OP&M had less control over the supply bureaus than did ASF, the navy faced an even greater challenge in its statistical work.

A year before OP&M was reorganized in 1943, Forrestal acted to bring greater unity to the navy's system of inspection. This vital function was dispersed among the supply bureaus and those examining costs, standards, performance, and the like. Lewis L. Strauss, a senior partner of Kuhn, Loeb, and Company who joined the Navy Department as a naval reserve officer, insisted that peacetime practices had to give way to a unified system. Under the massive demands of war, inspection was broadened to include production scheduling and expediting as well as policing the performance of contractors. Fearing that quality control would be compromised, various bureaus successfully blocked reform. After a management survey team reached the same conclusion as Strauss, Forrestal in May 1942 created in OP&M an Office of Inspection Administration to direct and consolidate inspection operations. Throughout the war years, this new office was always limited in what it could do because of bureau resistance. It gradually succeeded in bringing greater unity to and broadening the operations of inspections, but under conditions in which the Office of Inspection Administration only coordinated bureau activity.

Six months after inspection reform was under way, the PLD achieved the authority that it needed to institute radical contracting reforms. Set up in July 1941, the division had been hobbled by limited staff and running opposition, particularly from the Bureau of Supplies and Accounts. The bureau still prepared most navy contracts, and its bureaucratic ways emerged as a severe procurement bottleneck. Supported by Vice Chief of Naval Operations Horne,

PLD persuaded Forrestal in mid-December 1942 to issue a directive in which all bureaus could decide whether to let contracts on their own, through the Bureau of Supplies and Accounts, or through some combination of the two processes. Moreover, all bureaus had to organize an Office of Counsel, headed by a PLD appointee, and answerable both to the bureau chief and to the under secretary of the navy. Under this centralized/decentralized contracting procedure, procurement was both accelerated and improved as the bureaus increasingly chose to negotiate their own contracts and relied heavily on assistance and direction from PLD. The Bureau of Supplies and Accounts, however, continued to buy standard commodities such as food, clothing, petroleum products, and so forth. In August 1944, the PLD appropriately was renamed the Office of General Counsel of the Navy, and its chief became general counsel.

Up until that time, Forrestal and his staff were still perfecting their organization, and, in 1942, the navy struggled to negotiate contracts as quickly as possible without much regard for cost and saving. By mid-1943, the Office of the Under Secretary of the Navy's procurement structure had reached a level of stability. The office was then able to carry out the navy's vast business operations with a high level of competence.

The Procurement Branch of OP&M played a key role in supervising supply bureau operations. From the outset, its leadership was outstanding. Frank M. Folsom, an assistant to Donald M. Nelson who had been transferred from WPB to oversee navy buying and who later became president of Radio Corporation of America, headed the unit. In March 1942, Folsom established a Clearance Division, under Vincent Goubeau, purchasing agent for the United Fruit Company, to oversee bureau contracting. For the year 1942 alone, the division cleared 7,324 contracts totaling $24 billion in value. Unlike clearance that the NDAC and the OPM attempted, that which was performed by the navy itself worked. Goubeau's division covered a range of subjects in its reviews, among them price, specifications, minimizing the use of strategic materials, size, location, reliability, and the financial situation of contracting firms. Over time, the Clearance Division developed an internal checklist to be used along with one provided by WPB to guide its work. Whenever possible, the division relied on other units in OP&M, the Procurement Branch, the bureaus, and the PLD to complete its evaluations. This was particularly true in terms of pricing.

Actually, as the quality of bureau contracting improved, the Clearance Division's review functions became less critical. On the basis of work begun earlier with the Bureau of Supplies and Accounts, W. Browne Baker, a Folsom assistant and Texas businessman brought in to improve contracting procedures, organized a Negotiation Division at the end of 1942. It was located in the Procurement Branch, with subunits in each of the supply bureaus. The division was intended to introduce into bureau contracting the commercial dimension that only experienced businessmen could provide. Depending on bureau wishes, the duties of Negotiation Division personnel ranged from simply advising navy officers to actually negotiating contracts. With businessmen leading the way, firms were required to break down costs in setting prices and take other steps to ensure fair contracting. By mid-1943, many bureaus had assembled contracting teams made up of technical people from the bureaus, legal experts from the PLD, and business specialists from the Negotiation Division. Drawing on data from numerous sources grouped around the Office of the Under Secretary of War, the navy bureaus faced contractors on an equal footing, a situation that did not hold for most of 1942. As negotiating teams grew more proficient, they collected much of the information that the Clearance Division used in passing on contracts.

Encouraged by the WPB and other mobilization agencies, the Navy Department, along with the War Department, was quite successful in lowering prices for the goods it purchased and acquired through contracting. It accomplished that goal through improved contracting methods, incentive contracts and those instituting maximum prices subject to downward revision, and forward pricing and renegotiation to recapture excessive profits. These practices not only reduced prices and profits but also encouraged efficiency as contractors paid closer attention to costs, stressed output, consumed fewer materials, used less labor, and so on. Overall, in May 1945, the navy received around 25 percent more in goods per dollar spent than it had in 1942. According to another measure, the navy's general contract prices declined by 30 percent between January 1942 and the end of 1944.

The Office of the Under Secretary of the Navy never matched its success in pricing with success in quantity control. In part, this stemmed from OP&M reluctance to review and challenge bureau figures on the basis of requirements coming from the CNO. With the commander-in-chief and the chief of naval operations purposefully excluding the under secretary's office from strategic decisions and information, Knox, Forrestal, and their assistants were always at a disadvantage in evaluating demand. Only in the last months of the war was the secretary of the navy moving to coordinate effectively strategy, logistics, and procurement. Without such coordination, the navy inevitably built up astronomical surpluses as requirements were set at levels adequate to meet every possible contingency no matter how remote. Even if these circumstances had not existed, OP&M faced enormous odds. The navy lacked an effective system of inventory control. Without such information, any program for critically examining demand could not get far. Only in the last phases of the war was the navy beginning to make progress in gathering statistics on its holdings of supplies, equipment, and munitions.

The Navy Department's system of supply varied significantly from that of the War Department. Nearly all navy procurement was centered in Washington under the direction of OP&M, although decentralized to the several bureaus. By contrast, most of army buying and contracting took place in the field, often in and around the technical services' procurement districts. But the ASF had firmer and more fully established control over the supply bureaus than did the OP&M. On balance, the navy maintained a tighter rein on procurement than did the army in terms of managing prices and profits, building and financing facilities, and eventually even determining requirements. In part, this stemmed from the fact that, measured in dollars, the army's task was over twice the size of the navy's. Between July 1940 and August 1945, the two services spent $179.9 and $83.9 billion, respectively.[14] Navy procurement, however, particularly in terms of munitions, was more specialized and challenging than was army procurement.

Unquestionably, the navy's radically reorganized supply structure operated more harmoniously both within and outside the service than did the army's. Admiral Samuel M. Robinson, who headed the Bureau of Ships before being elevated to head the OP&M, led by persuasion and negotiation more than by dictation. He was also self-effacing and avoided lording OP&M's authority over the supersensitive supply bureaus, which for the first time had begun permanently and meaningfully to lose power within the navy structure. Robinson depended on OP&M winning over the shore establishment through the value of its performance more than by touting the office's virtues or stressing its necessity. OP&M relations with other government agencies were also agreeable. For the most part, it got along well with the WPB. Indeed, Folsom, a Nelson protégé, operated so successfully as head of the Procurement Branch in part because he was able to apply the vast knowledge of and experience with procurement and mobilization that he had gained in the NDAC and the OPM without arousing suspicion. Despite expectable differences, Robinson got along well with Somervell, his army counterpart, and OP&M worked with most other mobilization agencies in a reasonable manner.

Forrestal, more than Robinson, was the creative force of the navy's revamped material system. The under secretary of the navy chose Robinson as director of OP&M precisely because he wanted a leader who proceeded cautiously and worked through consensus. Unlike the Office of the Under Secretary of War, which had a supportive command system and twenty years of interwar planning to prepare it for the phenomenal procurement expansion of World War

II, the Office of the Under Secretary of the Navy faced daunting odds. It had practically to start from scratch in putting together piece by piece what became the PLD-OP&M structure. In doing so, Forrestal had to draw heavily on his extensive contacts in the legal, industrial, and financial worlds. While doing so, he had to battle the resistance of the supply bureaus below him and a hostile line above him. He succeeded, not only because of his own capabilities and the quality of his chosen assistants, but also because he was supported by Secretary of the Navy Frank Knox and, at key points, by Roosevelt. In the long run, Forrestal's deliberate and careful approach proved to be the right and successful one.

One of the best measures of Forrestal's work was that, unlike the ASF, OP&M survived the war years. With the end of hostilities, OP&M was transferred to the Office of the Assistant Secretary of the Navy and renamed the Material Division. In the Navy Reorganization Act of 1948—written largely by Forrestal's protégé, W. John Kenney, who served first as assistant and then as under secretary of the navy—the Material Division became the Chief of Naval Material, an office separate from the CNO even though both reported to the secretary of the navy.

Before those developments, Forrestal joined Secretary Knox in further strengthening civilian control in the Navy Department. With Admiral King making another attempt early in 1944 to place OP&M under his authority, Knox turned to corporate America for advice. A team headed by T. P. Archer, vice president of General Motors Corporation, and George W. Wolfe, president of the United States Steel Export Company, was tapped to analyze navy organization. Knox died before the study was far along, but Forrestal continued it as succeeding secretary of the navy.

Included in the Archer-Wolfe report of October 1944 was the call for the secretary of the navy to set up an Organization Control Board to act as his top policy council. Forrestal moved quickly to establish such a body, whose permanent members included himself (as chair), King, and their immediate deputies in the commander-in-chief's office, CNO, and OP&M. From the deliberations of this board, Forrestal created in February 1945 a Requirements Review Board assisted by a Requirements Review Committee, composed of representatives from the secretary's office, CNO, and OP&M, to scrutinize demand. Although just getting under way when the war ended, these new agencies set a crucial precedent for demand being determined under the secretary of the navy's authority and being based on considerations of strategy, logistics, and supply, with both military and civilian voices heard. This balanced approach was legally institutionalized with the Navy Reorganization Act of 1948.

CONCLUSION

World War II reemphasized one of the most critical points coming out of World War I: economic might was as important to victory as military strength, if not more so. That reality made control of the economy during wartime a crucial matter. During World War II, the navy was more respectful and appreciative of the need for civilian control of the economy than was the army. Hence, unlike the War Department, the Navy Department was not constantly at odds with civilian mobilization agencies. In a significant and paradoxical way, these realities grew in part out of the attitude and orientation of the military's civilian secretaries.

Frank Knox and James V. Forrestal had every reason to stress civilian roles in naval affairs. From the outset, they were forced to use legal, business, and financial talent in organizing systems to oversee massive wartime procurement. While doing so, they had to protect the new civilian units against the aggressive onslaught of Commander-in-Chief Ernest J. King and his associates (who knew little about the intricacies of supply and would no doubt have made a mess of it). The secretary and under secretary, however, were motivated by more than practical considerations. They never lost sight of the fact that the armed services served civilian purposes, not vice versa.

In sharp contrast, Secretary of War Henry L. Stimson and Under Secretary of War Robert P. Patterson came close to being more military than the officer corps. They defined their roles as protecting Chief of Staff George C. Marshall and his subordinates. They went along with Marshall dictating army reorganization early in 1942 even though their own authority was significantly diluted. They argued that civilian mobilization agencies existed to assist the army in carrying out its supply functions. They regularly castigated those agencies for lacking vigilance, for being too soft and too slow, and for being all but unpatriotic. And they regularly supported Somervell's blunderbuss, nearly irresponsible direction of the ASF, stepping in to check him only when he threatened chaos outside or inside the army. That ASF had more access to strategic planning than did OP&M resulted from Marshall's action, not from that of the secretary or under secretary of war. Marshall, Stimson, and Patterson notwithstanding, there is little evidence that Somervell advanced economic mobilization and considerable evidence that he retarded it or at least needlessly caused damaging disharmony. Under the genial but determined leadership of Admiral Robinson, Navy Department procurement operations were as good as or better than those of the War Department. Moreover, the way in which reforms were instituted and applied by Forrestal and Robinson led to continuous, permanent change, while Somervell's frontal assaults created a backlash that set back for years badly needed structural reforms in army supply and procurement.

Ironically, twenty years of procurement and industrial mobilization planning on the part of the War Department taught the wrong lessons. The planning convinced the army not only that it was fully capable of handling supply for war but also that it knew how to mobilize the civilian economy. (Bernard M. Baruch had feared such an outcome in the interwar years even though he sided with the armed services during World War II.)[15] Rather than building on the experience and institutional change that interwar planning had brought about to relate the War Department's material operations more effectively to civilian agencies, Stimson and Patterson encouraged the army to dominate the mobilized system. This flawed leadership resulted partially from the army's greater preparation for mobilization compared with the navy's. It also reflected the outlook of Stimson and Patterson, who, contrasted with Knox and Forrestal, revered the discipline, order, and role of the military. These very talented leaders came close to going through the looking glass; in the passions of war or impending war, they all but lost contact with the essentially civilian nature of American civilization.

Critical matters of wartime civil-military relations go higher than military departments, however. What of the views and actions of the president? Roosevelt was aware of the need to keep the military in its proper sphere, but he never seemed that concerned about the issue. His background and interest in the navy made him particularly knowledgeable about that service. He played an important role in preventing Admiral King from encroaching on the secretary of the navy's turf. Roosevelt also appeared to understand the army's dynamics and the strengths and weaknesses of Stimson and Patterson's leadership. The two were brought in as much for political as for military reasons and in order to compensate for the president's failure to provide strong leadership for the department in 1939–1940. Roosevelt also knew that the army was better prepared than was the navy to handle the greatly expanded procurement demands of war.

The president expected the services' civilian heads to work out the means for meeting the military's material needs. That left him to deal directly with Marshall, Arnold, and King in devising wartime strategy as an extension of the nation's foreign policy. By circumventing the secretaries of war and the navy, however, he violated civil-military canons. And the same was true in his allowing the armed services to gain a larger role in economic mobilization than was wise. Nonetheless, the president's first goal was victory. Time, energy, and priority limited his ability to maintain the proper balance in civil-military affairs. During the war, that task had to be largely left to the secretaries of war and the navy, with the president intervening only when necessary. In the long run, Roosevelt relied on the nation's deeply entrenched commitment to civilian domination of the military for withstanding the imbalance of war. While expecting a larger military establishment after hostilities compared with the interwar years, the president could not anticipate half a century of Cold War modifying radically the place of the armed services in American society.[16]

NATIONAL AND INTERNATIONAL MOBILIZATION AGENCIES

The War Production Board (WPB) and the armed services were affected by various mobilization agencies created during the defense and war years. Some of these were national, such as the War Food Administration (WFA); others concentrated on America's allies, like the Office of Lend-Lease Administration (OLLA); and a few worked in combination with Great Britain (to some degree Canada), as was the case with the Combined Production and Resources Board (CPRB). None of these agencies will be treated at length, but they need to be outlined so as to provide a fuller view of the mobilization system. Other agencies, like the War Manpower Commission, are analyzed in greater depth below.

A striking quality about the agencies to be reviewed is the degree to which they were based on existing, peacetime administrations. That was the case, for example, with the WFA. Agencies for foreign economic policy and combined boards designed to work in tandem with Great Britain also manifested this characteristic, although to a lesser degree than was true for domestically centered bodies. The various organizations analyzed below, therefore, differed from the strictly temporary agencies, such as the WPB, created to mobilize the economy. Actually, Roosevelt would have preferred using the national government's existing structure to an even larger extent than he was able.

THE WAR FOOD ADMINISTRATION

The Department of Agriculture implemented policies for the farmer during the war.[1] It was the only executive department that acted as a principal mobilization agency. That took place in part because the department over the years had set up extension services, research facilities, and like institutions, supplemented by the Agriculture Adjustment Administration and other New Deal planning agencies, that could be used in harnessing agriculture. A powerful

Farm Bloc in Congress and the American Farm Bureau Federation, the National Grange, and the National Farmers Union all also acted to ensure that wartime regulation of farmers was in friendly hands.

When President Franklin D. Roosevelt organized the National Defense Advisory Commission (NDAC) in May 1940, Chester C. Davis headed the Division of Farm Products. The division seldom went beyond studying subjects relevant to agriculture, and Davis concentrated more on general mobilization policies than on those relating specifically to farmers.[2] Hence, when the Office of Production Management (OPM) replaced NDAC in January 1941, no special agency for agriculture in or outside the new mobilization office was set up. Continuing surpluses took away any sense of urgency about farm goods, and the Agriculture Department seemed able to handle what needed to be done.

This reality changed once the United States entered the war. With demand exceeding supply and growing numbers of mobilization agencies becoming involved in farm output, more centralized direction of agriculture became necessary. Faced with the choice of creating a new agency, turning responsibility over to an existing one like the WPB, or enhancing the authority of the Department of Agriculture, the Roosevelt administration opted for the latter. But it implemented the decision only gradually and in a piecemeal fashion during 1942. Finally, in December 1942, by executive order, Roosevelt turned responsibility for war food output and distribution over to the secretary of agriculture. In March and April 1943, however, Roosevelt modified the December order so that the enhanced authority was exercised by the WFA, a new subdivision in the Agriculture Department headed by an administrator appointed by and answerable to the president. This awkward arrangement worked only because the administrator, Marvin Jones (replacing Chester C. Davis, who resigned in June 1943), and Secretary of Agriculture Claude R. Wickard worked well together.

WFA had vast and weighty responsibilities. Among other duties, it was to determine total requirements for food at home and abroad and devise programs for fulfilling and distributing demand according to priority. In performing these goals, it had to work with and divide responsibilities among numerous mobilization agencies, such as the WPB, the Office of Price Administration (OPA), the OLLA, the State Department, the Board of Economic Warfare (BEW), and the armed services. WFA always had trouble assembling reliable total requirement figures, with the military predictably a chronic problem. Nonetheless, WPA's relations with most war administrations were reasonable, even though it encountered difficulty with OPA in devising pricing and rationing programs.

At best the accomplishment of the Department of Agriculture/WFA were modest. The most serious failure was in terms of farm output. Between 1939 and 1944, total agricultural production increased 25 percent, around one-third of which can be attributed to unusually good weather. While that level of output was more than adequate for supplying the armed forces, the Allies, and the civilian population, it did not prepare the nation adequately for handling the overwhelming needs of liberated and underdeveloped areas facing great deprivation, even starvation, during the war and postwar periods. With existing allocation of resources, the American farm community could have conservatively produced 50 percent more than it did, and existing demand could have absorbed at least twice that which was marketed.

That the farm community was poorly harnessed for war is ironic. In terms of organization, in 1940–1941 Washington was better prepared to mobilize agriculture than any other economic sector. Yet, in 1941, the Agriculture Department's elaborate system for farm planning began to deteriorate. New Dealers who led so effectively in industrial mobilization did not play a comparable role in agriculture. Focused on farm surpluses and low prices for over a decade, the Department of Agriculture had great difficulty reorienting itself to conditions of war, in which output, speed, flexibility, and innovation counted. Bureaucratized and factionalized, the department operated in a confused, often contradictory, way. Facing a farm establishment determined to protect its constituents at all costs, WFA was timid. Particularly troublesome was the dominance of Southern Democrats in Congress. The legislative process was constantly used to micromanage agricultural policy in a way that preserved the status quo and that continued in the flush war years the parity or subsidy programs designed for depression. Instead of fighting back, the Department of Agriculture went along. That denied or reduced its ability to use price and other powerful economic tools for managing wartime farm output.

As a result, for example, surpluses of short-staple cotton were not cut back sufficiently to make way for more needed long-staple varieties or nutrient-rich crops like soybeans and peanuts. That same pattern was repeated with most basic crops. Farmers also continued to grow melons, buckwheat, sweet corn, and other luxury items unessential to the war effort but selling at high prices. Livestock herds were vastly overexpanded, keeping too much land in pasture, and absorbing an excessive amount of cereal crops. By comparison, the dairy industry was kept at too low a level of output. In general, farm machinery, labor, fertilizer, and credit sources were utilized according to prewar patterns in the least productive agriculture regions like the South, instead of being redirected to more efficient areas. Acreage was not expanded to the degree possible, and the potential of small farmers was neglected.

The congressional Farm Bloc and organizations such as the Farm Bureau always limited what WFA could do. Nonetheless, effective leadership using the urgency of war could have achieved a better record. There were those in the Agriculture Department who favored more efficient approaches, but either they were checkmated by opponents, or they lacked the will and power to push forward. Where the farm community did stand out during World War II was in augmenting its wealth. Net farm income went up from $5.3 billion in 1939 to $13.6 billion in 1944. Increased costs of production notwithstanding, the farmer received a greater share of consumer dollars than had probably ever before been the case.

THE OFFICE OF DEFENSE TRANSPORTATION

The Office of Defense Transportation (ODT) was an outgrowth of the NDAC's Transportation Division, headed by Ralph Budd.[3] Roosevelt phased out Budd's division only after creating ODT by executive order on December 18, 1941. Throughout 1941, Budd continued his NDAC practices of concentrating on railroads, proceeding cautiously, and depending on advice and assistance from railroad executives and their associations.

Beginning in the spring of 1941, the Bureau of the Budget and others began considering a new and stronger emergency transportation agency.[4] They concluded their work just before Pearl Harbor. The ODT took over shortly thereafter. Joseph B. Eastman, chairman of the Interstate Commerce Commission (ICC), was nearly everyone's choice to head the new body. A widely respected, progressive public servant, Eastman had served on ICC since 1919. ODT's responsibilities were vast. It was to oversee the operations of and set policies for all domestic transportation services, including railroads, motor vehicles, inland waterway and coastal and intercoastal traffic, pipelines, and air transport, so as to maximize their wartime use. ODT was also to represent transportation services before other government agencies, particularly the WPB. When necessary, the office could issue orders to achieve desired action.

Eastman never tested the limits of his vaguely defined but potentially broad authority. With a relatively small staff drawn heavily from the ICC, he was determined to meet war needs with the least disturbance to existing practices of privately owned transportation systems. Eastman consistently opposed any general program of priorities. Such an effort would require an enormous staff and, given the World War I record, was likely to do more harm than good. Throughout the war years, ODT stressed voluntary approaches, relying on the cooperation of involved industries and their executives and associations. ODT's director also recognized that his need to work with and through a host of other agencies, such as the armed services and the WPB, always limited and complicated whatever he did.

ODT appropriately concentrated most of its wartime attention on railroads. In ton miles, the railroads carried over 61 percent of the nation's freight in 1940; by 1943, the figure had jumped to 72 percent. Passenger miles increased even more dramatically, from around 9 percent in 1940 to 35 percent in 1944. But percentages alone do not convey the magnitude of the greatly expanded wartime load. Between 1939 and 1945, ton miles of freight more than doubled, and passenger miles increased over fourfold, even with track mileage declining somewhat between 1939 and 1945 and rolling stock and locomotion expanding only slightly. (Using the shortest and most direct routes during the war made gains even more substantial.) After 1942, WPB allowed a reasonable number of locomotives to be manufactured, but it kept freight- and passenger-car production at low levels. Over ODT protests, WPB chanced that railroads could constantly squeeze more from their operations without breakdowns. And they did so through the combined efforts of ODT and other government agencies, railroads, the American Association of Railroads, and shippers to increase efficiency through reducing freight-car turnaround time, maximizing passenger-car use, and other conservation measures. While the industry's profits skyrocketed from heavy railroad usage, wartime rates remained quite stable.

Little compulsion was used in achieving these impressive records despite steady pressure from WPB and other sources to institute priorities. Occasionally, ODT issued orders for more efficient use of freight and refrigerator cars, restrictions on changes in established services, or prohibition on non-essential uses. Under dire conditions, such as exceptionally heavy traffic to the West Coast in 1943 and again in 1945, ODT also implemented or prepared to use short-term priorities on freight. Although civilians experienced considerable inconvenience, some critical war programs were delayed, and various disasters were averted by narrow margins, the railroads met practically all the extraordinary demands of war.

ODT handled most challenges to its authority without disrupting operations. Conflict with WPB over priorities, turf, and railroad equipment was often great, but, on balance, board services and information assisted, more than thwarted, the office. The Army Service Forces (ASF) regularly claimed independence from Eastman's reach, sought exemption from ODT policies, or demanded the right to review ODT orders. Disputes also arose with the

War Manpower Commission and other mobilization agencies. Eastman relied on his accomplishments, flexibility, finesse, and support from the railroads to defuse, not feed, controversy.

Interwar developments largely account for the positive wartime record. Federal seizure and operation of the railroads during World War I convinced industry, the military, and the federal government separately and together to find solutions for avoiding such an outcome during future hostilities. With the outbreak of war in Europe in 1939, activities increased and, ultimately, became institutionalized in NDAC and ODT. The paralyzing port congestion and related crises of World War I were, thus, avoided.

The ODT was more an extension of the ICC than a new entity. Eastman continued to serve on the commission while he was ODT's director, and ICC Commissioner J. Monroe Johnson replaced Eastman as head of the office on the latter's death in March 1944. Principal staffing of ODT came from ICC and those serving with Eastman when he was federal coordinator of transportation in the 1930s. In addition, ICC continued peacetime regulatory and ratemaking roles along with exercising enhanced wartime statutory powers. At times ODT operated on its own, at others with or through ICC. The two agencies seldom differed because of shared personnel, outlooks, and goals. Relations between the ODT and the ICC resembled those between the WFA and the Department of Agriculture even though the first two operated on a much broader level.

ODT's record with other forms of wartime transportation was less impressive. It looked to water-borne traffic to relieve railroads, without much success. In 1940 and 1941, freight movement on inland and coastal and intercoastal water routes went up by over 20 percent from the base years 1935–1939. Thereafter, the figures dropped to as low as two-thirds of peacetime usage. The threat of submarines and a shortage of ships cut coastal traffic drastically. ODT used publicity, selective priorities, and availability of government-built tugs, barges, and other vessels to increase traffic on rivers, canals, and the Great Lakes, but with only gradual and limited results. Waterways were too slow, inconvenient, and, in some cases, costly in moving freight for most shippers or consignees, especially during the hurried plant buildup in 1942 and 1943. Nonetheless, increasing amounts of petroleum products gradually came to be transported by inland water routes. That gain, along with the expansion of pipelines for oil from the Southwest to the East Coast, reduced railroad burdens.

ODT never succeeded in handling motor vehicles effectively. It lacked the experience, staff, and initiative necessary for this massive undertaking, and voluntary methods would not work. To assist ODT, the OPA in 1942 instituted rationing for cars, tires, and gasoline. Throughout 1942 and 1943, ODT continued struggling to regulate millions of trucks and buses and hundreds of thousands of public carriers through cooperative methods and general rules. Facing continuing frustration, it finally turned the entire job over to OPA and, where farm vehicles were concerned, the Department of Agriculture.

Eastman's office did only marginally better with local transportation systems facing enormous stress. It issued a stream of regulations intended to conserve equipment and maximize usage. Until municipalities had stretched services to the limit, ODT would not distribute on a priority basis the minuscule number of streetcars, buses, and trollies that WPB allowed to be manufactured.

ODT's record was mixed. The office did well with rationalized national systems serving organized demand under familiar circumstances. The railroads stand out in that regard. ODT additionally handled water transportation and pipelines only acceptably. Air transport received little attention because it remained relatively inconsequential for moving freight or passengers. Despite considerable efforts, ODT made little headway in integrating transportation systems, particularly the operations of railroads and motor carriers. It ran into strong opposition among the industries involved. Failure with motor vehicles, a decentralized system on which the nation was heavily dependent, most clearly revealed ODT's serious limitations as a wartime regulatory body.

THE WAR SHIPPING ADMINISTRATION

The War Shipping Administration (WSA) was among the most successful mobilization agencies of World War II.[5] It made an indispensable and largely unrecognized contribution to Allied victory. Actually, WSA was a new and temporary agency set up within the United States Maritime Commission structure. In that sense, it shared some characteristics with the WFA/Department of Agriculture and ODT/ICC arrangements.

Global warfare made ocean transport central to all operations. Clearly recognizing that reality, the Axis powers attempted to neutralize Allied material and human superiority by turning to submarine warfare to make the Atlantic and related sea-lanes impassable. The U-boat attacks were devastatingly effective throughout 1941–1942 and into the early months of 1943. Only from April 1943 forward, with America and Britain effectively countering submarines and U.S. output of ships hitting stride, did the Allies have sufficient vessels to meet most critical demands. When the United States entered the war, the Allies had a total of around 45 million deadweight tons of shipping, most of which was British, with America's share around 12 million tons. The Axis powers destroyed in excess of 3 million tons in 1941 and nearly 10 million tons in 1942. Between 1941 and 1945, however, American shipyards constructed a total of 5,570 cargo and related vessels measuring over 55 million deadweight tons.

The United States had moved to expand its maritime fleet with the Merchant Marine Act of 1936. Replacing the U.S. Shipping Board, the U.S. Maritime Commission was charged with overseeing a program of subsidies for building and operating ships under the American flag and generally regulating the industry. In 1938, the commission set a ten-year goal of having constructed fifty ships a year of the most modern design. After war in Europe escalated in mid-1940, the commission upped the figure to two hundred ships a year. Even that was not enough.

The NDAC led in dealing with the growing crisis. Admiral Emory S. Land, chair of the Maritime Commission, joined NDAC as head of the Shipbuilding Section of the Production Division. Land and William S. Knudsen launched a crash program for building what came to be called the *Liberty ship* (later the *Victory ship*, an improved model): a stripped-down, simple, slow, steel cargo vessel patterned after the old British tramp steamer that could be mass-produced using subassemblies, prefabrication, and welding. In 1941, average time to deliver a Liberty was around 245 days, a figure cut to 39 days late in 1943, and a Henry J. Kaiser company completed a ship in 14 days. By the end of 1940, the Maritime Commission had contracted to finance and build nineteen yards with 131 shipways.

No production program could keep up with demand unless ships were maximally used. Here is where the WSA came in. Its creation was part of streamlining the U.S. Maritime Commission for wartime demands. With earlier reforms failing and the armed services attempting to gain control of water traffic, Pearl Harbor forced Roosevelt to move. Backed by the advice of Land, Harry L. Hopkins, the Bureau of the Budget, and others, the president concluded that direction of wartime shipping had to remain in civilian hands. By executive order in February 1942, consequently, he organized the WSA, its head reporting directly to him. While Land was appointed administrator, Lewis W. Douglas, who had been tapped earlier to assist with lend-lease operations, was designated as Land's adviser and, in May 1942, was made deputy administrator to run WSA. By then, ship construction and direction were in a crisis state. Land, whom Roosevelt in 1938 chose to head the five-person Maritime Commission, clearly lacked the administrative abilities to manage wartime shipping. Rather than replacing a friend who was generally well liked and who had good relations with Congress, the president and his advisers left Land nominally in charge while delegating critical functions to subordinates. Douglas took control of shipping, and two other admirals whom Roosevelt had earlier placed on the commission handled other major responsibilities: Admiral Howard L. Vickery assumed charge of all ship construction, and Captain Edward Macauley supervised merchant-shipping personnel.

Douglas was exceptionally well qualified to head WSA. (Close to Hopkins, he was recently reconciled with Roosevelt after resigning as Bureau of the Budget director in August 1934 over policy disputes.) Fully aware of the multiple challenges that he faced, Douglas accepted the appointment only after receiving Roosevelt's and Hopkins's commitments that they would keep Land out of his way and unequivocally back him in disputes. To carry out his duties, he continued the able services of those like Ralph Keating who had been with the Maritime Commission for some time. Douglas also brought in new talent such as a business colleague, Franz Schneider, and an old Washington hand, Fred Searls, Jr.

WSA had enormous responsibilities. It was to oversee every aspect of shipping except construction, including the purchase, lease, or requisition of any vessel for itself or any other government agency; repairing, arming, or converting ships for special purposes; arranging for crews; and providing for war risk and marine insurance. Most important, WSA controlled terminal and port facilities, the operation, loading, and discharge of ships, and the movement of vessels.

WSA ran no ships on its own; rather, it operated like an agency of assignment. The administration took title to or had unlimited right to use all American-owned or -controlled ships regardless of registry. As new, renovated, or repaired vessels became available, they were assigned to existing steamship companies. By avoiding the direct operation of vessels, WSA concentrated on allocating space on a priority basis. With a fluid pool of ships at its disposal, WSA constantly shifted vessels around to meet both the short- and the long-run exigencies of war. Key to WSA's success was having complete data on all ships, including availability, capacity, assignment, location, and the like. Devising procedures and working with still rather crude equipment for handling this information presented an enormous task. Requirements were a perennial problem throughout hostilities because of the ever-shifting nature of demand and the often-uncooperative armed services. Nonetheless, the WSA in time ultimately set up an exceptionally efficient operation.

WSA coordinated its activities with those of the British. Roosevelt and Winston Churchill had agreed that Britain would concentrate on building naval ships and the United States devote its attention to merchant ones. Douglas worked in close association with Sir Arthur Salter, Britain's representative for shipping in Washington, and Salter's London superior, Lord Leathers, minister of war transport. Indeed, in getting WSA under way, Douglas relied heavily on British knowledge and experience. Overall, WSA relations with Britain involving shipping were excellent.

That was not the case with interests at home. Douglas carried out an intricate juggling act in order to meet his multiple responsibilities. From the outset, he determined that presidential demands (such as aid to Russia) had first priority, with military needs coming second, Lend-Lease third, and civilian requirements last. For demand other than that of the armed services and Lend-Lease, WSA looked to the BEW for guidance. On imports, WSA took its directions from the WPB. To help guide his work, Douglas had the assistance of a Daily Operations Committee, made up of representatives from WSA, the War Department, the ODT, and the British Ministry of War Transportation.

While all claimants and related mobilization agencies struggled with WSA over policies and priorities, the army was the most persistent and difficult. The ASF commander, General Brehon B. Somervell, and chief of the Transportation Corps, General Charles P. Gross, from the outset were determined either to subordinate WSA operations to their will or to gain independence from the administration's control. In Douglas they more than met their match. While Douglas was willing to make reasonable compromises, he would not surrender his prerogatives to others, and, as promised, Roosevelt and Hopkins supported him.

Differences with the army revolved around the basic issues of loading and assigning ships. (WSA, of course, had no control over navy or army combat vessels or their limited fleets of cargo ships.) With never enough vessels, cargo space had to be used maximally. That meant that freight had to be loaded promptly and correctly and unloaded expeditiously for fast turnaround time. Outgoing and homecoming ships could never sail empty or with only a partial load. Ships returning from Europe, for example, would carry reverse Lend-Lease supplies or other goods heading to the United States. Without extensive maritime experience, army ships often were loaded poorly, sailed only partly loaded, and returned empty. To remedy this situation, WSA insisted on taking over or directing all longshoring activities. That would involve mixing military cargo with other freight in some instances. The army, and to a lesser degree the navy, demanded the right to handle its own cargo. On the issue of ship control, the army wanted vessels assigned to it for blocks of time. Douglas adamantly rejected this approach. WSA assigned ships a specific destination. Once voyages were completed, ships reverted to WSA's pool. Otherwise, WSA would lose flexibility in assigning ships according to priority, the military could hold ships for storage purposes, and the administration's general control over shipping would be significantly diluted.

The services were notorious for overstating requirements, harbored deep-seated antagonism toward Britain, and were suspicious of Lend-Lease in general and aid to Russia in particular. All these conditions, in Douglas's mind, militated against allowing them any more latitude in shipping than was absolutely necessary. Generally, the navy was easier to deal with; WSA's troubles were mostly with the army.

In June 1942, Douglas and Somervell hammered out a written agreement on relations between the WSA and the ASF. The accord began breaking down before long. In all areas, ASF attempted to encroach on WSA responsibilities, ignored administration policies and requests, and declared itself independent of Douglas's control. By the end of 1942, a frustrated and incensed Douglas finally went to Roosevelt to reassert WSA responsibility and authority. The president accommodated him, in the process setting off a firestorm of protest from the War Department, backed by the Navy Department. In a series of meetings in December 1942 and January 1943, under the watchful eye of Admiral William D. Leahy, chief of staff to the president, leading WSA and military figures negotiated the basis for a settlement. Douglas assisted the process greatly by consulting directly with Chief of Staff George C. Marshall. Although no formal agreement was reached, Douglas won out. While he gave some ground on the army loading its own equipment, weapons, and cargo, he maintained civilian control of shipping in his own hands. With the crisis in shipping starting to lift in April 1943, future conflict was more muted.

Douglas's battle in behalf of WSA was not simply a war for turf. Like the president, he realized that maximal use of limited shipping capacity depended on evenhanded civilian control guided by priorities set at the highest levels of government. Otherwise, the war effort could be seriously harmed, even lost.

Under Douglas's adroit direction, WSA throughout 1942 and 1943 managed to accomplish small miracles. Time and again, it readjusted schedules, reassigned ships, postponed deliveries, and took other steps to meet crises. At the Casablanca Conference in January 1943, for example, American and British military planners, without WSA represented, reached important agreements about the conduct of the war. The decisions included preparing for the pending invasion of Sicily, building up supplies in Britain for the cross-Channel invasion, and meeting minimum British imports to keep the nation fighting. Because of misunderstandings, miscommunications, and unsupplied information, negotiators made commitments that overstated shipping availability by 6 million deadweight tons. Learning of the massive blunder only in mid-February, Douglas worked furiously to solve the crisis. He had done so to nearly everyone's satisfaction by the end of March. All critical needs were met; delays occurred only in shipping for Britain's campaign to retake Burma. Even during the most severe shipping crunch in 1942–1943 WSA managed to meet most critical programs. In doing so, it had to take enormous risks on more than one occasion.

Once the shipping crunch began to ease in 1943, Douglas gradually cut back his time with WSA and finally resigned in April 1944. Land was happy to see him leave. Douglas had overshadowed the Maritime Commission–WSA head, a situation that the temperamental and proud Land found increasingly intolerable. More than most mobilization agencies, WSA was largely a Douglas creation. When he left, he had put in place an efficient civilian organization for directing the sailing and operations of merchant ships on a global basis. In 1942–1943, WSA had played a critical role in the Allies first surviving the Axis onslaught and then going from the defensive to the offensive.

WSA's extraordinary success depended heavily on Douglas's ability and Roosevelt's support. More than most wartime leaders, the two shared the realization that America's success depended on keeping the British and then the Russians fighting. In carrying out their goal, they had to battle constantly against numerous opponents at home.

THE PETROLEUM ADMINISTRATION FOR WAR AND THE SOLID FUELS ADMINISTRATION FOR WAR

The Petroleum Administration for War (PAW), created by executive order on December 2, 1942, replaced the Office of Petroleum Coordinator (OPC), which the president had set up on May 28, 1941, a day after declaring a state of unlimited national emergency. Secretary of the Interior Harold L. Ickes headed both agencies, which, while technically autonomous of his department, actually operated as part of his general domain.[6]

Separating petroleum from the WPB and predecessor agencies made it practically unique among industries. This outcome stemmed from precedent, oil's importance, and the complexity of and divisions within the industry. During World War I, petroleum was ultimately placed under the United States Fuel Administration. With the New Deal, oil was treated differently from most other industries. Ickes oversaw the writing and implementing of a National Recovery Administration (NRA) code for oil, not the agency's head, Hugh S. Johnson. After NRA's demise, an intricate federal-state, public-private pattern approaching cartelization was used to stabilize the industry. At the same time, the Roosevelt administration in the post-NRA years conducted an antitrust campaign against oil.[7]

Ickes reflected well the New Deal's contradictory approach to oil. He generally distrusted petroleum executives, especially those from the major firms, advocated greater state control over oil, yet worked effectively with industry leaders during times of crisis. Reform and change never clouded the Roosevelt administration's view of the centrality of the petroleum industry to America's political economy. With approaching war, oil's significance multiplied manyfold. On land, on water, and in the air, the armed services had become increasingly dependent on petroleum and its products, and practically every other facet of the economy had long before reached that stage. Yet harnessing the industry for war was a herculean task because of the complexity involved in extracting, refining, distributing, and transporting the product, often bitter divisions among majors, independents, and foreign as opposed to national operators, and the involvement of states and branches of the national government.

Of the 7 billion barrels of crude petroleum consumed by the Allies between the end of 1941 and mid-1945, the United States provided fully 80 percent. At the outbreak of war, the nation accounted for 60 percent of world output, with 45 percent of known global reserves. Between 1939 and 1943, U.S. consumption jumped by 28 percent, yet proven U.S. reserves increased by under 16 percent. These figures point to several realities concerning petroleum. First, the United States quite suddenly went from the need to control excess production to that to maximize output. A close working relation between government and industry was necessary to achieve that end—an end on which the Allies' victory depended. Second, war mobilization once again raised concerns about exhausting domestic oil reserves and emphasized the need for seeking new sources of petroleum abroad.

Roosevelt designated Ickes petroleum coordinator for national defense in mid-1941 after Congress failed to act on his request for legislation regulating oil and the NDAC and the OPM made little progress in the area. The secretary of the interior was to assemble information on demand and supply and recommend policies for meeting emergency needs to federal and state governments and industry. Roosevelt called on twenty interested government agencies, such as OPM and the Maritime Commission, to cooperate with the OPC.

Yet Roosevelt proceeded with great caution and in a most oblique way. Ickes received his new assignment by letter, not executive order or reference to any statute. While his responsibilities were great, his powers were slight. He could do no more than consult and advise. Roosevelt obviously was extending to industry a friendly hand backed by a threat. He was seeking industry's voluntary cooperation in mobilizing for war, and Ickes could follow that route. Known for his statist views and quest for power, however, Ickes could get tough if oil resisted national policies.

Ickes worked cooperatively and effectively with petroleum under terms practically dictated by the industry. Edwin W. Pauley, an independent California oil executive and Democratic Party treasurer, appeared to have a role in persuading Roosevelt to create OPC and place it in the Interior Department. Ickes selected Ralph K. Davies as deputy coordinator. At the time, Davies was senior vice-president of the Standard Oil Company of California. Some of OPC's staff was from the Department of the Interior, but about three-quarters of it came from oil firms. Davies attempted to balance majors and independents in recruiting personnel. He devised a system in which those coming from the petroleum companies received maximum government salary, with their employer making up the rest so as to avoid a cut in pay for government service. Davies served under such circumstances.

OPC was essentially structured along the lines of the petroleum industry. It had divisions for production, refining, transportation, and distribution and five regional and other offices patterned after the organization of the central office. Industry set up and financed a system of advisory committees paralleling OPC's central and regional structures, headed by a Petroleum Industry Council for National Defense (the Petroleum Industry War Council as of December 1942). Representatives from major oil firms and producing and marketing associations dominated the council, which met once a month at a minimum. To handle relations abroad and those with allies or potential ones, Ickes set up a Foreign Division in August 1941 and a Foreign Operations Committee in December. The committee was composed of chief executives from major oil firms and was to advise OPC on all foreign oil operations and oversee seven area committees. Meeting with over a thousand petroleum executives in June 1941, Davies and Ickes assured them that Washington was anxious to work voluntarily with oil in mobilizing the industry. To emphasize the point, Ickes explained that Acting Attorney General Francis Biddle had agreed to exempt oil advisory committees from antitrust prosecution, suspend pending antitrust suit activity against industry, and consult with OPC concerning any litigation involving oil. After hostilities, the Justice Department charged that, through advisory committees, industry had made basic wartime decisions that the government then accepted.

Once under way, OPC, in addition to its other duties, acted as an industry division for OPM and the WPB. In that capacity, it formulated policy for industry and reviewed and recommended action on priority decisions, preference ratings, and limitation and curtailment orders. Characteristically, Ickes was never satisfied with his essentially advisory powers and vaguely defined responsibilities. Before and after the nation declared war, he badgered the president to grant him the authority to determine national oil policy. Finally, in August 1942, with a positive nod from Roosevelt, Ickes spelled out in a draft executive order how he wanted OPC to operate. He proposed taking over from a dozen other agencies critical controls involving oil and in a way disruptive to mobilization.

After nearly four months of consideration, the Bureau of the Budget drafted an executive order that Roosevelt issued on December 2, 1942. It elevated OPC to the PAW, technically an independent agency under Ickes reporting directly to the president. Actually, little changed. PAW had more clearly defined responsibilities, but the authority of other agencies had not been reduced. PAW remained largely an administration for advising and making recommendations. Ickes's experience with and skill at bureaucratic infighting and support for his office from the petroleum industry, however, gave PAW more clout than the executive order indicated.

PAW and its predecessor took part in practically all action involving petroleum. Shortly after OPC was created, Ickes initiated a comprehensive survey of oil's producing, refining, distributing, and transporting capacities and facilities and what it had and needed in equipment and materials. Keeping these data current helped the agency make informed decisions.

The most immediate need facing Ickes in mid-1941 was transportation, particularly in District 1, which encompassed all states from Maine to Florida east of the Appalachians. Around 95 percent of the region's oil was brought in by coastal or intercoastal tankers. Ickes's office was put in place about the same time that the president diverted fifty tankers supplying the Atlantic Coast to provide for British petroleum needs. After Pearl Harbor, German submarines exacted a heavy toll on tankers, and a good part of the fleet was used to meet more urgent war demands of the nation and its allies.

These developments put District 1 in a state of almost perpetual crisis involving petroleum products until well into 1943. PAW had to team up with a host of other agencies to avert disaster. Ships that remained available were used as efficiently as possible. Every other conceivable means of transport was tapped in providing—often very narrowly so—the Atlantic Coast's minimal needs. These included railroad tank cars, barges and ships on inland waterways and the Great Lakes, existing pipelines, and trucks. Ickes realized that short-run solutions would never solve the problem.

Pipelines were essential for a long-run solution. Facing much opposition and priority restrictions, Ickes succeeded during 1942 and 1943 in having the Defense Plant Corporation finance the construction of two pipelines—one the world's longest, the other the world's largest—running from Texas oil fields to refineries around New York at a cost of $150 million. Between 1943 and 1945, the lines together carried nearly 380 million barrels of crude to District 1, pulling the area back from massive petroleum-shortage threats.

These were the most ambitious pipeline accomplishments of the war years.

In total during those years, 17,684 miles of pipeline were added, including relaying existing pipe and reversing the flow of others. Although government financing was involved, industry paid for most of the new or reworked lines other than the two massive ones.

The greatest single challenge faced by PAW during the war years involved 100-octane and higher-grade aviation gasoline. America's vast aircraft output created astronomical demand for high-octane gas. At the time of Pearl Harbor, the output of such fuel stood at around 40,000 barrels daily manufactured by about a dozen refineries. By the end of 1944, nearly four hundred refineries participated in producing approximately 514,000 barrels a day of a higher-quality fuel, almost a thirteenfold increase. Expenditures on equipment and reworked and new refineries reached $867 million with $260 million covered by government and the rest by private industry. In addition, the United States and its allies spent another $260 million on foreign facilities, principally in the Caribbean and the Middle East. The Defense Supplies Corporation, a subsidiary of the Reconstruction Finance Corporation (RFC), in collaboration with the armed services, purchased practically all high-grade aviation gasoline at prices adjusted to cover any unusual costs.

In achieving these goals, PAW overcame a host of formidable obstacles. From 1940 through 1942, the armed forces either could not estimate their needs or were chronically low in their calculations. Deputy Administrator Davies and his colleagues constantly had to fight for more realistic figures. In upping production, PAW faced the need to negotiate agreements covering licensing, patents, and royalties with the government and industry. Building new facilities ran into priority limitations. Only in July 1943 did aviation gasoline plant and equipment gain the highest priority rating. Even then, they competed for facilities and equipment with crash programs in synthetic rubber and naval vessels. These problems were solved to a degree only from mid-1943 onward with WPB programs for scheduling jointly for both high-octane gas and synthetic rubber facilities' component parts, raw materials, specialized equipment, and other items. Difficulties nevertheless continued to arise until practically the end of hostilities.

High-octane gasoline was not alone in straining the petroleum industry. The industry also had to handle the huge demand of a virtually new synthetic rubber industry heavily dependent on petroleum fractions for manufacturing. Refineries regularly had to adjust their facilities to often quickly changing demand for gasoline, fuel and heating oils, special diesels, and the like. Extensive research and development were essential for meeting the requirements, not only of synthetic rubber, but also of navy special fuel oil, army universal

80-octane gasoline usable throughout the world under widely varying temperatures, climates, and conditions, and other products.

To meet the extraordinary demands of war, PAW did what it could to push up production of crude, including exploration and conservation and other practices designed to maximize yield from existing sources. Between 1941 and 1945, crude output grew by 27 percent. Refinery runs jumped during the same time by 30 percent. This increase for the most part did not result from greater capacity to process crude. Only two completely new refineries were built during the war. Instead, existing refineries were expanded, ran more efficiently, and used new or modified techniques. PAW and oil firms were diligent in stressing research for new and better ways to advance industry's performance. Those approaches were necessary with the military absorbing unheard of amounts of oil, often of a specialized nature. In 1941, the armed services absorbed nearly 18 percent of total petroleum output; by 1945, the figure went up to over 33 percent.

PAW's accomplishments grew out of its willingness to follow industry's lead in most instances. That arrangement also acted to distort the judgment of Ickes, Davies, and some of their key advisers. Following the oil industry's lead, PAW fought against rationing gasoline and, when rationing was instituted, battled for inequitable procedures.[8] Ickes, Davies, and PAW also fought, unsuccessfully, with the OPA from 1942 through 1944 to increase the price of crude. The secretary of the interior, moreover, became oil's advocate for tax benefits and against unfavorable tax rulings.

Through persistence and bureaucratic battles, the PAW administrator won for his agency a significant say in policy and operations involving foreign oil. Unlike his forays into domestic operations, Ickes's ventures abroad were plagued with trouble and failed more than they succeeded. In 1942, PAW fought with the BEW to gain some control over petroleum exports and imports, even though PAW's responsibilities remained largely advisory. Ickes was more successful in ongoing turf wars fought with the State Department. With the strong backing of the president, for example, Ickes in 1942 and 1943 forced through a project allowing a group of independent oil companies to build a high-octane gasoline refinery in Mexico with the United States guaranteed a percentage of output.

The Middle East, however, emerged as the most important foreign petroleum area, identified as having the world's greatest oil deposits. With wartime demand drawing down American reserves, fears of domestic depletion and exhaustion grew, especially among those concerned with America's postwar international position. Attention naturally began to focus on the Middle East.

PAW was particularly interested in Saudi Arabia. As it did over Latin America, Ickes's administration often differed with the State Department over the Middle East. Operations abroad rekindled Ickes's statist tendencies, again with the president on his side, but also with the backing of the Joint Chiefs of Staff (JCS) and other military institutions.

To advance national security, Ickes led in attempting to have Washington, through the Petroleum Reserves Corporation, organized as a subsidiary of the RFC in June 1943, enter the international oil market. He proposed that the corporation buy out the vast and rich oil concession in Saudi Arabia jointly held by Standard Oil Company of California, Deputy Administrator Davies's employer, and the Texas Company. Fearing British antagonism, the State Department was opposed. Nearly all elements of the divided oil industry eventually came out strongly against the scheme. Forced to back off, Ickes took up the cause of the federal government building a pipeline from Saudi Arabia to the Mediterranean. Once more, widespread dissent killed the project.

PAW's record was made at home, not abroad. And its accomplishments were many and important. No military effort anywhere suffered from unavailability of oil, and homefront requirements were adequately met. The petroleum industry, however, benefited greatly from its wartime situation. It largely ran itself during hostilities under Ickes's aggressive protection. Besides the War Department, no other agency fought so frequently with so many agencies for such parochial goals. Oil also benefited handsomely from full-time use of an expanded plant, new pipelines, and new or vastly greater markets for synthetic rubber, high-octane gasoline, and other products manufactured in facilities financed in whole or part by the federal government.

Ickes also headed the Solid Fuels Administration for War (SFAW).[9] SFAW was established in the Department of the Interior by executive order on April 19, 1943. It was preceded by the Office of Solid Fuels Coordinator for National Defense, also set up in the Interior Department on November 5, 1941, and renamed the Office of Solid Fuels Coordinator for War on May 25, 1942. These agencies were intended to achieve some centralized government control of anthracite and bituminous coal and lignite. Despite growing competition from natural gas, fuel oil, and hydroelectric power, coal was still basic to the operations of the economy.

SFAW had a host of advisory committees, but, unlike petroleum advisory committees, they were not dominated by industry or major firms because bituminous was unconcentrated and badly fragmented. Moreover, the United Mine Workers of America (UMW) and public groups were represented as significant participants in mining operations. The NRA had brought a measure of stability to the chaotic bituminous coalfields, and the planning apparatus was kept going after the NRA's demise with what ultimately became the Bituminous Coal Act of 1937. The statute set up in the Interior Department the National Bituminous Coal Commission (reorganized in July 1939 as the Interior Department's Bituminous Coal Division) to work out a system of minimum prices for soft coal. Through various extensions by Congress, the act remained in effect until May 24, 1943. Up to that time, the Bituminous Coal Division had a role in regulating soft coal in cooperation with the SFAW, its predecessors, and other mobilization agencies such as the OPA.

SFAW resembled the PAW in its functions. It too served practically as an industry division of the WPB. On the basis of information obtained from public and private sources, it formulated policies to maximize coal output for essential war and civilian needs along with distributing, conserving, and using solid fuels most effectively. To accomplish those goals, the administration made recommendations to other agencies on prices, rationing, equipment, labor, transportation, and like areas for solid fuel industries. Beginning in early December 1943, the WPB additionally delegated to SFAW authority for regulating the distribution of coke as a domestic fuel. Working through SFAW or other specially created divisions, the Secretary of the Interior also carried out Washington's seizure of coal mines resulting from UMW strikes, threatened strikes, or job action between 1943 and 1946.

High wartime requirements for coal resolved to a degree the destructive competition chronically plaguing bituminous, by far the largest sector of the industry. Demand exceeded supply during the war years as industries and services expanded, military needs skyrocketed, various users converted to coal from other fuels in short supply, and exports grew. Bituminous and lignite output went from just under 395 million net tons in 1939 to an all-time high of nearly 619.6 million net tons in 1944. Even with anthracite production steadily increasing from slightly under 51.5 million net tons in 1939 to a wartime record approaching 64 million net tons in 1944, shortages became so severe that SFAW in 1943 introduced a program to ensure the equitable distribution of hard coal.

Overall, the Department of the Interior and its subdivisions had a much less demanding task with coal than with oil, and they performed well. The greatest challenges came from repeated strikes or possible work stoppages by the UMW between 1941 and 1946. These tense encounters were exaggerated manyfold by the personal feud between President Roosevelt and John L. Lewis, head of the UMW, and the exceptional stress and negative consequences of the union's action on organized labor and the Roosevelt administration.

AGENCIES FOR FOREIGN ECONOMIC POLICY

From mid-1939 through late 1943, agencies for carrying out foreign economic policies were decentralized, uncoordinated, and often at odds with one another. Policies basically divided into two major areas: materially assisting friendly nations or future allies; and weakening the economic strength of hostile nations or future enemies. Only in September 1943 were these two functions and related ones consolidated under one agency, the Foreign Economic Administration (FEA).[10]

Agencies for handling American assistance to Britain and France got under way when in mid-1939 Roosevelt authorized the Army-Navy Munitions Board (ANMB) to oversee skyrocketing munitions purchases at home. The president did not allow the armed services to exercise such review authority for long. He wanted this important function carried out by civilians, those anxious to assist potential allies even at the expense of America's military buildup, and those willing to follow his lead. Hence, by slow bureaucratic stages between the end of 1939 and late 1941, Roosevelt created the OLLA, set up by executive order in October 1941. Edward R. Stettinius, Jr., moved over from the OPM to head the administration. He had been acting informally in that capacity since September. Roosevelt delegated to Stettinius all his lend-lease authority except the critical matters of selecting countries for assistance (which was to be shared with the Economic Defense Board [EDB]) and negotiating master agreements with recipient nations (which the State Department would work out with the advice of the OLLA and the EDB). Nonetheless, Harry L. Hopkins remained involved with the aid program, as he had been from the outset.

OLLA was never an operating agency; it always had a relatively small, compact staff. The office depended on other permanent and wartime agencies to carry out procurement, production, and distribution functions under its general supervision. Munitions, for example, were handled through the War and Navy Departments and the Munitions Assignment Board (MAB); food and food products through the Agriculture Department/WFA. Overall, OLLA had enormous responsibilities. Through June 1945, it oversaw accounts in excess of $48 billion; reverse Lend-Lease and related programs netted nearly $8 billion. By the end of 1941, some thirty-eight countries had been certified for lend-lease assistance, although the overwhelming amount of aid throughout the war years went first to Britain and second to the Soviet Union; all other nations received crumbs by comparison.[11]

The Roosevelt administration took its first step involving international economic warfare in July 1940 by selecting Lieutenant Colonel Russell L.

Maxwell of the General Staff Corps as administrator of export control.[12] Maxwell's appointment was based on and took place almost immediately after the passage of the Export Embargo Act. This statute granted the president the authority to regulate the export of munitions and supplies, materials, and equipment involving national defense. Henceforth, all designated items, including most of the ANMB's lists of strategic and critical materials, could be exported only through licenses issued by the State Department's Division of Controls at the direction of Maxwell's office. While the statute acted to defend America's interests, it could be and was used to withhold needed goods from potential enemies. The Office of Export Control was largely staffed by military personnel, and it was influenced heavily by ANMB, which had been working steadily on the economics of defense and war throughout the interwar years. During over a year of activity, the office constantly broadened the list of munitions, supplies, and materials embargoed or regulated, particularly where Japan was involved. By 1941, however, it was becoming clear that a better administration capable of more aggressive action was needed. The armed services were particularly anxious to broaden their activity in the area, but civilian agencies generally opposed military control, and they were ultimately backed by the White House. After months of consideration, the Bureau of the Budget fashioned a new agency, the EDB.

Created by executive order at the end of July 1941, the EDB was chaired by Vice-President Henry A. Wallace and included the secretaries of state, the treasury, war, the navy, agriculture, and commerce along with the attorney general. All these departments or offices were concerned about or involved in international economics of defense. EDB would direct and coordinate their activity, which was defined to include exports, imports, the purchase and sale of goods (including preclusive buying), foreign exchange, foreign-owned or -controlled property, investments, credits, patents, transportation, communications, and other economic functions. With the organization of the Supply Priorities and Allocations Board (SPAB) in August 1941, the responsibility and authority of EDB grew: it now calculated total defense-related export requirements (excluding Lend-Lease), took over the duties of other offices operating in the area, and could license all exports falling within its jurisdiction. The board had become an operating agency as well as one for planning and coordinating.

Shortly after the United States entered World War II, the EDB by executive order became the BEW. Wallace's organization became much more active, as did the OLLA, the State Department, and other agencies involved in economics abroad. As long as the nation was preparing for hostilities, decentralization was not that consequential. Once the nation went on the offensive beginning with the North Africa invasion in November 1942, however, decentralization became a serious drawback to America's conduct of the war. As attempts to consolidate foreign economics in the State Department during 1943 broke down, the Roosevelt administration turned to setting up a new agency outside the department. An opening for doing so occurred in June 1943 when Henry A. Wallace, vice-president and director of the BEW, and Jesse H. Jones, head of the RFC, allowed a feud over foreign buying to become public. Removing both officials from dealing with policies abroad, the president by interim steps between July and September 1943 replaced the BEW with the FEA, administered by Leo T. Crowley. Besides BEW and RFC subsidiaries, the FEA took over the OLLA, appropriate parts of the State Department and the WFA, and a host of other offices. Economic warfare, Lend-Lease, export control, foreign procurement, and America's role in relief and rehabilitation were now all conducted from one office. FEA adapted its functions to foreign policy as determined by the State Department. In November 1943, FEA and the Department of State carefully defined the role of each agency in operations abroad and established procedures for resolving conflict between the two. While it took time for FEA to function effectively, no further changes were necessary. As American armies advanced and victory grew nearer, FEA shifted its role from conducting war to administering peace in liberated and conquered areas.

Although unification came late, the nation's economic policies abroad played a vital role in the Allied victory over the Axis powers. America's economic might was exercised principally through the national organizations sketched out briefly above. Britain was anxious to share in American economic decisionmaking through combined boards. Despite the creation of such administrations, none had much success outside the military area.

THE COMBINED BOARDS

The United States and Britain created five combined boards during World War II. The Combined Munitions Assignments Board (more commonly known simply as the MAB), the Combined Raw Materials Board (CRMB), and the Combined Shipping Adjustment Board (CSAB) were set up at the Arcadia Conference, which met in Washington in December 1941 and January 1942; the Combined Food Board (CFB) and the CPRB were organized in June 1942. For complex reasons, only the MAB worked well.

The MAB was charged with determining the best distribution of munitions produced collectively by the Allies for prosecuting the war.[13] It was an outgrowth of the Combined Chiefs of Staff (CCS), which was set up at the Arcadia Conference at Britain's urging to coordinate Allied strategy and to divide resources and services between the two nations. The CCS gained official standing when Roosevelt approved its charter in April 1942. By contrast, the JCS operated without an official directive: it more or less emerged so that America's army, air, and navy chiefs could deal as a collective whole with their British counterparts in the CCS. Once the JCS proved to be effective, Roosevelt increasingly relied on the agency, although denying the staff's request for an executive order enhancing its legitimacy and authority.

The CCS issued a charter for the MAB in February 1942. Consisting of representatives of the two nations' ground, air, and sea forces, MAB was chaired by Harry L. Hopkins. Although the board was subordinate to CCS, Hopkins's presence gave it a special status and indicated that the White House would remain active in channeling American assistance abroad. When announcing MAB's creation in January 1942, the president and the prime minister implied that the United States and Britain would oversee a common munitions pool as equals through boards in Washington and London. Nothing that dramatic took place. Washington dominated MAB since the United States overwhelmingly manufactured the greater share of weapons. That made MAB an agency for distributing lend-lease aid in the form of munitions. At the outset, Hopkins took an active role in directing the board, but, in time, illness and more pressing demands made his attendance at best sporadic.

Throughout hostilities, MAB was always subject to direction, not only from the CCS, but also from American civilian and military authorities reaching as high as the White House. The Army Service Forces, headed by General Brehon B. Somervell, assumed a particularly strong voice in determining how and under what circumstances finished munitions were allocated among the United States, Britain, and other involved nations. (Russia was handled by special protocols.) But the United States did not rely on fiat. The president's continued interest and involvement would not allow that to occur. Instead, MAB decisions were made through ongoing and often intense negotiations between the United States and Great Britain. An elaborate staff, secretariat, and series of committees and subcommittees evolved to carry out most of the board's critical work. MAB was the only combined agency, other than the CCS, that functioned even adequately throughout hostilities and had some defined powers for carrying out its vast responsibilities.

Compared with the MAB, the four other civilian combined boards performed poorly, a result of a common set of circumstances.[14] First, the United States was suspicious of and resistant to combined boards. Britain led in creating them because it was desperate for greater American assistance. At war for over two years, Britain's mobilization system was well perfected and ready to operate in combined structures. Still putting its mobilization structure together, the United States was not yet prepared for such responsibilities. Americans feared that the British would use crisis conditions and their experience, unity, and diplomatic skill excessively to drain American resources.

Second, Roosevelt and Hopkins largely shaped international economic operations. While fully committed to the Atlantic alliance, they remained guarded about British goals and methods. In addition, neither man functioned best in rigid institutional systems; both preferred working informally, often personally, and with the greatest latitude for maneuvering. If combined boards became necessary, the president and his unofficial chief deputy favored keeping them weak.

Third, if Roosevelt and Hopkins thought otherwise, they would probably have had to back off. MAB survived because it was under the CCS and, therefore, the several services. Combined agencies in the civilian sector could challenge the prerogatives of existing mobilization agencies. Hence, before such boards were set up or functioning, the WPB and other agencies moved swiftly to protect their administrative turf. Finally, the various combined boards might have achieved greater strength if they had been under central direction, or at least coordinated, since they shared similar goals and often overlapped or related in areas of interest and responsibility.

For those reasons and more, combined boards were set up only by announcement, not by executive order or some other official act, and their charges were vague and uncertain. None of the boards had much in the way of staff. They usually got along with a few people directing and handling what passed for a central office. Despite lengthy and sweeping declarations about duties, combined boards other than MAB remained advisory, not executive, agencies, restricted to studying, assisting, and recommending. On both sides of the Atlantic, mobilizing resources for war was basically carried out by national, not international, administrations.

Generalizations aside, each combined board had its own peculiarities and levels of success or failure. The most ambitious and least successful was the CPRB, created in June 1942.[15] Seeking to enhance its influence over American output, Britain proposed that the board combine American and British economic mobilization programs into one integrated system. Through collaboration with the CCS, the CPRB could then adjust total Allied production to the requirements of global strategy. Operating from such a broad base, CPRB could also absorb, create, or coordinate the activities of other combined boards. Overall, the board would provide the Allies with a totally rationalized mobilization structure. Donald M. Nelson, chair of America's WPB, and

Oliver Lyttelton, Britain's minister of production, along with their deputies, constituted the board, which was expanded in November 1942 with the addition of Canadian representatives.

CPRB was strongly and enthusiastically supported in certain American circles. Donald M. Nelson, Robert R. Nathan, Stacy May, and others from WPB, along with Bureau of the Budget staff, seized on the board as a means to advance at home something comparable to a supreme war production council of civilians and the military for comprehensively coordinating production and strategy.[16] At the outset, they had the critical endorsement of Roosevelt and Harry L. Hopkins. But, for CPRB, a war production council, or both to succeed, the American military had to cooperate. It would not do so because a strong CPRB or a strengthened WPB would diminish armed services prerogatives. As a result, CPRB essentially died before it was born. Even Churchill's personal intervention with Roosevelt could not save it.

Once it became clear in late 1942 that CPRB would not succeed, nearly all abandoned it, including Roosevelt, Hopkins, WPB, other U.S. mobilization agencies, and even the British. The board was not officially buried until December 1945, but, from 1943 on, it was always on the margins of World War II mobilization. In retrospect, Hopkins, Nelson, Nathan, and others were at best misguided in even thinking that they could use an extremely vulnerable combined board to assist them in making the American military more answerable to civilian authority.

The CRMB established a better record than any of the other combined agencies.[17] Set up in January 1942, the board was charged with maximizing the availability, distribution, and use of raw materials among the United States, Great Britain, various territories controlled by the two nations, and other allies. More than any other combined board, CRMB was tied into the WPB, which helps account for its gains. At the outset, William L. Batt represented the United States on CRMB while he also headed WPB's Materials Division and Requirements Committee. (He would later become vice chair for international supply.) Realizing that the board could threaten various agencies and departments, Batt restricted its range of activities. CRMB never tried going beyond studying, reporting, and recommending. What took place on this side of the Atlantic was carried out similarly on the other.

CRMB's accomplishments were modest but significant. While most of its attention was directed to immediate problems involving essential and critical products in short supply, such as manganese, rubber, and wool, CRMB ultimately came up with a reasonably comprehensive assessment of long-run Allied supply and demand for most raw materials. On the basis of these two approaches, it could and did recommend how supply could be expanded, demand cut back, and products best allocated. As Allied victories took place, it expanded its purview to include liberated areas. At a minimum, such data and advice were valuable to concerned mobilization administrations.

The CSAB was the most curious of all the combined boards.[18] Despite the desire of some Americans to have the board operate as charged, it became an agency for extracting from Washington all possible shipping assistance for Britain.

Organized in January 1942 with matching agencies in Washington and London, CSAB supposedly "pooled" the shipping resources of the two countries to handle the critical shipping crisis facing the Allies. Provisions were outlined for an elaborate bureaucracy to carry out weighty responsibilities. At the top of the proposed structure were Admiral Emory S. Land, chair of Maritime Commission, and Sir Arthur Salter, already in the United States as head of the British Merchant Shipping Mission. London shared practically no information with the Washington office, and Salter took over the latter as his lobbying base for Britain. Virtually no organization emerged under those circumstances, and the small American staff became enraged at its insignificance and impotence.

Meanwhile, U.S. shipping policy was shaped by the WSA and other civilian and military institutions. Practically all negotiations over shipping between Britain and the United States occurred away from CSAB. Lewis M. Douglas, WSA head, worked closely and well with Salter, but outside, not inside, CSAB. Salter returned to Great Britain in May 1943, after the shipping crisis had begun to lift. CSAB continued until the war's end as much a shadow as an actual organization.

In the CFB, created in June 1942, the United States reversed positions and treated Britain as the subordinate.[19] That reality grew out of the fact that, during hostilities, America produced or controlled a huge percentage of the world's food supply. Actually, CFB got off to a better start than most combined boards because it had roots in the past instead of having to start from scratch. After the passage of the Lend-Lease Act in March 1941, the United States and Great Britain set up an Anglo-American Food Committee in May to facilitate the flow of agricultural assistance to the latter. In a sense, CFB took over from and extended the work of this committee.

The board was led by Secretary of Agriculture Claude R. Wickard and the head of the British Food Mission in Washington, R. H. Brand, assisted by advisers, deputies, and other support staff. At the insistence of the United States, Canada was added to the board in October 1943. CFB proceeded with great caution during the first six months of 1942. It focused mostly on commodities in short supply and offered recommendations as to how they could best be allocated. Very little was done in terms of planning for overall output and how to increase it, general programs for conservation, and policies for procurement. The board recognized the need for comprehensive figures on Allied production and requirements and initiated surveys to obtain such critical data, but no basis for budgeting agricultural goods existed at the end of 1942. By then, all commodities except wheat were experiencing deficits. Although CFB made some gains, its overall record was at best modest.

By not achieving more in 1942, CFB lost whatever opportunity it had for becoming stronger in the future. Between December 1942 and March 1943, the Roosevelt administration moved to centralize control over the wartime production and distribution of food in the WFA. By then, however, power relations in CFB had shifted in a way unfavorable to Britain. WFA insisted that Britain was only one among many claimants for U.S. food supplies. It should not be operating as America's equal in CFB, and other nations should be included in board operations. Britain maneuvered to keep additional representatives limited to Canada, but it could not prevent the United States from looking on it as a subordinate within CFB. After October 1943, the combined board's pace quickened, but its focus was more on international food sources. That was the case because the WFA and other American mobilization agencies determined on their own how the nation's agricultural products, materials, equipments, and the like would be allocated abroad. This trend became more prevalent as emphasis began shifting in 1944 from war to relief and rehabilitation. CFB continued in existence until June 1946, when its responsibilities were absorbed by the International Emergency Food Council.

In general, the four combined boards of World War II were defined more by their limitations than by their strengths. Nonetheless, in differing ways, at a minimum each facilitated communication between the United States and Britain. The CRMB achieved the strongest record because the two nations approached equality in the vital area of raw materials. Since neither nation was willing to share national mobilization powers with the other, the CPRB accomplished the least. Britain's critical dependence on shipping made the nation ruthless in protecting its interests at America's expense. Realizing how vulnerable its ally was, the United States was willing to go along, particularly since the WSA was in such strong hands. America's overwhelming dominance in the agricultural sector allowed it to treat Britain in an offhand way.

The MAB was the one exception among the combined boards. Its relative success stemmed from direct ties to the Joint and Combined Chiefs of Staff and the White House. Roosevelt remained commander-in-chief almost until the war's end, and he and Churchill relied heavily on their chiefs of staff and the combined chiefs. Under such circumstances, the MAB could not fail. No other combined board had such underwriting.

When the other combined boards faltered or failed in crucial matters, America and Britain resolved problems on a higher or different plane. The success of war and peace depended on continued cooperation between the two nations.

11

CONVERTING AND EXPANDING INDUSTRY, 1942

The most immediate and pressing responsibility of the War Production Board (WPB) from January 1942 forward was converting the economy from peacetime to wartime production. Although this process got off to a slow and contentious start, it was largely completed by June 1942.

The Office of Civilian Supply (OCS) had been among the leading advocates for conversion in the Office of Production Management (OPM), and it continued to play that role during the first half of 1942. Once industry had completed modifying its facilities for war output and WPB increasingly emphasized munitions, OCS had to reorient its attention to protecting the civilian economy. In doing so, the office fought to maintain its power in altered circumstances and to improve its methods for representing civilians. Along those lines, OCS worked to encourage converted consumer goods industries to concentrated output in a few firms, to ensure availability of materials for the output of essential civilian goods, to maintain stable prices, and related activities. By mid-1942, however, the office's efforts in behalf of the civilian economy became more and more difficult to carry out.

Tied into conversion were programs for enlarging existing or constructing new plants for materials, semifinished products, and end items to meet the vastly expanded demands of modern warfare. Most of the facilities were built in 1942, but the process continued at a lessened pace throughout the war years.

At all times, plant expansion was troubled, and it generated a great deal of controversy. WPB had to move quickly to bring some order to a chaotic facilities program inherited from its predecessors. The board halted all nonessential building early in 1942, and, by slow stages, it forced the armed services to limit their facilities expansion to feasible levels. Most of the $26 billion spent on wartime industrial facilities went to the large corporate structure. Nonetheless, these expenditures brought about some change. The aluminum monopoly, for example, was broken up and industrialization in the Midwest,

West, and South accelerated. Disposing of government-financed or -built plant during and after World War II was conservative in nature and subject to a great deal of political pressure.

CONVERSION

When the WPB commenced operations in January 1942, it faced formidable production goals. On the basis of estimates and calculations of the Supply Priorities and Allocations Board (SPAB), the president set the War Munitions Program for 1942 at around $50–$55 billion, including 60,000 planes, 45,000 tanks, 20,000 antiaircraft guns, and 8 million deadweight tons of merchant ships. Such a level of output would total approximately 50 percent of the estimated GNP. Since overall munitions production and defense construction at the end of 1941 stood at only $14.7 billion, reaching Roosevelt's targets would require almost a fourfold increase in munitions output and building. WPB had to turn immediately to converting the civilian economy to war output and accelerating the construction of needed facilities and equipment.[1]

Conversion fell to the Division of Industry Operations, the most important subdivision of the board in the first half of 1942. It directed the Bureau of Priorities, other bureaus of consequence, and, most important, the Bureau of Industry Branches and the Bureau of Industry Advisory Committees. James S. Knowlson, president and chairman of the Stewart-Warner Corporation, a manufacturing firm, who had served under Donald M. Nelson in the OPM as deputy director of priorities, headed the Division of Industry Operations. The day-to-day work of conversion was overseen by Philip D. Reed, director of the Bureau of Industry Branches, who was also chairman of the board of the General Electric Company. The industry branches—totaling forty-two in March 1942—were the basic working units of the WPB and grew steadily in significance and power.

Authority resided with the branch chief, who could not be from the regulated industry. Those below him could be, however, and, in most industry branches, that was the case. To aid his work, the chief could call on WPB representatives, such as those from divisions and units for production, civilian supply, labor, and statistics, and the Office of the General Counsel. Ultimately, major claimants assigned personnel to most of the industry branches. Nearly all branches were assisted by one or more industry advisory committees. With such broad potential or actual representation, the branch served as the principal contact between the WPB and an industry in maximizing production. It dealt with conversion and curtailment, financing new or expanded facilities, obtaining materials, components, and equipment, labor supply, and related matters.[2]

To meet the astronomical production goals set by the president, WPB had to curtail and convert a huge portion of industry to munitions output. Prudence and the lack of time, facilities, equipment, and materials limited the amount of new plant that could be built. The process of curtailing and converting the economy was not done either methodically or expeditiously. At no time did the board draw up an overall plan or draft general policies for what to do. Instead, WPB improvised. Convinced that industrialists knew best how to adapt industries to war needs, Knowlson and Reed had the industry branches rapidly recruit hundreds of executives, with most serving for a dollar a year. The general, guiding idea was to match conversion with the availability of war contracts so as to keep facilities going and employees in place. With this approach, progress was slow. By mid-March, conversion was barely started.[3]

There were substantive reasons for the delay. With WPB just getting under way, confusion was rife and clear directions hard to establish. This limiting condition was complicated by the fact that conversion had to be guided by requirements and that none of the major claimants, particularly the armed services, could produce reliable figures about demand. Moreover, without conducting or controlling procurement, WPB could not effectively synchronize curtailment and conversion with placement of war contracts. Automobiles was one of the few industries converted in its entirety to war output. Most, such as refrigerators, farm equipment, bicycles, typewriters, and others, maintained partial output to fulfill civilian requirements as well as military and other wartime demand. Working out policies for converting only a part of an industry, even when a high percentage of capacity was involved, often presented numerous difficult, at times intractable, problems. Little experience existed to guide industry branches as they searched for solutions.

Still, industry was generally slow to give up business-as-usual outlooks and resisted rigorous conversion policies. Most conversion was carried out by the use of L or M orders. The former prohibited in part or whole the production of certain items, principally consumer goods; the latter limited how scarce materials could be used. These were very effective, flexible regulatory devices that could be adapted to practically any situation and combined with or replaced by priority, equipment, and conservation orders. The industry branches were exceptionally cautious in the use and enforcement of these orders.

Lagging conversion became headline news in mid-March 1942. Robert R. Gutherie, who had served in OPM, had been assistant chief of the Bureau of Industry Branches, and was currently heading the Textile, Clothing, and

Leather Goods Branch, resigned from the WPB, as did his primary assistants. In resigning, Gutherie publicly castigated Reed and dollar-a-year men in WPB for purposefully holding back conversion. Nelson called on the Senate Special Committee to Investigate the National Defense Program (also known as the Truman Committee) to investigate Gutherie's charges. The committee was already on record in opposition to the continued use of industry executives volunteering their services. While recognizing the complexity of conversion and the legitimacy of differing approaches, the committee still validated most of Gutherie's accusations, held Reed largely responsible for the poor record, pointed out that, in OPM, Reed had ignored the need to expand production of strategic metals, and reiterated its objections to dollar-a-year men.[4]

A few days after Gutherie's resignation, Knowlson stepped in to expedite curtailment and conversion. From mid-March 1942 on, the process began seriously and was fairly well accomplished in less than three months. In March and April, orders were issued to halt the production of domestic laundry equipment, metal windows, and other products and to curtail the output of typewriters, electric appliances, and the like. On April 7, Donald M. Nelson publicly declared that further orders would be immediately released shutting down completely consumer durable goods using critical metals, prohibiting the use of iron and steel in hundreds of products, and cutting off all nonessential construction. The various orders did not go fully into effect until midyear. By then, however, using total purchases in 1939 as a base, only 39 percent of production capacity was free of conversion, curtailment, or control. Manufacturers continuing peacetime output did not rely on critical materials or industries, particularly producers' durable goods, later classified as war related. Little actual new munitions production took place in the first half of 1942; this was the phase of preparation. But numerous firms sold more of their peacetime production for war uses. The vast output of converted facilities occurred in the last five months of 1942.

A war economy would obviously be different from that of peace, with certain characteristics and problems. Surveys as early as May 1942 indicated that most war and munitions work was concentrated among large firms. The majority of companies found a place once mobilization hit stride. Still, a great many companies were left out. Of the nation's approximately 184,000 manufacturing firms, around 78,700, or 43 percent, could not be used for war production and could not be spared critical materials for nonessential output at even curtailed rates. These firms were those principally in the small to medium-sized range. Special efforts were necessary to ensure that whole sectors of the economy were not wiped out and the shape of the economy not modified in significant and unwanted ways.[5]

Converting and curtailing the economy in the first half of 1942 also revealed an important pattern in the politics of mobilization. Once war production was seriously under way, the large corporate structure, which had held up conversion before hostilities, stressed the need for maximizing munitions and related output and minimizing production for civilian purposes. Conversely, the prewar all-outers argued that needlessly squeezing the civilian population would retard, not advance, mobilization. With the armed services joining the large corporate community, civilian supply subdivisions within WPB were thrown on the defensive in 1942 and remained in that position throughout the war years.

The major advocates of rapid, even radical, conversion and curtailment prior to Pearl Harbor came from nonbusiness sources. During 1941, the Office of Price Administration and Civilian Supply (OPACS)—later the Division of Civilian Supply in OPM—headed a drive for curtailment under the aggressive leadership of Director Leon Henderson and Deputy Director Joseph L. Weiner. WPB continued the Division of Civilian Supply—which, in July 1942, became OCS—under the same leadership. With Henderson preoccupied with the Office of Price Administration (OPA) and other duties, Weiner took actual charge of OCS.

OCS had less clout in WPB than it had had in OPM. In OPM, OCS directed industry branches not directly involved in munitions. In WPB, it controlled no industry branches. While OCS had civilian supply specialists serving in most industry branches, they were ultimately reduced to only advisory status, and various civilian mobilization agencies, such as the Office of Defense Transportation (ODT), insisted on stating their own requirements, not doing so through OCS. Increasingly, the office spoke only for otherwise unrepresented consumers.[6]

Despite its waning power, OCS still carried weight within WPB counsels during the first half of 1942.[7] Weiner was a respected and feared powerhouse who sat on the important Requirements Committee and who was determined to convert the economy as quickly as possible. His determination gave him an advantage in an organization that continued to hesitate about mobilization. Furthermore, Henderson was a member of WPB, and he still had close connections with the White House to which OCS could turn if necessary. OPACS/OCS had forced OPM to initiate a program for cutting back automobile production, and it began moving to curtail other consumer durable goods when war broke out. OCS played a significant role in the limited progress that WPB made in conversion and curtailment during the first three months. The office was strongly backed by the Labor/Labor Production Division and the Planning Committee. All these WPB subdivisions were led and staffed primarily by nonbusiness elements.

Under Weiner, OCS was so absorbed in conversion that the office neglected its critical duty of providing requirement figures for and protecting the interests of the civilian economy. Indeed, a staff member characterized OCS as "a war-making agency," "stripping" the economy for hostilities.[8] That was one of the reasons for the ODT and other civilian mobilization agencies fighting to break free of the OCS control. OCS appeared to be following Henderson's reasoning of 1941 that maximum mobilization met escalating munitions demand while also preparing to provide for civilian needs during a protracted war. Nonetheless, as early as January 1942, OCS began moving from the theoretical to the practical by devising programs for meeting civilian needs for critical materials in a war economy. But, up through spring 1942, OCS operated on what came to be called a residual supply principle: those producing for a civilian and indirect military market would receive whatever was left unclaimed by the armed services or for export. OCS would ensure that available materials and goods in short supply were equitably distributed among claimants within the civilian area.

With military requirements escalating exponentially, the residual approach began threatening to deny the civilian economy minimum needs. Under such circumstances, OCS early in June abandoned a leftover policy for one that broadly defined essential civilian and indirect military requirements: minimum goods and services for maintaining civilian health and morale and for ensuring production to meet war and essential civilian needs. These broadly defined categories, however, were not converted into specific programs. Unlike military, export, and ODT requirements, those for the economy as a whole were exceptionally difficult to calculate except in general terms and on the basis of historical usage.

Conversion, paradoxically, blunted OCS's offensive position and put it on the defensive. Once WPB was fully dedicated to production for war, it downplayed the significance of civilian and indirect military needs. Weiner was much less effective in his reversed role. When fighting for his sector, he began insisting that military requirements were too high and unexamined, that they needed to be thoroughly scrutinized by the Requirements Committee and its subdivisions for accuracy and balance. The army and navy denied WPB the right to review figures on the grounds of classified military strategy. Yet the services demanded that all civilian requirements be assessed and justified since OCS offered only generalities, not specific programs. Actively or passively, industrialists on the Requirements Committee, in the industry divisions, and in other WPB subdivisions backed the armed services' position. Nelson sided with Weiner, but, as the industry-military alliance began to solidify within the

WPB, OCS, along with other nonbusiness staff groupings, faced increasing opposition.

A. C. C. Hill, Jr., an assistant to Donald M. Nelson who served in mobilization agencies throughout the defense and war years, pointed to the ridiculousness of civilians being placed in the position of claimants on a civilian economy. He lashed out at America's "cockeyed" approach to fighting a war without the chiefs of supply and strategy closely coordinating their work. "The British knew they needed more safety pins," he noted, "so they made safety pins; we stopped making them, and had to argue with an Admiral Robinson or an Admiral Williams as to whether babies needed them, or whether the scarcity of clothing might not require more safety pins."[9]

Before it slipped into secondary status, OCS became a principal advocate of a highly controversial effort to concentrate production among firms in curtailed industries.[10] If, say, the stove industry was curtailed to 75 percent of normal output, many firms would turn to war production while a system was devised for concentrating reduced manufacturing among companies unsuitable or less suitable for conversion. These "nucleus plants" would usually be the smaller, undiversified companies unable to survive under drastically changed market conditions. Ideally, they would manufacture generic, simplified, and standardized models during the emergency.

The program originated late in 1941 as OPM struggled with the issue of converting industry to war. Once conversion was under way, concentration was pushed as a means to ensure minimal production for civilian and indirect military needs, to help maintain economic stability by holding down prices, and to ensure full and efficient use of plant, equipment, materials, and labor. Furthermore, with war production favoring large firms, smaller companies would be protected. Germany and Great Britain had implemented concentration programs. OCS began advocating this expedient in February 1942 when steel was in short supply.

With industry branches generally uninterested in or opposed to concentration, the OCS turned to Leon Henderson, who raised the issue with WPB late in April 1942. Henderson's advocacy set off an acrimonious debate in the board. Director of Industry Operations James S. Knowlson, speaking for most, but not all, industry branches, argued that the concentration process would naturally occur as curtailment took place, that it should not be made mandatory, and that it was not an unmixed blessing. Henderson was supported in general, although not in all details, by OCS, the Labor Production Division, OPA, and, ultimately, the Planning Committee, which later authored an elaborate plan for concentrating curtailed industries. With OCS refining its analysis of the process and Henderson continuing to insist on action, a reluctant WPB in July 1942 finally approved concentration in principle and spelled out various criteria for its application. The board may have been more favorable to proposals for concentration because Congress in June 1942 passed the Small Business Act, or the Murray-Patman Bill, aimed at WPB mobilizing small business more effectively for prosecuting the war. Also, Nelson was more open to examination of and experimentation with the program than was Knowlson.

Late in August, WPB created a Committee on Concentration. It was chaired by OCS Deputy Director Weiner, with members from the Labor Production Division, the Office of the Director General for Operations, what became the Smaller War Plants Division, and others as needed. The committee was to select industries for concentration and review plans for the process. The plans would be written by the industry branches under the supervision of the director general for operations. (Several informal committees led by OCS had been analyzing the problems of concentration since June.) By dividing responsibility for concentration between, in effect, OCS and the industry branches, WPB institutionalized stalemate. The Concentration Committee over a period of months designated thirteen industries for concentration. Industry branches wrote plans for only five: those for stoves, bicycles, and typewriters never got off the ground; and those for farm machinery and pulp and paper in the Pacific Northwest were full-blown programs implemented without much success. The farm machinery industry fiercely resisted concentration, while pulp and paper was much more amenable. At the end of December 1942, on the basis of earlier administrative arrangements, the director general for operations set up a Concentration Division. By then, however, the experiment had all but died.

The drive for concentration never stood a realistic chance of adoption short of a national and ongoing disaster. Industry branches were generally opposed and chronically dragged their feet. Concentration threatened existing and accepted industry practices, it radically disturbed competitive positions, and it brought the government into the day-to-day operations of industrial activity. WPB's top leadership either shared industry branches' opposition or remained uncertain, but it never insisted that the branches move expeditiously on planning or implementation.

There were enormous complications to concentration, problems that, at times, Henderson, Weiner, and some other advocates glossed over or ignored. Concentration plans often aimed at medium-sized and small firms and at moving civilian production out of labor-shortage areas. Yet, for various reasons, some large companies had difficulty converting to war production, and workers often could not or would not move readily from one job to another. Even more basic was the fact that reliable planning for concentrating production was extremely difficult in 1942 because military requirements were changing and OCS did not have detailed information on projected civilian and indirect military demand. A related problem was that, without controlling procurement, WPB could and did find itself in the position of curtailing production among firms with which the armed services and the Maritime Commission began placing a great many contracts. Additionally, plants selected for concentration could be among the most inefficient and limited in range in terms of production, thereby wasteful of scarce resources and unable dependably to meet varying demand. Also, since the United States is so large in size and transportation was so limited during the war, locating production far from raw materials and markets could significantly run up costs and the consumption of goods and services. Storage space, repair parts, and other difficulties complicated further concentration programs. Hence, what worked in Great Britain and Germany might not work in the United States with its difference in size, methods of mobilization, and peacetime industrial practices.

All these challenges could have been met had industry been interested in making concentration work. It was not, and that was the basic cause of the effort's failure. (That labor was a principal backer of concentration and that its advisory committees, along with those from industry, would be consulted on all or most programs probably acted to strengthen industry's resistance. The fact that the armed services either favored industry's position, intentionally or unintentionally undermined programs, or remained aloof from the debate lent further support to business's opposition.)

More immediately, the program went down because WPB was unable to solve the vexatious issue of compensating firms closed down by concentration. Some mobilization leaders, such as Under Secretary of War Robert P. Patterson, argued that companies adversely affected by concentrating production were, like draftees, forced to sacrifice for a larger cause and need not be compensated. Weiner at first supported the concept of compensation but later argued that its complexity was holding up progress and should be bypassed. Most war mobilizers, however, insisted that compensation was necessary practically and in terms of equity and justice for involved companies and industries. Henderson held to that position from the beginning, and so did most of industry and WPB executives. Closing down firms by government fiat created too many adverse precedents. Moreover, national interests, a sense of fair play, and postwar competitiveness within various industries required that plant and equipment be preserved during the war years. Without some form of compensation, few firms could afford to keep their facilities intact on their own.

Compensation could take various forms. Government-financed programs were ruled out. WPB lacked the resources, and the Treasury Department and other agencies were uninterested. Any program would have to be privately covered. With a number of variations, there were two possible approaches. The first involved an industrywide compensation fund in which, according to approved formulas, operating firms made payments to reimburse companies forced to close down. The second was based on closed plants selling their quota of production manufactured by operating firms.

When the WPB approved concentration in July 1942, it purposefully avoided the issue of compensation. Without clear guidance from the top, WPB subdivisions could not arrive at a generally acceptable approach. Most agreed that, without WPB making private compensation mandatory, industry would not move. In an attempt to break the compensation stalemate, WPB on December 1, 1942, took up the contentious issue only to sidestep it again. With the board continuing to divide over the compensation issue, Nelson finally turned to General Counsel John Lord O'Brian for a legal opinion as to whether the board could require corporations to participate in a compensation scheme. Late in January 1943, O'Brian concluded that WPB did not have the authority to institute compulsory programs and that even voluntary arrangements were questionable and would have to pass the scrutiny of the WPB, the Justice and Treasury Departments, OPA, and the Office of Economic Stabilization.

To go forward, therefore, privately based compensation required legislation. WPB never explored that option. By early 1943, the war was looking more favorable for the Allies, production was starting to improve, and the WPB was in the process of solving critical problems of materials control and production scheduling. Without a sense of urgency, the cause of concentration stalled, and, despite attempts to reorient and revive it, WPB finally abandoned the controversial proposal in February 1943.

OCS—PROTECTING THE CIVILIAN ECONOMY

During the height of the struggle over concentrating production in certain industries, OCS entered the most intense phase of its fight for authority and effectiveness within the WPB.[11] A series of events late in 1942 and early in 1943 triggered the crisis. In December 1942, Leon Henderson, who had led in mobilizing the economy since 1940 along reform lines, resigned as director of both OPA and OCS. For varying reasons, Congress was growing antagonistic toward him, and he had lost favor in the White House. Henderson's departure in December 1942, even more than Roosevelt's declaration in December 1943, loudly proclaimed that "Dr. New Deal" had given way to "Dr. Win-the-War." Henderson and Weiner, who took over as OCS head, were a close team in OPM and WPB, but Henderson was the undisputed, irreplaceable giant. OCS had lost a formidable defender.

Around the same time, the new materials allocation system—the Controlled Materials Plan (CMP)—was being phased in. Under it, OCS lost significant ground to the industry divisions—its principal rivals in WPB—in the critical areas of determining, programming, and scheduling indirect military requirements such as those necessary for the maintenance, repair, and operation of industry. Additionally, independent agencies for materials, goods, and services like petroleum, food, and transportation were allowed to determine and handle their own requirements free of OCS supervision. OCS was left to speak only for the consumer. Even in this area, however, Weiner's leadership of the office came under criticism, not only from other WPB officials, but also from the Planning Committee. OCS, it was charged, weakened efforts in behalf of consumers by not coming up with specific requirements for items like stoves, laundry equipment, clothing, food, etc. Definite numbers were needed to work out programs, allocate materials, and schedule production.

Late in 1942 and early in 1943, Weiner launched an intense, no-holds-barred attack to strengthen OCS. He argued that the agency's loss of authority and its unclarified authority, along with the fragmentation of control over civilian supply, prevented OCS from fulfilling its duties. The general population was left exposed and the economy inadequately protected, threatening the war effort by reducing the nation's production potential. By focusing almost exclusively on munitions and neglecting civilian needs, WPB was inviting the public's wrath.

In the latter part of January 1943, Weiner finally concluded that the civilian economy required an agency separate from and equal to the armed services. He was not alone. In and outside WPB, concern, even alarm, was growing over the neglect of the civilian sector. Congress had considered the possibility of setting up an administration for the civilian economy early in 1942, without result. With tensions mounting, several congressional committees were investigating the subject in January 1943, the most important of which was the Senate Special Committee to Study and Survey Problems of Small Business Enterprise, headed by Senator James E. Murray (the Murray Committee). Surveys and hearings revealed high levels of discontent among retailers, wholesalers, their organizations, and other consumer-associated groups with WPB's treatment of civilian supply. In mid-March 1943, the Murray Committee had a bill introduced in the Senate for creating a strong Civilian Supply Administration to serve under the Office of Economic Stabilization.

After hearings, the bill was passed by the Senate on May 10, 1943, and then referred to the House of Representatives.

Although wavering for a time, Donald M. Nelson decided that civilian supply must remain in WPB. In April 1943, he moved quickly to head off congressional action. He elevated OCS's status within WPB, placed the office under its own vice chair, and changed its name to the Office of Civilian Requirements (OCR). He then set out to recruit a nationally prominent and powerful new leader, not an easy task. After Roosevelt extended an invitation and Nelson met his demands, Arthur D. Whiteside, president of Dun and Bradstreet, Incorporated, who had previously served in the OPM, reluctantly accepted the post. OCR's mission was narrowed from the entire civilian economy to include only consumer goods and services. In dealing with those areas, the office's functions and authority were clearly spelled out. Moreover, OCR reported directly to Nelson. At least on paper, civilian needs would no longer be treated as an afterthought within WPB. To emphasize the point, Nelson also simultaneously organized the Civilian Requirements Policy Committee in the board, chaired by him, with Whiteside as his deputy, and composed of representatives from the Department of Agriculture, the War Manpower Commission, the Petroleum Administration for War, and ODT. This new board was designed to coordinate within WPB the policies of various agencies affecting consumers. Nelson's action had the anticipated effect of killing in the House of Representatives the Senate bill for a separate civilian supply administration.

Whiteside's formal appointment to OCR occurred on May 1, 1943; he resigned from the post on February 19, 1944. Following the turbulence of the Henderson-Weiner period, this was a prosaic phase. No longer was the office focused on the whole economy and stressing civilian sacrifice. Instead, it concentrated on what the civilian population required to maintain its "productive efficiency, health, and morale."[12] So reoriented, academic and professional leadership gave way to that principally from business and sales.

Under Whiteside's leadership, OCR stressed collecting factual data about civilian requirements. Weiner and his assistants had estimated civilian requirement on the basis of past consumption patterns, population trends, availability of materials, and minimum needs. Whiteside had his organization survey the population in addition to wholesale and retail sources to determine civilian needs. Such information was then combined with Weiner's theoretical approach to arrive at projected civilian demand. With those calculations, OCR provided what had been seriously missing under Weiner's leadership: programs for specific end products, particularly for goods in short supply. Compared with its focus in the earlier period, OCR also paid more attention to rationing, price controls, the equitable geographic distribution of consumer goods, and the availability of consumer services, such as repair shops, restaurants, and construction trades.

OCR became a more effective agency for protecting consumer interests than it had been under Weiner's stormy direction. Congress and other critics were reassured that civilians were receiving adequate, although hardly ample, goods and services. Weiner and Henderson, however, had been fighting a larger battle. They were aiming at mobilizing the economy while maintaining New Deal, reform values. Within that larger framework, civilian supply tended to become obscured or subordinated. Whiteside made OCR perform better by narrowing its focus. But that also meant that the office lost much of its importance in WPB operations.

Nonetheless, OCR still operated in an unfriendly, if not hostile, environment. In an agency devoted to munitions output and coming under the domination of an industry-military production team, civilian supply was treated as secondary, even frivolous. For that reason, among others, Whiteside practically surrendered his direction of the office to his deputy, A. C. C. Hill, Jr., in December 1943 and resigned on February 19, 1944. Hill, a Nelson protégé, was fully qualified to take over from Whiteside. He had taught economics, spent time with the Brookings Institution, and left the Guaranty Trust Company in 1940 to join the National Defense Advisory Commission (NDAC). Unable to recruit a prominent name for a thankless job, Nelson passed over Hill to appoint William Y. Elliott as the new vice chairman for civilian requirements in early May 1944. Nelson did so in part because his relations with Charles E. Wilson were deteriorating. Hill was in Nelson's camp and known to be anti-Wilson. Elliott, a Harvard University professor of government who had been involved in mobilization since NDAC and knew WPB thoroughly, worked well and easily with the board's industrial leadership.

Elliott recruited an excellent staff that, like that of Weiner, had a definite academic orientation. With some success, the new vice chair attempted to reduce industry's hostility directed at OCR by his straightforward leadership, free of hidden agendas. Along those lines, he set up a business advisory group to better inform and support OCR policies. Elliott also improved on and, in some instances, went beyond techniques and procedures introduced by Whiteside. Under Elliott's direction, OCR became a persistent, vociferous, and effective advocate for the general population. Nonetheless, civilian needs remained secondary, and industry was unwilling to give any ground to OCR. Indeed, the office's responsibilities grew more challenging in 1944–1945 as manpower shortages and reconversion policies made production for civilians among the most controversial issues. America ended the war as it had begun it, fighting over the level of civilian production.

Compared, however, with the populations of other belligerent nations, Americans on the whole fared well during hostilities. Consumers spent more (in constant-dollar terms) for goods and services during the war years than they had in 1939. By 1944, the figure was about 10 percent higher.[13] Nonetheless, there was still privation, shortages, and deterioration in quality. The civilian population was probably squeezed more than was necessary. That resulted from decisionmaking by an industry-military production team excessively focused on mutual interests rather than on those of the nation as a whole.

FACILITIES EXPANSION

Curtailing and converting civilian industries by itself never met the material demands of war, particularly in view of the nation's limited munitions capacity. Building and equipping new plants got under way no later than 1939, and the pace steadily grew during 1940 and 1941. At the time of Pearl Harbor, nonetheless, America still had a long way to go. Most wartime construction took place in 1942. The process of building facilities, however, always had a decentralized, improperly organized, and haphazard quality to it that at times threatened to destabilize the entire economic mobilization effort.

Several reasons account for this state of affairs. First, a firm and feasible war munitions program was not adopted until the end of 1942, after the bulk of facilities had already been built, were being built, or were scheduled to be built. After 1942, military requirements and other demands continued to change because of war exigencies. Without reliable requirement figures, the quantity, nature, and pace of facilities expansion could not be intelligently set, let alone properly programmed and scheduled. Second, authority over new facilities was divided between the WPB and the armed services, and, within those institutions, various subdivisions formulated and implemented construction policies without adequate coordination. Finally, the construction industry consisted of numerous relatively small, individualistic firms that were difficult to regulate and control.[14]

Despite all these limitations, the amount of new and expanded plant put in place during the defense and war years was vast and impressive. Between June 1940 and December 1944, total spending for facilities at home and abroad reached a figure just short of $68.9 billion, 47 percent of which was federally financed.[15] Manufacturing plant and equipment expansion totaled nearly $26 billion, around 61 percent of which was federally financed. These figures increased the dollar value of the nation's industrial plant by nearly two-thirds in unadjusted terms from what it was in the beginning of 1940. In actual value, the figure is probably closer to between one-quarter and one-third.[16] During 1942 alone, overall facility expansion was somewhat under $22 billion, and that for manufacturing reached nearly $8.7 billion. The bulk of manufacturing plant was financed directly or indirectly by the War and Navy Departments, the U.S. Maritime Commission, and the Defense Plant Corporation (DPC).[17]

In 1940 and 1941, most munitions output took place in newly constructed plant since the nation had very limited facilities for such production and industry was reluctant to convert peacetime manufacturing capacity. At the outset, a high percentage of the construction and equipping of facilities was privately financed, but, as defense demands escalated, increasing amounts were financed by the government. Once the nation entered hostilities, Washington became the principal financier. In 1942, for example, over three-quarters of all manufacturing facilities expansion was federally financed.[18]

Throughout the defense and war years, constructing and equipping new and expanded plant always generated controversy. During the NDAC and OPM periods, disputes repeatedly erupted over whether additional facilities were necessary and where they should be located. In the last months of 1941, the SPAB began concentrating as well on limiting construction in order to conserve steel, aluminum, copper, and other materials in short supply. Between August and October 1941, it started using priorities to limit construction not tied to national defense or necessary to maintain public health and welfare.[19]

Rapidly escalating demand after Pearl Harbor forced the WPB to struggle with construction and facilities policy throughout 1942.[20] After extended deliberation and debate, the board on April 9, 1942, issued Limitation Order L-41, "one of the most basic orders issued by the War Production Board."[21] The order was intended to halt all building not essential to the war effort, including where necessary projects already under way. All residential construction over $500, agricultural structures exceeding $1,000, and private or public industrial, commercial, recreational, institutional, and other construction such as roads, utilities, and the like costing more than $5,000 required special permits. L-41 was amended in 1942 in a way that generally made it even more restrictive. Although not easy to enforce, the order largely stopped nonessential building for the duration of hostilities.

L-41 was administered by the Construction Bureau, organized on May 8, 1942, in the Production Division. While the bureau unified a number of WPB functions involving housing, plants, and related operations, it did not and could not achieve the broad centralized control over construction that many WPB executives felt to be essential. The bureau's authority was too limited, and it faced too many competing sources of power in and outside the WPB, to do more than handle non- or less essential construction. In carrying out its responsibility, the Construction Bureau turned to the negative controls of issuing limitation and conservation orders, administering priorities, and halting construction projects when necessary. Its reach was restricted even more when the bureau was moved from the center of wartime authority in Washington, DC, to New York because of the lack of space and available personnel in the capital.

Curbing or eliminating nonessential construction was relatively easy compared with regulating wartime building programs, which, in 1942, grew so frantic and chaotic that they nearly overwhelmed WPB. The board inherited from OPM a badly fragmented system for overseeing new and expanded facilities. All the industry branches in addition to the Purchase, Production, Labor, and Materials Divisions had a role in such construction. Outside WPB, conditions were equally bad or worse. L-41 exempted from WPB control construction carried out by the army, navy, Maritime Commission, and other government agencies, along with facilities for mining and petroleum production. In March and April 1942, Donald M. Nelson signed bilateral agreements with the under secretaries of war and the navy that granted the services the right to handle their own facility programs. War housing programs were also carried out under a number of government agencies. WPB officials complained that they lacked statistics on overall demand for facilities and materials used in construction. Without that information, they could not arrive at a balanced facilities program in which projects were rated according to importance. Matters were made worse by lack of uniform procedures, improper clearance, duplication, and related conditions.

From the outset, the Statistics Division, headed by Stacy May, and Robert R. Nathan's Planning Committee led in attempting to bring some order to the critical but badly disorganized war construction program. Their efforts were a continuation of SPAB/OPM statistical analyses that produced in December 1941 the Victory Program (later the War Munitions Program). The Planning Committee's work with facilities was part of its larger, controversial, and more important struggle in behalf of a feasible munitions program that went on throughout 1942 and was resolved only late in the year after an intense mobilization battle.

The Statistics Division in January 1942 became concerned that the munitions program (and construction as part of it) was getting out of hand. A December 1941 goal of $40 billion, with $6.5 billion earmarked for facilities, had grown by February 1942 to $62 billion, with $14.9 billion, as a low estimate, designated for construction and plant. Figures on construction grew even greater within a few months. Combining its analysis with the Planning

Committee's feasibility study, the Statistics Division joined the committee in March to warn Donald M. Nelson that the proposed overall facility expansion program would have to be cut nearly in half. Otherwise, it would adversely affect the entire mobilization effort. Although calculating plant and equipment for munitions output was a challenging and undeveloped procedure, the Planning Committee was making progress in the field with the pioneering work of Simon Kuznets. He was concerned that facilities construction would outpace the available supply of machine tools. If that took place, not only would new and expanded plant be delayed, but also munitions production would suffer.

The analysis of the Statistics Division and the Planning Committee was supported by the findings of the Priorities Division of the Army-Navy Munitions Board (ANMB). Colonel J. L. Philips and Commander H. G. Sickel, joint heads of the division, insisted to the board and to Nelson that drastic cuts in the facilities program were essential to avoid a major breakdown in the output of munitions. Because of inadequate planning, the two argued, there was not enough equipment, materials, and other items to meet military demand while constructing facilities in the amounts called for. Trying to do both would result in a paralyzing imbalance:

> If we continue as at present, we shall have plants standing useless for lack of equipment or raw materials, or other things. Other plants will be turning scarce materials into items which cannot be used to oppose the enemy because of the lack of other things which should have been made instead. We shall have guns without gun sights, tanks without guns, planes without sights, ships held up for lack of steel plate, planes which we cannot get to the field of battle because of lack of merchant bottoms.[22]

With the Planning Committee, Statistics Division, and ANMB all calling for action, Nelson in April 1942 created a Committee on Industrial Facilities and Construction, chaired by Nathan and including Philips and Sickel, to review and recommend policy on war facilities. Reporting in May, the committee found that the total construction program for 1942 was around $18 billion, with $16.3 billion federally financed, far beyond both need and feasibility. It recommended that that portion financed by Washington should be cut by about one-third in order to meet munitions requirements while avoiding waste and shortages. The committee further recommended that Nelson, in agreement with the War and Navy Departments, set up a Facilities and Construction Board with full responsibility and authority for maintaining a building program that was essential, economical, and feasible. Such a board, the committee pointed out, could operate effectively only if it was guided by a "higher [mobilization] body" that, on the basis of strategy and production, set overall goals for the economy and determined how the nation's resources should be used.

The Committee on Industrial Facilities and Construction encountered difficulties even before its work was concluded. Only Nathan and Sickel signed the report. Although Philips had played a leading role in committee deliberations and agreed with the committee's findings and recommendations, the army ordered him to file a minority report. In it, the colonel argued that any checks on construction would delay the war effort. Moreover, the War Department rejected outside review, insisting that it was fully capable of managing mobilization activities and that it answered only to the president and Congress.

The War Department felt confident in undermining the committee because it had successfully maneuvered to receive the president's support. Writing to Nelson on May 1, 1942, Roosevelt insisted that all facilities essential for meeting production goals earlier set by the White House and more fully developed by the Joint Chiefs of Staff (JCS) must be built. Most knowledgeable officials recognized that the president's goals were highly inflated.[23]

Acting on the recommendations of the Committee on Industrial Facilities and Construction and White House instructions, Nelson on May 11, 1942, established a Committee on Facilities and Construction, headed by William H. Harrison, director of the Production Division, and including representatives from the military. Harrison, who had been vice-president and chief engineer of the American Telephone and Telegraph Company, had overseen defense construction since NDAC. Following the lead of William S. Knudsen, Harrison viewed civilian mobilization agencies as facilitators for the armed services. At the beginning of July 1942, Harrison left the WPB to serve as a general in the Army Service Forces. Nelson directed the so-called Harrison Committee to review all new facilities projects and those authorized but not yet under way, with the intent of cutting them back to practical, essential, and feasible levels. No construction, excepting synthetic rubber, was to go forward unless it would be producing for the munitions program by July 1943. The committee solved nothing and actually made conditions worse by failing to reduce significantly new facilities for the armed service while curtailing WPB-sponsored construction for the production of strategic materials already in short supply.

Resolution of the growing construction crisis came only late in 1942 through the continued efforts of Nathan's Planning Committee and May's Statistics Division, with the added support of Ferdinand Eberstadt. The latter left ANMB in September 1942 to become a leading WPB executive. The Planning Committee argued to Nelson that, if the military's inflated facilities program was left unmodified, it would seriously harm mobilization. Of particular concern was not only the shortage of machine tools but also the fact that they were poorly distributed. Munitions programs that were on schedule were receiving tools at the expense of those that were behind.

Through constant prodding, and as part of its larger goal of reducing military requirements to feasible limits, the Planning Committee gradually succeeded in reducing a 1942 federally financed construction program that had risen as high as $16.3 billion to $14 billion.[24] Although program costs were still higher than what the Planning Committee considered to be wise, the cuts were substantial. Moreover, at the insistence of WPB, JCS in November 1942 curtailed military munitions programs for 1943 in a way that reduced federally financed facilities for 1943 to an estimated $9.9 billion. On the basis of those figures, construction for 1943 absorbed around 13 percent of the year's wartime spending, compared with nearly 33 percent in 1942.

The Planning Committee had always insisted that, in addition to cutting back on construction, facilities had to be programmed and scheduled for proper balance. While that end was never fully achieved during the war, construction was more carefully planned beginning late in 1942. When becoming program vice chair in November 1942, Eberstadt was intent on eliminating all unnecessary construction, both civilian and military. He had reached that conclusion as chairman of the ANMB, and the report of Sickel and Philips in March 1942 on the chaotic consequences of uncoordinated facilities expansion both helped shape and reflected Eberstadt's thinking. His position put him at odds with various members of the armed services who anxiously sought to halt civilian construction while leaving that for the military unchecked.

In seeking to implement his construction goals, Eberstadt devised a structure intended to assess total facilities requirements as part of the whole mobilization program and rank projects according to their strategic and economic importance. Although still flawed, his was the best scheme for regulating construction put in place during the war years. Drawing on structures that were created before he joined WPB and that ultimately consolidated or replaced various units dealing with facilities in WPB, ANMB, and the War Department, Eberstadt in November 1942 established the Facilities Bureau as a staff service within his Office of Program Vice Chair. The new bureau was directed by Fred Searls, Jr., a tough-minded, no-nonsense mining engineer who was a member of the Planning Committee, had earlier served in the Ordnance Department, and shared the committee's and Eberstadt's views on construction. The Facilities Bureau operated through the Facility Clearance Board (which cleared construction projects valued at $500,000 and above) and the Facility Review Committee (which had responsibility for facilities costing between

$100,000 and $500,000). Searls's bureau was to centralize WPB control over all construction, determine requirements of and programs for facilities, and report its findings to the Requirements Committee. The Facilities Bureau concentrated its efforts on the most critical of the generally lagging construction programs, including those for aluminum, carbon and alloy steel, synthetic rubber, and aviation gasoline. To hasten the construction of these facilities, the bureau scheduled their materials and components and acted as a claimant agency on their behalf under the CMP. It went one step further by ranking critical facilities on the basis of JCS determinations so that such projects would benefit from priority deliveries.

The Facilities Bureau made significant progress in regulating wartime construction. Its major accomplishments involved the most critical projects, but the bureau still managed to bring greater order to the badly disorganized general facilities program. What the bureau failed to do, however, was achieve meaningful programming in which all new and expanded facilities were ranked according to their significance and coordinated with scheduled end-item output. The Facilities Bureau still dealt with construction on a project-by-project basis. Under that approach, armed services representatives who dominated review agencies generally avoided critically examining military proposals, fought for their projects, and resisted WPB efforts to expand its authority over facilities at the expense of procurement agencies.

Some mobilizers had argued from the beginning that, unlike end items, construction could not be programmed. Fully developed and stable requirements were unavailable and too many variables involved for close and careful planning. The most that could be done, these critics insisted, was to handle facilities case by case. Although such claims remained in dispute throughout the war years, the experience of Eberstadt and Searls suggested that WPB lacked the will or the skill, and probably both, to program construction meaningfully. Whatever the case, at the end of 1942, urgent handling of facilities for alloy steel, carbon steel, synthetic rubber, and aviation gasoline had improved. But machine tools, the major bottleneck for war output, had an eight-month backlog of unfilled orders. And facilities in general were still running two to three months behind schedule on average.

Structures and policies for handling facilities in 1943 and beyond did not change much, but the urgency of new and expanded plant did. Construction peaked in 1942, dropped by nearly one-third in 1943, and fell even lower thereafter. By mid-1943, almost three-quarters of industrial facilities for war had been built. Nonetheless, as late as March 1943, the Planning Committee was still calling for an integrated, programmed facilities approach. By that time, the chances of achieving this goal were even less than they had been earlier. In February 1943, Eberstadt left WPB, and with him went the team most devoted to and probably most capable of coordinating construction effectively. Those who followed were sincere in their desire to control building, but they had little experience in the field. Attempting to streamline organization for handling facilities proved to be largely inconsequential. Some gains were probably made with greater stress on full utilization of existing facilities, interchange of critical tools and equipment, and industrial conservation programs emphasizing substitution, standardization, and simplification.

Already in 1943, however, along with the procurement agencies, WPB began facing problems raised by contract termination and cancellation. Combining its efforts at first with the armed forces to use or adapt plants for continued war purposes when demand dropped, designs changed, or contracts ended, WPB later faced a more difficult task. In what turned out to be highly contentious negotiations, the board had to devise with the procurement agencies uniform contract termination or cancellation clauses and procedures. Even more controversial was Donald M. Nelson's insistence late in November 1943 that the time had arrived, not only that policies should be set forth for a smooth transition from war to peace, but also that reconversion should favor smaller firms to compensate for larger corporations dominating conversion and war production. Battles over reconversion, including facility utilization, raged throughout a good part of 1944 and 1945.[25]

Facilities and construction programs do not lend themselves to simple yardsticks for evaluation. Nonetheless, a number of salient points stand out about these wartime developments.

Defense and wartime industrial facilities expansion totaled nearly $26 billion. Of that amount, $8,623 billion was paid for by corporate America and $17,169 billion federally financed, with government agencies (principally the War and Navy Departments) either operating arsenals and like plants valued at $5.6 billion themselves or paying private management a fee to do so.[26] While private firms built and operated plants exceeding $11.6 billion, they were financed by Washington: the DPC accounted for almost $7.4 billion, the War Department nearly $1.7 billion, the Navy Department over $1.4 billion, and other sources short of $1.1 billion. With the nation's gross industrial plant valued at around $40 billion in 1939, defense and wartime facilities growth between mid-1940 and mid-1945 increased America's productive capacity by about 65 percent.

No one proposes that the $26 billion investment maintained that value after hostilities. Significant adjustments must be made to account for peacetime use, location, inflation, quality of construction, efficiency of operation, and other relevant factors. Estimates of postwar worth vary greatly. In 1946, the Smaller War Plants Corporation argued that $20 billion of the $26 billion for defense and war plant could be used during peacetime and was properly priced. Going by these calculations, American manufacturing facilities grew by 50 percent, a figure obviously much too high.[27] Historian Gerald T. White, analyzing DPC in 1980, argued that only around 15 percent of the defense and war plant enriched the peacetime economy, a number that is much too low.[28] Roughly one-quarter to one-third of the $26 billion figure seems to be a more accurate and reasonable estimate.

There is much less controversy over who benefited economically from the defense and war building: predictably, it was the large corporate structure that dominated both prime and subcontracting. From June 1940 through September 1944, $175 billion in prime contracts were let to 18,539 firms. Of this total, over two-thirds, or $117 billion, went to the leading 100 corporations, nearly half to the top 30 corporations, including General Motors Corporation, Curtiss-Wright Corporation, Bethlehem Steel Company, and General Electric Company. Available evidence indicates that subcontracting did not substantially change this picture: it was not that extensive, and most of it took place among large firms with over five hundred employees.[29]

New and expanded facilities had to follow these contracting patterns. Of the $11.2 billion in publicly owned, privately operated plants built through June 1944 (and excluding government-operated and management-fee plants), over 83 percent were run by 168 corporations. The largest 100 corporations accounted for 75 percent, and 25 major corporations were in charge of almost 50 percent, including giants such as General Motors, Ford Motor Company, Aluminum Company of America, United States Steel Corporation, and Curtiss-Wright. Of the $8.6 billion of privately financed manufacturing plants built between 1940 and 1945, $4.8 billion were war plants and $3.8 billion war related. Among the war plants, 250 large corporations accounted for almost 60 percent of this growth, 100 top corporations over 50 percent.[30] Whether offering incentives for industry to build factories on its own or providing the financing itself, Washington consistently and logically turned to the "industrial ability and know-how of the giant concerns" in mobilizing industry for war.[31] Hence, the war years did not change appreciably patterns of concentrated economic power. With only a slight rise during the years of hostility, the top 250 corporations accounted for two-thirds of total manufacturing capacity in both 1939 and 1945.

Numbers aside, defense and war spending brought meaningful change in some sectors of the large corporate structure. Besides the dramatic example of the aircraft industry, that trend is most clearly seen in aluminum, synthetic rubber, and natural gas. The DPC played a critical modifying role in all three industries. Its financing of new aluminum plants, for instance, helped break Aluminum Company of America's monopoly with the rise of two strong competitors in Reynolds Metals Company and Henry J. Kaiser's Permanente Metals Corporation. Working with a collection of major corporations, DPC and its parent body, the Reconstruction Finance Corporation, provided indispensable financing for the transformation of synthetic rubber from a minor industry into a giant one. The two major oil pipelines from Texas to the East Coast that DPC financed between 1942 and 1944 were ultimately acquired by Texas Eastern Transmission Company for transporting natural gas from Texas to the Eastern Seaboard, a new trend that benefited producers and consumers alike.[32]

Achieving maximum efficiency in the use of new, converted, and existing facilities was during the war years a constant and never fully successful endeavor. The WPB reported in January 1942 that utilization of plant in key war industries was relatively low. While facilities for engines and propellers, for example, were running at around 61 percent of capacity, those for airframes, machine tools, and ordnance were only at about 50 percent, and shipbuilding was not even up to 43 percent.[33] With mobilization starting to hit its stride at the end of the year, the board reported significant progress in facility usage. Using a plant-utilization index based on total hours of plant operations and the number of workers per shift, metal products industries in general, excepting aircraft and shipbuilding, had reached 72, miscellaneous industries were at the low end at around 57, and automobiles and aircraft were at the high end at nearly 85 and 100, respectively.[34] Other sources of information were less sanguine. The Planning Committee, advocates of small business, labor spokesmen, and others constantly charged that existing facilities were passed over in favor of new or expanded plant, that smaller business units were underutilized, and that labor was inefficiently used.[35]

Excessive new construction, especially on the part of the military services, was a continual source of concern to WPB subdivisions charged with regulating facilities. Until the end of 1942, even into 1943, the army and navy, especially the former, drove relentlessly forward in maximizing output without clearly defined goals. The Planning Committee and the Statistics Division led in forcing the armed services to scale back their production drive, including the construction of new plant.[36] Yet building still went on.

Alarmed about charges of waste and partially used or unused facilities, the Truman Committee investigated. Reporting in March 1944 that the army and navy had already canceled $13 billion in contracts, the committee examined the consequences of these changes for new plant. As of March 1943, it found, the War Department had directly or indirectly arranged for the financing of

234 plants employing more than a thousand persons at a cost of nearly $4.5 billion. Of these facilities, 84 were operating at capacity or were scheduled to do, 46 were producing at rates between 60 and 100 percent of their goal, 64 functioned at less than 60 percent of their potential or not at all, and 40 had been converted to production different from their original intent. Although unable to obtain information on the use of 1,666 other plants with fewer than a thousand employees that the War Department built or financed at a cost of about $5.1 billion, Truman and his colleagues suspected that findings on those plants would resemble those on the other 234 facilities.[37] Actually, the War Department between 1940 and 1945 accounted for plant expansion totaling $11.9 billion: $4.3 billion paid for by the department; over $3 billion financed under DPC and like programs; and $4.6 billion financed privately but certified as necessary by the War Department for accelerated amortization.[38]

Although mobilization for World War II did not alter America's concentration of economic power, it had some effect on the distribution of manufacturing among regions and states. Following established patterns, most of the new large factories were located in or near major metropolitan areas, such as New York, Chicago, Detroit, St. Louis, and Los Angeles. Around half of all facilities producing for war were situated in the most industrialized prewar regions, the East North Central and Middle Atlantic.

For varied reasons, including security, labor pools, raw materials, available land, uncongested conditions, and weather, the Midwest, West, and South experienced unusual industrial growth. In 1939, for example, the West South Central received only 6 percent of overall national capital expenditures. By 1943, the figure had jumped to almost 11 percent, with Texas accounting for over half this gain on the basis of synthetic rubber, chemicals, and petroleum output. While the West North Central, East South Central, and Mountain regions attracted under 10 percent of industrial capital in 1939, in 1943 they were at almost 18 percent. By the war's end, Kansas, Oklahoma, and Texas had major aircraft centers. The Pacific region started higher, with 6.8 percent of national capital expenditures in 1939, but, in 1943, it still grew to 8.8 percent. California's prewar aircraft facilities in the south and its shipyards in the north grew vastly along with other industries, and aircraft, shipyards, and aluminum plants in the Pacific Northwest accounted for a high level of war-induced manufacturing. Considerable industrial growth in the less advanced areas involved munitions with limited peacetime utility. Even where that was the case, however, populations expanded, management and labor were trained, and some regions were introduced to large-scale industrialization for the first time. Stimuli for manufacturing did not end with the war, as subsequent economic development of various regions establishes.[39]

SURPLUS PROPERTY DISPOSAL

Most of the industrial facilities built and equipped by Washington during the defense and war years were sold, some were retained by government agencies, especially the War and Navy Departments, and others were maintained in reserve status for future emergencies.[40] Debate over how to dispose of so-called surplus property began in 1943. It was largely settled along conservative lines by the February 1944 report on reconversion of Bernard M. Baruch and John Hancock to James F. Byrnes, director of the Office of War Mobilization (OWM). Surplus property would be handled in a way meant to support society's existing patterns and institutions, not to bring about social and economic change. Following the lead of the elder statesmen, Roosevelt by executive order in February 1944 established in OWM a Surplus War Property Administration (SWPA) headed by William L. Clayton, a colleague and friend of Jesse H. Jones. Between October 1944 and March 1946, the SWPA was gradually transformed into the War Assets Administration (WAA), an independent agency. By mid-1949, the momentous task involved in disposing of nearly $17.2 billion worth of government-titled industrial plant and equipment had been largely completed.[41]

Assessing how well the public interest was served in the disposal of surplus industrial property is extremely difficult. WAA oversaw property from numerous agencies using different and varying accounting methods. In general, wartime record keeping was lax, especially so for the DPC. Postwar sales were at best complex and messy. Among other practices, plants were often sold separately from equipment. WAA at first aimed for prices equal to the cost of postwar construction, minus depreciation and conversion; it later stressed fair value. Both these approaches were subjective, and fair value depended on a host of considerations, including the location of property, the number of prospective buyers, time pressure, and such nonmarket considerations as supporting small business, providing employment, and strengthening competition.

The most valuable government-titled assets were the $7.4 billion of DPC-financed property that was closest to commercial, peacetime usage. From the facilities and equipment that were sold, according to Gerald T. White, a thorough and careful scholar of the subject, the government recovered roughly 35 percent of costs.[42] WAA and its predecessors did best with synthetic rubber and pipelines, in which Washington's investment was nearly matched or slightly exceeded. Machine tools also did reasonably well but returned less than 50 percent of costs. Aircraft plants, which constituted DPC's largest percentage of investment, did not do as well. With demand for planes dropping to a small fraction of wartime figures, industry could not absorb a good part of the growth. Most of the huge factories had to be emptied of equipment and sold to giant corporations, such as General Motors, General Electric, and International Harvester Company, for whatever price they would bring. Similar conditions existed with high-octane gasoline plants. Uncertain postwar markets and Washington's desire to encourage competition led to the sale of aluminum plants at around 30 percent of cost. WAA did not do much better with steel since the industry was still resistant to expansion. The government's $428 million investment in vastly augmented wartime magnesium output was largely lost. Without much growth in demand, a huge plant in Nevada was sold for a pittance, and most other facilities were held in reserve or destroyed. Around $1 billion of facilities that WAA could not sell or lease, along with large amounts of machine tools and other plant, were placed in custodial or industrial reserve. Since DPC held the best, most marketable property, White's estimate of a 35 percent cost-recovery figure for wartime government-titled facilities may be optimistic.

White also points out that public building and financing protected the public interest better than it had been under accelerated depreciation. At least that was the case with the DPC. Industry used accelerated depreciation for expanding facilities totaling about $8.6 billion, $1.2 billion more than that expended by DPC.[43] Industry designed the plants and determined where they were located. As much as half the amount went to huge corporations for large plant; the remainder was for smaller facilities or the expansion of existing ones. The postwar value of rapidly depreciated plants was usually much higher than was true with DPC projects. In addition, such facilities benefited from generous tax provisions. Nonetheless, considering accelerated amortization to be a fast and convenient method of financing desired plant without any expenditures on their part, the armed services usually certified such facilities for 100 percent depreciation without verifying whether the plants would be used solely for defense and war purposes or whether they would have postwar value. In the spring of 1944, the WPB finally instituted policies for setting depreciation rates at 35 percent and adjusting the figure upward or downward on the basis of estimated postwar value and wartime use. By then, however, most wartime construction was completed. One WPB official estimated that full as opposed to partial depreciation from 1940 to 1944 resulted in "windfall gains," costing the federal government as much as $3 billion.[44]

Overall, defense and war facilities programs were seriously flawed. Centralized control was never achieved, and proper programming and scheduling never took place. Perhaps careful facilities planning could not have been achieved; if such planning had been possible, industry and military elements constantly thwarted it, actions based on perception and interests. As a result, excessive plant was built, existing facilities were inadequately used, and industry ended up with elaborate plant acquired with little or no risk. Attempting to measure with precision exactly what took place is nearly impossible since critical information in usable form is hard to come by and analyze as well as being subject to varying interpretation.

Within the context of the basically flawed general mobilization system, however, what occurred with facilities was probably unavoidable, even predictable. Although the price was high, perhaps extraordinarily so, the American economy produced the munitions and goods essential for defeating formidable enemies, the ultimate goal of war. Furthermore, facilities extravagance was balanced to a degree by manufacturing gains for less industrialized regions, greater competition in some industries such as aluminum, nurturing new industries like synthetic rubber, and helping strengthen economic foundations for postwar prosperity.

12
REFINING WPB ECONOMIC CONTROLS, 1942

Once conversion and facilities expansion were under way or completed, the War Production Board (WPB) faced the task of rationalizing a war production program in which demand far outdistanced supply. This process turned out to be a lacerating one. Only after great effort and much controversy was a planning system devised for maximizing output while maintaining economic balance. For that to take place, three major, related functions had to be worked out.

The first involved setting military demand at a level that was feasible for the economy in terms of its potential and output for civilians. Without feasible requirements on the part of the armed services, no production program could be properly managed. Such calculations were all the more complicated because the WPB was always slow and deficient in defining carefully what were basic civilian needs during wartime.

After feasibility had been resolved, a program for allocating materials had to be devised. Raw materials—steel, copper, rubber, and so forth—were the principal limiting source for output in 1942 and into 1943. Under such circumstances, a priorities system would not work. To handle a shortage of materials, an allocation system became necessary. Under such an approach, blocks of materials are assigned directly or indirectly to producers according to the urgency of need determined by a centralized authority. In 1942, the WPB went from a horizontal allocation system, called the Production Requirements Plan (PRP), to a vertical one, the Controlled Materials Plan (CMP).

Allocating materials according to a feasible war production program still did not guarantee maximum orderly output. Production had to be scheduled so that facilities were properly used, inventories were not excessive or short in supply, and raw materials, machinery, components, and the like flowed according to a set and synchronized pattern.

Not only were calculations for feasibility and programs for allocations and production scheduling exceptionally demanding for the largest and most complicated economic system in the world, but they also involved vital matters of power and control both within the WPB and among the claimant agencies. The military services, and particularly the War Department, as the major procuring agencies, fought against these regulations, which could limit their latitude as well as restrict their authority. Numerous industrialists serving in WPB sided with the armed services. They did so in part because they feared excessively strengthening government agencies and they resisted planning devices originating with and/or supported by academics, economists, other professionals, and New Deal reformers.

So intense did the battles of production controls become that they were often referred to the White House for resolution. From those circumstances, James F. Byrnes began emerging as practically an assistant president for the homefront, appointed director of the Office of Economic Stabilization at the end of 1942 and then head of the Office of War Mobilization in mid-1943.

Turmoil aside, by late 1942 and early 1943, the mobilization system had been refined to the point that munitions began flowing at an accelerated rate. Nonetheless, intense conflict continued.

FEASIBILITY

Feasibility was the central issue facing the WPB in 1942. What was the maximum immediate and long-run wartime demand that the mobilized economy could meet without threatening its stability? Until that critical concept was accepted and applied, balanced programs for facilities and construction, along with priority and allocation controls and production scheduling, could not be formulated and instituted.

Feasibility generated enormous tension because it left no part of economic mobilization unaffected. It was made more contentious by the fact that the analytic tool originated with economists, statisticians, and academics, who were resented, perhaps even feared, by industry and the military. Businessmen and soldiers for the most part appeared uninformed about and uninterested in feasibility. If accepted, the concept could limit and shape their decision-making and empower outsiders, impractical theorists, those not sharing the views and values of industry and the military. Animosity toward professionals and specialists not serving directly under and answerable to industrialists can be traced back to the National Defense Advisory Commission (NDAC). Stacy May's Bureau of Research and Statistics and successor agencies were constantly under attack and fighting to preserve their existence.[1]

The Planning Committee was at the heart of the feasibility dispute. Nelson created the committee in February 1942 to advise him on long-range prospects and problems involving economic mobilization. In a little over thirteen months, the committee studied and made recommendations on a host of long- and short-run mobilization matters dealing with construction and facilities, aircraft, small business, transportation, and related topics. Defining, analyzing, and fighting to implement policies on feasibility, however, was its greatest achievement.[2]

Robert R. Nathan chaired the Planning Committee. He was a statistician who had been chief of the National Income Division, Bureau of Foreign and Domestic Commerce, Commerce Department. In June 1940, he joined Stacy May in NDAC's Bureau of Research and Statistics and remained with May in the Office of Production Management (OPM) and the Supply Priorities and Allocations Board (SPAB). The second committee member was Thomas C. Blaisdell, Jr., an economist with the National Resources Planning Board who had previously served, among other posts, with the Temporary National Economic Committee. Fred Searls, Jr., the third member, vice-president of Newmont Mining Company, was a tough, conservative mining engineer who in 1941 became a consultant to the Ordnance Department. For conducting the committee's feasibility analyses, Nathan recruited Simon Kuznets, a pioneering and leading authority on national income and its composition who was in Stacy May's Statistics Division. Nathan had studied under Kuznets at the University of Pennsylvania. The three members of the committee, along with Kuznets and others, were not fuzzy theoreticians. Most were hardheaded, knowledgeable professionals, thoroughly familiar with economic mobilization and power operations in Washington.

The Planning Committee was closely tied to the Statistics Division and the Office of Progress Reports. Stacy May headed both these agencies, Nathan was assistant director of the Office of Progress Reports, and Kuznets served simultaneously on the Planning Committee and in the Statistics Division. From NDAC through SPAB, May and Nathan had joined Leon Henderson as leading all-outers fighting to prepare the nation economically for war. That gave them prestige and clout after Pearl Harbor.[3] In a sense, the feasibility dispute was the last mobilization battle fought by Henderson and his New Deal brigade. Henderson had acted as mentor for May, who recruited Nathan, Kuznets, and others. Late in 1942, when the fate of the Planning Committee's feasibility proposals hung in the balance, Henderson played a significant role in their acceptance. Henderson led in the push for full-blown mobilization in 1940–1941; when his aspirations became reality in 1942, he acted to ensure that newly converted industry and military enthusiasts did not act to undermine the harnessed economy. Once achieving success, Nathan, Henderson, and other feasibility advocates were pushed to the side, making way for mobilization under industry-military domination.

The feasibility issue actually originated with the SPAB's Victory Program of December 1941, which called for expenditures of between $110 and $115 billion by September 1943 for defeating the Axis powers.[4] Starting with SPAB's figures, Roosevelt in January 1942 set forth a War Munitions Program for 1942 of about $50–$55 billion to include "must items" (those in the highest-priority category and essential for a balanced war program) of 60,000 planes, 45,000 tanks, 20,000 antiaircraft guns, and 8 million deadweight tons of merchant ships; in 1943, figures would rise to $60–$65 billion, with specified weapons increasing proportionately. On the basis of SPAB's analysis, Nelson and his advisers agreed that these goals were within achievable realms.[5]

Fulfilling Roosevelt's War Munitions Program would require extraordinary, unprecedented efforts. When war broke out, OPM's peak production aims stood at $27 billion for 1942, $34 billion for 1943. WPB's daunting challenge was made much greater by the fact that the army and navy, particularly the former, used the president's War Munitions Program to recalculate their requirements to coincide with his "must items." By doing this, the military increased projected production for 1942 and 1943 to impossible numbers. Roosevelt had included in his general dollar figures munitions aid for the Allies, not just national demand, making his estimates an improper guide for army and navy expansion. The Army Supply Program of February 1942 called for outlays of around $63 billion through 1943. Such requirements pushed the War Munitions Program up to $62.6 billion in 1942 and $110 billion in 1943, far beyond what was considered to be feasible for the economy.[6]

Once organized, the Planning Committee turned to the feasibility of the War Munitions Program as its first and primary concern.[7] It quickly concluded that escalating requirements would undermine mobilization, particularly with material shortages, a defective priority system, and the lack of adequate production scheduling. To better grasp what was feasible, the Planning Committee called on Kuznets. By mid-March, Kuznets had completed a preliminary analysis of production potential based on GNP, raw materials, industrial facilities, and labor. He concluded that $48 billion was the maximum in munitions and construction that the mobilized economy could meet in 1942. Alarmed about what was occurring, Nathan and May wrote Nelson on March 17, 1942, summarizing Kuznets's findings, arguing that immediate action was necessary to reduce military demand, and warning that the economy could not be pushed too far without dire consequences:

Any attempt to attain objectives which are far out of line with what is feasible will result in the construction of new plants without materials to
keep them operating; vast quantities of semi-fabricated items which cannot be completed; production without adequate storage facilities; idle
existing plants due to lack of materials; and similar disrupting situations.[8]

Convinced by Nathan and May's argument, Nelson sought corrective action. He first proposed that the army and navy work with WPB in lowering
requirements. The Navy Department was unresponsive, and the War Department said that it would cut demand after Nelson persuaded Roosevelt to lower
"must-item" figures. Calling on the president, the WPB chair laid out the
Planning Committee's case for feasible demand. Roosevelt gave Nelson verbal, but not written, permission to work with the army and navy to reduce
munitions and facilities spending for 1942 from $62 to approximately $45
billion. WPB's second feasibility round with the military was only slightly more
successful than the first. By the end of April, munitions figures had been cut by
$4.5 billion but construction and facilities increased by $1.6 billion. Overall
projected spending by the armed services remained at over $59 billion for
1942, still nearly one-third higher than the Planning Committee's maximum.
Although both the president and the military conceded in effect that the War
Munitions Program had been pushed too high, Nelson's attempts at remedi-
ation in March and April had not gotten very far.

By May 1942, feasibility had become a major source of conflict. General
Brehon B. Somervell, commanding general of the Army Service Forces (ASF),
emerged as the principal opponent of feasibility as a concept and of WPB acting on it to limit military demand. Beginning in April, when Nelson, pressured by both the Planning Committee and the Army-Navy Munitions Board
(ANMB), was attempting to cut back construction and facilities programs for
feasibility purposes, Somervell was instrumental in undermining the effort.[9]
In part, the ASF commanding general wanted maximum latitude for meeting
the supply needs of a vastly expanding army preparing for worldwide hostilities. Consequently, he refused to consider limits on his supply goals. But
Somervell's instinctive competitiveness also came into play. He bristled at the
idea of WPB having a say in military requirements, and he strove to prove his
worth by achieving the seemingly impossible.

Acting from a subordinate position, Somervell was able to act as mobilization spoiler because he had support, or at least tolerance, in high places. All
the top civilian and military War Department leaders, including Secretary of
War Henry L. Stimson, Under Secretary Robert P. Patterson, and Chief of
Staff George C. Marshall, to varying degrees considered WPB and other civil-

ian institutions as at best coordinate service units for the army.[10] They also believed that the military had to have direct control and authority over its supply operations with the least amount of civilian interference.

These same views, however, were present among industrial executives in WPB. Dating back to the NDAC and OPM, Knudsen and those in his circle argued that civilian mobilization agencies existed to serve the armed services.[11] In WPB, William H. Harrison, director of the Production Division, shared this outlook, and he was far from alone. Various WPB executives, like those in positions of power in the armed services, did not understand or accept feasibility. The idea that there were restraints on what a war economy could produce was to them a new and unwelcome one. They, along with Somervell, preferred to rely on "incentive scheduling": the higher the production goals, the better the performance.[12] Additionally, for numerous WPB executives and military officers, feasibility was suspect because its authors and advocates were academics, theorists, New Dealers, and planners. Since Nelson chose to heed their counsel, he too became suspect and was ultimately charged with being ineffectual, even incompetent.

Early in 1942, opponents of feasibility benefited from the apparent support of Roosevelt. The president resisted any attempt to modify his War Munitions Program and "must items" announced in January for purposes of both aspiration and inspiration. Although he had agreed to Nelson's request for lowering escalated War Munitions Program totals in March, his commitment was at best lukewarm, he had not been educated on feasibility, and he had too many other critical matters demanding his attention. Besides, with WPB slow in converting industry to war production, lowering requirements hardly seemed to be the most pressing mobilization priority.

Somervell was able to exploit all these conditions to strike a heavy blow against feasibility. He seems to have used his connections with Harry L. Hopkins to obtain Roosevelt's signature on a letter addressed to Nelson that was written in the ASF. Dated May 1, 1942, the president's correspondence reaffirmed his War Munitions Program of January, increased some of the "must items," said that his goals included all complementary weapons and other supplies that the armed services required, and insisted that necessary construction and facilities expansion be expedited. This officious communication was followed by another on May 4 asking the WPB chair what could be done to speed up the lagging production record.[13]

With such missives emanating from the White House, Nelson took another approach. At Nathan's suggestion, he set up a Committee on Feasibility, consisting of Nathan and directors of the principal operating divisions. The committee shortly reported that a complete feasibility report was essential and that it would require time and effort. On the basis of those findings, Nathan brought Kuznets into the Planning Committee to head a section on Program Analysis and Research to conduct the study. Out of the spotlight, Kuznets and his assistants worked on a full-scale feasibility analysis for around four months.

While Kuznets was carrying out his analysis, Nathan began an extended educational campaign. Day after day, he met informally, alone and in the company of others, with numerous well-placed friends and mobilization officials. An intense, persuasive, and engaging personality, Nathan explained how feasibility was determined and why it was so critical for setting mobilization parameters. He was carefully preparing for the next feasibility round.

On August 12, 1942, Kuznets delivered to the Planning Committee a lengthy feasibility report. Similar to his preliminary study of March, it was based on a four-part analysis. Since 1942 was fast closing, Kuznets concentrated on 1943. Nonetheless, he estimated, projected munitions and war-related construction and facilities, which had risen to nearly $60 billion for 1942, would fall around $15 billion short. He was off by $1 billion since output approximated $44, not $45, billion. In August 1942, munitions, construction, and facilities for 1943 were set at about $93 billion, almost 20 percent too high according to Kuznets, who estimated maximum 1943 capacity for those categories at $75 billion. (If 1942 shortfalls were carried over to 1943, the feasibility discrepancy would be even greater.)[14]

Kuznets explained that unfeasible requirements need not be an insurmountable obstacle to stable economic mobilization as long as war production was properly programmed and scheduled. But even those controls required complete and realistic requirements to be effective. Feasible demand was the sine qua non for a stable mobilized economy operating at or near maximum output.

Kuznets did not stop there; he went on to argue that, as long as strategy and supply were set by different and uncoordinated sources, feasibility would remain a critical problem. Along with the president, the Joint Chiefs of Staff (JCS) set strategy and outlined requirements to carry it out, but the staff did not review, adjust, or consolidate detailed demands forwarded to WPB by the army and navy's supply services. (The ANMB had been intended to perform this vital function, but, for complicated reasons, it failed to do so.) Instead, WPB received from separate services and, at times, their supply subdivisions requirements, often in a rough, incomplete, and unrefined state. Without WPB dealing directly with JCS on production, difficulties with requirements would persist, probably get worse.

Kuznets proposed to close the gap between the production agency and the joint chiefs through creating a "supreme war production council" made up of representatives for military strategy, economic mobilization, and political practices. Guided by what was economically feasible, the armed services could soundly determine strategy. Along those lines, the council would have the authority to determine requirements, adjust demand to changing circumstances through continuous deliberations, and enforce decisions among institutions and agencies involved in the conduct of the war. The Planning Committee accepted this recommendation.

Kuznets and the Planning Committee were addressing a crucial subject that had plagued economic mobilization beginning with NDAC. Leon Henderson and others had made similar proposals for relating strategy and economic policy beginning in 1940.[15] Since March 1942, Nathan had favored such an approach, and in April 1942, an interagency committee on facilities and construction, which included representatives from the ANMB, insisted that an institutional arrangement along those lines was necessary.[16] Nelson and others initially saw the Combined Production and Resources Board, created in June 1942, as another opportunity to coordinate requirements. When that outcome did not materialize, Nelson in August proposed to Roosevelt that the JCS establish a Requirements Section for working directly with WPB to ensure that military demand was balanced and feasible. The president had Hopkins explore this option. The latter ran into strong opposition from the armed services. Both Nelson's latest approach and the Kuznets–Planning Committee supreme production council were on the table for consideration at the same time.

Dealing directly with JCS would not solve major problems that WPB faced with military requirements. Under any organizational structure, the armed services' supply services were basic to all material operations. Yet, late in 1942, the statistical and reporting systems of ASF and its navy counterpart were grossly inadequate. Too often the board had to grapple with requirements passed on from supply bureaus that were uncollated and unintegrated or wrong, piecemeal, or nonexistent.

The navy was both more and less troublesome than the army. It resisted repeated WPB requests for usable statistics on need or the board's attempts to scale down requirements. The newly created Office of Procurement and Material, headed by Admiral Samuel M. Robinson, protected the supply bureaus and moved very slowly in getting from them data for providing WPB with consolidated demand figures. The naval bureaus preferred working directly with appropriate WPB subdivisions. By contrast with the aggressive bureaucratic imperialism of ASF's General Somervell, however, Robinson was generally accommodating. Moreover, the navy, unlike the army, appeared satisfied with mobilization, and it did not constantly challenge WPB policies and practices.

On its part, the army did have centralized statistical services; ASF provided WPB with overall requirement figures, and it engaged the board when deficiencies or differences arose. Nonetheless, data flowing to the board were frequently poor. Tables of allowances by which the bureaus determined need could be obsolete, statistical offices were often poorly manned, and amounts were padded or guessed. ASF frequently did not understand or bother to learn the importance of WPB controls and assign enough qualified personnel to the board for carrying out vital functions such as materials allocations. WPB struggled with the navy to obtain requirement figures; it struggled with the requirement figures that the army presented.

No member of the WPB or predecessor agencies advocated a role for its members in formulating strategy. Instead, Nelson, Nathan, Kuznets, and others insisted that strategists had to have reliable information on economic resources in order properly to perform their duty. In turn, production officials had to know what the armed services needed in order of urgency and adjusted to current conditions. Tenaciously guarding their strategic independence, the military in general and the JCS in particular never seriously considered dealing directly with WPB. That being the case, neither Roosevelt nor Hopkins showed any inclination to push the armed services in a direction that they so intensely opposed. On the army's part, Kuznets's supreme war production council encountered other difficulties. In the midst of the feasibility conflict, ASF's chief, Somervell, was engaged in a battle to become the principal army representative for logistics in the JCS structure. Kuznets's council appeared to ignore or bypass ASF completely. Such a proposal strengthened further Somervell's intense hostility toward the Planning Committee.

The Planning Committee adopted Kuznets's study and, on September 4, forwarded it to Donald M. Nelson. Displaying unusual administrative guile, Nelson sent full copies of the report under Nathan's name to Harry L. Hopkins, Admiral Robinson, and General Somervell. The first two did not respond; Somervell quickly fired back a handwritten reply on September 12 that bristled with anger and contempt. Since Kuznets admitted that his analysis was subject to a wide margin of error, and since those who were now calling for retrenchment not long ago pressed ASF to increase requirements, Somervell lectured Nathan, he found it hard to take the study seriously. In addition, the sections of the report that dealt with industrial facilities, military construction, and merchant ships were uninformed. The proposal for a production strategy council was "an inchoate mass of words." "I am not impressed with either the character or basis of the judgments expressed in the reports," the ASF commander concluded, "and recommend they be carefully hidden from the eyes of thoughtful men."[17]

Nelson allowed the Planning Committee to answer Somervell, and Kuznets gladly wrote Nathan's reply on September 17. "In view of the gravity of the problem discussed in these Documents," he opened, "I hesitate to take your memorandum seriously." The call for higher requirements a year ago hardly justified setting demand at totally unrealistic levels today. By providing WPB at best with piecemeal requirement figures, the armed services forced the Planning Committee to work with unreliable statistics. "I regret that the memorandum which spells out the significant problems in relation to objectives and production was not phrased so as to be comprehensible to you," Kuznets went on. He continued by reminding the ASF chief that the suggested supreme war production council was similar to an arrangement that Somervell had proposed to Nelson on May 15, 1942. Noting Somervell's declaration that he was unimpressed with the feasibility analysis, Kuznets pointed out: "Your conclusion from it . . . that these judgments be carefully hidden from the eyes of thoughtful men is a non-sequitur." As a parting shot, the economic analyst lamented that the basic points of his study had been overlooked "in favor of minutiae." If intelligent and thoughtful men did not "forthrightly and aggressively" mobilize the economy along feasible lines, adverse effects could be so great as to disrupt the national effort.[18]

Feasibility now had to be faced. Nelson placed it on the agenda for the October 6 meeting of WPB. By then, the dispute had hit the Washington gossip circuit, was in the press, and was being dramatized as a showdown between civilians and the military. The White House was alerted, instructing Nelson that the conflict be taken up as scheduled, not postponed. Nathan prepared by conferring with additional mobilization officials. After a thorough review, Leon Henderson endorsed Kuznets's work, and Nathan spent over an hour at the White House going over the analysis with Harry L. Hopkins and his aide, Isador Lubin, who was also an assistant to the president and commissioner of labor statistics. Nathan also continued his educational efforts among WPB officials.

The WPB meeting of October 6 was extraordinary. Besides the regular board members, alternates, and staff, seventeen others were invited, including all members of the Planning Committee, Kuznets, Stacy May, Somervell, Robinson, various representatives from the Maritime Commission, and Paul V. McNutt, chair of the War Manpower Commission. Somervell had lined up support from Patterson, Robinson, and others, and he had a letter from Chief of Staff Marshall, which the ASF chief clearly had written himself, designating him as the army's spokesman on strategy before the WPB and opposing a supreme war production council as superfluous. Nathan presented the case for feasibility, backed in various ways and emphasizing different points by Nelson,

Assistant Director of the Bureau of the Budget Wayne Coy, Lubin, Henderson, and McNutt. Nelson and McNutt hit at the military's serious and continuing statistical lapses, and Henderson emphasized the army and navy's inability to schedule their production. Somervell lauded the benefits of incentive over feasible goals and scoffed at any gains from a war production council. He was supported by Robinson and Patterson, although the latter was somewhat flexible on the need for coordinating strategy and production.

In the give and take that lasted three hours, instead of the usual one and a half, the advocates of feasibility made the better case. However, almost all the debate centered on feasible requirements, not a supreme war production council for handling military demand. Arguing against Kuznets, Somervell inadvertently ended up strengthening the Planning Committee's case. He admitted that strategy and production had to be related, that all 1942 production requirements could not be met, and that ASF and the supply services were not constantly recalculating their needs according to the ongoing flux of strategy and mobilization. As the meeting reached its end, however, the War Department refused to give any ground. Quite suddenly, Leon Henderson took over. At first speaking softly and referring to total war demand for 1943, he mused that, if the JCS could not fight a war on $90 billion, maybe they should be replaced by those who could:

> The statement was received in dead silence. Then Henderson turned to Somervell and proceeded to make the most violent personal attack ever heard in a meeting of the War Production Board. He was disgusted, he said, with Somervell's repeated obstinacy, overbearing manner, and ignorance of production problems. He stated flatly his belief that Somervell had always padded his requirements, and that he had no idea of the disastrous implications of infeasible goals. For a considerable period Henderson gave vent to every grievance he had accumulated throughout the first year of war. . . . When W. L. Batt attempted to assuage Henderson by pointing out that Somervell did not, after all, make strategy, Henderson replied: "Ain't he got a letter?"[19]

After embarrassed attempts at continued deliberations, and without formal action on feasibility, WPB adjourned.

Shortly after the October 6 meeting, a solution was fashioned for the JCS to reduce requirements. The official record is barren about how the settlement was devised. No doubt Roosevelt directed what was to be done. Most likely, Hopkins and Admiral William D. Leahy—chairman of the JCS and presidential chief of staff—negotiated terms with Nelson, who was advised by the

Planning Committee, and the War and Navy Departments.[20] Patterson informed Somervell on October 7 of the approximate terms. WPB's October 13 meeting was carefully scripted for the board to reemphasize the importance of feasibility and for Somervell to back off while saving face. By agreement or tacit understanding, the supreme war production council was dropped as too controversial and as an obstacle to settling feasibility differences.

The feasibility dispute that began in March ended in November. Nelson wrote JCS on October 19 explaining why $93 billion in 1943 for weapons, construction, and facilities was not possible and what would occur if programs were not lowered to $75 billion as the probable maximum output achievable. On November 26, the JCS returned to Nelson a revised program that reduced requirements to a total of $80.15 billion, with the navy absorbing approximately one-quarter of the cuts and the rest coming at the expense of the army. The final figure still exceeded the Planning Committee's ceiling by $5 billion, but both Nathan and Kuznets considered it to be within acceptable limits.

While the Planning Committee won the battle of numbers in the feasibility struggle, it did not even come close to having a supreme war production council set up. Presumably responding to Nelson's August request that JCS create a Requirements Section to work with WPB, Leahy wrote Nelson on October 16, 1942, that the joint chiefs would appoint military officers to keep WPB abreast of strategic needs for men and materials—a sop, not a compromise.

With feasibility behind it, WPB quickly took major steps late in 1942 and early in 1943 to use a new allocation system meant vastly to improve programming. That change was followed by the institution of elaborate methods for scheduling production. These advances forced the army and navy to refine their supply and procurement operations and provide WPB with current, reliable, and consolidated requirement figures. Sound mobilization processes were, thereby, achieved without direct contact being established between WPB and JCS.

Nelson and the Planning Committee had to win the feasibility conflict in order for economic mobilization to proceed in an effective and stable way. However, the WPB chair and the Planning Committee were forced to spend enormous amounts of political capital in achieving their goal. The War Department never forgave Nelson, Nathan, and their group for victory and the way they won it, and most WPB industrialists were more than willing to join in punishing the victors at the opportune time. Up until September 1942, Stacy May was prominent in WPB meetings and operations; after that, he rarely appeared. By early 1943, the Planning Committee was slipping in importance and influence, and, by the end of March, it was shut down. Around the same time, Nelson lost control of WPB, slowly becoming a lonely, sad captain commanding his ship more in form than in reality and treated with disrespect by the majority of his nominal subordinates. Before most of these developments occurred, Leon Henderson had already left Washington, out of favor at the White House, resented and attacked in Congress. New Dealers increasingly disappeared from the ranks of the powerful in wartime Washington mobilization circles, replaced by those from industry and the military, representing the principal producers and consumers of the once-again-mighty American economic machine.

FROM PRIORITIES TO ALLOCATIONS

Feasible requirements ultimately made possible an allocation system for directing scarce materials to the most urgent usage. Throughout most of 1942, however, the WPB had to rely on priorities for achieving that end. Those priorities began with the NDAC and grew in coverage and importance under the OPM. Since neither NDAC nor OPM had the staff or the inclination to administer a priority operation that in 1940–1941 dealt primarily with military production, the ANMB took over most of this critical regulatory function. As defense demand grew during 1941 and shortages became more extreme, OPM supplemented priorities with other related and, at times, overlapping controls, such as prohibiting the manufacture of various products. The office also started to experiment with total, integrated allocation systems, the most important of which was the PRP.

As WPB got under way, however, priorities still remained the basic means for channeling materials and equipment according to need. That was the case despite the fact that priorities were fatally flawed. Unrelated to available supply of resources, priorities became the less meaningful the more of them the armed services issued. As that occurred, increasing amounts of goods were pushed to the highest levels, threatening the output of lesser-rated munitions, cutting out indirect and essential civilian products, and generally disrupting economic mobilization. Before OPM gave way to WPB, the priority system was in an advanced state of distress.[21]

Limitations notwithstanding, WPB at the outset had to use priorities.[22] Between February and April 1942, Nelson officially delegated to ANMB, under WPB direction, responsibility for determining general priority categories and for issuing priorities to military goods. Both WPB and ANMB recognized that, without reform, priorities procedures would not be useful. Accordingly, with Nelson's concurrence, Ferdinand Eberstadt late in February requested from what became the JCS a new directive that, on the basis of strategic need, established military requirements for 1942 rated according to urgency. Those figures, he argued, would allow WPB and ANMB to reconfigure priorities in a way that worked.

By early April, the JCS completed its review, including the president's "must items," and forwarded the program to Roosevelt. Approving it, the president instructed JCS to direct ANMB to revise priorities for armed services procurement. Roosevelt then went one step further. On May 1, he informed Nelson of his directions to JCS, asked him to assist ANMB in reforming priorities, and, most important, instructed WPB to obtain ANMB's concurrence when issuing priorities and allocations in facilities expansion for basic materials. On May 20, ANMB presented WPB with a new priority directive in which military production, along with facilities for manufacturing it, was rated according to five categories. These ratings were to take precedence over all other priorities. ANMB's consent was required to add items or to allocate materials essential to armed services programs.

The military, and particularly the army, was aggressively moving to take control of economic mobilization. About the same time that the priority system was being revamped, WPB was struggling to have the armed services reduce their overall demand, including inflated facilities and construction projects, to feasible levels. To strengthen its hand against WPB in emerging battles over feasibility, facilities, and priorities, the War Department maneuvered to have Roosevelt support its position. As chair of ANMB, Eberstadt had since Pearl Harbor tried to increase the board's authority at the expense of WPB. With Somervell becoming commanding general of ASF in March 1942, the army and ANMB became even more aggressive. The War Department may have convinced the president that the May 1 communication to Nelson was an emergency measure necessary to get a lagging munitions program under way.[23]

ANMB's May 20 priority proposal was positive in that it was the first effort to issue priorities quantitatively and for a set period. The highest ratings were balanced and restricted to the most urgent requirements, and the five-category approach was limited to the JCS program for 1942. Heretofore, priorities had been issued only qualitatively and without regard to time. Otherwise, ANMB's directive was negative. It was based only on end items since the board could not translate finished products into materials essential for their manufacture. Much more significant, the proposal was silent on indirect military, civilian, and Lend-Lease and other export requirements. Since ANMB dealt only with the services, that was logical. But the May 20 directive gave ANMB the right to block WPB in extending or modifying military priorities to cover other areas. In his May 1 letter to Nelson, Roosevelt gave ANMB veto power over priorities and allocations involving only munitions facilities; according to the

May 20 directive, which was vague at critical points, ANMB could extend its reach to include all priorities and allocations.

In June, Nelson approved the May 20 ANMB directive after it was modified to provide better coverage for Merchant Marine needs and other matters. Nelson, with the president's backing, also insisted that essential civilian requirements had to be included in ANMB's highest priority rankings. The WPB chair accepted the ANMB's work despite intense resistance from chief lieutenants and the Planning Committee. By going along, they argued, Nelson tacitly granted ANMB coordinate, even superior, status vis-à-vis WPB. The military agency could use the priority directive to try to dictate overall mobilization policies. Moreover, and regardless of verbal declaration, essential civilian needs were left unprotected. Finally, the Planning Committee pointed out that an unqualified ANMB had interjected itself between the WPB and the JCS. Such a crucial coordinating role required an agency like a supreme war production council.

Nelson reluctantly approved the ANMB document because he saw few other options. The president's involvement made rejection very difficult. Additionally, no overall program for essential civilian needs or indirect military ones existed. That reality weakened Nelson's bargaining hand. Finally, the WPB chair felt that further delay in reforming priorities was out of the question. Besides, he informed his staff that he had accepted the ANMB proposal as only a statement rating the urgency of military demand. Civilian requirements were a WPB responsibility, and the board would act accordingly.

The ANMB directive never worked well. While Nelson was working on priorities for civilian needs, the Office of Civilian Supply negotiated directly with Eberstadt in setting up a new rating band for essential nonmilitary goods. ANMB challenged Nelson when he directed other WPB subdivisions to ignore the board in making priority determinations for indispensable civilian needs. With neither Eberstadt nor Nelson backing off, a tense and unsettled conflict was left unresolved. More to the point, in mid-1942, WPB began switching from a failing priority to a mandatory allocation system.

Nelson finally tired of the armed services' freewheeling priority operations. On August 22, 1942, he informed the War and Navy Departments that he was ending ANMB's independent functions. As of September 9, WPB would supervise the system. Alarmed at the loss, Eberstadt led the way in working out with the endlessly patient Nelson a solution in which the military committed itself to abiding by WPB decisions in exchange for WPB personnel operating through the army and navy's procurement offices. In that way, the armed services maintained direct contact with their contractors in the issuance of priorities.

At about the same time that WPB took back priority authority, Eberstadt left ANMB to become WPB's vice chairman for program determination. With Eberstadt's departure, ANMB no longer had a meaningful role in economic mobilization.[24]

Throughout the period from February through June 1942 and beyond, as WPB struggled with priorities it simultaneously moved to put in place the PRP, a comprehensive, integrated system for allocating scarce materials. Desperately seeking levers to control economic mobilization, Donald M. Nelson late in May authorized the mandatory implementation of PRP for the third quarter of 1942. The plan involved distributing basic metals under conditions of scarcity in what was designated as horizontal allocation.

Very generally, the PRP worked in this way: manufacturers reported to WPB what munitions and essential civilian orders they held or would hold for the coming three months, the metals required to complete these contracts, and their metals inventory. On the basis of that information and other data, WPB calculated overall metals demand. From its materials branches such as steel and additional sources, the board established metals supply. With information on demand and supply, top WPB policy bodies divided available metals among industries, and lower-echelon WPB and claimant agencies rated the urgency of contractors' production and provided for the delivery of metals during the coming quarter. Various metals could carry a different priority rating for the same manufacturer. Theoretically, demand for metals would not be allowed to exceed supply, and priorities would become only a means for timing the delivery of metals, not a claim on them. Of incomparable value to WPB was the fact that PRP would provide the board with nearly complete information on wartime industrial load essential for maintaining economic stability.

A number of forces pushed a somewhat reluctant Nelson to make the PRP compulsory when he did. His principal lieutenant, Director of Industry Operations James S. Knowlson, and Chief of the Bureau of Priorities C. H. Matthiessen, Jr., insisted that the existing system for distributing materials had broken down and could not be salvaged. Priorities issued by the armed services and WPB, blanket priorities for particular industries, allocations of steel, aluminum, and other metals by WPB materials branches, and related regulations were all unsynchronized, and most had no quantitative controls. Unless WPB centrally distributed materials, mobilization would become increasingly chaotic. The OPM had introduced PRP on an experimental and voluntary basis in December 1941, the WPB continued the plan with some compulsory features, and, by June 1942, around seven thousand firms were already participating. When fully implemented, PRP would cover most metal fabrication by eighteen thousand large corporate users.

Knowlson waited until May 4 before recommending to Nelson that PRP be made mandatory. He would have moved earlier except for strong opposition to the plan from the military and elements within the board. The armed services adamantly opposed PRP because they believed that war production should be centered in military, not civilian, agencies. Moreover, PRP was aimed at industrial plants, not munitions. With PRP, the services could lose the direct control over weapons supply that they currently held. WPB materials branches, such as those for steel and copper, also argued fervently against PRP. They had a host of theoretical reasons for objecting, but, since they were already allocating the output of their industries, the essential reason was that they would lose power and position under PRP. Since industry dominated the materials branches through its representatives serving in WPB and on advisory committees, it was reluctant to surrender clout and control already in hand. The materials branches' position was favored by a substantial number of WPB corporate executives.

The military, the materials branches, and others in WPB preferred vertical controls over the horizontal controls of PRP. With PRP, WPB made allocations to metal-fabricating facilities whether those plants manufactured semifinished goods, parts, or finished products; metals were distributed on a single plane without regard to stages of production. A vertical system would follow the procurement-production chain. WPB would allocate materials to claimants, like the army, that would divide them among their contractors, the contractors among their subcontractors, and so on. In this way, the distribution of metals was tied directly to end products, production to strategy.

Informally, a decentralized, uncoordinated vertical system operated with the NDAC, the OPM, and the initial WPB. Once the military granted priority ratings to its contractors, the contractors could extend those claims to their subcontractors. The same was true for whole industries benefiting from blanket priorities like airframes and ship hulls. With metals industries under allocation, including steel, copper, aluminum, nickel, and synthetic rubber, materials branches often ignored or modified assigned priorities in which they lacked confidence. They then worked directly with the military and industry in distributing metals and other products according to established urgency. Most industries and firms benefiting from these practices, along with claimant agencies, materials branches, and WPB executives, saw no need for centralized allocations as long as less structured methods were working. At most, they favored improving what existed. If basic change was necessary, they did not want a cumbersome horizontal allocation system that they believed to be unsound and that would reduce their power and might threaten their materials supply.

With controversy over materials control growing and WPB divided over the matter, Nelson early in May reconstituted the Committee on Feasibility as the Committee on Control of the Flow of Materials. Robert R. Nathan chaired the committee, which was made up of representatives from key WPB divisions. Working intensely under nearly impossible pressures, the committee grudgingly advised Nelson on May 26 that WPB had to implement PRP for the third quarter to improve materials distribution. Nelson, then, authorized Knowlson to proceed. On May 30, WPB took the first formal step in instituting a slightly modified PRP. With some exceptions, all firms consuming over $5,000 in scarce metals in any three-month period were included. Eventually, all enterprises were brought within PRP's reporting system so as to provide WPB as complete data on materials use as possible.

PRP was an extremely ambitious project. It was designed to track and direct the flow of 90 percent or more of thirty-six metals basic to manufacturing. If the allocation system worked as intended, it would place in WPB's hands for the first time very specific control over the entire economy. Its immediate challenges, however, were immense. PRP was new, demanding, and not fully understood at any level. The paperwork was staggering and the job of tabulating, classifying, and analyzing myriad reports and data monumental. Months of educating, training, and accumulating staff, setting up procedures, writing manuals, and other steps were essential for initiating the endeavor with any hope of success. Knowlson and his assistants did not have that luxury. They were forced to devote the months between February and May to battling to have PRP accepted. With only June left before implementing PRP in July, time had all but run out.

Under those circumstances, the PRP was defeated before it started. The plan plunged WPB into extreme administrative tumult. Once it was under way, there was no turning back. By necessity, the third quarter became an experimental one in which the new system was worked out, not to be fully applied until the fourth quarter, preparations for which also had to begin in July and early August. Third-quarter confusion was rife as various units struggled to complete only partially understood assignments, competing WPB units fought over turf, and industry struggled with perplexing forms. Adding to the confusion was the fact that deadlines were regularly missed, industry classifications did not work as intended, massive statistical errors were made, and guesswork and arbitrary decisions by unqualified persons were commonplace. A sense of disarray was furthered by continuing in effect priority and related controls to assist the transition to allocations and by the ANMB introducing in June revamped priority regulations.

All the missteps convinced PRP's opponents that they were right, and the gross fumbling tended to turn those who were skeptical against the plan. By

September 1942, opposition to PRP was so widespread that Nelson turned to an alternate approach.

Although PRP was replaced by the CMP, devised late in 1942 and fully implemented in July 1943, it was not an unqualified failure. PRP was WPB's basic allocation approach for almost a year. This was the most critical period in getting economic mobilization for World War II fully under way. PRP was largely responsible for the vast acceleration of munitions production, which peaked in the fall of 1943. In that sense, PRP was a success. PRP succeeded in another critical way. It made unmistakably clear the imperative need for a full, integrated allocation system. Resistance to that reality throughout WPB and the armed services vanished. Furthermore, PRP graphically demonstrated that the extraordinary complexities of a full-blown allocation system required months of preparation and education. The success of the CMP owed a great deal to what was learned from PRP.

The CMP also had the benefit of mobilization conditions denied PRP. When the latter was put into effect, feasible requirements and production scheduling did not exist. That meant that PRP became practically the sole regulatory device for guiding mobilization. Unable to fulfill impossible goals, PRP was blamed for the failure of larger mobilization policies. With feasibility and production scheduling instituted late in 1942 and early in 1943, CMP worked well because it was expected to do less. Indeed, the single most important reason for the failure of PRP was the armed services' refusal to scale back their demand in accordance with the availability of scarce metals documented by the plan. No mode of allocations can succeed if demand for materials chronically and grossly exceeds supply. When Nelson took back priority authority from ANMB in September 1942, he began setting the mobilization stage for successful allocation of materials with CMP.

Despite its various positive attributes, PRP had definite negative ones. Knowlson complained that "there was never any real pressure exerted either upon the branches of WPB or upon the Services to get behind [PRP] and push it."[25] Such an effort would have been largely futile. The military refused to be separated from its contractors, as PRP proposed. Most of industry resisted the plan because it opposed centralizing WPB power in a way not fully answerable to industry and materials branches dominated by corporations. Corporate America was no more willing to free its grip on the production process than the armed services were ready to dilute their procurement authority. The two power groups combined their strength to protect themselves against a potentially independent state. This pattern had been evident since the NDAC.

In terms of power and practice, PRP taught another vital mobilization lesson. David Novick, who was a member of WPB and who had fought in behalf of PRP, articulated that truth. If controls "disturb industrial practices too much," he argued,

> there is grave danger that manufacturing activity may be impeded so that it will not reach maximum production goals. If they do not interfere enough, there is equally grave danger that materials, labor, and industrial plant and machinery urgently required for war production will be diverted to other uses, and again the attainment of maximum output for war will be interfered with or made impossible.[26]

Priority and other controls preceding PRP did not go far enough along those lines; PRP went too far. The CMP achieved what Novick considered to be the "go-between role." It centralized materials distribution by formalizing the informal vertical controls that had emerged over two years and that were based on the operations of industry and armed services procurement. By drawing on existing institutions and patterns, CMP was simpler to administer than PRP was, and it won the support and cooperation of most involved in mobilization. Concentrating on the vertical production chain, CMP, unlike PRP, related materials to end products and output to the fighting front.

Donald M. Nelson took a major step away from PRP and toward CMP on September 20, 1942, when he appointed Ferdinand Eberstadt, head of ANMB, to be WPB's vice chair for program determination, replacing James S. Knowlson. Eberstadt would design a new system for controlling materials. Since March, he had been a leading advocate of vertical, as opposed to horizontal, allocations, and, in May, Major James Boyd and Commander John D. Small of the ANMB worked out the details for such an approach, which came to be known as the warrant plan. It was based in part on what was successfully used in England and what had been outlined by the Office of the Assistant Secretary of War's interwar planning.[27] By the time Eberstadt joined WPB, proposals for modifying PRP were being advocated, along with a host of vertical systems offered by the steel industry, automobile firms, and others.

The Committee on Control of the Flow of Materials ended its tenure in August by favoring but not formally recommending vertical methods to Nelson. During the same month, however, the Planning Committee, which Nathan also chaired, began concentrating on allocations, and, in September, it officially came out in favor of a vertical approach. Indeed, advised and assisted by Charles J. Hitch, a specialist on British economic mobilization techniques, the Planning Committee on September 1 sketched out to the WPB chair the essentials of what became the CMP.

From the time he joined WPB in September until he left in February 1943,

Eberstadt brought to WPB a driving, determined leadership style to which it was unaccustomed. Enormously talented, Eberstadt recognized and used the ability of others. After due deliberation, however, he insisted on decisions being followed by action. To an agency too often characterized by discord and drift Eberstadt introduced a welcome interlude of movement and direction.

Eberstadt quickly set about fashioning a vertical materials allocation system, the CMP. It was a composite that incorporated and blended the best and most suitable aspects of various proposals before WPB. In formulating CMP, Eberstadt worked through a Committee on Materials Control Plan, composed of WPB officials and representatives from claimant agencies, that met first on September 30. On October 27, Eberstadt presented WPB with a final draft of CMP, and it was released to the public on November 2.

CMP stressed simplicity, the use of existing institutions and practices whenever possible, and methods familiar to industry. It tied materials to the end products for which they were used. As the plan was set up, both claimant agencies and contractors were encouraged to make the most of allotted materials, avoid waste, and minimize inventories. The entire plan revolved around three controlled metals: steel (carbon and alloy); aluminum; and copper. These were basic to practically all munitions and war-related manufacturing, facilities, and construction. Sixteen other materials were carefully monitored but were not formally part of the plan. All materials were expected to flow in the approximate channels established by the three controlled ones.

When fully developed, CMP functioned in the following way. Claimant agencies—the army, navy, Maritime Commission, Office of Civilian Supply, Office of Lend-Lease Administration, etc.—stated their requirements for military and civilian goods. On the basis of bills of materials provided by their contractors, claimants would then specify the amounts of the three controlled materials required to produce their goods. The requirements for the controlled materials were to be broken down by major programs (tanks, planes, freighters, and the like) and monthly production schedules for a year, with the following six months covered by lump-sum needs. The three metals were to be given in forms and shapes as well as divided according to use for production, construction and facilities, or maintenance, repair, and operating needs. The composite of requirements from all claimants constituted total demand, which was compared with the estimated total supply of the three metals provided by divisions for steel, aluminum, and copper.

These divisions did the initial screening of claimant demand. Any problems unresolved at that level were referred to the Requirements Committee (on which sat major WPB officials and claimant representatives), which was the final review source and which made the allotment of the three controlled materials to claimants. Conflicts among military agencies were usually referred to JCS, and those among civilian and military claimants that the Requirements Committee could not settle could be appealed to the WPB chair. At this point, in theory, with three controlled materials matched in terms of demand and supply and all other materials following suit, the WPB would have achieved a balanced war mobilization program.

Once claimants received their allotments, they would reconcile their programs and schedules to their shares and, accordingly, distribute the three materials among their prime contractors. After taking his portion, the principal contractor either let subcontractors divide the remainder or divided it among them himself.

While basically vertical, CMP also involved horizontal allocations. Civilian goods, industrial equipment and machinery, products using slight amounts of controlled materials, and standard components usually produced in advance were not easily handled by vertical procedures. Consequently, they were serviced horizontally as "B" goods, as distinguished from "A" products, handled vertically. The total of controlled materials allowed for B products was charged to the general allotments of the responsible claimant agency. Although WPB tried to keep the B list limited, pressure constantly increased to expand the horizontal features of CMP.

Critical to the entire operation of CMP were allotment numbers. These numbers identified the claimant agency, the production program and schedule, and the month in which the shipment of the controlled material was authorized. All stages and inputs of production along with all orders and other paperwork, carried such numbers. With controlled and other materials directly identified with end products, monitoring, analyzing, and adjusting materials distribution was greatly facilitated. Just as important, allotment numbers were a sure guarantee of delivery. They took precedence over any priority.

CMP did not make priorities in general irrelevant, however. For noncontrolled materials or parts, claimant agencies and WPB industry divisions assigned priority rating or ratings. With rare exceptions, any priority rating was inferior to an allotment number.

To facilitate the administration of CMP, and to emphasize that materials control was the WPB's most important responsibility, Eberstadt, with Nelson's approval, reorganized the board in November 1942. He became program vice chair, with the director general for operations serving under him. Such an arrangement allowed Eberstadt to supervise practically the entire operating structure of WPB. Of critical importance to Eberstadt's November reorganization was elevating the industry branches to divisions and making them the basic operating units in WPB.

Acting as small WPBs, the divisions made decisions and spoke for the industry or industries they represented. To fulfill such extensive duties adequately, division membership was expanded. The divisions were then expected to handle requirements, production, distribution, conservation, and other policies and practices relevant to their realm. For example, not only did the Controlled Materials Divisions pass on requirements coming from claimant agencies and inform the Requirements Committee of industry's output capacity; they also directed and scheduled mill production in terms of quantity, shapes, and forms and oversaw industry's delivery of its products.[28]

Eberstadt's reorganization resulted in the creation of new board subdivisions and the rising prominence of existing and new executives. As program vice chair, Eberstadt himself headed the Requirements Committee, the one most important WPB subdivision responsible for materials allocations. Immediately below Eberstadt was Ernest Kanzler, formerly of the Ford Motor Company and currently board chair of the Universal CIT Credit Corporation. Kanzler was committed to elevating the status and increasing the responsibility of the industry divisions and appeared both to influence and to support Eberstadt in that regard. Julius A. Krug, a career civil servant who joined economic mobilization with OPM, served in Kanzler's office as deputy director general for distribution. The Distribution Bureau, which Krug headed, was central to all CMP operations. Also of critical importance was the Controlled Materials Plan Division, also under Krug, which worked out the details for implementing the new allocation system. Two new faces were brought in to head the division: Harold Boeschenstein, president and general manager of Owens-Corning Fiberglass Corporation, as director, and Walter C. Skuce, previous supervisor of materials procurement, priorities, and inventory control for General Electric Company, as assistant director. The CMP workhorses were the three Controlled Materials Divisions, with steel headed by Hiland G. Batcheller, president of Allegheny-Ludlum Steel Corporation, copper directed by Harry O. King, president of Munson Lines, and aluminum and magnesium under Arthur H. Bunker, a partner in Lehman Brothers.[29] Generally speaking, Eberstadt turned to manufacturing executives as his chief assistants.

Unlike the PRP, CMP benefited from a lengthy and extended period of explanation, education, and training for WPB, claimant agencies, and industry. Efforts at the national level were ultimately extended to regional and local areas. Ample time was also allotted for assembling staff, writing and publishing regulations, and working out procedures and techniques. Five months passed between the announcement of CMP in November 1942 and the process of phasing it in that began in April and continued until July 1, 1943. Actually, Eberstadt began taking preparatory steps for activating the plan shortly after announcing it in November, and he quickened the introductory pace during the early months of 1943. From November 1942 through June 1943, WPB modified and adjusted various aspects of CMP on the basis of criticism, insight, and experience. For the crucial area of inventory control, CMP was in theory inferior to PRP. In fact, however, CMP significantly reduced inventory concerns after July 1943. Once learning that the new allocation system reliably delivered controlled materials on schedule and in the right amounts, industry was much less likely to hoard.

Compared with the PRP, CMP more closely matched peacetime economic patterns, and it directly utilized existing practices and institutions. CMP centralized policymaking in WPB but decentralized operations among procurement agencies and their contractors; it structured, formalized, and vastly improved materials distribution methods emerging since the origins of the NDAC. For all its complexity, CMP was relatively simple in concept and application. In time, most of industry accepted it as necessary and successful. And it remained the basic means for allocating materials until the end of the war.

CMP was not a mobilization marvel. Charles J. Hitch and others proclaimed that the plan would make the economy into a vast munitions assembly line, integrating strategy, production, and materials flow, and allowing WPB to regulate the wartime economy efficiently at whatever level the agency desired. Nathan, Novick, and like-minded associates were more realistic. Maximizing the plan's potential, they insisted, depended on the entire procurement-production chain operating according to the dictates of feasibility. Ideally, claimant agencies would adjust their end-product requirements in terms of both quantity and time of delivery to the controlled materials they were allotted. Prime contractors, subcontractors, and suppliers would then base their scheduling of noncontrolled materials (e.g., nickel), parts (e.g., bearings), and components and subassemblies on the revised and refigured demand of the procurement agency. A balanced and stable economic mobilization program would emerge.

CMP never realized its promise, for a number of reasons. The armed services were partly to blame because they did little to reduce requirements to feasible levels as indicated by controlled materials allocations. Instead, they continued to schedule incentively, and WPB failed to force them into line. Prime contractors, in turn, frequently ordered beyond CMP-dictated needs for noncontrolled materials, components, and the like, to the detriment of overall output. As a result, munitions programs were, on paper, chronically behind schedule. More seriously, to meet the military's elevated demand, WPB's Requirements Committee reduced controlled materials flowing horizontally to manufacturers of parts, components, and subassemblies, at times decreasing their output below the demand level for important end products. Indeed, some noncontrolled materials in time became scarcer than those that were controlled. Unless controlled materials were coordinated with uncontrolled ones, no over-all production program could be kept in balance.

Most involved in allocations expected other materials to be added to CMP as shortages arose. That never took place. Correlating uncontrolled materials with controlled ones was blocked by industry divisions strenuously resisting further encroachment on their turf. As a result, the divisions could interfere with programs approved at the highest levels of WPB and claimant agencies. Under certain circumstances, the divisions could withhold materials that they managed from CMP-scheduled production. Such circumstances made CMP vulnerable to multiple forces over which its administrators had no control or of which they perhaps had no knowledge. More significant, those conditions stood in the way of CMP achieving an integrated, scheduled war production program.

Despite the negatives, CMP still realized a better balance between materials flow and end-product output than had existed before. During the last half of 1943, controlled materials were no longer the primary manufacturing bottleneck. The fact that raw materials capacity had been expanded was a definite plus. Still, the superiority of CMP as an allocation system, the quality of its administration, and the confidence that it engendered were of great importance. Also, by strongly emphasizing feasibility, CMP, albeit subtly and gradually, moved both claimants and manufacturers toward lowering demand to the level of supply. The production scheduling that CMP did not attain was achieved in another way.

PRODUCTION SCHEDULING

The WPB worked out the basis for scheduling wartime munitions production late in 1942. Even if the CMP had worked perfectly as intended and all claimant agencies had cooperated fully, WPB would still have had to become involved in scheduling. Procurement agencies at times competed for scarce materials, parts, and assemblies. WPB was the only agency with the authority, staff, and experience to direct the flow of materials and components in a way that maximized munitions manufacturing.

From the outset, the Planning Committee insisted that, without proper scheduling, even feasible requirements would disrupt mobilization.[30] Stacy May illustrated the committee's point. Beginning in mid-1942, the WPB's chief statistician warned that wartime production was in trouble. By August, munitions output had reached only half of annual goals, and production rates were dropping, not rising. Follow-up reports in September and October confirmed these alarming trends. May stated that, from January through July, munitions output had grown at an average monthly rate of 13 percent but that, since August, the figure had dropped to an average of 4 percent. At such a low level, production would not meet even feasible goals.[31] Improper production scheduling was to blame.

May and Robert R. Nathan, backed by the Truman Committee and others, provided ample evidence of fundamentally flawed scheduling on the part of the army and navy.[32] Production delays stemmed less from materials shortages than from the fact that steel, aluminum, and other key supplies did not flow to the most important projects at the right time. Along these lines, various shipyards stored steel needed eighteen months down the line at the same time as construction of escort vessels for handling German submarines suffered from steel shortages. Besides misusing steel, such conditions wasted storage space, cluttered job sites, misused transportation systems, and disturbed all other factors of output. The same outcome resulted from the standard military practice of stockpiling ammunition and other items far in advance of need and usage.

Critically needed machine tools, additionally, went to firms not needing them, while those firms that did saw their production adversely affected. Some components or parts were underordered, others grossly overordered. Numerous contractors delayed placing orders for inputs, confident that procurement agencies would ensure that their needs were met. And manufacturers faced hosts of claimant-agency expediters intent on rushing production for their benefit, even at the expense of others.

Even as production rates were dropping, the services claimed that they were rising. Gross production figures were misleading. Output of easily manufactured items such as clothing and motor vehicles was far ahead of demand, but difficult end items like combat planes and signal equipment were far behind.

Most of these practices resulted from flawed procurement methods. The various claimants did not follow uniform scheduling policies, including determining amounts of materials and components for specific items, setting production lead times, converting and utilizing facilities, and handling changes in design and specifications. Of enormous importance was the fact that no agency acted to coordinate and reconcile competing demands for materials, parts, tools, and the like. Under such circumstances, production inevitably declined, and it would continue to do so without fundamental change. Not only did WPB have to take up production scheduling, May, Nathan, and others averred, but, in doing so, the board also had to get away from annual projections to deal in quarters, months, and even shorter periods to avoid or clear manufacturing bottlenecks.

Nelson moved to correct the situation in September 1942 by recruiting Charles E. Wilson, president of General Electric Company (GE). Wilson would serve as vice chair of production and head the newly created Production Executive Committee (PEC), made up of the heads of procurement for the army, the Army Air Forces (AAF), the navy, and the Naval Bureau of Aeronautics, along with the vice chair of the Maritime Commission and Eberstadt as the WPB's program vice chair. Nelson announced that Wilson would be the board's top production authority with responsibility for ensuring that all manufacturing goals were met. Exactly how Wilson would carry out such vast responsibilities was left unspecified. Indeed, the new vice chair took a number of months to familiarize himself with WPB.

Nelson brought Wilson into WPB to regain control over production, which the army and navy claimed under agreements negotiated with the board in March and April 1942. Nelson had begun reasserting the board's authority about the same time that he spelled out WPB's relations with the armed services, indicating that the WPB chair never intended to grant the military the free rein that it asserted. In March 1942, Nelson took up feasibility; in July, he made the PRP mandatory; in September, he reclaimed priority power and invited Eberstadt to join the board in reworking materials allocations; and, in September, he secured Wilson's services. The intense struggles between WPB and the military over feasibility, priorities/allocations, and production scheduling occurred simultaneously and interacted; their resolution also took place simultaneously, in the last few months of 1942.

As the last step, Wilson's appointment was troubled from the beginning. It ultimately cost Nelson his job. Wilson would not accept Nelson's initial offer to join WPB, believing that he was needed at GE because of its vast war contracts. Also, the company was reluctant to have its president serving in Washington while antitrust suits were still pending. Secretary of War Henry L. Stimson negotiated directly on the matter with Owen D. Young, GE's board chair, and eventually Roosevelt intervened, insisting that Wilson owed the country his service.

Wilson was not the mobilization savior that many in and outside WPB, including New Dealers, had hoped for. Knowing little about him, most expected Wilson, who had just taken over as GE president, to be in the enlightened corporate mold of Young and the past president, Gerard Swope. That was not the case. Narrow, cautious, and conservative, Wilson was a capable industrialist but an ineffective public leader. Having risen from the bottom to the top of GE, he functioned well only within the GE environment. He never mastered or even fully understood WPB operations. While powerful and shrewd,

Wilson was insecure, petty, and ruthless. He surrounded himself with yes-men, constantly threatened to resign in order to get his way, and avoided the tough decisions that Nelson had in his own way made. Few in the board had confidence in Wilson, and the executive chair maneuvered to get rid of those of ability who threatened him, such as Hiland G. Batcheller. Positive assessments of Wilson are all but missing from the wartime records, and criticisms, often bitter attacks, abound.

Nelson wanted Wilson in WPB for the obvious reason that the board needed a production specialist at the vice chair level. Since William S. Knudsen left OPM, the principal mobilization agency had no top leader familiar with the nuts and bolts of mass output. With conversion, feasibility, and allocations behind it, WPB faced one remaining challenge, managing production. Another reason explains Wilson's appointment. Eberstadt and Wilson joined the board at the same time. The former was identified with the armed services, and Wilson was considered to be a civilian advocate balancing Eberstadt's influence.

At the outset, Wilson was welcomed by the armed services. Increasingly antagonized by Nelson, whom they perceived as weak, the army, and to a degree the navy, believed that Wilson, along with Eberstadt, would bring order and direction to WPB. In part, the military supported Wilson's appointment because it believed that he would facilitate production without disturbing its procurement operations.

For two months or so, Wilson's presence in WPB had little impact. Exactly what he and PEC would do remained uncertain. As May and Nathan began tightening production-scheduling screws, Wilson's role became clearer and much more controversial. Early in November 1942, the Planning Committee completed an analysis of scheduling problems and set forth in detail what WPB should do to correct the situation.[33] Drawing heavily on the Planning Branch's work, Wilson on November 11 laid out to the PEC his policies for correcting the scheduling tangle.

He would appoint a director general of production scheduling to head a PEC subcommittee. All procurement agencies would create scheduling units in each bureau or branch along with a central office to direct agency activities. A representative from the latter body would sit on the scheduling subcommittee. On the basis of PEC policies and rules, each procurement agency would submit to the subcommittee monthly production schedules for all items consistent with JCS goals. The committee would review the schedules for internal consistency, availability of facilities, critical materials, common components, complementary items, and manpower; and it would resolve conflicting programs and ensure that overall demand was balanced and feasible. Wilson's proposal was unanimously endorsed by PEC members, who were designated to "advise and assist" the chair.[34]

Almost immediately, General Brehon B. Somervell, who was not at the meeting but had sent General Lucius D. Clay as his alternate, rejected Wilson's proposal and rallied the navy and Under Secretary of War Patterson to his cause. This set off a nearly two-month battle between the WPB and the military over production scheduling—in Nelson's own words, "the bitterest fight I ever had with the War Department people."[35] Issues aside, Somervell was determined to protect his turf, and Patterson did not step in to check him, as he had done during the feasibility struggle.

Writing for the ASF, the AAF, and their navy counterparts, Somervell on November 16 informed Wilson that his proposed role for PEC was unacceptable: the committee could not accomplish Wilson's goals; and, if it tried, PEC would be abrogating the armed services' March and April agreements with Nelson, violating CMP procedures, and taking over JCS responsibilities. At regular and special meetings of the WPB, Somervell directed an assault on the need for WPB scheduling, claiming that the military was performing well, and insisting that declining munitions output resulted from WPB's failures in distributing scarce materials.[36]

Determined to hold his ground, Wilson worked with Nelson in drafting preliminary WPB orders that spelled out PEC's functions, including a section that terminated those parts of Nelson's agreements with the War and Navy Departments that conflicted with Wilson's responsibilities. Somervell and Patterson carried their case to Secretary of War Stimson and, through Harry L. Hopkins, to the White House.

Instead of stepping in to aid the military, Roosevelt offered his assistance to Nelson. The latter, knowing that the fight would end only when he convinced the War Department that he was right, simply asked Roosevelt not to back the armed services. At that point, the president ordered Nelson, Stimson, and Secretary of the Navy Knox to settle their differences. Through meetings and correspondence, the WPB and the War Department in December resolved the matter. Stimson largely determined the War Department's position, considering Patterson, and behind him Somervell, lacking sensitivity and flexibility about the dispute. About the same time, the secretary expressed his disdain for Nelson and his growing doubts about Wilson.[37]

With Nelson and Wilson assuring Stimson that they never intended to take over procurement duties or to interfere with JCS prerogatives, the conflict was settled largely along the lines earlier outlined by Wilson. With Knox's consent, Stimson insisted on a "bill of rights for the practices of the services."[38]

Of principal importance were agreements that any downward revisions of requirements would be handled by JCS and that PEC would carry out its responsibilities by working with the military's existing supply and procurement structures. Nonetheless, in issuing the administrative order defining PEC functions on December 9, Nelson stressed Wilson's authority, not limitations on it.[39]

Wilson's duties fell into two related areas. Nelson specifically directed Wilson to oversee the production of aircraft, radio and radar equipment, and escort vessels, ensuring that the president's production goals for 1943 were met. For aircraft, Wilson would work through an Aircraft Production Board made up of civilian and military officials directing armed forces aircraft procurement. In this instance, WPB continued practices reaching back to the NDAC. For the larger task of scheduling war production in general, Wilson would operate along the lines that he set forth to the PEC in November 1942.

Before the PEC could get fully under way, Wilson and Eberstadt had to work out a division of labor between production scheduling and materials distribution. Largely at Eberstadt's initiative, the two in November arrived at an agreement dealing with the review of and appropriate action concerning military, civilian, and foreign requirements. With the arrangement made, new systems for materials and production control got under way.

Production scheduling came into its own in 1943 and was adjusted to mobilization realities as needed until WPB was disestablished at the end of 1945. Initial scheduling began with materials distribution under the CMP. PEC then reviewed claimants' individual and collective procurement programs for feasibility, consistency, and priority. In performing these functions, the committee relied heavily on industry divisions. The divisions knew or made themselves aware of manufacturing cycles for end items, lead times, and so forth in order to devise proper input flow. In addition, they worked with manufacturers to maximize production and to check claimants' efforts to get specialized treatment for their contractors at the expense of other procurement agencies.

PEC's most important scheduling duties involved components. With materials becoming more plentiful, components were becoming the major obstacle to maximum production late in 1942. Components were the parts essential to completing end products. They varied all the way from the smallest jewel bearings to mammoth steel castings and forgings; in the case of trucks, for example, internal combustion engines were a major component, requiring such subcomponents as values, crankshafts, and dozens of other parts. Heat exchangers, turbines, blowers, pumps, and bearings were all in short supply, with multiple claimants in the most critical production programs for ships, aircraft, and synthetic rubber.

Desperate need forced WPB early in 1942 to schedule the production and distribution of key items such as machine tools, compressors, turboblowers, and other products. The board was able to do this with relative success using rudimentary methods because manufacturers and consumers were relatively few in number. More typically, common components had hundreds of producers and thousands of users. Successfully scheduling them required sophisticated techniques. During peacetime, common components were "off-the-shelf" items readily obtained as needed.[40] Chronic wartime shortages changed that reality and required contractors to adjust their attitudes and practices accordingly, a process often difficult to do.

At the end of 1942, PEC compiled a list of thirty-four common components and arranged with Eberstadt for their manufacturers to receive materials for meeting 100 percent of their known requirements. In January 1943, the committee went further, requiring all contractors to place designated common component orders for the first two quarters of 1943 by February 6 and for the remainder of the year by March 1. PEC also divided components into three categories, compiling data on supply and demand, and instituting regulations based on levels of urgency. Once approved by the committee, component orders could be altered only by WPB.

In June 1943, PEC went further with a Components Scheduling Plan (CSP) for the most important munitions facing production delays. Manufacturers of ships, tanks, and rubber fell into this category. Under the plan, components were tabulated, verified, and tracked much like materials under CMP. Voluntary at the outset, selectively mandatory for a time, CSP had to be diluted in 1944 because of objections to cumbersome procedures and demanding paperwork. Component scheduling in general became less onerous as production increased, even though some items remained in short supply even at war's end.

Absent before PEC's creation, these practices helped solve the production crisis developing in the last half of 1942. Combined with feasibility and materials allocation, production scheduling distributed the industrial load among firms in a balanced fashion.

Before PEC was fully under way, a crisis over scheduling arose in WPB in December 1942, grew in intensity for two months, and ended in a destructive eruption in February.[41] At the center of the conflict were Production Vice Chair Charles E. Wilson, Program Vice Chair Ferdinand Eberstadt, and the industry divisions.

The industry divisions had gradually evolved as WPB's principal operating units, particularly after Eberstadt's reorganization in November 1942. The program vice chair controlled almost all the divisions. While this arrangement made some sense when materials were the principal limiting production factor, it was less logical with materials scarcity easing as CMP was phased in. The new emphasis for WPB was production scheduling. To fulfill his responsibilities, Wilson needed selected industry divisions under his direction. At first he had de facto, and later formal, control of the Aircraft Division along with the Radio and Radar Division. In December 1942, Wilson argued that he required jurisdiction over all industry divisions related to military end items and their components. Later, he expanded the list of divisions to include those that affected the production vice chair, including the Aluminum and Magnesium Division. While potentially all divisions in one way or another involved production scheduling, most also dealt with materials distribution, and that was certainly the case with the Controlled Materials Divisions, of which Aluminum and Magnesium was one. Eberstadt presented a forceful case to Nelson for maintaining jurisdiction of the industry divisions that he needed. After months of growing strain, Nelson on February 4 transferred to Wilson's office key industry divisions and stated that the production vice chair could claim any other organizational units that he required.

Nelson's action created a major crisis within WPB and mobilization circles. While industry divisions were of great importance, an even larger issue was at stake. Eberstadt and Wilson were in coordinate positions under Nelson. Equally ambitious and driven, the two could remain in WPB only if they agreed to work side by side; one would not accept a subordinate position to the other. Matters of power were further complicated by personalities. Different in background, approaches, and temperament, the two never appeared to relate well. While attempting to work out accords with Wilson, Eberstadt did so from a position of strength where the industry divisions were concerned. Dividing industry divisions between the two might have been possible, but Wilson appeared to be uninterested in that solution.

Taking the role of the aggressor, Wilson was intent on domination, even at the cost, possibly the intent, of driving Eberstadt from WPB. Although evidence is incomplete, Wilson was probably in contact with the White House and insisted on controlling all industry divisions as his price for remaining on the board. For various reasons, the president disliked Eberstadt and favored Wilson. With Nelson failing to move forthrightly in resolving the growing tension between Wilson and Eberstadt, Roosevelt decided to replace Nelson with Wilson at the opportune time. He appeared to have reached that decision no later than January 1943. Nelson was probably acting under direct orders from the president when he transferred all industry divisions to Wilson early in February. Whatever the situation, Nelson was favoring Wilson over Eberstadt aware that, at some point, the latter would resign from WPB.

Director of Economic Stabilization James F. Byrnes, conservative and close to the armed services, used these dramatic circumstances to persuade Roosevelt that he should replace Nelson at once, but with Bernard M. Baruch, not Wilson. If the president of GE was put in charge, Byrnes reasoned, Nelson's supporters would be alienated, further harming economic mobilization. Stimson, Patterson, and Somervell, with some support from the Navy Department, had favored Baruch's elevation at the expense of Nelson for quite some time, had been pushing Byrnes along those lines, and joined him in pressuring the president on Baruch's behalf.[42] Eberstadt was identified with the military and considered to be the best executive in WPB. In directing WPB, Baruch's age and health would require him to rely heavily on assistants. These would most likely include his close associate John M. Hancock and Eberstadt, whom he knew well and respected.

A hesitant and frustrated Roosevelt finally agreed to offer Baruch the post—a move that he had been resisting for over two years—but the elder statesman took several days to make up his mind. Learning of the intrigue, Nelson on February 16 quickly fired Eberstadt. By doing so, he saved his job since the president could not replace Nelson without appearing to favor Eberstadt. Furthermore, for various substantive and symbolic reasons, Roosevelt was no doubt relieved not to be elevating Baruch to serve as WPB chair. Without official action, the earlier offer to Baruch was tacitly withdrawn, ending one of the more bizarre intrigues in the wartime capital.

Acting on his own or on instructions from the White House, Nelson on February 16 also elevated Wilson to executive vice chair and, by administrative order, turned over to him operating control of WPB.[43] The WPB chair ultimately was left directing only a few offices. In March 1943, Wilson implemented the final major reorganization of the board. He kept directly under his control the board's production-scheduling apparatus, CMP units, and several other key offices. Otherwise, WPB was directed by four vice chairs, all of whom reported to Wilson: Julius A. Krug, as program vice chair, was the most important; the operations vice chair changed frequently; Ralph J. Cordiner, president of Schick, Incorporated, and a former associate of Wilson's in GE (as vice chair without portfolio), served as the executive vice chair's assistant; and William L. Batt occupied the position for international supply.

Critical to the March 1943 reorganization was loss of the Planning Committee. Nelson had always kept the committee as a staff agency to the chair. Inexplicably, he turned the committee over to Wilson. Uncomfortable with the committee, and unappreciative of its significance, Wilson did not welcome Robert R. Nathan and his associates. Furthermore, Wilson and Cordiner felt that they had to placate the military, which had lost out in the fight to oust

Nelson and keep Eberstadt. Controlling procurement, the armed services' cooperation was essential to Wilson's success. The armed services, particularly the War Department, were intensely hostile toward the Planning Committee because of the battles over facilities, feasibility, production scheduling, and other matters. Consequently, Wilson first placed the committee under Cordiner and then even lower in the hierarchy. Nathan and other members resigned before the shuffle was completed, ending the committee's tenure as of April 1, 1943.

Almost as great a loss to WPB was Stacy May, who into 1943 had headed the Statistics Division and the Office of Progress Reports. May had fought side by side with the Planning Committee in behalf of a rationalized mobilization system. Krug had the opportunity to have both the Planning Committee and the Statistics Division under his direction, but he rejected the offer. Bernard L. Gladieux pointed out that both agencies were associated with academic "long-hairs," "New Dealers," theorists who were resented, not only by the military, but also by industry.[44] Exceptionally ambitious, Krug did not want to carry the taint of their cause. Ultimately, May's services were retained by a Bureau of Planning and Statistics that served under Cordiner. It was a mere shadow of what the former Planning Committee and Statistics Division had been.

By March 1943, WPB had passed through its most important phase of development. It had worked out the controls essential for managing wartime growth. Tension between Nelson, Wilson, and their bureaucratic allies was high, but WPB had advanced to the point where essential functions could be performed even within a suspicious, hostile environment. Also, Byrnes as director of economic stabilization began to act as assistant president for the homefront late in 1942, and that role became more definite when he became director of the Office of War Mobilization in May 1943. Conflict within and among mobilization agencies would now be settled outside the Oval Office as Roosevelt increasingly concentrated on the war abroad.

WPB IN MARCH 1943

For many contemporaries and future scholars, WPB conflict and missed opportunities stand out in 1942. Yet, during its first year, the board devised methods that made the production record of 1943 and after possible. Between 1939 and 1944, GNP grew by 52 percent in stable dollars, and manufacturing output trebled. With some validity, those accomplishments are often attributed to the economy's vast potential rather than to the means for mobilizing it. Nonetheless, wrong policies or the lack of right ones can deter the growth of the strongest economic system. America's massive wartime production did not just happen; proper guidance and planning played a major role in what took place.

Donald M. Nelson deserves a great deal of credit for the mobilization system implemented in 1942. Yet he is often portrayed as an amiable, well-intended, but weak leader. With virtually no one fully satisfied with how WPB functioned, Nelson is usually faulted for its real or perceived failures. New Dealers were disappointed because the board did not adequately strengthen the state; labor, small business, consumer advocates, and others were angered by their exclusion from WPB's inner circles and by policies that they opposed; civil servants were distressed by WPB's constant strife and its chaotic administration; and most of these critics were convinced that WPB was too attentive to big business and not tough enough with the military. Industry wanted WPB to operate like the World War I War Industries Board (WIB), and it distrusted Nelson because of his reliance on New Deal advisers such as Leon Henderson and Robert R. Nathan. The armed services, and especially the army, were outraged that WPB set parameters for carrying out procurement. All these positions were reflected in one way or another in Congress, where Nelson had more friends than enemies. Still, since few on Capitol Hill were genuinely satisfied with WPB, Nelson received tepid sympathy rather than strong backing.

Nelson was in an unenviable position. He had to contend with two powerful forces greatly limiting what WPB could do. First was the large corporate community. The American political economy based on a government-business regulatory partnership had changed in substance and tone during the Great Depression. Washington expanded massively, frequently at business's expense, and relations between corporate and government structures grew increasingly antagonistic. Mobilization for World War II altered the dynamics of the nation's political economy in a way favoring industry. Although the federal government grew rapidly in the 1930s, it did not develop a higher civil service capable of harnessing the economy. As during World War I, Washington had to turn to industrialists, assisted by economists, attorneys, and other professionals, to do the job. Through dollar-a-year men and industry divisions, corporations kept control of the central mobilization agencies in their own hands, ensured that labor and other interest groups were checked, and undermined or prevented New Deal–type experiments. Industry seized on Washington's dependence and war-induced prosperity to reclaim the power and prestige lost during a decade of depression.

The second force of great consequence was the armed services. Conducting their own procurement, they had a vast impact on the wartime economy. Unlike the civilian sector of government, the military's officer corps, and, below it, non-commissioned officers, constituted a career, policymaking elite—one that was greatly expanded by recruits and supplemented by volunteer businessmen, professionals, and others to handle the emergency. Until World War I, the armed services had controlled their own buying in peace and war without major difficulty. Resisting civilian-directed mobilization methods during World War I, the military came close to losing its procurement authority. That did not take place because of the nature of America's political economy. Since the WIB was dominated by industrialists, the Woodrow Wilson administration refused to place military buying in WIB hands because of the potential conflicts of interest. Through procurement and economic mobilization planning during the interwar years, the armed forces prepared themselves for World War II. With the NDAC and the OPM remaining weak in 1940–1941 and the WPB slow in getting started in 1942, the military challenged civilian mobilization agencies instead of merging with them, as interwar planning had proposed.

Many analysts and World War II participants charge that Donald M. Nelson's first major error was allowing the army and navy to continue conducting their own procurement. In retrospect, the WPB chair had few options. A WPB that had trouble fully converting industry to war production was hardly prepared to take on massive military buying responsibilities. If it had tried to do so, the board would have encountered the conflicts-of-interest dilemma. And the military would have strenuously fought any such attempt.

Had Nelson moved to absorb armed services procurement, corporate America had every reason to oppose him. Between June 1940 and December 1941, industry and the military had worked out relations within and outside NDAC and OPM that were mutually supportive. As the loosely structured OPM was replaced by the more centralized WPB, corporations were not anxious to have the board accrue too much power. A WPB buying for the armed forces would have been less dominated by industry. Such a development could have led to a strengthened New Deal state, an outcome that business in general was intent on avoiding.

During 1942, as WPB struggled to devise effective mobilization methods, industry and military leaders often shared outlooks. Various industrialists were as opposed to feasibility constraints as the army was. Neither business nor the armed services saw any urgency in replacing the hodgepodge of priority, allocation, and related controls with comprehensive materials allocation. When Nelson forced such a system on them, they helped undermine horizontal methods that they did not want in favor of the vertical ones that they did. The industry divisions moved cautiously toward production scheduling, and, once it was implemented, they joined the armed services in limiting its application.

In 1942, then, Nelson fought a two-front bureaucratic war involving industry within WPB and the armed services outside it. Under such adverse circumstances, he could do little more than develop and implement general policies for ensuring the successful mobilization of the economy. Few business leaders were better qualified to achieve those ends. Throughout his years in NDAC and OPM, Nelson demonstrated a sophisticated grasp of the economic system and how it could best be harnessed for war. He consistently turned to Leon Henderson and his group for policy guidance because of their expertise and bold, farsighted advocacy. In doing so, he was fully aware that he estranged industry and the military.

The Planning Committee, the Office of Progress Reports, and the Statistics Division, along with a few businessmen such as James S. Knowlson, either led or initiated the drive for feasibility, what became the CMP, and production scheduling. Without Nelson's steady support, those critical controls would not have been adopted or would have been delayed, disrupting, perhaps disastrously, the mobilization effort. Nelson preferred to lead by agreement rather than fiat or power play. He avoided conflict whenever possible, and he displayed other like characteristics that frustrated many. These traits may have been exaggerated by Nelson's sense that he could not always depend on Roosevelt's support in a crunch or that the president could act to WPB's detriment at the urging of other mobilization agencies. Yet he had the intelligence to see the need for and the courage to insist on policies that he was convinced were indispensable for successful mobilization.

The drawn-out, often brutal mobilization battles of 1942 had a devastating effect on Nelson. Milton Katz, who had been with the mobilization structure since 1940 and served as WPB solicitor during 1942–1943, pointed out that, by late 1942 and early 1943, Nelson was burned out and ill. Those conditions, made worse by a complicated personal life that distracted the WPB chair and made him vulnerable to political attack, reduced Nelson to periods of practical paralysis. Bernard L. Gladieux, who in January 1943 moved over from the Bureau of the Budget to direct WPB's organization and administration, reported that the normally sanguine Nelson was in a dark mood after fighting off James F. Byrnes and the army's attempt to oust him in favor of Bernard M. Baruch early in 1943. Dispirited, he willingly turned over control of the WPB to Wilson, only later deciding to keep a few offices under his authority. From then on, Gladieux notes, most WPB executives treated him without respect, even with derision.[45] Along with the Planning Committee and Stacy May's offices, the WPB chair was being shoved aside.

With WPB more tightly structured, exercising greater economic control, and having clearer goals, industry and the military by March 1943 could return to the cooperative patterns established under NDAC and OPM. But now they would do so under leaders such as Charles E. Wilson and Julius A. Krug. Nonetheless, WPB operations and accomplishments in 1943 and after were made possible by what Donald M. Nelson and his mobilization team had achieved in 1942.

13
THE WPB AT FLOOD TIDE, 1943–1944

Under the direction of the War Production Board (WPB), the economy late in 1943 reached its highest levels of munitions output. From then on, direct or indirect military requirements generally remained on a plateau or declined, although the armed services' needs fluctuated according to the immediate exigencies of the battlefronts. Having devised and implemented the means for harnessing the massive American economy for war, WPB in 1943 and after turned to the task of adjusting the mobilized system to the multiple changes and crises that arose with the demands of global warfare.

A growing economy in 1943 also allowed the WPB to increase the flow of products to civilians. Continued scarcity of such goods could adversely affect war production after the drastic reduction in nonmunitions output in 1942. With its responsibility reduced from the civilian economy in general to only consumer goods, the Office of Civilian Requirements (OCR) was better able to represent and to act on behalf of civilians. Despite its gains in 1943, OCR still encountered a great deal of resistance, even hostility, in the WPB, which concentrated on war production. These unfavorable conditions became much worse in 1944 and 1945, when the reconversion controversy all but halted greater production for civilians even though the economy's potential had grown and military demand was decreasing.

The issue of small business was always closely related to that of civilian supply. As a group, small businesses were more involved in output for civilian markets. Absorbed in converting and expanding the economy for war output during 1942, WPB had not paid as much attention to small business as it might have. Led by legislative advocates of the "little fellow," Congress in mid-1942 passed legislation setting up the Smaller War Plants Corporation (SWPC), which was tied into WPB. While this approach yielded some benefits for its clients in 1943 and 1944, WPB and claimant agencies never awarded small business what many of those firms, their congressional advocates, and other supporters felt to be a fair share of war work. WPB and the military, various small-unit spokesmen insisted, were wedded to the interests of large corporations. Nonetheless, many smaller business units ended up doing reasonably well during the war years, although small business as a group lost market share to larger corporations.

Throughout most of 1943 and 1944, WPB politics were exceptionally tumultuous. The board in effect divided between those favoring the chair, Donald M. Nelson, and those aligning with the executive vice chair, Charles E. Wilson. Since Wilson controlled the principal subdivisions for policymaking and operations, he dominated WPB. Wilson increasingly shaped and implemented economic mobilization through the Production Executive Committee (PEC), staffed heavily with representatives from the armed services. A bifurcated board performed as well as it did because most key mobilization functions had been worked out under Nelson in 1942 and early 1943. With clearly defined policies and procedures, the board's subdivisions continued operating well even when top-level management was at loggerheads.

But these conditions could not go on indefinitely. Nelson moved to break the deadlock and take back WPB leadership beginning late in 1943 and early in 1944 in a battle over defining and implementing reconversion policies. Wilson resisted Nelson's move, and the armed services in and outside the board went beyond Wilson in aggressively blocking the chair's attempt to regain control of WPB. The ensuing conflict brought WPB divisions out into the open, with battles raging throughout a good part of 1944. Finally, in August 1944, the divided board was once again united after both Nelson and Wilson were forced out. Thereafter, WPB entered a more prosaic phase, but with the board following conservative lines favored by many WPB executives and the military.

The large corporate interests and the armed services had their way on reconversion policies at least in part because James F. Byrnes supported their position. Byrnes had begun to act as assistant president for the homefront while serving as director of the Office of Economic Stabilization (OES) late in 1942. This role was made more formal and more authoritative when President Franklin D. Roosevelt elevated him to director of the newly created Office of War Mobilization (OWM) in May 1943. In that position, Byrnes became arbiter among the numerous and often conflicting war mobilization agencies. He had to mediate, not only between WPB and the military, but also among those agencies and various functional and commodity "czars," such as those for manpower and rubber. As Roosevelt focused more of his attention abroad, Byrnes was left to handle the troublesome scene at home. On balance, the OWM director sided with corporate and military interests in the numerous and growing disputes over economic mobilization and demobilization.

PRODUCTION ACHIEVEMENTS

In November 1943, the nation produced over $5 billion in munitions ($60 billion on an annual basis), a level exceeding all future weapons needs. War production (munitions, government-financed war construction, and nonmunitions expenditures such as pay, food, transportation, and the like) went from $3.6 billion in the last half of 1940 to $93.4 billion in 1944. Output for war increased nearly fivefold between 1940 and 1941, over threefold between 1941 and 1942, more than half between 1942 and 1943, and over 8 percent between 1943 and 1944. Where America was devoting around 3.6 percent of its GNP to defense and war in 1940, by 1943–1944 that figure had jumped to just short of 45 percent, based on the peaks achieved in the last two months of 1943. Overall, from July 1940 through August 1945, American war production totaled $315.8 billion; munitions output for the same period reached $184.5 billion. In 1943 and 1944 alone, the nation accounted for around 40 percent of the world's munitions output. With Allied output totaling another 31 percent, the United States and its allies far exceeded the logistic strength of their enemies.

By the end of 1943, then, the United States had won the battle of production at home. It could manufacture and supply the tools of war for itself and its allies at needed levels. That goal was reached without excessively squeezing the civilian population, which in 1944 spent roughly 10 percent more on consumer goods than it had in 1939.[1]

PRODUCTION RESTRAINTS

By mid-1943, WPB had fairly well perfected its mobilization techniques; by the end of the year, it had reached a level of stability that continued with only minor fluctuations until the war's end. Within limits set by feasibility, the board implemented and refined materials allocation and production scheduling. Those economic controls allowed the board to adjust output to the frequently and often rapidly changing military requirements dictated by strategic needs and battlefield conditions. In instances requiring more detailed attention, WPB combined its efforts with claimants and other mobilization agencies to expedite production.

Increasing supplies of basic materials in 1943 greatly eased WPB planning. Materials shortages had been the principal factor limiting production in 1942. Of particular importance were the controlled materials: steel; aluminum; and copper.

Of the three controlled materials, aluminum made the greatest gains. Output of the metallic element was scheduled to increase from 1.65 to 2.9 billion pounds between 1942 and 1943, a gain of over 75 percent. Surplus ingot supply developed during summer 1943 as aircraft output was significantly cut back. Those reductions brought relief to an unbalanced aluminum program in which, most important, shortages of facilities for fabricating shapes and forms required by the aircraft industry caused problems. By September 1943, WPB was well along in diverting excess aluminum to government stockpiles, easing restrictions on the metal's use, and halting the completion or start-up of new capacity. Between January and November 1944, monthly aluminum output was cut from a peak of 188 million pounds (reached in October 1943) to 88.5 million pounds. In August 1944, WPB lifted all restrictions on aluminum use. Although some shortages of shapes and forms developed with military emergencies, aluminum ceased to be critical in mid-1943.[2]

Steel made only modest gains compared with aluminum, and it failed to reach surplus levels. Ingot output grew less than 5 percent between 1942 and 1944, going from 86 to 90 million net tons annually, still a 33 percent gain over 1940 production. By limiting the use of steel elsewhere, WPB increased its availability for war purposes by as much as 20 percent. As the war went on, gross production would be less important than specialized steel and shapes and forms required by the armed services. By the end of 1943, problems in these areas had been largely solved, although capacity for plate production had to be expanded. Throughout 1944, there were periodic shortages of steel fabrications, such as rails, sheets, tubing, and wire. Only with Victory in Europe (VE) Day in May 1945 did steel realize surpluses as military demand fell off sharply.[3]

Copper remained a critical metal throughout the war years. That was the case in 1943 even though output increased around 7 percent (compared with a 25 percent rise between 1941 and 1942), imports grew, and civilian usage continued to be curtailed. In 1944, production dropped and had to be offset by even greater imports. Brass was also in short supply for a good part of the war. Together, copper and brass were tied closely to direct military requirements, especially ammunition. The output of copper mines and brass mills was limited by labor shortages, not basic capacity. Various war mobilization agencies repeatedly combined their efforts to maximize labor and avoid harming the war effort. Although copper and brass fell out of the urgent category in 1945, neither ever reached the surplus stage during hostilities.[4]

Supply conditions for a host of other noncontrolled metals also improved significantly by the end of 1943. That was the case with magnesium, zinc, lead, tin, and primary nickel. Because of either improved supply or a drop in demand, or a combination of the two, they were never again a major bottle-neck to war output, even though relatively minor problems could develop in emergency situations.[5]

While most metals were removed from the critical list, shortages of other, previously uncritical materials replaced them. Such was the case with lumber, pulp and paper, leather, and textiles.

Lumber reached crisis levels in 1943 and remained in that status practically until the war's end. Demand actually exceeded supply as early as 1942 and was offset by drawing down inventories. The same pattern continued at even more exaggerated levels in 1943 when output dropped nearly 12 percent; similar results were expected in 1944. Mill capacity was not the source of difficulty. A number of problems plagued lumber. The principal one was a chronic shortage of labor in a low-wage, high-risk industry that used its manpower poorly. While production dropped, requirements grew as claimants shipped more abroad using increasing amounts of wooden containers, crates, and dunnage, the armed services built bases abroad, and essential civilian usage had to be met. As with aluminum and numerous other materials, WPB had great difficulty planning for lumber since claimants' requirements estimates were crude and unreliable. What the board did in 1943 was to combine its efforts with those of the War Manpower Commission (WMC), the Selective Service System, the War Labor Board (WLB), and the military to maximize production by alleviating severe and growing labor deficits. Progress was slow and relief temporary. At the end of 1943, the lumber situation was still dire. Lumber's troubles inevitably carried over to pulp and paper, which by mid-1943 were facing growing problems from diminished wood-product supplies.[6]

As 1943 opened, drastic shortages of hides and leather existed because of reduced kills at home and abroad. To curtail civilian demand, the Office of Price Administration (OPA) instituted comprehensive shoe rationing in February 1943. The armed services also reduced their requirements, which seemed excessive in any case. On the supply side, the United States and the United Kingdom, with some Canadian participation, by the end of 1943 worked out a program for dividing world hide supply and regulating it to the degree possible. Through these acts, WPB stabilized the hide and leather situation, which, nonetheless, remained critical into 1945.[7]

A serious shortage of cotton broad-woven goods developed by mid-1943. As with copper and other materials, a labor deficit, not inadequate facilities, was the main difficulty. Better, higher-paying, and less onerous work was readily available in other industries. Between 1942 and 1944, cotton textile output dropped by over 15 percent. At the same time, demand increased as the armed services expanded in size and their replacement rates went up under combat, relief programs in liberated areas grew, and civilians wanted more goods. The imbalance in cotton textiles continued until practically the war's end.[8]

Growing and persistent manpower shortages in 1943 moved WPB beyond efforts to improve labor availability and use in addressing materials difficulties. It usually turned to allocations appropriate for the severity of the problem and the nature of the industry and claimants. Beginning in January 1944, for example, wood pulp was placed under total allocation, a situation that continued into 1945. While the selective allocations list was quite long in mid-1943, it had become quite short by the end of 1944. Most specialized allocation plans achieved at least a modest level of success.[9]

Micromanaging production increasingly occupied WPB as materials supply improved. The year 1943 opened with growing concern about "must" programs.[10] These were products designated by the president as critical to the outcome of the war. The list changed from time to time. In 1943, it included synthetic rubber, high-octane gasoline, aircraft, and destroyer escorts. The board's headaches stemmed from a number of complicating conditions, including increased requirements, late contracting, and competition for the same materials, machine tools, and components. Conditions were made worse by lack of proper guidance from the president and the Joint Chiefs of Staff (JCS) and driving, outspoken advocates, such as Rubber Director William M. Jeffers. Conflict among various claimants became so intense that, in April 1943, it broke out in the press. The Special Senate Committee to Investigate the National Defense Program (or Truman Committee) had to step in to restore harmony.

More lasting solutions to "must" programs resulted from progress in WPB controls. By mid-1943, the Controlled Materials Plan (CMP) was already well advanced, and production scheduling, particularly of common components, was implemented and being refined. These systems allowed WPB to manage general and specific production programs with a level of effectiveness not possible before. As a result, both claimants and contractors became more confident about board operations. As they did so, procurement agencies and industry tended to become more flexible and less aggressive in pursuing their goals.[11]

Short "must" lists in 1943 gave way to very long ones in 1944. Partly this stemmed from production falling behind schedule. A number of factors accounted for the falloff. Most significant was accelerated military requirements during emergencies or unanticipated crises, like the Normandy invasion in mid-1944 and the Battle of the Bulge at the end of the year. Changes in weapons and equipment design were another major source of difficulty. Furthermore, growing labor shortages adversely affected most production programs, some quite severely. Finally, in a few areas such as chemicals and ammunition, inadequate facilities persisted as late as 1944.

The "must" list also expanded because the armed services basically took it over. As Roosevelt shifted his attention to the international scene after mid-1943, WPB's PEC began highlighting the critical programs.[12] Beginning modestly late in 1943, the selection process got out of control. Toward the end of 1944, fully one-quarter of total war production had been tagged as critical, including trucks and buses. A form of priority inflation again set in, severely weakening the system. In October 1944, a new approach was introduced that significantly pared down the "must" category. Nonetheless, the list again began to stretch out.

In breaking bottlenecks and speeding production in critical programs, WPB had to supplement its own expediting efforts with assistance from claimant agencies, the WMC, the Selective Service System, the WLB, the OPA, and other government agencies. Teamwork was essential in going beyond materials, component parts, facilities, and equipment to address labor, transportation, housing, and community problems.[13]

With so many weapons and products on the "must" list in 1944, WPB created procedures for singling out the most urgent programs for priority attention through a Special Rating Division. On the basis of approaches worked out late in 1943, the division could issue priority directives for jumping a distressed program ahead of all others. Only twelve such directives were issued in 1944, for landing craft, naval rockets, and other weapons. In instances where emergencies demanded immediate attention, the Special Rating Division could issue onetime, nonextendable, and temporary AAA or top-priority ratings, as occurred with specialized equipment involved with the Normandy invasion.

Great munitions requirements, "must" programs, and special-directive items continued into 1945. Only after Germany was on the verge of collapse did armed services demand enter a phase of major and final reduction.

OFFICE OF CIVILIAN REQUIREMENTS

Although war production remained the WPB's primary focus from 1943 into 1945, the civilian economy required, and received, more attention during that period than it had in 1942.[14] As 1943 opened, the Office of Civilian Supply (OCS), the Planning Committee, and other WPB subdivisions, supported by Donald M. Nelson, emphasized two central points: efficient war production depended on maintaining a sound civilian sector; and resources should not be diverted to military uses excessively or to impose sacrifice on the population.

The Planning Committee in February 1943 warned that meeting civilian needs required comprehensive programming. Nelson moved in that direction in May 1943 by upgrading OCS to the OCR and putting Arthur D. Whiteside in charge. In doing so, he restricted the elevated office largely to consumer goods. It would no longer deal with indirect military requirements or those covered by WPB industry divisions and independent agencies such as the Office of Defense Transportation.

OCR was now better positioned to act in behalf of civilians because its scope was more manageable and the office had access to required information. Since early 1942, OCS had had to rely on industry divisions for data in order to carry out its duties. As OCS's rivals for power and turf in WPB, the divisions generally were unhelpful. When setting up OCR in May, Nelson required industry divisions to provide the office requested statistics on supply and demand and assist it in fulfilling responsibilities. No longer competitors with OCR, industry divisions became reasonably cooperative.

Combining OCS methods with surveys and other techniques, OCR in mid-1943 launched a major effort to determine consumer requirements precisely. Within months, it compiled fifteen hundred commodity programs and was well along in setting overall demand for 1944. By October 1943, OCR had achieved a level of planning for essential civilian needs that, although never as complete as that for the armed services, far exceeded anything done before. With food, housing, farm machinery, and railroad equipment covered by separate agencies, OCR dealt with nearly all other products basic to the functioning of the urban and rural workaday world. Consumer durables were emphasized since, by 1944, expenditures for such items had fallen to around one-third the 1941 level. The demand for refrigerators, stoves, washing machines, electric irons, and like products was always great. In 1944, the most urgent civilian requirements included oil burners and storage tanks, commercial laundry machinery, light trucks, and farm freezers. The most frequently cited items of need were clothing and standard household supplies: children's shoes; diapers; flashlight and radio batteries; and alarm clocks.

Programming gave the OCR a level of authority that its predecessors had lacked. When the office identified civilian goods as indispensable, that identification carried the same weight as military demand. Shortly after OCR was created, for example, it took charge of farm supplies other than machinery, including fencing, sprayers, binding material, etc., the unavailability of which was claimed to be harming output. To achieve immediate relief, the armed services and the Office of Lend-Lease Administration had to surrender part of their assigned materials and resources, and various manufacturers were required to sell to designated firms. Going further, military requests under the CMP for the fourth quarter of 1943 were cut substantially to allow a 21 percent increase in materials to OCR. William Y. Elliott, who replaced Whiteside as vice chair for civilian requirements in May 1944, insisted that essential civilian services such as transportation and products like clothing had to be treated the same as less urgent military programs. As manpower shortages became the principal factor limiting output in 1944 and 1945, OCR successfully demanded representation in WPB field offices and WPB–War Manpower Commission (WMC) labor supply structures to ensure access to critical information and a voice in decisions vital to the welfare of the general population.

In carrying out its responsibilities, OCR had to go beyond programming. By mid-1943, critical conditions developed in distributing nonrationed supplies and in operating services such as laundries. Enormous population shifts resulting from migration, selective service, and other wartime effects caused some areas to suffer more than others. Geography and class could exaggerate such trends. To achieve more equitable product availability, OCR used existing regulations or instituted new or modified ones to enhance output and improve distribution of essential goods and to check excessive inventories, hoarding, and like practices. Similar goals were pursued through cooperation with other government agencies and the extensive use of trade conferences.

In dealing with inadequate and deteriorating services from laundries, repair shops, hotels, restaurants, office and apartment buildings, and recreation facilities, OCR had to combine its efforts with those of the OPA, the WLB, the OES, the Office of Defense Transportation, and the armed services. In that way, it could deal with low prices and wages, which drained away labor, provide needed supplies, equipment, and facilities, and take related action to address the multiple problems plaguing businesses catering to the public. OCR never alleviated all or even most distributive and service ills. But its efforts brought needed relief and often acted to halt further deterioration.

OCR's success in protecting civilian interests in 1943 and after cannot be precisely measured. Certainly, the office had a role in the reasonably positive record that was achieved. In adjusted dollars, consumer spending was slightly higher in 1943 than in 1942; in 1944, it rose about 7 percent over 1943, around 10 percent above 1939. Gross figures, of course, conceal inflated prices, a decline in the quality and availability of goods and services, and reduced choices faced by families and individuals working long hours under frequently trying circumstances. In some instances, acute shortages of products and services, such as children's shoes and medicine, were real. For the most part, however, the American population in the war years experienced more inconvenience than outright deprivation.

Statistics aside, OCR's job grew more, not less, demanding over time. As civilian needs mounted and the office became more insistent in pursuing goals, it often encountered greater resistance. Although industry divisions cooperated more fully with OCR than with its predecessors, they were never fully reliable. The office was also treated as a second-class citizen by many WPB executives, was excluded from critical policymaking bodies, and was forced to defend and justify what it was doing.

All these conditions became greatly exaggerated from late 1943 forward when Donald M. Nelson took up and began formulating policies for reconversion.[15] OCR was among the few offices in WPB that supported Nelson and that the WPB chair in turn just as regularly backed. A gradual transition to a peacetime economy would increase civilian supply and strengthen OCR's role in the board. Nelson, however, was no longer the major source of power in WPB. The PEC, chaired by Executive Vice Chair Charles E. Wilson and staffed primarily by representatives of the armed services, was. Practically from the time he joined WPB in September 1942, Wilson was either uninterested in or hostile toward civilian production and toward what became OCR. As the executive vice chair filled key WPB positions with his own men, the entire upper echelon of WPB outside those in Nelson's orbit reflected Wilson's views.

Wilson and his lieutenants opposed or looked askance at OCR for a number of reasons. A strong office could threaten not only industry divisions but general WPB operations as well. Also, greater output for consumers could reduce that going to the armed services. Like William S. Knudsen and others, Wilson considered WPB primarily an agency for furthering munitions output.

Finally, the executive chair and his followers were obsessively concerned about competitive industry positions. With major corporations tied up with military contracts, civilian output was carried out mainly by small to mid-sized firms. If civilian production increased as armed services demand dropped, those manufacturing for a peacetime economy could have an advantage once hostilities ceased. The large corporate structure consistently insisted on all or most firms beginning the transition from a war to a peacetime economy at the same time.

Relations between OCR and PEC were especially tense throughout the period that Whiteside oversaw civilian requirements, May 1943–February 1944. As an elder business statesman with great prestige, Whiteside was treated cautiously by Wilson and his staff. On his part, the president of Dun and Bradstreet, Incorporated, all but held Wilson in contempt. Increasingly distressed by the tensions and frustrations of a position that he never genuinely wanted, Whiteside withdrew from WPB in December 1943 and resigned in February 1944. William Y. Elliott was elevated from within WPB to the directorship. A talented, pragmatic, exceptionally ambitious, and rather devious academic, Elliott recognized that his success in heading OCR depended on Wilson's goodwill. Consequently, as he fought in behalf of consumers, he courted the WPB's executive vice chair and the growing industry-military production team that he led. In the process, he turned against Nelson, who had nurtured his WPB career, a tactic that was all but necessary in dealing with Wilson, who demanded unquestioned loyalty.

Elliott's maneuvering worked up to a point. Once reconversion became a central issue, OCR suffered. WPB rejected practically all new civilian production favored by that office or others. Those conditions prevailed throughout most of 1944 and well into 1945. OCR looked on helplessly as growing and often urgent consumer needs were held back despite easing military demand.

SMALL BUSINESS AND ECONOMIC MOBILIZATION

One of Donald M. Nelson's arguments for gradually resuming civilian output as military demand eased was that the process would assist small business.[16] Smaller firms never did well under the WPB's predecessors, and WPB inherited a barely functioning Division of Contract Distribution. Congress stepped in to try to remedy the situation.

Members of Congress kept their eyes on the fate of small companies under the National Defense Advisory Commission (NDAC) and the Office of Production Management (OPM). The principal small business proponents were Senator James E. Murray (D-MT) and Representative Wright Patman (D-TX). Murray persuaded the Senate in October 1940 to create the Special Committee to Study and Survey Problems of American Small Business (the Murray Committee), which he chaired. In the House of Representatives, Patman headed the Select Committee on Small Business, organized in December 1941.[17] Strong adherents to New Deal principles, both legislators were motivated by ideology and partisan politics.

Murray and Patman ushered through Congress between February and June 1942 the Small Business Act. The bill passed both houses of Congress unanimously because its authors compromised where necessary and took Nelson's advice. That meant that any new small business offices would be controlled by, and, therefore, not a threat to, WPB. The legislation created a dual structure for advancing small business's interests (limited to firms in manufacturing, not retail or service, and aimed at those with fewer than five hundred employees). A Smaller War Plants Division (SWPD) was set up within WPB; independent of the board was the SWPC. Nelson bridged the two units by having the deputy chair of the SWPD also head the SWPC. Lou E. Holland filled both posts. He was a friend of Senator Harry S. Truman (D-MO) who had successfully led an organization devoted to solving the problems of lesser manufacturing plants in Missouri and Kansas.

Holland would oversee inventorying facilities, converting plants, analyzing procurement agencies' reports on contracting and subcontracting, and informing claimants of small business potential and certifying to them a firm or collection of companies capable of fulfilling a contract. SWPC had a capital stock of $150 million, and it consisted of five directors who were appointed by Nelson and who selected their own chair. The corporation could make loans or advances to small businesses, acquire for or lease or sell to such firms plant, equipment, materials, etc. necessary for producing war or essential civilian goods, and obtain prime contracts from procurement agencies that would be met by subcontracting with small businesses. The armed services were alarmed about the last provision. They were obligated to award SWPC those contracts that WPB chair certified it was competent to perform. WPB could use this provision to encroach on military procurement. No such threat materialized. Nelson made only limited use of the provision, and congressional attempts to transfer certifying authority from WPB to SWPC were unsuccessful.

As it worked out, SWPD served as staff for SWPC in implementing the Small Business Act. Holland also elected to use WPB's existing field organization for carrying out his duties at regional and local levels. All in all, then, SWPD/SWPC fit into WPB along lines that predecessor small business offices had followed in the NDAC and the OPM.

SWPD/SWPC got off to a slow start. A host of administrative and jurisdictional details, along with a lack of enthusiasm in WPB, held up an administrative order for the new division until September. With Holland having trouble recruiting staff, Nelson stepped in to assist. Using WPB's weak field organization also held back SWPD. The new structure did not take hold until mid-November.

Travails aside, Holland in January 1943 reported optimistically to Nelson about accomplishments. He highlighted October agreements with the War and Navy Departments and the Maritime Commission and affirmed that they were cooperating with his division. During his months in office, small firms had received contracts totaling $1 billion. Congress was unimpressed. Murray and Patman were furious with delays in getting SWPD/SWPC under way, accused Holland of not aggressively using prime-contracting power, financial resources, and other authority contained in the Small Business Act, and dismissed as inconsequential and misleading Holland's $1 billion contracts claim. WPB and the armed services had manipulated and diverted the deputy chair at the cost of aiding small business.

Holland's support from Nelson and the armed services was not enough to save him. Although Congress, and especially Patman, had been excessively critical of SWPD's deputy chair, he was a poor administrator and probably beyond his depth. Nelson replaced him in January 1943 with Robert Wood Johnson, chief of the New York Ordnance District and chairman of the board of Johnson and Johnson.

Unlike Holland, Johnson had experience with small and big businesses and knew how to operate in huge government bureaucracies. He quickly reorganized his office and its place in WPB, revamped the field structure, and restored a sense of direction and esprit de corps to the system. A consistent innovator, Johnson worked with large corporations, procurement agencies, the National Association of Manufacturers, and others to enlarge the number of contracts going to lesser manufacturers and to increase subcontracting. All these efforts paid off in terms of SWPC functioning more effectively. Nonetheless, the number of direct military contracts awarded to small businesses grew only slightly.

Several problems also plagued Johnson's tenure. Shortage of staff was one. Insisting that he needed twenty-five hundred employees, he had only eleven hundred in May 1943. His effort to recruit qualified personnel from within WPB was blocked by cries of raiding. The use of dollar-a-year men was limited by restrictions and red tape. Shortage of funds was another major headache for the SWPC chief. Finally, Johnson, like Holland, found that WPB in general and the industry divisions in particular were indifferent to or hostile toward SWPC.

A frustrated and ill Johnson resigned in September 1943. Nelson held off replacing him for months. With an acting head unable to provide effective leadership, the corporation inevitably deteriorated. The WPB chair finally tapped Maury Maverick, the colorful, populist former representative from Texas, for the position. Maverick quickly restored morale in and a sense of direction to the neglected organization. Proclaiming that he spoke for all small businesses, not just those in trouble, Maverick launched a publicity drive in their behalf. He also restructured SWPC and liberalized its lending policies. Joining Murray, Patman, and others, he picked up the theme that small manufacturers faced a reconstruction crisis; government in general, and SWPC in particular, had an obligation to help the "little fellow." For the first time, SWPC and the congressional small business committees spoke with the same fervor and language.

From June 1942 through 1943, SWPC was unclear over whether its primary goal was to mobilize small business for war or to protect it from the distorting effects of hostilities. Conflict over this basic issue played an important part in the failure of Holland and the disillusionment of Johnson. By late 1942, Holland began tentatively to conclude that small manufacturers on their own had successfully adapted or were adjusting to a war economy. In a mobilized system, the strong and able smaller manufacturing firms survived, even prospered. Johnson went further. He insisted that Holland's tentative conclusions had already become fact.

SWPC surveys indicated that, of the nation's 165,000 small manufacturers, fewer than 2,500 could be classified as distressed, meaning that they were operating at less than two-thirds of prewar levels.[18] Other studies by the Commerce Department, the Office of War Information, and Dun and Bradstreet appeared to support SWPC's findings. That meant—as Holland suspected and Johnson insisted—that there was no overall small business crisis, even though shortages of materials and labor continued to be a problem. Increasingly, Johnson, like Holland before him, concentrated on firms that were in distress. SWPC sought out contracts or subcontracts for them, offered financial assistance, and negotiated higher prices at which they could compete.

Holland's doubts about and Johnson's denial of a small business crisis were never accepted by Murray, Patman, and Congress's small business supporters. Critical of large corporate structures, and favoring antitrust solutions, they viewed small business as the backbone of American democratic capitalism. WPB and its predecessors, along with the armed services' procurement system, were dominated by and favorable to big business. The Small Business Act was aimed at balancing the mobilization scales so that smaller manufacturers received a fair share. By accepting existing mobilization trends, Holland and Johnson were defeating the principal purpose of the statute.

Depending on how the problem was defined, Murray and Johnson could both be correct. Such a paradoxical situation underlined the challenges of dealing with small manufacturers in a mobilized corporate capitalist system. Murray was right in that lesser firms collectively were harmed by World War II. Two-thirds of all prime war contracts, totaling $175 billion between June 1940 and September 1944, went to the top hundred corporations. Small firms reaped only 22 percent of prime contracts and 8 percent of subcontracts. Small companies, therefore, ended up losing market share. In 1939, small manufacturers with fewer than five hundred employees accounted for around 52 percent of total manufacturing employment, those with fewer than a hundred employees 26 percent. By 1944, the percentages had dropped to 38 and 19 percent, respectively, within a context of a 55 percent increase in employment for the entire period. The very largest firms, employing ten thousand or more, were the principal beneficiaries. Where they accounted for 13 percent of manufacturing workers in 1939, their share jumped to 30 percent in 1944. Big business compared with smaller manufacturers was also the primary beneficiary of government disposal of plant and surplus property after hostilities.[19] And, while reconversion was not the disaster for small business that many had feared, the postwar decline in small manufacturers' market share continued. The total share of real value added manufacturing by single-plant firms between 1947 and 1954 dropped from 41 to 32 percent and continued to shrink thereafter.

Declining market shares did not add up to a crisis for small firms, Johnson argued. Evidence supports his position. It has been estimated that, between 1939 and 1944, the number of small manufacturers grew from 7 to over 11 percent. Studies also showed that smaller firms may have reaped higher profit rates than did giant corporations because of greater flexibility, less government regulation, and other conditions. Most of these small companies depended on their own resources or their connections with larger corporations or prime contractors to handle wartime challenges. Government programs, particularly SWPC, appeared to play a limited role in the outcome. The SWPC aided small firms in securing around $6 billion in war contracts (approximately 3 percent of wartime totals), accounted for leases and loans equaling $500 million, and took charge of twelve prime contracts valued at around $35 million. SWPC's efforts with major procurement agencies, especially the armed services and the Maritime Commission, however, did improve the value of contracts going to small manufacturers in 1943 and 1944. Nonetheless, Johnson, like Floyd B. Odlum before him, began stressing the role for those firms in the production of essential civilian goods, tacitly conceding the difficulty of protecting small business in a war economy.

A major challenge facing Murray, Patman, and their congressional allies was that no major organization spoke for small manufacturers. These firms identified more with their industries, trades, and regions than they did with their fellow small firms. Attempts to establish such associations in the 1930s and the war years never produced the desired results. SWPC and its predecessors did not benefit from an effective lobby. Moreover, small businessmen were usually conservative, displaying an aversion to large, active government. During World War II, they complained about wage, price, and priority controls and numerous other restrictions and regulations. Reflecting such views, Johnson proclaimed that SWPC came to view itself as "an agency to defend small business from government."[20] Liberally oriented members of Congress, many of whom were Democrats, often found themselves conducting a crusade for small manufacturers who were Republican and did not want Washington's help.

The SWPC, like its predecessors, faced intractable odds. The failure of the efforts to concentrate production in essential civilian industries indicates that even a well-developed program for integrating small manufacturers into a harnessed economy would not have gone far.[21] The huge corporate structure was too dominant, military procurement agencies naturally turned to big corporations for weapons output, and small manufacturers were unorganized and usually saw big government as a greater threat than big business. The emergency facing the nation, furthermore, was not sufficiently strong to break down existing power patterns. The United States was the only major belligerent whose homeland was not under attack. And the nation met all its own demand and most of that of its allies without fully mobilizing small manufacturing potential. Those realities defied congressional campaigns in behalf of small business led by Senator Murray and Representative Patman.

What was true during war remained true in preparing for peace. Nelson was supportive of small business during mobilization without urgently pressing its case. Late in 1943, he changed tactics. Planning for reconversion had to begin, he insisted, and smaller manufacturers should be allowed the opportunity to make up for big businesses' advantages during the war. His enthusiastic supporters included the Truman, Murray, and Patman Committees and SWPC's new head, Maury Maverick. The public also seemed to be on the side of the WPB's chair. None of that seemed to matter. The large corporate structure, combined with the military and backed by Byrnes, first held back Nelson's demobilization efforts and then drove him from office. Small business was given no greater favor in reconversion than it had received in conversion.

FIELD OFFICES

As the WPB began shifting emphasis late in 1943 from expanding production to managing and modifying it according to changing war conditions, the board's field offices assumed greater importance. When organized in January 1942, WPB inherited a host of differing and uncoordinated local structures that had been building up since the NDAC. Seeking to bring some order to these decentralized services, WPB set up a Bureau of Field Operations in February 1942 and established thirteen (later twelve) regional offices in April 1942. Although various executives favored decentralizing as much of the board's operations as possible, such efforts ran into strong opposition from industry divisions and other units. Repeated attempts to improve localized operations throughout 1942 and well into 1943 became sidetracked for one reason or another.

From late 1943 on, however, more effective field services became essential for dealing with production expediting and scheduling, materials allocation, crisis management, manpower problems, contract cancellation, expansion of civilian production, and, ultimately, reconversion. Under such pressures, the board gradually began to reform and restructure its field service system. The effort culminated in July 1944 with the creation of a vice chair for field operations.[22]

THE RISE AND DOMINANCE OF
THE PRODUCTION EXECUTIVE COMMITTEE

The rise of the PEC in 1943 overshadowed all other WPB developments. Two principal and interrelated consequences ensued. First, the armed services as the principal claimants on the wartime economy were fully integrated into the policymaking and operating structure of WPB. The lack of such a critical development prior to 1943 had aggravated relations between the board and the military. Second, the industry-military production team that had been emerging in the mobilization system since the NDAC was consolidated and strengthened.

The armed services' interwar Industrial Mobilization Plan (IMP) had provided for integrating civilian and military mobilization systems through the Army-Navy Munitions Board (ANMB). That did not take place because the board never unified army and navy supply operations as intended and the NDAC and the OPM remained weak. Under those circumstances, a civilian and military mobilization structure emerged: neither functioned well; the two setups competed at points; and they were inadequately coordinated. Through feasibility controls, materials allocation, and production scheduling, WPB took major steps in strengthening its operations and integrating armed services members into its structure. Ferdinand Eberstadt's transfer from ANMB to WPB in September 1942 was an important step in that direction.

Eberstadt's appointment reportedly set off a mass transfer of personnel from ANMB to WPB late in 1942 and early in 1943. The assertion is more fiction than reality. Beginning in 1940, both services had officers serving in industry divisions and other units of NDAC, OPM, and WPB to facilitate procurement. They were usually officers from the army and navy supply bureaus who might be serving in a dual capacity as ANMB members since the board had no independent staff. While relations among military and civilian mobilizers were usually cordial at the lower, contrasted with the top, level of WPB and its predecessors, the system of representation was irregular and unstructured. After WPB instituted the CMP and production scheduling, more officers from both services formally joined the board.[23]

When the PEC got fully under way early in 1943, military participation in WPB policymaking and operations became thoroughly systematized.[24] This development was a consequence of the committee's membership and responsibility. With Charles E. Wilson as chair, PEC consisted of General Brehon B. Somervell, commanding general of the Army Service Forces; Admiral Samuel M. Robinson, director of the navy's Office of Procurement and Material; General Oliver P. Echols, assistant for procurement, Army Air Forces; Admiral Ralph A. Davison, assistant chief, Bureau of Aeronautics; Admiral Howard L. Vickery, vice chairman, U.S. Maritime Commission; and Program Vice Chair Eberstadt. Such high-ranking military and other officials serving together in a key subdivision gave unity and direction to numerous army and navy officers scattered throughout WPB.

With PEC dealing principally with military procurement and production, Wilson could tap the assistance of industry divisions, the CMP structure, and other sections of the board under the general oversight of Nelson as WPB chair. In that way, the committee could coordinate armed services functions with those of WPB in a much more direct and accomplished fashion than it had previously.

But the WPB blowup in February 1943 pushed PEC far beyond being a vehicle for coordinating armed services supply operations with the civilian system. It became an agency for dominating the board through an industry-military production team. As executive vice chair, Wilson directed all WPB operating subdivisions. In theory, Nelson and his small staff concentrated on policy. In fact, divorced and isolated from day-to-day functioning, the WPB chair lost contact with and control of the agency that he headed. Under such circumstances, Wilson by stages began determining and implementing overall WPB policy. Had the executive vice chair done so by expanding his own office, relations within WPB would have been awkward but not exceptional. Many organizations are directed by lieutenants serving under a nominal chief. Wilson, however, chose to direct the board through PEC. PEC was dominated in numbers by the armed services, who considered Nelson to be incompetent and antimilitary. On their part, the WPB chair and his supporters looked on the military as an aggressive rival, if not an administrative enemy. Such an arrangement created nearly intolerable tensions within WPB, eventually reducing the board to a subordinate status within the mobilization structure.

Wilson used PEC as an executive committee to run WPB for a number of reasons. He needed a cooperative military to succeed in directing economic mobilization in a stable and effective way. With feasibility calculations, materials allocation, and production scheduling, WPB completed organizing effectively the supply side of economic mobilization; the system would work only if the demand side went along. After the lacerating battles of 1942, the armed services had to be accommodated. Even without that imperative, the executive chair would have worked closely with the military. Wilson in 1943 and 1944 formally returned to the leadership principle of William S. Knudsen, John D. Biggers, William H. Harrison, and other industrialists in NDAC and OPM: the civilian mobilization agencies existed to serve the armed services. With the military supporting the status quo, corporate America had nothing to fear from that strategy.

Donald M. Nelson differed basically from Charles E. Wilson over economic mobilization because the two viewed government differently. The WPB chair welcomed a large federal government as a societal overseer, economic regulator, and welfare agent. In this sense, he was a moderate New Dealer. To the degree possible, he believed, war mobilization should be carried out in a representative way and with proper regard for society as a whole. Such views made it possible for Nelson to turn to and work in harmony with Leon Henderson and Robert R. Nathan.

By contrast, Wilson was an unquestioned advocate of big business who responded to large government—particularly second New Deal directions—skeptically. Washington had to create agencies for mobilizing the economy. Like the World War I War Industries Board, however, those agencies should combine industry, finance, and business with the armed services and other claimants to oversee the harnessing of the economy. The blueprint for such an approach was laid out in the IMP.[25]

Among industrialists and businessmen in WPB, Nelson spoke for a minority, Wilson for an overwhelming majority. Their views reflect responses to the early New Deal (1933–1935), particularly the National Recovery Administration (NRA). The Business Advisory Council (BAC) of the Department of Commerce was created by the joint efforts of Secretary of Commerce Daniel C. Roper and business statesmen such as Gerard Swope, president of General Electric Company. BAC helped lead in the direction of what became NRA and, after its creation, the organization of the Industrial Advisory Board (IAB) to NRA. Swope and those in his circle attempted to use BAC and IAB to move industry in the direction of greater cooperation with the New Deal and its antidepression measures, including more support for organized labor and welfare reforms. BAC had conservative, moderate, and progressive elements. Swope and his associates were at the left end of the business political spectrum, Pierre S. DuPont, retired head of the DuPont empire, and his allies at the right end, and most others probably in the center. Many leading WPB executives were BAC members and had served in NRA, including Nelson and Wilson. Nelson followed, even went beyond, Swope's aims, while Wilson was definitely on the conservative side, opposing any active role for government in economic planning. Swope and his fellow progressives had trouble encouraging industrialists to be flexible toward Roosevelt during the height of the depression, when corporations were on the defensive. Nelson and those sharing his views faced much greater challenges with war-induced prosperity and the success of mobilization dependent on industry.[26]

Wilson and his associates used PEC to ensure that WPB pursued conservative policies. The military became an effective, aggressive partner in maintaining that goal. The impact of the alliance would have been less consequential if PEC had dealt only with production scheduling. By mid-1943, however, the committee expanded its purview to include critical production programs, manpower shortages and selective service deferments, facilities policy, cutback and cancellation of contracts, and, ultimately, reconversion. By 1944, James F. Byrnes communicated directly with Wilson on fundamental WPB policies, bypassing Nelson. Wilson was directing WPB through PEC. In doing so, the executive vice chair treated PEC as a collegial body, not as one advisory to him. That gave the armed services a dominant voice in WPB operations. Within PEC, General Lucius D. Clay, sitting in for General Somervell, and Admiral Samuel M. Robinson, as the navy's representative, were the outstanding, forceful, vocal leaders.

As PEC expanded its decisionmaking range, it gradually and grudgingly increased its membership to include greater civilian representation. By early 1944, the operations vice chair and a WMC member were included; the civilian requirements vice chair was admitted in mid-1944; and, after much agitation, the vice chair for labor production joined the committee at the end of December 1944. All these new additions, with the exception of the WMC and the labor spokesman, were Wilson subordinates disinclined to challenge his leadership. According to Bernard L. Gladieux, an informed and reliable observer of WPB—he had been the Bureau of the Budget's economic mobilization specialist since 1940 and transferred to WPB as an administrative assistant to Nelson early in 1943—Wilson included in his inner circle only those whom he "owned."[27] Hence, William L. Batt, William Y. Elliott, and, ultimately, Sidney J. Weinberg—of Goldman, Sachs and Company and a former Sears, Roebuck and Company director—surrendered any loyalty to Nelson, who had advanced their mobilization careers, to serve under Wilson and his chief lieutenants. In addition to PEC, Wilson also worked with his own staff, but the most important members were already serving on the committee.

Although PEC generally spoke with one voice, that was not true of WPB as a whole. Nelson may have been eclipsed, but he was still the legal chair, and he was not easily waylaid when convinced of the need for action. Additionally, he had intensely loyal, often formidable lieutenants within WPB, along with a great deal of support outside it, particularly in Congress, and especially from the Truman Committee.

From early 1943 on, WPB in effect split. Conditions were tense but still manageable. Wilson plotted to get rid of Nelson, the WPB chair waited for Wilson to resign, as he frequently threatened to do, but both stayed on. General and staff meetings of WPB continued to be held, but these were more informational or formal, not substantive, gatherings. The personal staffs of Nelson and Wilson met separately with only a few executives crossing the line. Roosevelt avoided seeing either Nelson or Wilson throughout most of 1943 and into 1944. The chair depended on Harry L. Hopkins to communicate with the White House; Wilson relied on Robert P. Patterson and James V. Forrestal for the same purpose.

The standoff could not go on indefinitely. Tensions began mounting late in 1943 and 1944 as selective manpower shortages grew, some munitions programs were cut back, and contract cancellation policies began to be formulated. Gladieux tried to heal the WPB breach so that the board could better handle these multiplying challenges. In doing so, he conferred regularly with Nelson, Wilson, and their staffs, in addition to John Lord O'Brian, Harold D. Smith, Wayne Coy (special assistant to the president and assistant director of the Bureau of the Budget), and Vice President Henry A. Wallace. Little progress took place.

Fighting broke out openly early in 1944 when Nelson insisted on proceeding with reconversion planning over the opposition of Wilson, PEC, and most WPB executives. At that point, Nelson recalled Luther Gulick, who had served in WPB during 1942–1943, to board service in March 1944 in an attempt to improve his relations with Wilson. The latter rejected the approach. Sidney J. Weinberg, a former close assistant of Nelson's, returned to WPB in June as peacemaker. Before very long, he deserted Nelson for Wilson. The WPB chair then tried to persuade William E. Levis, the respected chairman of the board of Owen-Illinois Glass Company who had served in OPM and had good relations with the army, to join the board to mediate the ongoing struggle between himself and Wilson. After a brief visit to the capital, Levis declined, no doubt sensing the futility of such a thankless mission.

By mid-1944, although the WPB lower echelons kept operating, the highest executive level became caught up in what was properly perceived as a last-ditch struggle to determine whether Nelson or Wilson would direct the board.

Although White House counsels remained divided, Roosevelt ultimately concluded that Nelson had to go. The news of his pending departure created an uproar on Nelson's behalf among the public, the media, and Congress. Under those circumstances, Wilson could not continue to serve in WPB. In August 1944, both Nelson and Wilson left the board, with Julius A. Krug taking over as acting chair. He was expected to reestablish mobilization harmony after over a year of nearly unending disruption. The acting chair, who became chair in September 1944, returned to Wilson's pattern of running WPB through the PEC, with the armed services practically having veto power concerning WPB policy.

THE OFFICE OF WAR MOBILIZATION

President Roosevelt began organizing a formal executive system to supervise a fragmented mobilization system with the OES, created in October 1942. Relying on a small White House staff and the Bureau of the Budget, Roosevelt had overseen the homefront up until then. With growing domestic complexity and the war abroad demanding more of his attention, the president required greater assistance. Conflict between the WPB and the armed services needed to be settled, along with the clashing interests of the numerous functional (e.g., OPA) and commodity (e.g., petroleum) "czars." And all these agencies had to be coordinated for the purpose of a common goal.

Roosevelt chose James F. Byrnes as director of OES.[28] While charged with checking inflation, Byrnes was told by the president to go beyond the economic realm, and the OES head declared his intention of coordinating the entire mobilization scheme. Actually, Byrnes had been assisting Roosevelt with mobilization matters from the outset, uninterrupted even by his appointment to the Supreme Court in July 1941. He had served as a representative from South Carolina from 1910 through 1924, was elected to the Senate in 1930, and quickly rose to prominence as a shrewd and able legislator. The Roosevelt-Byrnes relationship predated World War I.

Byrnes had an important part in an economy harnessed for war. As OES director, he began to be seen as assistant president for the homefront, and the distinction grew after his elevation to director of OWM in May 1943. The president turned to Byrnes for a number of reasons. Byrnes was a valuable supporter of the New Deal throughout the 1930s, and he and the president worked comfortably together. As a Washington insider, ideologically in the center, more likely to the right, Byrnes could operate effectively in the increasingly conservative political climate of the capital. All these factors weighed in the South Carolinian's favor; none would have been enough had Roosevelt, so hesitant in delegating unchecked authority, not been convinced that Byrnes could be relied on to use his vast powers prudently and in a way that relieved the president of responsibility without threatening his authority. Byrnes knew what Roosevelt wanted without going beyond what he would tolerate.

Neither bold nor innovative, Byrnes was a cautious mediator, a talented compromiser, a referee. Roosevelt tried him out first as economic stabilizer and then promoted him to OWM. In both offices, Byrnes pushed his powers to the limit, won respect for and deflected challenges to his authority, and helped keep the awkward, confused mobilization structure on track, albeit with great difficulty at times. None of the other key presidential advisers and assistants, including Harry L. Hopkins, Harold D. Smith, and Samuel I. Rosenman, had Byrnes's special talents. He was a gifted second-tier leader.

Byrnes's success as assistant president for the homefront stemmed in part from his determination to avoid operations. His staff was always kept purposely small. In that way, he, not assistants, made decisions, and agencies like WPB and WMC were left to implement, and, hence, take responsibility for, controversial matters that Byrnes had mediated. After OWM was organized, some favored merging OES with it. Roosevelt and others opposed the idea, arguing that it was better "spreading the heat" of disputed decisions rather than concentrating them all in one place.[29]

From October 1942 to May 1943, while concentrating on economic stabilization, Byrnes was involved at some level with most mobilization decisions. That was the case in devising formulas for dividing a very short supply of rubber among squabbling claimants and trying to harmonize incessant WPB-military feuding. Nonetheless, until well into 1943, the president remained engaged in the homefront, and disputes still came to the White House. But, by mid-1943, most of the mobilization machinery was in place, and more of Roosevelt's attention was drawn abroad. Under those circumstances, the president turned domestic policy increasingly over to Byrnes. Setting up OWM was the last major administrative step in harnessing the economy for war. In part, Roosevelt's hand was forced by Congress. Since late 1942, the national legislators grew more critical of the fragmented mobilization system. By early 1943, the so-called Tolan-Kilgore-Pepper Bill for centralizing mobilization gained in strength, along with other, related legislation. The president headed off these legislative challenges by establishing the OWM.[30]

Under the executive order of May 27, 1943, OWM had vast powers. The director was authorized to issue directives to and require reports from all involved federal agencies and departments for the purpose of unifying and maximizing war mobilization. Only OES was excepted from the order. In July

1943, OWM's reach was extended to include foreign economic policy and operations. With his authority more explicit than it was under OES, Byrnes included in his purview nearly all economic war policies. No fine line divided the jurisdiction of OWM and that of OES. Byrnes cooperated with the latter office in handling policy and disputes dealing with OPA, the WLB, the War Food Administration, and like organizations. He also dealt with taxation and fiscal policy, particularly as they involved Congress. When various "must" programs clashed, the OWM director worked with WPB and claimant and other agencies in determining order of production. Strikes, especially those threatening and occurring in coal mines and railroads, received the director's careful attention, as did the vexatious issue of national service. During 1944 and 1945, the intensely controversial and related matters of manpower and reconversion absorbed more of the OWM director's time than did any other issues. He also had to help settle disputes in the State Department and between the Board of Economic Warfare and the Reconstruction Finance Corporation as well as help set up what became the Foreign Economic Administration. The list of Byrnes's activities was lengthy and encompassed practically all phases of economic mobilization.

Military requirements were among Byrnes's most significant area of oversight. Since armed forces demand shaped the entire mobilization program and generated such intense controversy, he took up the task almost immediately after being appointed OPM director. In June 1943, Byrnes instructed claimants to organize top-level procurement review boards that were independent of contracting functions and included a member of his office. These boards would survey requirements with an eye to setting realistic goals, reducing duplication within or between agencies, eliminating waste, reducing excessive inventories, and like practices. While including all procurement administrations in his order, Byrnes centered attention on the armed services as the main purchasers and as the most difficult to regulate.

Despite clearing his project with the secretaries and under secretaries of war and the navy, Byrnes quickly encountered resistance from the armed services. They insisted that sensitive strategic information could not be shared with civilians. After Byrnes threatened presidential intervention, the army was more forthcoming. The navy differed. Secretary Frank Knox and Under Secretary James V. Forrestal were reasonably flexible, but Commander-in-Chief of the United States Fleet Admiral Ernest J. King led the officer corps in resisting civilian intrusion into naval affairs. Byrnes made some headway with the navy, but he had to proceed cautiously. At no time throughout the war years did OWM have unlimited access to military data essential for doing its job.

Byrnes's procurement reviews began to be completed in August 1943, with varying results. Few problems were encountered with the Office of Lend-Lease Administration, the Maritime Commission, and OCR. OWM's representative on the army board, Frederick Pope, reported that the service cooperated and that its procurement was carried out in an accomplished way. Nonetheless, significant problems existed. Requirements were inflated, inventories were lax, supply experience gained in one combat area did not carry over to others, bureaucratic inertia kept programs like the construction of coastal batteries in the Western Hemisphere going despite radical strategic change, and Army Air Forces procurement was badly out of balance in terms of planes, bombs, fuel, ammunition, and so forth.

The navy remained a problem. Byrnes appointed William Francis Gibbs, an experienced manufacturer of naval supplies, to serve on the service's review board. The navy invoked rules of secrecy to obstruct his work. Hence, Gibbs did not participate in writing the review, which he characterized as vague and elusive. On the basis of information that he gathered and other data available to OWM, Gibbs concluded that the navy was building unneeded escort vessels, patrol craft, and minesweepers, that its aircraft program was badly out of balance, and that inventory control was especially weak. Summarizing these findings for the president in September 1943, Byrnes pointed out that, by July 1944, navy schedules required a 22 percent increase in shipyard workers, most of whom had to be recruited on the West Coast, where dire labor shortages were developing. Cutting back on construction would save massive amounts of both manpower and materials. If current building programs continued, Byrnes warned, by the end of 1946 the navy's total tonnage would be 3.6 times greater than that which currently existed. Gibbs also informed the OWM's director that navy operations involving ordnance, bases, the Marine Corps, and other areas were troubled as well.

Extravagant claims exist about the results of the reviews. One estimate places the dollar savings for the army at $8 billion. There is no reliable evidence to support such conclusions. At best, modest reductions in demand took place, and some supply reforms resulted. Since military procurement had not been subject to examination by an outside agency before, OWM's action probably made the armed services more cautious about requirements and encouraged procurement reforms that the services might not have pursued on their own.

Future gains aside, the reviews concerned OWM. The reports turned up meaningful deficiencies with no guarantees that they would be corrected. An analysis of the collective surveys pointed to huge, unexamined procurement projects, overlapping purchasing, inadequate divisions of labor, and other difficulties. Most important, the armed services denied Byrnes's office full requirement statistics. The OWM head could not, therefore, determine whether military demand was feasible and reasonable. The army's review, for example, established that firm strategic plans were made for only six months in advance, yet procurement planning was projected for eighteen months, almost inevitably leading to inflated figures.

Fred Searls, Jr., insisted that Byrnes's success in overseeing the wartime economy depended on his getting tough with the military. Addressing Byrnes in mid-September 1943, the seasoned mobilization executive argued that Donald M. Nelson had squandered WPB's right to analyze military requirements and adjust them to the needs of the economy: "The people in uniform have successfully reduced [Nelson's] authority. I am very much afraid that, within the next 30 days, they will accomplish the same end with respect to yours."[31]

To head off such an outcome, Byrnes sought the president's assistance in having his chief of staff and the presiding officer of the JCS, Admiral William D. Leahy, suggest ways to review military demand on an ongoing basis. With Leahy uninterested in the project, Byrnes persuaded Roosevelt to act on his own. On September 24, 1943, the president ordered the creation within JCS of a Joint Production Survey Committee (JPSC).

Made up of senior officers, JPSC was to advise JCS on procurement as it related to the war program, changes in strategy, and the economy's potential. By working with OWM, the committee would act for JCS in helping coordinate civilian and military mobilization systems. Specifically, the committee would inform the joint chiefs of problems raised by OWM and seek to reduce military requirements when possible. Byrnes attended meetings of both JPSC and JCS, and he appointed Searls as OWM's observer on the committee. Although not a member of the committee and without voting rights, Searls could attend all meetings, including those dealing with strategy, and participate in deliberations. JPSC's conferences were supplemented by Byrnes consulting with Leahy. Since both had offices in the White House and were in regular contact with the president, they frequently worked out among themselves issues needing attention or in conflict.

OWM-JPSC activity was the closest the nation came to a structure for coordinating strategy and production. The Planning Committee and others had advocated a supreme war council or a war cabinet for achieving that goal. In practice, the JPSC had some positive results; overall, it was a flawed, improvised arrangement more ceremonial than substantial in nature.

Along positive lines, Byrnes used JPSC to keep an eye on military procurement and critical developments shaping it. In some instances, OWM was able to institute corrective action or head off abuses. Late in 1944, for example, the military claimed that labor shortages on the West Coast were denying the armed services needed ships. In addressing the problem, Byrnes investigated the use of the vast merchant-ship fleet. He discovered that numerous vessels had become floating warehouses, tied up in foreign ports through neglect or unloading delays. By calling the armed services' attention to these facts, OWM encouraged reform, checked the building of unneeded bottoms, and tempered complaints.

OWM (as of October 1944 the Office of War Mobilization and Reconversion [OWMR]) discovered that it could never drop its guard. In February 1945, the JCS requested approval from the president and the Maritime Commission to build twenty-eight Victory ships beyond those authorized earlier by OWM. Both Byrnes and his successor, Fred M. Vinson, argued that no rationale existed for such an increase. Moreover, since JCS was not basing its request on military need, the staff was encroaching on civilian turf, particularly that of the War Shipping Administration. Although Leahy attempted to defend JCS action, both Byrnes and Vinson emphatically dismissed all challenges and successfully held their ground.

About the same time, OWMR took up a battle with the navy over combat vessels, clearly in the service's realm. In January 1945, the secretary of the navy, at the request of Admiral King, asked the president to approve construction of eighty-four additional ships totaling 644,000 tons. After a quick review, Roosevelt said that the proposal appeared to have merit. Director of the Bureau of the Budget Harold D. Smith strongly urged Roosevelt to change his mind since costs would run close to $2 billion, no apparent need for the ships existed, and, if there was, much of the new construction would not be available until 1947. With the president still appearing favorable, Smith asked for Byrnes's assistance. The OWMR director was able to get both King and Secretary Forrestal to concede that the ships were not necessary and that advocacy for them originated with Representative Carl Vinson (D-GA), chair of the House Naval Affairs Committee. Marshaling all arguments against more ships, and pointing out that some officials supported the proposal to keep labor in shipyards and ensure a large postwar fleet, Byrnes ultimately succeeded in having the president reject the project. As a face-saving move, the navy was allowed to go forward with twelve of the eighty-four ships it wanted.

OWM/OWMR gains in dealing with armed services requirements actually were limited and peripheral. More often than not, the office encountered uncertainty, frustration, or defeat. During Byrnes's first meeting with the JPSC early in October 1943, committee members resisted the idea of cutting back superfluous programs, arguing that such action would lead to the loss of plant, equipment, and labor for future production. In late 1943 and early 1944, JPSC ran interference for nearly every program that it examined, including coastal fortifications and Canol, General Brehon B. Somervell's folly for drilling and refining Alaskan oil. Byrnes's staff protested that they could not obtain reliable data on demand because the army, navy, Maritime Commission, and War Shipping Administration all joined in justifying each other's projects as a way of protecting their turf. To illustrate the charge, it pointed in mid-1944 to an eightfold increase in requirements by the army and Maritime Commission for cargo vessels that could be converted to troop ships at the same time that JCS was releasing troop ships to the Maritime Commission for use as postwar passenger vessels.

In November 1943, Byrnes insisted that JPSC act on the earlier charges of the army review that there was profligate waste of military equipment in North Africa. Only in April 1944 did JPSC indicate that it had corrected the situation and taken steps to prevent similar developments in the future. Byrnes had to accept the military's word because his office had no way of verifying what was done. A similar development occurred in terms of airpower. When OWM asked JPSC to analyze reports of unbalanced programs, duplication between the services, and excess procurement, the committee responded late in 1943 that all was proceeding properly; nearly a year later, JCS reported substantial cutbacks in aircraft. Yet, throughout much of 1945, OWMR remained in the dark about its insistence that the services' air arms either reduce their requirements or justify exceptionally heavy demand despite the transition to a one-front war.

OWM staff expressed extreme impatience at what it perceived as military obfuscation and dodges. Reflecting that distress, Byrnes in March 1944 complained to Roosevelt that JPSC and the navy were not cooperating with his office. Without strong backing from the president, he could not do his job. OWM/OWMR's running battles with the military in 1944 and early 1945 indicated that the president either would not or could not strengthen Byrnes's hand.

A larger truth existed about OWM's interaction with JPSC. No matter what information OWM had or what questions it posed, if the army or navy at any point invoked strategic necessity in defending procurement, Byrnes automatically backed off. He trusted the armed services out of either conviction or need. If he challenged them, Byrnes would be risking a fundamental power struggle that he could not be sure of winning. The OWM director's charges from the commander-in-chief and his access to the president, JCS, and JPSC had not basically changed civil-military relations as they existed before OWM was set up.

Also of critical importance, JPSC came into being late in 1943, about the same time Donald M. Nelson started his drive for reconversion. On a plateau, or declining for a time, in 1944, armed services requirements started rising as the struggle over demobilization grew. By August 1944, Bureau of the Budget Director Smith complained to the president that, instead of "tapering off," the military was calculating its needs "as if the war in Europe was expected to go on for years."[32]

To thwart reconversion, the armed services throughout 1944 and into 1945 blocked or restricted practically all increases in civilian output. The WPB went along, and so did Byrnes, who by mid-1944 was all but dictating board policy. By then, WPB was accepting military requirements without question. Indeed, Byrnes, who explained that he worked out the details of JPSC with Chief of Staff General George C. Marshall and Admiral Leahy, may have agreed to block demobilization efforts as the price for setting up the committee. When announcing the creation of the committee and later, the OWM director explained that any reductions of military programs would not enrich civilian supply but would be necessary for other armed services needs.

Additionally, Byrnes went on to warn that reconversion rumors could delay winning the war. Deviations from this line led to quick rebuke. In July 1944, with the army and navy engaged in public charges that munitions shortages could threaten the war effort, Stacy May's Progress Division issued a report to WPB indicating that ordnance supplies at home and abroad and scheduled for output provided for an eighteen-month reserve during the remaining seven months of 1944 and that small arms ammunition stored in the United States totaled a five-year supply. With the army protesting the accuracy of the report, Executive Vice Chair Charles E. Wilson ordered May to withdraw it immediately. Calculations in the study were vulnerable to army attack because WPB had only limited information on the service's demand. Once Nelson entered the fray, Leahy referred the matter to JPSC. By then, parts of the report had been leaked to and made public by the media and the Truman Committee. JPSC finessed the issue to cover the army, but, in September 1944, the army began reducing its inventories.

Nonetheless, with the Battle of the Bulge in December 1944, military requirements suddenly shot up drastically. Some WPB executives were convinced that stated demand bore little resemblance to actual need, that the armed services were setting their demands at levels intended to block reconversion. This suspected condition persisted well into 1945. Protesting to Vinson in May 1945 that the armed services were proposing few requirements reductions in the transition from a two- to a one-front war, WPB Chair Julius A. Krug went on: "It appears that the Air, Naval, and Army Ground Forces are each developing production plans for winning the war practically singlehanded."[33] OWMR declined to investigate the situation, claiming that the JCS was conducting a major procurement review. Prior to Krug's May complaint, the WPB chair had warned OWMR in February and March 1945 that it did not have detailed military procurement plans for a one-front war. Without that vital information, the board could not go forward with efforts to prepare for peace. When WPB finally and publicly proceeded with its reconversion plans in April, the board had to caution readers about their tentative nature since armed services requirements remained uncertain.

Overall, then, Byrnes proved to be an able umpire and arbitrator in keeping the tangled and contentious mobilization system running. In doing so, he freed the overextended president from the never-ending homefront turmoil. Moreover, and of great importance, in handling the details of the Roosevelt administration's transition from Dr. New Deal to Dr. Win-the-War, the OWM/OWMR director absorbed enormous political heat on Roosevelt's behalf. Despite the rightward shift, Byrnes was exceptionally evenhanded in helping shape manpower, labor, and other policies affecting the people in the street, at least until mid-1944. Thereafter, he became more conservative. Exactly why is difficult to determine.

Several reasons suggest themselves. With the war winding down and the general population growing restless, Byrnes may have felt that it was essential to tighten controls in order to maintain the course until hostilities ended. Another basic characteristic of the OWM/OWMR head could have reinforced such a decision: he worked with, instead of trying to alter, power realities. Operating through the PEC, the industry-military production team had consolidated its hold on the WPB. With the battle over reconversion growing more intense in and outside WPB, Byrnes lined up with and acted to protect PEC and the status quo. In a sense, Byrnes's ongoing struggle with the military over requirements strengthened his hand by making the OWM/OWMR director appear to be an authentic neutral. Finally, Roosevelt had passed over the ambitious and anxious Byrnes to tap Harry S. Truman as his running mate for the 1944 presidential election. Bitter and resentful, Byrnes may have felt freer to manifest his essentially conservative side. Whatever the case, Byrnes resigned as director of OWMR in April 1945 when victory in Europe was certain and close. His successors faced a different, less urgent set of problems.

14

ORGANIZED LABOR IN A MOBILIZED ECONOMY, 1940–1945: LABOR SUPPLY

The defense and war years were frustrating for organized labor. Massive growth for the American Federation of Labor (AFL) and the Congress of Industrial Organizations (CIO) during the 1930s and 1940s did not convert into significantly enhanced power in a mobilized economy. From 1940 through 1945, unions remained a distinctly secondary power group in a system increasingly dominated by industry and the military.

Sidney Hillman headed the Labor Division in the National Defense Advisory Commission (NDAC), the Office of Production Management (OPM), and, initially, the War Production Board (WPB), and he served as associate director of OPM. In NDAC and OPM, Hillman's division generally sided with the New Deal faction led by Leon Henderson, which aimed to accelerate mobilization and carry it out along liberal lines. When after Pearl Harbor WPB was created, New Deal influence declined, and Hillman was all but pushed out of the board in April 1942. Thereafter, labor's influence in WPB was minimal.

Throughout the defense and war years, union influence was largely confined to the areas of labor supply and labor relations. Once America entered hostilities, labor's powers even in these areas became more restricted. Unions achieved a significant voice in the operations of the War Manpower Commission (WMC), organized in April 1942. The commission, however, turned out to be relatively weak, excluded from determining the size and recruitment of the armed services, the placement of contracts, and the utilization of labor. By slow stages, WPB and the armed services reduced WMC to acting as a service agency for their production and procurement functions. Unions, furthermore, had to fight steadily to keep WMC limited to voluntary methods for directing workers and to beat back attempts to enact national service legislation, even though there was never a general labor shortage.

In the labor relations area, Hillman's Labor Division always competed with a host of other administrations and was never able to define and enforce a general labor policy. The lack of such a policy increased the likelihood of strikes, especially in industries directly or indirectly involved in munitions output. Work stoppages threw unions on the defensive and invited other agencies, particularly the military, into labor relations.

With America at war, organized labor officially shelved the strike weapon, surrendered much of its collective-bargaining rights, coped with the armed services intruding into labor supply and labor relations matters, and experienced rigid economic controls overseen by what labor felt to be unsympathetic conservatives. Although during the war there were few actual strikes, growing pressures inevitably led to work stoppages, which tarnished labor's image and resulted in punitive countermeasures. For varying reasons, union leaders faced growing difficulty in controlling their restive members in the last years of the war.

Stronger than it had ever been before, organized labor discovered the limits of its power in a corporate capitalist economy harnessed for war.

MOBILIZING LABOR

Between 1940 and mid-1943, the national labor supply was largely distributed by market forces.[1] Millions of workers migrated to defense and war production centers, attracted by new and lucrative employment opportunities. Unlike with facilities and materials, the government did not become heavily involved with manpower management until mobilization was well advanced. Since depression-based unemployment was still high, a sense of urgency was missing. In June 1940, 9 million Americans were without jobs—4 million at the time of Pearl Harbor, nearly 10 percent of the civilian labor force. Workers began to become scarce only in 1943.[2]

Roosevelt charged Hillman's Labor Division in NDAC and OPM with defense manpower issues, which included coordinating the activities of numerous federal agencies, such as the Federal Security Agency, the Labor Department, and the Civil Service Commission. Hillman's division failed to establish itself as a center for overseeing labor supply. Never accepted by the industry-dominated mobilization agencies, it remained isolated within NDAC and OPM. More particularly, neither the industry divisions nor the procurement agencies would cooperate with Hillman's attempts to have labor supply considered in placing contracts and constructing facilities. And other federal agencies dealing with manpower refused to follow the lead of a new and temporary body operating without clearly established authority.

Organized labor also acted to weaken Hillman. Neither the AFL nor the CIO fully supported the Labor Division head since he was appointed without their approval. Competition and suspicion between the two labor federations additionally made Hillman's job of appointing labor officials to various positions difficult and often resulted in poor or inappropriate representation. Moreover, within the Labor Division, the Labor Relations Branch was staffed with trade union officials, the Labor Supply Branch with economists and other professionals. The former wanted to determine policy to suit unions, while the latter favored a broader approach. Although feuding between the two branches disrupted the division's employment operations, Hillman failed to resolve the conflict. A poor administrator, the president of the Amalgamated Clothing Workers of America never succeeded in molding his multibranch division into a smoothly functioning whole.[3]

Once America entered hostilities, a more effective manpower agency became imperative. Labor supply problems were becoming evident, and they would grow as mobilization expanded. With intense controversy surrounding a new agency, the Roosevelt administration held off creating the WMC until April 1942.

With the Labor Division transferred to the WPB in January 1942 and a new manpower agency in the making, Hillman insisted that all labor supply functions be placed under him. Donald M. Nelson did not go along. When given the choice by the president, he elected to have manpower handled outside, not inside, WPB. Disgusted with what they perceived to be Labor Division impotence, the AFL and the CIO united in advocating that all civilian and military manpower programs be centered in a restructured and revitalized Labor Department. Others favored setting up a Labor Division–type organization outside WPB. Facing conflicting advice, Roosevelt turned first to a cabinet committee and later to an advisory group headed by Samuel I. Rosenman. On the basis of further consultation, the president in April established WMC and selected Paul V. McNutt, head of the Federal Security Agency, as its chair.[4]

On paper, WMC had broad powers. It was to direct the mobilization, allocation, and utilization of manpower for industry, agriculture, and the military and to recommend legislation for achieving those goals if necessary. Executive authority rested with McNutt, who was advised initially by representatives from the War, Navy, Agriculture, and Labor Departments, the WPB, the Selective Service System (SSS), and the Civil Service Commission. Basic to the operation of WMC was the United States Employment Service (USES). Housed in the Federal Security Agency, the USES was essentially a state-based system consisting of thousands of local offices scattered throughout the country. The president federalized the structure after Pearl Harbor, but it maintained a state orientation, suffered from uneven, often low-grade personnel, and was chronically underfunded. USES weaknesses plagued WMC throughout the war years.

WMC was intended to carry out massive responsibilities through coordinating powerful permanent and wartime administrations. It quickly became clear that the commission had to be an operating, not just a coordinating, agency to carry out its duties. The transformation took place over a number of months in 1942. In September, USES and various Federal Security Agency subdivisions transferred to WMC. The biggest step occurred in December 1942. By executive order, the SSS was placed under WMC authority. Henceforth, the armed services were required to consult with McNutt on their size, and voluntary enlistment for the army and navy was ended. Additionally, the commission would regulate all recruitment of labor in areas designated as critical by the chair, and all other federal agencies were required to cooperate with WMC in enforcing its rules. WMC now had the organization and authority to mobilize manpower among military and civilian users for the purpose of maximizing the war effort.[5]

Another development of critical importance between April and December 1942 was the decline of the WMC in McNutt's organization and the rise of the Management-Labor Policy Committee (MLPC). Aware that, without the support of industry and unions, his organization would be severely handicapped, McNutt in May 1942 appointed the MLPC to advise him on policies and practices. In short order, MLPC replaced WMC as the commission's principal advisory body. For a time, War Department representatives had considerable influence in WMC. Sensing that the army was attempting to dominate WMC, McNutt reduced military membership to a minimum. His action in part accounts for the War Department's hostility toward WMC.

In time, MLPC developed a separate staff, was broadened to incorporate agriculture, and, ultimately, included representatives from the AFL, the CIO, the Order of Railway Conductors, the United States Chamber of Commerce, the National Association of Manufacturers, the American Farm Bureau Federation, and the National Farmer's Union. The committee's status was enhanced in December 1942 when the executive order reorganizing WMC required the commission to continue and to consult MLPC. Operating through consensus, management and labor used the committee to protect their mutual interests. Since WMC was one of the few wartime agencies in which organized labor had an authentic voice, MLPC was more important to unions than to management. Accordingly, labor was the more dynamic element. McNutt set no major policy or took any important step without first consulting the committee.[6] "Rarely had a group of private citizens," observes one scholar, "had as much direct authority in the conduct of the affairs of a government agency."[7]

A strengthened WMC never realized its potential. Since manpower was basic to all aspects of the war effort, WPB and the armed services separately and together acted to limit commission authority and to subordinate the agency to themselves. Overall, McNutt had more trouble with the military, particularly the War Department, than with any other mobilization body. That was the case in terms of both raising fighting forces and procurement practices.

Once America entered hostilities, the size of the armed forces and how their ranks were filled became a matter of growing concern. If the military grew too large or recruited its personnel carelessly, economic output could be adversely affected.

When WMC was created in April 1942, most assumed that it would have a voice in determining how large the military would be, a matter that was formalized with the executive order of December 1942.[8] By late 1942, the armed forces' size had become a subject of great controversy. In September 1942, the Joint Chiefs of Staff (JCS) approved a figure of just under 11 million officers and men for the army, navy, Marine Corps, and Coast Guard to be reached by the end of 1943. Both the WMC and the WPB challenged these estimates as too large. WMC argued for total forces not exceeding 9 million, while WPB set the figure at 7.6 million on the basis of Planning Committee studies. As the numbers were debated, the Senate Special Committee to Investigate the National Defense Program (the Truman Committee), the House Select Committee Investigating National Defense Migration (the Tolan Committee, after its chair, John H. Tolan [D-CA]), and members of Congress, business leaders, and labor spokesmen all joined the fray, usually in support of the military's critics. Secretary of War Henry L. Stimson went public in defense of the joint chiefs, arguing that the army was trying to shorten the war, "to save the lives of thousands of young Americans," while its opponents were unwilling to tolerate "inconveniences and relatively minor sacrifices."[9] Throughout the conflict, JCS insisted that, although willing to confer with WMC and WPB, it answered only to the president on how large the army and navy would be.

After a period of uncertainty, Roosevelt in February 1943 backed JCS figures and, by implication, the military's right to determine its size. To lend greater weight to his ruling, the president in March appointed a special committee to review his decision; that committee consisted of Harry L. Hopkins, James F. Byrnes, Samuel I. Rosenman, Admiral William D. Leahy, and Bernard M. Baruch. In short order, the committee reported that, while manpower was becoming scarce, the armed services could safely go slightly over the 11 million figure. As it turned out, WMC, WPB, and other sources questioning JCS projections were too pessimistic. In May 1945, the armed forces reached their maximum strength at somewhat over 12 million, causing stress, but not harm, to the homefront.

The battle waged by civilians over the military's size was not fought in vain. JCS planners proposed overall military forces for 1944 of around 14 million. Unwilling to accept such inflated numbers, both Chief of Staff George C. Marshall and Commander-in-Chief Ernest J. King required their subordinates to rework calculations until, in November 1943, total strength was reduced to under 11.3 million, not much above the 1943 goals. In doing so, the JCS relied on the findings of a number of special committees that it had appointed as well as estimates from the WMC. The extended controversy had convinced Marshall and King—particularly the former—that the army and navy had to consider the impact of their numbers on munitions output, on civilian views, and on the analysis of economic experts. The fact that the WPB had recently forced the armed services to accept the concept of feasibility for requirements probably also affected JSC's outlook.

Ironically, Marshall in 1944 had to resist the persistent attempts of Secretary of War Stimson to increase the army's size. Not pushing for a larger army, argued Goldthwaite H. Dorr, an assistant to Stimson with responsibility for manpower, was to chance a letdown on the homefront. "The American people respond best when they see before them an unattained and desperately difficult goal," he insisted.[10] In part, Stimson, Dorr, and others in the War Department were maneuvering to create manpower problems so as to strengthen the case for national service and to help block Donald M. Nelson's drive to begin implementing a reconversion program.

The military's methods of raising and selecting its manpower affected WMC operations more than the numbers involved. Throughout 1942, all the armed services conducted extensive recruitment campaigns that indiscriminately reduced manpower pools. Areas already experiencing labor deficits and a shortage of skilled workers were particularly hard hit. WMC attempts to curb recruitment drives were unsuccessful, and the practice continued even after being prohibited by the executive order of December 1942.[11]

Selective service, however, was the most important method of raising millions of men for the armed services, especially the army. Created by Congress in September 1940, SSS by the end of 1942 had registered nearly 30 million individuals aged eighteen to forty-five and had inducted over 5 million of them. It was the major and most powerful manpower agency of World War II.[12]

Theoretically independent, and reporting only to the president, SSS was always dominated by the War Department. On the basis of World War I precedent, the army and navy in 1926 had created in the General Staff a Joint Army-Navy Selective Service Committee (JANSSC). From then until World War II, JANSSC planned and prepared for another selective service system to meet an emergency, including the recruitment and training of a national staff. Except for a few months late in 1940 and early in 1941, SSS was directed by General Lewis B. Hershey, a regular army officer who had become JANSSC secretary in 1936. Nearly every significant position within SSS was filled by an army officer. At its base, the system consisted of around sixty-five hundred local boards. While these boards could and did act independently at times, their latitude was consistently reduced as manpower grew scarce in 1943.

Practically all SSS acts affected WMC. Of most immediate importance were draft quotas. These quotas, which were based on army and navy manpower requirements, were set in Washington and worked their way down to the local boards. As more men were inducted, naturally, fewer were available for civilian employment. Except for efforts to keep the size of the armed forces within feasible ranges, WMC had little control over induction numbers. The commission's impact was greater in the sensitive area of draft deferments. SSS's enabling legislation provided for occupational deferments where appropriate. Operating under general directions from Washington, local boards initially passed over married men, fathers, and others with dependents, inducted otherwise eligible single men, and deferred those considered to be essential to the war effort.

From the outset, WMC attempted to rationalize the deferment process. Operating under vague national guidelines, thousands of local boards could not implement uniform or even reasonably consistent policies. The commission first sought better to inform the SSS deferment process by providing it with a *List of Essential Activities.* WMC's more sophisticated and preferred method involved "manning tables." On the basis of the analysis of its utilization experts, WMC sketched out how a plant could most efficiently use its workforce. From such a breakdown, management could prioritize the process of releasing men for military service. Widespread use of manning tables could bring order to an otherwise capricious SSS. The use of manning tables, however, was minimized by the opposition of the War Department and, to a degree, management and even unions. Manning tables elevated WMC's role in war industries—particularly among military contractors. Intent on minimizing commission power, the department insisted on the use of "replacement schedules," in which management provided local boards with preference lists for drafting, deferring, or exempting workers. Such an approach kept WMC out of factories, even if the exclusion of WMC utilization experts meant less efficient use of labor. Out of expediency, Hershey followed the War Department lead. Management favored replacement schedules over manning tables because they meant less government intervention, and, if collective-bargaining contracts became involved, unions backed the employer. As labor shortages grew, manpower utilization became an intensely contentious issue among WMC, the armed services, and WPB.

WMC's argument that its responsibilities required directing military as well as civilian manpower mobilization persuaded Roosevelt to place SSS under the commission's control during the December 1942 reorganization. The transfer was bitterly opposed and never accepted by the War Department. According to Stimson, McNutt's staff was "feeble," consisting of "callow New Dealers with more ambition than brains."[13] In actuality, shifting SSS to WMC changed little. A tightly structured bureaucratic system that had been operating for more than two years before WMC was fully under way, SSS was beyond the commission's reach. Hershey's organization was further strengthened by the fact that, unlike WMC, it had powerful backers in Washington and was popular in Congress. Moreover, SSS had the sanction of law, while WMC operated only through an executive order.

Nonetheless, McNutt's determination to make selective service policies more rational and consistent led to SSS breaking free of WMC control. Politically shrewd, Hershey made sure that his organization minimized any conflict with Congress. Such an approach was not easy since the nation's legislators were quick to meddle in SSS affairs. In November 1942, for example, Congress passed the so-called Tydings Amendment emphasizing the need to defer agricultural workers. Fully cognizant of Farm Bloc intent, Hershey interpreted discretionary language in a way granting farm workers a virtually blanket exemption throughout most of the war.

McNutt was less willing to placate national legislators. With labor supply growing tight, he concluded that husbands and fathers could no longer be free from selective service. In March 1942, dependency accounted for 65 percent of all deferments, and, a year later, 11.7 million men were so exempted. Late in January 1943, WMC directed SSS to terminate all such exemptions for eligible men between eighteen and thirty-eight not in deferrable occupations. Occupation, not dependency, would, henceforth, guide SSS operations. The new and radical departure created a firestorm of opposition. McNutt's order was acrimoniously debated, local boards often refused to go along with it, and, in December 1943, Congress passed legislation in effect rescinding the WMC directive. In the same act, Congress reestablished SSS as an autonomous agency. Although basically agreeing with McNutt's stand on dependency deferments, Hershey allowed his staff to use the unpopular measure to strengthen Congress's jaundiced view of WMC.

WMC began losing authority over deferment policy even before Congress removed SSS from its sphere. In dealing with the West Coast manpower crisis that erupted during the late summer of 1943, WMC ordered a sixty-day deferment for all critical aircraft workers while corporations devised a replacement system; the War Department insisted that six months, not two, were required. Concerned about setting a precedent, WMC stood firm. To get their way, the armed services bypassed the commission and went to James F. Byrnes, director of the Office of War Mobilization (OWM). Agreeing with the military, Byrnes in October 1943 ordered into effect—until permanent programs could be implemented—a plan in which army and navy procurement officers, working with aircraft firms, certified to the SSS irreplaceable workers for six-month deferments. The War and Navy Departments now had more authority than previously in determining who was drafted and who was deferred.

Variations of the West Coast approach were soon applied to the entire nation. In 1944 and 1945, a declining pool of men between the ages of twenty-two and twenty-nine eligible for the draft required severely restricting deferments in that category. The crude, inexact methods of the SSS were not up to the challenge. To meet the growing crisis, the War and Navy Departments proposed solutions controlled either by them or by the WPB's Production Executive Committee (PEC), on which they had a dominant voice. WMC insisted that deferment policy had to be made in an informed and careful way to avoid adversely affecting critical production programs. Refusing to bend to military pressure, and backed by the president, the commission pushed through a compromise measure that set up an Inter-Agency Committee on Occupational Deferments. Chaired by WMC, and including members from WPB, the procurement agencies, and other administrations, the new body determined deferrable occupations, in some instances assigning quotas to claimant agencies. The arrangement kept WMC involved in deferments. If major disagreements arose, however, the armed services could usually have their way, turning to Byrnes and the JCS for support when necessary.

Overall, then, WMC at best had a subordinate, indirect influence over determining the size of, and the process of selecting millions of men, for the armed services. The peculiarities of the SSS, the capricious methods for determining deferment and enlistment, and the arrogance of the military services all acted to distort badly the way in which the nation raised its fighting forces. Nonetheless, and despite the huge size of the army and navy, the numbers involved in the fighting forces were substantial, but not great. It was in the production area that man- and womanpower grew to enormous proportions. Here, as with its own ranks, the military hand was heavy, powerful, and distorting.

The basic pattern of mobilizing the American economy for World War II was determined by the distribution of contracts and the conversion, expansion, and construction of facilities to fulfill them. From the beginning, the armed forces and the United States Maritime Commission let the majority of contracts and made decisions about production facilities. Both contracts and facilities went in overwhelming numbers to giant corporations, which acted to tie together military and industrial America in a union dominating the harnessed economy.

Concentration in contracting and facilities construction had an enormous impact on labor supply. Most plant expansion was under way or completed by mid-1943, before manpower emerged as a significantly limiting factor. That was the case with 70 percent of War Department–authorized facilities. WPB reported that, between May and November 1942, over 80 percent of contracts measured in dollars went to areas with manpower problems. By July 1943, over half those employed in the final assembly of aircraft, aeronautical engines, and propellers and more than two-thirds of the manpower hired by shipyards were located in labor-deficient places. Cities such as Detroit, Baltimore, and Los Angeles were overloaded with war business, while others like New York and Scranton, Pennsylvania, had production capacity to spare. Similar trends were evident for entire regions of the nation.[14]

The NDAC and the OPM had tried, without much success, to achieve more balance in plant expansion. The WPB did little better, except toward the end of 1942 and the beginning of 1943, when most facilities had already been constructed or commitments for them made. There were some good reasons, of course, for locating plants in a limited number of areas, including the availability of reliable management, the adequacy of transportation, the location of raw materials, required weather conditions, and even strategic considerations. Much of what took place, however, resulted from expediency, not necessity. Procurement officers invariably turned to the experienced large firms for munitions output. These were usually situated in a relatively few metropolitan areas, and their executives insisted on expanding existing plants or building new ones in their immediate localities. In time, cities and regions had contracts exceeding available labor. And, if men and women in needed numbers could be hired, they could not be retained because of inadequate community facilities, including housing, stores, restaurants, medical, dental, and child-care centers, various other services, transportation systems, and the like.

Maldistributed contracts and facilities resulted principally from the procurement operations of the armed services. Seven technical services in addition to the Army Air Forces procured for the army, five supply bureaus for the navy. Prior to Pearl Harbor, neither service adequately controlled its supply units. After entry into the war, the Army Service Forces for the army and the

Office of Procurement and Material (OP&M) for the navy centralized direction to a degree, but letting contracts and providing for facilities remained largely decentralized. What ASF, OP&M, and the War and Navy Departments did do, however, was protect their bureaus from meaningful oversight by civilian mobilization agencies. With contracts and facilities authorizations pouring into the economy from thirteen poorly coordinated sources, unbalanced results were probable. That outcome was almost assured by the general belief among procurement officers that labor supply was either not a problem or the responsibility of WMC. Labor offices in both the army and the navy, and especially the former, knew better, but their views were ignored.[15]

The principal civilian mobilization agencies were hardly blameless. Neither NDAC nor OPM had the experience, staff, authority, or sense of urgency to insist on manpower considerations in procurement. WPB should have anticipated labor supply difficulties, but it did not. Moreover, in March and April 1942, Nelson signed agreements with the War and Navy Departments in which he surrendered any meaningful control over their buying, contracting, and facilities functions. By encouraging the Roosevelt administration to establish WMC outside WPB, Nelson indicated his lack of interest in or concern about manpower. Thereafter, various WPB policies acted to the detriment of WMC. WPB was both late and perfunctory in emphasizing the importance of labor supply in contracting and facilities operations, and it consistently refused to use its priority and related powers to enforce WMC policies. By not acting more forcefully in curtailing less and nonessential industries or in concentrating essential production among a few firms in an industry, WPB passed up opportunities for freeing more workers for munitions or essential civilian output. In not doing more for small business, the board failed to maximize use of existing facilities and to achieve a better distribution of contracts, thereby easing labor supply problems.[16]

WPB's most significant impact on WMC involved two related issues: data on contracting to guide commission activities;[17] and policies for ensuring maximum utilization of manpower. Shortly after being created, WMC requested WPB to provide it with lists of plants in order of importance so that the commission could prioritize the recruitment of labor. In doing so, the commission would determine whether firms used their labor in the most effective way. WPB balked at WMC's proposal. Nelson argued that, as the agency responsible for production, the board, not the commission, would establish such priorities. WMC would then simply follow WPB determinations. Led by the War Department, the procurement agencies backed WPB. The army categorically denied the right of WMC to have any voice in its contracting prerogatives. McNutt rejected the notion that the commission was a service agency for

WPB and the military, delivering labor as directed without evaluation. Before acting, WMC had to ensure that requirements were sound, workers were utilized efficiently, and other such matters.

In time, Nelson appeared to accept the validity of McNutt's argument. However, WPB could not provide WMC the information it wanted. The industry divisions did not have adequate, usable data. As the principal procuring agencies, the army and navy had the most complete statistics, but, with operations spread out among numerous services and bureaus, the armed forces either could not or would not provide the required information. Furthermore, without assuming any control over subcontracting, the army and navy never had full data on the contracts they let. The inadequacy of reliable figures on overall manpower requirements created problems throughout the war years. WMC, WPB, and other agencies had to rely on estimates instead of hard data in formulating labor supply policy. Such an approach always created uncertainty, and, when projections were off, WMC's dependability came under attack.

WMC-WPB relations involving manpower were further complicated by conflict within the board over the role of the labor office. When Sidney Hillman left WPB in April 1942, the president replaced the Labor Division with the Labor Production Division. Unable to agree on someone from their own ranks, the AFL and the CIO compromised on Wendell Lund, an obscure, career government official, to head the labor office. Not having been consulted about its creation, Nelson neither welcomed nor knew what to do with the new division. When WMC requested production data to assist its operations, the Labor Production Division jumped at the opportunity. Since a number of its members served in WMC and WPB, the Labor Production Division insisted that it was ideally suited to coordinate functions between the two administrations. Nelson resisted the proposal, but, desperate to placate restless trade union members, he finally agreed to transfer the Labor Requirements Committee into the labor office.

The move satisfied no one. The Labor Production Division did not have access to WPB's contract information because it was spurned by the industry divisions and barred from the board's decisionmaking councils. WMC ended up without the data it wanted but with the Labor Production Division trying to push into its area in a frantic search for something to do. In mid-1943, a beleaguered Nelson replaced the Labor Production Division with Joseph D. Keenan of the AFL as vice chair for labor production and Clinton S. Golden of the CIO as vice chair for manpower requirements. The latter was more acceptable to WMC, but his virtual isolation within the board and the statistical deficiencies of WPB still left WMC without the assistance it needed.

As important to WMC as reliable statistics on manpower requirements was the critical issue of labor utilization.[18] Throughout the war years, the commission hammered at the theme that demand for labor could not be considered separate from its use. When properly using labor, plants could increase output while reducing workforce. Drawing on WMC analyses, McNutt estimated that 20–25 percent of the workforce was underutilized. Consequently, he insisted that WMC could not take at face value employers' requests for workers as represented by WPB or the procurement agencies. When deemed necessary, the commission had to be able to survey facilities to ensure that labor was not being hoarded, underutilized, or wasted, that programs to train and upgrade employees, simplify jobs, and the like were in place, and that sound labor relations existed. With variations of cost-plus contracting widespread, management had little incentive to use its workforce most effectively.

Repeatedly throughout the war years, congressional investigations, trade union reports, and other studies documented WMC's claims. In time, even WPB grew more flexible on the subject. But not the claimant agencies. Led by the War Department, they adamantly maintained that manpower utilization was a management responsibility. If questions arose about labor use, the procurement administrations, alone or with assistance from others, would handle matters. Even in the midst of crises, the army, navy, and Maritime Commission beat back WMC attempts to provide for utilization studies, and, declarations to the contrary, the procurement agencies were uninterested in conducting or unable to conduct investigations on their own. At best, organized labor was equivocal on the subject. Collective bargaining could be involved, and unions were unwilling to antagonize management members of the WMC's MLPC.

Overall, then, WMC got under way inauspiciously. Contract distribution and facility expansion shaping mobilization patterns were already fairly well set before the commission had the authority to act with the reorganization of December 1942. Furthermore, WMC was forced to operate without proper manpower data and without the ability to enforce efficient labor-usage policies. Most significantly, without the clout that industry provided WPB and that contracting gave the procurement agencies, WMC was in a secondary power position. Consequently, WPB and the armed services looked on WMC less as an equal and more as a service agency. Questionable status increased the difficulties that the commission faced in trying to fulfill vast responsibilities.

By August 1942, WMC had devised an employment stabilization plan for distressed areas.[19] Employers agreed to recruit labor only through the USES and to use manpower in the most efficient manner. Employees would not leave jobs or be hired for new ones without a certificate of availability provided by USES or their employer. WMC supplied USES offices with a *List of Essential*

Activities to guide their referral services. The commission's MLPC went along with the program only after ensuring that workers were properly protected and that management-labor policy committees were used at local levels.

The stabilization plan was first applied in September 1942 for the nonferrous metal, logging, and lumbering industries in the twelve Western states. Plagued by low wages, abominable working conditions, deteriorating community facilities, and tumultuous, violent labor histories, workers in these industries were easily lured away by the promise of higher pay and more suitable living arrangements. Alarmed by the migration, the armed services wanted to freeze existing labor in all three industries, but MLPC persuaded WMC not to go along. Instead, representatives of government, management, and labor adapted the commission's stabilization program to the region. The adapted program was never very successful. Throughout the war years, emergency measures were constantly required to avert crises without bringing about long-term solutions.

The Western states were an anomaly. Throughout 1942 and 1943, employment stabilization plans were usually applied on a local basis. During 1942, such plans were implemented in cities like Baltimore, Buffalo, Louisville, and Detroit. By March 1943, around forty-four such programs were in effect. They were uneven in nature and generally limited in impact. Since the plans revolved around USES offices, that outcome was inevitable. The understaffed, often poorly staffed, offices tended to be inefficient and lacked priority guidance in referring workers. Furthermore, plans were voluntary and without enforcement mechanisms. Certificates of availability were easy to acquire, and employers could hire without them. Those conditions persisted even after the president's anti-inflation "Hold-the-Line" Order of early April 1943 sanctioned freezing workers in existing jobs through the commission's employment stabilization plan.

Most important, employment stabilization plans dealt more with symptoms than with causes. Labor availability was less the problem than labor turnover, which was up to around 75 percent per year nationally in September 1943 and went much higher in some industries and areas. Some "job shopping" was involved, but most shifting resulted from unsatisfactory working and living conditions over which WMC had no control. Community problems could be very stressful. The president by executive order in April 1943 appointed a Committee for Congested Production Areas, but progress was always slow. A subcommittee of the Senate Military Affairs Committee in 1943 reported that "many thousands of workers on the Pacific Coast, with their families, are living under conditions that must be characterized as abominable."[20] Absenteeism was also high. Some of it stemmed from poor attitudes.

Reliable studies, however, established that workers failed to report for work principally because of sickness, transportation difficulties, long hours, bad nutrition, wives visiting inducted husbands, and bad weather.

Another weakness of WMC's approach was workers' resistance to moving from non- and less essential employment to that which was critical. Draft-age men usually transferred in order to avoid induction. That motivation was missing for older men and women. Even under pressure, many would not transfer because stabilization plans failed to protect seniority in existing jobs.

WMC Regional Director Anna Rosenberg led in modifying the stabilization plan for Buffalo in mid-1943 in a way that proved promising. Representatives from WPB, WMC, and procurement agencies combined efforts to devise a priority system for referring workers. Employers and employees ignoring the program or violating its rules were boycotted by USES and other approved employment agencies. While the approach remained voluntary, the instituted changes made it much more effective.

A variation on what took place in Buffalo ultimately became the basis for a national manpower approach.[21] Throughout most of 1942, and well into 1943, labor continued to be distributed by market forces tempered by WMC's modest approaches and the impact of other mobilization agencies. A manpower crunch on the West Coast late in the summer of 1943 led to significant change. San Francisco, Portland, Seattle, and Los Angeles and areas around them became major centers for shipbuilding and ship repair, aircraft, and other war industries. Military contractors were falling behind schedule, with the inadequacies of labor supply highlighted as a major cause. Several investigations ensued, the most important of which Bernard M. Baruch and John Hancock conducted for Byrnes as director of the OWM. In August, the two investigators reported that the manpower crisis stemmed from

> the lack of any system of labor priorities and the hopelessly unbalanced production demands that have been imposed on the Pacific Coast. These demands for the next six months are so far in excess of the available labor supply that a disastrous breakdown of vital production programs all through the region is threatened.[22]

In order to avoid such a calamity, Baruch and Hancock insisted that contract placement, military recruitment, labor utilization and standards, and community facilities must be more effectively handled. To accomplish that end, the two elder statesmen appended remediating proposals for WMC to implement.

The plan recommended by Baruch and Hancock was authored by WMC and provided for the commission to direct WPB and procurement agencies in devising a system of priorities for referring labor, for placing, cutting back, and removing contracts, and for ensuring maximum labor utilization. In carrying out these programs, WMC would be guided by local, regional, and national management-labor policy committees.

WMC's proposal met with fierce opposition from the procurement agencies led by the War Department. Although divided, the WPB basically came down on the side of the procurement administrations. The War Department insisted that solutions to the West Coast labor supply crisis had to be controlled by WPB's PEC, the armed services, and the Maritime Commission, with WMC acting in only a supporting role.

A long and acrimonious negotiation process led by Byrnes resulted in a compromise solution that was unveiled early in September 1943 and came to be known as the Byrnes Plan. It was designed more effectively to regulate and to prioritize the flow of contracts into and out of the industrially impacted West Coast, to provide contractors with the required labor force, and to take other steps to alleviate labor shortages.

The heart of the plan consisted of two committees, the Area Production Urgency Committee (APUC) and the Area Manpower Priorities Committee (AMPC). Chaired by an official from WPB who worked through the board's PEC and with members of the procurement agencies and WMC, APUC would determine whether new contracts and facilities would be allowed into the Pacific Coast region, whether existing contracts had to be moved within or outside the area, and whether civilian output had to be reduced. Additionally, the committee would rate the urgency of all war production so as to inform WMC labor referrals. AMPC, headed by a WMC member or a prominent citizen of the region and made up of the same members as APUC, would prioritize all plants in the area on the basis of APUC data, set "employment ceilings" for various establishments, and determine worker referrals to plants on the basis of level of urgency. To assist APUC and AMPC, West Coast localities were classified from Group I (critical labor shortage) through Group IV (labor surplus). USES, or agencies selected by it, would be the sole source for referring labor, and management was prohibited from hiring through other sources. SSS was to cooperate in deferring key workers, and the armed services were to cease recruitment campaigns.

Although the Byrnes Plan was presented as a compromise, WMC actually lost ground. PEC and the procurement agencies dominated both APUC and AMPC. With the War Department leading the way, Byrnes had been persuaded, practically forced, to all but prohibit WMC from conducting labor-utilization surveys and to eliminate MLPC participation. SSS was required to follow War Department over WMC directives. Finally, although Baruch and

Hancock had backed the commission in emphasizing the importance of improving community facilities, that part of the program was neglected.

Organized labor was particularly distressed by Byrnes's solution. WMC was one of the few wartime agencies in which it had achieved some genuine influence. Not only was the commission being downgraded in its functions, but MLPC was also belittled. More than WMC was involved, however. In WPB, PEC bypassed Clinton S. Golden's Office of Manpower Requirements to set up a Program Adjustment and Requirements Committee under PEC to handle the board's role in the West Coast program. Golden's office gained representation on the new committee in January 1944, but only after a long struggle, and, even then, its influence remained slight. A similar development took place in the War Department. The labor offices within the department were ably staffed and well informed and maintained good relations with unions. Once manpower reached the critical stage, General Lucius D. Clay, who directed procurement, pushed these offices aside so that his staff could handle labor supply policy.

Byrnes's program had more weaknesses than strengths. Although WMC and MLPC were downgraded in West Coast manpower activities, they still had enough influence to keep the plan voluntary. They were strengthened in their resolve by great apprehension on the West Coast over the Byrnes Plan, necessitating its cautious implementation. Old practices also continued. The issuance of certificates of availability remained lax, management continued hiring outside USES (which was not substantially strengthened), workers could not be required to transfer from unessential to essential jobs, unessential industries were not forced to cut back or shut down, and, without substantial improvement in community facilities, turnover and absenteeism remained high. Additionally, APUC and AMPC provided only fragmentary data on contract urgency and manpower requirements, reducing WMC's ability to devise reliable labor supply budgets. The commission had to fall back on past practices of estimating demand.

Procurement agency behavior also did not change in any meaningful way. Few projects were reduced or removed from tight labor markets, new contracts continued to flow into the area, and some additional construction even started. Since the army, navy, and Maritime Commission dominated the West Coast labor supply committees, and since they were usually supported by WPB personnel, they easily voted through each other's projects. If that did not work, the armed services could and did ignore APUC in contracting—or claim that the committee did not have jurisdiction because no new labor was required or unique or vitally needed facilities were involved, conditions provided for in the Byrnes Plan. When criticized for such practices, procurement agencies pointed out that change on their part could not be expected as long as the WPB failed to stop, reduce, or move less and nonessential industries. Moreover, often management and members of Congress, even at times unions, opposed moving contracts from or restricting their flow into glutted areas.

For all its limitations, the Byrnes Plan still had some merit. It prevented conditions from getting worse, and it improved conditions in certain circumstances. First, combining in APUC and AMPC representatives from procurement, production, and manpower agencies emphasized labor supply and, to a degree, facilitated its handling. Second, rating areas according to stringency highlighted those facing the worst conditions, improved referrals, and reduced turnover and absenteeism. Third, the threat of cutting back contracts to or removing them from the West Coast forced management to be more realistic in estimating manpower needs and to use its labor more effectively. Trade unions also became more attentive and flexible. Finally, and despite their resistance, procurement agencies diverted some production and facilities to less impacted regions, and they also tended to examine more critically their requirements and schedules for fulfilling them.

Had labor supply conditions deteriorated further in 1944, the Byrnes program would have been tightened and modified to bring about better results. That proved to be unnecessary. Despite continued problems in some industries and localities, manpower pressures generally eased in 1944 after war production peaked, selective service calls fell off, and WPB and industry operations improved.

Indeed, the manpower program worked out on the West Coast expanded beyond it. During late 1943 and early 1944, various regions and localities implemented some, all, or modified parts of the plan. By May 1944, ten areas had fairly well duplicated what was done on the Pacific Coast. Then, by order of WMC in June 1944 and OWM in August, the Byrnes Plan was implemented throughout the nation and became the basic method for mobilizing manpower until the war's end. Since the program was put into effect by locality and area, it varied in nature and effectiveness.

Seeking greater uniformity, WPB in 1943 set up a Coordinating Area Production Urgency Committee to oversee area committees. Convinced that labor supply was fundamentally local in nature, WMC resisted centralization. In 1944, it finally established a National Manpower Priorities Committee to guard against WPB invading commission turf:

> Thus it was near the end of 1944 that for the first time there appeared to be significant close working relationships among the multiplicity of agencies with some responsibilities in the manpower field and also for the first

time personnel with such responsibilities in the field recognized themselves to be part of a unified national system for handling such problems.[23]

As on the West Coast, the Byrnes Plan applied nationally worked well enough to be continued despite its often piecemeal and awkward quality. Limited experiments for making regulations more stringent and even using some compulsion were conducted, with at best qualified success. In Philadelphia, Allentown, Pennsylvania, Dayton, Ohio, and elsewhere, for example, desperate conditions allowed WMC to work with management, labor, and others to force non- and less essential industries to release workers to essential ones. Early in 1945, however, in the face of intense and growing resistance from an entire community, WMC's dogged and persistent efforts to compel workers to transfer from textile mills to tire firms producing for critical military programs were unsuccessful.[24]

Where the Byrnes Plan, and, before it, even less developed employment stabilization approaches, was unequal to various labor supply crises, mobilization officials turned to a variety of temporary, short-term expedients. The most frequently used measure was the release of conscripted troops.

Although the army detested and resisted using soldiers to solve manpower problems and the navy refused to cooperate in such endeavors, draftees were throughout the war either furloughed for specific lengths of time or transferred to the enlisted reserve to work in civilian industries. Before 1943, soldiers were used primarily in nonferrous mines and to harvest crops. During 1943, some were released to assist in the maritime and aircraft industries. To deal with critical conditions in 1944 and 1945, the army provided troops for five "must" industries: tires; forge and foundry; cotton duck; heavy ammunition; and aluminum. Soldiers were generally used in instances where jobs were exceptionally difficult, working conditions poor, and pay low. The War Department took great care to ensure that the practice did not disturb existing labor relations, such as union security arrangements. Around seventeen thousand troops served in release programs.[25]

From almost the beginning of the war, the United States imported labor—Mexicans, Bahamians, and Jamaicans—and employed prisoners of war. Pressure for using these men increased as emergencies arose. Because of organized labor's objections, however, their use was minimized. When conditions were especially challenging, unions would organize special recruiting efforts to provide skilled labor in industries considered to be among the most critical.[26]

Army crisis teams were also used to try to solve urgent labor supply problems. With Boeing Aircraft Company falling behind on its production schedules, the War Department labor offices in June 1943 dispatched several of their most talented officers to Seattle with instructions to do whatever was necessary to deal with company difficulties. Their action was often beyond War Department authority, and it intruded on the duties of other agencies. But results ensued, including ridding Boeing of an abusive labor relations official, improving management-labor relations, recruiting employees from outside the Seattle region, persuading the War Labor Board to increase wages, and expediting a host of projects involving housing, transportation, child-care centers, and other community facilities. By these acts, the War Department assisted the firm in meeting its production schedules.

Success with Boeing led the War Department to establish a Special Projects Section for dealing with future emergencies. From 1943 into 1945, the army sent out sixteen such teams to handle crises ranging from whole communities to single firms. WPB at first opposed the approach, later grudgingly accepted it, and, in time, even encouraged War Department intervention. WMC never accepted the affront to its responsibility. Although the teams helped solve some immediate problems, their long-run usefulness was, commission members pointed out, questionable. After teams departed, their quickly imposed remedies frequently fell apart, with a return of old problems.[27]

The last labor supply crisis erupted with the Battle of the Bulge in December 1944. Declining production and canceled contracts had lessened manpower pressures throughout most of the year. With military procurement suddenly accelerated after December, labor supply problems inevitably arose. WMC, WPB, procurement agencies, labor unions, and others all went into action to meet the worker demands of "must" programs. Along with other approaches, soldiers were released, labor imported, and prisoners of war used. Although some schedules had to be reduced because of manpower shortages, no harm to the fighting front ever occurred. By early March 1945, the war's final labor supply emergency had passed.[28]

Raw numbers graphically set forth the dramatic wartime changes in the nation's workforce.[29] A growing economy and military service reduced unemployment from approximately 9 million in June 1940 to 4 million in December 1941. Significant labor reserves still existed for massive munitions output at the time of Pearl Harbor, and the pool could be supplemented by normal population growth, women, minorities, and those in less essential jobs. The equivalent of additional labor could result from longer hours of work.

In December 1941, around 51.6 million Americans held jobs or were in the armed services. Two years later, in December 1943, at or near the peak of the war effort, that figure stood at 61.3 million, approaching a 20 percent increase. Unemployment, at less than 800,000, was all but eliminated. Next to the unemployed, women constituted the biggest addition to the workforce, their numbers rising from about 13.8 million in July 1940 to 18.7 million in July 1943. When the war began, women accounted for around 25 percent of the laboring population; before hostilities ended, they accounted for about 33 percent.[30] In 1942, 4.2 percent of blacks held war jobs; by 1945, 8.6 percent were so employed.[31] The forty-hour workweek also stretched out to the forty-eight-hour one. In May 1940, the average manufacturing workweek was 37.3 hours; by May 1943, it had risen to 45.3 hours. In some industries, such as shipbuilding, workers were typically employed sixty hours or more per week.

By mid-1943, labor supply had fairly well reached its limits within the voluntary mobilization methods that WMC used. Predictions in July 1943 that 1.7 million additional workers would be needed in six months set off alarms that more stringent regulations and/or more compulsion would be required. That was not the case. Demand did not rise much and soon began to fall. Estimates were off for several reasons. Military requirements were reduced, management overstated its labor requirements, and output per worker went up as production techniques improved and corporations drew on hoarded labor.

While statistics indicate the magnitude of what occurred during hostilities, they do not capture the enormous impact involved. Unprecedented migration reaching into the millions took place, which affected the nation in ways ranging from obvious to subtle. Transformations in the workforce involving location, gender, ethnicity and race, and other factors were not passing episodes but the beginnings of fundamental change.

Returning to the war years, much more could have been done with the expanded workforce that existed in mid-1943. In many respects the nation was profligate in the use of its labor. That becomes clear when reviewing military recruitment and selective service operations along with the mismatch between contract and population distribution, labor utilization, the neglect of community facilities, and other matters. Rather than merely improved labor usage through better mobilization techniques, the need was, some insisted, for greater regimentation of America's working population through a labor draft.

NATIONAL SERVICE LEGISLATION

The drive for national service legislation is an odd and troubling wartime development. It was the swan song of the "old Plattsburg crowd," patrician New Hamiltonians dedicated to elitism, social control, and nationalism. In 1915–1916, they had organized the Military Training Camps Association (MTCA) which played a basic role in recruiting and training officers for America's vastly expanded World War I army. While the association continued after hostilities, its activity and importance gradually waned, only fully to come alive again in mid-1940. Alarmed by the nation's unpreparedness as World War II ignited and spread across Europe, MTCA in May–June 1940 formed what came to be called the National Emergency Committee (NEC). Through an intense, well-organized campaign, NEC led in pushing through Congress America's first peacetime draft, the Selective Service and Training Act, or Burke-Wadsworth Bill, of September 1940.[32]

Grenville Clark, who had played an instrumental role in the World War I Plattsburg Movement, was NEC's initiator and indispensable leader. Born, raised, and educated as an American aristocrat, Clark joined Elihu Root, Jr., during 1909 in organizing what became the high-powered law firm of Root, Clark, Buckner and Ballantine. His passion, however, was serving the public interest as he defined it from an informal and independent base. Familiar, if not friendly, with most of the nation's economic and political elite, Clark knew how to make his voice heard. Before and during World Wars I and II, he became consumed by the issues of preparedness and mobilization. Prior to plunging ahead in the drive for what became the Burke-Wadsworth Bill, Clark teamed up with Supreme Court Justice Felix Frankfurter in persuading Roosevelt to put the War Department under the direction of Henry L. Stimson and Robert P. Patterson. Once Stimson and Patterson were in place, he led in writing what became the Selective Service and Training Act and organized the campaign in and outside Congress for having it enacted.[33]

After selective service was under way, Clark turned his attention to national service: a mandatory system for inventorying and registering male and female adults and directing them to jobs in such a way as to maximize munitions and essential civilian output.[34] Where Clark's direction of NEC appeared flawless, his four-year campaign for national service never succeeded. NEC's membership and finances regularly exceeded anticipated goals. By contrast, the Citizens Committee for a National War Service Act, which Clark organized in December 1942, constantly struggled to hang on, faced chronic financial problems, never had many members even without dues or other obligations, and, in the end, consisted of little more than Clark and a few loyal lieutenants as active participants. On April 15, 1944, the Citizens Committee's National Council, which constituted its total membership, numbered 501 men and 28 women, most of whom came from New England or the Middle Atlantic states. A membership drive, combined with setting up a Women's Division in 1944 to counteract the opposition of women to a labor draft, pushed figures up to 699 men and 352 women by July 11, 1944.[35] Between December 22, 1942, and December 31, 1944, Clark's group raised $41,032, 76 percent of which came from New York, 18 percent from Boston, and only the remaining 6 percent from elsewhere. On more than one occasion, Clark had to tap his own funds to meet organization expenses.[36] The Citizens Committee essentially remained an increasingly ingrown enclave within America's social and economic elite.

Despite adverse circumstances, the Citizens Committee remained active practically until the war's end. Clark's connections and tenacity partly explain why. Just as important, if not more so, was the avid support of Secretary of War Stimson and Under Secretary Patterson. Stimson and Patterson both had participated in the Plattsburg Movement and favored preparedness. Patterson had been a member of Clark's law firm, Clark and Stimson knew each other well, and, before his health deteriorated, Clark had an office in the War Department as an informal consultant to the secretary. All three were passionate in their dedication to national defense. Stimson and Patterson (more subtly so in Clark's case) became engrossed with the wartime need for order, discipline, and sacrifice.

Stimson, Clark, and others manifested a definite antilabor bias. Representative James W. Wadsworth (R-NY), who sponsored the principal labor draft bill, wrote Clark in March 1942: "Incidentally, it may amuse you to realize that when we have reached that stage [assignment of labor under national service legislation] there can be no such thing as a closed shop or union dues applicable to men who take orders and go where they are sent."[37] Stimson constantly lamented Roosevelt's "coddling" of unions,[38] and Clark remained convinced that only the ulterior motives of union leaders prevented the working population from supporting his cause.[39] During the War Department's drive to subordinate WMC to WPB and enact national service legislation, General Lucius D. Clay insisted that "initiative and responsibility" for determining manpower policy had to remain with management: "Labor must be treated from a production standpoint along the lines of material control."[40]

Many industrialists, financiers, attorneys, and other prominent leaders dissented. In June 1944, for example, Irenee DuPont pointed out to Charles Whitney Dall, a key Clark colleague, that workers, along with industry, were performing remarkably; forced labor, he went on, never did as well as volunteers. Samuel Sloan Duryee, of the New York law firm of Parker and Duryee, resigned from the Citizens Committee in February 1944, complaining that the group seemed more intent on punishing labor than on solving manpower problems. Insisting that the national service bill was wide open to abuse, George Fielding Eliot told Clark in February 1943 that he and his group failed to understand the nature of the American people.[41]

As hostilities drew to a close and labor supply problems eased, Clark, Stimson, Patterson, and others became frantic. The national service end became so important that practically any means appeared justified to advance it. The secretary of war and his manpower adviser, Goldthwaite H. Dorr, with Clark's knowledge, late in 1943 and 1944 began pressing Chief of Staff George C. Marshall to increase the size of the army in order to heighten the need for a labor draft. Marshall refused to go along.[42] After three years of dogged effort, the civilian heads of the War Department, Clark, and their advisers were desperate for some national service victory. In pursing their goal, they were willing to manipulate statistics, switch arguments according to circumstances, and, ultimately, settle for practically any bill carrying the national service label. In January 1945, Stimson confided in his diary:

> It seems funny that in such a situation [end of the Battle of the Bulge] I should be distressed by our successes and our good fortune. But the true fact is that these things are going to make it more difficult than it would have been to get the necessary legislation through our Congress which we had in view at the time when everybody was scared. . . . I never had a more vivid viewpoint of some of the curious characteristics of our noble people in the United States that [*sic*] have no more notion that they are in a war or the sacrifices which are involved or needed— that is, the great bulk of them do not—just so many children.[43]

NEC succeeded with the Burke-Wadsworth Bill despite strong opposition to it because of the obvious need for the legislation. The fact that selective service was already known and tried also assisted in re-creating the system. Drafting men and women for private employment was not only intensely controversial and untried but also of questionable need. For that principal reason, combined with a fear of even larger government, no industry or business group ever supported national service. An essentially conservative and rebellious Congress consistently turned back Clark and the military. Despite differences, the AFL, the CIO, and other unions united solidly in opposing any legislation even suggesting a labor draft. The American Legion, which had led the interwar movement for universal service, could muster only tepid support for Clark's work. Public opinion surveys consistently indicated overwhelming support for national service if essential. When controversy erupted over the need for and type of labor draft involved, Congress never sensed any compelling pressure from the general population to act.

Clark began considering methods for controlling the civilian workforce shortly after Pearl Harbor. In doing so, he worked principally with Lewis Sanders, a reserve field artillery colonel serving in SSS national headquarters who had played an active role in NEC, and Howard C. Petersen, from a prestigious Manhattan law firm, who served as Clark's principal NEC aide and, in January 1941, became a special manpower assistant to Under Secretary of War Patterson.

From December 1941 until April 1942, as the Roosevelt administration agonized about methods for handling the wartime labor force, Clark strategized with Sanders and Petersen over how to achieve the best system. None of the three wanted Paul V. McNutt, whom they characterized as an ambitious, pandering politician, to head a labor supply agency. Instead, they preferred creating a Manpower Board or Council, made up of the chairman of WPB and the secretaries of war and the navy.

This new board would remain small and make policy. It would appoint an executive officer to oversee SSS handling of military personnel and USES handling of civilian labor. The director of the SSS would serve as the board's secretary. Since the War Department dominated selective service and the army and navy would have controlling votes in the new Manpower Board, the entire system would be answerable to the military. To ensure that outcome, the Manpower Board executive officer would report to the board, not to the president.

Petersen argued that labor, like resources and transportation, had to be controlled by producers. Additionally, through Clark's instigation, Congress in December 1941 amended the Selective Service and Training Act to require the registration of all men eighteen to sixty-five. SSS could now collect and share with USES vital information on most workers concerning occupation, training, experience, and the like. Sanders pointed out that, by subjecting all men eighteen to sixty-five to induction, civilian labor allocation could be made compulsory through deferments, work-or-fight orders, and government labor battalions. He envisaged an elaborate selection process in which, at sixteen to seventeen years of age, all men would be designated as officer or nonofficer candidates, educated and trained accordingly, and used for industry or the armed services according to priorities. Universities and colleges would be closed or integrated into the system as needed. With such an approach, national service could be achieved simply through modifying existing statutes and agencies.[44]

Once WMC was created with McNutt in charge, Clark concentrated his efforts on drafting national service legislation. A rather crude bill was first endorsed by a WMC subcommittee in the summer of 1942 and then all but rejected by the commission's MLPC. Roosevelt encouraged McNutt to gauge the public's response to the issue of national service, which the latter did throughout most of 1942, indicating that he thought that such legislation would ultimately be necessary.[45] Emerging as a principal and determined opponent of national service and a supporter of voluntary manpower controls,

MLPC, along with various WMC staff members, convinced McNutt in November 1942 to tell the president that a labor draft was unnecessary. Henceforth, MLPC, and, less stridently, WMC, became a major bastion of opposition to compulsion applied to workers. With opposition to national service widespread in and outside his administration, Roosevelt decided to stick with voluntary methods. He institutionalized his decision in December 1942 by strengthening WMC.[46]

Throughout World War II, Roosevelt was more enigmatic about national service than he was about most other aspects of mobilization. The issue was so volatile that he personally made key decisions on labor controls right up to the end. All interested parties looked to the White House for signals, cognizant of the fact that what the president said or left unsaid would largely determine the fate of national service. From 1942 into 1945, the armed services, backed by Clark and his group, were the only consistent, strong advocates in the administration of mandatory labor regulation. Most others opposed a labor draft, wavered, or avoided the issue. The president—in Clark's circle "His Excellency" or the "Great White Father"—most likely wanted to avoid compulsion applied to the labor force and sensed that it was unnecessary. With the War and Navy Departments—and particularly the former— emerging as the administration's principal power centers, Roosevelt probably felt that he had to give ground. That proclivity was strengthened by pressures from the president's growing involvement in war and diplomacy abroad and mounting homefront disputes. When finally giving a nod to national service early in 1944, the president did so in a way that undermined it, and he became less equivocal only in 1945 when enactment of such legislation would have occurred too late to matter.[47]

With Roosevelt definitely turning down a labor draft in December 1942, Clark organized the Citizens Committee for a National War Service Act and refocused his attention from the White House to Congress. By then, a number of manpower bills were already pending.[48] Clark chose to work with an old ally, Representative James W. Wadsworth (R-NY), and the author of a proposed mandatory statute, Senator Warren R. Austin (R-VT), conservative legislators who were international in outlook. After several months of review and revision, a bill that Clark had started writing early in 1942 was simultaneously introduced in both houses of Congress in February 1943. The Austin-Wadsworth Bill was brief and vague. From their own and past efforts, Clark and his supporters learned that a detailed bill would be hopelessly long and open to endless dispute. But allowing administrators wide latitude in a matter as critical as labor supply weakened the position of proponents, as opponents warned of numerous potential abuses.

Granting authority to the president and designating the WMC chair as administrator, the proposed legislation called for SSS to register and classify all men eighteen to sixty-five and women eighteen to fifty for national service, with specified groups exempted. If voluntary methods failed to provide the workforce necessary for essential industries, local boards would draft the required numbers. People would be assigned as close to their homes as possible, protected against unsuitable housing, and ensured existing wages and hours, some transportation costs, reasonable reemployment and seniority rights, and other safeguards. Convicted violators could be fined and/or jailed. Responding to widespread criticism, the authors later modified the bill to remove the WMC chair as administrator in favor of a director of national service, appointed by the president with the consent of the Senate. A troublesome issue was resolved by amending the act further to allow workers to decide whether they would join a union in plants to which they were assigned. Consistent with the views of Clark and associates, practically all Austin-Wadsworth Bill obligations fell on labor, not management.[49]

Roosevelt covered his political flanks in February 1943 by having Samuel I. Rosenman reassess the need for national service through an informal group that included Harry L. Hopkins, James F. Byrnes, William D. Leahy, and Bernard M. Baruch. In March, Rosenman's panel concluded that, while mandatory measures were eventually inevitable, they were not needed now. The public had to be educated about such a radical departure, and, if such a move was considered, capital, industry, and other resources should be obligated along with labor.[50]

Congress kept the prospects of a labor draft alive. Brief House Military Affairs Committee and extended Senate Military Affairs Committee hearings on the Austin-Wadsworth Bill started in March 1943 and stretched out to the summer months. Other than for the War and Navy Departments, the Maritime Commission, and the American Legion, there was not much support for the bill. Equality of sacrifice and total mobilization of the nation's resources were the principal reasons offered in the bill's defense. Organized labor became the most vociferous opponent of the Austin-Wadsworth measure. Union leaders hit at the bill's grave dangers for the worker and also argued that manpower problems resulted from chaotic mobilization programs, not labor shortages. They pointed to the findings of the Truman and Tolan Committees and insisted that, unlike the piecemeal Austin-Wadsworth Bill, the Tolan-Kilgore-Pepper Bill for integrated mobilization would produce the needed change.[51] The War Department's own labor offices were never enthusiastic about and usually opposed to a labor draft.[52]

With little support and waning interest, the Austin-Wadsworth Bill died without a vote in the Military Affairs Committees of both houses. By modi-

fying, yet reaffirming, a voluntary approach, the Byrnes West Coast labor supply program worked out in August–September 1943 put an end to the first
congressional effort in behalf of national service.

With firmer support from the Navy Department and Maritime Commission, the Citizens Committee and War Department used a rash of strikes or
threatened ones beginning late in spring 1943, especially those of John L.
Lewis's United Mine Workers, to revive their demands for a labor draft. Although some advocates had doubts about using national service to combat
work stoppages, most went along because wartime strikes generated strong
responses and invited retaliatory measures. After army seizure had precluded
a railroad strike in December, Stimson told the president that, unfair though
they might be, charges were circulating to the effect that White House
favoritism toward unions invited strikes. National service was the solution for
troubled times. "Goddess opportunity" had knocked earlier with the mine
workers' strikes, the secretary of war went on. Another chance was at hand,
one that Roosevelt should not pass up.[53]

After visiting the troops abroad and participating in the Teheran Conference during November–December 1943, the president was more responsive
to military pressure. Wavering until the end, and without informing any mobilization officials, including an irate Byrnes, Roosevelt on January 11, 1944,
called on Congress in his State of the Union Address to enact legislation to
conscript civilian labor. In doing so, he admitted that such legislation was not
imperative, emphasized the need to handle strikes as a possible rationale, and
proposed that fairness required that national service be balanced by a better
tax law, more rigorous contract renegotiations, and firmer economic stabilization measures. No follow-up occurred. Roosevelt refused to endorse any
particular bill, withheld "must" designation from national service, and allowed
departments and agencies to respond to his proposal as they wished.[54]

Austin and Wadsworth agreed to reintroduce their revised bill immediately,
and the Senate Military Affairs Committee began a new set of hearings. Proponents had to shift their arguments in favor of national service since labor
supply was improving as production programs were cut back and work stoppages were having a minimal effect. Stimson and others insisted that strikes
and slack worker practices pointed to a letdown, a souring, of the homefront
that threatened the war effort and undermined the esprit de corps of the
troops abroad. National service was essential for lifting the morale of the fighting forces and rekindling a sense of urgency among the American people.[55]

Opposition to conscripting civilian workers was stronger and more vociferous in 1944 than it had been in 1942 or 1943. Through WMC's MLPC,
major labor, business, industrial, and agricultural organizations or federations

were on record against national service as unnecessary and unwise.[56] Secretary of the Navy Frank Knox convened a meeting in his office on April 20 to drum up support for Austin-Wadsworth. It included the senator and the representative, civilian and military heads of the armed services and Maritime Commission, and members of the Citizens Committee and the American Legion, along with representatives from the U.S. Chamber of Commerce, the National Association of Manufacturers, and the Association of American Railroads. Even with Chief of Staff Marshall, Commander-in-Chief Ernest J. King, and Secretary of War Stimson providing off-the-record briefings about the war front, no views were changed.[57]

While they had before been hesitant to attack the armed services, unions went on the offensive in 1944. "The War Department is not satisfied with running the war effort," cried the AFL's *Weekly News Service*. "It wants to run America too. . . . The military mind, apparently, can never be satisfied with anything less than absolute power."[58] The Truman Committee's *Third Annual Report,* issued in March, contained a stinging rebuke of those arguing for a labor draft and a glowing report of homefront accomplishments.[59]

Although less stridently, most members of Congress seemed to share Truman's sentiments. Support for the Austin-Wadsworth Bill was virtually nonexistent among the national legislators. Stimson informed Clark late in May that they should accept temporary defeat. Efforts for national service had to wait "until we really have a disaster or something like that which makes it more evident to these dumb-headed congressmen that it is necessary."[60]

The Battle of the Bulge in December 1944 was the perceived disaster that initiated the last campaign for national service. Prior to that, the military had been waging psychological warfare on the homefront to kill reconversion planning and to create the right atmosphere for labor conscription. For months, despite indisputable evidence to the contrary, the War and Navy Departments and the Maritime Commission insisted that work stoppages, labor shortages, men and women leaving war work, and the like were jeopardizing output. The propaganda campaign intensified with the German offensive and when Byrnes appointed General Clay as his chief assistant in December. That month, the Office of War Mobilization and Reconversion (OWMR) placed a 12:00 P.M. curfew on all places of amusement, took other action to create a crisis atmosphere, and, most important, issued a "work-or-fight order." Henceforth, any male under thirty-eight not in essential employment or transferring between such jobs without his local selective service board's permission would be drafted. If physically unqualified for military service, he could be deferred back to private industry or be assigned to an army work battalion after undergoing abbreviated basic training. As critics had warned, including those from the War

Department labor offices, industry received no assignees, and the army ended up with twelve thousand men it neither needed nor wanted.[61]

Meanwhile, the armed services also turned up the heat on the White House. Early in January 1945, Marshall and King, albeit indirectly, for the first time joined Stimson and Knox in insisting on the need for conscripting labor. Shortly thereafter, in his 1945 State of the Union Address, Roosevelt unequivocally called for a comprehensive national service law and, as an interim step, recommended that Congress pass a statute obligating 4 million 4-Fs to assist war production. The president based his decision on the military's recommendation, production requirements, and the need for repledging the people to maximum war effort.[62]

The final drive for civilian labor conscription was also the most curious one. It engaged Congress from January through April.[63] With the president now more firmly on their side, national service proponents concluded that the chances of passing a bill would improve under Democratic sponsorship. Hence, Austin and Wadsworth stepped aside in favor of Representative Andrew J. May (D-KY) and Senator Josiah W. Bailey (D-NC). The two quickly introduced a modified 4-F bill that would be administered by SSS. All men between eighteen and forty-five had to remain in or transfer to essential employment. The May-Bailey Bill at first provided for violators to be drafted; later, as the War Department had urged, they were subject to criminal prosecution. Variations of this act had been before Congress since late 1943.[64] To the chagrin of Clark, Stimson, and others, legislators ignored Roosevelt's stated goal of full-blown national service legislation to concentrate exclusively on the May-Bailey Bill.

The White House required all departments and agencies to support May-Bailey, a first for national service legislation. Although few labor-draft advocates were satisfied with the measure, the War Department rallied proponents in support of the bill as the most that could be achieved at the time. Under those circumstances, and after a short but bitter debate, the House of Representatives passed the act by a vote of 246 to 165 on February 1, 1945.

The Senate was less compliant. Congressional hearings established that no troops suffered from a lack of weapons, production was not threatened, and no overall manpower shortage existed.[65] Management and labor members from the advisory committee to OWMR joined WMC's MLPC in lining up against the need to conscript labor. Both the AFL and the CIO reported that, when seeking to provide workers for plants that the army said were in dire need, they usually found numbers to be exaggerated, no employees needed, layoffs occurring, or firms cutting back production.[66]

To make the May-Bailey Bill more palatable, Byrnes proposed amending it so that it could be administered by WMC, not SSS. Before such a compromise could be secured, Byrnes joined Roosevelt at the Yalta Conference during critical weeks of February 1945. Without the leadership of the president or the OWMR director, the legislative struggle over national service became bitter and confused. McNutt convinced the commission's MLPC that the best way to combat May-Bailey was to support an alternate measure. For the first time, earlier opponents of national service united behind legislation, a bill sponsored by Senators Harley M. Kilgore (D-WV) and Joseph C. O'Mahoney (D-WY) that would do little more than give legislative sanction to WMC's manpower controls.[67] On March 8, the Senate passed the Kilgore-O'Mahoney Bill 63 to 16. From then until April 3, the two houses of Congress wrangled over versions of the May-Bailey versus the Kilgore-O'Mahoney Bills without final agreement, despite Roosevelt's repeated intervention, Byrnes's maneuvering, and the War and Navy Departments' frenzied activities on behalf of May-Bailey. Trying to salvage what they could from the wreckage, some War Department leaders at the end were even willing to settle for the Kilgore-O'Mahoney Bill, but they were denied even that token measure.

Although the push for national service legislation from 1942 into 1945 failed, it kept the WMC and organized labor on the defensive. The commission and the unions repeatedly had to justify voluntary approaches as adequate for meeting wartime production requirements. In doing so, they pitted themselves against the armed services, which held the high ground, often distorted or misused facts, and hid behind alleged strategic necessity and the welfare of the troops. Without strong supporters, such as the Truman Committee, and absent the overwhelming opposition of management, opponents probably would have been unable to hold off Congress from enacting some form of national service. The lack of need for compulsion, particularly the methods proposed in the Austin-Wadsworth Bill, was the best argument against compulsory labor controls. Not even the president could overcome that unassailable fact. Despite the claims of Clark and others, no evidence exists that the failure of national service prolonged the war or even impeded substantially any munitions or other production.[68]

WMC's flawed but adequate method for regulating World War II labor supply highlighted a major reality: the commission's approach was consistent with the general pattern for mobilizing the World War II economy. America's plenty allowed the nation to harness its system for hostilities without altering in any basic way peacetime power operations. Hence, industry and business basically controlled WPB and related agencies, farmers the War Food Administration, railroads and other carriers the Office of Defense Transportation, and so forth. Within that general approach, more neutral civil servants, academics, and professionals assisted in devising mechanisms and controls necessary for maximizing production while maintaining stability. Such help aided, without threatening, interest-group control.

WMC followed the principal mobilization outline. McNutt institutionalized it through the MLPC. Industry went along. Although denying organized labor any meaningful voice in WPB operations, business leaders teamed up with unions in WMC fundamentally to protect their interests by guarding those of labor.

The World War II mobilization pattern was tacit but consensual. It was constantly criticized for inefficiency, waste, and conflicts of interest, but there was no serious attempt to change the pattern, including efforts by the Truman Committee and supporters of the Tolan-Kilgore-Pepper Bill. The same was true for the highly contentious relations during the war years between Congress and the Roosevelt administration.

The War and Navy Departments' drive for national service threatened the mobilization accord. Most recognized that no part of the gradually devised system could be changed without unbalancing the whole. Industry and its allies who opposed national service constantly argued that employees could not be regimented without compulsion ultimately reaching employers. A quiet animosity built up during the war years against the armed services for arrogantly trying to introduce compulsion against workers to protect what often appeared to be the military's own profligacy. Since the army and navy wielded such enormous power, their demands for national service were never rejected outright; instead, they were consistently thwarted. Out of that curious set of circumstances, McNutt, unfairly in a sense, became the whipping boy of the War and Navy Departments and other national service advocates.

The sustained drive for national service during World War II was not a sideshow, a minor episode. Its nature, advocates, opponents, and defeat reveal a great deal about the complexity and intricacy of power in America. The labor-draft movement certainly highlighted the authoritarian strain brought out by heightened concerns about national security, war, and a large military.

15

ORGANIZED LABOR IN A MOBILIZED ECONOMY, 1940–1945: LABOR RELATIONS

Unions played a greater role in shaping defense and war labor relations than they did labor supply. Nonetheless, organized labor was steadily restricted in carrying out its functions, and unions experienced increasing numbers of government agencies becoming involved in management-labor relations. Labor leaders, hence, experienced growing pressure from mobilization authorities above and their burgeoning membership below.

Organized labor made great gains during the war years.[1] Union membership shot up from about 9 million in 1940 to around 14¾ million by 1945. At the time of Victory in Japan (VJ) Day, unions accounted for around 35 percent of the nonagricultural workforce and were well established in all mass production industries. In another sense, however, labor lost power and status. In 1939, unions were generally viewed as a progressive social force; by 1945, they were considered by much of the public as at best unruly, at worst a threat. Management received credit for the so-called miracles of war production. Corporate America, which entered the war with a depression-tarnished image, emerged from hostilities with a positive reputation. The unions' experience was exactly the opposite.

The hard realities of war mobilization hardly justified such judgments. No "miracles of production" took place, and industry held up munitions output and economic conversion before and after Pearl Harbor, often acting in parochial ways. Nonetheless, with war-induced flush times and the nation serving as the world's principal arsenal, corporate capitalism took on an almost invincible glow.

Strikes hurt unions in the public eye. From 1939 through 1941, and into the war years, the American Federation of Labor (AFL) and the Congress of Industrial Organizations (CIO) mounted massive organizational drives that were frequently messy and violent. During 1940–1941, union activity and conflict halted munitions output in more than a few cases. While strikes during the war years were relatively few and usually of short duration, they did occur. Management's behavior was largely hidden from the public; union activity was always highly visible. Moreover, wartime strikes of any kind were quickly and loudly condemned by Washington—particularly by the armed services. That was particularly so as the struggle for national service and against reconversion planning intensified in 1944–1945.

In part, labor's wounds were self-inflicted. Wartime jurisdictional disputes— petty wrangling between the AFL and the CIO—could end in strikes and weakened or threatened to undermine the effectiveness of the National Labor Relations Act. A shrewd observer of the union scene noted: "When William Green proclaim[ed] that there [were] Communists in the CIO and Philip Murray [said] that there [were] racketeers in the AFL, the public conclud[ed] that unions [were] a breeding place for Communists and racketeers."[2] Unions had no time for such divisions. While still adjusting to the rapid expansion of industrial organizations, the AFL and the CIO faced the challenge of even greater growth with a shortage of capable leaders and collective-bargaining procedures fundamentally altered. Significant tension, even internecine warfare, between the two federations distracted their harried leaders from central concerns and created numerous openings for labor's numerous enemies.

The cruelest blow faced by the two federations was John L. Lewis's feud with President Franklin D. Roosevelt, which began as early as 1936. It reached a turning point in 1940 with the CIO president pitting himself against the president's third-term reelection. Roosevelt's victory led to Lewis stepping aside as the federation's head, leaving the CIO, and conducting guerilla warfare as head of the United Mine Workers of America (UMW) against the Roosevelt administration and, indirectly, the rest of the union movement. While Lewis's personality quirks, massive ego concerns, and differing priorities all became involved in his destructive battles with the president, a larger issue was at stake. The UMW president in the 1930s already perceived that Roosevelt's relations with organized labor were more expedient than principled, that the president would use more than serve unions. Temperamentally unwilling, perhaps even unable, to accept a co-opted position for labor in a liberal state, Lewis appears purposefully and resentfully to have isolated himself and the mine workers' union. If that was the case, one of America's most talented, yet most enigmatic, labor leaders simply refused to accept the realities of power in America: even at their strongest, unions could never go beyond secondary power status in America's corporate capitalist system.

Roosevelt was hardly blameless in his running dispute with Lewis. With war declared and Lewis attempting to regain lost power, the president in January 1942 intervened to ensure that the UMW president's shadowy maneuvering to unify the AFL and the CIO did not succeed. Although the possibility of unity was always remote, Roosevelt was taking no chances. Unified federations formally or informally controlled by Lewis constituted too great a threat to the president's leadership.[3]

SIDNEY HILLMAN'S LABOR DIVISION, 1940–1942

Labor's own destructive tendencies aside, the AFL and the CIO faced trying circumstances that grew increasingly difficult as the war years stretched out. What occurred during 1942–1945 was foreshadowed by what took place during 1940–1941.

Roosevelt's support for Sidney Hillman's Labor Division in the National Defense Advisory Commission (NDAC), Office of Production Management (OPM), and War Production Board (WPB) was at best uncertain.[4] The selection of the president of the Amalgamated Clothing Workers of America (ACWA) was both logical and unfortunate. With a divided labor movement, Roosevelt explained that Hillman was "half-way between John L. Lewis and William Green."[5] However, Hillman was appointed without consulting either federation, and in part he became a pawn in maneuvering between Roosevelt and Lewis.

The UMW president viewed the ACWA president as a rival, and the AFL regarded him as a renegade. In the words of Lee Pressman, the CIO's general counsel, Hillman was "a Government representative in the ranks of labor, rather than a representative of the ranks of labor in the field of Government."[6] Without solid support from either federation, Hillman lacked adequate backing for the enormous responsibilities that he faced. Additionally, coming from the needle trades instead of heavy industry, Hillman's appointment was more political than economic. Moreover, a poor administrator, Hillman failed to establish effective centralized direction for what became a fragmented and conflicted Labor Division.

The division's troubles were complicated by the fact that it competed with a host of other agencies. The Labor Department, for example, dealt with nearly all the responsibilities assigned to Hillman, and Secretary of Labor Frances Perkins looked on the Labor Division as an intruder on her turf. Hillman, of course, had no authority over the National Labor Relations Board (NLRB). As the principal procurement agencies, the War and Navy Departments also created offices to oversee labor relations and supply for their contractors. By

early 1941, new administrations were being organized to quell strikes and regulate collective bargaining.

Operating from a weak base, the Labor Division faced great challenges.
Hillman was supposed to speak for organized labor in formulating mobilization policies in general, a role further emphasized when the president of the
ACWA was made codirector of OPM. To a degree, Hillman had some influence on the process of harnessing the economy, but he did so in an indirect
way. He was a reliable supporter of Leon Henderson, Donald M. Nelson, and
other all-outers. The Labor Division head also pushed for, and achieved labor
advisory committees to match those of industry, but, since the former never
advanced much in NDAC, OPM, and WPB, his accomplishment was not significant. In truth, Hillman never seriously tried to extend the reach of his division beyond labor and manpower policies, as is evident in his tepid and
ambiguous response to the Murray and Walter Reuther plans for tripartite
conversion and mobilization councils. Hillman probably kept his purview
restricted because he had his hands full with labor, he was acting as he thought
the president wanted him to, and he ran into a wall of resistance from industry and the armed services when attempting to go beyond union and workforce matters.

Even without a voice in larger mobilization policy, Hillman's division could
have made a substantial contribution by formulating and enforcing a national
defense and war labor policy. It made little progress in that regard. Hillman
struggled from May through September 1940 to persuade the reluctant
NDAC and the armed services to endorse a relatively moderate defense labor
policy. According to this policy, unemployment patterns would be a major
consideration in building defense facilities and distributing contracts. In addition, the forty-hour workweek and standard overtime compensation should
be generally observed and all defense work carried out in accordance with
local, state, and federal labor laws.

Hillman could not enforce the policy. At no time before or during World
War II did labor supply significantly affect the location of defense plants or
the letting of contracts. In the massive cantonment construction projects, the
Quartermaster Corps during 1940–1941 insisted that its contractors disregard standard hours of work and pay for their employees.

Hillman suffered his worst and most humiliating defeat over interpretations of the National Labor Relations Act. Could federal contracts be awarded
to firms violating the Wagner Act? The question became critically important
when billions of dollars of contracts went to labor's sworn enemies, such as
the Ford Motor Company. With the adoption of the NDAC policy, Hillman
got the War and Navy Departments and the attorney general committed to

an interpretation denying further contracts to Wagner Act violators. Business representatives in and outside the mobilization agencies and antilabor forces in Congress figuratively screamed their defiance. From September 1940 to June 1941, Hillman fought a spirited battle for labor. At crucial points, Roosevelt either opposed him or equivocated. The military services eventually lined up with the industrial community. In the end, Hillman lost the struggle. Throughout the years 1940–1945, neither the civilian mobilization agencies nor the armed services would use their vast powers to enforce labor laws.[7]

The Labor Division's failures eroded its prestige, left the nation without an enforced defense labor policy, and added to the forces creating industrial unrest. Neither the AFL nor the CIO would shelve the strike weapon during a national emergency without having its interests protected. Consequently, as industrial mobilization advanced, so too did the strike record. By 1941, the incidence of strikes—involving organizational campaigns, jurisdictional disputes, wages, hours, and working conditions, and, for some left-wing unions, political purposes—alarmed numerous government officials.

Initially, the Labor Division did quite well in either avoiding or settling strikes. When the Labor Department's United States Conciliation Service did not satisfactorily deal with labor disputes involving national defense in 1940, Hillman's division stepped in through what eventually became the Labor Relations Branch. Having 241 potential strikes called to their attention, Hillman and his associates were able to prevent all but two of them from occurring. The tactics used were often quite rigorous, with AFL's Joseph D. Keenan, chief of the Labor Relations Branch, acting forcefully in dealing with recalcitrant labor leaders.[8]

In the eyes of the armed services, the actions of the Labor Department and Hillman's division were never enough. These agencies appeared to be too concerned about union rights and labor standards. That being the case, with the War Department leading the way, the military advocated that it be allowed directly to intervene in strikes. Of particular concern to the army was the burgeoning West Coast aircraft industry. It inevitably experienced labor tumult, which threatened to halt production. Under pressure, Hillman in August 1940 invited a War Department labor adviser to assist in heading off a strike at Boeing Aircraft Company in Seattle. The army's participation was instrumental in satisfactorily settling management-labor conflict. In November 1940, the War Department's participation in mediating a strike at Vultee Aircraft, Incorporated, in Los Angeles, by contrast, turned out disastrously, needlessly prolonging the dispute. Only with the recall of the War Department representative were Conciliation Service and union officials able to end the work stoppage.

The Vultee fiasco led the War Department to regularize its labor relations program. It recruited Edward F. McGrady—a former AFL union official and assistant secretary of labor who was in his seventies and serving as a labor consultant to the Radio Corporation of America—as a labor adviser to Under Secretary Robert P. Patterson. Simultaneously, the department established centralized procedures for dealing with the civilian workforce as well as arranging for close liaison with the Navy Department and Maritime Commission.

Shortly after these reforms, a storm of industrial conflict swept the nation. In 1941, there were over forty-two hundred strikes, causing the loss of more than twenty-three thousand man-days of work. Some of the most critical plants for munitions were hit, including Allis-Chalmers Manufacturing Company, Aluminum Company of America, and San Francisco shipyards. Strikes grew rapidly around the first quarter of 1941, reached a peak in June, tapered off slightly during the third quarter, and all but stopped after war broke out.[9]

Antistrike legislation proliferated in Congress as the number of strikes grew in 1941, but no bill ever passed both houses. Over the protest of Hillman, the War Department began a publicity blitz against work stoppages. Secretary of War Henry L. Stimson also stepped up his pressure on Roosevelt to create a World War I–type war labor board to regulate industrial strife, a proposal that he had been advocating since late 1940. Finally, in March 1941, the president set up by executive order the National Defense Mediation Board (NDMB). The board was to mediate labor disputes certified to it by the secretary of labor after the Conciliation Service was unable to work out a settlement.[10]

Although NDMB's operations were quite successful, with industrial conflicts multiplying beyond the board's ability to keep up, strikes continued to take place. Convinced that Communists were behind much of the agitation, Stimson in September 1940 called on John J. McCloy to direct the War Department's antisubversive program in a way similar to that in which he had headed a War Department antisubversive effort during World War I. Secretary of the Navy Frank Knox joined the secretary of war in proposals that could have led to a witch-hunt, but Roosevelt, backed by Attorney General Robert H. Jackson and Hillman, blocked such moves. The president informed his military advisers that strikes in general were inhibiting defense production by somewhere between 1 to 5 percent at the most and that subversives were by no means the cause of all labor disputes.[11]

Despite being burned by the Vultee episode, the armed services could not stay away from strikes involving their contractors. In some instances, their intervention was beneficial, as with Bethlehem Steel Corporation late in 1940 and early in 1941; in other cases it was detrimental, as with the Allis-Chalmers strike in Milwaukee between January and April 1941.[12]

By April, Stimson began insisting that Roosevelt use troops to break up work stoppages adversely affecting national defense. That outcome was realized in the airframe industry on the West Coast in mid-1941.[13] When negotiations over wages and union status broke down between the United Automobile Workers (UAW)–CIO and the North American Aviation, Incorporated, in Inglewood, California, the dispute was certified to the NDMB. Violating earlier commitments, local Communist union leaders precipitated a strike early in June that resulted in rioting and other forms of violence. When local officials rejected direction from UAW international headquarters, the War Department persuaded the union, the secretary of labor, Hillman, and other administration officials to support a military seizure. With a united front, and with a national emergency declared on May 27, 1941, the president went along since conditions at the plant were deteriorating and going beyond the control of the local police. On June 9, the president signed an executive order for the War Department to seize the facility.

For Stimson, June 9 was "one of the most important days of my service here."[14] Over twenty-five hundred troops with fixed bayonets moved in to disperse the picket lines and opened the North American facility. Over War Department objections, the president assigned a member of Hillman's division to the staff of the commander in charge and ordered that the situation be kept as "fluid" as possible in order for management and labor to reach a settlement. Ultimately, local UAW leaders were permanently removed from their posts, and selective service regulations were amended to permit canceling the deferments of striking employees. With the local in UAW international hands, the NDMB worked out an agreement that ended the seizure. All unions and federations regretted military intervention. The AFL was sullen, the CIO indignant, and John L. Lewis outraged.

On the War Department side, the North American seizure went as well as it did largely because of the wise counsel of Edward F. McGrady and other labor advisers, who acted to check the military's instinct for crushing opposition. When their influence did not prevail, other government labor agencies and the president stepped in. Probably none of these restraints would have prevented a disastrous outcome had the army been allowed to intervene in the "captive coal mine" strike.

Demanding a union shop in coal mines owned by steel firms, Lewis called out over fifty thousand miners in September 1941, when the UMW was turned down.[15] The NDMB intervention returned the coal miners to work, but, after another brief walkout in October, they were ready to go out again in mid-November unless Lewis's demands were met. With the NDMB ready to rule against the UMW, Secretary of War Stimson went into action. On November

7, he, the chief of staff, and others met with the president to review plans for the army to seize all mines. The secretary of war recorded in his diary:

> I told him . . . that I did not want him to call out the Army unless he was prepared to let us go through with it and do a good job, even if it was a stern job; that the Army should not be called out unless it was allowed to win a complete decision. It must not have its prestige affected by a misfire or being called back when the job was half done. . . .[16]

War Department plans called for dividing authority between the troop commander and the director of operations, with final authority in the hands of neither. Large numbers of soldiers supported by tanks and heavy artillery would move into scattered mining areas.

Such plans alarmed War Department labor advisers. On November 14, McGrady wrote Under Secretary of War Patterson:

> The idea is currently widespread that troops are being used as part of a military operation or a campaign to take physical objectives. Such an approach to the problem would be fatal. The miners will not return to work because of any intimidation or because of any overpowering show of force. I know this because I have lived and worked with the miners during many of their struggles, often bloody ones, to gain recognition and strength.

Army plans, McGrady complained, were intended to crush a civil war rather than return men to work, the only possible rationale for seizure.[17] The labor advisers' protests went unheeded. Supporting army plans up until the day before Lewis would call the miners out again, Roosevelt pulled back at the last moment, thereby ending the War Department's impending action. When the president announced his decision at a cabinet meeting, Stimson launched "the hardest and hottest" debate the gathering had ever heard.[18] "Almost with tears in his eyes," he pleaded for War Department seizure of all the mines, but he could not sway the president.[19]

To end the series of walkouts, Roosevelt agreed to a mediating procedure that Lewis could not lose. The wily UMW president had maneuvered the president and other unions into a position in which disciplining the UMW would seriously harm the entire labor movement as America was about to enter the war. Not only did Lewis get what he wanted, but he also succeeded in killing off NDMB, which appeared to have lost its objectivity during the coal-mining crisis.

When war broke out, Roosevelt summoned a management-labor conference that produced the no-strike, no-lockout pledge and created the tripartite National War Labor Board (NWLB) for settling disputes. Unions responded to the board with mixed emotions. By rejecting management's desire to freeze union security for the war's duration in favor of the maintenance-of-membership formula, NWLB granted labor a significant victory. As a modified form of the union shop, the decision allowed labor to continue its organizational drives. Both the AFL and the CIO, as well as other unions, were less satisfied with the NWLB's "Little Steel" decision of July 1942, which, along with other government directives, froze wages. The decision created endless strife throughout the war years.

By the time NWLB began functioning early in 1942, the Labor Division was fading from the mobilization scene. Hillman's service in NDAC and OPM had not been completely without accomplishment. His Labor Division had begun training and retraining programs, played a major role in working out labor stabilization agreements, assisted in having the AFL and CIO work together, and helped contain growing union unrest. However, Hillman neither made his division the center of national labor policy nor won for it a place in shaping industrial mobilization policy. In a meaningful sense, both goals were always beyond what was possible for him and his division. Hillman's major failure was in not accepting that harsh reality and assisting organized labor to adjust itself accordingly.

LABOR AND THE MILITARY

After the departure of the Amalgamated Clothing Workers of America's head from WPB, more and more union activity came under government regulation, particularly from NWLB, NLRB, and the War Manpower Commission, but also from the Office of Price Administration, the Office of Economic Stabilization, and the Office of War Mobilization (OWM) (as of October 1944 the Office of War Mobilization and Reconversion [OWMR]). But practically every mobilization agency in one way or another affected and was affected by organized labor. That was certainly the case with the military.

As the major consumers in the planned wartime economy, the armed services played an important part in Washington's extensive involvement in labor affairs. The relationship between unions and the military was always potentially explosive. Union leaders identified the military with management because of prewar developments, the services' role in the World War II economy, and the inclusion of many business executives in the armed services' procurement systems. On their part, the War and Navy Departments continued to view organized labor as an obstruction to full production, and antilabor attitudes prevailed among the officer corps of both the army and the navy.

Despite their differences, unions and the armed services worked together in labor relations areas with reasonable harmony. That was the case principally because the largely civilian-staffed War Department Labor Branch (WDLB) maintained its role as a buffer between unions and the army.[20] Since the army was the largest and most powerful procurement agent and had the most capable personnel, the navy and Maritime Commission usually followed its lead in labor matters.[21]

The military's antilabor stance and the ameliorating role played by the WDLB were most manifest when the armed services and unions came into direct contact. The operation of government-built plants, ships, and port facilities and the security programs and plant guards for military contractors are outstanding examples.

Prior to and during World War II, the War Department financed the construction of numerous giant plants costing billions of dollars and employing hundreds of thousands of workers. Most of the plants were built under the Ordnance Department's auspices. The department devised a system, designated "government owned, privately operated" (GOPO), whereby firms like Atlas and Hercules Powder Companies, along with E. I. du Pont de Nemours and Company, would operate the facilities as private contractors and be guaranteed all management prerogatives consistent with government interests. Specifically, the companies would be solely responsible for hiring personnel. Where organized labor was involved, Ordnance, having apparently made some commitments to Atlas and other firms, maintained that the facilities should be considered as government owned and operated with unions practically prohibited for purposes of security and optimum production.[22]

In October 1941, the Ordnance Department attempted to implement its antiunion policy. The War Department Labor Branch initially blocked Ordnance, but the latter ultimately converted the War and Navy Departments to its point of view. The NWLB and NLRB reluctantly agreed to go along with the policy if organized labor approved. During extended negotiations with the armed services, the AFL and the CIO, over the vehement opposition of the Navy Department and some members of the War Department, successfully insisted that the Wagner Act, modified only to protect the government's investment, must apply to GOPO plants. By mid-1942, the new policy was implemented. Throughout the war, the WDLB worked closely with union leaders to maintain amicable labor relations in GOPO plants.[23]

Labor problems involving the GOPO facilities were minuscule compared with what developed in the maritime industry. The army's difficulties in this industry stemmed largely from lack of experience and the incompetent and antiunion staff that it recruited, mainly from marginal areas of the shipping and waterfront industries. Starting late in 1940, the Army Transportation Corps (ATC), the Army Air Forces, the Quartermaster Corps, and other bureaus began leasing port facilities and operating fleets of ships for the movement of freight. On the West, East, and Gulf Coasts, the army's operation of docks and warehouses produced great confusion. Although the army usually continued to hire union longshoremen, it replaced union freight checkers, shipping clerks, warehousemen, and others with inexperienced personnel hired as civil servants. The practice tended to break down the unity and coordination between the docks and the warehouses. Port operations in general became hopelessly tangled, facilities were improperly used, and ships sailed only partially or poorly loaded.[24]

The army's management of ships caused as many problems for unions as did its operation of port facilities. When the ATC took over ships, it informed crew members that, henceforth, they would be civil servants, denied union rights, suffer a cut in pay, and work unlimited hours without overtime pay. The general response was for crews to walk off en masse. In recruiting new crews, the army largely avoided union and government hiring halls, with the result that it often ended up with low-grade or inexperienced personnel. If union members remained on an army ship and proved to be troublesome, they were usually fired as subversives.[25]

Longshore and maritime unions, AFL and CIO alike, all bitterly protested the antiunion policies. Beginning late in 1941, the War Department labor office attempted to reform army practices, but it was unable to initiate forthright action until mid-1942. In August 1942, and continuing until February 1943, the department employed a group of labor relations experts, under the direction of Professor Douglass V. Brown of Princeton University, to conduct a thorough investigation of army port and maritime operations.

The Brown Committee investigation revealed that not all problems in the maritime industry originated with the army. The International Longshoreman's Association (ILA), along with many employers on the East Coast, was hopelessly corrupt and unstable. Furthermore, unions from the two major federations added to the industry's instability by competing with one another. Brown and his associates also established that army-labor relations were not uniformly bad. In Baltimore and Hampton Roads, the ATC and ILA worked cooperatively to solve mutual problems. Despite these observations, the Brown Committee established beyond question that the army's practices were intensely antiunion and generally incompetent.[26]

The investigation and the efforts of the WDLB led to reform. The department removed or downgraded inexperienced and antiunion personnel; it eliminated whenever possible the practice of forcing workers into the civil service; and it instituted recognized wages, hours, working conditions, and grievance and discharge procedures. These reforms produced results varying from good to poor.

Plant guards and security programs for military contractors, both of which were under armed forces auspices, also caused some serious labor problems. The military tenaciously fought the unionization of the guards. "Permitting the condition to be brought about," insisted an Army Air Forces colonel, "is as preposterous as the thought of surrendering our defense effort to the forces we are trying to destroy."[27] Abuse of the security programs also prevailed. Labor leaders charged that they were not given the chance to transfer suspected individuals to nonsensitive employment and that management and the military discharged undesirable employees as subversives. Also, there were no adequate provisions for review, appeal, reemployment of cleared suspects, or protection of seniority rights. By late 1943, under the constant prodding of unions, the effort of the military labor offices, and rulings of the NLRB, most of labor's complaints had been met. Plant guards could be unionized under conditions consistent with the war effort, and procedures protecting employees' interests were adopted in the security programs.[28]

Military participation in labor affairs during the war, as before it, did not stop at the point where unions and the armed services came into direct contact. After Pearl Harbor, the Navy Department, the Maritime Commission, and, with some hesitation, the War Department attempted to persuade the president to support a national labor policy that included freezing union security and wages. In addition, the workweek would be increased from forty to forty-eight hours and most overtime pay eliminated. Roosevelt turned thumbs down on the policy except for the premium pay proposal. With the president's backing, the military services and the Maritime Commission during 1942–1943 pressured the Labor Department into restricting standard overtime pay to work over forty hours per week or on the seventh consecutive day and a few holidays. Operating through an Interdepartmental Committee on Wage Control, the armed services also joined forces with the Office of Price Administration to block various potentially inflationary wage plans and to keep pressure on the NWLB, which undoubtedly expedited the adoption of the Little Steel formula in mid-1942. Additionally, the military attempted to change most labor laws that might inhibit production, but it met a wall of opposition from unions and other government agencies.[29]

The War and Navy Department labor offices also continued to be involved in labor relations through attempts to settle or prevent strikes that would disrupt military production and through the seizure of facilities at the order of the president. At the Washington level, military labor advisers tried to maintain strict neutrality in dealing with both management and unions. This meant that they often had to restrain field personnel, who tended to be inexperienced, mediocre, or biased toward management, from provoking or aggravating labor unrest.[30]

Despite the skillful performance of the WDLB and, to a lesser degree, its Navy Department counterpart, labor-military relations became increasingly strained from 1943 onward. As strikes grew in number, the armed services, usually over the objection of their labor advisers, launched a publicity campaign against work stoppages, stepped up their efforts in behalf of national service, and, within the Roosevelt administration, became the leading advocates of the War Labor Disputes Act of 1943.[31] That bill was intended to prevent strikes but, among other provisions, sanctioned them after a thirty-day cooling-off period and a favorable union vote.

LABOR RELATIONS, 1943–1945

Support for the War Labor Disputes Act was based on the assumption that irresponsible labor leaders drove their membership to the picket line—an assumption proven erroneous when the act was implemented. The rank and file usually voted overwhelmingly for strikes.[32] Rather than encouraging strikes, union leaders faced increasing difficulty controlling their membership. Philip Murray constantly fretted about "an attitude of rebellion on the part of the workers generally."[33] Numerous local union leaders lost their elected positions during 1944–1945 because they had demanded moderation on labor's part.[34]

Labor's unrest stemmed largely from conservative domestic policies. Union spokesmen believed that the traditional Southern Democrats, whom the president had selected to oversee the economy, were principally responsible for such policies. They were thinking first of James F. Byrnes, who had been appointed director of economic stabilization late in 1942 and later served as head of the OWM, and then of Fred M. Vinson, Byrnes's successor in the stabilization office.

The Byrnes-Vinson leadership prevented runaway inflation by holding a tighter rein on wages than on prices. The Bureau of Labor Statistics (BLS) calculated that the cost of living had risen 23.4 percent between January 1941 and December 1943; labor set the figure at 43.5 percent. Yet NWLB, acting under directives from the stabilization office, generally held wage increases to

15 percent in order to offset a commensurate rise in prices from January 1941 to April 1942. Using the low BLS estimates, the average real spendable income of a manufacturing worker with three dependents went up slightly over 30 percent between 1941 and 1943.[35] But, quite clearly, most of labor's income gains resulted from full employment, overtime work, and the upgrading of workers. Averages, moreover, do not account for the many instances where wages remained substandard and gross inequities existed. Even when wages were good, American workers did not receive the protection afforded, for example, their British counterparts, including a guaranteed forty-hour workweek, separation and relocation pay, and preservation of peacetime seniority for those transferring to war work. Furthermore, millions of workers and their families needlessly suffered from substandard living conditions and inadequate community facilities and services.[36]

Other interest groups were protected to a far greater degree than labor was. The farmer had the benefits of the parity system. Industry, and especially large corporations, experienced high profits and directly and indirectly received elaborate facilities and research financed at public expense.

Although prices remained remarkably stable from December 1943 to VJ Day, agitation among the working population grew rather than diminished because of the absence of adequate plans for reconversion. As the least protected economic interest group, labor faced the prospect of peace with foreboding. Predictions of a postwar depression were rife; a few years of war prosperity had not erased the painful memories of the depression decade. To avoid a postwar crash, union spokesmen were among the leading advocates of a carefully planned reconversion program—one in which they participated and that included the welfare benefits denied the worker during the war. Their proposals were ignored.[37]

Spokesmen from the large corporations and the military services who dominated WPB were mainly responsible for the nation being unprepared for peace. During 1944, the president and Congress designated the OWM—now the OWMR—as the agency to determine demobilization policy. Among OWMR's most significant acts was resolving the reconversion controversy that racked WPB in favor of the conservative industry-military production team and against the liberal plans of WPB chair Donald M. Nelson and his allies.

The postwar depression feared by many did not materialize, but the lack of planning for peace had its consequences. A quick end to the war caught the Harry S. Truman administration unprepared for maintaining stable economic conditions during demobilization. One result of that failure was the massive explosion in industrial relations—an explosion that had been building up slowly for almost two years.

UNIONS IN THE DEFENSE AND WAR YEARS

The CIO, and the AFL as well, recognized no later than 1940 that traditional American "business unionism" in an economy mobilized for war would cruelly trap organized labor. In order to protect their power and maintain the loyalty of their members, unions had to go beyond collective bargaining to participate in operating a planned economy. Hence, both federations insisted that labor be granted an equal voice with management in mobilization agencies. Philip Murray's National Industry Council Plan, made more specific by industrial unions in automobiles, steel, aluminum, nonferrous metals, and farm equipment, spelled out more clearly what labor had in mind. A practical way to start expanding labor's participation was for union officials to serve alongside industrialists in mobilization agencies and for labor advisory committees to match those of industry. Proposals for such an approach began with the NDAC and continued with the OPM and the WPB.[38]

Labor's proposed tactic was as perceptive as it was futile. The futility was based on a harsh reality: Washington needed industry to mobilize the economy; it could persuade or force labor to go along with what mobilization required. Industrialists and industry advisory committees, although criticized by many, were accepted as essential and legitimate in WPB and its predecessors. Union leaders, however, were looked on by numerous mobilization officials as representing special, not public, interests. As a result, labor never entered the mainstream of policymaking in NDAC, OPM, or WPB, regardless of its contribution, testimony about its excellence, or proof of its impartiality. Union representation was always minimized, kept separate and unequal, or isolated. The Labor Production Division (LPD), which replaced Sidney Hillman's Labor Division in WPB, was farcical; the vice chairman for labor production and vice chairman for manpower requirements taking over for LPD in June 1943 had more prestige but little more power or influence. Labor did have a meaningful voice in NWLB and the War Manpower Commission, but those agencies dealt exclusively with the workforce and were ultimately subordinated to WPB and the OWM/OWMR.

The fate of labor advisory committees in OPM illustrates the point of labor's subordination. With New Dealers ascendant and industry on the defensive, a few aggressive labor advisory committees such as that in rubber and, later, Reid Robinson's International Union of Mine, Mill, and Smelter Workers, a CIO affiliate, made some headway, but most failed. Once WPB was organized, mobilization seriously under way, and industry, backed by the military, taking charge, the surviving labor advisory committees were simply shoved aside. By mid-June 1942, most ceased to function. In the words of a disgruntled labor spokesman, the committees had always been "undigested lumps in the stomachs of the management people."[39] After much agitation, WPB in 1944 finally issued regulations for the operation of labor advisory committees, and a substantial number were appointed at the end of 1944. By then, WPB was preparing for reconversion under policies that labor opposed. Its committees again quickly fell into disuse.

While management was the major roadblock to the success of labor advisory committees and union leaders operating in NDAC, OPM, and WPB, labor was hardly blameless. To maximize their contribution, unions needed the expertise of the economists, statisticians, and academics serving in the Labor Division. Yet Sidney Hillman never succeeded in working out harmonious relations among these professionals and labor leaders. Furthermore, the two federations quarreled over representation, some unions wanted the prestige of OPM or WPB membership without devoting time to production matters, and most unions lacked or were unwilling to assign qualified representatives to labor advisory committees. With most unions growing rapidly, many unions factionalized, and all unions adjusting to industrial organization, officials could not absent themselves for any length of time without threatening the stability of their organizations or their positions in them. Few labor leaders had the security that allowed Sidney Hillman to serve in NDAC, OPM, and WPB as he did.

Even had labor succeeded in correcting all these weaknesses, no evidence suggests a different outcome. Adamantly opposed to flawed labor advisory committees, industry would have been more hostile to stronger ones. Donald M. Nelson could not get very far even with his modest "War Production Drive" of early 1942. This program called for the voluntary formation of management-labor shop committees to expedite production. Industry's widespread suspicions undermined the effort.

Consistently throughout the defense and war years, management overreacted, manifesting its own insecurities. Industry had little to fear from tripartite planning, labor advisory committees, and the like. Below the Washington and headquarters levels, the Murray-type plans appeared to have limited appeal. As collective-bargaining latitude narrowed, shrewd labor leaders recognized that alternate plans for mobilization allowed them to go on the offensive against industry and the state in defending the workforce. They did not appear to expect their proposals to be accepted, and they seemed unprepared to fulfill new responsibilities had they been proven wrong.

Advocacy for labor advisory committees, calls for more coherent mobilization policies, and like initiatives strengthened labor's arguments against national service and for workers getting a greater share. In a similar vein, members of Congress were not seriously determined to alter the mobilization structures radically in the midst of war through the Tolan-Kilgore-Pepper Bill. Instead, they were using the proposed legislation to force the White House to rein in industry and the military and to coordinate better a chaotic mobilization system. So too, labor seemed less interested in invading management prerogatives than it was in advancing union interests. Had labor leaders intended otherwise, they probably would not have carried the rank and file with them. Most of the working population appeared less interested in changing the economic system than in having it operate in a more equitable and just way.

Other than insisting on a greater mobilization role, the options for organized labor were not promising. Consistently to follow main trends, in the Sidney Hillman mold, invited the scorn and lost the respect of unions. To challenge the wartime state, along the lines of John L. Lewis, endangered the nation and threatened retaliation of terrible proportions. The AFL and the CIO truly had a Hobson's choice. They did what they had to do. Returning to the main point, in America's corporate capitalist system mobilized for war, organized labor's secondary power status even after great change and massive growth became glaringly and painfully obvious.

16

ECONOMIC STABILIZATION

The Franklin D. Roosevelt administration devised a reasonably sound program for maintaining economic stability during the defense and war years. That was the case despite expenditures far exceeding the expectations of most public officials. Although stabilization policy evolved piecemeal from 1940 into 1942, a comprehensive program was in place by late 1942 and early 1943. Carried out by a number of wartime agencies, all coordinated by the Office of Economic Stabilization (OES), the program included fixing prices and wages, rationing consumer goods, and raising revenue through relatively heavy taxation and borrowing designed to tame rather than feed inflationary pressures.

World War II was America's most expensive war to date by a wide margin. It was also the most successful one in terms of distributing scarce consumer goods in an equitable fashion, controlling inflation, and paying for nearly half of war costs through taxation. The record could have been better, particularly in terms of taxes.

Several reasons explain the strength of the wartime record. The World War I developments were still fresh in the minds and the experience of numerous wartime leaders, including the president. Throughout the interwar years, past and future wartime economic policy was a constant source of study and debate. Furthermore, the New Deal brought into government a host of economists, statisticians, and other academics, many of whom were inspired by the theories of John Maynard Keynes. As defense and war spending gradually turned depression into prosperity and threatened inflation, New Dealers adjusted their thinking to achieving massive munitions output while maintaining economic stability. In short, the New Deal state was better equipped to handle the economics of World War II than the Progressive state was to handle the economics of World War I.

Wartime economic policy was largely an executive matter. Congress almost automatically authorized the president to spend as he and his principal civilian and military advisers saw fit. Although differences developed, the nation's legislators also generally accommodated the administration in passing statutes sanctioning price and wage policy, rationing, and borrowing. How these controls and devices were applied was left largely to the executive. Taxation was the one major exception. Congress regularly denied the president, especially in the last years of war, the more stringent and progressive taxation policies that he sought. To grasp better the accomplishments and limitations of stabilization policies requires at least a brief analysis of executive-legislative relations.

PRICES, WAGES, AND RATIONING

Monitoring prices as defense spending increased began with the National Defense Advisory Commission (NDAC) in May 1940.[1] Leon Henderson headed the Division of Price Stabilization. Advisory powers limited what he could do. The Price Division, therefore, relied on persuasion, appeals to patriotism, public pressure, and threats to hold prices down, as was the case in the summer of 1940 with pulp and paper, lumber, and other products. Actually, Henderson's tasks were made easier by the fact that substantial inflationary pressures did not appear until early spring 1941. Between August 1939 and March 1941, wholesale prices had risen by less than 9 percent and consumer prices by less than 3 percent.

By March 1941, however, prices began to increase more rapidly as both defense and peacetime output grew. In December 1941, wholesale prices had risen nearly 25 percent and consumer prices more than 12 percent over those of August 1939. In the face of such inflationary pressures, the Division of Price Stabilization initiated a policy of "selective price control."[2] This approach continued from the NDAC period through the early months of America's entry into the war. Roosevelt strengthened Henderson's hand in April 1941 when the Division of Price Stabilization was replaced by the Office of Price Administration and Civilian Supply (OPACS). In August 1941, the Office of Price Administration (OPA) was set up as a separate agency and continued as the basic body for administering prices throughout hostilities. Until January 1942, OPA and its predecessors depended on the president's delegated powers, not statutory authority, to regulate pricing. That reality denied Henderson and his colleagues direct means with which to enforce their decisions. A member of Congress explained that OPA's price-fixing authority rested on the solid constitutional right of free speech.

A strong advocate of controlling prices, Henderson ignored legal doubt about his ability to act. In February 1941, his NDAC division issued Price

Schedule No. 1, setting maximum prices on used machine tools. Aluminum and scrap aluminum came next in March 1941. In general, the Price Stabilization Division proceeded cautiously, OPACS acted more boldly, and OPA became even more active. Between 1940 and the end of January 1942, Henderson's organization placed controls on around 50 percent of all wholesale prices through 53 price schedules, 120 voluntary agreements, and several hundred warnings and suggestions. Retail prices were left unpoliced. Even with a weak legal base, OPA performed reasonably well. The public and most businesses supported the idea of regulating prices, although differences existed over how it should be done.

The OPA had been seeking a legal basis for its actions since early in 1941. After much debate, an administration-sponsored bill introduced in the House of Representatives in August 1941 became law at the end of January 1942 as the Emergency Price Control Act. What emerged from Congress was considerably weaker than Henderson, the president, and others desired. OPA was granted wide latitude in setting prices to maintain stability and to control rents in areas affected by war production. It could enforce its decisions through criminal prosecution resulting in such punishments as fines and imprisonment, writs, licensing, or suits resulting in pecuniary losses. The law provided for protest against and appeal of OPA decisions, and it set up a special court system to expedite hearings and to guard against lengthy and crippling judicial action. Henderson was not given the power to ration goods; that vital function remained with the War Production Board (WPB) and other agencies having allocation authority, even though OPA implemented rationing under their direction. Wages were also outside the administrator's purview, and his authority over farm prices was coordinated with that of the secretary of agriculture. Moreover, through complicated formulas, OPA could not set farm prices below 110 percent of parity.

Once the bill became law, OPA progressed from selective price controls to general ones. The administration inaugurated the new phase in April 1942 by issuing the General Maximum Price Regulation, or General Max, freezing virtually all retail prices at maximum levels existing in March 1942. As it turned out, General Max was more a desired than a realizable goal. If implemented as announced, the regulation would have institutionalized gross inequities and inefficiencies; more important, merchants were left to set their own prices on the basis of extremely complex rules, and consumers had no way of verifying that OPA directives were being followed. What was needed instead was an approach sufficiently flexible to achieve realistic pricing and to set prices in "dollars-and-cents"[3] so that consumers could discern merchant violations. Unable to meet those criteria, OPA during 1942 had to depend on business cooperation and public support to enforce its decisions. The results were disappointing. Between April 1942 and April 1943, the consumer price index rose 7.6 percent, and evasion and abuse probably pushed the figure higher.[4]

OPA functioned poorly because its national office was awkwardly organized and inefficient. As a result, policies and processes for administering prices, rents, and rationing were greatly retarded. Conditions were made worse by an exceptionally weak field staff. Actually, a number of field offices emerged without adequate coordination and centralized direction. Gradually in 1942, eight thousand local boards and forty-eight state ones were created to handle rationing, twenty-five district offices, approximating industrial and commercial lines, were set up to deal with pricing, and numerous area boards came into being for rent-control purposes. All these structures were to be directed by eight regional offices. Such a layered, duplicative, and basically unsupervised system could not and did not work well. The field system and OPA in general began functioning effectively only in 1943, when the administration turned to unified price control and rationing boards organized at grassroots levels, run principally by volunteer housewives, and kept informed by graspable and sensible regulations. Such an approach worked well in Canada and had been recommended but rejected earlier for the United States.

Wages, unlike prices, were basically unregulated in 1940–1941. An exception existed with the Shipbuilding Stabilization Committee, which worked out zonal wage rates for the shipbuilding industry in 1941–1942. Although this voluntary approach was attempted by several other industries, its overall impact was limited. The National Defense Mediation Board (NDMB), created in March 1941, was intended to settle industrial disputes, but it had no authority over wages. When mediation efforts broke down, the most the board could do was to have special investigators, operating without established guidelines, make recommendations about fair wages to facilitate management-labor negotiations. Nonetheless, while rising, wages were not skyrocketing. Between August 1939 and March 1941, they went up less than 6 percent. From then on, wage rates rose faster along with inflationary forces, reaching a level nearly 17 percent above that of August 1939 by December 1941. The take-home pay of the average employee, however, went up faster than wage rates with longer hours of work, premium pay for overtime, upgrading, and like practices.[5]

The potential for greater control over wages existed with the organization of the National War Labor Board (NWLB) in January 1942. Clearly, the board had to deal with wages in disputes referred to it. But it did so without guidance since wages were not included in its charges. Moreover, NWLB had no say in wage rates set by management and labor in uncontested negotiations. Slowly and methodically, the board worked its way toward the Little

Steel Formula of July 1942: straight-line hourly wages could rise 15 percent above the relatively stable rates of January 1941. In that way, labor would be compensated for increases in the cost of living taking place before the administration announced its stabilization plan in May 1942. Through legislation followed by an executive order in the first days of October 1942, NWLB's jurisdiction was expanded to include all wage adjustments, and the board was authorized to hold wages at the September 1942 level except to "correct maladjustments or inequities, to eliminate substandards of living, to correct gross inequities, or to aid in the effective prosecution of the war."[6] Thereafter, the NWLB, using the Little Steel Formula as its base, worked out principles with which to stabilize wages in the wartime economy.

Controlling prices and wages was only part of a broader plan for stabilizing the wartime economy. Consideration of such an approach began before Pearl Harbor and became more focused and urgent thereafter.[7] As early as July 1941, the Bureau of the Budget advocated a comprehensive anti-inflation program and, with the president's approval, began formulating specific proposals. For various reasons, bureau efforts did not lead to action until March–April 1942. Combining its economic experts with those from the Treasury and Agriculture Departments, OPA, the Federal Reserve Board, and other agencies, the bureau headed up the informal Anti-Inflation Committee. Late in March, the committee forwarded to the president an integrated plan for maintaining economic stability. It proposed freezing prices (including farm prices), wages, salaries, and rents. The committee further recommended rationing, stringent credit restrictions, and a general increase in taxes and social security deductions along with compulsory savings. All these measures were intended to pay maximum war costs out of current income while reducing spending power. Early in April, Samuel I. Rosenman joined the committee, and the president designated Vice President Henry A. Wallace to oversee the group.

The rigorous program was significantly watered down before being adopted. Conferences early in April, some of which took place at the White House and included the president, revealed "irreconcilable disagreement among the 'top policy' group."[8] Secretary of the Treasury Henry J. Morgenthau, Jr., intensely opposed parts of the plan, particularly those involving taxes, compulsory savings, and a wage freeze, and he insisted on greater reliance on strict, across-the-board rationing. Other Anti-Inflation Committee members joined Morgenthau in rejecting various proposals. The president's unwillingness to support a wage freeze, however, was the most important factor in undermining anti-inflation policies. Without agreement on rigidly controlling wages, the administration could not achieve unity on a tough stabilization policy.

Rosenman took over the task of formulating what became the seven-point anti-inflation program that Roosevelt sent to Congress on April 27, 1942. The program constituted the most that could be salvaged from the deliberations of the Anti-Inflation Committee. Often in general and vague terms, the president called for stabilization through heavy taxation, price-fixing, wage and salary restraints, tighter controls on agricultural pricing, voluntary savings, rationing, and credit restraints and debt reduction. In the face of divided counsel, Roosevelt typically was signaling the need for forceful action but waiting for the circumstances to compel agreement.

Accordingly, the seven-point program initiated the administration's gradual movement toward a firm stabilization program. OPA took a step in that direction by almost immediately issuing its General Max order and beginning rigorously to expand rent controls. At this point, OPA was hampered, not only by the weakness of its structure and policymaking, but also by Congress's parity-plus and other statutory limitations on its ability to control food prices. NWLB acted next with the Little Steel Formula. In May, the Federal Reserve Board additionally strengthened measures to restrict credit. All these acts were helpful, but not enough to curb inflation through squeezing consumer purchasing power. Particularly harmful were inadequate increases in taxation. The Anti-Inflation Committee favored new taxes of $11.6 billion plus $2 billion more in those for social security, the Treasury Department cut the figure to $7.6 billion, and Congress in the Revenue Act of October 1942 provided for only $3.6 billion. Furthermore, war bond purchases in 1942 were dismally disappointing.

Firmer stabilization policies were essential to check growing inflation. Once again, OPA led in the drive for a more effective approach. Late in July, it began calling for a stabilization board that could hold down wages and agricultural prices as indispensable for implementing the seven-point program. The White House and Bureau of the Budget staff in August proposed creating by executive order the OES to achieve OPA goals. Roosevelt ultimately concluded that such a crucial step required legislation. Hence, in September 1942, he called on Congress to amend the Emergency Price Control Act of January 1942 in a way allowing him effectively to move on all parts of his seven-point program. The president warned that the consequences of inflation were so great that he would proceed on his own if Congress did not respond positively by October 1.

After intense, extended debate and parliamentary maneuvering, Congress on October 2 sent the president the bill that he had demanded. He was essentially authorized to stabilize prices, wages, and salaries on the basis of the highest rates reached between January 1 and September 15, 1942, with flexibility allowed for necessary adjustments. While lifting the earlier requirement for farm prices to rise to 110 percent of parity, Congress practically restored or exceeded it by including farm labor costs in parity calculations.

To implement the expanded anti-inflation powers, Roosevelt by executive order created on October 3, 1942, the OES, with James F. Byrnes designated as its director. Byrnes was advised by an Economic Stabilization Board made up of representatives from key departments and agencies and two members each for labor, management, and agriculture. Acting for the president, the director would define comprehensive policies for achieving economic stability, and he would resolve any conflicts among numerous agencies involved in controlling inflation, including OPA, NWLB, the Department of Agriculture, etc. All proposed wage increases now had to be filed with the NWLB, and those requiring an upward adjustment in OPA price ceilings had to be approved by both the board and OES. The director of economic stabilization was also instructed to hold salaries to $25,000 after taxes. OPA was additionally ordered to extend rent controls throughout the entire nation. Greater emphasis was also placed on rationing.[9]

Creating OES and stiffening anti-inflation measures slowed but did not stop the rise of prices. Between September 1942 and April 1943, the cost of living went up 6.2 percent.[10] OPA came under withering attack from Congress, elements within the Roosevelt administration, affected interest groups, and the public. Conditions were temporarily made worse by Henderson being forced out of OPA in December 1942. Under first Prentiss M. Brown and then Chester Bowles, the agency became more effective by unifying its subdivisions, simplifying its rules and methods, and making itself more friendly and accessible to consumers, business, and Congress. But that took time. Furthermore, with prices still rising, John L. Lewis in March 1943 began his guerilla warfare against the Roosevelt administration, seeking increased wages for miners. Around the same period, the powerful Farm Bloc in Congress maneuvered to achieve greater latitude for agricultural prices to go up. Without checking wages and food prices, economic stabilization simply could not be achieved.

In the face of another inflation crisis, Roosevelt on April 8, 1943, issued the "Hold-the-Line" Order to halt further increases in the cost of living. This was to be done through better coordination of wage and price controls and more explicit guidelines for the operations of OPA, the War Food Administration, and NWLB. With the president delegating to the OES director his full powers and directing him to act forcefully, Byrnes moved from a passive to an active role. Between October and April, the OES director intervened when conflicts and problems came to him; after April, he was out front in the fight against inflation. Indeed, Byrnes and his advisers, including Bernard M. Baruch, were the principal authors of the Hold-the-Line Order.[11]

On the basis of White House instructions, NWLB was to hold wages to May 1942 levels except to correct substandard conditions. Under Byrnes's watchful eye, workers were allowed some increases in the light of existing rules, new procedures, and fringe benefits. Overall, however, manufacturing wages were placed in an iron grip. From April 1943 to August 1945, they rose only 10.6 percent, the lowest monthly average rate of increase for the entire period from January 1941 through August 1945.[12]

Under new rules, OPA entered its most active and effective phase. Brown initiated and Bowles continued a comprehensive drive, not only to hold, but also to roll back consumer prices. Price controls were extended to cover practically all consumer goods. Where obvious gouging took place, prices were rolled back; a program of subsidies, principally for food but also for some manufactured goods, was instituted to ensure adequate output of essential goods where violations were not involved. Additionally, controls on food prices went from vague ceilings to dollar-and-cents amounts that were graspable by shoppers and subject to their complaints. Control of rents in particular was accomplished under efficient OPA administration from mid-1942 onward. Some rents remained practically stable from 1942 to the war's end; others experienced a rise of around 23 percent between April 1940 and November 1945. Evasion and other abuses, however, appear to have been quite common.

Rationing, which had started in January 1942 and slowly expanded, became much more widespread and effective as OPA improved its techniques. Tires and other products were rationed through special authorization, while food, fuel, gasoline, and the like were subject to stamps or coupons. Food was ultimately under a very sophisticated point system devised by OPA that allowed consumers some choice in their buying patterns. Under the Hold-the-Line Order, OPA and other agencies increased their policing efforts against rule violations, black market activity, and similar practices.

The Hold-the-Line period, from April 1943 to August 1945, finally accomplished the tight inflation controls that Leon Henderson and others had been pushing since 1941. During the twenty-eight-month period, consumer prices went up only 4.2 percent, wholesale prices a mere 1.9 percent. Average monthly consumer prices from October 1942 to April 1943 rose 0.72 percent and from April 1943 to August 1945 only 0.15 percent.[13] The key to success was moving forcefully and on many fronts to hold down prices, especially for food, and keep wage increases to a bare minimum. Overall, by the calculations of one scholar, consumer prices from January 1941 through

August 1945 rose a total of 26.8 percent, wholesale prices 29.5 percent.[14] Other scholars arrive at figures both higher and lower than these.[15]

Controls under the Hold-the-Line Order did not go unchallenged. Organized labor claimed that Bureau of Labor Statistics (BLS) figures on inflation were too low. To investigate union charges, Roosevelt appointed the Presidential Committee on the Cost of Living in December 1943, headed by William H. Davis, NWLB chair, and two members each from management and labor who served on the board. Labor members R. J. Thomas and George Meany insisted that the BLS calculation of a 23.4 percent rise in the cost of living from January 1941 to December 1943 was far off the mark; the increase was as high as 43.5 percent. BLS distortion, they argued, arose from relying excessively on food items that were controlled or subsidized, ignoring quality deterioration or the disappearance of more cheaply priced items, using large cities where prices were lower, and other relevant factors.[16]

For a more disinterested analysis, Davis called on a high-powered committee of economists, chaired by Wesley C. Mitchell, to review the BLS work. The committee found the bureau's statistical calculations to be sound but estimated that the cost of living for the time period in dispute had risen somewhere between 26.8 and 28.5 percent.[17] An authoritative study by Hugh Rockoff in 1984 found the Mitchell study to be off by at least 4.8–7.3 percent when the analysis was extended to June 1946, and Rockoff and a coauthor in 1987 revised the figures further upward, considering factors that labor raised and the consequences of black market operations and rationing restrictions.[18] Robert Higgs, working with the analyses of Simon Kuznets, Milton Friedman, Anna Jacobson Schwartz, and others, provocatively arrives at conclusions about the cost of living that could be interpreted in a way placing him closer to Thomas and Meany than to their detractors.[19]

Controversy aside, labor never succeeded in breaking the Hold-the-Line Order on wages, although NWLB had enough latitude to grant some direct or indirect wage increases and, thus, provide an outlet for growing worker discontent. Moreover, despite decline in the manufacture and availability of various goods, prices were holding according to traditional measurements; rationing assured a reasonable distribution of products in short supply; and in 1944, civilian consumption (measured in 1939 prices) was around 5 percent higher than in 1939, about the same as in 1940, and only slightly less than in 1941.[20] Organized labor argued to union members that, through representation on the OPA, OES, and the Office of War Mobilization and Reconversion, it insisted on policies protecting the public.[21] Nonetheless, restlessness among workers over real or supposed wartime economic inequities generated enormous tensions for union officials and led to strikes.[22]

OPA controls involving military purchasing were significantly attenuated.[23] During the defense years, OPA and predecessor agencies were only partially successful in controlling armed services pricing. With war declared, the secretaries and under secretaries of war and the navy requested first from Congress and then from the president exemption of all military procurement from OPA regulations. Munitions, they argued, could not be handled like other products without unending delays and obstacles to contracting. Furthermore, cost-plus-fixed-fee (CPFF) and similar contracts, along with operations of government-owned, privately operated (GOPO) plants, caused further problems. Elevated profits stemming from high prices could be recaptured through renegotiation and excess profits taxes. Relying on the recommendations of Leon Henderson, both Congress and the president rejected the appeals.

Continuing to press its case, the military ultimately won out. Realizing the enormity of trying to work out prices for the armed forces and the fact that many OPA rules were being ignored, Henderson gradually gave way. Between July and November 1942, the office and the military negotiated the Henderson-Patterson-Forrestal Agreement. Under the accord, all strictly military products, such as tanks and naval vessels, would be exempt from OPA controls, with the army and navy rigorously policing pricing and reporting results to OPA. Around 35 percent in dollar value of army purchasing, and probably a comparable proportion for the navy, remained subject to OPA regulation. The buying included civilian goods typically acquired by the Quartermaster Corps and the Bureau of Supplies and Accounts, common components, and raw materials.

Although the largest wartime procurers, the armed forces did not significantly affect the cost of living directly since their purchases of civilian goods were subject to OPA policies and bulk buying usually kept prices below allowable maximums. More important, most of military expenditures went to weaponry, which was outside normal civilian channels. Indirectly, of course, military contracting had an enormous impact on inflationary pressures.

Recognizing that fact, Congress, beginning early in 1942, required the War and Navy Departments and the Maritime Commission closely to monitor the pricing of all their buying. While armed services and commission pricing was lax in 1942 and early 1943, by mid-1943 and after it was becoming more stringent under close, progressive, forward, and company pricing, the use of cost analyses and pricing indexes, restricting, terminating, or modifying CPFF contracts in favor of fixed-price ones, and better liaison with OPA, WPB, and other agencies.

From the war's outset, cost and price analysis among government procurement agencies was always tied in with reducing or eliminating excess profits, especially through renegotiation of contracts. Henderson consistently maintained that the services' claim of correcting pricing abuses through excess profits taxation and renegotiation was never foolproof. Those practices could reduce but never eliminate unjustified wartime gains. How successful military control of costs, prices, and profits was is exceptionally difficult to determine and still remains a matter of controversy.

WAR FINANCING

Methods of financing the war both added to and subtracted from inflationary forces.[24] "If one assumes that all government debt acquired by commercial banks was financed by money creation," observes Hugh Rockoff, "and that none of the debt held by the public was so financed, then we get the following results":

> On average during the years of large wartime deficits (1942–5) taxes accounted for 47 per cent of total spending, money creation 26 per cent, and borrowing from the public 27 per cent. The monetary share can be further divided into spending financed directly by government-created money (6 per cent) and spending financed indirectly by money created by the banking system (20 per cent).[25]

Since the money supply was growing much faster throughout the war years than either prices or GNP, the administration's anti-inflation program overall was working reasonably well.

Had the Bureau of the Budget–led Anti-Inflation Committee of early 1942 had its way, heavy taxation and compulsory saving from the outset would have paid for more of war costs out of current income and tamed inflationary forces by reducing consumer spending power. Secretary of the Treasury Morgenthau opposed committee recommendations in several areas. He was against a sales tax, felt that Congress could not be pushed far on income taxes, and favored voluntary, over compulsory, savings. These and added objections, supported in part by the president and others, slowed the administration's anti-inflation program.

As prices continued to rise in 1942 and 1943, however, and despite hesitation in the executive branch and resistance in the legislature, taxation loomed large in economic stabilization. Corporate income and excess profits taxes and individual income taxes combined constituted the principal source of federal revenue. In 1940, out of gross receipts totaling nearly $6.9 billion, corporate taxes accounted for 17 percent and income taxes 14 percent, for a combined amount of 31 percent. By 1944, government revenue amounted to about $47.8 billion, with around 38 percent coming from income taxes and 31 percent corporate taxes, the two equaling 69 percent. Individual income taxes permanently surpassed those for corporations in 1944 as the principal source of federal revenue.[26]

Growing sums from individuals were extracted by reducing exemptions for joint returns in 1940 to $2,000 and single returns to $800; by 1944, the amounts had been pushed even lower, to $1,000 and $500. As the income tax reach was expanded, rates were made increasingly progressive. In 1944, the lowest brackets were taxed at an effective rate of just under 3 percent, while the highest-income earners went up to nearly 65 percent. Of great significance was the fact that, in 1943, Congress, after bitter debate, provided for a system in which all taxpayers had 20 percent of their wages and salaries withheld and were required to make quarterly estimated payments on other sources of income.[27] In 1940, around 7.5 million taxable returns were filed; by 1944, the figure had jumped to nearly 42.4 million. Stated another way, around 7 percent of the population paid income taxes in 1940; by 1944 over 64 percent did so.[28]

Corporate taxes between 1940 and 1942 had been pushed up from 24 to 40 percent; in 1943, the excess profits tax rate reached 95 percent. While excess profits taxes produced only $166 million in 1941, after 1943 they accounted for over half of all corporate receipts. Unlike personal returns, those from corporations dropped around 14 percent between 1940 and 1944, although the number of firms reporting net income rose by nearly 30 percent.[29] Other taxes, including those on estates, gifts, alcohol, and luxuries, were also raised and/or modified. Congress considered but never advanced far with proposals originating mostly in the executive for a national sales tax, forced savings, and so forth.

Despite dramatic tax increases, Congress consistently lagged behind the administration on wartime financing and economic stabilization, generating growing tension between the two. Reasonably cooperative in 1940 with two revenue acts, the nation's legislators thereafter consistently, often drastically, reduced the president's revenue goals. They also delayed a withholding system, quickly reversed executive action to cap after-tax salaries at $25,000, refused to increase social security taxes, and rejected a host of new or revised taxes. Animosity peaked in February 1944 when Congress slashed White House–recommended additional revenue of $10.5 billion (already cut from the administration's initial estimates of $12 billion) to a little over $2 billion and incorporated retrogressive features in the revenue bill. For the first time in history, the president vetoed a tax bill; Congress quickly and decisively overrode the executive's action. In the process, the majority leader, Senator Alben W. Barkley (D-KY), resigned, forcing Roosevelt to take time out and coax him into running for reelection. Thereafter, other than for a tax simplification act later in 1944, no other war taxation of significance was passed during hostilities.

While no major taxation breakthrough took place during the war years other than a permanent withholding system, the general impact was dramatic, even transforming. A steady decrease in exemptions from levies and increase in effective rates of income taxes, along with heavy corporate normal and excess profits taxes, produced unprecedented federal revenue to match unprecedented federal spending. Although federal taxes in general were reduced after the war, they never again returned to prewar levels in terms of revenue produced and the number of people and institutions affected. Most important, during hostilities, individual income taxes became and remained the principal source of national revenue.

Vast World War II spending also required huge borrowing on Washington's part, resulting in a level of federal debt never before seen. Gross debt grew from $43 billion on June 30, 1940, to almost $270 billion on June 30, 1946, for the first time in history exceeding GNP. Interest on the debt amounted to 3.5 percent of national income, and federal securities accounted for 43 percent of all liquid assets of nonbank investors. "All this meant," in the words of Paul Studenski and Herman E. Krooss, "that henceforth the management of public debt was going to be a potent instrument in influencing the entire economy."[30]

The Treasury Department was flexible and innovative in marketing public securities. In addition to its day-to-day procedures, the department between November 1942 and December 1945 sponsored one Victory and seven War Loan Drives of around three to six weeks in duration, netting nearly $157 billion in bond sales. Marketing was maximized by offering three varieties of savings bonds plus traditional long-term bonds to meet the differing needs. In addition, the Treasury sold a host of short-term paper in the form of certificates of indebtedness, Treasury bills, and tax savings notes.

From the outset of hostilities, the Roosevelt administration aimed at selling securities in a noninflationary way and including as much of the population as possible. Neither objective was ever met. Selling bonds and other issues without expanding the money supply (which fed inflationary forces) required minimizing sales to commercial banks, discouraging securities purchased directly or indirectly through bank loans, and related practices. Efforts along these lines were made, but they never went much beyond exhortation, and, without commercial bank purchases, loan drives and sales in general would never have met their goals. In 1946, consistent with patterns beginning in 1940, ownership of total government interest-bearing securities of around $270 billion broke down as follows: individuals 23 percent; nonbank investors such as insurance companies and corporations 37 percent; and commercial banks 40 percent. To minimize government expenses and maximize sales, the Treasury Department kept interest rates exceptionally low: under 1 percent for short-term paper and 2.5 percent for long-term bonds. Those goals were met, but low lending costs added to inflationary borrowing in a number of ways. Government securities were key to expanding the money supply, by conservative calculations, from $48.4 to $125.3 billion between June 1939 and June 1945.

Limited evidence also points to the fact that sales were not heavy among lower-income groups. That was the case even though the Roosevelt administration set up widespread voluntary payroll savings plans for purchasing U.S. savings bonds by government and civilian employees and members of the armed forces. Still, bond sales in the $10–$100 range were not great, and a relatively high percentage of those sold were redeemed before hostilities ended.[31]

In terms of finances and economic stabilization, the record was much better in World War II than in World War I. The Woodrow Wilson administration had neither a clearly defined policy for maintaining economic stability nor an agency to oversee such a program. Price setting was crude, rationing did not exist, control of wages was experimental, and taxing and borrowing practices left much to be desired. As a result, although the years of World War I hostilities were less than half and total costs around one-eighth those of World War II, wholesale prices rose by 81 percent and cost of living by about 83 percent during the first war, compared with approximately 38 and 27 percent, respectively, during the second. Additionally, World War I taxes, generously calculated, paid for around 36 percent of war costs, those for World War II around 47 percent.[32]

The principal architects of World War II economic stabilization were centered in OPA and the Bureau of the Budget. Leon Henderson was usually out in front. Consequently, as with mobilization policies for conversion and expansion, feasibility, materials allocation, and production scheduling, New Dealers led the way. Once their programs were in place, reformers and their allies were replaced by more pragmatic and politically acceptable executives. Similar patterns and overlapping personnel, therefore, characterized both economic mobilization and stabilization.

A good record on finances and stabilization could have been even better. Differences within the administration delayed achievements, the president was slow in moving to restrict wages, and the Treasury Department could have pursued more effective and noninflationary borrowing policies. Nonetheless, Congress was more responsible than the executive branch for weakening economic stabilization, particularly tax and price control policies. The national legislators were more than conservative; they became obstructionist at times, especially in protecting the farmer and resisting higher and varied forms of taxation.

Nearly all scholars studying World War II finance consider it of great significance for the future. Hugh Rockoff asserts: "The most long-lasting legacy may have been intellectual and institutional." He points to "a new macroeconomic regime which reshaped monetary and fiscal policy and profoundly influenced employment and inflation for decades afterwards." Rockoff explains that the war "played a major role in converting American macroeconomists to Keynesian economics." While Keynes emphasized fiscal policy, he did not totally neglect monetary policy, and Friedman and Schwartz's seminal, *A Monetary History of the United States* established the importance of that approach.[33]

WARTIME PROFITS, FARM INCOME, AND WAGES

Throughout the defense and war years, war profits were a prominent and sensitive issue. The real and rumored gross profiteering of World War I, magnified by the antibusiness attitudes of the Great Depression, largely accounts for the concern. Overall corporate after-tax profits in 1917 reached as high as 70.4 percent above the base year 1913. Steel companies, excepting United States Steel Corporation, in 1917 made profits of over 23 percent. Such lavish returns resulted more from rising prices than from increasing production. Only in 1918 did taxes and other conditions reduce overall corporate returns to more reasonable levels.[34]

Repeated investigation and agitation about World War I economics kept the issue alive throughout the interwar years. "Taking the Profits Out of War" became a rallying cry for many. This plea peaked in 1934–1936 with the Senate Special Committee to Investigate the Munitions Industry (the Nye Committee, after its chair, Senator Gerald P. Nye [R-ND]).[35] When Congress authorized an expansion of the fleet in 1934 with the Vinson-Trammel Act, it included provisions restricting profits on naval vessels and aircraft to 10 percent of contract price; amendments to the statute in 1936 and 1939 and further changes in 1940 made for greater flexibility and extended coverage to army aircraft. The Merchant Marine Act of 1936 followed the Vinson-Trammel Act in limiting profits on ship construction for the U.S. Maritime Commission, along with limitations on corporate salary allowances. In a complex legislative package enacted by Congress in October 1940, Vinson-Trammel and related laws were suspended in favor of the Excess Profits Tax Act of 1940, which was subsequently altered.[36]

The nation's legislators did not stop with taxation in their quest to limit profits; they also provided for the renegotiation of war contracts before taxation. Action along this line was precipitated by a Supreme Court ruling in February 1942 to the effect that Bethlehem Steel Corporation's World War I profits on government shipbuilding contracts were exorbitant but nonetheless legal. Explicit legislation was necessary to regulate returns to contractors. Hence, on the basis of the Second War Powers Act of March 1942, the president designated the War and Navy Departments, the Maritime Commission, WPB, and other agencies to inspect the plants and audit the books of war contractors with an eye to restricting profits. In April 1942, Congress went further with the Renegotiation Act. Under this legislation, the War and Navy Departments and Maritime Commission, and, later, other agencies, were required to include in all contracts or subcontracts exceeding $100,000 renegotiation clauses to retain or recover excessive profits. After a number of amendments, the 1942 legislation was superseded by a law of 1943 (enacted in February 1944). The new statute provided more guidance than the earlier one, met some complaints of industry and procurement agencies, raised the renegotiation level from $100,000 to $500,000, and placed renegotiation under a War Contracts Price Adjustment Board made up of representatives from contracting departments, other mobilization units, and a WPB designee. None of the legislation ever spelled out what constituted excessive profits. The general assumption was that they should be *fair,* another critical term left undefined.[37]

The armed services, particularly the War Department, along with some scholars, laud renegotiation as a major step in reducing profits to reasonable levels, at times below peacetime years. While profits were not taken out of war, they claim, corporate returns were held to levels about which few could complain.[38] No doubt, renegotiation helped reduce contracting prices to a degree and saved the federal government somewhere in the vicinity of $3–$4 billion. Of total war contracts in the vicinity of $300 billion, around 118,000 contracts or contractors were subjected to renegotiation. As a result, average profits on wartime contracting before taxes were reduced by around 25 percent, leaving contracting or subcontracting firms with profits generally in the 10–14 percent range. Although impressive, these figures are still far above the generally accepted guidelines for war profits: on greatly expanded sales, such profits should not exceed one-third to half of peacetime rates.

More important in a sense, the figures conceal more than they reveal.[39] Congress intended the Renegotiation Act of 1942 primarily to reduce prices so as to lower war costs, improve efficiency, hold down wages, and so on. In that way, inflationary pressures would be moderated, government outlays reduced, and firms kept competitive for postwar conditions. Many of the benefits of capitalism would be preserved despite the exigencies of war. Through wartime tax levies, Washington would reclaim excess profits resulting from earlier contracting. But, with readjusted prices, current and future returns would remain in the lower, desirable range.

Those aims never worked out in fact. Practically from the outset, and furthered by minor changes in the 1943 act, renegotiation was separated from procurement and acted principally to reduce profits, not prices. Indeed, upper administrative circles began setting profit ranges for distributors, assemblers, and manufacturers in ascending order from about 5 to 13 percent. Under this approach, all industries and businesses were treated alike, with only slight variation. For example, the most efficient firm in an industry might received 10.3 percent profits, as opposed to the average firm receiving 10 percent and the marginal company 9.7 percent. Such an approach violated the intent of the Renegotiation Acts by failing to encourage or reward corporations for lowering costs. And, since profits were calculated on sales, inefficient companies could end up making more profits on net worth than more efficient ones. Firms with high sales and those with certificates of necessity were favored under renegotiation formulas.

Standardization of profit margins was furthered by often low-grade, unqualified personnel directed by superiors with flawed goals. Richards C. Osborne, a careful scholar of renegotiations, points out that the success of the program depended on "good business judgment."[40] Yet, by the time renegotiations began, talented people were difficult to recruit and retain. Those familiar with the production process, engineers, and accountants were in short supply. Less able individuals had to be relied on, coming predominantly from the ranks of salesmen, brokers, and bankers. Additionally, too often they did not understand the purpose of the laws; or, if they did, poor administration and red tape stood in the way. But even an average group can be made to operate effectively if inspired by good leaders and guided by proper system.

Those qualities were lacking. The principal thrust of renegotiation became selling the virtue of the approach to industry, government, and the public: "The failure [of renegotiation] must be shared by the top administrators who appeared to those in the field to be more interested in convincing Congress and business that a good job was being done than in doing a good job."[41] While industry intensely resented renegotiation, it generally responded favorably to those running the program. And well it might. Most reviews were conducted in offices, not the field, with the primary aim of securing agreement and avoiding conflict. That meant treating industry generously, not harshly or even rigorously. Firms objecting to renegotiation proposals found that they could usually get their way by sticking to their position instead of seeking common ground. Nonetheless, throughout the renegotiation bureaucracy and the procurement agencies, the process was lauded for holding down prices, encouraging savings, and promoting and rewarding efficiency. To prove the case, the armed services submitted to the OPA indexes of falling prices. The office was neither impressed nor taken in.[42] No one denies, however, that World War II corporate profits, unlike those of World War I, resulted from vast output, not skyrocketing prices.

Using renegotiation for the ceremony of removing excess profits without harming production, argues Osborne, wasted the time and energy of busy executives and pressed government officials. Taxes could have been devised to achieve the same purpose. While Osborne's critique of renegotiation is trenchant, he fails to push his analysis to its logical conclusion. Renegotiation basically turned out as it did because that outcome was consistent with the mobilization scheme fashioned around the WPB. From beginning to end, industrialists who dominated the board, backed by the armed services, acted to harness the economy for war with the least disturbance to the status quo. Had the armed services or War Contracts Price Adjustment Board tried to use renegotiation authority to reduce prices meaningfully so as to avoid excess profits, they would have intruded on industry prerogatives. Renegotiation was acceptable to corporate America only because it was used in the inappropriate way to which Osborne objects; otherwise, it probably would have run into intolerable levels of obstruction and resistance from industry.

What renegotiation, along with excess profits taxes, did was prevent the unconscionable profit levels of World War I. Nonetheless, returns to industry were more than generous. Furthermore, corporate profits were higher, perhaps much higher, than official figures record. From its interwar investigations, the Nye Committee warned that there was no way to remove war profits or even reliably reduce them to agreed-on levels. Industry essentially determined what information Washington received, and the government had neither the time, the personnel, nor the resources significantly to challenge corporations determined to have their way. Calculations of net worth, costs, prices, profits, and other factors are so subjective and open to challenge that business could figuratively run circles around the government.

Besides relying heavily on corporate figures, Washington in terms of both taxes and renegotiations seldom had the opportunity to challenge what Osborne calls *hidden profits:* inflated salaries; unmodified peacetime formulas for corporate reserves; goodwill advertising; customer rebates; lavish travel and entertainment expenses; exaggerated and improper use of outlays designated as maintenance and repair; and outright fraud and falsification. Additionally, profit figures frequently do not take into account the "carryback" and "carry-forward" provisions of the tax code. These features allowed corporations to adjust wartime gains against postwar losses and to reclaim up to 10 percent of wartime excess profits taxes. In addition, industry benefited from acceler-ated depreciation of facilities and government-built or -financed plant acquired below market value.[43]

Total annual corporate profits rose from about $7.2 billion in 1939 to $26.5 billion in 1944; even after taxes that was an increase in 1943 of nearly 105 percent. For twenty-five hundred leading industrial corporations, returns on net worth for the years 1940–1945 averaged slightly over 10 percent, with the highest year, 1941, bringing in over 12 percent and the lowest year, 1945, measuring 8.3 percent. Before-tax profit rates for the six years averaged nearly 22 percent, meaning that corporate and excess profits taxes reduced industry returns by over 50 percent; for all corporations, the figure was just over 47 percent. By comparison, for the last full peacetime year of 1939, the leading twenty-five hundred corporations had before-tax profit rates of 9.8 percent and after-tax rates of 8.1 percent. The only industries realizing rewards close to those of World War I were shipbuilding and aircraft. In 1943, these firms had returns based on net worth after taxes ranging from 13 to 33 percent, with most closer to the higher figure. For aircraft, federal outlays converted an infant industry into one of America's giant ones; and, for shipbuilding, it vastly expanded an old industry. Aircraft and shipbuilding, along with machine tools, were among the few industries at the end of hostilities favoring contin-ued high levels of military spending.

High profit rates during World War II were not confined to war industries. Numerous industries catering primarily to civilian markets that were able to maintain output often made profits higher than those producing munitions or related goods. Such was the case with beverages, soaps, and drugs. Small businesses could also do well in terms of profits, and they tended to be granted a larger earning percentage in renegotiations.[44]

Actually, agriculture, not industry, came closer to duplicating the World War I–type returns. And, similarly to manufacturing during World War I, agri-culture gained principally from rising prices, not increasing output. Total farm output grew by only 25 percent during the war years and not always in ways most beneficial to the war effort. Prices between 1940 and 1945 shot up by 102 percent and were at 119 percent of parity in 1943. Net farm income in

1945 stood at 182 percent of the base year 1940, and, since the agricultural population declined from around 30 to 25 million between 1940 and 1945, per capita agricultural income grew to 223 percent above 1940. Agriculture was, of course, starting from a low base coming out of the depression. Still, and despite cries of anguish from and for the farmer in and outside Congress, agriculture outperformed all other sectors of the economy in terms of elevated income.[45]

Labor also did well, but it matched neither agriculture nor industry. Gross average weekly earnings for manufacturing workers went up from $23.64 in 1939 to $45.70 in 1944, or a 93 percent increase in unadjusted dollars; in 1939 dollars, the figures were $23.64 and $36.16, respectively, or a 53 percent increase. Average annual family earnings before taxes, measured in 1954 dollars, grew from $3,343 in 1935–1936 to $5,268 in 1944, or almost 58 percent; after-tax figures are $2,895 and $4,133, respectively, or nearly 47 percent. By 1947, family income had dropped around 7 percent before taxes and 4 percent after.[46] Whatever the figures, the average worker was comparatively well-off. In the words of one labor historian: "The purchasing power of average weekly wages was higher than ever before in American history. The primary reason for shortages in meats, fats, oils, fruits, and vegetables was *not* a reduction in civilian supply, but an increase in effective demand."[47]

General figures aside, surveys by the Office of Civilian Requirements established that many congested communities suffered from a serious deprivation of goods and services. Furthermore, with employment available for practically anyone, around 25 percent of families and individuals still remained mired in poverty during 1944.[48]

Interest group benefits and returns during World War II involve two related subjects: the war's effect on economic concentration of corporate power and income distribution. Concentrating economic power in the traditional sense of mergers and acquisitions did not take place at a significant level during and immediately after the war. But the wealth acquired by corporations and financial institutions during the war no doubt helped create the conditions for the economic consolidation that began in the mid-1950s and, with varying degrees of intensity, continues right to the present day.[49]

The war years were significant for what they both did and did not do in terms of income distribution. Those tending toward a more positive view of the homefront often assert that, from 1939 or 1941 to 1945, there was a lessening of economic inequality in that the top 5 or 20 percent of the population received less of the national income. That is correct. This type of focus took on new importance with the now-classic study of Robert J. Lampman, *The Share of the Top Wealth-Holders in National Wealth*.[50]

While it is true that the top 1, 5, 10, or 20 percent of the population saw its share of the national income shrink, several points about the phenomenon need to be made. First, the trend began in 1929, not 1939 or 1941. Second, the redistribution process stopped in 1944, and that development has held rather consistently until the last few decades, when the turn toward greater inequality set in. Finally, and perhaps most important, the beneficiaries of the redistribution in the depression and war years were not the bottom fifth of the population; their gain was minimal. Most of the shift in income went to those in the upper 50 percent of the population. Moreover, when all forms of taxation are taken into account, taxes do not appear to have meaningfully altered patterns of income distribution.[51]

WHITE HOUSE–CONGRESS RELATIONS, 1940–1945

In formulating policies for economic stabilization and war finance, the Roosevelt administration faced periodic difficulties with the nation's legislators but little outright obstruction. This characterization holds for the president's relations with Congress in general during the war years: they were troubled but avoided deadlock.

Along those lines, James MacGregor Burns, in his study of Roosevelt's World War II presidency, observes: "Congress was surly and prickly on minor issues, generally acquiescent on the big." Burns, however, is almost taken aback by the "atmosphere of conflict" within which Roosevelt was forced to operate—"political bitterness, industrial discord, racial tension, press opposition, Democratic party defections," and "intense and persistent . . . enmity against him."[52]

The poisonous rancor frequently manifested itself in Congress.[53] Yet the nation's legislators never acted in a way that undermined the conduct of the war. Policies for stabilizing the economy illustrate the point. Congress was slow to act on what became the Emergency Price Control Act of January 1942. But the United States was not yet at war, and the administration was hesitant over the proposed legislation. Once the president made it clear in September 1942 that he required greater powers to contain inflationary forces, resentful legislators went along. With the Hold-the-Line Order of April 1943, the administration turned to the Commodity Credit Corporation and the Reconstruction Credit Corporation to finance subsidies, soon totaling over $1 billion a year, to roll back and stabilize food prices. Under pressure from the farm community and related interests opposing subsidies, and disturbed by the administration using vast sums without explicit authorization, Congress in

1943 and 1944 twice voted indirectly to halt them. Roosevelt vetoed the congressional action both times, and the legislators failed to override him. Despite intense criticism of the OPA, Congress renewed its legislative mandate without crippling amendments in mid-1944, and it readily extended price controls and subsidies in 1945.

Patterns for financing the war were more troubled but still not that different. National legislators regularly agreed to administration recommendations on debt ceilings even though the amounts reached unprecedented levels. They also did not attempt to interfere with or influence Treasury Department borrowing practices. Revenue, particularly taxation, however, was a constant source of irritation between the executive and the legislative branches. Reasonably cooperative with the administration between 1940 and 1942, Congress became obdurate after an extended battle within its own chambers and with the administration over the form and nature of an income tax withholding system, finally enacted in June 1943.

The nation's legislators also largely left economic mobilization to the executive. However, Congress was quick to criticize the layered and sprawling bureaucracy. Through committee scrutiny, Congress sought legislative remedies for what it considered to be missing from or necessary for policies involving synthetic rubber, civilian supply, coordinating mobilization, and national service. Except for small business and organized labor, however, no legislation resulted because one chamber failed to act, the two houses could not agree, Congress as a whole backed off, or a presidential veto was not overridden.

The threat of congressional interference was usually enough to persuade the president and his assistants to address problems and bring about needed changes. Furthermore, Congress's power of the purse allowed it to review the record of war agencies. The critical function was usually performed with predictable give-and-take between the executive and the legislative branches. But various agencies that antagonized congressional elements faced rough handling, as occurred with OPA, the War Manpower Commission, the Office of Civilian Defense, the Civilian Branch of the Office of War Information,[54] and the Committee on Fair Employment Practices.

The nation's legislators proceeded cautiously with the armed services. Huge and growing military budgets were passed with little difficulty. Congress, however, did scrutinize expenditures that became controversial, such as the Canol Project (extracting and refining Alaskan oil), learned to detect hidden funding (like that for the Manhattan Project), and developed techniques for generally reviewing requests for massive military outlays.

Legislators dug in their heels during a long and bitter battle with the Roosevelt administration before the 1944 election over maximizing armed services voting at home and abroad through the use of a federal ballot. In the end, Congress won. With only minor concessions, states maintained control over voting. But Congress stayed away from the volatile issue of the armed forces' size, even though it did involve itself in the Selective Service System and deferment policies. Military strategy and the course of the war also remained beyond legislators' purview. Nonetheless, methods were worked out for briefing Congress on sensitive matters, including the Manhattan Project. Some flare-ups still occurred over the Pearl Harbor attack, fighting the war in Asia as opposed to Europe, Britain and the Soviet Union as allies, alleged regular army discrimination against the National Guard, and other peripheral matters.

Various New Deal agencies, unlike the armed services and most mobilization administrations, faced congressional hostility, which began before and grew in intensity after the Republicans' substantial gains in the 1942 midterm elections. In 1942, Congress ended the Civilian Conservation Corps (CCC) and the Works Progress Administration (WPA); in 1943, it cut off funding for the National Youth Administration (NYA) and drastically cut back the Farm Security Administration (FSA) and the Rural Electrification Administration (REA). Most significant, the nation's legislators terminated the National Resources Planning Board (NRPB), which was on record for postwar prosperity and security achieved through an activist state along New Deal lines. With jobs plentiful and full employment approaching, CCC and WPA were hard to defend, but NYA was still usefully training labor, FSA and REA served small and threatened farmers, and NRPB in an informed and professional way addressed critical postwar issues.[55]

On its part, the Roosevelt administration failed to maximize some opportunities to tie social advances to national security. Representative John H. Tolan's Select Committee Investigating National Defense Migration insisted that millions of people migrating to production centers and military installations required extensive federal attention with regard to housing, community facilities, transportation systems, and related services.[56] Despite conservative resistance, Congress could usually be persuaded to pass legislation for and/or fund such projects. Moreover, the armed services and the Maritime Commission could be counted on for support if their interests were directly involved.

Scattered, unfocused leadership, an inadequate sense of urgency, bureaucratic complexity, and the tangled nature of federal-state-local relations all acted to limit national assistance to areas that were or would be inundated with migrating workers and their families.[57] The National Housing Agency (NHA) and its predecessors oversaw the completion of over 2 million housing units between July 1940 and September 1945. Despite this considerable accomplishment, Senator Harry S. Truman's Senate Special Committee to Investigate the National Defense Program found NHA to be conflict ridden and inefficient, WPB complained that it was chronically behind schedule, and labor and other groups protested that living quarters in congested areas were grossly deficient.

If wartime housing left much to be desired, community assistance was even more lacking. No one agency existed to coordinate federal programs with those on state and local levels. At the outset, the NDAC's Consumer Protection Division and Division of State and Local Cooperation initiated studies and worked with states and localities on practically every major issue resulting from mass migration. Also, NDAC in September 1941 persuaded Roosevelt to set up in the Federal Security Administration what eventually became designated the Office of Community War Services (OCWS) to assist urban areas with health, medicine, nutrition, and recreation. When the Office of Production Management (OPM) replaced NDAC in January 1941, commission progress suffered. In April 1941, the newly created OPACS, later the Office of Civilian Supply (OCS), absorbed and overwhelmed the Consumer Protection Division. The Division of State and Local Cooperation was replaced by the Office of Civilian Defense (OCD) in May 1941. With OPACS, OCS, and OCD directing their efforts elsewhere, NDAC's promising initiatives involving congested communities were lost, never again to achieve such focused attention.

Although the American civilian population fared well compared with those of other belligerents, the availability of adequate housing and the whole range of community facilities and services could and should have been better. Not only would improvements in these areas have served the war effort, but also some, maybe even most, would have carried over into the postwar years to improve general standards of living.

Although such committees as the Truman and the Tolan were supportive, although critical, of the Roosevelt administration, others were corrosive and disruptive. In that regard, Senator Howard W. Smith's (D-VA) Special Committee to Investigate Acts of Executive Agencies beyond the Scope of Their Authority and Representative Martin Dies's (D-TX) Special Committee to Investigate Un-American Activities stand out.[58] Smith ruthlessly hounded OPA and other wartime agencies. Through his crusades against alleged subversives, Dies exacerbated already tense congressional relations with the Roosevelt administration. Smith and Dies exemplified the venomous and frequent assaults in Congress on the president, his advisers, New Dealers, and bureaucrats. Republicans had no monopoly on vitriol; conservative Democrats, particularly from the South, matched or went beyond them on more than one occasion.

All this divisive, ugly activity took place while the nation was at war against formidable opponents. While America reached the zenith of munitions output and saw the war turn in its favor during 1943, hostility toward the White House was only a degree less poisonous then than in 1942, when conditions at home and abroad ranged from discouraging to threatening. Promises of eschewing politics by both parties after Pearl Harbor were broken practically while they were being uttered.

Reasons for the highly charged political atmosphere were both immediate and basic. America had latitude for politics as usual because the mainland was never violated or even seriously threatened. Even then, however, rancor seemed to go beyond normal levels. Tension generated by fundamental and ongoing change was involved. Within less than a decade, a primarily conservative, isolationist, and majority Republican Party had faced the trauma of adjusting to minority-party status, New Deal regulatory-welfare reforms, and an interventionist-internationalist foreign policy. Simultaneously, numerous conservative Southern Democrats were torn over their support for collective security, basic opposition to much of the New Deal, and growing anxiety about race relations and diminishing power within the Democratic Party. Late in the 1930s, there began to appear the political curiosity of Southern Democrats joining Republicans to thwart Roosevelt and domestic reform.[59]

Regardless of positions on policies abroad, conservative Republicans and Democrats alike looked with disfavor on an activist foreign policy and war inevitably strengthening further presidential powers and the state.[60] Their frustration and bitterness grew as the enormously talented, elusive, and manipulative Roosevelt achieved unprecedented reelection for third and forth terms. In that regard, the emerging Republican–conservative Democrat coalition responded to the process of harnessing the economy in mixed ways. It was alarmed by New Dealers, labor, and other all-outers shaping principal mobilization policies between 1940 and 1942. At the same time, it was comforted by the growing presence in Washington of industrialists, financiers, and attorneys who worked in harmony with the armed services. With such a conservative alliance increasingly dominating the wartime economy in 1943 and after, New Dealers, economists, and academics could be subordinated in or removed from mobilization administrations.

Major transformations wrought by depression, reform, and war roiled the party system and frayed political nerves, accounting for much of the rancor that characterized Washington. Despite the tumult, the conservative coalition that came to dominate Congress did not and could not try to undo basic New Deal reforms. Indeed, in 1940 and 1944, the Republican Party and its candidates no longer ran against and even tacitly endorsed the New Deal.

Assessing Congress's overall performance during the defense and war years is difficult. Despite a great deal of reluctance and hesitation, Congress acted responsibly in the majority of instances. Many, probably most, permanent, special, and select committees of both houses worked diligently in writing legislation, conducting hearings, and taking other steps to inform Congress's work and oversee executive action. The nation's legislators also fulfilled a vital role in maintaining contact with and voicing the attitudes of their constituents.

All that said, however, Congress was far from inspiring, and too often its conduct bordered on the disgraceful. Overrepresenting rural areas, the nation's legislators not only acted in ways that served parochial agricultural interests but also threatened the operations of mobilization agencies such as OPA.

Although the comparison is not totally apt in terms of the war's length, Congress during World War I performed better, although it was hardly above reproach. With the Woodrow Wilson administration practically paralyzed over economic mobilization, for example, the legislators moved to force needed reform. And congresses of World War I faced nearly as much change and transformation as those of World War II did.

Returning to James MacGregor Burns's "atmosphere of conflict" within which the Roosevelt administration operated during World War II, several points stand out. First, in terms of formulating and enforcing a program for sound wartime finances and economic stabilization, both Congress and the administration recognized an invisible line of conflict that both attempted to avoid crossing. From that tacit agreement, generally successful economic policies emerged. Second, Congress, like industry and the military, accepted New Dealers formulating policies both for successful economic mobilization and for stabilization despite often-shared fears and resentment of those associated with Leon Henderson. Conservatives in and out of Congress followed New Dealers because they had to. No other person or group so consistently led in first pushing forward the program for economic preparedness and then fashioning policies and mechanisms for ensuring mobilization success. Finally, and ironically, the New Deal and New Dealers acted as model and theorists for adjusting and adapting the crude mobilization system of World War I to meet the nearly overwhelming demands of World War II.

That fundamental reality, and the contradictions that it involved, goes a long way in accounting for both the success of World War II economic mobilization and the unending conflict concerning it both within and outside Congress.

17
RECONVERSION

Formulating and implementing policies for reconversion stretched from around April 1943 until the war's end and became extremely controversial. In a sense, demobilization created more problems than mobilization because greater choice was involved. After Pearl Harbor, Washington struggled with how best to maximize munitions output in the shortest possible time, not with whether such production should be undertaken. Such an imperative was missing with reconversion. Once hostilities ceased, munitions and related contracts could be canceled, mobilization agencies and controls ended, and the economy allowed to readjust on its own to peacetime conditions. That is approximately what took place after World War I.

Few advocated such an approach. World War I policies helped precipitate a brief but severe postwar depression, the Great Depression had increased vastly the state's size and economic sophistication, and American participation in World War II dwarfed its participation in World War I in every way. Nearly all agreed that demobilizing the economy required early and extensive preparation. But consensus stopped there. Disagreements always existed over policy, roles for government vis-à-vis industry and civilian versus military agencies, and, most immediately, when reconversion should commence.

While all these issues had a practical dimension, they also involved intensely ideological matters. Liberal New Dealers, supported by organized labor, some small business and farm elements, and consumer groups, favored reconversion that ensured economic stability, equity, and the short- and long-run welfare of the population. Such goals could best be achieved through careful planning and gradual relaxation of wartime controls. Although its views varied in terms of size, product, geography, and like considerations, industry generally agreed that demobilization should disturb least the economic status quo, not serve as a vehicle for reform, and be guided by businessmen in government service. While planning was necessary, industry increasingly supported demobilization that was short in duration and quickly lifted War Production Board (WPB) regulations.

These differing conceptions were complicated greatly by divisions within WPB, which became the primary reconversion agency. Donald M. Nelson, the board chair, favored the liberal approach. He intended to use it in reclaiming control of the board, which he had largely lost to Charles E. Wilson, the executive chair and head of the Production Executive Committee (PEC). Wilson became identified with industry's demobilization outlook. Neither Nelson nor Wilson and their respective supporters alone could prevail in disputes over returning the economy to peace. An emerging stalemate was broken by the armed services siding with the Wilson forces. They were able to break the stalemate because of their vast procurement powers and their dominant position within PEC. Insisting that the central concern was not policy but when reconversion was implemented, the War and Navy Departments and United States Maritime Commission, supported or at least not opposed by most WPB industrialists, blocked demobilization movement until nearly the war's end. As a result, WPB minimized public planning, quickly lifted multiple wartime controls, and terminated its operations in November 1945.

Consistency of sorts characterized the roles of New Deal elements, industry, and the military involving both conversion and reconversion. Leon Henderson and his supporters had steadily pushed for maximum munitions output from 1940 into 1942 over industry's resistance and the military's confusion. Henderson's protégés and successors were again in the forefront of those calling for the careful direction of the economy from war to peace. The difference was that necessity ensured the success of New Dealers with conversion; choice gave the advantage to industry and the military with reconversion. In a larger sense, however, basic decisions for conversion and reconversion always rested with industry and the military, the principal sources of supply and demand. It was that reality that dictated the wartime alliance between the two. At best, New Dealers never did more than influence the direction of events under the right circumstances.

FROM THE KANZLER REPORT TO NELSON'S FOUR-POINT PLAN, APRIL 1943–JUNE 1944

With munitions output reaching peak levels in 1943, Nelson turned his attention to reconversion.[1] In April 1943, he recalled Ernest Kanzler to conduct for the WPB a preliminary study of what demobilization would require and how the board could begin preparing for it. A well-known member of corporate America, Kanzler was a former Ford Motor Company executive, related by marriage to Henry Ford, and board chair of the Ford-related Universal Credit Corporation of Detroit. He had served in the Office of Production Management (OPM), the Supply Priorities and Allocations Board, and WPB between 1941 and 1943. After completing his study, Kanzler late in June submitted his findings and recommendations to Nelson.[2]

Kanzler's report touched on most of the significant issues involved in reconversion. He emphasized the need for centralized control and pointed out that WPB was the logical agency for that role. In terms of specifics, he recommended that the board's Procurement Policy Board lead in formulating uniform contract termination clauses, take an active role in contract cancellations, and coordinate financial settlements with contractors. Government-owned plant and machinery had to be divided into appropriate categories for retention or disposal and excess civilian supplies and munitions held by the armed services liquidated in an orderly way. Most critically, the transition from a war- to a peacetime economy should be programmed through the use of WPB's allocation, limitation, conservation, and priority powers. The process would begin gradually and accelerate as munitions output was cut back. As long as resources remained scarce, the board should use quotas in dividing resumed civilian output among firms in an industry and determine whether and when new producers would be allowed into the field. The Office of Civilian Requirements (OCR) and industry divisions, advised by industry advisory committees, could provide data for determining the order and magnitude of industries returning to their normal production patterns. If small business needed assistance, that could be provided by the Smaller War Plants Corporation (SWPC).[3]

Kanzler, in effect, proposed that, for purposes of demobilization, WPB reverse its mobilization operations in stages. On the basis of the report, Nelson prepared a memorandum for the president in late August 1943 explaining what reconversion involved, WPB's qualifications for handling the task, and that the board should take preliminary steps at once. Apparently receiving Franklin D. Roosevelt's overt or tacit approval, Nelson in September directed the Planning Division of Stacy May's Bureau of Planning and Statistics to undertake a full-scale study of reconversion policy. Simultaneously, he had the operations vice chair begin reviewing the myriad limitation, conservation, and similar orders that WPB had issued in converting the economy so that they could be rationally modified or lifted for demobilization.[4]

While his action was ultimately blocked by Wilson's forces within WPB and the military outside it, Nelson first encountered criticism from sympathetic elements within the board. Leon Henderson, still unofficially involved in mobilization, pointed out in July that, in writing his report, Kanzler had relied too heavily on industrialists, neglecting numerous economists and other professionals, and that he had offered too little to the public, consumers, and labor.[5] William L. Batt, vice chair for international supply, wrote Nelson at the end of August that, in converting the economy, WPB emphasized maximum output in the shortest time with little regard for cost or means. Maintaining public confidence during demobilization required different priorities. Specifically, he joined Henderson in warning that the dominant voice of industry advisory committees would have to be greatly toned down. Furthermore, he agreed with Kanzler that "the Military point of view" had to be diminished. "As we go back into peace," Batt insisted, "the Military naturally has less and less interest and influence, and social and economic considerations have more and more."[6] Robert E. Johnson, chief of the Military Requirements Section, Materials Branch, in June 1944 went even further. For reconversion, he maintained, the strength of the economy as a whole and the highest levels of employment must be the gauge, not the armed forces' exclusive concentration on winning the war. That meant not only overruling narrow military judgments but also overcoming "the effect of habit-forming associations between WPB personnel and the Military over the past several years. The authoritarian point of view is now so deeply ingrained in many of our people that nothing short of a basic reorganization can be expected to correct it."[7]

Well aware of the validity of his critics' charges, Nelson first had to stake out WPB's reconversion turf. Kanzler had encouraged him to move quickly: "Activity along this line is beginning to break out all over as if by spontaneous combustion."[8] The board could lose out to other agencies if it dallied. In November 1943, the Senate created a Special Committee on Post-War Economic Policy and Planning (the George Committee, after its chair, Walter F. George [D-GA]), and, in the spring of 1944, the House of Representatives set up a special committee of the same name chaired by William M. Colmer (D-MS). The Senate Special Committee to Investigate the National Defense Program (the Truman Committee) and other congressional committees were also focusing on both general and specific aspects of demobilization.[9] Furthermore, Harold D. Smith, director of the Bureau of the Budget, began angling to have his office act as demobilization coordinator.[10] Most significantly, James F. Byrnes, director of the Office of War Mobilization (OWM), soon to become by statute the Office of War Mobilization and Reconversion (OWMR), began consulting appropriate officials on reconversion and arranged for the president to instruct him "to take charge of the consideration of demobilization."[11] The War Mobilization and Reconversion Act of October 1944, which expanded OWM to OWMR, established statutory authority for Byrnes's office. "From this point on," notes the Bureau of the Budget history, "preparation for peace was largely initiated and guided by the new agency."[12]

Nonetheless, WPB was still the basic organization for formulating and implementing reconversion policy. OWM/OWMR remained a policymaking and coordinating body. Nelson made his first formal reconversion move at the November 30, 1943, meeting of the WPB. With munitions production peaking and military demand beginning to drop, surplus facilities, materials, and labor would become available. When that occurred, the chair asked the board whether it believed that greater civilian output should be permitted as long as more urgent production was not deterred. With Secretary of Commerce Jesse H. Jones and War Manpower Commission (WMC) Chair Paul V. McNutt answering in the affirmative and no one dissenting, Nelson declared that that would be official WPB policy.[13]

Nelson had seized the reconversion initiative. However, his position was not yet secure. On November 4, 1943, Byrnes announced that he had called on the elder statesmen Bernard M. Baruch and John M. Hancock to direct a Reconversion Unit in his office and to write a report on demobilization. Byrnes noted that Baruch and Hancock would not replace the WPB but simply outline a plan for various agencies to follow. Despite the disclaimer, Washington's rumor mill speculated about Nelson being elbowed aside or the WPB chair and Baruch competing for power and position.[14]

In fact, Nelson moved quickly in attempting to establish amicable relations with Baruch and Hancock. He and Wilson met with Byrnes's assistants, and Nelson forwarded to them board memoranda, reports, and studies, including the Planning Division's work, which covered most aspects of demobilization.[15] Nelson went even further. In a candid letter to Baruch of December 29, 1943, he expressed his distress over "external forces driving a wedge into our personal relationship" through false stories fed to the press about rivalry and treachery. Nelson was reported to be alarmed and hurt by what he perceived to be Baruch's cool response of January 7.[16] His concern was not imagined. On January 3, Baruch informed Secretary of War Henry L. Stimson that he now agreed with the War Department that Charles E. Wilson had to replace Nelson and that he would so inform the president.[17]

Actually, the Nelson-Baruch relationship had been strained since 1942, if not before. After all, earlier in 1943, Baruch had participated in a War Department–Byrnes plot to oust Nelson from his position in favor of Baruch. The enormously egotistical and sensitive Baruch felt that Nelson and his principal lieutenants in the Henderson circle ignored his advice, considered him to be outdated, and denied him the deference he deserved. Such was not the case with the armed services. Beginning in 1940–1941, the War and Navy Departments welcomed, even courted, the elder statesman. His relations were especially close with Under Secretary of War Robert P. Patterson and Under Secretary of the Navy James V. Forrestal, somewhat less so with Chief of Staff George C. Marshall and Stimson. A partnership of mutual benefit grew. It was based in part on shared views. Both Baruch and the army and navy command structure accepted the need for and the operations of the emerging industry-military mobilization alliance. That was the case despite Baruch's interwar fears that War Department procurement and economic mobilization planning could lead to the military dominating a wartime economy.[18]

But more was involved. As a Washington insider with great influence among congressional conservatives, particularly Southern Democrats, and important contacts with the press, Baruch was a valuable ally. For that reason, Roosevelt tolerated the self-important, often trying South Carolinian. For his part, Baruch received from the military the respect and adulation denied him by Nelson and WPB. As tension increased between WPB and the War Department in 1942–1943, Baruch drew ever closer to the armed services. As a shrewd calculator of power, Baruch was able to discern that, in the "Battle of Washington," the armed services would win. Not only did Baruch want to be among the victors, but he also luxuriated in associating with military leaders, who inevitably outshone economic mobilizers during war.

Baruch's positive association with the War and Navy Departments was complicated by his temperamental relations with Byrnes. The two were very similar in that they both had massive ego needs and sought recognition in their own right. Baruch resented Byrnes not consulting him regularly or following his advice as director of first economic stabilization and then war mobilization. On his part, Byrnes tired of Baruch's constant and frequently unwelcomed flow of exhortatory memoranda and the unending need to have his pride assuaged. Whenever possible and appropriate, Byrnes turned to Baruch, as was the case with the West Coast manpower crisis and reconversion. However, the OWM/OWMR director did so as much out of desire to occupy the elder statesman and use his prestige as to benefit from his knowledge and experience. Tension between Byrnes and Baruch disturbed the War Department. The latter looked to using Baruch, in Stimson's words, as its "backstairs operator" for influencing OWM.[19]

The Baruch-Hancock Report on reconversion was submitted to Byrnes on February 15, 1944. It was shaped significantly by the studies of WPB and thereafter served as the overall guide for demobilization. The two elder statesmen recommended against a new agency for guiding the nation from war to peace and instead for a more sharply focused OWM carrying out policymaking and coordinating functions in that regard. Anticipating the sudden collapse of Germany, the armed services and WPB together should prepare plans for a smooth transition from a two- to a one-front war. Working with the procurement administrations, the WMC, and other agencies, WPB would use and adapt its structure and controls for guiding the increase of civilian production as munitions contracts were cut back.

The principal thrust of the report was maintaining economic stability through expeditious demobilization. "Speed in shifting this productive capacity from war to peace," asserted Baruch and Hancock, "is our most effective attack against the two enemies which threaten in the transition and post-war period—unemployment and inflation." To accelerate the process to "peacetime enterprises," the report emphasized uniform termination articles to be included in all prime and subcontracts. Working with established rules, trained procurement agency settlement teams could quickly and finally reimburse firms when contracts ended or were terminated. Tying up funds through extensive preaudits advocated by the comptroller general "would quibble the Nation into a panic." Additionally, a surplus property administrator should be appointed to inventory and dispose of surplus facilities and equipment in useful and orderly ways. Government property should be removed from private plants within sixty days after being inventoried to facilitate firms resuming peacetime production.

Baruch and Hancock emphasized productive capacity. Human factors received some attention. The two advisers recommended that a "Work Director" be established in OWM to assist all workers, particularly returning veterans, in job placement. Also, they advised that various public works be readied in the event of extensive unemployment.

Finally, Baruch and Hancock suggested that their programs gain legislative sanction. Executive orders should serve only as a temporary expedient until Congress acted.[20]

Roosevelt indirectly endorsed Baruch and Hancock's handiwork by quickly issuing executive orders in February 1944 setting up in OWM a Surplus War Property Administration (SWPA) and a Retraining and Reemployment Administration. Byrnes selected William L. Clayton, assistant secretary of commerce and right-wing Texas cotton broker, to head the first and General Frank T. Hines, the conservative head of the Veterans Administration, to be in charge of the second.[21]

Congress had been examining various aspects of demobilization since early in 1943 and moved to the legislative stage beginning in mid-1944. On July 1, 1944, the Contract Settlement Act, creating the Office of Contract Settlement (OCS), became law. The nation's legislators combined their work with that of

OWM in this regard. Since 1942, the WPB's Procurement Policy Board had been working with the procurement agencies in behalf of a uniform contract termination clause. The issue became quite urgent in 1943 as contracts began to be canceled without any set pattern, a matter that distressed industry. Under WPB pressure, progress was made, but no final solution emerged. Intense disagreements arose between the army and the navy, and the two services resisted a civilian agency directing termination settlements. Breaking the impasse, the War Department succeeded in having OWM remove the issue from WPB in October 1943 and place it under a Joint Contract Termination Board (JCTB), headed by Hancock as an OWM representative, in November. By January 1944, the new board had devised a uniform contract termination clause that Byrnes ordered into effect for all procurement agencies as well as procedures for shutting down contracts. Baruch and Hancock incorporated the essence of JCTB's efforts in their report, and the Contract Settlement Act was consistent with the elder statesmen's recommendations.

By all accounts, OCS was an unqualified success. It guided the settlement of billions of dollars of contracts with exceptional efficiency and speed. By the end of 1945, 83 percent of canceled contracts had been settled, and, by mid-1946, the office's work was all but done. Throughout its existence, OCS was praised by most and criticized by practically none.[22]

The handling of surplus property was less successful and harmonious. The SWPA was absorbed by the congressionally created Surplus Property Board in October 1944, then by the Surplus Property Administration in September 1945, and finally, in effect, by the War Assets Administration in November 1945. Unlike terminating existing contracts, disposing of surplus property generated a great deal of attention, controversy, and congressional involvement.[23]

The Baruch-Hancock Report was silent on the critical issues of how WPB would formulate reconversion policy, which subdivisions of WPB would make key decisions, and when a program should commence. By February 1944, those matters had already reached a point of great contention within the board and between it and the armed services, especially the War Department.

In obtaining on November 30, 1943, WPB's support for increasing civilian production when conditions permitted, Nelson did not address the vital matter of how industries and firms would be selected. Programming that was used for military and essential civilian production seemed the logical means. Kanzler had proposed that solution. Planning for civilian goods would increase as military demand declined until a point was reached where resources were ample to lift controls and phase out programming. The Planning Division in its preliminary report of January 1944 advocated an approach similar to Kanzler's but more flexible. Along those lines, Vice Chair Julius A. Krug's Program Bureau and its subdivision, the Requirements Committee, in November began implementing plans for greater essential civilian output by inviting proposals from the OCR and other claimant agencies. Most WPB executives agreed that, as long as production was programmed, prewar producers would be granted quotas and new firms restricted to residual output.[24]

The programmed approach ran into difficulty almost from the outset. Late in 1943, Nelson had WPB begin adjusting the restrictive controls necessary for such production to take place, but the process turned out to be extraordinarily complex and agonizingly slow. By mid-1944, only modest progress had been made. Even when additional civilian goods gained approval and were in conformity with WPB regulations, the armed services representatives on the divisional requirement committees blocked their approval because the War and Navy Departments were determined to halt Nelson's program. Facing these realities, the WPB chair by slow stages and on the advice of various sources decided on a different approach, one that was incorporated in his four reconversion orders of June 1944. According to these orders, all manufacturers could begin to prepare for peacetime production, and, in certain instances such production could commence immediately through exemption from all existing WPB restrictions—a nonprogrammed, open-ended approach. Nelson's decision to cut through various obstacles to greater civilian output led to a major mobilization blowup, resulting in both himself and Wilson leaving WPB in August 1944.[25]

Of more immediate importance than the methods used to expand civilian production was the WPB subdivision to be in charge of reconversion. Intent on regaining control of the board from Wilson and the PEC, Nelson favored Julius A. Krug's Program Bureau. Krug supported Nelson's reconversion policies, and, as one of the few nonbusiness vice chairs in the board, he, as well as his bureau, staffed principally with economists and professionals, would be more disinterested in handling the multiple and sensitive readjustment issues. Nelson wanted to restrict PEC's reconversion role to that of cutting back military contracts.

In December 1943, the WPB chair had Bernard L. Gladieux draft an organizational plan for handling demobilization. Gladieux proposed that the PEC be expanded to include in its membership the vice chair for civilian requirements and that the committee would have final authority over contract terminations. In determining companies, industries, and areas for cutbacks, PEC would operate through a subcommittee, the Production Adjustment Committee. The armed services and the Maritime Commission would have representatives on this new committee, but the committee would be headed by the program vice chair and include the vice chairs for operations, civilian requirements, manpower requirements, and labor production, and without portfolio. Unlike PEC, this subcommittee would be dominated by civilians. Moreover, and more important, the program vice chair would have overall direction of reconversion, relating the work of PEC to that of the board as a whole and determining how much, when, and where civilian production would take place as military output dropped. To facilitate its work, the Bureau of Planning and Statistics, the program and requirement functions of the Facilities Bureau, and the Procurement Policies Division would be transferred to the Program Bureau. Furthermore, the Program Bureau would rely heavily on industry divisions in carrying out its readjustment duties.[26]

Significantly, Gladieux's plan was countered, not by Wilson or another WPB official, but by General Lucius D. Clay, the Army Service Forces (ASF) representative on PEC and a driving force on the committee. In December 1943 and January 1944, Clay advocated that PEC make decisions on expanded civilian production and that it set up a structure for doing so. At Clay's initiative, a drafting committee was organized in January to work out the details. At the end of February, the committee recommended that PEC create a Production Planning and Adjustment Committee (PPAC) chaired by Wilson and made up of nearly an equal number of WPB vice chairs and representatives from the armed services and the Maritime Commission. The committee was to recommend to PEC policies on cutbacks, on increased nonmilitary output and how it would be implemented, and on demobilization plans following VE and VJ Days. Stacy May's Bureau of Planning and Statistics would act as the technical staff for PPAC, and May would serve as its executive officer.[27]

The plan was largely that of the War Department, and it had several outstanding features. First, in terms of contract modification or termination, PEC would have only advisory powers with full authority continuing with the armed services; for expanded civilian output and partial and full reconversion, the committee would have total control over both policy and the details of implementation. Second, not only would the Program Bureau and the Requirements Committee be denied any reconversion role, but their existing policies of programming expanded essential civilian goods as military demand declined would also be halted. The War Department considered Krug and his staff to be untrustworthy because of their identification with Nelson. All in all, Clay's approach would practically end Nelson's ability to shape demobilization; PEC and the armed services would take charge.

With the Gladieux and Clay proposals on the table, WPB stalemated over reconversion from March to May 1944 because Nelson would neither approve the latter plan nor move to implement the former. Had the WPB chair attempted to put in place the approach that he favored, he would most likely have precipitated a showdown with PEC and the armed forces that he did not want and had no confidence that he could win. Yet he was not about to turn demobilization over to Wilson. The executive vice chair claimed that he wanted to leave WPB, but the president, probably at the urging of the military, persuaded him to hold off. With Wilson still intending to resign during the summer, Nelson appeared to be waiting for his departure before deciding on the organizational structure for handling reconversion.

Despite the insistence of Byrnes in March and Baruch and Hancock in May that action was essential, Nelson held off. His resolve appeared to be strengthened, rather then diminished, by a frustrated Krug resigning in April as program vice chair. Wilson and PEC were determined to ban him from any meaningful demobilization role, and Krug was unwilling to challenge them. Indeed, in April, Nelson appointed a Policy Committee for Civilian Production that he would chair and that was composed of prominent leaders from the government, media, banking, industry, business, and labor to advise him on reconversion. The WPB chair worked out the arrangement with Arthur D. Whiteside, former vice chair for civilian requirements. He intended to use the clout of this group to offset the armed services' influence in formulating reconversion policies, convinced that these were primarily civilian, not military, responsibilities. Before Nelson could get the committee under way, a crisis forced the WPB chair to go in directions that he had previously resisted.[28]

Late in May 1944, the navy suddenly canceled a fighter plane contract at the Brewster Aeronautical Corporation on Long Island on short notice and without arranging for a replacement contract or the transfer of the workforce to other facilities. Outraged workers staged a "stay-in-strike" until they were assured employment. To deal with the immediate situation, a new contract was rushed to the corporation. More important, the episode gained national exposure and highlighted the necessity of dealing with contract modification in a more rational fashion. Nelson was now forced to act. He reluctantly instructed Wilson to set up a structure under PEC for handling munitions cutbacks. Wilson did so by creating the Production Executive Committee Staff (PECS), made up of representatives from appropriate subdivisions of WPB, WMC, and the procurement agencies and intended to advise PEC on contract curtailments. Probably because of growing conflict between Nelson and Wilson, official instructions to the staff and the role of PEC in cutbacks and increased civilian output remained especially vague. On June 5, Byrnes stepped in to clarify the situation. Bypassing the WPB chair, he directed Wilson to have PECS determine uniform policies for contract cancellations and required the procurement agencies to clear all cutbacks and terminations with the staff.[29]

Both Wilson and Nelson interpreted Byrnes's action as encouraging PEC to seize the reconversion initiative. Accordingly, Wilson on June 7 selected Arthur H. Bunker as director of PECS and vice chair of PEC and, shortly thereafter, as deputy executive vice chair of WPB. Bunker, along with John M. Hancock, was from Lehman Brothers, had been vice chair of Metals and Minerals, and was now Wilson's principal assistant. Around the same time, Samuel W. Anderson, an investment banker who was closely associated with Bunker in WPB and who would join Lehman Brothers after the war, was appointed program vice chair, replacing Krug. Anderson assumed a significant reconversion role. The same was true for Operations Vice Chair Lemuel R. Boulware, vice-president and general manager of Celotex Corporation, a trusted Wilson assistant who joined the General Electric Company after the war and pioneered its policies for countering labor unions. Ephraim F. Jeffe, on leave from his position as vice-president of the Consolidated Edison System Companies, who became in June 1944 an army reserve brigadier general, transferred from ASF headquarters in February 1943 to serve as Wilson's executive assistant, replacing New Dealer Mordecai Ezekiel. In June 1943, Jeffe took over as executive secretary of the PEC. Gladieux describes him as being more military than the military. He played an important role in PEC operations and obviously transferred from ASF to WPB as part of the board's accommodation of the army as it took over the critically important production scheduling. Also, Stacy May and William B. Murphy, deputy vice chair for production, were appointed deputy directors of PECS. Wilson was streamlining PEC for reconversion purposes and selecting for key slots capable executives known and loyal to him.[30]

Of additional significance in economic mobilization and demobilization was not just the corporate, financial, or legal connections of leading WPB officials but the future business positions to which high military officers were destined. After retiring from the army, for example, General Brehon B. Somervell, ASF commanding general, was recruited by the Mellon group and took over in 1946 as Koppers Company's president and board chair; and Clay on retiring in 1949 became chair of the board of Continental Can Company and, in 1963, a senior partner in Lehman Brothers. Circulation among the armed services and corporate America had begun before World War II, but, with the large wartime military then and during the Cold War, the practice became much more prevalent and important.[31]

Nelson realized that he had to move quickly and effectively to maintain authority over reconversion. By mid-1944, he had abandoned the idea of programmed increases in civilian output as military curtailment occurred. The complexity involved was overwhelming, and the process could break down at a number of points. Drawing on ideas from the Planning Division, the advice of other WPB officials, and the enthusiastic support of Maury Maverick, head of the SWPC, Nelson decided on a four-point reconversion program. The program could be implemented with minimal revision of existing WPB regulations and controls and without much action on the part of WPB in general and PEC in particular.[32]

Nelson issued his plan on June 18 after the Normandy invasion and once assured that the munitions program was sound. The plan consisted of the following: (1) lifting restrictions on the use of aluminum and magnesium; (2) allowing firms to make a working model of a product for postwar production; (3) permitting manufacturers to purchase surplus machine tools and dies, or place unrated orders for them, for peacetime output; and (4) granting WPB regional offices the power to authorize production of any nonmilitary goods as long as resources were available and such output did not interfere with the war effort. The last point, known as spot authorization since it would be handled by WPB field officials, was by far the most controversial. Nelson intended for the plan to go into effect on July 1. Instead, it was first stretched out over a six-week period and then all but blocked in its entirety.

Nelson's opponents never fought him on the issue of reconversion per se; instead, they insisted that their opposition stemmed from differences over timing, or when demobilization should be implemented. The armed services—and particularly the War Department—led the challenge to the WPB chair, but most of the board executives ultimately followed the military's lead. Why they did so became and remains as controversial as the issue of reconversion itself.

The War Department took and maintained the lead in opposing the WPB on reconversion, particularly Nelson, but also Julius A. Krug after Nelson left and Krug returned to the board. General Brehon B. Somervell, commanding general of ASF, Clay, director of material, ASF, and Under Secretary of War Robert P. Patterson were the principal department spokesmen, but they operated with the obvious approval and, when necessary, the support of Secretary Henry L. Stimson. Clay, as the army's representative on PEC, and Patterson, speaking for the War Department on WPB, were the principal combatants. Taking his signals from Somervell, Clay was the official most involved on a day-to-day basis, acting as the driving, aggressive prosecuting or defense attorney. The Navy Department followed the War Department's lead with Secretary and Under Secretary of the Navy Frank Knox and Forrestal and Admiral Samuel M. Robinson, chief of the Office of Procurement and Material (OP&M), always more flexible and manifesting less ardor. The Maritime Commission lent its voice when such seemed essential. Chief of Staff Marshall, Commander-in-Chief Ernest J. King, Chief of Staff to the President William D. Leahy, and the Joint Chiefs of Staff (JCS), separately or together, were called on for backup as necessary.[33]

The armed services were motivated by a number of concerns. Most directly, with a worldwide war to conduct, they wanted to ensure that logistics did not undermine strategy. It was always better to have too many than too few tools of war. Allowed to set their own requirements free of outside review from the outset, the military resented civilians intruding on its territory. That was certainly the case during the feasibility dispute and was evident in the struggles over materials allocations and production scheduling. With reconversion policy tied to estimated military demand, civilians again appeared to be moving in on armed services prerogatives. A natural inclination to resist set in. Moreover, especially with the War Department and Patterson in particular, too high a level of homefront comfort could threaten public awareness of and support for the war. Civilian want served military interests.

More with the army than with the navy, legitimate concern for ample supply blended over into arrogance and abuse. Stimson, Patterson, and Somervell assumed, not only that they were right in their battles with Nelson, but also that their opponents were misguided, even unpatriotic. That being the case, the War Department leaders repeatedly used strategic necessity to cut off debate, twisted truth to suit their purposes, and sought support from a harried and exhausted president increasingly detached from the homefront and depending excessively on militarily oriented advisers. A growing dislike of and disdain for Nelson on the part of the armed services, particularly among War Department leaders, made matters worse and gave the dispute a personal quality.

All that said, the armed services would not have been allowed to go beyond their proper sphere without the support of or a lack of resistance from corporate America. The business community's opposition to national service played an important part in blocking the military's drive for such legislation; industry's ultimate support for feasible requirements, a proper allocation system, and production scheduling was essential for their adoption. Discerning why so many industry leaders bowed to the army and navy's views on reconversion remains both an intriguing and an enormously significant matter.

Motives aside, War Department challenge to Nelson's November 30, 1943, decision to allow increased civilian output under the right circumstances was quick to develop. Obviously, the WPB chair's announcement created great concern among the military and led to the department organizing forces against him. At the next meeting of WPB on December 28, Patterson questioned the chair's desire to ease restrictions on nonwar facilities. When Nelson at the January 11, 1944, board meeting proposed officially allowing greater latitude for essential civilian construction and facilities involving railroads, schools, roads, and the like as the growing availability of resources allowed, he encountered general opposition. Most on the board believed that any change in policy should await a clarification of the military situation. The public might misread WPB action as an indication that the end of the war was in sight and respond accordingly. Furthermore, the projects that Nelson had in mind could be brought under existing WPB regulations on essential non-military requirements. Patterson was among those strongly opposed to the chair's move, while others were more conciliatory. Bowing to board views, Nelson supported a unanimous decision temporarily postponing any change in policy on construction and facilities.[34]

The armed services appeared to have won their first reconversion victory. Although the January 11 decision related only to facilities and construction, it was usually taken as involving demobilization policy in general. Nelson seemed to endorse such an interpretation when he informed the press on January 17 that any increase in less essential civilian output would have to wait until the invasion of Europe. In retrospect, Nelson was responding characteristically. Arguments during the WPB meeting were cogent, urgent civilian needs could be met under existing policies, and planning would go forward. Delaying a formal decision was not that consequential. Compromise made sense. Had reconversion been handled along the lines of Nelson's January response, the bitter battles that ensued could have been avoided. The major difficulty was that the military and most WPB corporate leaders sought, not compromise, but domination. As that became clear, Nelson grew more determined to institute policies he believed to be in the public interest.

From December 1943 through Nelson's departure from WPB in August 1944, the War Department led in an unrelenting drive to halt reconversion action. The armed services argued that they had no objection to and even encouraged planning. It was overt acts that they opposed. Such acts could set off a stampede for peacetime production, denying the military needed munitions. Firms could be distracted from completing existing contracts or refuse new ones, workers could leave or decline munitions employment, and the public could lose its sense of urgency. As long as hard and unpredictable combat existed anywhere, all threats to production had to be minimized. The morale and welfare of the fighting forces demanded nothing less.

Of particular concern to the armed services was labor. It had been the principal factor limiting output since mid-1943. No overall shortage of workers existed, but specific skills were in high demand, congested areas faced problems, and foundries, tire factories, and other industries were stressed. With contracts being cut back, pockets of unemployment began to appear and would grow in number. Patterson, Somervell, and others insisted that holding back reconversion would force workers without jobs to migrate to where they were needed. New York should not increase civilian output if war contractors were hiring in St. Louis.[35]

The armed services' campaign against reconversion took place within and outside WPB and grew increasingly shrill. At meetings of the WPB from January to June 1944, the War and Navy Departments insisted that no further expansion of nonmilitary output should be countenanced regardless of positive reports on munitions programs, availability of resources, or level of civilian need. Patterson followed up a tense WPB meeting of February 22 with a letter to Nelson:

> The principal reason why no considerable resumption of civilian goods should now be undertaken is because any such program would inevitably draw manpower from essential war production. Those who say that production of consumers' goods should be commenced for the sake of providing employment at any place where workers happen to live, despite the overall need of additional workers for direct war work, place the ease and preference of a particular person above the needs of the armed forces for munitions and supplies. I know that you do not countenance any such proposition.[36]

The armed services could do more than exhort; they had the ability to act. Late in January, Krug alerted Nelson that military representatives had tied WPB in knots:

> At the present time, the entire programming machinery of Industry Division Requirements Committees is bogging down due to Army and Navy instructions to their Committee members to protest all nonmilitary expansions whatsoever. No one, including the military, is happy with this situation. It is causing a great deal of administrative friction and vexation.[37]

The military's practice of blocking additional civilian output continued even after Normandy, making the division requirements committees "practically useless." Clay explained in August 1944 that, as long as manpower shortages existed for munitions and essential goods, the army would continue to veto more civilian output requiring additional labor. The War Department's tactic interfered with, not only industry divisions, but also the Program Bureau's scheduling of essential civilian needs, OCR's efforts to prevent inadequate supplies of consumer goods and community services from hurting the war effort, the Redistribution Division's ability to handle bulging inventories of surplus materials and equipment, and SWPC's attempts to aid small business as contracts and subcontracts were reduced.[38]

Actually, the War Department was holding divisional requirement committees hostage as it attempted to block additional nonmilitary production on a higher level. Thwarted by Nelson until May 1944 in having PEC take over reconversion policy, Clay began to achieve piecemeal what he was denied on a larger scale. At the February 23 meeting of the PEC, the ASF representative persuaded the committee to hold civilian production to the first-quarter 1944 level. Since the Program Bureau had already arranged for selected output beyond that range, the military backed off only when Krug pointed out that PEC was intruding on Requirements Committee responsibilities. Nonetheless, the intervention of both Nelson and Wilson was required to move forward the specially authorized manufacture of laundry, dairy, and bakery machinery and other goods.[39]

But PEC efforts to restrict resumed or expanded civilian production went on. With labor the principal factor restricting production, WMC early in March 1944 adopted policies for minimizing essential civilian contracting in labor-tight areas or allowing it only under carefully regulated conditions. The commission asked Nelson to take the necessary action to enforce the directives. Proceeding on its own with Nelson out of Washington, the PEC early in April virtually prohibited all civilian production beyond the first-quarter 1944 level from labor-short locales. A hue and cry almost immediately arose from SWPC, OCR, and the Senate committee specializing in small business. Such an arbitrary and inflexible policy, it was argued, would hurt small business, deny civilians vitally needed goods, and waste national resources. Returning to Washington, Nelson revoked PEC action and required the committee to make its orders more consistent with WMC policies.[40]

Operating on a number of levels, the armed services kept additional civilian output limited during the first half of 1944. Some added production took place, along with the authorization in the third quarter of more farm machinery, telephones, cooking equipment, water heaters, and a few other products. In general, however, civilian goods were largely restricted to the first-quarter of 1944 level, as Clay had demanded.

Throughout the months of conflict, December 1943–June 1944, Donald M. Nelson continued to perfect his reconversion approach.[41] From the outset, the WPB chair envisaged demobilization occurring in three phases: first, planning for and some expansion of civilian production as military requirements declined; second, an accelerated pace in returning the economy to peacetime standards after Germany's defeat; and, finally, total reconversion with the war's end. Failure to prepare for and implement a gradual transition from war to peace, Nelson was convinced, could lead to economic calamity and undermine mobilization. An abrupt end to munitions and related output involving nearly half the economy would thrust the vast American economy into a severe decline reminiscent of the Great Depression. More immediately, without assurance that civilian production would pick up as military demand contracted, employers and employees alike would become distracted from the war effort and begin concentrating on their own welfare.

Expanded output for the general population, furthermore, would assist, not detract from, fulfilling munitions demand. General services in heavily industrialized areas were suffering from limited or prohibited production, goods ranging from washing machines to gloves were in short supply, and repair and replacement parts were badly needed. Addressing such essential needs would raise civilian morale and reduce absenteeism, turnover, and worker inefficiency. Additionally, war production had gone mostly to large firms. With reconversion, the smaller companies could and should be protected. They would be the first to lose contracts and subcontracts. Allowing them to resume civilian output as resources became available would benefit the nation's diverse business community, the civilian population, and workers.

Moreover, labor problems could not be solved by creating pools of unemployment. The job market had to be approached on a local and an area, not on a national, level; age, marital status, gender, class, attachment to community, training and education, and skills were all involved. With the availability of jobs reduced, most women and older workers would leave the workforce instead of migrating to centers that were hiring, and others would seek out secure peacetime employment. Labor was not a commodity, and its mobility was limited. Purposefully leaving people jobless would end up diminishing the ability to increase emergency munitions output by reducing the available workforce.

In Nelson's mind, gradually guiding the economy from war to peace maximized opportunities for ensuring stability and prosperity after hostilities ceased. WPB would be irresponsible in not pursuing those goals. Furthermore, the board had to act expeditiously. Its mandate, argued General Counsel John Lord O'Brian, ended with the surrender of Japan. By then, WPB should begin terminating its operations as the economy entered the third stage prepared for peace.

By the early months of 1944, the WPB chair and his principal assistants had gone from general to specific ideas about reconversion. Queries from Senator Francis J. Maloney (D-CT) provided Nelson with the opportunity to address critical demobilization matters in his written reply of March 7, 1944.[42] Before responding to the senator, Nelson first submitted his answers to and received the approval of all WPB vice chairs. Nelson explained, first, that, as war contracts were cut back, civilian production would be resumed according to essentiality when resources were available and the military situation secure. WPB's first responsibility remained meeting all armed services requirements and not adversely affecting morale either at home or abroad.

Second, Nelson went on, conditions would not permit all firms in an industry to resume production simultaneously or at the same relative prewar level. With regions, localities, industries, and companies released from war output at different times, public interest required nonwar production to begin when feasible, despite effects on competitive situations and hardship faced by some firms. As long as restrictive WPB controls were operative, however, expanded civilian production would be programmed along with all other military and essential output. Companies beginning peacetime production could be required to share their output with competitors in an industry still absorbed in war work. In that way, all firms could benefit from the sales of resumed civilian products. But serious obstacles made such an approach impractical in some industries. Each industry had to take up the matter separately.

Third, firms desiring to enter an industry for the first time once peace returned, Nelson affirmed, must be free to do so. Otherwise, WPB or a comparable organization would have to plan the postwar economy to protect competitive positions of prewar firms. Such a result "would do irreparable injury to the free enterprise system in the United States." However, as long as wartime controls existed and critical components were in short supply, new firms should be held back until established companies able to resume prewar output were permitted to get under way.

Fourth, according to the WPB chair, all WPB "controls should be relaxed whenever they cease to be necessary to war production." Fifth, in directing various industries, WPB would turn to representative industry advisory committees as long as their assistance was consistent with the interests of the fighting forces and the public. Finally, Nelson concluded:

> Maximum employment of workers, which lies at the heart of the public interest in peacetime, must be the essential test of any government policy affecting industrial readjustments, and the most far-sighted elements in industry accept that plain fact as a basis for their planning and expectations. There will be no deviation from this policy so long as I have responsibility for the Board's activities.

Nelson's four-point reconversion program (involving peacetime models, spot authorization, etc.), announced more than three months later, on June

18, 1944, deviated from his statement to Senator Maloney of March 7 in only one crucial way: so-called spot authorization entirely ignored prewar producers. Under the right conditions, all firms were free to enter any industry they chose as long as they gained approval from WPB regional officials. While in theory latitude was great, in fact it remained very limited. All the orders were hedged with so many safeguards and restrictions that only gradual movement could take place. Companies manufacturing an experimental peacetime model, for example, operated under the threat of losing their deferred staff of engineers and technical personnel. Spot authorization was even more encumbered. It required, in effect, the approval of WMC, and it depended on the availability of materials, components, equipment, and so forth. Nonetheless, once under way, spot authorization could grow in importance as war production declined and greater nonmilitary output was permitted.[43]

The precedent that spot authorization could set and its potential impact on competitive positions disturbed industry. Despite flush times, corporate America manifested considerable anxiety throughout the defense and war years. For a number of reasons, including fear of excess capacity, industries had hesitated to convert their facilities or devote their full efforts to war output as late as 1942. Facing reconversion several years later, many, if not most, industries displayed exceptional concern about postwar conditions. If they had their way, all firms would resume normal peacetime operations at the same time. Since that was not possible, companies reconverting early should be held to quotas based on prewar market shares with various arrangements suggested for protecting the interests of corporations still involved in war output. New entrants would be barred from an industry until existing firms claimed or declined their past level of participation, or else some percentage of estimated total production would be allotted to newcomers. To achieve and maintain such policies, control over demobilization had to be maintained at the Washington level, not delegated to the field, as spot authorization proposed.[44]

Maury Maverick, the Truman Committee, and authors such as Bruce Catton charged that, in opposing Nelson's four-point reconversion plan, giant corporations feared small business gaining a competitive edge in postwar markets, as the WPB chair intended.[45] Evidence supports the case of Maverick and others in part, but the subject is much more complex. Certainly, the corporate community showed little regard for small business's welfare, as indicated by the meager achievements of various subdivisions created for such concerns in mobilization agencies, the outcome of efforts to concentrate essential civilian industries, and the hostility aimed at OCR and its predecessors. What distressed industry was the perception of special privilege offered to small business rather than any direct challenge coming from such firms. Those same advantages could ultimately be claimed by medium-sized and even large companies; if giant corporations in the same industry returned to civilian production at different times and paces, oligopolistic patterns and practices built up over years could start to break down. Without the right policies, a competitive economic jungle threatened as hostilities began to wind down. Hence, the widespread desire in and outside WPB for uniform, national policies formulated by the board and including mobilization quotas, restrictions on new entrants, and related measures designed to start the race for postwar markets among all firms at the line existing in 1939 or thereabouts.[46]

Corporations in general saw as many dangers as opportunities in returning to economic normality. The war had vastly expanded industries and plants, changed financial markets dramatically, created huge capital reserves among war contractors, placed in workers' hands enormous buying power, opened up nearly unmeasurable opportunities for new products at home and trade abroad, and enlarged greatly and permanently the national government and the armed services. During the war, mavericks such as Henry J. Kaiser had moved into shipbuilding, steel, and other industries, and the Aluminum Company of America lost its monopoly to Reynolds Metals Company and other firms. After hostilities ended, potential competitors would abound, and established corporations would be looking to diversify into other industries.

When conversion was just getting started in 1940, the airframe firms agreed to allow the automobile companies (some of which were heavily invested in the industry) to undertake airplane output only if Detroit would commit to leaving the field at the end of hostilities. To protect their interests in the wartime creation of a virtually new synthetic rubber industry, rubber, oil, chemical, and other firms individually and collectively maneuvered in skillful and ruthless way to guard their varied interests. Worried about postwar markets and an expanding New Deal state, many corporations individually and collectively conducted extensive, imaginative advertising campaigns throughout the war years designed to keep their names before the public eye, to associate them with the public interest, and to emphasize the virtues of free enterprise over collectivism.[47] With the end of hostilities in sight, corporate America anxiously sought a transition to peace that would help quiet instead of further disturb its concerns about competitive position.

Kanzler's preliminary reconversion study and report early in 1943 appeared a reasonable reflection of WPB attitudes. Demobilization would be centralized in the board and programmed with adequate attention paid to "pre-war industry competitive relations."[48] However, just as Nelson and his supporters came to realize the potentially paralyzing complexity and vulnerability of carefully planned reconversion, so too did the corporate executives who dominated

WPB.[49] Furthermore, they began to realize that, at best, industry-directed readjustment would be intensely controversial and that, at worst, the corporate community could lose control of the process. Over substantial opposition, big business had largely had its way in converting and running the wartime economy because its plant, expertise, and personnel were indispensable. With the end of the war in sight, that was no longer necessarily true. Despite various safeguards, dollar-a-year men and industry advisory committees were coming under attack. WPB General Counsel O'Brian remained uncomfortable with WPB powers used for guiding the transition to peace. And the Justice Department began again considering the use of antitrust laws to limit business's latitude. Labor demanded a greater role in industry divisions and industry itself during and after reconversion. Maury Maverick attacked the corporate structure for its shabby treatment of small business, and the Special Committee to Study and Survey the Problems of American Small Business (the Murray Committee, after its chair, Senator James E. Murray [D-MT]), along with the Truman Committee, criticized WPB's approach to demobilization.[50]

Industrial America had never been at ease with WPB and its predecessors. That was the case principally because of the Roosevelt administration and the New Deal, professional and academic, consumer, and labor elements in the mobilization agencies. Business's concerns about WPB were further aggravated by postwar initiatives propounded by the National Resources Planning Board and all but endorsed by the president in his 1944 State of the Union Address. Fearing a resurgence of New Deal forces as peace approached, big business had an additional reason collectively to decide against a planned return to normality and for a quick end to WPB.[51] For different reasons, industry reached the same conclusions as Nelson had.

The decision was obliquely articulated by Operations Vice Chair Lemuel B. Boulware in a March 1944 plan concerning what should take place between VE and VJ Days. The thrust of Boulware's conclusion was that programming should be restricted to military requirements and a few critical civilian needs and that all WPB controls should be lifted as expeditiously as possible. Extended planning for nonmilitary items (as proposed by the Program Bureau) was criticized and warned against. Policies had to be framed on the location of postwar industry, production models, the status of prewar firms and new producers, how goods were to be distributed, and assistance to small business. In settling these matters and deciding on the resumption or expansion of civilian output, Boulware advised, guidance should come from industry and be subject to market forces.[52] Implied more than stated in Boulware's proposal were ideas becoming increasingly prevalent in WPB: minimize WPB control over reconversion; return industry to normal peacetime relations as quickly as possible; and rely on oligopolistic, trade association, and other practices to manage competition and tame economic forces unloosed by mobilization.

Industry became more confident about handling reconversion on its own once Washington accepted or began instituting key aspects of the Baruch-Hancock Report. Those included procedures for terminating war contracts, settling accounts, handling surplus equipment and plants, and offering financial assistance in a quick and orderly way.

Two other conditions tended to reassure big business. Only about one-quarter of industrial capacity had to be fully reconverted, as was the case with automobiles and most consumer durable goods. The rest faced only partial or no reconversion, except, perhaps, for cutting back output and adjusting to peacetime markets. Many firms had gone on manufacturing their regular products along with munitions or alternated between the two, as was true with farm machinery and typewriters. Fully half the nation's plant had continued operating in war as it had in peace (albeit often at an expanded and accelerated pace), including basic metals, chemicals, machine tools, electric motors, food products, textiles, clothing, and lumber. Furthermore, as Nelson pointed out in June 1944, many firms, and usually the larger ones, had already begun preparing for peace by manufacturing models and taking other steps that were technically in violation of WPB policies. Even more important, under WPB auspices, and with its encouragement, practically all industry divisions were well along by 1944 in writing plans for the transition to peace. The level and quality of the planning varied from rudimentary to advanced.[53]

Preparations for demobilization also took place outside WPB. All business federations and organizations, including the still-traditional National Association of Manufacturers, the more moderate United States Chamber of Commerce, and the quite enlightened Business Advisory Council (and its spinoff the Committee for Economic Development), encouraged and guided planning for peace down to the local level. Their aim was not only to ensure a smooth transition but also to head off or temper efforts by New Dealers and other planners to dominate reconversion. Control by the latter elements would enhance the strength of an already expanded state at the expense of private power.[54]

In short, while battles over demobilization raged in and outside WPB in 1944 and 1945, industrial America was hardly drifting helplessly toward the shoals of unprepared reconversion. In the midst of turmoil, a great deal of planning for peace was taking place.

The armed services became central to demobilization's pace and policy. There was never a clear division between military supply structures and the business community. ASF, its Army Air Forces counterpart, and the navy's OP&M were heavily staffed with civilians in and out of uniform who were industrialists, attorneys, engineers, financiers, and so forth. The real muscle of the automobile industry, for example, went into the army's Ordnance Department, which, among other products, handled motor vehicles and tanks; WPB's Automotive Division was staffed heavily with those involved in sales. Armed forces representatives were well represented throughout WPB; and, in PEC, industry and the military forged a partnership. Consequently, the War and Navy Departments were well aware of corporations' anxieties about reconversion and their shifting position concerning it. The military was genuinely fearful about being denied the nearly unlimited supply to which it had become accustomed as demobilization loomed. It was particularly concerned that, if industry's fears about reconversion were not stilled, corporations could become hesitant to take contracts or not give them their full attention. Furthermore, if demobilization took the wrong turn, corporate executives throughout the mobilization structure might begin leaving for or being recalled by their firms.

That being the case, the armed services seriously began objecting to Nelson's demobilization approaches early in 1944, and their opposition grew as corporate America became alarmed about Nelson's plan. By slow stages, industry and the military appeared to agree that their mutual interests would best be served by delaying major reconversion steps until hostilities were practically over. Business could not argue that its competitive anxieties justified delay, but the military could insist that labor shortages at home threatened the welfare of the troops abroad. That approach not only held off the transition to peace but also added pressure in behalf of the military's drive for national service legislation.

In that regard, the military demonstrated consistency. With the conversion efforts slow to get under way in 1940–1941, the army blamed unions and strikes, not corporations, for holding back. Dependent on the productive power of corporate America to fulfill their mission, as well as sharing with industry class and ideological outlooks, the armed services never turned on the business community as they did on workers and their organizations.

The reconversion debate, expectably, centered on Donald M. Nelson and Charles E. Wilson as the WPB's two principal executives. The chair's role in the conflict is clearer and less contradictory than is that of the executive vice chair. Wilson acted very differently on the WPB than he did on the PEC. This paradoxical situation grew out of two circumstances: first, Wilson was directing the board, not from the chair's office, but as head of PEC; second, Wilson favored, perhaps in part shaped, corporate conservative aims, while Nelson insisted on open, liberal policies.

When Nelson at the November 30, 1943, WPB meeting indicated his intent to allow more civilian output as resources became available, Wilson was the only one to voice concern:

> Mr. [Jesse H.] Jones expressed the firm conviction that manpower, facilities, and materials could not be allowed to stand idle. Mr. Wilson inquired whether Mr. Jones would approve local reconversion even though such a policy had the effect of throwing previously established commercial relationships out of balance. To this question Mr. Jones answered in the affirmative; Mr. McNutt concurred, provided the manpower is available. While expressing the belief that the implementation of such a policy would disturb competitive relationships within the industry affected, Mr. McNutt thought the need for utilizing available resources for the increased production of civilian goods should be the governing consideration.[55]

That was the last time that Wilson at a WPB meeting questioned the chair, let alone doing so on the basis of competitive considerations. More often, Wilson stood by Nelson's proposals and supported his action. At PEC meetings, however, the executive vice chair, frequently without comment, went along with increasingly blatant challenges to Nelson's position on reconversion. Indeed, when the military began moving in December 1943 to have demobilization policy centered in PEC, it did so in part, echoing Wilson, to ensure "equity to industry."[56]

Paradox and puzzlement in mobilization circles over reconversion were furthered by WMC. Paul V. McNutt supported Nelson's decision late in 1943 to expand nonmilitary output when feasible, and WMC had been butting heads with the military since its creation. Yet, as the reconversion struggle heated up in 1944, WMC increasingly sided with the armed services in opposition to Nelson. It did so more to protect the commission's interests than to support the military's charges. WMC knew well that existing labor shortages did not constitute a crisis and that reasonable demobilization plans would make conditions better. Nonetheless, the commission itself was under attack. It had recently lost control of the Selective Service System, was out of favor with OWM and Congress, and faced the war's most sustained drive for national service legislation. Once labor supply surfaced in mid-1943 as the principal factor limiting mobilization, WMC faced greater pressure, especially from the armed services. At the same time, the military and WPB maneuvered the commission into the position of acting as their service agency.

WMC relations with WPB were only slightly better than those with the military. The board would not use its authority to enforce commission policies, refused to support WMC use of manpower utilization surveys, and isolated labor's representatives, who best understood worker issues, in the board. Vulnerable, and on the defensive, McNutt had no reason to join Nelson's losing cause. Instead, he concentrated on solving manpower problems as best he could and on protecting whatever was left of WMC's prestige. At the same time, WMC strove to hold off a labor draft and demonstrate that there was no need to go beyond voluntary manpower controls. In doing so, McNutt and his lieutenants documented without exaggerating existing labor supply problems. To oppose the administration's emerging line on reconversion would serve only to weaken WMC further and sully even more McNutt's damaged reputation.

Finally, of course, the president's influence must be considered. In his State of the Union Address in January 1944, he carefully balanced Dr. Win-the-War with Dr. New Deal because he needed a continued sense of both war urgency and postwar promise to maximize his and the party's fortunes in the upcoming election. Moreover, as it turned out, Roosevelt was more accurate in his estimation of when Germany would surrender than were most military and civilian leaders. That led him to approach proposing a reduction in military supply programs with care. He informed Bureau of the Budget Director Smith at the end of August 1944 that the war in Europe would probably go on for another six months, perhaps even a year; in October, he speculated that guerilla warfare could preclude VE Day. Such pessimism, his distance from domestic developments, his reliance on conservative advisers such as James F. Byrnes and Admiral William D. Leahy, and the political need to calm controversy among mobilization agencies all led the president to be cautious about reconversion. The military's willingness to carry its case to an uncertain and ill-informed White House further hurt the WPB chair. (Throughout the war years, Nelson, wisely or unwisely, refused constantly to involve the president in his mobilization battles, even when Roosevelt offered to intervene.) All these factors created conditions in which Roosevelt would turn against Nelson if demobilization tensions gave way to a public brawl. That was the case, ironically, despite the fact that the president's reconversion views were closer to those of Nelson than to those of his detractors.[57]

NELSON AND WILSON DEPART WPB, JUNE–AUGUST 1944

The intricate maneuvering over reconversion between April 1943 and May 1944 gave way to political warfare in June 1944. Events triggering the fighting took on a curious aspect, suggesting that, at least initially, WPB corporate executives were more determined to halt Nelson's four-point reconversion program than were the armed services. Exceptionally anticipatory and edgy before Normandy, the army and navy appeared to relax somewhat with the campaign's success.

Waiting until after the invasion and a positive assessment of the munitions situation, Donald M. Nelson at the June 13 meeting of the WPB outlined generally the four-point reconversion program that he intended to implement. Before the WPB chair informed the board of his proposed action, Paul V. McNutt reviewed labor supply conditions. He explained that there was no national manpower deficit. Nevertheless, he was ordering into effect throughout the nation on July 1 the West Coast Manpower Program (the Byrnes Plan) for handling local worker shortages threatening critical war production. The program had dealt successfully with past crises. Relying on WMC's operations to control the labor situation, Nelson insisted that WPB had to begin modest preparations for the transition to peace. All the major mobilization officials or their surrogates were at the meeting. Several members of the War and Navy Departments warned that any moves toward demobilization had to be taken with the greatest of care. McNutt was concerned about perceptions of impending peace creating greater difficulties for WMC. However, no one directly challenged Nelson's proposal, Wilson went along with it, and Under Secretary of the Navy Ralph A. Bard said that he had no objection to the plan if war production was unaffected.[58]

Despite the surface calm, the WPB meeting was obviously a tense one with all in attendance aware that Nelson was cautiously entering a veritable minefield. By mid-1944, the WPB chair and his opponents had concluded that programming for demobilization would be kept to a minimum and WPB controls lifted as quickly as possible without adversely affecting the war effort. The key issues in dispute were when reconversion would begin and whether competitive positions within industries would be protected. Nelson addressed the areas of conflict directly:

> The Chairman recognized the hardship that will be imposed on firms located in tight labor areas and those that will for the duration of the war devote entire facilities to war production. However, it would be against the public interest to delay reconversion until all firms in a given industry could resume peacetime production on an equal competitive basis.[59]

The challenges began shortly after the June 13 WPB meeting. On June 16, Nelson had circulated among the board's executives the press release announcing his four-point reconversion plan to take effect on July 1. Unlike in the past, all vice chairs now objected to his plan, with the exception of Clinton S. Golden, Manpower Requirements, Joseph D. Keenan, Labor Production, and Maverick, Smaller War Plants. The other vice chairs based their dissent on Nelson's approach and his timing. There should be no public release, but, if the chair insisted on going forward with his plan, he must explain that urgent war production programs would delay any demobilization for a considerable period. As with feasibility, materials allocation, and production scheduling, Nelson, who usually avoided confrontation but persisted when convinced that a decision was sound, agreed to change only the packaging, not the product. Public relations personnel worked out a compromise of sorts in which Nelson on June 18 outlined to the press his four-point plan after first warning the public that dedication and diligence had to remain high since heavy fighting was ahead, critical munitions programs were behind, and labor supply problems loomed.[60]

A *Washington Evening Star* editorial of July 7, 1944, asked why most WPB vice chairs, led by Wilson, were opposing Nelson's four-point program when they had raised no objection when the chair presented his proposal to WPB on June 13. The editorial speculated that the source of conflict involved "the fact that Mr. Nelson's plan would tend to give new and old nonwar enterprises a competitive advantage over established manufacturers whose war contracts keep them from resuming peacetime production."[61] Programming was not the point of contention since both Nelson and his opponents ultimately deemphasized that approach. Instead, spot authorization and the other three points (free use of aluminum and magnesium, postwar models, and retooling for peacetime production) that would advance it appeared to be at the heart of the conflict. They would allow firms to resume civilian output at different times and decentralize critical decisions to field offices. Perhaps a definite, not a proposed, plan, one that would be made public, was what stirred the WPB vice chairs to overt opposition. Military demand and war uncertainties seemed to have little to do with their challenge. Nelson was fully committed to moving forward only when he felt that it was safe, and his program included all practical precautions. Wilson and his group could not say no to Nelson arguing that they were determined to maintain the status quo. Maverick, who provocatively questioned industry's motives in and outside WPB, was, according to Gladieux, met with fury in Wilson's circle. The vice chairs appeared to turn to military necessity to explain the legitimate question raised by the *Evening Star*.[62]

Once Nelson's reconversion proposals had been made public, the military took the lead in opposing them. On June 23, Under Secretary of War Patterson wrote Nelson that the War Department was alarmed about "positive steps toward reconversion at this most critical phase of the war when our troops in ever-increasing numbers are in actual contact with the enemy" and the demand for munitions mounted daily. Stringency of workers, Patterson went on, limited and will continue to retard war output. Yet Nelson's demobilization proposals would divert labor to noncritical civilian areas, and WMC controls were unreliable.[63] In a public announcement on June 29, JCS went beyond Patterson:

> A dangerous state of mind which cuts war production by causing people to throw up their war jobs is just as harmful as desertion on the fighting front. No effort required in the home-front battle should be diverted by any element in the production machine, whether it be ownership, management, rank and file workers, or those in the service of Government.[64]

Speaking for JCS in a July 7 letter to Nelson that was made public, Admiral Leahy became even more strident:

> We are disturbed over the existing lag in war production, which, if it continues, may necessitate revision in strategic plans which could prolong the war. In view of the major offensive operations under way on every front, it is essential at this time that there be no relaxation in war production, and that deficits in deliveries be made at the earliest possible date. The issuance of orders at this time which will affect our ability to produce war materials is not consistent with the all-out prosecution of the war.[65]

Although the battle of reconversion had begun, it became further complicated by Nelson's unexpected hospitalization with pneumonia on June 23. He would not directly participate in WPB deliberations again until July 26. Wilson automatically became acting WPB chair with instructions from Nelson to implement his reconversion program on July 1 as had been announced. These developments placed the executive vice chair in an extremely awkward position. WPB meetings to the contrary, he had never favored the chair's plan, almost all the vice chairs opposing Nelson were either Wilson appointees or in his loyal circle, and PEC, which he headed, had succeeded in wrestling from the chair major responsibility for demobilization. Nonetheless, and under scrutiny from all sides, Wilson felt obligated to follow Nelson's bedside instructions. Despite unrelenting and growing pressure, Nelson basically stood by his four-point reconversion approach, giving ground only slightly.

The first formal challenge to the WPB chair's plan originated in PEC on June 28, where the armed services, backed by WMC, attempted to prevent Nelson's orders from going into effect on July 1.[66] Unwilling to defy his superior, and prevented by medical doctors from seeing Nelson to urge flexibility, Wilson delayed issuing the four-point plan until the WPB could meet in emergency session on July 4. Once again, the military and WMC maintained that lagging war output, labor shortages, and a declining sense of public urgency necessitated postponing any reconversion activity. During meetings of PEC and WPB, Wilson regularly pointed out that Nelson was fully familiar with the arguments against his plan and yet elected to proceed.[67] Indeed, in answering Leahy's July 7 letter, Nelson on July 10, after reviewing and rebutting criticism of his proposal, declared:

> I have given careful attention to representations made both within the WPB, and by the Armed Services, the War Manpower Commission and other agencies, in opposition to the lifting of restrictions at this time. Although I have over and over again opened my mind to the objections raised, I am unable to find any real substance in them.[68]

With Wilson unwilling to delay or revoke Nelson's orders without his consent, both the War and the Navy Department representatives insisted that they would carry their case to Byrnes.

Nelson was not without his supporters. At the July 4 meeting of WPB, Wilson noted that no action of WPB had received such wide acclaim in Congress and the press as Nelson's recent policies, validating the WPB chair's assertion that the public expected and approved of preparing for reconversion. The Truman and Murray Committees stood staunchly behind the WPB chair, and the Truman Committee threatened public hearings unless Wilson moved expeditiously to implement Nelson's reconversion orders. In a July 5 memorandum to all members of WPB, Keenan and Golden argued that the chair's approach in behalf of more civilian production was appropriate, that labor available for nonmilitary output could not, their studies established, be transferred to war production, and that armed services requirements were being met. "So long as this duty is performed," the labor vice chairs went on, "the military are not in any position to oppose action by the WPB for the benefit of the civilian economy."[69] Months earlier, Robert W. Johnson, former SWPC chair and a reserve Ordnance general, had warned the military away in practically the same terms. He wrote Patterson: "The War Department has a place—a vital place—but it is not qualified to direct the American economy. Undue influence in that direction is neither appropriate nor in the course of wisdom."[70]

While Keenan and Golden were among the few WPB executives willing to charge the armed services with jurisdictional violations, Nelson's assistants Edwin A. Locke, Jr., and David M. Noyes, working with Director of Information Bruce Catton, took on the large corporations. Locke, who among other duties oversaw relations with the Truman Committee, had been an executive with Chase National Bank, Noyes had a public relations background, and Catton was a journalist. As Wilson and others were attempting to persuade a convalescing Nelson to hold off on issuing his four directives, Locke and Noyes on July 7 composed a memorandum for Nelson that they proposed he send to all WPB vice chairs. In it, Nelson reaffirmed his decision to go forward with the orders and, in effect, charged big business with blocking reconstruction over concern about competitive positions. After Wilson prevailed on Nelson to modify the incendiary parts, Nelson decided against signing or sending the correspondence. Nonetheless, the original memorandum was quickly in the hands of the media, which generally favored Nelson. The episode enraged Wilson and his executive team, creating divisions within WPB that became irreconcilable.[71]

With the controversy spinning out of control and both Nelson's supporters and his detractors using the press to strengthen their cases, Byrnes stepped in. On July 10, he announced that any further reconversion conflict would be handled by his office. Nelson had earlier agreed to the OWM director's proposed compromise that the four orders be staggered, and Byrnes now forced the reluctant armed services to accept his solution. After a testy WPB meeting on July 11 in which some of Nelson's directives were subject to even further safeguards, it was decided that they were to be implemented alternately: on July 15, the use of aluminum and magnesium would be relaxed; on July 22, work on experimental models could commence; on July 29, unrated machine tools could be ordered; and, on August 15, spot authorization could go into effect. With this action taken, the Truman Committee again threatened public hearings unless it saw progress within a week. Wilson also went out of his way to assure the public that WPB was unified on reconversion policy, that differences existed on timing only because of concern for the war effort, and that all vice chairs agreed that competitive positions within industry would not deter resumption of peacetime production.[72]

Nelson's return to WPB on July 26 set in motion a series of events making it clear that neither Nelson nor Wilson could any longer direct WPB. The executive vice chair and the chief operating executives who followed his lead were intent on taking away Nelson's authority or driving him out. While the chair might not fight Wilson, his devoted and able staff would. A public airing of fundamental and bitter divisions within the principal mobilization agency would necessitate the departure of both the chair and the executive vice chair.

On Nelson's first day back, Wilson and the vice chairs insisted on a restricted and secret staff meeting. Among Nelson's supporters, only Bernard L. Gladieux was present; Clinton S. Golden, Joseph D. Keenan, and Maury Maverick were not. The executive vice chair and the vice chairs in attendance launched a harsh and sustained attack on Noyes, Locke, Catton, Gladieux, and Maverick either for failing to respect their authority or for charging that their opposition to the four-point reconversion was based on protecting big business. The vice chairs aggressively protested that they had been slandered and that Nelson had not publicly refuted his staff. Although the fierce criticism was leveled at the chair's assistants, Nelson himself was the target. Wilson and his lieutenants made it clear that, without a virtual surrender to their demands, the chair faced a revolt. Before the meeting was over, Nelson agreed that, henceforth, he would take no official action without first having the approval of the appropriate vice chair, but he made no commitments about firing his staff or exonerating WPB executives from the big business allegations.[73]

By the end of July, the White House, not WPB, had determined Nelson's fate. Roosevelt and his advisers had already concluded that the WPB chair's removal was essential to settle the politically and economically damaging imbroglio. Nelson's popularity and his appeal to liberals, however, necessitated that his departure be handled with the greatest of care. Between July 13 and August 18, the White House arranged for Nelson to join a presidential mission traveling to China. The WPB chair willingly accepted the offer, probably believing that he would be gone for about five weeks while Wilson took over as acting WPB chair. Roosevelt met with Wilson several times during this period and, along with Byrnes, seems to have indicated to Wilson that Nelson's departure was permanent and that Wilson would be made board chair after a decent interval.

For over a month, Harry L. Hopkins and others had been trying to get Nelson out of Washington before a WPB blowup. They did not succeed. A press leak forced an irate president to announce Nelson's trip to China on August 19. When a close Nelson associate informed an inquiring reporter that, contrary to what was said by the president and Nelson, the departing chair was being forced out, the White House was inundated with protests from Congress, labor, and other sources. Attempting to quell the uproar, the White House had to come to the defense of Nelson and his reconversion program, and Byrnes had to tell Wilson that his elevation to WPB chair would be too controversial. Wilson had suffered his final indignity. He resigned on August 23. On August 24, both the chair and the executive vice chair met with assembled WPB executives for the last time. Nelson insisted that all was well; WPB would be ably handled in his absence. A fuming Wilson exploded. Both to the stunned WPB group and afterward to an equally amazed press corps, he blasted the chair and his staff for defaming him and making it impossible for him to continue leading WPB under a poisonous cloud of suspicion. A few days thereafter, Roosevelt made it clear that Nelson would not return to WPB.[74]

The reconversion strife could not have taken place at a more politically sensitive time. Early in July, Roosevelt announced his fourth-term candidacy for the presidency; later in the month, the Democratic Party held its convention and went through the wrenching process of selecting a vice-presidential candidate. From then on, presidential politics took on increasing importance until the November election. These circumstances both benefited and harmed the contending parties, in different ways. Certainly, the president and his party could not allow the mobilization struggle to go on because it would adversely affect Roosevelt's reelection chances. On balance, however, the demobilization conflict was being settled by power positions, not political considerations. That the blowup occurred when it did probably acted to Nelson's detriment, as did his untimely illness, but only in an immediate, not a fundamental, way. Nelson, his staff, and a few isolated vice chairs were up against the industry-military mobilization team that had shaped the harnessing of the economy in ways overt and subtle since 1940. The WPB chair and his associates could, as they did, embarrass and expose the corporate executives and military brass over demobilization without ever having a chance of winning against them.

WPB AND RECONVERSION UNDER KRUG, AUGUST 1944–NOVEMBER 1945

On the basis of Nelson's recommendation, the president appointed Julius A. Krug as acting WPB chair; after Nelson resigned on September 30 on his return from China, Krug became chair. An able, ambitious public servant for many years, Krug had served in both OPM and WPB. He was very familiar with both the processes and the politics of the board. What instructions he received from the White House and Byrnes are unknown, but he unquestionably understood that he was to stabilize WPB operations and keep from the public domain any further conflict within the board or between it and other agencies.[75]

The new chair moved quickly to reorganize WPB's governing structure (see chart 6). Doing away with the executive vice chair's position so as to avoid a repetition of the Nelson-Wilson discord, Krug centralized control in his own

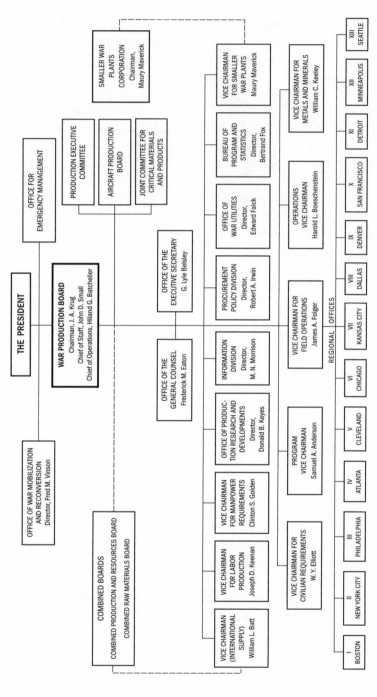

Chart 6.   Organization of WPB, June 1945. *Source:* Civilian Production Administration, *Industrial Mobilization for War: History of the War Production Board and Predecessor Agencies, 1940–1945* (Washington, DC: Civilian Production Administration, 1947), p. 867.

office and also took over direction of PEC and the Aircraft Production Board. Directly under him were three principal deputies: former Deputy Executive Vice Chair Arthur H. Bunker took over as chief of staff; Hiland G. Batcheller, a talented and enlightened corporate executive in the Nelson mold, was called back to the board to serve as chief of operations; and John D. Small, a respected official from the navy's procurement structure, acted as executive officer. A few other organizational changes were also made. With most of the vice chairs continuing in office, Krug quickly reestablished the board's equilibrium and focus. At the end of 1944, and in 1945, various executives began leaving WPB. By then, their departure was less consequential than it would have been had they left when Krug first took over.[76]

Once restructuring the board was under way, Krug had to deal with the volatile reconversion matter. After months of battle, confusion was widespread about where WPB stood on the issue; industry, labor, other agencies, and the general public had to be reassured that the board was prepared to handle decreased war production and the transition to peace. Besides Nelson's short-term proposals for dealing with increased civilian output as munitions requirements declined, the Planning Division, along with other board sources, had since late 1943 been studying and writing plans for demobilization after the defeat of Germany. The planning was always tenuous because it had to take place without reliable figures or estimates on when Germany and Japan would be defeated, levels of military demand, availability of resources, and other vital data. Moreover, and of great significance, the Planning Division had to reflect changing ideas about reconversion among WPB's high officials. Under these circumstances, the periodic reports of the division increasingly favored a nonprogrammed approach for the transition from war to peace. Nevertheless, controversy still continued since, both within and outside the board, voices rose in favor of planning the demobilization process to varying degrees.[77]

Shortly after his selection as acting chair of WPB, Krug, backed by army and navy officials, rejected his earlier espousal of programmed reconversion in favor of lifting all but essential board controls after VE Day. As quickly as possible, industry would be freed of wartime regulations to pursue readjustment to peace on its own. On the basis of Krug's instructions, the Planning Division on September 2 issued its fourth and final plan, which, with a few revisions, became WPB's official policy for reconversion. Assuming a 40 percent reduction in munitions requirements within a year after VE Day, the report called for rapidly lifting most controls on civilian production. Priorities would remain where necessary for military output and, if direly needed, for some civilian goods. Additionally, the few materials still in short supply would be regulated, as would the construction industry. All restrictions on labor supply would be dropped. To handle any unanticipated problems, WPB would be kept in a state of readiness. The acting chair set up a committee to give greater specificity to the Planning Division's document. By October 3, 1944, the reconversion proposal had received the unanimous support of the WPB. Although the plan explicitly stated that it would not be used to maintain prewar competitive positions, it practically guaranteed that most, if not all, corporations could begin the transition to peace together.[78]

The plan reflected an emerging consensus among WPB's top policy group, the vice chairs, and their subdivisions, particularly the industry divisions. Significantly, it was emphatically endorsed at WPB meetings by the under secretaries of war and the navy and by General Clay. Even McNutt and Isador Lubin, economic adviser to the president who was sitting in for Hopkins, went along, albeit with some reservations. Krug's plan for reconversion appeared to have been approved, perhaps even suggested or directed, by Byrnes with White House clearance. To the degree that the acting chair was moving on his own, he appeared to have concluded that WPB had become discredited by allowing the reconversion controversy to get out of control. Putting a quick end to the board was the most expedient solution to this awkward state of affairs. In reaching that conclusion, Krug had to overcome the opposition of a number of WPB executives who wanted to maintain various controls for handling unexpected difficulties and/or protecting some or all industries.[79]

Not all in WPB went along, although outright opposition went unexpressed at WPB meetings. The SWPC protested that small business was left without protection; the Offices of Manpower Requirements and Labor Production argued that restrictions should be more judiciously lifted so that they could be used to avoid mass unemployment; and the OCR protested that low-cost consumer goods would disappear without proper regulations. OCR was joined by the Office of Price Administration (OPA) head Chester Bowles. WPB controls, Bowles insisted, must be used to protect essential civilian production as well as to help to maintain stable prices, wages, and production costs. Krug attempted to meet Bowles's criticisms by arranging for a committee to resolve differing views between the WPB and OPA. Some progress was made before reconversion planning was all but suspended at the end of 1944.[80]

In hammering out reconversion policies, Krug and his associates had to address the inadequacy of PEC to handle the cutback of military contracts. The PECS—set up in May 1944 and intended to become central to reconversion— had never functioned well. Lack of proper staff work, unavailable information on subcontracts, and excessive focus on replacing one military contract with another all acted to undermine its effectiveness. Additionally, the armed services insisted on placing contracts in industrially impacted areas because of nonoptional or unique facilities, performed their own reviews, or ignored WPB policies. In an attempt to improve conditions, PECS was replaced in November 1944 by a Production Readjustment Committee that directed a series of subcommittees. The overall results of the reorganization were disappointing. Patterns set by PECS could not be reversed. Consistent with the placement of armed services contracts during defense and war conversion from 1940 through 1943, the military largely canceled its contracts during 1944 and 1945 with only slight influence from civilian mobilization agencies. As it turned out, the armed services had an even freer hand in terminating obligations than industry would have in resuming civilian output.[81]

Although concentrating his early effort on longer-run demobilization issues, Krug also had to deal with Nelson's four reconversion orders, which had been issued in a staggered way before he took over as acting chair. A War Department propaganda campaign against the approval of Nelson's program began in June 1944 and intensified in July once the orders were accepted and issued. For months, Robert P. Patterson, General Brehon B. Somervell, and others made headline news by charging that declining production was threatening the war effort and soldiers' lives, that labor was leaving munitions plants in droves or engaging in strikes, and that, lacking a sense of urgency, the general public was concentrating on peace, not war. News releases, radio programs, and movies featured frontline commanders relating how deficits in munitions, equipment, and supplies endangered battlefield success.

On the basis of the data available to him, Nelson realized that the military was misrepresenting the situation. There was no production crisis, workers were not fleeing war plants, and any lags in war production were either in the normal range or created by suddenly increased orders or design changes. Chief of Ordnance Levin H. Campbell reassured him that such was the case with his department. The WPB chair also knew that military cutbacks in requirements preceded reconversion action, not vice versa. Moreover, optimism about an impending end to the war came principally from top civilian and military heads of the armed services. Indeed, early in July 1944, General George C. Marshall informed Baruch that the Allies had Germany boxed in, and, a month later, Patterson predicted the nation's imminent collapse. Looking back, Nelson ruefully observed that the "War Department deliberately tried to make the people believe" that frontline shortages resulted from homefront production failures, "but the accusation was never once made directly":

> The Army's technique was to go into great detail about shortages at the front then, in the same breath, to draw attention to the fact that war production programs at home were behind schedule. But the record

shows that in not a single instance—after the critical early period of 1942—did an American fighting man at the front have to go without munitions because of any failure in production. Front-line shortages in the summer of 1944 were a question of logistics, and were not due to production shortages. The Army's deliberate attempt to create a contrary impression was one of the most dangerous bits of double talk I ever heard of.

The Truman Committee—now the Mead Committee, Senator James M. Mead (D-NY) having assumed the role of chair in 1944—validated Nelson's claims. After investigating army charges on August 16, it announced to the public: "The picture presented at the closed session was not the one that had been given to the public."[82]

His patience worn thin, the WPB chair finally appealed to Byrnes at the end of July about War Department behavior. After a reported August 2 meeting with Patterson, Nelson, and Wilson concerning the matter, Byrnes elected to join the War Department rather than temper its attack on the four-point reconversion program, particularly spot authorization, scheduled to be implemented on August 15. Why the OWM director, who up until this time had played a moderating role, aggressively joined the anti-Nelson elements is unclear. Perhaps his being passed over as the candidate for vice-president and his intense resentment about the outcome freed him to act more forcefully and candidly on his basically conservative views. Whatever the case, on August 4, he declared publicly that War Department charges were valid. To deal with the situation, he was stiffening the West Coast Manpower Program, made nationwide by the WMC in July, in a way in which additional civilian output under Nelson's pending spot authorization order would be practically impossible. Spot authorization now had to have PEC approval and be based on written certification by WMC that any such production would not interfere with local or interregional labor recruitment for essential military and civilian output.[83]

WPB created further problems for spot authorization by claiming just before the order went into effect that no steel was available for the program. Eventually, a small amount of steel was allocated, justifying the claims of OCR, SWPC, and labor offices that the Steel Division and the program vice chair were manipulating estimated supply and demand statistics for the purpose of nullifying spot authorization.[84]

When Krug took charge of WPB at the end of August, antagonism to all Nelson's demobilization orders and especially to spot authorization had not diminished on the part of the armed services or most top WPB officials. However, it is necessary to keep in mind that, from mid-1944 through April 1945, the War Department led the most fervent and unremitting drive for national service occurring during World War II. That goal necessitated a constant emphasis on labor shortages, workers leaving war plants, production programs falling behind, lack of urgency, a homefront gone sour, a betrayal of troops abroad, and similar charges.

Attempting to sort out whether the military was more intent on defeating reconversion efforts or pushing through a labor draft is neither possible nor significant. The armed services' psychological warfare campaigns simultaneously served both ends. Few WPB officials supported national service, but their general silence in the face of military propaganda aided the drive for national service as well as their desire to obstruct reconversion. By their inaction, WPB industrialists also contradicted their counterparts on the WMC's Management-Labor Policy Committee who steadfastly opposed national service in any form.

Despite the adversity that Nelson's reconversion program faced, Krug went on record in favor of it and appeared to take steps toward its implementation. When complaints increased that spot authorization was not making much headway, the acting WPB chair appointed a task force to improve its operation and listened to the recommendations that he received. Nonetheless, with Allied progress against Germany slowing down in September and military orders going up, prospects for getting reconversion under way also dimmed.

Krug was no Nelson. Although he might resist pressure from the armed services and Byrnes, he would not, and knew he could not, allow differences to break out into a public brawl. Hence, when Patterson in September began working for suspension of spot authorization and various board vice chairs advised similarly, Krug did not comply, but neither did he push forward with increasing optional civilian output. Furthermore, he would not challenge military representatives using their WPB positions to block spot authorization even when WMC had granted its approval. As pressure mounted, the acting chair early in November ultimately lent support to those determined to hold back spot authorization.[85]

Perhaps Krug believed that an unbiased report on production lags would allow him more latitude in dealing with Nelson's four orders. Most likely acting for the War Department, Byrnes late in October asked the acting chair to investigate the cause of production delays. Krug assigned the task to Chief of Operations Hiland G. Batcheller. Batcheller reported to WPB on November 14 that 40 percent of total war programs were behind schedule and that 28 percent of those programs were in the critical area. Batcheller explained as follows: 40 percent of the delay resulted from rapid jumps in orders, 26 percent from model or design changes, 22 percent from labor shortages, and 12 percent from unavailable facilities. The chief of operations noted that problems were aggravated by the armed services not alerting WPB expeditiously so that it could prepare for change. Furthermore, he went on, each troubled program could and should be handled separately; there was no production crisis. In the present and future, as in the past, critical requirement shortages were inevitable during a war of high technology and changing tactics.[86]

The War Department was unsatisfied with Batcheller's proposed solutions; it wanted spot authorization along with the rest of Nelson's four orders suspended. Krug, Isador Lubin, and others pointed out that the opponents were unable to specify a single case of spot authorization interfering with war output in fact or in worker attitudes; the labor shortages that existed were caused by specific, not general, causes, such as low pay, poor working conditions, and inadequate housing and community facilities. When Byrnes also refused conditionally to halt spot authorization, the army once again upped the level of its psychological warfare, with General Marshall and Admiral King, joined by the president, exhorting the population not to desert the men abroad. Soldiers were returned from battle zones to relate to the public the consequences of ammunition shortages. No argument, no factual information could prevail in persuading the armed services to give up the crusade against spot authorization. With Byrnes and Krug finally joining them, spot authorization was all but suspended early in December, and programmed civilian production was limited to the level authorized for the last quarter of 1944.[87]

Even then, the army kept hammering away on the need to create a sense of dedication to and urgency about war production. Determined once more to give the public a balanced analysis, the Mead Committee on December 4 called Somervell, Krug, and others to testify about the so-called production crisis. What the committee established was what Nelson had concluded earlier: any battlefront shortages stemmed, not from production breakdowns, but from logistic complications. The bizarre nature of the army's campaign against Nelson's program is illustrated by a communication from Patterson to Baruch early in November 1944 in which the under secretary of war reported that his own inspection in the field discredited Somervell/ASF reports about production lags and diminished civilian morale. Furthermore, Baruch early in September 1944 assured Marshall that all was well with war production, only to argue at a November 1944 WPB meeting that the military should be listened to about frontline shortages.[88]

Nevertheless, and despite growing and vocal objection to military scare tactics even from a friendly press, Byrnes on December 11, 1944, selected General Clay as deputy director of the OWMR and declared that his, Byrnes's, office would become more active in formulating policy. With the Battle of the Bulge starting on December 16, Byrnes and Clay led OWMR in closing racetracks, setting curfews for amusement centers, and taking other measures to bring home to apparently distracted and uncaring civilians that the nation was at war. To make sure that no one doubted that an early start on reconversion was a bad blunder, Byrnes's annual report of January 1, 1945, to Congress and the president, probably written under Clay's direction, all but in name blamed Nelson for current production failures. Simultaneously, munitions requirements, which were escalating before mid-December, now shot up even further, reaching levels nearly 15 percent above those of 1944. By January 1945, all of Nelson's reconversion program in fact or in effect had been suspended; even post–VE Day planning was halted. In such a hostile atmosphere, the former chair's staunch supporters hesitated to defend moves toward demobilization. WPB appeared to be taking instructions directly from Byrnes and Clay.[89]

The onslaught ultimately tapered off when the German advance was halted early in February and the Reich was about to surrender in March. By then, the WPB was beginning to show more independence in reviewing military requirements, and Nelson's supporters were again willing to speak out. Clay left OWMR at the end of March. Byrnes had allowed WPB quietly to resume reconversion planning on February 1, and, in mid-March, Krug announced that the board would soon unveil a revised demobilization plan when VE Day arrived. At nearly the end of April, spot authorization was finally reinstated. By then, with VE Day all but achieved and VJ Day quickly to follow, spot authorization had become at best secondary.[90]

From late 1944 through August 1945, various WPB officials were convinced that the armed services purposefully kept their requirements excessively high to prevent WPB from moving forward with demobilization. Evidence and common sense validate the judgment.[91]

Munitions production and war construction peaked in 1943 at $64.8 billion and dropped to $64.3 billion in 1944. Actually, munitions output in 1944 increased by $5 billion, but a reduction in construction brought annual war expenditures down. Military demand began rising toward the end of 1944 and then skyrocketed with the Battle of the Bulge. On January 1945, war budgets for the year were projected at $61.1 billion; within a few weeks, they grew to $64.6 billion, nearly matching spending in 1943. In October 1944, the annual program had stood at $56.6 billion, escalating by almost 15 percent within a matter of months. After the German advance was checked and reversed, some decline in military requirements took place. But military requirements were still scheduled for over $4.6 billion in May 1945 (an annual rate of almost $55.4 billion), with an approximate projected decline of 15 percent to above $3.9 billion in August (or around $47 billion annually), when, as it turned out, Japan capitulated.[92]

Requirements for a projected one-front war were, therefore, not much below those for a two-front one. As troops were transferred from the European to the Asian front, the army, among other things, spoke of the need to reequip totally and rearm them. Furthermore, cutbacks from March 1945 on did little to assist additional civilian output, for a number of reasons. Most reductions involved projected, not immediate, cutbacks, meaning, according to an authoritative source, that, "when Japan surrendered, munitions production was down little more than 10 percent from the spring peak." Also, heavy cuts in aircraft and other munitions did not free facilities and materials needed for nonmilitary output, particularly steel, and reductions spread out among many producers failed to release plants for civilian use.[93]

High War Department officials directly and indirectly stated that military demand was being used to shape demobilization decisions. Reviewing production plans late in February 1945, Secretary of War Stimson and Under Secretary of War Patterson agreed to keep requirements for 1945 at a two-front level. Reduced demand in 1943–1944, they concluded, had opened the door to Nelson's reconversion drive, a mistake that they would not repeat.[94] (Stimson and his manpower assistant Goldthwaite H. Dorr had earlier attempted to persuade Chief of Staff Marshall to expand the army's size to increase pressure for national service legislation and, perhaps, to check Nelson's reconversion efforts.) General Clay had signaled the secretary and under secretary of war's approach much earlier. After Nelson announced his four-point reconversion plan on June 13, 1944, the general told PEC on June 21 that future military requirements would most likely go up, not down, "as the South Pacific Area is extended and as the forces increase."[95] Six months earlier, the general had informed PEC that the army estimated that its requirements would drop around 45 percent with VE Day.[96] Late in 1944, and early in 1945, the armed services candidly admitted that they were once again engaging in "incentive," rather than realistic, scheduling so as to push WPB on to greater efforts. When such goals went unmet, military representatives expressed no distress because legitimate need was not involved.[97]

Byrnes's attempt beginning late in 1943 to review military requirements and to coordinate production and strategy through the Joint Production Survey Committee had achieved very little. Indeed, during 1944 and 1945, while the military insisted that production failures were undermining the war effort and that demobilization programs were making or would make conditions worse, OWM/OWMR and WPB documented that armed services demand was inflated, that unneeded munitions were being ordered, and that waste, duplication, and mismanagement were rampant. When early in 1945 JCS proposed that it participate directly in determining civilian demand so as to ensure adequate military supply, even Byrnes said no, and his successor, Fred M. Vinson, was even more emphatic in his denial. Neither Byrnes nor Vinson, however, would act on the complaints of Krug, Bureau of the Budget Director Harold D. Smith, and others in 1944 and 1945 that military requirements were grossly out of line.

Beginning with the commander-in-chief, civilians had allowed the military to get out of control on mobilization issues as early as 1940; by 1944, they either would not or could not reassert their authority over the army and navy. Indirectly, therefore, the armed services were setting levels for civilian demand by having a virtually free hand in determining their own supply needs. By late 1944 and into 1945, ironically, basic civilian requirements, such as clothing, household items and equipment, and transportation, had been squeezed to the point that war production was being adversely affected by such factors as labor turnover and absenteeism. Labor, OCR, WMC, and others had repeatedly warned that such was or would be the case.[98]

In retrospect, all the disharmony caused by and energy expended on spot authorization were needless. So many safeguards limited its use that, under the best of circumstances, only a small amount of production could take place. By February 1945, almost five thousand applications for production totaling around $710 million had been approved, most involving badly needed household items. By late 1944, spot authorization never engaged more than about twenty-five thousand workers. Investigations of selected plants operating under spot authorization indicated that firms used it to hold together their workforce when war output was reduced for various reasons and that it had no adverse effects on labor supply.[99]

When Byrnes allowed Krug to resume planning for reconversion on February 1, 1945, he insisted that the planning be kept secret. Not only was the public kept in the dark, but most members of WPB were also excluded. Finally, in mid-March, Krug announced publicly that the board was updating its earlier demobilization plans for dealing with the period after Germany's surrender, but he provided no specifics. In April, the chair and OWMR went a step further by spelling out in general terms how the board was proceeding. WPB was either concerned about adversely affecting war production if it emphasized reconversion or fearful of opening itself up to another publicity blast by the armed forces.[100]

WPB felt compelled to reexamine post–VE Day plans completed and approved in October 1944 because, among other considerations, these were based on the expectation that military requirements would decline by 40 percent. That assumption was no longer valid since the armed forces were indicating that a drop-off in their demand could be slight. As late as June 1945, however, WPB had to work with its own estimates because the military could not or would not come up with set and reliable figures. Nonetheless, planning had to go forward since Germany's collapse was imminent. Ultimately, Krug centered preparations for reconversion in a Committee on Period One— Period One being that between VE and VJ Days—headed by John D. Small, now WPB's chief of staff. Previously, the program vice chair had directed such planning, but he, along with the labor offices, SWPC, OCR, and OPA, believed that WPB controls should be used to oversee and protect essential indirect military and civilian needs as well as those of the armed services during the transition to peace. Krug was determined to limit board regulations to a minimum and lift them as quickly as possible. Small shared the chair's views and was willing to follow his direction in that regard.[101]

By the end of April, the Committee on Period One had fairly well completed its post–VE Day proposals. They did not differ markedly from plans formulated in September 1944. The board's first priority remained fulfilling military requirements and maintaining a sound wartime economy. WPB would work with the procurement agencies to cut back contracts in a way that minimized unemployment. To facilitate industry's reconversion, WPB would modify regulations, sparingly use priorities and other restrictions, assist small business, and protect opportunities for new producers. Since shortages of materials required continued limitations on construction, the board would prioritize nonwar projects that were most urgently needed. With these goals in mind, WPB would simplify and eliminate all board controls as quickly as possible. Detailed proposals were worked out as to how WPB would implement various phases of its plans.[102]

With the defeat of Germany in May, WPB almost immediately began modifying and lifting its various restrictive orders, and the process was accelerated in June and July. Controls were kept on materials and goods still in short supply such as textiles, lumber, and machine tools. Consumer durables like automobiles, refrigerators, and electric ranges were also restricted. By absorbing huge quantities of resources, those goods would excessively distort the transitional market. Early in July 1945, the Committee on Period One was already well along in planning for VJ Day and working to coordinate WPB demobilization with those of other agencies. The filing of the committee's final report practically coincided with the surrender of Japan. With the armed services quickly canceling contracts wholesale, WPB followed suit in lifting its mobilization orders. By November, only a few residual restrictions remained on items and materials like clothing, leather, tin, and rubber. During his period as chair, Krug became increasingly determined to close down WPB operations soon after hostilities terminated. He achieved his goal. On November 4, the Civilian Production Administration took over remaining responsibilities as the WPB ended nearly four years of tumultuous operation.[103]

In quickly closing down the WPB, Krug faced a great deal of opposition. OCR, SWPC, the labor offices, and other WPB subdivisions were not the only ones opposing a fast end to the board. OWMR also objected. Byrnes departed in April 1945 and was replaced by the former head of the Office of Economic Stabilization, Fred M. Vinson. The latter selected Robert R. Nathan, former chair of the WPB's Planning Committee, as deputy director for reconversion. Along with Nathan came a host of young professionals in the New Deal mode who looked favorably on planning and centralized controls. In time, Nathan and his cohort might have had a greater impact on demobilization policy. However, Vinson departed in July 1945; his successor was John W. Snyder, a conservative businessman with close ties to President Harry S. Truman. The new OWMR director favored neither an active role for his office nor policies advocated by Nathan. In December 1945, the latter resigned in frustration, and with him went the last opportunity for the OWMR significantly to influence reconversion policy along the lines established by Byrnes and picked up for a few months by Vinson.[104]

Actually, the most concerted and enduring challenge to Krug and WPB in quickly removing board controls came from Chester Bowles, the OPA chief. By comparison with the opportunistic Krug, who saw his future with the rising interests of business, Bowles, who was from the world of advertising, tenaciously fought to protect the consumer. He began challenging WPB's determination rapidly to lift restrictions late in 1944 and never let up until OPA virtually died in 1946.

Bowles and his assistants insisted that, if a smooth transition to a peacetime economy was to take place, WPB had to limit demand to available supply, protect essential production, and ensure that industry did not take the easy and profitable path of producing expensive lines and models while neglecting inexpensive goods. Furthermore, smaller businesses had to be assured access to scarce materials in the face of big business's ability to dominate the market. OPA was particularly concerned about the continuing output of inexpensive textiles and clothing, which were in desperately short supply, and about maintaining regulations on construction so as not to make the housing crisis worse. Without WPB's varied controls, Bowles insisted, OPA's ability to help maintain price controls and economic stability would be greatly weakened. Experience and common sense led him to dismiss pledges from Krug and industry that all or most materials would be in ample supply shortly after VE Day, that larger producers would not squeeze out smaller competitors, and that a free market was the quickest, best route to demobilization.

Despite support from President Truman, backing from some existing and former war mobilizers, and encouragement from various members of Congress, Bowles was less outmaneuvered than he was overwhelmed. He too often fought alone without the consistent support of liberals, small business, or consumers. Those circumstances allowed Krug, WPB industrialists, and OWMR Director Snyder to have their way.[105]

Even before Bowles began his running encounter with WPB and other mobilization agencies, some members of Congress favored OWMR having a central role in directing the economy from war to peace. In August 1944, as the nation's legislators began focusing more seriously on reconversion, Senators Murray and Truman joined forces with Senator Harley M. Kilgore (D-WV) to sponsor a reconversion bill not dissimilar to one that a like group of senators had proposed for taking over the troubled mobilization program in 1943. A single administration, advised by representatives from industry, labor, and agriculture, would devise and implement demobilization policy. Specifically included in the proposed legislation were provisions for extended unemployment pay for labor and discharged veterans along with financial assistance for workers who had been transferred to war production centers. Significantly, the army was strongly opposed to the bill because a reconversion agency would have review powers over the cutback of military contracts and the War Department considered proposed unemployment benefits to be too generous.[106]

Passing over the so-called Kilgore-Truman-Murray Bill, Congress in October 1944 enacted instead the War Mobilization and Reconversion Act, or the George Bill, which, essentially on the basis of the Baruch-Hancock Report, turned reconversion over to OWM (now expanded to OWMR). While the Office of Contract Settlement was unusually successful, SWPA and its successors were less so, and the Retraining and Reemployment Administration and subsequent offices were a grave disappointment. The unimaginative, backward-looking General Frank T. Hines concentrated his efforts on veterans.

That left the working population at a time of uncertainty and fear of depression with little or no added protection. The Baruch-Hancock Report, the George Bill, and OWMR generally neglected or downplayed the human factor in policies for the transition to peace. To remedy the situation, Senators Robert F. Wagner (D-NY) and James E. Murray teamed up with Representative John D. Dingell (D-MI) to introduce in Congress a bill in 1943, 1945, and again in 1947 to federalize the unemployment system, extend and liberalize unemployment, old-age, and survivor benefits, create a national employment placement service, and devise a national health insurance system. Even Byrnes favored revising the outdated unemployment schedules, and Roosevelt supported such an approach before Congress. Conservative legislators were willing to go no further than setting up a reserve to assist states that had exhausted their funds. One of the major congressional stumbling blocks to action was federalizing the unemployment compensation system.[107]

What Congress did do was to pass the Employment Act of 1946. The act originated in the War Contracts Subcommittee of the Senate Military Affairs Committee, sponsored by Senator Murray. As originally introduced in January 1945, it would have obligated the federal government to adopt economic policies guaranteeing all workers employment. After extended and heated debate, a significantly altered bill emerged from Congress in February 1946. No longer was labor assured jobs; instead, the federal government would maximize employment, production, and purchasing power through unspecified policies consistent with national goals. To facilitate those ends, a Council of Economic Advisers would assist the president in presenting an annual report on the state of the economy to a congressional Joint Committee of the Economic Report.[108]

The most significant social service legislation passed by Congress addressing the postwar years was the Serviceman's Readjustment Act (the GI Bill). With provisions for health, unemployment, and job assistance, along with financing for homes, farms, and businesses, Congress helped ease the transition from war to peace for millions of fighting men. Probably the educational benefits were the most important. They kept many men out of the workforce while providing for their eventual upward mobility.[109]

Despite the rapid removal of production controls, the postwar collapse anticipated and feared by many did not materialize. Consumer demand was so high, as various analysts had predicted, that industry could not produce enough. Moreover, quickly settling war contracts and clearing plants of government property so that industry could expeditiously resume peacetime pursuits represented exceptionally sound policy. The index of industrial production stood at 211 in July 1945, just before VJ Day. By February 1946, it had fallen to a low of 152 but rose to 180 in September 1947.[110] To say that those supporting the rapid removal of controls and those delaying reconversion planning were farsighted is to argue from hindsight. Respected economists had warned that a postwar downturn was likely. Had a downturn occurred, Washington would have been ill prepared to meet it, particularly with the unexpectedly early end to the war in the Pacific. Besides, those advocating a more judicious lifting of restraints were concerned that inflation as well as deflation be avoided.

Rampant postwar inflation did occur. It resulted from the premature collapse of the stabilization program.[111] With most WPB restraints removed, wage and price controls became all the more essential, particularly with deferred demand great, pent-up buying power vast, yet supply still very restricted. The administration, however, had worked out plans for only gradually relaxing wage and price regulations during the anticipated year between VE and VJ Day. With a quick end to the war, programs had to be devised rapidly for correcting wartime distortions of prices and wages. Maintaining economic stability would have been difficult under the best of circumstances; conditions in the last months of 1945 were not auspicious. The OPA, the National War Labor Board (NWLB), the Office of Economic Stabilization, and OWMR—together responsible for stabilization—all had recently experienced turnover in leadership, were understaffed, and had to work with confusing formulas. Most postwar planning assumed the continued existence of NWLB. Yet, in September, the board began terminating its operations in favor of a National Wage Stabilization Board that took over on January 1, 1945. The former agency had compulsory powers; the latter did not.

Under this ominous state of affairs, labor and management began maneuvering to test their mutual strength. Union ranks had been growing ever more restless during the last year of war. On its part, industry was both flush and confident. As the Truman administration early in November 1945 urgently sought to have both sides step back from industrial conflict, time had run out. Strikes began to occur in the last months of 1945, and, as the nation entered the new year, 2 million workers had shut down many of the biggest corporations and smaller ones as well. Nonviolent for the most part, the strikes involved numbers exceeding anything seen in the past. By necessity, reconversion was virtually at a standstill. In time, the work stoppages ended through what became a three-way bargaining process. Unions made their demands, management waited to see how much of the increase Washington would let them cover with higher prices, and, when acceptable proportions were reached, settlement occurred. Labor began demanding $0.30 more an hour and ultimately settled on an average of about $0.185.

As the turmoil began to calm in March 1946, John L. Lewis and the United Mine Workers upped the ante, forcing the federal government again to seize mines and negotiate terms with the burly union leader. Truman halted a threatened railroad strike only by seizing the lines and, ultimately, preparing to draft into the army any worker threatening the national interest.

By June 1946, the administration faced an even more far-reaching crisis: OPA's statutory authority expired. Always having a New Deal aura and resented by many, particularly farm elements and the National Association of Manufacturers, OPA had few friends despite its outstanding wartime performance. Congress predictably returned to the president legislation inadequate for maintaining the stabilization program, prompting Truman's veto. After three weeks of further deliberation, the national legislators could do no better. Reluctantly, the president signed the bill. Any hope for economic stability was gone as various interest groups challenged further restrictions. By October 1946, the administration's stabilization policies, such as they were, had completely given way.

Prices skyrocketed as controls were removed. Between March 1945 and March 1947, consumer prices went up 23.3 percent—nearly matching the increases of all the defense and war years. From June (the end of effective price controls) to December 1946, prices shot up 15 percent—the steepest increase for such a limited period ever recorded by the consumer price index.

Although the United States was entering a period of unequaled growth and prosperity, its transition from war to peace was needlessly tumultuous. The choice was never between continuing a planned economy or lifting all restraints as quickly as possible. What thoughtful, nondoctrinaire leaders, such as Chester Bowles, intended was to maintain enough controls long enough that the economy could be eased through the inevitable period of shortage and dislocation. In that way, reasonable stability could have been maintained.

CONCLUSION

World War II reconversion contrasted sharply with that of World War I. In 1918–1919, leading industrialists, backed by some Woodrow Wilson administration officials, attempted to have Washington institute a planned transition from war to peace. The president himself squelched the controversial endeavor. Such an outcome resulted from institutional weakness at all levels. A growing federal government was just beginning to get its footing as an economic regulator and social welfare agent. Industry was struggling to stabilize its own structure while adjusting to the emerging power of an activist state. And the armed services' supply and procurement structures had been nearly overwhelmed by the demands of modern warfare. With widespread uncertainty, quickly closing down a makeshift, undeveloped mobilization system turned out to be prudent, probably even unavoidable.

By the time of World War II, national institutions had changed dramatically. In combating the Great Depression, Washington grew vastly, took on a new level of professional expertise, and benefited from mass support for the Roosevelt administration. On its part, the corporate community had to become more proficient economically and politically in dealing effectively with chronic hard times, expanding government, and the challenge of organized labor. Not only was the military steadily modernizing its supply system, but it was also the center of planning for mobilizing the economy for a future war.

This far-reaching transformation became almost immediately obvious when the nation formally began harnessing its economic system in mid-1940. An industry-military mobilization team began forming in the National Defense Advisory Commission (NDAC), became more focused in OPM, and reached maturity in WPB. It was professional state bureaucrats, however, who devised most of the necessary controls for making a harnessed economy reach its potential and operate efficiently.

Many of those same professionals or their adherents, who were usually also reformers and were supported by spokesmen for labor, small business, and consumers, favored a careful transition to peace as calibrated by WPB. The industry-military mobilization alliance blocked such a development. Donald M. Nelson's unfortunate fate resulted from the power dynamics among government, industry, and the military. More enlightened, ideologically flexible, and economically sophisticated than most members of business, Nelson successfully bridged the gap between industry and the Roosevelt administration from 1940 into 1943. He did so by relying on those in the Leon Henderson–Robert Nathan circles and like-minded industrialists such as James S. Knowlson and William L. Batt. These officials were key to devising the basic controls essential for successfully mobilizing the economy, particularly feasible requirements, a workable allocation system, and production scheduling, along with policies for financing the war while maintaining economic stability. Ironically, what made the command economy work effectively also made Nelson and his professional team less important. When they attempted to shape reconversion as they had conversion, they were shoved aside by the industry-military production team that they had helped create.

Industry and the military did not want carefully planned demobilization because the process could further enhance a reformist state, something that both saw as a threat. Since the armed services are part of the state, their opposition to strengthening it is both curious and almost uniquely American. The paradox grows out of the American political economy centered around a government-business regulatory partnership and the nation's pattern of controlling the military.

Without a high-level, professional civil service to conduct its affairs, Washington largely depended on temporary recruits from the corporate structure and the financial and legal worlds to do so. The practice became more exaggerated during a time of war, when the economy had to be planned.

Almost from its origins, America depended on managing its military by keeping it small, except during periods of hostility. Starting before World War I, and culminating with World War II, the nation built a massive and permanent military establishment. As the nation expanded the size and nature of its armed forces, it did not simultaneously create the institutional structure or gain the experience necessary to control its new military effectively. Those conditions were bound to result in a serious problem.

Twentieth-century America's problem with the military has been multiplied manyfold by the growing ties between the armed forces and the corporate system. Basic to the effectiveness of the armed services has been the industrial system that supports them. This new institutional development began in the late nineteenth century with the building of a modern fleet. It took on added significance with the mobilization of the World War I economy and the interwar military procurement and industrial mobilization planning. During World War II, however, a full-blown industry-military alliance came into being, an alliance that dominated economic mobilization.

The alliance was as interesting as it was consequential. Corporate America was the dominant power group of the partnership. Without public arsenals and weapons centers of significance, the armed services have depended heavily on the private economic sector for supplying weapons, equipment, and goods. During periods of hostility, however, the military has become critically important to industry. The massive requirements of modern warfare have made the armed services the economy's major consumers during hostilities. A military unprepared to exercise such great economic power effectively and responsibly threatened corporate interests, as occurred during World War I. But armed services ready to carry out their massive procurement operations in an accomplished and dynamic manner became extraordinarily useful to the business community, as World War II demonstrated.

As the principal sellers and buyers of a wartime command economy, industry and the military were able to combine their power to minimize the effects of a strengthened state on their operations. Such an extraordinary outcome was possible because WPB and its predecessors, established to organize sellers, were staffed primarily by industrialists on temporary duty. Additionally, the armed services were statutorily authorized to purchase their own weapons and supplies. Since a wartime economy is basically centered on procurement and production functions, military and industry managed to carry out their exchange in the name of the state without significant interference from other power groups and even the state itself.

Neither the corporate structure nor the armed forces favored a strengthened New Deal state. Corporations wanted no further advances in New Deal regulatory and welfare reforms. Besides sharing business's conservative and class values,

the military also opposed a stronger liberal state, because by more closely overseeing industry, such a state would also establish greater control over the armed
services. Leon Henderson and his associates in NDAC, OPM, and WPB were
intent on subordinating buyers as well as sellers to the rule of the civilian mobilization agencies. Indeed, they had to establish authority over both procurer and
supplier in order firmly to establish state control of mobilization.

In holding off state control, the military provided the corporate structure
with a nearly indispensable service: a high-level civil service system. Indeed,
throughout American history, the officer corps of both the army and the navy
have been the only extensive, professionalized civil service that the nation has
ever had. From the beginning of economic mobilization for World War II,
the military had the staff in Washington and the field, which the civilian mobilization agencies lacked in numbers and quality, for handling critical functions
such as priorities. If the WPB had had available to it the staffing of the ASF
or the OP&M, the board could have made the Production Requirement Plan
work. Such an allocation system would have provided WPB the wherewithal
centrally to direct the wartime economy.

Another critical attribute of the armed services was their command system,
which allowed them to speak with one voice despite the existence of varied
outlooks. That was the case even when they brought into their supply systems
great numbers of highly trained and capable civilians. The divisions and disputes that characterized all the mobilization agencies and the strife that all but
tore apart WPB were largely absent from the supply operations of the army
and navy, interservice rivalry notwithstanding. Furthermore, the military did
not have to tolerate state prerogatives, the National Guard notwithstanding,
interfering with their operations, as was the case with WMC. A state-oriented
and congressionally protected United States Employment System weakened
fundamentally WMC's effectiveness. Additionally, and of the greatest significance, the armed forces could invoke strategic necessity in protecting their
interests, which usually coincided with those of the corporation. And that was
the case whether national security was being used legitimately or for purposes
of convenience.

Under such circumstances, once PEC was established and running, Charles
E. Wilson and his corporate associates willingly allowed the military, and especially the War Department, to lead in mobilization. This trend became even
more exaggerated in the battle over demobilization. Unwilling and unable to
oppose Donald M. Nelson's modest reconversion plans based on preserving
competitive positions and limiting New Deal initiatives, corporate America
allowed an anxious War Department to do so under the nearly unassailable,
yet highly questionable, banner of battlefield need and troop welfare.

The armed services, of course, were supposedly under the civilian direction of the secretaries of war and the navy and their assistants and staff. Reality hardly matched theory during World War II. As commander-in-chief, Roosevelt bypassed his secretaries to deal directly with JCS on strategic matters. In terms of economic mobilization, Secretary of War Henry L. Stimson and Under Secretary Robert P. Patterson acted to protect military, not public, interests. On Stimson's part, that mode of action was exaggerated manyfold by an intense anti–New Deal bias. While Secretary of the Navy Frank Knox and Under Secretary James V. Forrestal usually followed the War Department's lead, they did so without either the fervor or the certainty of their War Department counterparts. The face of militarism in America during World War II manifested itself, not only in the officer corps of both services, but also in the secretary and under secretary of war's offices.

A huge military equipped with technologically advanced weaponry in the post–World War II years continued many of the patterns of the industry-military alliance of the war years, albeit at a lesser and different level. Nonetheless, World War II mobilization, and particularly the running encounter involving reconversion policy and timing, signaled trouble for America. The corporate community–armed forces partnership repeatedly demonstrated that it could operate in ways that served the interests of the partners at the expense of the nation's immediate and long-run interests. Certainly, the industry-military alliance would continue to act after the war, as it had during hostilities, as a powerful influence opposing reform.

18
MOBILIZING THE WORLD WAR II ECONOMY

THE PRODUCTION RECORD

Viewed in gross figures and in isolation, the American production effort during World War II appears impressive. GNP in 1939 dollars grew by 52 percent between 1939 and 1944, 124 percent in unadjusted dollars. Munitions production went from about 10 to 40 percent of total output between 1940 and 1943–1944. Manufacturing industries trebled their output during the period 1939–1944. All that was accomplished while consumer expenditures in 1944 were somewhere in the region of 10 percent above the 1939 mark. Going from national to international calculations, the United States in 1944 produced in excess of 40 percent of total world munitions output and around 50 percent more than either all its allies or all its enemies combined.[1]

From these or similar figures has grown the notion of wartime "miracles of production," "prodigious production," and like characterizations.[2] Such observations hold up only if the nation's prewar production potential and the achievements of other belligerents are ignored.

When placed in the proper context, the American production record does not appear exceptional, unless the characterization applies to all other belligerents. Gauged by the percentage distribution of the world's manufacturing production for the period 1926–1929, the United States in the peak year 1944 was producing munitions at almost exactly the level it should have been. Great Britain is modestly high, Canada low, Germany high, Japan very high, and the Soviet Union spectacularly high. If the period 1936–1938 is taken instead, the United States and Great Britain are reasonably high, Canada is still low, Germany and Japan are both high, but the Soviet Union is now somewhat low (see tables 1–3).

Of course, these figures are crude. But they are corroborated by Raymond W. Goldsmith, an economist serving on the War Production Board (WPB)

Table 1.   Percentage Distribution of the World's Manufacturing Production (excerpted)

Period	United States	Canada	United Kingdom	Soviet Union	Germany	Japan
1926/1929	42.2	2.4	9.4	4.3	11.6	2.5
1936/1938	32.2	2.0	9.2	18.5	10.7	3.5

Source: National Industrial Conference Board, *The Economic Almanac, 1953–1954* (New York: National Industrial Conference Board, 1955), pp. 600–601.

Table 2.   Volume of Combat Munitions Production of Major Belligerents (billions of dollars, 1944 U.S. munitions prices)

Country	1935–39	1940	1941	1942	1943	1944
United States	1.5	1.5	4.5	20	38	42
Canada	0	0	.5	1	1.5	1.5
Great Britain	2.5	3.5	6.5	9	11	11
Soviet Union	8	5	8.5	11.5	14	16
Germany	12	6	6	8.5	13.5	17
Japan	2	1	2	3	4.5	6

Source: Raymond W. Goldsmith, "The Power of Victory: Munition Output in World War II," *Military Affairs* 10 (1946): 75.

Note: In comparing manufacturing production before the war with munitions production in 1944, I am assuming a production level of about $100 billion, even though for the six countries listed the total comes to $93.5 billion. Table 3 below is a much more accurate gauge of what actually took place.

Table 3.   Prewar and Wartime Productivity in Major Belligerent Countries (production per manpower in United States = 100)

	All Prewar Manufacturing Industries, 1935–1938	War Munitions Industries, 1944
United States	100	100
Canada	71	57
Great Britain	36	41
Soviet Union	36	39
Germany	41	48
Japan	25	17

Source: Raymond W. Goldsmith, "The Power of Victory: Munitions Output in World War II," *Military Affairs* 10 (1946): 75. The prewar figures are taken from War Production Board Release TP-178. The 1944 data are rough estimates based on the figures for total combat munitions production given in table 2 above (increased by estimates of merchant vessels and motor vehicles), number of workers in the metal and basic chemical industries, and average hours per week. The data on number of workers and hours are taken from official sources for the United States, Canada, and the United Kingdom but based on rough estimates for the Soviet Union, Germany, and Japan.

Note: Robert Sobel, *Age of the Giant Corporation: A Microeconomic History of American Business, 1914–1970* (Westport, CT: Greenwood, 1972), p. 177, observes: "Big business was far stronger in 1938–1939 than most contemporaries had realized. Small- and medium-size firms suffered greatly during the depression, but the large concerns emerged without undue difficulty, and often stronger than they had been in 1929." Relatively few huge corporations constituted the basis of the American economic mobilization effort.

Planning Committee who later headed the Planning Division and specialized in the munitions output of America's allies and enemies. According to his principal finding:

> The munitions production of the major belligerents at full mobilization was roughly proportional to the size of their prewar industrial labor force combined with the prewar level of productivity in industry. This is hardly an astonishing result, but one which confirms the belief that basic economic factors rather than accidental developments or sudden changes in elementary economic relationships—more familiar under the names of "secret weapons" and "miracles of production"—have determined the course of munitions production.[3]

Goldsmith also found that about two years were required to convert fully from peace- to wartime production even if a nation started from scratch. Finally, he observed that, in 1944, all belligerents except for the United States, and perhaps Canada, had stretched themselves to the ultimate with a dropoff imminent for both Great Britain and Germany. For the United States, full mobilization had not been achieved, and an additional 10–20 percent increase in munitions production could have been implemented within a short period of time and without excessive strain "through some curtailment of civilian consumption even if only down to the prewar level, through a labor draft, and through a tighter control over the efficiency of munitions production."[4]

THE MOBILIZATION SYSTEM

In the absence of drastic interwar developments, World War II mobilization most likely would have picked up where World War I mobilization left off. Significantly affecting America's political economy, however, the Great Depression and the New Deal had far-reaching consequences for harnessing the World War II economy. As a result, beginning in mid-1940, both a civilian and a military mobilization structure came into being, and the two systems were not fully integrated until early in 1943.

President Franklin D. Roosevelt took a major step leading to that outcome in mid-1940 by appointing Henry L. Stimson and Frank Knox to head the War and Navy Departments, respectively. With the nation divided badly over American policy toward the outbreak of war in Europe and the Republican Party dominated by isolationists, Roosevelt was seeking to strengthen interventionist forces with the appointments. Stimson and Knox were both prominent

Republican internationalists. The new secretary of war recruited a high-powered team featuring Wall Street attorneys and financiers to run the department, and he turned to Robert P. Patterson to serve as under secretary. Knox tapped James V. Forrestal as under secretary of the navy, and the latter also turned primarily to Eastern elite circles in selecting his assistants. The top civilian staffs of the two principal departments for conducting the war were predominantly Republican in a Democratic administration.

These developments were most consequential for the War Department. Stimson was a military-oriented neo-Hamiltonian who was intensely elitist in outlook and strongly anti–New Deal. Although not as ideological as the secretary of war, Patterson shared Stimson's military mind-set and was ardent in his insistence on the need for wartime sacrifice. By comparison, Knox and Forrestal were much less martial in nature, more flexible, and rather open-minded about the New Deal.

The War Department led in mobilization matters. It did so because the army was the largest procurement agency, interwar procurement and industrial mobilization planning familiarized the department with the economics of warfare, and Stimson knew his way around Washington and was among the most prestigious wartime leaders. The Navy Department either hung back on mobilization or followed the War Department's lead. Knox and Forrestal may also have been more hesitant about the economics of war because the navy was less prepared for wartime supply operations than was the army and the civilian heads of the department constantly had to ward off Admiral Ernest J. King's attempts to undermine their authority.

These realities led to the emergence between mid-1940 and January 1942 of competing and, at times, contradictory mobilization structures that were only partially related. The first consisted of the serial agencies set up by the Roosevelt Administration, the National Defense Advisory Commission (NDAC), the Office of Production Management (OPM), and the Supply Priorities and Allocations Board. The second was the War Department, backed to a degree by the Navy Department, which attempted, without much success, to coordinate the supply and procurement operations of the two services through the Army-Navy Munitions Board (ANMB). The complexity of the situation was compounded by the fact that the civilian mobilization agencies were temporary in nature and created by executive orders; the armed forces were permanent government entities statutorily authorized.

Both mobilization systems were basically flawed because they were decentralized: the NDAC and OPM among functional divisions; the armed services among supply bureaus. Leaders in both structures worked for centralization, but that was not achieved until after Pearl Harbor with the creation of WPB and the sweeping reforms of the armed services' supply and procurement organizations. For successful mobilization, the two systems then had to be integrated. The contradictions that had grown among them between 1940 and 1942 made that accomplishment extremely difficult, leading to the ongoing conflict that racked WPB throughout its existence.

From 1940 through 1942, the two systems related most harmoniously in the negotiation of contracts between the army and navy supply bureaus and the corporations. The Production Division in both NDAC and OPM coordinated and facilitated the process on the basis of the idea that civilian mobilization agencies existed to assist the military. The day-to-day operations of the Production Division and others were carried out by what came to be called industry divisions, staffed by dollar-a-year men from the industries involved and assisted by industry advisory committees. This had also been the approach devised during World War I for mobilizing a corporate capitalist system that lacked a higher civil service system capable of doing so. Efforts were made during World War II to reduce and better police the rampant conflicts of interest involved in the industry-division structure during World War I, but the progress made was at best problematic.

The industry divisions became the foundation of agencies harnessing the economy. They were mainly responsible for keeping the mobilization system going in the face of the constant controversy roiling NDAC, OPM, and WPB. Moreover, they were a critical component of the corporate community–armed services nexus that dominated the wartime economy. That connection was in time furthered and deepened by businessmen recruited to serve in the military's supply operations and by the armed forces appointing representatives to the industry divisions.

Without the New Deal, a perfected form of the World War I industry-military mobilization nexus would probably have gone unchallenged. Because of the New Deal, that alliance was constantly under attack beginning in 1940. Hard-nosed reformers such as Leon Henderson and representatives for labor, agriculture, consumers, and small business rejected the idea of William S. Knudsen, Edward R. Stettinius, Jr., and most other corporate executives on temporary duty that NDAC and OPM existed for the benefit of the army and navy. They insisted that those agencies had a duty to ensure that mobilization maximally met public interests and was carried out for purposes of efficiency, stability, and equity. That meant that NDAC and its successors would approve and clear the armed services' contracts, oversee their requirements, administer priorities, and perform related functions. With NDAC and OPM divided between corporate advocates and reformers, the military largely remained free of mobilization agency control. It did so by ignoring NDAC and OPM, only nominally going along with their requests and directives, or maneuvering successfully to take over mobilization agency functions such as priorities. That left the army and navy to deal with the corporate structure as they chose.

The complicated dynamics of economic mobilization in the defense years were further confused by the fact that Leon Henderson, Donald M. Nelson, Stacy May, and others in their circle assisted the military in numerous and vital ways. They pressured a reluctant industry to expand and convert its plant for defense output, devised creative means, like the Defense Plant Corporation, for financing facilities when corporate America balked at doing so, worked for more effective agencies to harness the economy, and insisted that the armed services increase greatly their requirements and present them to the mobilization administrations in a usable and reliable way.

While recognizing the positive mobilization aims of New Dealers, the War and Navy Departments never lost sight of the fact that the reformers' contributions were short-run expedients and that those such as Leon Henderson often antagonized industry, as in the disputes over contract distribution, excess profits taxation, and strengthening state functions at the expense of the private sector. The military remained acutely aware that its long-run interests rested with the corporate structure, on which it was dependent for the output of munitions and supplies. Industry reciprocated since the army and navy negotiated and let contracts. Consequently, more often than not, the armed services and corporate America stood together on mobilization policy even though, at times, their immediate interests differed.

By mid-1941, the tension and contradictions multiplying within and between the two systems for harnessing the economy had reached the point where mobilization was stalling. Not yet ready for basically reorganizing the structure, Roosevelt turned to an ingenious solution for breaking the growing stalemate. He created the Supply Priorities and Allocations Board. It was dominated by high-level liberal all-outers on whom the president could depend to restore mobilization momentum. In that way, the corporate community–armed services contractual connection was left undisturbed, but industry and the military were forced both to move forward and to raise their sights in preparing for war.

The WPB, organized shortly after Pearl Harbor, never succeeded in resolving the conflicts and inconsistencies characterizing the NDAC and OPM. In order for it to accomplish that goal, fundamental change was essential. There were basically two ways to straighten out the tangled mobilization patterns once America entered war: have WPB take over military procurement; or create a high-level administrative body to coordinate economic output with armed forces requirements. Neither solution was feasible because of the peculiarities of

American political economy and power operations. WPB, therefore, came up with a third alternative. After a turbulent year devising basic regulatory devices, it merged the civilian and military mobilization structures in a way allowing industry and the armed forces to dominate the board. Although clumsy and contentious, the expedient worked, and it was continuous with NDAC and OPM procedures.

Proposals by members of Congress, wartime mobilizers, and scholars that WPB absorb army and navy wartime purchasing apparatus were unrealistic. That was the case not because, as the armed forces insisted, such an act would threaten the integrity of their supply operations. To varying degrees, most other countries created civilian munitions ministries with positive results. Instead, procurement remained with the military because America lacked reliable civilian structures for carrying out such operations. Without a higher civil service, industrialists serving for nominal salaries would end up awarding billions of dollars of contracts to their own companies. Such blatant conflicts of interest would be politically intolerable. Even if the practice were acceptable, civilians did not have the personnel to perform such vast transactions. Under NDAC, OPM, and, for a time, WPB, priorities fell to the military by default because those agencies lacked the organization and staff to perform on a national scale such complex and demanding functions. Placing military buying in civilian hands sounded like a good idea; as became evident during World War I, the nature of the American political economy made the proposition all but impossible.

A war production council headed by the president and consisting of members from the WPB, the political structure, and the Joint Chiefs of Staff and meant to synchronize economic mobilization and military strategy was theoretically possible. That was the solution proposed by the Planning Committee during the feasibility crisis. While insisting on feasible military requirements and realizing the need for a war production council, WPB chair Donald M. Nelson withheld support for a council because it was too controversial. Opposition to excessively increasing state power even in times of war stood in the way. The New Deal strengthened that tendency. Industry was intent on using the national emergency to check further reform, refurbish its depression-tarnished reputation, and reclaim its dominant place in American society. It could expect support from a conservative, obstructive Congress. More important, corporations and the military by 1942 had forged close ties. Together, they could thwart any mobilization system that was perceived as threatening or reducing their latitude, as would be the case with a high-level council. In that regard, the United States was all but unique. Practically every other industrialized nation during World Wars I and II relied on some variation of a war production council. Without such a system, the World War II American military assumed levels of power that were unusual, and unwise, in a democratic country.

In the early months of 1942, WPB appeared to be getting off to a slow but reasonable start. A closer look, however, revealed extremely volatile developments. The corporate structure was on the defensive because it had not yet found its mobilization footing and was still resisting full conversion. New Dealers had the offensive because they had been the chief preparedness advocates. The armed services ended up assisting industry in regaining the initiative in WPB operations. That resulted from the War and Navy Departments continuing to operate largely free of WPB controls, as they had in NDAC and OPM, in setting requirements, awarding contracts, building facilities, granting priorities, and other areas.

Realizing the economic havoc that would ensue, Nelson moved to rein in the armed services. In doing so, he was encouraged and supported by a few corporate leaders (such as James S. Knowlson), Stacy May, and the Planning Committee. Headed by Robert R. Nathan, a smart and tough statistician in the Leon Henderson mold, the committee emerged as the aggressive New Deal planning unit in WPB. Its members became major policy advisers to Nelson in 1942.

WPB first attempted to bend the military to its will over facility construction. Although failing in that endeavor, the Planning Committee won a significant victory in forcing the armed services to reduce their overall requirements to a feasible range. However, with WPB then reclaiming priorities control and switching to an allocations system, industry and the military together began reasserting their dominance within WPB. They did so by defeating the Production Requirements Plan, which would have centralized mobilization controls under the WPB chair and his lieutenants at the expense of the industry divisions and the procurement agencies. Instead, they pushed through the Controlled Materials Plan (CMP), which formalized and rationalized industry division–armed services mobilization operations reaching back to NDAC and OPM. Moreover, CMP brought into WPB Ferdinand Eberstadt, who epitomized the emerging industry-military mobilization alliance.

Although an enormously talented executive, Eberstadt was too aggressive and too intent on dominating WPB. In those circumstances, the Planning Committee won one last victory. It convinced Nelson of the need to schedule armed services production in order to maintain economic balance. In moving to implement the process, the WPB chair ran into the greatest resistance that he had yet encountered from the military because the stakes were so high. Roosevelt had to step in personally to resolve the imbroglio, and Nelson was compelled to fire

Eberstadt. The blowup led to Charles E. Wilson in effect taking over WPB and managing it through the military-dominated Production Executive Committee (PEC). As a result, the Planning Committee and other New Deal elements were either eliminated from or subordinated within WPB.

WPB had returned to the principal patterns of the NDAC and OPM. But now the two mobilization systems were integrated through the operations of the PEC and strengthened industry divisions on which the armed services were more fully represented. Additionally, WPB could now run effectively and stably because its operations were based on feasible requirements and guided by a proper allocations system and production scheduling, controls basically worked out by New Dealers before they were eclipsed.

Donald M. Nelson was the principal victim of the WPB's mobilization battles in 1942. Basic to his troubled and perplexing years as chair of WPB was his opposition to the emerging industry-military wartime alliance. Nelson's years in NDAC and OPM had exposed him fully to the parochial qualities of corporate America and the armed forces; his battles in behalf of feasibility, allocations, and production scheduling strengthened his negative views.

Although from the corporate world and fully devoted to the American business system, Nelson in the defense and war years increasingly allied himself with those like Leon Henderson, Robert R. Nathan, and Stacy May. He did so because their analysis of and recommendations concerning economic mobilization were broad, informed, and astute; they were also consistent with public, over special, interests. His affinity for reformers, however, made Nelson suspect among corporate executives, limiting his ability to win and maintain their support. Those circumstances generated terrible tensions for Nelson. Uncomfortable with confrontation, he constantly searched for middle ground, making himself appear weak and vacillating. Beyond question, Nelson could be frustrating as he denied or sugarcoated obvious conflict or delayed making troublesome decisions. Nonetheless, once he had made up his mind on an important issue, the WPB chair stood his ground, as demonstrated during the struggles over feasibility, allocations, production scheduling, and, even more, demobilization. Alarmed by the distorted decisionmaking in the WPB under the influence of industry and the military during 1943, Nelson began viewing mobilization from the perspective of reformers, labor, small business, and consumers. Acting on his concern, he aggressively attempted to reassert his control of the board early in 1944 so as to shape reconversion. Facing overwhelming odds, the Roosevelt administration finally had to ease Nelson out of WPB.

Perhaps Nelson was imprudent in not accepting emerging power patterns in WPB. However, he seemed no more capable of joining the industry-military juggernaut than did Henderson and Nathan. (The price that Nelson paid for his integrity was great since he was exiled from elite corporate circles and has been treated harshly by history.) The only New Dealer who might have accepted the system as a managing participant was Secretary of the Interior Harold L. Ickes, if his directorship of the Petroleum Administration for War is any indication. Given how that administration was staffed and run, Ickes probably would have remained in charge as WPB chair, but with approximately the same outcome as occurred under Charles E. Wilson.

Despite serious limitations, Nelson was one of the few high-ranking business mobilizers who had the wit and the courage to insist that mobilization be carried out for the benefit of the entire economic system and the population as a whole, not principally for the corporate giants alone. Others sharing his views either left or were pushed out of WPB, including Knowlson, Arthur D. Whiteside, and Hiland G. Batcheller. Survivors, like William L. Batt and Julius A. Krug, remained silent or switched their positions and allegiance. Too often, leading corporate executives tended to be narrowly focused on corporate welfare, excessively devoted to military values, driven by ambition and greed, well meaning but ineffective, or insecure and petty. Industrial leaders performed best at the industry-division level, dealing with areas closest to their peacetime pursuits. President Roosevelt, Bureau of the Budget Director Harold D. Smith, and the bureau's mobilization specialist and, for a time, a WPB official, Bernard L. Gladieux, repeatedly complained about the apparent inability of corporate executives to deal with the complexities of public service effectively.

World War II mobilization, of course, elevated the military to a position of extraordinary power and influence. In analyzing that situation, various scholars insist that the armed services were little more than lackeys for corporate-financial America during hostilities. In arguing their case, they point to civilian elites recruited by Secretary of War Stimson and Secretary of the Navy Knox for managing their wartime departments. Additionally, they hold that the procurement structures of both services were staffed heavily with business executives in or out of uniform. Claims are also made to the effect that army, navy, and air forces officers were directly or indirectly offered corporate or financial positions on retiring from the armed services. The postarmy careers of Generals Brehon B. Somervell and Lucius D. Clay and the general pattern of officers joining firms after leaving the military are cited. Finally, these analysts maintain that, as long as business interests were being served, corporations had no reason to challenge military mobilization policies.[5]

These points are true to varying degrees without validating the larger assertion that the armed services lack an independent power base. Industry and the military were using one another during the defense and war years for separate and shared purposes. Nonetheless, the two are distinct, although not equal, power groups. Industry is clearly the dominant one. The aims of the two power groups also differ. The armed forces' principal goal is defending the nation; the corporation looks to maximizing profits.

The military, however, did provide the corporate structure with a number of invaluable, protective practices during hostilities. They included a large and expandable higher civil service system that constituted a disciplined hierarchy for making and enforcing decisions; extensive experience with bureaucratic infighting, particularly at the Washington level; and, most important, strategic necessity as a rationale for implementing controversial policies. Those characteristics were already evident in 1940–1941, but they became much more exaggerated when General Brehon D. Somervell took over as commanding general of the Army Service Forces (ASF) shortly after WPB was created in January 1942.

The general's great talents were matched or exceeded by grave shortcomings. Acting at times as if he bordered on emotional imbalance, Somervell was the economic mobilization counterpart of General George S. Patton, Jr. Like Patton, he required close supervision. Instead, Chief of Staff George C. Marshall, who neither knew much about nor indicated any desire to become involved in procurement and economic mobilization, gave his ASF chief free rein and usually provided him with unquestioned support. Stimson and Patterson also allowed the freewheeling general to proceed without restraint. The only time that they interfered was during the feasibility dispute (probably at White House insistence) and when Somervell, with Marshall's backing, attempted to push through reforms including the consolidation of the supply bureaus. Marshall, Stimson, and Patterson appeared to welcome Somervell's blunderbuss approach since it served their purposes without dirtying their hands.

There were other possibilities in terms of ASF leadership. The most promising was General James H. Burns. He served for a time as Patterson's executive officer and was thoroughly familiar with the War Department's procurement and industrial mobilization planning. He led in a drive at the Washington level for increasing army requirements while the rest of the service, including Marshall, was holding back. Burns also had served in various capacities in the civilian mobilization agencies, including assisting Harry L. Hopkins with what became the Office of Lend-Lease Administration. Why Burns was not considered for the position as ASF commanding general is unclear. Not liking and appearing to fear Burns, Somervell maneuvered to deny him the position as chief of the Ordnance Department.

Had Somervell concentrated more of his ample energies on improving War Department supply operations, including requirements calculations, facilities programs, and inventory control, and less on warding off or encroaching on the prerogatives of civilian mobilization agencies, he would have made a greater contribution. His navy counterpart, Admiral Samuel M. Robinson, faced a different but equally challenging assignment, which he performed without creating such turmoil. Military waste and unnecessary expenditures were massive. How much is hard to say since the subject has not been researched in depth. On the basis of the findings of the Senate Special Committee to Investigate the Defense Program, reviews of the Office of War Mobilization (OWM)/Office of War Mobilization and Reconversion (OWMR), and other sources, waste among the armed services probably was somewhere in the region of one-quarter to one-third of total wartime military outlays.

The industry-military mobilization alliance manifested its worst proclivities during the reconversion controversy. Nelson began seriously looking at reconversion at the end of 1943 when the converted economy had hit its stride and could meet all feasible requirements. The person in the street as well as those in official positions could sense that such was the case. Otherwise, the WPB chair would not have had the widespread support that he did. For the military and industry to hector a population, most of which had relatives in the armed services, for letting down the troops was more than presumptuous. No explanation of the running battle over demobilization makes any sense other than military arrogance combined with corporate insecurities. Behind both was the fear of a liberal resurgence if Nelson and those in his circle regained control of the WPB.

What took place with reconversion was anticipated earlier by the seriously flawed corporate community–armed services leadership. Civilian supply was needlessly and capriciously restricted. Greater attention to housing, transportation systems, medical services, and community facilities would have added to, not distracted from, war output. Smaller business units were never adequately tapped. On a broader plane, few serious shortages in the workforce would have occurred had selection for the armed services and manpower mobilization been rationally handled. Instead, the military recruited in a reckless fashion, the Selective Service System ran illogically, contracts were distributed without concern for congesting communities, and efforts to utilize manpower maximally were blocked. The War Manpower Commission (WMC) was vilified for not overcoming such obstacles, and national service legislation was relentlessly pushed by the armed forces as a panacea for labor woes. Facing much worse conditions with far fewer resources, Britain did a great deal better than the United States did in these areas.

Growing conflict within the wartime economy forced the Roosevelt administration in May 1943 to set up the OWM, headed by James F. Byrnes. The new office was not a war production council but rather a coordinating and mediating body for minimizing strife within the enormously complex and fragmented mobilization system. Increasingly absorbed in military strategy and diplomacy, and declining in health, the president could no longer manage the homefront largely on his own, as he had done from 1940 through 1942. Byrnes had begun assuming some domestic responsibilities late in 1942 as director of the Office of Economic Stabilization. An experienced, cautious political leader, Byrnes performed his task well. In doing so, he served Roosevelt and provided him political cover in gradually guiding the administration away from New Deal standards and toward the traditional values of the industry-military mobilization alliance dominating the capital. Basically conservative, Byrnes was well suited for and comfortable with the task that he faced, which no doubt played a large part in the president's selecting him for such a critical post.

Byrnes spent a good part of his time acting as arbiter among contending forces in the WPB, settling disputes between the board and the armed services, and dealing with the multiple problems of the WMC. Nevertheless, he also intervened in the operations of the numerous other wartime agencies when that became necessary. His skill helped keep the makeshift mobilization system running as it faced greater strain.

The numerous other agencies for harnessing the economy had a mixed record. Overseen ultimately by the Office of Economic Stabilization, the combined leadership of the Bureau of the Budget, the Office of Price Administration, the Treasury Department, and the National War Labor Board financed the war in a reasonably successful manner and held down inflationary pressures in a very accomplished way. Many reform elements in the Leon Henderson circle, who played such a critical role in devising the controls for successful economic mobilization, also participated in formulating the administration's economic stabilization and war-financing policies.

By comparison with agencies for war finance and economic stabilization, the Agricultural Department/War Food Administration performed poorly because of bureaucratic ossification and parochial intervention on the part of the Farm Establishment. For railroads, the Office of Defense Transportation performed exceptionally, but, when it came to motor and water transport, it fell down. Few wartime agencies equaled the high quality of the War Shipping Administration. The Munitions Assignment Board functioned in a creditable way. But, with the United States unwilling to share its authority and wealth on an equal basis with Britain, the other combined boards withered. The tangled bureaucracy for foreign economic policy accomplished a great deal and was rationalized to a degree only late in 1943 with the creation of the Foreign Economic Administration.

Central to economic mobilization was the president. That was the case even after Byrnes's elevation to OWM. Practically until his death, and even when events abroad absorbed most of his time and diminishing energy, the president's attention was required on homefront matters. By any measure, Roosevelt's leadership during the defense and war years was remarkable, all the more so since he relied on a small White House staff, the Bureau of the Budget, and, later, OWM/OWMR to manage the war at home and abroad.

From the outbreak of hostilities in Europe until Pearl Harbor, the president at times seemed to stand almost alone in his conviction that the American economy could meet all the demands of a global war. Although the mobilization system emerged slowly and awkwardly, it met and could even have gone beyond the president's goals. Roosevelt did not appear to welcome corporations and the armed forces taking over the process of harnessing the economy. But he was realistic enough to know that that is what would take place. At the same time, the president seemed to encourage or at least not to discourage challenges to that power grouping from labor, small business, consumers, and New Deal elements and their supporters in Congress.

All that said, two major questions remain: Was Roosevelt concerned about the growth of military power and influence during the war and its likely continuance at a high level after the war? And did the president, political rhetoric and platitudes aside, have meaningful intentions or plans for continuing reform in the postwar years? The first question is easier to answer than the second.

The president never seemed overly concerned about the armed services achieving excessive power, although he did not dismiss the issue as unimportant. Several decisions point to presidential caution about the armed services. In mid-1939, for example, Roosevelt placed the ANMB directly under his authority as the board prepared to take on mobilization functions. And, in February 1942, he ordered that a reorganized ANMB operate under the WPB. He purposefully refused to grant the Joint Chiefs of Staff greater status and security through confirming its organization with an executive order. He also repeatedly stepped in to prevent Admiral King from taking over supply operations from Secretary Knox and Under Secretary Forrestal. Additionally, by creating the War Shipping Administration, the president kept a critical service away from the narrowly oriented military command and under the direction of the broadly oriented Lewis W. Douglas.

Nonetheless, Roosevelt both allowed military influence at the White House to grow during hostilities and guarded the armed services against proper civilian scrutiny. In July 1942, he appointed Admiral William D. Leahy as chief of staff to the president. As illness sidelined Harry L. Hopkins in the last years of the war, Roosevelt turned increasingly to the conservative Leahy for advice. (Hopkins himself had grown more and more conservative as the war progressed.) Although on a lesser scale, General Edwin M. ("Pa") Watson, as the president's appointments secretary, provided the War Department with an additional entry to and a source of information about the White House. By 1944 and 1945, War Department influence at the White House had grown so strong that the president endorsed first tentatively and then unequivocally unneeded and terribly divisive national service legislation.

In January 1942, the president, on the advice of Hopkins, agreed to Chief of Staff Marshall's ultimatum that the Munitions Assignment Board had to remain answerable to the Combined Chiefs of Staff, not to Roosevelt and Winston Churchill. Marshall insisted that he had to have control of supply to fulfill his mission. The president also failed to back Byrnes in persuading Leahy to assist in reviewing military requirements or in making the Joint Production Survey Committee work effectively in critically examining questionable army and navy demands. Indeed, in January 1945, the Bureau of the Budget had to call on Byrnes's assistance in persuading Roosevelt to back off in supporting eighty-four additional and unneeded naval ships. Without at least the president's tacit support, Byrnes would never have embraced so completely the military's furious assault on Nelson's reconversion program.

On balance, Roosevelt was reasonably comfortable with an expanding military and its growing power, and he seemed confident of his ability to manage the services effectively. As the war went on, his dependence on the armed services grew, and his concern about that development appeared to lessen. Although the president could not anticipate the specifics of the massive military establishment of the Cold War years, he knew that the postwar services would be larger and better armed and equipped than had been the case in the interwar years. That reality raised no alarm with him, although he did begin to think about issues of service unification and reorganization.

The critical matter of modern warfare drawing together industry and the military never seemed to bother Roosevelt before or during the war. In the interwar years, the Senate Special Committee Investigating the Munitions Industry (the Nye Committee, after its chair, Senator Gerald P. Nye [R-ND]) analyzed in depth what it called "an unhealthy alliance" between business and the armed services, and the committee focused a great deal of attention on the expanding navy. Not only did the Roosevelt administration ignore the committee's findings and recommendations, but it also consistently sought to undermine Nye and his colleagues. In 1940 and 1941, the president was troubled by industrialists in the mobilization agencies, and he kept the clearance process for appointing dollar-a-year men at the White House level. After Pearl Harbor, however, such worries were dropped. The president was reluctant to replace Nelson with Bernard M. Baruch in February 1943, and he took a strong dislike to Ferdinand Eberstadt, both of whom came to epitomize what would later be labeled the military-industrial complex, but his motivations were personal, not institutional. Along those lines, Roosevelt personally recruited Charles E. Wilson for service in the WPB, and he intervened throughout 1943–1944 to strengthen Wilson's position vis-à-vis that of Nelson. By that time, Wilson embodied the principles of the industry-military alliance in an even more direct way than either Baruch or Eberstadt.

The president's record on the future of reform is no better than his apprehension about the role of an expanding military in American life. During 1940–1941, as the economic mobilization system was being fashioned, Roosevelt took pains to guarantee that interest group and class interests appeared to be balanced in NDAC and OPM. He made sure that New Dealers were in positions of power, labor was represented, small business received attention, the civilian population was protected, and war profits legislation was enacted. With war declared, the president continued many of these efforts, most important of which was the selection of Donald M. Nelson to head the WPB. He appears to have intervened personally to ensure the success of the Planning Committee's drive for feasible military requirements.

Once the mobilization structure operated properly and produced at a level meeting demand, the president downplayed reform. New Dealers were removed from or disempowered within most mobilization agencies. The selection of James F. Byrnes to act as assistant president for the homefront loudly signaled that the administration was stressing output, not reform. This dramatic shift to the right became so strong that a conservative and recalcitrant Congress considered or enacted legislation to protect the civilian population, guard the interests of small business, and temper the blatant behavior of corporate structures involved in synthetic rubber. Agencies for housing, consumer welfare, and community services were scattered, uncoordinated, poorly funded, and generally neglected. More and better attention to congested areas would have led to improved mobilization conditions. That being the case, Congress most likely would have supported, even welcomed, greater appropriations for improved conditions if requests for them had been properly presented. They were not.

The Senate Special Committee to Investigate the Defense Industry and other progressive congressional committees raised the alarm about the reactionary behavior of the industry-military mobilization alliance in the face of

Roosevelt administration silence. Attempts to address the human side of reconversion came from Congress, not the Roosevelt administration, which went headlong in pursuit of Baruch and John M. Hancock's conservative polices. The Truman administration was unable to maintain stable postwar economic conditions in large part because the Roosevelt administration had allowed the industry-military alliance to block meaningful planning for demobilization and reasonable increases in civilian output even after the end of the war was at hand.

The issue of reform was revived only with the presidential election campaign of 1944. The outcome of that election turned out to be reasonably positive for the president and congressional Democrats, not because the Roosevelt administration's record was that good, but because the Republican Party alternative was that bad. Moreover, labor and especially the Congress of Industrial Organizations's Political Action Committee had mobilized voters effectively because of the hostile atmosphere in which unions operated.

The truth of the matter is that the New Deal as a reform movement was largely spent no later than 1938. From then on, foreign and military policy took precedent. No wonder, then, that the Roosevelt administration had little to offer in the way of progressive advance during the defense and war periods. The slight gains made were forced on the administration, as occurred with militant blacks insisting on what became the Fair Employment Practices Committee. The unhappy aspect of the New Deal in this period is that, while the reform movement was exhausted, reformers were still numerous, but they had become excessively dependent on one overextended, increasingly exhausted, and ultimately dying leader. Without a movement or a leader, reformers grew increasingly dispirited and disoriented. Such being the case, the future of reform in April 1945 appropriately looked bleak.

A sad and ironic legacy of the New Deal was that it helped create the partnership between corporate and military America that was so destructive to reform. In the defense and war years, New Dealers took the lead in preparing the nation for World War II. Once hostilities ensued, the same reformers were at the center of devising the structure and controls essential for successfully harnessing the economy for war under stable economic conditions. Many of those same New Dealers, along with Donald M. Nelson, who came to embody some of the New Deal's better attributes, became victims of the industry-military alliance that their mobilization policies and methods had assisted in bringing into being.

With its reform energies low, the Roosevelt administration in 1942 began relying on plenty to direct the nation: the vast potential strength of the American economy that the administration in years of peace never had been able fully to stimulate. Nevertheless, New Deal government had greatly advanced the nation's ability to maximize its might under the right conditions. With industry dragging its heels, Washington stepped in to finance the expansion of munitions output and basic industries like aluminum. Practically unlimited demand, guaranteed profits, new and augmented plant at bargain prices, and the other benefits of a war economy regenerated corporate confidence and revived industry's creativity and drive. Farmers were literally bought off with undeserved subsidies. Nearly unlimited employment opportunities at relatively high wages allowed the Roosevelt administration to rely essentially on market forces for mobilizing workers. Growing unions assisted by a weak WMC and the threat of national service legislation were relied on to keep in line migrating masses facing inadequate community facilities and services. Ultimately, severe price, wage, and related controls were used to tame inflationary pressures more than steep taxes, profit restraints, or forced savings. Bulging corporate treasuries and accumulated worker savings held out the promise of at least temporary plenty in the postwar years.

Relying on plenty for mobilizing a war economy had one fundamental drawback. Unmatched prosperity was brought about by direct and indirect spending for the armed forces. That acted to elevate an authoritarian military to a dominant power position in a democratic society and contractually tied it to the corporate structure. Since massive military expenditures were expected to be temporary with the armed forces returned to modest size as occurred after World War I, potential wartime dangers seemed remote. The Cold War, of course, proved those prognostications wrong. Large financial outlays for the armed forces became permanent. The result was the military-industrial complex. As during World War II, that complex operated to the immediate economic benefit of most within the society. In the long run, however, it created profound problems for America.

The four factors shaping the political economy of warfare help put in historical perspective how the World War II economy was harnessed for hostilities. The maturity of the economy, as the first factor, allowed the Roosevelt administration to use plenty as the driving force for economic mobilization. In terms of the second factor—the size, strength, and scope of the federal government—more complicated considerations come into play. New Deal government in its quest for recovery grew in size, sophistication, and quality of staffing, and it encouraged organization among business, agriculture, and labor. All these developments contributed to the mobilization process. Yet, in antagonizing industry, the reform movement limited mobilization by making corporate leaders suspicious of and resistant to government controls and agencies. The New Deal also heightened class and interest group tensions, which added to the tumult of the wartime economy.

Civil-military relations, as the third factor, had an overwhelming impact on harnessing the economy for war. Prepared for mobilization by years of planning, and fortified by civilian elites, the armed services refused to integrate their procurement apparatus into civilian mobilization agencies except on their own terms. When those conditions were met, the military allied itself with the anxious corporate community to formulate conservative mobilization policies that protected the welfare of both. In part, the growing sophistication of weaponry—the fourth factor—acted to draw industry and the military together and enhance their clout. During World War II, however, the quantity of munitions and the intricate economic controls essential for producing them are what stood out.

NOTES

ABBREVIATIONS USED IN ARCHIVAL CITATIONS

AFL, *Annual Proceedings:* American Federation of Labor, *Report of the Proceedings of the . . . Annual Convention* (various years)

Amberg Collection: Julius H. Amberg Collection, Records of the Office of the Secretary of War, RG 107, National Archives, College Park, MD

ANMB: Records of the Joint Army and Navy Boards and Committees, RG 225, National Archives, College Park, MD

ASF: Records of the Army Service Forces, RG 160, National Archives, College Park, MD

Baruch Papers: Bernard M. Baruch Papers, Princeton University, Princeton, NJ

BofB: Series 39.27, Bureau of the Budget, RG 51, National Archives, College Park, MD

Booz Report: Booz, Fry, Allen and Hamilton, "Survey of the Office of the Under Secretary of War," 2 vols., file 310, "Business Methods," General Correspondence of Under Secretary of War Robert Patterson, 12/40-3/43, Under Secretary of War, Records of the Office of the Secretary of War, RG 107, National Archives, College Park, MD

CIO, *Annual Proceedings:* Congress of Industrial Organizations, *Proceedings of the . . . Constitutional Convention* (various years)

Clark Papers: Grenville Clark Papers, Dartmouth College, Hanover, VT

Coy Papers: Wayne Coy Papers, Franklin D. Roosevelt Library, Hyde Park, NY

Dorr Collection: Goldthwaite H. Dorr Collection, Records of the Office of the Secretary of War, RG 107, National Archives, College Park, MD

Eberstadt Papers: Ferdinand Eberstadt Papers, Princeton University, Princeton, NJ

Emmerich Papers: Herbert Emmerich Papers, University of Virginia, Charlottesville, VA

FDR Papers: Franklin D. Roosevelt Papers, Franklin D. Roosevelt Library, Hyde Park, NY

Fesler Papers: James W. Fesler Papers, 1965 Accession, Yale University, New Haven, CT

Gladieux Reminiscences: "The Reminiscences of Bernard L. Gladieux," 1951, Oral History Collection of Columbia University (for further information on the Gladieux

Reminiscences, see Elizabeth B. Mason and Louis M. Starr, *The Oral History Collection of Columbia University* [New York: Oral History Research Office, 1979])

Green Papers: William Green Collection, Wisconsin State Historical Society, Madison, WI

Greenbaum Collection: Edward S. Greenbaum Collection, Records of the Office of the Secretary of War, RG 107, National Archives, College Park, MD

Henderson Papers: Leon Henderson Papers, Franklin D. Roosevelt Library, Hyde Park, NY

Hertz Collection: John D. Hertz Collection, Records of the Office of the Secretary of War, RG 107, National Archives, College Park, MD

McGrady Collection: Edward F. McGrady Collection, Records of the Office of the Secretary of War, RG 107, National Archives, College Park, MD

McReynolds Papers: William H. McReynolds Papers, Franklin D. Roosevelt Library, Hyde Park, NY

Murray Papers: Philip M. Murray Papers, Catholic University, Washington, DC

Nelson Papers: Donald M. Nelson Papers, Huntington Library, San Marino, CA

OF: Official File

Ohly Papers: John H. Ohly Papers, Harry S. Truman Presidential Library, Independence, MO

OSW: Records of the Office of the Secretary of War, RG 107, National Archives, College Park, MD

OWMR: Records of the Office of War Mobilization and Reconversion, RG 250, National Archives, College Park, MD

PEC: Production Executive Committee

Petersen Collection: Howard C. Petersen Collection, Records of the Office of the Secretary of War, RG 107, National Archives, College Park, MD

PSF: President's Secretary's File

Rosenman Papers: Samuel I. Rosenman Papers, Franklin D. Roosevelt Library, Hyde Park, NY

RWA, BOB: Series 41.3, Division of Administrative Management, War Records Section and Committee on Records of War Administration, Records 1941–1947, Bureau of the Budget, RG 51, National Archives, College Park, MD

Smith Papers: Harold D. Smith Papers, Franklin D. Roosevelt Library, Hyde Park, NY

Stimson Diary: Henry L. Stimson Diary, January 1939 to September 1945, 23 vols., Yale University, New Haven, CT

Truman Committee: U.S. Congress, Senate, Special Committee to Investigate the National Defense Program (called the *Truman Committee* after its chair, Senator Harry S. Truman [D-MO])

USW/OSW: Records of the Under Secretary of War, Records of the Office of the Secretary of War, RG 107, National Archives, College Park, MD

Wadsworth Papers: James W. Wadsworth Papers, Library of Congress, Washington, DC

WMC: Records of the War Manpower Commission, RG 211, National Archives, College Park, MD

WPB: Records of the War Production Board, RG 179, National Archives, College Park, MD

CHAPTER ONE. ORIGINS, STRUCTURE, AND STAFFING
OF THE NDAC

1. For the tangled history of the Reorganization Act of 1939, see Luther Gulick, *Administrative Reflection from World War II* (University: University of Alabama Press, 1948); Louis Brownlow, *A Passion for Anonymity: The Autobiography of Louis Brownlow, Second Half* (Chicago: University of Chicago Press, 1958), pp. 313–455; Barry D. Karl, *Executive Reorganization and Reform in the New Deal: The Genesis of Administrative Management, 1900–1939* (Cambridge, MA: Harvard University Press, 1963); Richard Polenberg, *Reorganizing Roosevelt's Government: The Controversy over Executive Reorganization, 1937–1939* (Cambridge, MA: Harvard University Press, 1966); Herbert Emmerich, *Federal Organization and Administrative Management* (University: University of Alabama Press, 1971), pp. 46–81; and Peri E. Arnold, *Making the Managerial Presidency: Comprehensive Reorganization Planning, 1905–1980* (Princeton, NJ: Princeton University Press, 1986), pp. 81–117. See also Larry Berman, *The Office of Management and Budget and the Presidency, 1921–1979* (Princeton, NJ: Princeton University Press, 1979); Frederick C. Mosher, *A Tale of Two Agencies: A Comparative Analysis of the General Accounting Office and the Office of Management and Budget* (Baton Rouge: Louisiana State University Press, 1984); Matthew J. Dickinson, *Bitter Harvest: FDR, Presidential Power, and the Growth of the Presidential Branch* (New York: Cambridge University Press, 1997); and Herman M. Somers, "Coordinating the Federal Executive" (Ph.D. diss., Harvard University, 1947), pp. 1–42. Primary sources are also helpful. See Hester to Rosenman w/enc., 9/3/38, Reorganization (Folder 2), and McReynolds to Rowe, 3/18/41, and other documents, Reorganization of the Executive Office, Box 41, Rosenman Papers; and Brownlow to Neustadt, 9/16/63, Louis Brownlow, 1933–1963, Box 4, and Fesler to Emmerich, 3/23/42, Herbert Emmerich; Employment, War Production Board, 1942, Box 8, Emmerich Papers.

2. The following analysis of the OEM is based on Conference with the President, 8/28/39, 8/29/39, 8/30/39, 9/4/39, 9/28/39, 10/13/39, and Daily Record, 9/4/39, 9/5/39, 9/7/39 (two memoranda), Smith Papers; and "Notes on Interview with Louis Brownlow," 11/13/41, Box 12, Unit 138, RWA, BOB.

3. The WRB and the IMP are analyzed in depth in Paul A. C. Koistinen, *Planning War, Pursuing Peace: The Political Economy of American Warfare, 1920–1939* (Lawrence: University Press of Kansas, 1998), chap. 15. See also Fesler to Krug, 9/10/45, 9/12/1945, and Wiltse to Fesler (on A. C. C. Hill, Jr., interview), 1/17/46, 1–4/1946, Box 2, Fesler Papers; and Joanne E. Johnson, "The Army Industrial College and Mobilization Planning between the Wars," Special Collections, National Defense University, Fort McNair, Washington, DC.

4. Daily Record, 9/7/39, Smith Papers.

5. McReynolds's qualities are evident throughout the documents on the National Defense Advisory Commission. See, e.g., "Notes on Interview with Sidney Sherwood," 10/22/41, Box 12, Unit 138, Milton to Herring, 10/28/42, Box 12, Unit 139, and Laurence E. Radway, "The Advisory Commission to the Council of National Defense: An Administrative History," 1943, pp. 37–38, 106–14, Box 13, Unit 145, RWA, BOB; and Emmerich to Brownlow, 7/30/40, 11/6/40, U.S. Industrial Mobilization; Office for Emergency Management, 1940–1956, Box 30, Emmerich Papers.

6. Daily Record, 5/22/40, and Conference with the President, 5/22/40, 5/23/40, 5/25/40, Smith Papers; Roosevelt to Johnson, 12/17/37, and other documents, OF: Council of National Defense, FDR Papers; Fesler Memorandum (on Louis Brownlow interview), 5/20/46, 5–6/1946, Box 2, Fesler Papers; memorandum "Origins of the NDAC," Box 13, Unit 147, RWA, BOB; Bureau of the Budget, *The United States at War: Development and Administration of the War Program by the Federal Government* (Washington, DC: Bureau of the Budget, 1946), pp. 14–25; and Civilian Production Administration (CPA), *Industrial Mobilization for War: History of the War Production Board and Predecessor Agencies, 1940–1945* (Washington, DC: Civilian Production Administration, 1947), pp. 3–22.

7. CPA, *Industrial Mobilization for War*, p. 17.

8. Conference with the President, 5/30/40, Smith Papers. See also Hamm to Henderson, 7/16/40, National Defense Advisory Commission: Organization, Etc., WPB Papers, Box 34, Henderson Papers.

9. Memorandum "Appropriation Acts" and two memoranda on "Committees," Box 13, Unit 147, and Radway, "Advisory Commission," pp. 96–106, Box 13, Unit 145, RWA, BOB. In the face of opposition from the White House, the Bureau of the Budget, and McReynolds, the NDAC also began to develop field offices. This theme is explored by Arthur F. Lucas, "Field Relations of Advisory Commission of National Defense Council," Box 13, Unit 148, RWA, BOB.

Many of the administrative details of the NDAC and also its dynamics are made manifest in the introduction to and the early minutes of the commission: Civilian Production Administration, *Minutes of the Advisory Commission to the Council of National Defense, June 12, 1940, to October 22, 1941* (hereafter *NDAC Minutes*) (Washington, DC: Civilian Production Administration, 1946), pp. iii–iv, 1–5. These well-indexed minutes are much more extensive and valuable for research purposes than the minutes of subsequent civilian mobilization agencies. The two principal official histories—Bureau of the Budget, *United States at War;* and CPA, *Industrial Mobilization for War*—do not adequately cover either the NDAC or the Office of Production Management (OPM), although the second publication is much better than the first on these agencies. The Bureau of the Budget did the research for a thorough coverage of the period 1940–1941, but, apparently, space restraints forced it to pay little attention to pre–Pearl Harbor developments. WPB scholars were not as well versed on the NDAC and OPM period, but the bureau would not share its work with them. See memorandum Key for Files, 7/31/45, Box 11, Unit 131, RWA, BOB. WPB scholars produced numerous "Special Studies" and "Brief Surveys" (all enumerated in CPA, *Industrial Mobilization for War*, pp. 989–92) that cover in great detail numerous aspects of NDAC and OPM activity and that WPB authors relied on heavily in writing their history. Around half these studies are published in the sense that they received official sanction and were mimeographed for limited distribution. The rest are rough-draft typescripts in varying stages of completion. Those that were published are usually quite cautious since they were subject to challenge by individuals or firms involved in mobilization. (See memoranda Auxier to Hechler, 11/7/46, and Wiltse to Auxier, 10/21/46, Box 11, Unit 131, RWA, BOB.) In that regard, the unpublished manuscripts can be more valuable since they are usually unedited and, therefore, often more candid.

10. Radway, "Advisory Commission," pp. 200–238, Box 13, Unit 145, "Notes on Interview with Don Riley," 10/30/41, Box 12, Unit 138, and memorandum "Re-

search and Statistics," Box 13, Unit 147, RWA, BOB; and *NDAC Minutes,* pp. 5, 10–11, 39, 58, 64, 65, 79, 93, 96, 113.

11. Wiltse to Fesler (on Hill interview), 1/17/46, 1–4/1946, Box 2, Fesler Papers; and Radway, "Advisory Commission," pp. 115–26, Box 13, Unit 145, RWA, BOB.

12. The following discussion of the Production Division is based on B. L. G., "Division of Industrial Production," 11/12/40, "Hearing on the 1941 Budget Estimates of the Division of Industrial Production of the Advisory Commission to the Council of National Defense, November 15, 1940," 11/26/40, and memoranda "Knudsen" and "Division of Industrial Production," Box 13, Unit 147, and Radway, "Advisory Commission," pp. 126–33, Box 13, Unit 145, RWA, BOB; *NDAC Minutes,* pp. 29, 32, 63, 76, 86, 88, 89, 92, 94, 99, 105; Joseph P. Harris, "The Emergency National Defense Organization," *Public Administration Review* 1 (Autumn 1940): 10–12; James A. McAleer, *Dollar-a-Year and without Compensation Personnel Policies of the War Production Board and Predecessor Agencies, August 1939 to November 1945* (Washington, DC: Civilian Production Administration, 1947), pp. 1–20; Edythe W. First, *Industry and Labor Advisory Committees in the National Defense Advisory Commission and the Office of Production Management, May 1940 to January 1942* (Washington, DC: Civilian Production Administration, 1946), pp. 1–54; and CPA, *Industrial Mobilization for War,* pp. 31–32.

For a convient list of dollar-a-year appointments in most NDAC subdivisions as of November 1940 by name, former association, and address, see the file Dollar-a-Year Appointments, Box 24, McReynolds Papers.

13. The following analysis of the Materials Division is based on B. L. G., "Division of Industrial Materials," 11/13/40, and "Hearing on the 1941 Budget Estimates of the Division of Industrial Materials of the Advisory Commission to the Council of National Defense, November 14, 1940," 11/25/40, Box 13, Unit 147, and Radway, "Advisory Commission," pp. 134–51, Box 13, Unit 145, RWA, BOB; *NDAC Minutes,* pp. 11, 34, 54, 55, 57, 63, 74, 77, 79, 86, 88, 99, 103, 116, 118, 132, 134, 142–43; Harris, "Emergency National Defense Organization," pp. 8–10; McAleer, *Dollar-a-Year Personnel,* pp. 1–20; First, *Industry and Labor Advisory Committees,* pp. 1–54; and CPA, *Industrial Mobilization for War,* p. 30.

14. The military's industry advisory committees designed to assist its procurement planning, are covered extensively in Koistinen, *Planning War, Pursuing Peace,* chaps. 1–11.

15. "Hearing on the 1941 Budget Estimates of the Division of Price Stabilization of the Advisory Commission to the Council of National Defense, Nov. 26, 1940," 12/3/40, Box 13, Unit 147, RWA, BOB.

16. The following section on the Labor Division is based on memorandum "Division of Employment," 11/27/40, "Hearing on the 1941 Budget Estimates of the Division of Employment of the Advisory Commission to the Council of National Defense, November 28, 1940," 12/12/40, and memoranda "Hillman," "Labor Division," and "Labor Policy," Box 13, Unit 147, and Radway, "Advisory Commission," pp. 151–64, Box 13, Unit 145, RWA, BOB; *NDAC Minutes* (see extensive index references under *labor, Labor Department, Labor Division, labor statistics, training-in-industry program, Sidney Hillman,* and other specific topics); R. Burr Smith, "Labor and Manpower Administration in War Production, May 1940 to March 1943," Special Study No. 1, 1943, pp. 1–6, and R. Burr Smith, "The Training-within-Industry Program, July 1940

to December 1943," Brief Survey No. 6, 1944, pp. 1–5, Policy Documentation File, WPB; Richard J. Purcell, *Labor Policies of the National Defense Advisory Commission and the Office of Production Management, May 1940 to April 1942* (Washington, DC: Civilian Production Administration, 1946), passim; Paul A. C. Koistinen, *The Hammer and the Sword: Labor, the Military, and Industrial Mobilization, 1920–1945* (New York: Arno, 1979), pp. 79–103, 124–96, 341–58, 553–73; Harris, "Emergency National Defense Organization," pp. 12–13; McAleer, *Dollar-a-Year Personnel*, pp. 1–20; First, *Industry and Labor Advisory Committees*, pp. 55–64; CPA, *Industrial Mobilization for War*, p. 32; Steven Fraser, *Labor Will Rule: Sidney Hillman and the Rise of American Labor* (New York: Free Press, 1991), pp. 452–80; and Francis X. Gannon, *Joseph D. Keenan, Labor's Ambassador in War and Peace* (Lanham, MD: University Press of America, 1984), pp. 35–51.

17. The following discussion of the Price Stabilization Division is based on "Notes on Interview with David Ginsburg," 12/2/41, Box 12, Unit 138, memorandum "Division of Price Stabilization," 11/20/40, "Hearing on the 1941 Budget . . . Division of Price Stabilization," and memoranda "Henderson," "Price Stabilization," and "Price," Box 13, Unit 147, and Radway, "Advisory Commission," pp. 165–74, Box 13, Unit 145, RWA, BOB; *NDAC Minutes*, pp. 7, 55, 63, 64, 73, 86, 93, 96, 123, 132, 138, 140–141, 144, 145, 148; Harris, "Emergency National Defense Organization," pp. 13–14; First, *Industry and Labor Advisory Committees*, pp. 41–45; CPA, *Industrial Mobilization for War*, p. 33; Hugh Rockoff, *Drastic Measures: A History of Wage and Price Controls in the United States* (New York: Cambridge University Press, 1984), pp. 85–90; Andrew H. Bartels, "The Politics of Price Controls: The Office of Price Administration and the Dilemmas of Economic Stabilization, 1940–1946" (Ph.D. diss., Johns Hopkins University, 1980), pp. 2–170; and John Kenneth Galbraith, *A Theory of Price Control* (Cambridge, MA: Harvard University Press, 1952).

18. The following analysis of the Farm Products Division is based on memorandum "Division of Farm Products," 11/19/40, "Hearings on the 1941 Budget Estimates of the Division of Farm Products of the Advisory Commission to the Council of National Defense, November 19, 1940," 12/7/40, and memorandum "Davis," Box 13, Unit 147, and Radway, "Advisory Commission," pp. 186–94, Box 13, Unit 145, RWA, BOB; *NDAC Minutes*, pp. 2, 78, 89, 104, 115, 123, 127, 146, 148, 154, 155, 157; Harris, "Emergency National Defense Organization," p. 14; CPA, *Industrial Mobilization for War*, pp. 33–34; Walter W. Wilcox, *The Farmer in the Second World War* (Ames: Iowa State College Press, 1947), pp. 1–50; Bela Gold, *Wartime Economic Planning in Agriculture: A Study in the Allocation of Resources* (New York: Columbia University Press, 1949); and Theodore W. Schultz, *Agriculture in an Unstable Economy* (New York: McGraw-Hill, 1945).

19. The following section on the Transportation Division is based on memorandum "Division of Transportation," 11/27/40, "Hearing on the 1941 Budget Estimate of the Division of Transportation of the Advisory Commission to the Council of National Defense, November 27, 1940," and memorandum "Budd," Box 13, Unit 147, and Radway, "Advisory Commission," pp. 194–200, Box 13, Unit 145, RWA, BOB; *NDAC Minutes* (see the numerous index entries under *transportation, transportation-air, Transportation Division,* and *transportation-railroads*); Walter L. McMurtry, "Wartime Problems of American Railroads, 1939–1945," 3 vols. (Ph.D. diss., University of New Mexico, 1983), 1:1–152; Harris, "Emergency National

Defense Organization," pp. 13–14; First, *Industry and Labor Advisory Committees,* pp. 32–33; and CPA, *Industrial Mobilization for War,* p. 33.

20. The following analysis of the Consumer Protection Division is based on "Notes on Interview with John Cassels," 12/16/41, "Notes on Consumer Representation," ca. 12/41, and "Notes on Gladieux's Talk on Consumer Organization," 10/23/41, Box 12, Unit 138, B. L. G., "Division of Consumer Protection," 11/18/40, and "Hearing on the 1941 Budget Estimates of the Division of Consumer Protection of the National Defense Commission, November 18, 1940," 12/6/40, Box 13, Unit 147, Gladieux Notes, "Consumer Relations," 11/21/41, Box 19, Unit 200, and Radway, "Advisory Commission," pp. 175–86, Box 13, Unit 145, RWA, BOB; *NDAC Minutes,* pp. 20, 23–24, 29, 36, 51, 55–56, 68, 88–89, 90, 92, 124, 146; Harris, "Emergency National Defense Organization," pp. 14–15; Emmerich to Brownlow, 7/30/40, U.S. Industrial Mobilization; Office for Emergency Management, 1940–1956, Box 30, Emmerich Papers; First, *Industry and Labor Advisory Committees,* p. 25; and CPA, *Industrial Mobilization for War,* pp. 34–35.

21. The following discussion of the coordinator of national defense purchases is based on B. L. G., "Office for Coordination of National Defense Purchases," 11/13/40, "Hearing on the 1941 Budget Estimates of the Office for Coordination of National Defense Purchases of the Council of National Defense, November 15, 1940," and memorandum "Coordinator of National Defense Purchases," Box 13, Unit 147, and Radway, "Advisory Commission," pp. 115–26, Box 13, Unit 145, RWA, BOB; *NDAC Minutes* (see numerous index entries under *contracts, Coordinator of National Defense Purchases, Donald M. Nelson, small business,* and other related and specific topics); Harris, "Emergency National Defense Organization," pp. 17–18, 23–24; McAleer, *Dollar-a-Year Personnel,* pp. 9–10; First, *Industry and Labor Advisory Committees,* pp. 24–25, 47–54; and CPA, *Industrial Mobilization for War,* pp. 35–36.

22. "Hearing on the 1941 Budget . . . Office for Coordination of National Defense Purchases," "Hearing on the 1941 Budget . . . Division of Industrial Production," and "Hearing on the 1941 Budget . . . Division of Price Stabilization," Box 13, Unit 147, RWA, BOB; and Harris, "Emergency National Defense Organization," pp. 23–24 (quotation p. 23).

23. The best sources on the organization, operation, and staffing of the NRA include Leverett S. Lyon et al., *The National Recovery Administration: An Analysis and Appraisal* (Washington, DC: Brookings Institution, 1935); and Leverett S. Lyon, Myron W. Watkins, and Victor Abramson, *Government and Economic Life: Development and Current Issues of American Public Policy,* 2 vols. (Washington, DC: Brookings Institution, 1939), vol. 2, chap. 27.

24. McAleer, *Dollar-a-Year Personnel,* pp. 1–20; and James A. McAleer, "Policies and Procedures on Dollar-a-Year and Without-Compensation Employees of the War Production Board and Predecessor Agencies, May 1940 to March 1944," Brief Survey No. 8, 1944, Policy Documentation File, WPB.

25. Memorandum "Department of Justice" and related documents, Box 13, Unit 147, RWA, BOB; First, *Industry and Labor Advisory Committees,* pp. 1–64; and J. Carlyle Sitterson, "Industry and Labor Advisory Committees, May 1940 to April 1944," Brief Survey No. 10, 1944, Policy Documentation File, WPB.

26. Emmerich to Bock, 1/11/56, U.S. Industrial Mobilization; Office for Emergency Management, 1940–1956, Box 30, Emmerich Papers. The operation of the

divisions headed by Knudsen and Stettinius, and particularly the attitude and activity of John D. Biggers, highlights these points. This outlook in its extreme form was articulated by C. W. Carroll, a Philadelphia publisher who served both on the World War I War Industries Board and in the World War II Office of Production Management. Writing to Bernard M. Baruch in 1942, he lashed out at Stacy May as a "radical," Sidney Hillman as a "communist," and Harry Hopkins as the White House's "Rasputin" and longed for leadership that would "punch in the nose and throw down the stairs" the "loafing bums" tolerated in the mobilization agencies. He concluded: "As a matter of fact big business has stolen the ball from the WPB and we are going to win the War inspite [*sic*] of, rather than on account of, WPB." See Carroll to Baruch, 4/8/42, 5/1/42, and other correspondence, and also the curious and revealing 1941 exchanges between Baruch and George N. Peek, in Selected Correspondence, Baruch Papers. Frederick M. Eaton, Knudsen's NDAC counsel, arrived at the same conclusion, albeit less belligerently, by observing: "When the New Dealers were in power they didn't include us; now that we are in power we won't include them." Quoted in Fraser, *Labor Will Rule*, p. 483. A very subtle and insightful analysis of this theme is presented in Robert Griffith, "The Selling of America: The Advertising Council and American Politics, 1942–1960," *Business History Review* 62 (Autumn 1983): 388–412.

27. New Deal bibliography is reviewed in Koistinen, *Planning War, Pursuing Peace*, pp. 376–78 n. 2. Alan Brinkley, "The New Deal and the Idea of the State," in *The Rise and Fall of the New Deal Order, 1930–1980*, ed. Steve Fraser and Gary Gerstle (Princeton, NJ: Princeton University Press, 1989), pp. 85–121, is particularly insightful concerning the above analysis. Brinkley develops his ideas more fully in *The End of Reform: New Deal Liberalism in Recession and War* (New York: Alfred A. Knopf, 1995). Economic mobilization for World War I is covered in Paul A. C. Koistinen, *Mobilizing for Modern War: The Political Economy of American Warfare, 1865–1919* (Lawrence: University Press of Kansas, 1997), chaps. 6–13.

28. "Hearing on the 1941 Budget . . . Division of Price Stabilization," and memorandum "Housing, Executive Session [of NDAC], January 14, 1941. Informal notes," Box 13, Unit 147, RWA, BOB (quotations are contained in these sources). Sources on executive reorganization, the OEM, and McReynolds are cited in nn. 1–5 above. Memoranda in the Bureau of the Budget files related to the bureau's historical project shed exceptionally good light on the thinking of Smith and his staff. See memoranda "NDAC General," "Social Philosophy," "Organization of NDAC," "Notes on interview with Gladieux, April 23, 1942," and "Notes on Interview with Staats, April 17, 1942," Box 13, Unit 147, RWA, BOB. Joseph P. Harris worked with the President's Committee on Administrative Management and served as a consultant on administration to the NDAC. His "Emergency National Defense Organization" in subtle ways illustrates the thinking of pubic administration specialists. See also William H. McReynolds, "The Office for Emergency Management," *Public Administration Review* 1 (Winter 1941): 131–38. This issue of the *Review* constituted "The Executive Office of the President: A Symposium," with articles by Smith, Louis Brownlow, Luther Gulick, Charles E. Merriam, and others, and provides good insight into the thinking of an influential group helping shape and staff the office of the president under Roosevelt.

29. The divisions and discord in the NDAC can be traced in the *NDAC Minutes*. Radway, "Advisory Commission," treats the subject at length. The role of the military in NDAC activities is analyzed in chaps. 2–3 below.

CHAPTER TWO. THE MILITARY AND ECONOMIC MOBILIZATION

1. This planning is covered in great detail in Paul A. C. Koistinen, *Planning War, Pursuing Peace: The Political Economy of American Warfare, 1920–1939* (Lawrence: University Press of Kansas, 1998), chaps. 1–11.

2. Erna Risch and Chester L. Kieffer, *The Quartermaster Corps: Organization, Supply, and Services,* vol. 2 (Washington, DC: Office of the Chief of Military Services, 1955), p. 121.

3. Constance McLaughlin Green, Harry C. Thomson, and Peter C. Roots, *The Ordnance Department: Planning Munitions for War* (Washington, DC: Office of the Chief of Military History, 1955), pp. 65–90, 105–20; and Harry C. Thomson and Lida Mayo, *The Ordnance Department: Procurement and Supply* (Washington, DC: Office of the Chief of Military History, 1960), pp. 24–67, 104–6, 465–76. See also Levin H. Campbell, Jr., *The Industry-Ordnance Team* (New York: McGraw-Hill, 1946); Chester Mueller, *The New York Ordnance District in World War II* (New York: New York Post/Army Ordnance Association, 1947); and William B. Fitzgerald, "The Ordnance Program under the War Production Board and Predecessor Agencies, May 1940 to April 1944," Brief Survey No. 4, 1944, Policy Documentation File, WPB.

4. Dulany Terrett, *The Signal Corps: The Emergency (to December 1941)* (Washington, DC: Office of the Chief of Military History, 1956); George Raynor Thompson et al., *The Signal Corps: The Test (December 1941 to July 1943)* (Washington, DC: Office of the Chief of Military History, 1957), pp. 21–33, 147–85, 315–52, 491–565; and George Raynor Thompson and Dixie R. Harris, *The Signal Corps: The Outcome (Mid-1943 through 1945)* (Washington, DC: Office of the Chief of Military History, 1966), pp. 1–26, 144–73, 351–506, 611–32.

5. Blanche D. Coll, Jean E. Keith, and Herbert H. Rosenthal, *The Corps of Engineers: Troops and Equipment* (Washington, DC: Office of the Chief of Military History, 1958), pp. 1–63, 88–108, 132–45, 175–92, 216–40, 498–580; and Lenore Fine and Jesse A. Remington, *The Corps of Engineers: Construction in the United States* (Washington, DC: Office of the Chief of Military History, 1972), pp. 3–476.

6. Leo P. Brophy and George J. B. Fisher, *The Chemical Warfare Service: Organizing for War* (Washington, DC: Office of the Chief of Military History, 1959), pp. 3–62, 88–90, 93–141; Leo P. Brophy, Wyndham D. Miles, and Rexmond C. Cochrane, *The Chemical Warfare Service: From Laboratory to Field* (Washington, DC: Office of the Chief of Military History, 1959), pp. 1–48, 226–380; and Brooks E. Kleber and Dale Birdsell, *The Chemical Warfare Service: Chemicals in Combat* (Washington, DC: Office of the Chief of Military History, 1966), pp. 3–35, 636–57.

7. Clarence McKittrick Smith, *The Medical Department: Hospitalization and Evacuation, Zone of Interior* (Washington, DC: Office of the Chief of Military History, 1956).

8. Chester Wardlow, *The Transportation Corps: Responsibilities, Organization, and Operations* (Washington, DC: Office of the Chief of Military History, 1951), pp. 1–94, 406–14; Chester Wardlow, *The Transportation Corps: Movements, Training, and Supply* (Washington, DC: Office of the Chief of Military History, 1956), pp. 462–525; and Joseph Bykofsky and Harold Larson, *The Transportation Corps: Operations Overseas* (Washington, DC: Office of the Chief of Military History, 1957), pp. 605–19.

9. Erna Risch, *The Quartermaster Corps: Organization, Supply, and Services,* vol. 1

(Washington, DC: Office of the Chief of Military History, 1953), pp. 3–74, 208–82; Risch and Kieffer, *Quartermaster Corps,* pp. 120–36; and George E. Mowry, "The Procurement of Quartermaster Supplies, May 1940 to April 1944," Brief Survey No. 7, 1944, Policy Documentation File, WPB.

10. Irving Brinton Holley, Jr., *Buying Aircraft: Materiel Procurement for the Army Air Forces* (Washington, DC: Office of the Chief of Military History, 1964); and Wesley F. Craven and James L. Cate, eds., *Men and Planes,* vol. 6 of *The Army Air Forces in World War II* (Chicago: University of Chicago Press, 1955), pp. 171–424. An extensive bibliography on aircraft is provided in Koistinen, *Planning War, Pursuing Peace,* chap. 10, nn. 9, 10, 14, 15, 16, 20.

11. For background on the World War I preparedness movement, see Paul A. C. Koistinen, *Mobilizing for Modern War: The Political Economy of American Warfare, 1865–1919* (Lawrence: University Press of Kansas, 1997), chap. 6.

12. Stimson and his leadership during World War II are covered in depth in Paul A. C. Koistinen, *The Hammer and the Sword: Labor, the Military, and Industrial Mobilization, 1920–1945* (New York: Arno, 1979). The annual reports of the secretary of war provide a rich source of information on War Department operations. See War Department, *Report of the Secretary of War to the President,* 1939–1946. Rudolph A. Winnacker, "The Office of the Secretary of War under Henry L. Stimson, Part I: The National Emergency, July 1940 to December 1941," ca. 1946, U.S. Army Center of Military History, Washington, DC, is a helpful study. A recent, valuable biography is Godfrey Hodgson, *The Colonel: The Life and Wars of Henry Stimson, 1867–1950* (New York: Alfred A. Knopf, 1990). See also David F. Schmitz, *Henry L. Stimson: The First Wise Man* (Wilmington, DE: Scholarly Resources, 2001).

13. R. Elberton Smith, *The Army and Economic Mobilization* (Washington, DC: Office of the Chief of Military History, 1959), pp. 106–12.

14. Koistinen, *Hammer and Sword,* chaps. 2–8; Henderson to Roosevelt, 10/14/40, OF: Council of National Defense, FDR Papers; Troyer S. Anderson, "Introduction to the History of the Under Secretary of War's Office," 1947, chap. 6, pp. 100–120, U.S. Army Center of Military History, Washington, DC; and Smith, *Army and Economic Mobilization,* pp. 106–12.

15. Coll, Keith, and Rosenthal, *The Corps of Engineers,* p. 99.

16. There are many fewer sources on the Navy Department and economic mobilization for World War II than on the army. Those that exist are of varying quality. The following account of Navy Department activities related to economic mobilization is based on Duncan S. Ballantine, *U.S. Naval Logistics in the Second World War* (Princeton, NJ: Princeton University Press, 1949), chaps. 1–2; Walter Millis and Eugene S. Duffield, eds., *The Forrestal Diaries* (New York: Viking, 1951); Robert H. Connery, *The Navy and the Industrial Mobilization in World War II* (Princeton, NJ: Princeton University Press, 1951); Robert G. Albion and Robert H. Connery, *Forrestal and the Navy* (New York: Columbia University Press, 1962); Arnold A. Rogow, *James Forrestal: A Study of Personality, Politics, and Policy* (New York: Macmillan, 1963); Townsend Hoopes and Douglas Brinkley, *The Life and Times of James Forrestal* (New York: Alfred A. Knopf, 1992); Jeffrey M. Dorwart, *Eberstadt and Forrestal: A National Security Partnership, 1909–1949* (College Station: Texas A&M University Press, 1991); Calvin L. Christman, "Ferdinand Eberstadt and Economic Mobilization for War, 1941–1943" (Ph.D. diss., Ohio State University, 1971); and Robert C. Perez, *The*

Will to Win: A Biography of Ferdinand Eberstadt (Westport, CT: Greenwood, 1989). The annual reports of the secretary of the navy are also helpful. See *Annual Report of the Secretary of the Navy,* 1939, 1940–1946. See also U.S. Navy Department, Naval History Division, Office of the Chief of Naval Operations, "United States Naval Administration in World War II: Office of the Secretary of the Navy, Civilian Personnel," 3 vols. (Washington, DC). Other relevant sources on the navy and industrial mobilization will be cited below. See also the relevant sources on the navy cited in Koistinen, *Mobilizing for Modern War,* chap. 3.

Robert G. Albion, *Makers of Naval Policy, 1798–1947,* ed. Rowena Reed (Annapolis, MD: Naval Institute Press, 1980), is a valuable source. The editor's preface and the book's bibliography cite most of Albion's publications relevant to this subject and also provide information about the hundreds of unpublished manuscripts from the navy's history program, which Albion supervised during World War II. The substance of those manuscripts is summarized in Julius A. Furer, *Administration of the Navy Department in World War II* (Washington, DC: Naval History Division, 1959), an excellent synthesis and analysis that is also based on additional research and provides citations for many of the unpublished studies broken down by subject matter.

17. The ANMB during the interwar years is analyzed and documented in Koistinen, *Planning War, Pursuing Peace* (as recorded in the index), in chap. 5 below, and in subsequent chapters dealing with the War Production Board.

By a military order of July 5, 1939, the president placed the ANMB—along with the Joint Army and Navy Board, the Joint Economy Board, and the Aeronautical Board—directly under his authority as commander-in-chief of the army and navy. This was done at the instigation of the Bureau of the Budget as part of the process of reorganizing the executive branch and was further evidence that Roosevelt intended to direct all aspects of the defense and war effort personally. Indeed, the president took this action before he approved the board's June request that it oversee foreign buying related to national defense. See the section on the ANMB in chap. 5; and Thurman Arnold memorandum, 6/27/39, OF: Army and Navy Munitions Board, and Acting Secretary of War and Acting Secretary of the Navy to the President, 8/14/39, and related correspondence, OF: Educational Orders, FDR Papers.

CHAPTER THREE. THE NDAC IN OPERATION

1. Civilian Production Administration (CPA), *Industrial Mobilization for War: History of the War Production Board and Predecessor Agencies, 1940–1945* (Washington, DC: Civilian Production Administration, 1947), pp. 39–44.

2. Stettinius to Roosevelt, 12/19/40, PSF: Council of National Defense—Report to President, FDR Papers; "Hearings on the 1941 Budget Estimates of the Division of Research and Statistics of the Advisory Commission to the Council of National Defense, November 18, 1940," 12/13/40, and memorandum "Relations with Armed Services," Box 13, Unit 147, and Laurence E. Radway, "The Advisory Commission to the Council of National Defense: An Administrative History," pp. 50–52, Box 13, Unit 145, RWA, BOB; Nathan D. Grundstein, "Programming of Defense Production by the National Defense Advisory Commission and the Office of Production Management, May 1940 to December 1941," Special Study No. 31, 1947, and Maryclaire

McCauley, "The Conversion of the Consumer Durable Goods Industry to War Production, May 1940 to December 1944," Special Study No. 33, 1947, Policy Documentation File, WPB; Civilian Production Administration, *Minutes of the Advisory Commission to the Council of National Defense, June 12, 1940 to October 22, 1941* (hereafter *NDAC Minutes*) (Washington, DC: Civilian Production Administration, 1946), pp. 12, 65; and CPA, *Industrial Mobilization for War,* pp. 55–56.

3. The following analysis of contract clearance is based on memoranda "Relations with Armed Services" and "Contract Powers under Appropriation Act" and related documents, Box 13, Unit 147, and Radway, "Advisory Commission," pp. 55–58, Box 13, Unit 145, RWA, BOB; Curtis W. Garrison, "Procurement Policies of the National Defense Advisory Commission and Office of Production Management, May 1940 to December 1941," Special Study No. 39, 1947, Policy Documentation File, WPB (this manuscript is in rough-draft form and covers the full range of procurement policies and problems); *NDAC Minutes,* pp. 16–17, 82–83, 89, 95, 102–3, 115–17, 120, 121–23, 126, 128–29, 131, 134, 147–48; and CPA, *Industrial Mobilization for War,* pp. 24–25, 35, 56–61.

4. This subject is explored fully in Paul A. C. Koistinen, *The Hammer and the Sword: Labor, the Military, and Industrial Mobilization, 1920–1945* (New York: Arno, 1979), pp. 132–44.

5. Memorandum "Relations with Armed Services," Box 13, Unit 147, and Radway, "Advisory Commission," pp. 58–61, Box 13, Unit 145, RWA, BOB.

6. The following analysis involving plant location is based on Radway, "Advisory Commission," pp. 58–70, Box 13, Unit 145, and memoranda "Relations with Armed Services," "Determination of Site for Emergency Facilities," and "Site Location," Box 13, Unit 147, RWA, BOB; Roosevelt to Davis, 7/29/40, OF: Council of National Defense, FDR Papers; and *NDAC Minutes* (numerous index entries under plant sites; see also *Minutes* citations in n. 3 above). The process of clearing contracts and approving plant sites for military contractors was often combined.

7. The following analysis of facilities expansion is based on memoranda "Materials Division," "Mr. Stettinius," "Stettinius," "Relations with Armed Services," "Aluminum," "Rubber," "Criticism of NDAC's Efforts to Expand Production," "Small Business Participation," and "Small Business" and other relevant documents, Box 13, Unit 147, and Jesse Burkhead, "Reconstruction Finance Corporation Loans," 12/42, Box 19, Unit 191, RWA, BOB; *NDAC Minutes,* pp. 6–10, 17–23, 30–32, 37–39, 40–42, 44–50, 58, 60–62, 66–67, 69–74, 78–79, 82, 85, 86, 87, 89–90, 94–95, 100, 101, 104–7, 109–11, 113, 115–18, 121, 125–26, 129, 131, 133, 135–36, 137, 139, 140, 141–42, 147, 149, 164; Civilian Production Administration, "Industrial Mobilization for War: History of the War Production Board and Predecessor Agencies, 1940–1945," vol. 2, "Materials and Products," 1947, pt. 2, chaps 4, 5, Policy Documentation File, WPB; Reginald C. McGrane, *The Facilities and Construction Program of the War Production Board and Predecessor Agencies, May 1940 to May 1945* (Washington, DC: Civilian Production Administration, 1945), pp. 1–36; Ethan P. Allen, *Policies Governing Private Financing of Emergency Facilities, May 1940 to June 1942* (Washington, DC: Civilian Production Administration, 1944), pp. 1–89; J. Carlyle Sitterson, *Aircraft Production Policies under the National Defense Advisory Commission and the Office of Production Management, May 1940 to December 1941* (Washing-

ton, DC: Civilian Production Administration, 1946), pp. 1–6, 22–49, 102–62; Charles M. Wiltse, "Aircraft Production under the War Production Board and Predecessor Agencies, May 1940 to April, 1944," Brief Survey No. 2, 1944, pp. 1–8, Policy Documentation File, WPB; Frederic C. Lane, *Ships for Victory: A History of Shipbuilding under the U.S. Maritime Commission in World War II* (Baltimore: Johns Hopkins University Press, 1951); Charles H. Coleman, *Shipbuilding Activities of the National Defense Advisory Commission and Office of Production Management, July 1940 to December 1941* (Washington, DC: Civilian Production Administration, 1945), pp. 1–139; George E. Mowry, "The Naval and Maritime Shipbuilding Programs, May 1940 to June 1944," Brief Survey No. 13, 1944, Policy Documentation File, WPB; Charles M. Wiltse, *Aluminum Policies of the War Production Board and Predecessor Agencies, May 1940 to November 1945* (Washington, DC: Civilian Production Administration, 1945), pp. 1–35; George W. Auxier, *Rubber Policies of the National Defense Advisory Commission and Office of Production Management, May 1940 to December 1941* (Washington, DC: Civilian Production Administration, 1947), pp. 1–92; Frederick W. Harrison, "Steel Policies of the National Defense Advisory Commission, May–December 1940," Special Study No. 40, 1947, Reginald C. McGrane and Jerome Thomases, "Machine Tool Policies of the War Production Board and Predecessor Agencies, May 1940 to November 1945," Special Study No. 35, 1947, and Virginia Turrell, "High-Octane Aviation Gasoline Program, 1940–44," Brief Survey No. 12, 1944, Policy Documentation File, WPB; George W. Auxier, *Copper Policies of the War Production Board and Predecessor Agencies, May 1940 to November 1945* (Washington, DC: Civilian Production Administration, 1947), pp. 1–12; Charles M. Wiltse, *Lead and Zinc Policies of the War Production Board and Predecessor Agencies, May 1940 to March 1941* (Washington, DC: Civilian Production Administration, 1946), pp. 1–11; Maryclaire McCauley, "Evolution of the Metals and Minerals Policy of the War Production Board, September 1939 to August 1943," Special Study No. 2, 1943, pp. 1–9, and Reginald C. McGrane, "Defense and War Housing Policies of the War Production Board and Its Predecessor Agencies, May 1940 to July 1944," Brief Survey No. 14, 1944, Policy Documentation File, WPB; CPA, *Industrial Mobilization for War,* pp. 25–27, 44–50, 56–60, 68–81; Gerald T. White, *Billions for Defense: Government Financing by the Defense Plant Corporation during World War II* (University: University of Alabama Press, 1980), pp. 1–49; R. Elberton Smith, *The Army and Economic Mobilization* (Washington, DC: Office of the Chief of Military History, 1959), pp. 437–502; Irving Brinton Holley, *Buying Aircraft: Materiel Procurement for the Army Air Forces* (Washington, DC: Office of the Chief of Military History, 1964), pp. 290–329; Wesley F. Craven and James L. Cate, eds., *Men and Planes,* vol. 6 of *The Army Air Forces in World War II* (Chicago: University of Chicago Press, 1955), pp. 299–361; Troyer S. Anderson, "Introduction to the History of the Under Secretary of War's Office," 1947, chap. 6, pp. 157–91, U.S. Army Center of Military History, Washington, DC; Robert H. Connery, *The Navy and the Industrial Mobilization in World War II* (Princeton, NJ: Princeton University Press, 1951), pp. 89–92, 344–53, 366–70; and Robert G. Albion and Robert H. Connery, *Forrestal and the Navy* (New York: Columbia University Press, 1962), pp. 72–74.

8. For critically important background information on the National Advisory Committee for Aeronautics, see Paul A. C. Koistinen, *Planning War, Pursuing Peace: The*

Political Economy of American Warfare, 1920–1939 (Lawrence: University Press of Kansas, 1998), pp. 184–85 and passim (for extensive primary and secondary sources that are relevant to aircraft mobilization for World War II, see pp. 371–74 nn. 9–20).

9. The analysis of priorities is based on Gilbert Convers, "Priorities and Allocations Systems under the National Defense Advisory Commission, Office of Production Management, and War Production Board, May 1940 to November 1942," Special Study No. 36, 1947, pp. 5–79, and James W. Fesler, "Relations between the Armed Services and the Advisory Commission to the Council of National Defense, May to December 1940," Special Study No. 3, 1943, pp. 5–23, Policy Documentation File, WPB; Letter to McNutt, 10/25/40, OF: Government Contracts, FDR Papers; Baruch to Roosevelt, 5/7/41, Selected Correspondence, Baruch Papers; memoranda "Conversion," "Priorities under the NDAC," and "Priorities," Box 13, Unit 147, and Radway, "Advisory Commission," pp. 70–76, Box 13, Unit 145, RWA, BOB; *NDAC Minutes*, pp. 4, 50, 57, 77, 80, 98–99, 102, 104, 112, 122, 134; and CPA, *Industrial Mobilization for War*, pp. 28, 54, 64–68.

10. The emerging alliance between the armed services and the corporate community in the operations of the NDAC was not without its tensions and contradictions. This subject can be profitably explored through the activity of Bernard M. Baruch. See Baruch's extended correspondence in 1940 with James F. Byrnes, Forrestal, Henderson, Harry Hopkins, George C. Marshall, Patterson, George N. Peek, Stettinius, and numerous other public and private figures. Of particular importance is Baruch's exchanges with Lewis H. Brown in 1942. All these exchanges can be found in Selected Correspondence, Baruch Papers. See also Baruch's extensive correspondence with the White House, which can be found in PSF: General Correspondence, FDR Papers.

11. Foreign aid and its significance have been discussed above and will be more fully analyzed and documented below.

12. The following account of the transition from the NDAC to the Office of Production Management is based on Conference with the President, 11/30/40, 12/18/40, 12/20/40, 12/21/40, 12/31/40, 1/3/41, 1/6/41, 2/5/41, 2/6/41, 2/15/41, White House Memoranda, Smith to Roosevelt, 5/15/41, and Roosevelt to Smith, 5/20/41, and Daily Record, 12/1/40, 12/21/40, Smith Papers; Henderson to Roosevelt, 10/14/40, OF: Council of National Defense, FDR Papers; memorandum "Notes on Interview with David Ginsburg," 12/2/41, and other documents, Unit 138, Box 12, and memorandum "Reorganization—Nov. 25, 1940 Stone's Memo on Organization Problem" and numerous other documents, Unit 147, Box 13, RWA, BOB; Entry, 12/21/40, Henderson, Leon: Diary Notes and Memos to Himself, WPB Papers, Box 36, Henderson Papers; Baruch to Knox, 12/20/40, and Knox to Baruch, 12/21/40, Selected Correspondence, Baruch Papers; Koistinen, *Hammer and Sword*, pp. 567–73; Radway, "Advisory Commission," pp. 252–324, Box 13, Unit 145, RWA, BOB; Bureau of the Budget, *The United States at War: Development and Administration of the War Program by the Federal Government* (Washington, DC: Bureau of the Budget, 1946), pp. 50–55; and CPA, *Industrial Mobilization for War*, pp. 89–95.

13. In Koistinen, *Planning War, Pursuing Peace*, chap. 14, I deal with the president's response to the Senate Special Committee Investigating the Munitions Industry (the Nye Committee). Roosevelt was principally intent on undermining the committee and minimizing its potential damage. Nowhere in the primary sources (including the FDR Papers, the Smith Papers [which provide excellent insight into

Roosevelt's thinking], and the elaborate files of the Bureau of the Budget collected to write the agency's history of economic mobilization, *United States at War*) have I encountered any concern on the president's part about the possible consequences of modern warfare drawing together industry and the military.

The president worried about business and bankers dominating mobilization agencies and trying to take over his authority. He also expressed concern about and took steps to monitor war profiteering, the use of dollar-a-year men, and related issues. The growing power of the military within the government, on the other hand, did not appear to bother him. However, he repeatedly intervened in the operations of the navy to preserve civilian control.

Roosevelt's principal concern seemed to be preparing the nation for and moving it toward war in order to check the numerous threats to American interests abroad. A weak, not a strong, military was the biggest hindrance to the success of that policy. Moreover, as a former assistant secretary of the navy, the president claimed an expertise about the armed services that provided confidence that he could control them. Certainly, his determination to act in many respects as his own secretary of war and navy indicated that the armed services per se were no major source of anxiety for him. In an economic mobilization alliance of industry and the military, the former seemed to be the partner that needed watching. Finally, Roosevelt devoted considerable time and energy to economic mobilization only from 1939 into 1943. Once the War Production Board was fully under way, his emphasis was the war abroad, not the mobilization program at home. In the earlier years, Roosevelt's chief aim was getting a mobilization system going without unduly strengthening the antipreparedness and antiwar forces. This returns me to my central point: the president was interested in immediate results, not long-run consequences.

CHAPTER FOUR. STRUCTURE AND STAFFING OF OPM, OPACS, AND SPAB

1. Executive Order 8629, dated 1/7/41, which created OPM, is reproduced in Civilian Production Administration, *Minutes of the Council of the Office of Production Management* (hereafter *OPM Minutes*) (Washington, DC: Civilian Production Administration, 1946), pp. 89–90. The executive order did not provide for a council. The decision to distinguish the council as the policymaking organ from the OPM as the operating agency is obscure but appears to have been made by Knudsen, perhaps advised by Stimson and Knox.

There is no well-integrated history of the OPM. A number of sources, however, are helpful in tracing its course. See Ernest C. Mossner, "An Administrative History of the Office of Production Management, 1941," 1943, Box 19, Unit 204, RWA, BOB. The fullest published account is found in Civilian Production Administration, *Industrial Mobilization for War: History of the War Production Board and Predecessor Agencies, 1940–1945* (Washington, DC: Civilian Production Administration, 1947), pp. 89–205, which draws heavily on numerous "Special Studies" and "Brief Surveys" produced by the War Production Board and Civilian Production Administration, many of which are cited in this and subsequent chapters. See also Bureau of the Budget, *The United States at War: Development and Administration of the War Program by the Fed-*

eral Government (Washington, DC: Bureau of the Budget, 1946), pp. 53–95. For the limitations of the CPA and Bureau of the Budget volumes, see chap. 1, n. 9, and the Bibliographic essay.

2. Emmerich claimed that he had a "confidential arrangement" with Knudsen in which either party could end his appointment after a sixty-day trial. See Emmerich to Brownlow, 2/12/41, Herbert Emmerich; Employment, PACH, 1937–1945, Box 8, Emmerich Papers. A *New York Post* piece of 2/14/41 asserted that those favoring Emmerich used the unchallenged appointment of O'Brian (a Buffalo corporate attorney) as leverage to help secure their candidate the job. Eaton was the son-in-law of the late Frederic W. Allen, senior partner of Lee, Higginson and Co. See Clipping, Scrapbook, Box 3, 1940–1943, Public Administration Papers, Emmerich Papers. See also Conference with the President, 2/5/41, 2/6/41, Smith Papers; and Mossner, "Administrative History of OPM," pp. 38–39, Box 19, Unit 204, RWA, BOB.

3. OPM, *Minutes,* pp. 2, 3, 6, 15, 19, 24, 35, 73, 74, 88; Report of Special Committee to Knudsen and Hillman, 5/28/41, and other documents, U.S. Industrial Mobilization; Office of Production Management, 1941–1944, Box 30, Emmerich Papers; Edythe W. First, *Industry and Labor Advisory Committees in the National Defense Advisory Commission and the Office of Production Management, May 1940–January 1942* (Washington, DC: Civilian Production Administration, 1946), pp. 65–168; and James A. McAleer, *Dollar-a-Year and without Compensation Personnel Policies of the War Production Board and Predecessor Agencies, August 1939 to November 1945* (Washington, DC: Civilian Production Administration, 1947), pp. 21–40.

4. See the sources cited in n. 3 above.

5. *OPM Minutes,* pp. 1, 2, 4, 8, 16, 19, 20, 28, 46–47, 49, 50–53, 57, 58, 60, 72–73.

6. Ibid., pp. 1–4, 6, 8, 19, 25, 27, 28–29, 31–32, 34–36, 39, 41–43, 45, 46–49, 51–57, 60–64, 67–69, 72–73, 75–76, 78, 80, 82, 86, 88.

7. Ibid., pp. 1–3, 8, 28, 36, 50, 58, 60, 66; and Mossner, "Administrative History of OPM," pp. 42–50, Box 19, Unit 204, RWA, BOB.

8. *OPM, Minutes,* pp. 7–8, 10, 20–21, 37, 40, 56, 68–69, 88; R. Burr Smith, "Labor and Manpower Administration in War Production," Special Study No. 1, 1943, Policy Documentation File, WPB; Richard J. Purcell, *Labor Policies of the National Defense Advisory Commission and the Office of Production Management, May 1940–April 1942* (Washington, DC: Civilian Production Administration, 1946), pp. 15–33, 66–238; Mossner, "Administrative History of OPM," pp. 64–67, 79–80, Box 19, Unit 204, RWA, BOB; Paul A. C. Koistinen, *The Hammer and the Sword: Labor, the Military, and Industrial Mobilization* (New York: Arno, 1979), pp. 80–158, 554–630; and Steven Fraser, *Labor Will Rule: Sidney Hillman and the Rise of American Labor* (New York: Free Press, 1991), pp. 452–94.

9. "Notes on Interview with Don Riley," 10/30/41, Box 12, Unit 138, and Mossner, "Administrative History of OPM," pp. 59–64, Box 19, Unit 204, RWA, BOB; Entry, 8/29/40, Henderson, Leon: Diary, July 1938–December 1940, WPB Papers, Box 36, Henderson Papers; First to Fesler (on Frederick F. Stephan address), 11/18/44, 11–12/1944, Box 1, Fesler Papers; *OPM Minutes,* pp. 9, 28; and Nathan D. Grundstein, "Programming of Defense Production by the National Defense Advisory Commission and Office of Production Management, May 1940 to December 1941," Special Study No. 31, 1947, pp. 225–35, Policy Documentation File, WPB.

10. A small but significant collection of documents exists on the PPB, including files 015.711 (establishment), 015.712 (personnel), 015.716 (functions), 015.717 (organization), 015.715M (minutes, 2–6/41, minutes, 6–7/41, and verbatim minutes, 3/10/41), and 015.715R and 015.718 (reports, which must be considered along with the minutes), Box 30, file 211 (production planning), Box 963, and file 221 (facilities), Box 984, Policy Documentation File, WPB. Other sources on the board include Fesler Memorandum (on Emmerich-Key interview), 2/2/45, 1–3/1945, Box 2, and "The Production Planning Board," War Production Board, Box 6, September 1978 Addition, Fesler Papers; *OPM Minutes,* pp. 16, 25, 30; Grundstein, "Programming of Defense Production," pp. 239–67; First, *Industry and Labor Advisory Committees,* pp. 96–99, 105; and CPA, *Industrial Mobilization for War,* pp. 98, 100.

11. The following analysis of OPM reorganizations relies on a number of sources. See Conference with the President, 7/10/41, Smith Papers; "Notes on Interview with Stephen E. Fitzgerald," 12/23/41, Box 12, Unit 138, Gladieux Notes, "Meeting of Smith and Coy with Nelson," 11/26/41, and numerous other documents, Box 19, Unit 200, and Mossner to Herring, "Interview with Mr. Herbert Emmerich," 10/6/43, Box 19, Unit 202, RWA, BOB; Rosenman to Patterson, 8/14/41, and other correspondence and documents, Office of Price Administration and Civilian Supply, Box 13, Rosenman Papers; Production Planning Board, Minutes, 4/10/41–7/9/41, file 015.715M, and Emmerich et al. to Biggers, Nelson, and Stettinius, 5/28/41, and other documents, file 015.715R, Box 30, Policy Documentation File, WPB; Emmerich et al. to Knudsen and Hillman, 5/28/41, 1941, Box 1, and Fesler Memorandum (on Emmerich-Key interview), 2/2/45, 1–3/1945, Box 2, Fesler Papers; and *OPM Minutes,* pp. 12–14, 27, 31, 33, 35–37, 43, 45, 55, 58–59, 60, 86, 89–90. Secondary sources are rich and essential: Mossner, "Administrative History of OPM," pp. 68–74, Box 19, Unit 204, RWA, BOB; Civilian Production Administration, "Industrial Mobilization for War: History of the War Production Board and Predecessor Agencies, 1940–1945," vol. 2, "Materials and Products," 1947, pt. 1, chap. 3, pp. 7–35, Policy Documentation File, WPB; CPA, *Industrial Mobilization for War,* pp. 96–114; and Bureau of the Budget, *United States at War,* pp. 60–84.

12. Emmerich et al. to Knudsen and Hillman, 5/28/41, and related documents, U.S. Industrial Mobilization; Office of Production Management, 1941–1944, Box 30, Emmerich Papers; and Grundstein, "Programming of Defense Production," pp. 239–67. See also the PPB documents cited in n. 10 above, particularly the minutes and reports.

13. The following analysis of industry advisory committees is based on Smith to Emmerich et al., 5/20/41, file 015.717, and Levis, Weinberg, and Reed to Biggers, Nelson, and Stettinius, 6/13/41, and Doherty to Emmerich, 6/18/41, file 015.715R, Policy Documentation File, WPB; Belsey to Emmerich, 11/28/44, and related documents, U.S. Industrial Mobilization; Office of Production Management, 1941–1944, Box 30, Emmerich Papers; Mossner to Herring, "Interview with Mr. Herbert Emmerich," 10/6/43, Box 19, Unit 202, RWA, BOB; First to Fesler (on O'Brian address), 12/16/44, 11–12/1944, Box 1, Fesler Papers; Whiteside to Baruch, 12/26/41, Selected Correspondence, Baruch Papers; and *OPM Minutes,* pp. 15, 19, 20, 24, 35, 37, 46, 61, 73, 88. In analyzing industry advisory committees, a number of secondary sources are invaluable: Mossner, "Administrative History of OPM," pp. 176–84, Box 19, Unit 204; RWA, BOB, J. Carlyle Sitterson, "Industry

and Labor Advisory Committees, May 1940 to April 1944," Brief Survey No. 10, 1944, pp. 1–8, Policy Documentation File, WPB; First, *Industry and Labor Advisory Committees,* pp. 65–168; Koistinen, *Hammer and Sword,* pp. 585–89; and CPA, *Industrial Mobilization for War,* pp. 105–7.

14. Rowe to President, 2/6/41, and numerous other correspondence and documents, PSF: Dollar-a-Year Men, and Roosevelt to Secretary of the Treasury et al., 10/30/41, and other correspondence, OF: Dollar-a-Year Men, FDR Papers; Mossner to Herring, "Interview with Mr. Herbert Emmerich," 10/6/43, Box 19, Unit 202, RWA, BOB; Rowe to Rosenman, 12/1/41, Rowe, James Jr., Box 4, Rosenman Papers; *OPM Minutes,* pp. 74, 78; McAleer, *Dollar-a-Year Personnel,* pp. 21–40; and James A. McAleer, "Policies and Procedures on Dollar-a-Year and without-Compensation Employees of the War Production Board and Predecessor Agencies, May 1940 to March 1944," Brief Survey No. 8, 1944, pp. 1–17, and exhibit A ("Dollar-a-Year Employees and Temporary Dollar-a-Year Appointments Pending Investigations"), Policy Documentation File, WPB (on exhibit A, see chap. 8, no. 2, below).

15. Truman Committee, *Hearings, Investigation of the National Defense Program,* 77th Cong., 1st sess., 1941–1942, pt. 10, pp. 4025–47, and *First Annual Report,* 77th Cong., 2d sess., 1942, S. Rept. No. 480, pt. 5, pp. 7–10; and Donald H. Riddle, *The Truman Committee* (New Brunswick, NJ: Rutgers University Press, 1964), pp. 41–43, 64–66, 71–73, 143–44.

16. First, *Industry and Labor Advisory Committees,* p. 167.

17. Henderson to Roosevelt, 7/19/41, and numerous related correspondence and documents, Supply Priorities and Allocations Board, Box 16, Rosenman Papers; *OPM Minutes,* pp. 12–14, 27, 31, 33, 35–37, 45; and CPA, *Industrial Mobilization for War,* 102–5.

18. "Hearings on the 1941 Budget Estimates of the Division of Price Stabilization of the Advisory Commission to the Council of National Defense, November 26, 1940," Box 13, Unit 147, RWA, BOB; Roosevelt to Hillman, 7/9/41, PSF: Sidney Hillman, FDR Papers; Conference with the President, 6/19/41, 7/10/41, Smith Papers; Henderson to President, 8/16/41, and other documents, Office of Price Administration and Civilian Supply—Office of Production Management, Box 13, and Ginsburg to Rosenman, 8/8/41, and numerous other documents, Supply Priorities and Allocations Board, Box 16, Rosenman Papers; Drummond Jones, *The Role of the Office of Civilian Requirements in the Office of Production Management and War Production Board, January 1941 to November 1945* (Washington, DC: Civilian Production Administration, 1946), pp. 1–35; and Maryclair McCauley, "The Conversion of the Consumer Durable Goods Industry to War Production, May 1940 to December 1944," Special Study No. 33, 1947, pp. 8–211, Policy Documentation File, WPB.

19. Smith to President, 7/2/41, and numerous other correspondence and documents, Supply Priorities and Allocations Board, Box 16, and Rowe to Rosenman, 8/29/41, Rowe, James Jr., Box 4, Rosenman Papers; "Notes on Interview with Stephen E. Fitzgerald," 12/23/41, Box 12, Unit 138, RWA, BOB; *OPM Minutes,* p. 55; Civilian Production Administration, *Minutes of the Supply Priorities and Allocations Board* (Washington, DC: Civilian Production Administration, 1946) (the entire *Minutes* is one of the best sources for tracing the board's activities); Mossner, "Administrative History of OPM," pp. 117–28, 141–44, Box 19, Unit 204, RWA, BOB; and CPA, *Industrial Mobilization for War,* pp. 109–14.

CHAPTER FIVE. THE MILITARY AND OPM

1. Booz Report, vol. 1, p. 9; Troyer S. Anderson, "Introduction to the History of the Under Secretary of War's Office," 1947, chap. 6, p. 36, U.S. Army Center of Military History, Washington, DC; and R. Elberton Smith, *The Army and Economic Mobilization* (Washington, DC: Office of the Chief of Military History, 1959), p. 6. The first full-length study of Patterson's War Department service was recently published: Keith E. Eiler, *Mobilizing America: Robert P. Patterson and the War Effort, 1940–1945* (Ithaca, NY: Cornell University Press, 1997). Chapters 2–12 of *Mobilizing America* cover the years 1940–1941 in considerable detail. From July to December 1940, Patterson was assistant secretary of war. In December, he was elevated to under secretary. Nonetheless, for purposes of clarity, I will refer to the Office of the Under Secretary of War, even through it was the Office of the Assistant Secretary for a number of months. The change in title in no way affected the office's functions. See also the sources cited in chap. 2 above and the extensive analysis of and documentation concerning the War Department in Paul A. C. Koistinen, *The Hammer and the Sword: Labor, the Military, and Industrial Mobilization, 1920–1945* (New York: Arno, 1979).

2. Booz Report, vol. 1, app. 1, pp. 16–28; and Anderson, "Under Secretary of War's Office," chap. 6, pp. 81–89.

3. Booz Report, vol. 1, app. 1, pp. 28–34; and Anderson, "Under Secretary of War's Office," chap. 6, pp. 89–93.

4. Booz Report, vol. 1, pp. 87–125 (quotation p. 117), and app. 1, pp. 34–40; and Anderson, "Under Secretary of War's Office," chap. 6, pp. 93–98.

5. Booz Report, vol. 1, app. 1, pp. 3–16; Anderson, "Under Secretary of War's Office," chap. 6, pp. 74–81; and Smith, *Army and Economic Mobilization,* pp. 106–7. The Planning Branch is also discussed in chap. 2 above and its operations during the interwar years analyzed at length in Paul A. C. Koistinen, *Planning War, Pursuing Peace: The Political Economy of American Warfare, 1920–1939* (Lawrence: University Press of Kansas, 1998).

6. Booz Report, vol. 1, pp. 83–84; and Anderson, "Under Secretary of War's Office," chap. 6, pp. 98–99.

7. Booz Report, vol. 1, pp. 144–72; and Anderson, "Under Secretary of War's Office," chap. 6, pp. 120–22. See also Joanne E. Johnson, "The Army Industrial College and Mobilization Planning between the Wars," Special Collections, National Defense University, Fort McNair, Washington, DC.

8. Booz Report, vols. 1–2.

9. Anderson, "Under Secretary of War's Office," chap. 6, pp. 34–39, 70–71, 100–119; and Koistinen, *Hammer and Sword,* pp. 93–96. These assistants and others are discussed in Eiler, *Mobilizing America* (consult the index).

10. Booz Report, vol. 1, unnumbered page between p. 40 and p. 41; Anderson, "Under Secretary of War's Office," chap. 6, pp. 72–74; and Smith, *Army and Economic Mobilization,* pp. 129–39.

11. Anderson, "Under Secretary's Office," chap. 6, pp. 67–68 (quotation p. 68).

12. Ibid., pp. 100–124. See also Edward S. Greenbaum, *A Lawyer's Job: In Court, in the Army, in the Office* (New York: Harcourt, Brace and World, 1967), pp. 125–79. Bernard M. Baruch became an informal adviser to Patterson, and to a lesser degree Forrestal, offering suggestions for filling civilian slots in the departments. See the exten-

sive 1941 correspondence among Baruch, Patterson, and Forrestal in Selected Correspondence, Baruch Papers.

13. Smith, *Army and Economic Mobilization,* p. 6.

14. Robert H. Connery, *The Navy and the Industrial Mobilization in World War II* (Princeton, NJ: Princeton University Press, 1951), pp. 11–23; and Julius A. Furer, *Administration of the Navy Department in World War II* (Washington, DC: Naval History Division, 1959), pp. 18–19, 36–44, 124–25. The secondary literature on the navy and the Navy Department is extensive. In an earlier volume, I have cited not only the most recent surveys but also the more specialized work, much of which deals with or is relevant to World War II: Paul A. C. Koistinen, *Mobilizing for Modern War: The Political Economy of American Warfare, 1865–1919* (Lawrence: University Press of Kansas, 1997), pp. 306–9 n. 1. See also the sources cited in chap. 2 above.

15. Connery, *Navy and Industrial Mobilization,* pp. 23–30; and Furer, *Navy Department Administration,* pp. 124–25.

16. Brief summaries of Edison's and Knox's years in office are presented in Allison W. Saville, "Charles Edison, 2 January 1940–24 June 1940," and George H. Lobdell, "Frank Knox, 11 July 1940–28 April 1944," in *American Secretaries of the Navy,* vol. 2, *1913–1972,* ed. Paolo E. Colletta (Annapolis, MD: Naval Institute Press, 1980), pp. 669–74, 677–727. For introductory information on King, see Robert W. Love, Jr., "Ernest Joseph King, 26 March 1942–15 December 1945," in *The Chiefs of Naval Operations,* ed. Robert W. Love, Jr. (Annapolis, MD: Naval Institute Press, 1980), pp. 137–79.

17. Furer, *Navy Department Administration,* pp. 69, 70–71, 72, 135n, 265n, 309, 364–67, 408, 442–43, 461, 503–6, 558, 893; and Connery, *Navy and Industrial Mobilization,* pp. 113, 146–47, 323.

18. The discussion of the movement for and the creation of the OP&M is based on Daily Record, 10/18/40, Smith Papers; Connery, *Navy and Industrial Mobilization,* pp. 130–34, 143–53, 160–62, 179–224; Robert G. Albion and Robert H. Connery, *Forrestal and the Navy* (New York: Columbia University Press, 1962), pp. 59–108; Furer, *Navy Department Administration,* pp. 838–46, 870–79; Duncan S. Ballantine, *U.S. Naval Logistics in the Second World War* (Princeton, NJ: Princeton University Press, 1949), pp. 135–44; and Townsend Hoopes and Douglas Brinkley, *Driven Patriot: The Life and Times of James Forrestal* (New York: Alfred A. Knopf, 1992), 136–80.

19. Edison and Johnson to President, 6/30/39, Roosevelt to Collins, 12/13/39, Roosevelt to Callaghan, 4/6/40, and other related documents, OF: Army and Navy Munitions Board, FDR Papers; and Connery, *Navy and Industrial Mobilization,* pp. 82–84. For the War Resources Board, see Koistinen, *Planning War, Pursuing Peace,* chap. 15.

20. Bureau of the Budget, *The United States at War: Development and Administration of the War Program by the Federal Government* (Washington, DC: Bureau of the Budget, 1946), pp. 32, 63–69, 421–28; and Civilian Production Administration, *Industrial Mobilization for War: History of the War Production Board and Predecessor Agencies, 1940–1945* (Washington, DC: Civilian Production Agency, 1947), pp. 71–73. Koistinen, *Planning War, Pursuing Peace,* chaps. 4–10, covers the OASW and ANMB interwar commodity committee work in depth.

21. Smith, *Army and Economic Mobilization,* pp. 602–4; and Connery, *Navy and Industrial Mobilization,* pp. 84–87. Stockpiling and related activities during World

War II are covered from a broad base in Alfred E. Eckes, Jr., *The United States and the Global Struggle for Minerals* (Austin: University of Texas Press, 1979), pp. 57–119.

22. The following analysis of machine tools is based on Roosevelt to Nelson, 2/11/42, OF: Army and Navy Munitions Board, FDR Papers; Civilian Production Administration, *Minutes of the Advisory Commission to the Council of National Defense, June 12, 1940, to October 22, 1941* (Washington, DC: Civilian Production Administration, 1946), pp. 89, 111–12; Civilian Production Administration, *Minutes of the Council of the Office of Production Management* (Washington, DC: Civilian Production Administration, 1946), pp. 2, 20, 21, 23, 26, 38, 45, 50, 62, 66, 69, 75, 76; and Civilian Production Administration, *Minutes of the Supply Priorities and Allocations Board* (hereafter *SPAB Minutes*) (Washington, DC: Civilian Production Administration, 1946), pp. 10, 11, 13, 25, 26–27, 30, 33; Reginald C. McGrane and Jerome Thomases, "Machine Tool Policies of the War Production Board and Predecessor Agencies, May 1940 to November 1945," Special Study No. 35, 1947, and Maryclair McCauley, "The Conversion of the Consumer Durable Goods Industry to War Production, May 1940 to December 1944," Special Study No. 33, 1947, pp. 95–101, Policy Documentation File, WPB; Calvin L. Christman, "Ferdinand Eberstadt and Economic Mobilization for War, 1941–1943" (Ph.D. diss., Ohio State University, 1971), pp. 35–38; Robert C. Perez and Edward F. Willett, *The Will to Win: A Biography of Ferdinand Eberstadt* (Westport, CT: Greenwood, 1989), p. 2; Connery, *Navy and Industrial Mobilization*, pp. 165–70, 302–3; Smith, *Army and Economic Mobilization*, pp. 512–13, 564–66; and Albion and Connery, *Forrestal*, pp. 77–78. Background and bibliography on the machine tool industry and the military's interwar planning for it are presented in Koistinen, *Planning War, Pursuing Peace*, pp. 150–55 and relevant notes.

23. See chap. 3 above.

24. The operations of priorities under OPM are covered and documented at length in chap. 7 below.

25. Eberstadt to Patterson and Forrestal, Report on the Army and Navy Munitions Board, 11/26/41, pp. 31–34, file 723, Policy Documentation File, WPB; and Smith, *Army and Economic Mobilization*, pp. 145, 259, 453–55, 493, 507–49, 551–64, 578–80. Also consult other secondary sources cited in the notes above.

26. Daily Record, 5/22/40, 10/22/40, Smith Papers; Baruch to Pershing, 4/22/40, 5/15/40, Selected Correspondence, Baruch Papers; "Hearings on the 1941 Budget Estimates of the Division of Industrial Materials of the Advisory Commission to the Council of National Defense, November 14, 1940," ". . . the Office for Coordination of National Defense Purchases . . . November 15, 1940," and other hearings, Box 13, Unit 147, RWA, BOB; Nathan D. Grundstein, "Programming of Defense Production by the National Defense Advisory Commission and Office of Production Management, May 1940 to December 1941," Special Study No. 31, 1947, pp. 62–67, Policy Documentation File, WPB; Mark S. Watson, *Chief of Staff: Prewar Plans and Preparations* (Washington, DC: History Division, Department of the Army, 1950), pp. 172–82; Smith, *Army and Economic Mobilization*, pp. 126–33; and Russell F. Weigley, *History of the United States Army* (New York: Macmillan, 1967), pp. 423–26. The Munitions Program was at least temporarily cut in half (to two million men and eighteen thousand planes) because of NDAC concerns about expanding industrial capacity rapidly enough to meet the higher numbers.

27. *SPAB Minutes,* p. 24; Watson, *Chief of Staff,* pp. 331–66; Smith, *Army and Economic Mobilization,* pp. 133–42; Richard M. Leighton and Robert W. Coakley, *Global Logistics and Strategy, 1940–1943* (Washington, DC: Office of the Chief of Military History, 1955), pp. 117–40; CPA, *Industrial Mobilization for War,* pp. 125–29, 138–40, 274–75; James A. Huston, *The Sinews of War: Army Logistics, 1775–1953* (Washington, DC: Office of the Chief of Military History, 1966), pp. 461–67; Harry C. Thomson and Lida Mayo, *The Ordnance Department: Procurement and Supply* (Washington, DC: Office of the Chief of Military History, 1960), pp. 55–67; and Erna Risch, *The Quartermaster Corps: Organization, Supply, and Services,* vol. 1 (Washington, DC: Office of the Chief of Military History, 1953), pp. 221–25. The Victory Program is analyzed at greater length in chap. 7 below.

28. Connery, *Navy and Industrial Mobilization,* pp. 88–89, 103–4, 130–32, 144–46, 180–82; and Albion and Connery, *Forrestal,* p. 81.

29. The following analysis of converting military requirements into materials and components is based on Daily Record, 10/18/40, Smith Papers; Mossner to Herring, "Interview with Mr. Herbert Emmerich," 10/6/43, Box 19, Unit 202, and Ernest C. Mossner, "An Administrative History of the Office of Production Management, 1941," 1943, pp. 129–44, Box 19, Unit 204, RWA, BOB; Grundstein, "Programming of Defense Production," pp. 99–225, 235–38, 268–303; CPA, *Industrial Mobilization for War,* 150–52; Smith, *Army and Economic Mobilization,* pp. 143–54; Connery, *Navy and Industrial Mobilization,* pp. 143–46, 179–99; and Ethan P. Allen, *Hide and Leather Policies of the War Production Board and Predecessor Agencies, May 1940 to December 1943* (Washington, DC: War Production Board, 1944), pp. 7–8.

30. Eberstadt, Report on ANMB, 11/26/41, file 723, Policy Documentation File, WPB. See also Henderson to Roosevelt, 10/14/40, OF: Council of National Defense, FDR Papers; Grundstein to Fesler, 2/16/45, 1–3/1945, Box 2, Fesler Papers; Johnson to Baruch w/ encs., 4/18/40, and Baruch to Kent, 10/19/40, Selected Correspondence, Baruch Papers; and memorandum "Army and Navy Munitions Board vs Office of Production Management," 1/13/42, and Gladieux Notes, "OPM-Civil-Military Relations," 12/18/41, Box 19, Unit 200, Mossner to Herring, "Interview with Mr. Herbert Emmerich," 10/6/43, Box 19, Unit 202, and "Notes on Interview with Louis Brownlow," 11/13/41, Box 12, Unit 138, RWA, BOB.

31. Roosevelt to Hopkins, 1/11/42, and numerous other documents and correspondence, OF: Army and Navy Munitions Board, FDR Papers; Hill to Nelson, 1/23/42, 1–8/1942, Box 1, Fesler Papers; and CPA, *Industrial Mobilization for War,* pp. 216–17.

32. The following analysis of the ANMB is based on Army Section, ANMB, "Proposed Organization ANMB" w/ enc. (appendices and exhibits), and related documents, file 370.26/200-18.00, ANMB, Minutes, 4/18/42–7/9/43, and related documents, file 370.26/200-13.7, and ANMB Executive Committee Minutes, 10/26/42–1/1/43, Executive Committee Minutes, Box 5, ANMB; Entries, Diary, 10/30/41–11/12/41, Paget and Cresar to Eberstadt w/ enc. ("Report on the Organization of the Army and Navy Munitions Board"), 6/15/42, Commodities Division to Eberstadt (on recommendations to WPB), 5/8/42, and numerous other correspondence and documents, Hines, "The Army and Navy Munitions Board" (address to the Army Industrial College), 8/8/41, and other correspondence, Box 12, Army and Navy Munitions Board, and Gulick to Eberstadt, 7/17/42, and numerous other

correspondence and documents, Box 163, War Production Board, 1941–1942, Eberstadt Papers; CPA, *Industrial Mobilization for War,* pp. 221–22, 293–302, 334–38; Bureau of the Budget, *United States at War,* pp. 107–9, 126–27, 129–31, 280–81; Connery, *Navy and Industrial Mobilization,* pp. 154–78, 352–54; Smith, *Army and Economic Mobilization,* 452–55, 493, 537–39, 567–96; Christman, "Ferdinand Eberstadt," pp. 59–250; Perez and Willett, *Will to Win,* 1–9; and Jeffery M. Dorwart, *Eberstadt and Forrestal: A National Security Partnership, 1909–1949* (College Station: Texas A&M University Press, 1991), pp. 30–68. The ANMB will be analyzed in greater depth, and on the basis of additional primary documentation, in the chapters on the WPB below.

33. Gilbert Convers, "Priorities and Allocations Systems under the National Defense Advisory Commission, Office of Production Management, and War Production Board, May 1940 to November 1942," Special Study No. 36, 1947, pp. 37–148, Policy Documentation File, WPB; Mossner, "Administrative History of OPM," pp. 55–58, Box 19, Unit 204, RWA, BOB; and CPA, *Industrial Mobilization for War,* pp. 65–68, 171–74. The priorities systems in both the NDAC and the OPM are analyzed and documented in chap. 7 below.

34. As early as October 1940, Leon Henderson explained to Roosevelt that NDAC's troubles with the War Department stemmed from old line officers who wanted no outside interference with their procurement responsibilities and from new civilian structures headed by Stimson and Patterson. The latter were the greater threat. "My guess," Henderson stated, "is that the War Department is organizing its own version of a War Resources Board." See Henderson to President, 10/14/40, OF: Council of National Defense, FDR Papers. See also the numerous documents cited in n. 30 above.

35. This critically important theme will be further developed and documented in the chapters below on the WPB.

CHAPTER SIX. OPM, OPACS, AND THE STRUGGLE TO EXPAND PRODUCTION

1. Civilian Production Administration, *Minutes of the Council of the Office of Production Management, December 21, 1940, to January 14, 1942* (hereafter *OPM Minutes*) (Washington, DC: War Production Board, 1946), lists attendance at the council's meetings and provides a very basic outline of its deliberations. Other sources are essential for understanding fully what transpired at council sessions. Some of the best sources on the inner workings of the OPM are Ernest C. Mossner, "An Administrative History of the Office of Production Management, 1941," 1943, pp. 75–83, Box 19, Unit 204, Mossner to Herring, "Interview with Mr. Herbert Emmerich," 10/6/43, Box 19, Unit 202, and "Notes on Interview with Stephen E. Fitzgerald," 12/23/41, Box 12, Unit 138, RWA, BOB.

2. This is a major theme of chap. 3 above.

3. Mossner to Herring, "Interview with Mr. Herbert Emmerich," 10/6/43, Box 19, Unit 202, RWA, BOB. While the collection contained in the Emmerich Papers is extensive, it is disappointing in terms of material on the operations of the OPM. Nonetheless, there is some information of value on Emmerich and his role in economic mobilization. Also helpful are Mossner, "Administrative History of OPM," pp. 75–83,

Box 19, Unit 204, RWA, BOB; and Civilian Production Administration, *Industrial Mobilization for War: History of the War Production Board and Predecessor Agencies, 1940–1945* (Washington, DC: Civilian Production Administration, 1947), p. 101.

4. For background information on Amberg, see Troyer S. Anderson, "Introduction to the History of the Under Secretary of War's Office," 1947, chap. 6, pp. 102, 106–7, U.S. Army Center of Military History, Washington, DC; and Keith E. Eiler, *Mobilizing America: Robert P. Patterson and the War Effort, 1940–1945* (Ithaca, NY: Cornell University Press, 1997), p. 52. The Julius H. Amberg Collection is included as part of the Records of the Office of the Secretary of War, RG 107, National Archives, College Park, MD. Information on Dulles and Detmar is available in Robert H. Connery, *The Navy and the Industrial Mobilization in World War II* (Princeton, NJ: Princeton University Press, 1951), pp. 57–58; and Robert G. Albion and Robert H. Connery, *Forrestal and the Navy* (New York: Columbia University Press, 1962), pp. 33–35.

5. Fuller to Biggers, 3/31/41, file 015.715R, Box 30, and Doherty to Biggers, 5/16/41, and other documents, file 221, Box 984, Policy Documentation File, WPB; *OPM Minutes,* pp. 2, 37, 42; Civilian Production Administration, *Minutes of the Supply Priorities and Allocations Board* (hereafter *SPAB Minutes*) (Washington, DC: War Production Board, 1946), pp. 9, 11, 13–14; Reginald C. McGrane, *The Facilities and Construction Program of the War Production Board and Predecessor Agencies, May 1940 to May 1945* (Washington DC: War Production Board, 1945), pp. 37–70; Reginald C. McGrane, "Defense and War Housing Policies of the War Production Board and Its Predecessor Agencies, May 1940 to July 1944," Brief Survey No. 14, 1944, Policy Documentation File, WPB; Ethan P. Allen, *Policies Governing Private Financing of Emergency Facilities, May 1940 to June 1942* (Washington, DC: War Production Board, 1944); Charles H. Coleman, *Shipbuilding Activities of the National Defense Advisory Commission and Office of Production Management, July 1940 to December 1941* (Washington, DC: War Production Board, 1945); George E. Mowry, "The Naval and Maritime Shipbuilding Programs, May 1940 to June 1944," Brief Survey No. 13, 1944, pp. 1–6, Policy Documentation File, WPB; J. Carlyle Sitterson, *Aircraft Production Policies under the National Defense Advisory Commission and Office of Production Management, May 1940 to December 1941* (Washington, DC: Civilian Production Administration, 1946); Charles M. Wiltse, "Aircraft Production under the War Production Board and Predecessor Agencies, May 1940 to April 1944," Brief Survey No. 2, 1944, pp. 1–13, Policy Documentation File, WPB; CPA, *Industrial Mobilization for War,* pp. 160–61; and Gerald T. White, *Billions for Defense: Government Financing by the Defense Plant Corporation during World War II* (University: University of Alabama Press, 1980). See also chap. 3 above.

6. Mary McCauley, "The Conversion of the Consumer Durable Goods Industry to War Production, May 1940 to December 1944," Special Study No. 33, 1947, pp. 8–184, Policy Documentation File, WPB; and CPA, *Industrial Mobilization for War,* pp. 89–92, 121–40, 150–52, 185–86.

7. The following analysis of the struggle over curtailment of industry for defense production purposes is based on "Notes on Interview with David Ginsburg, OPA General Counsel," 12/2/41, and "Notes on Gladieux's Talk on Consumer Organization," Box 12, Unit 138, and Gladieux Notes, "Consumer Relations," 11/21/41, Box 19, Unit 200, RWA, BOB; Conference with the President, 2/6/41, and Daily Record, 7/6/40, Smith Papers; Production Planning Board, Minutes, 2/21/41–6/4/41,

6/9/41–7/23/41, file 015.715M, Policy Documentation File, WPB; Weinberg to Henderson w/ enc., 9/13/41, and other documents, Automobile Curtailment, and Automobile Defense Industry Advisory Committee, Verbatim Transcript of Proceedings, 10/15/41, Automobile Defense Industry Advisory Committee (to January 1942), WPB Papers, Box 31, Entries, 6/30/41, 7/2/41, 7/9/41, 7/16/41, Office of Price Administration and Civilian Supply: Staff Meetings, Box 34, and Conference with Mr. Knudsen on Industry Committees, 7/1/41, Henderson, Leon: Personal Correspondence, Misc., Box 36, Henderson Papers; Walter Reuther, "Tooling Program for Conversion of the Automobile Industry to War Production," 1/42, Box 10, Unit 1, No. 5, Nelson Papers; Searls to Baruch, 7/1/41, Selected Correspondence, and Chambers to Baruch w/ enc., (Chambers to Kuznets, 11/3/42), 11/14/42, Washington File, 1942–1945, Box 35, Sec. 2—Government Agencies: War Production Board, Baruch Papers; *OPM Minutes,* 2, 12–14, 17, 19–20, 27, 31, 33, 34, 35, 36–37, 39, 45, 51, 53, 55; *SPAB Minutes,* pp. 8–9, 40, 55–56; McCauley, "Consumer Durable Goods Industry," pp. 8–211; J. Carlyle Sitterson, "The Automobile Industry in War Production, May 1940 to December 1943," Brief Survey No. 1, 1944, pp. 1–12, Policy Documentation File, WPB; Drummond Jones, *Role of the Office of Civilian Requirements in the Office of Production Management and War Production Board, January 1941 to November 1945* (Washington, DC: Civilian Production Administration, 1946), pp. 1–56; Edythe W. First, *Industry and Labor Advisory Committees in the National Defense Advisory Commission and the Office of Production Management, May 1940 to January 1942* (Washington, DC: Civilian Production Administration, 1946), pp. 108–14; CPA, *Industrial Mobilization for War,* pp. 175–77, 185–97; Paul A. C. Koistinen, *The Hammer and the Sword: Labor, the Military, and Industrial Mobilization, 1920–1945* (New York: Arno, 1979), pp. 597–630; Steven Fraser, *Labor Will Rule: Sidney Hillman and the Rise of American Labor* (New York: Free Press, 1991), pp. 473–76; Nelson Lichtenstein, *Labor's War at Home: The CIO in World War II* (New York: Cambridge University Press, 1982), pp. 40–42, 84–89; Lichtenstein, *The Most Dangerous Man in Detroit: Walter Reuther and the Fate of American Labor* (New York: Basic, 1995), chap. 8; and Stan Luger, *Corporate Power, American Democracy, and the Automobile Industry* (New York: Cambridge University Press, 2000).

8. The following analysis of aluminum is based on ANMB, Executive Committee Minutes, 12/9/42, and other entries, Executive Committee Minutes, Box 5, and Havemayer to Chairman of the Army and Navy Munitions Board, 10/20/42, and other entries, file 370.26/200-13.7, ANMB; Ickes to Baruch w/ enc. (Ickes to Jones, 9/2/41), 9/22/41, Selected Correspondence, Baruch Papers; *OPM Minutes,* pp. 21, 25, 33–34, 38, 39, 41, 45, 59, 69, 74, 87; *SPAB Minutes,* pp. 3, 7, 9–10, 14–15, 26, 31, 33, 47–48, 49, 56, 66; Civilian Production Administration (CPA), "Industrial Mobilization for War: History of the War Production Board and Predecessor Agencies, 1940–1945," vol. 2, "Materials and Products," pt. 2, chap. 4, pp. 122–45, Policy Documentation File, WPB; Charles M. Wiltse, *Aluminum Policies of the War Production Board and Predecessor Agencies, May 1940 to November 1945* (Washington, DC: War Production Board, 1945), pp. ii, 1–165; Maryclaire McCauley, "Evolution of the Metals and Minerals Policy of the War Production Board, September 1939 to August 1943," Special Study No. 2, 1943, pp. 1–15, Policy Documentation File, WPB; CPA, *Industrial Mobilization for War,* pp. 76–77, 150–53, 638–41; White, *Billions for Defense,* pp. 9, 43–45, 70, 72–73, 97, 106–7, 123, 144–45; and Robert F.

Lanzillotti, "The Aluminum Industry," in *The Structure of American Industry: Some Case Studies* (3d ed.), ed. Walter Adams (New York: Macmillan, 1961), pp. 185–232. See also Paul A. C. Koistinen, *Planning War, Pursuing Peace: The Political Economy of American Warfare, 1920–1939* (Lawrence: University Press of Kansas, 1998), pp. 116–20 (for the army's interwar planning for aluminum), 358, n. 1 (for the citation of other secondary sources on aluminum).

Also important are Truman Committee, *Report on Aluminum Investigation,* 77th Cong., 1st sess., 1941, S. Rept. No. 480, pt. 1, pp. 1–7; Truman Committee, *First Annual Report,* 77th Cong., 2nd sess., 1942, S. Rept. No. 480, pt. 5, pp. 15–17; Truman Committee, *Third Annual Report,* 78th Cong., 2nd sess., 1944, S. Rept. No. 10, pt. 16, pp. 65–68. (There are forty-three parts to the committee's published public hearings, held between April 1941 and November 1947. The committee also held executive hearings between February 1942 and February 1948.) Donald R. Riddle, *The Truman Committee: A Study in Congressional Responsibility* (New Brunswick, NJ: Rutgers University Press, 1964), pp. 188–191, conveniently lists all public hearings by parts, subject matter, and dates (see app. 5, pp. 188–91) and itemizes all executive hearings by date and subject matter (see app. 6, pp. 192–94). The committee itself failed to itemize its work or to provide an index concerning it. In the case of aluminum, e.g., Riddle clearly indicates that the subject is treated in public hearings, pts. 3, 7. The committee investigated and reported on practically every topic of significance for mobilizing the economy. In the process, it compiled an extensive and invaluable collection of documents on numerous subjects.

9. As the OPM was reorganized between June and December 1941, the subdivision dealing with aluminum became a branch and moved among divisions. Wiltse, *Aluminum Policies,* pp. 65–67, traces these changes and their significance and also provide a record of the unit/branch's staffing.

10. Ibid., p. 31.

11. The following analysis of steel is based on Production Planning Board, Minutes, 3/28/41, 6/9/41, 6/18/41, file 015.715M, Policy Documentation File, WPB; Williams to Hopkins, 5/29/41, Alphabetical File, Box 8, Hopkins, Harry L., Administrative Assistant, Coy Papers; Entry, 6/5/41, Notes and Memos to Himself, WPB Papers, Box 36, Henderson Papers; James W. Fesler's unpublished "Memoir," in author's possession; ANMB, Executive Committee Minutes, 10/26/42, and numerous other entries, Executive Committee Minutes, and Minutes, 4/18/42, and numerous other entries, file 370.26/200-13.7, ANMB; Replogle to Baruch, 5/15/41, and related documents, Selected Correspondence, Baruch Papers; *OPM Minutes,* pp. 2, 24, 42–43, 53, 66, 71, 74, 75, 76; *SPAB Minutes,* pp. 3–4, 6, 7–8, 11–12, 15–16, 17, 21, 22, 24, 30, 33–34, 62; Frederick W. Harrison, "Steel Policies of the National Defense Advisory Commission, May to December 1940," Special Study No. 40, 1947, Policy Documentation File, WPB; McCauley, "Consumer Durable Goods Industry," pp. 101–8; CPA, "Industrial Mobilization for War," vol. 2, pt. 2, chap 4, pp. 10–121a; Truman Committee, *First Annual Report,* 77th Cong., 2d sess., 1942, S. Rept. No. 480, pt. 5, pp. 27–29; Truman Committee, *Interim Report on Steel,* 78th Cong., 1st sess., 1943, S. Rept. No. 10, pt. 3, pp. 1–18; Truman Committee, *Third Annual Report,* 78th Cong., 2d sess., 1944, S. Rept. No. 10, pt. 16, pp. 91–96; CPA, *Industrial Mobilization for War,* pp. 69, 75–76, 153–54, 359–83, 641–642, 779; David C. Motter, "Government Controls over the Iron and Steel Industry during World War

II: Their Development, Implementation, and Economic Effect" (Ph.D. diss., Vanderbilt University, 1958); Richard A. Lauderbaugh, *American Steel Makers and the Coming of the Second World War* (Ann Arbor, MI: UMI, 1980); Walter Adams, "The Steel Industry," in *Structure of American Industry*, ed. Adams, pp. 144–84; Philip E. Brown, "The American Steel Industry: An Analysis of Its History, Strategies, and Market Control" (Ph.D. diss., Union Institute, 1994); and Mary A. Yeager, "Trade Protection as an International Commodity: The Case of Steel," in *Survival of Corporatism during the New Deal Era, 1933–1945*, ed. Robert F. Himmelberg (New York: Garland, 1994), pp. 401–10. For the army's interwar planning for steel and the citation of other secondary sources on steel, see Koistinen, *Planning War, Pursuing Peace*, pp. 105–15, 356–57 n. 15.

12. Harrison, "Steel Policies of NDAC," p. 18.

13. Priorities, allocations, and other distribution controls are analyzed below.

14. The following analysis of copper is based on Wiltse to Fesler (on Douglas interview), 11/1/44, 11–12/1944, Box 1, Fesler Papers; ANMB, Executive Committee Minutes, 11/2/42, and other entries, Executive Committee Minutes, and ANMB, Minutes, 9/4/42, and other entries, file 370.26/200-13.7, ANMB; *OPM Minutes*, pp. 2, 33, 59; *SPAB Minutes*, 3, 7, 9–10, 12, 14, 16–17, 20, 23–24, 31, 35–36, 43, 66–67; Truman Committee, *First Annual Report*, 77th Cong., 2d sess., 1942, S. Rept. No. 480, pt. 5, pp. 19–25, 212–13, 220–21; U.S. Bureau of the Census, *Historical Statistics of the United States, Colonial Times to 1970* (Washington, DC: U.S. Government Printing Office, 1975), pt. 1, p. 602; CPA, "Industrial Mobilization for War," vol. 2, pt. 2, chap. 4, pp. 219–338; McCauley, "Metals and Minerals Policy," pp. 10, 18, 22–23, 25–33, and exhibits 1–2; George R. Kinzie, *Copper Policies of the War Production Board and Predecessor Agencies, May 1940 to November 1945* (Washington, DC: Civilian Production Administration, 1947); Charles M. Wiltse, *Evolution of Premium Price Policy for Copper, Lead, and Zinc, January 1940 to November 1943* (Washington, DC: War Production Board, 1943); CPA, *Industrial Mobilization for War*, pp. 69, 154, 642–44, 779; Charles K. Hyde, *Copper for America: The United States Copper Industry from Colonial Times to the 1990s* (Tucson: University of Arizona Press, 1998); and Koistinen, *Hammer and the Sword* (parts of the entire volume are relevant to copper and other nonferrous metals since it treats with labor relations and supply as well as industrial mobilization). For the army's interwar planning for copper and relevant secondary sources, see Koistinen, *Planning War, Pursuing Peace*, pp.134–35, 361 n. 8. See also Charles M. Wiltse, *Lead and Zinc Policies of the War Production Board and Predecessor Agencies, May 1940 to March 1944* (Washington, DC: War Production Board, 1944); Edythe W. First, "Tin Smelting in the National Defense Program, April 1939 to August 1944," Brief Survey No. 15, 1944, Policy Documentation File, WPB; Charles M. Wiltse, *Mercury Policies of the War Production Board and Predecessor Agencies, May 1940 to March 1944* (Washington, DC: War Production Board, 1944); and Vernon H. Jensen, *Nonferrous Metals Industry Unionism, 1932–1954: A Story of Leadership Controversy* (Ithaca, NY: Cornell University Press, 1954).

15. The following analysis of rubber is based on a number of primary and secondary sources. Primary sources include Conference with the President, 6/5/42, 6/13/42, 8/6/42, Smith Papers; Gladieux Notes, Rubber Rationing Order, 9/18/42, and numerous other memoranda and related documents, Box 20, Unit 208, RWA, BOB; Stettinius to Roosevelt w/ enc., 10/23/40, OF: Council of National Defense, "Allot-

ment of Materials in Connection with the Rubber Program," 12/8/42, OF: Office of the Rubber Director, and Jeffers to President, 12/1/42, and other correspondence and documents, OF: Joint Chiefs of Staff, FDR Papers; entry, 4/2/42, Alphabetical File, Box 3, Telephone Transcripts, April 1942, Conference of Director and Assistant Director with President, 6/18/42, Alphabetical File, Box 13, Roosevelt, Franklin D.— 1943, and Coy to President, 7/20/42, and memorandum, 8/6/42, Alphabetical File, Box 13, Roosevelt, Franklin D.—Conference with Director and Assistant Director, Coy Papers; Auxier to Fesler, 10/9/45, and numerous other memoranda, 9–12/1945, Box 2, Fesler Papers; ANMB, Executive Committee Minutes, 11/2/42, and numerous other entries, Executive Committee Minutes, and ANMB, Minutes, 9/12/42, and numerous other entries, file 370.26/200-13.7, ANMB; extensive correspondence and documents in Baruch's Selected Correspondence, 1942 (with Batt, Bush, Byrd, Byrnes, Carroll, Chadborne, Cowden, Forrestal, Gillette, Hauser, Hirsch, Johnson, Rosenman, Roosevelt, and Wallace), 1943 (with Compton, Dewey, Jeffers, Perkins, Roosevelt, and Wallace), 1944 (with Dewey), and 1945 (with Dewey, and Hancock), and Lubell to Baruch, 4/3/43, and other memoranda, Washington File, 1942–1945, Box 43, Sec. 3—Special Subjects: Rubber Survey Committee, and Swope to Baruch, 2/4/43, and Jeffers to Baruch, 6/24/43, Washington File . . . Alcohol, Baruch Papers; *OPM Minutes,* pp. 19, 21, 59; *SPAB Minutes,* pp. 8, 38, 39, 41, 47, 49, 50, 56, 58, 62–63, 64–65; and congressional hearings and reports and the report of the Rubber Survey Committee, all cited below separately.

Secondary sources are indispensable for understanding the enormously complex and at times highly technical synthetic rubber program during the defense and war years. The most thorough study of rubber and synthetic rubber has been prepared by the Division of Information, Reconstruction Finance Corporation: Brendan J. O'Callaghan, "Rubber in World War II: A History of the U.S. Government's Natural and Synthetic Rubber Programs in World War II," 2 vols., 1948, rev. 1954 and 1955 (vol. 1 deals with natural rubber, vol. 2 with synthetic rubber), Entry 26, Office of the Secretary, Records of the Reconstruction Finance Corporation, RG 234, National Archives, College Park, MD. Entry 26 is a rich collection that includes numerous other reports, studies, and documents involving rubber. This monographic treatment, however, skirts the numerous controversies generated by synthetic rubber and casts the Rubber Reserve Company, its sponsor, in the best possible light. The outstanding, nongovernment scholar on wartime synthetic rubber, and hence perhaps the most reliable one, is Robert A. Solo. His work in this field is based on his "The Development and Economics of the American Synthetic Rubber Program" (Ph.D. diss., Cornell University, 1952) and includes *Synthetic Rubber: A Case Study in Technological Development under Government Direction,* U.S. Congress, Senate, Subcommittee on Patents, Trademarks, and Copyrights of the Committee on the Judiciary, Study No. 18, 85th Cong., 2d sess., 1959, which is reprinted with a twenty-eight-page introduction as *Across the High Technology Threshold: The Case of Synthetic Rubber* (Norwood, PA: Norwood, 1980); "The Sale of the Synthetic Rubber Plants," *Journal of Industrial Economics* 2 (November 1953): 32–43; and "Research and Development in the Synthetic Rubber Industry," *Quarterly Journal of Economics* 68 (February 1954): 61–82. Solo served in various government mobilization agencies during the defense and war years, including OPM. He wrote his dissertation under the direction of Professor

Melvin deChazeau, an economist serving in various capacities in the NDAC, OPM, and WPB and referred to above.

Other important work on synthetic rubber includes Paul Wendt, "The Control of Rubber in World War II," *Southern Economic Journal* 13 (January 1947): 203–27; William M. Tuttle, Jr., "The Birth of an Industry: The Synthetic Rubber 'Mess' in World War II," *Technology and Culture* 22 (January 1981): 35–67; David R. B. Ross, "Patents and Bureaucrats: U.S. Synthetic Rubber Development before Pearl Harbor," in *Business and Government,* ed. Joseph R. Frese, S.J., and Jacob Judd (Tarrytown, NY: Sleepy Hollow Press, 1985), pp. 119–55; and Peter J. T. Morris, *The American Synthetic Rubber Research Program* (Philadelphia: University of Pennsylvania Press, 1989). The notes in Ross, "Patents and Bureaucrats," contain an excellent bibliography on the subject, which is further broadened in Morris, *American Synthetic Rubber.* Other volumes are significant. In *Buna Rubber: The Birth of an Industry* (New York: D. Van Nostrand, 1947), Frank A. Howard, president of the Standard Oil Development Co., presents Standard's case, providing invaluable information, but in a way that misleads both by what is said and by what is left out. A much more subtle and effective defense by Standard officials is Vernon Herbert and Attilio Bisio, *Synthetic Rubber: A Project That Had to Succeed* (Westport, CT: Greenwood, 1985). Jesse H. Jones, *Fifty Billion Dollars: My Thirteen Years with RFC* (New York: Macmillan, 1951), pp. 396–433, is worth perusing, but not much more. There is some useful information in "The Emergency Rubber Project," in *Public Administration and Policy Development: A Case Book,* ed. Harold Stein (New York: Harcourt, Brace, 1952), pp. 635–48; and White, *Billions for Defense,* pp. 18, 23–24, 39–41, 57, 61, 64, 77–78, 108–9, 122, 127, 147–48.

Official government studies other than O'Callaghan's work are disappointing for the most part. Their coverage is usually brief and superficial but nonetheless helpful at points: CPA, "Industrial Mobilization for War," vol. 2, pt. 2, chap. 5, pp. 5–115; Virginia Turrell, "Rubber Policies of the War Production Board and Its Predecessor Agencies, May 1940 to March 1944," Brief Survey No. 11, 1944, Policy Documentation File, WPB; George W. Auxier, *Rubber Policies of the National Defense Advisory Commission and the Office of Production Management, May 1940 to December 1941* (Washington, DC: Civilian Production Administration, 1947); Bureau of the Budget, *The United States at War: Development and Administration of the War Program by the Federal Government* (Washington, DC: Bureau of the Budget, 1946), pp. 164–69, 293–97, 425; CPA, *Industrial Mobilization for War,* pp. 44, 73, 255–57, 377–79, 564–67, 646–48, 697–98, 743–44. However, Virginia Turrell, *Alcohol Policies of the War Production Board and Predecessor Agencies, May 1940 to January 1945* (Washington, DC: War Production Board, 1945), does make a valuable contribution. Joseph Borkin, *The Crime and Punishment of I. G. Farben* (New York: Free Press, 1978), provides good information on American synthetic rubber development within an international context. In the following analysis, I have purposefully kept discussions of the science and technology of synthetic rubber brief and uncomplicated.

16. Statistics on rubber during the defense and war years vary considerably at least in part because authors often fail to state whether they are using the U.S. short ton (2,000 pounds) or the U.K. long ton (2,240 pounds), a difference of 12 percent. Whenever possible, I have taken my figures from Wendt, "Control of Rubber in World

War II," because his calculations appear to be among the most thorough, consistent, and reliable. Wendt uses the long ton.

17. Koistinen, *Planning War, Pursuing Peace,* pp. 120–28 (the relevant notes cite additional secondary sources on rubber and synthetic rubber).

18. James B. Conant, Karl T. Compton, and Bernard M. Baruch, *Report of the Rubber Survey Committee, September 10, 1942* (Washington, DC: U.S. Government Printing Office, 1942). For developments leading up to the appointment of the committee, see the series of Bureau of the Budget memoranda between June and September 1942 on gasoline rationing, interagency disputes over it, and the president's response in Box 20, Unit 208, RWA, BOB.

19. The best secondary source on the Justice Department's suit against Standard, including the citation of primary sources, is Tuttle, "Synthetic Rubber 'Mess,'" pp. 40–43 (Arnold quotation p. 42). Howard, *Buna Rubber,* pp. 188–211, provides Standard's response to its legal problems.

20. Truman Committee, *Additional Report,* 77th Cong., 2d sess., 1942, S. Rept. No. 480, pt. 7, pp. 1–57 (committee quotations p. 28).

21. Weidlein served in the Chemicals Division of the War Industries Board during World War I. Basic biographical information on Weidlein is available in *The National Cyclopaedia of American Biography* (New York: James T. White, 1930), C-82. Union Carbide was a major sponsor of Mellon Institute research projects, particularly the use of natural gas and petroleum as feedstocks for chemicals. Weidlein's strength was more as a scientific administrator than as a scientist. For background on the Mellon Institute and Weidlein, see John W. Servos, "Changing Partners: The Mellon Institute, Private Industry, and the Federal Patron," *Technology and Culture* 35 (April 1994): 221–57.

22. Solo, *Synthetic Rubber,* p. 45.

23. U.S. Congress, Senate, Committee on Agriculture and Forestry, Subcommittee on S. Res. 224, *Hearings, Utilization of Farm Crops: Industrial Alcohol and Synthetic Rubber,* 77th Cong., 2d sess., pts. 1 and 2, 1942, and *Report to Accompany S. 2600,* 77th Cong., 2d sess., 1942, S. Rept. No. 1516, pp. 1–4; and *Cong. Rec.,* 77th Cong., 2d sess., 1942, 88, pt. 5:6433–43, 6481–95, 6538–39 (quotation p. 6434).

24. See n. 23 above. For the Roosevelt administration's reaction to this proposal, see memorandum "Rubber," 7/20/42, Box 20, Unit 208, RWA, BOB.

25. Conant, Compton, and Baruch, *Report of the Rubber Survey Committee,* quotations pp. 6, 17. For the Roosevelt administration's work with the Baruch Committee and bureaucratic infighting about implementing committee recommendations, see the Gladieux and other memoranda of 8–9/42 and Roosevelt to Nelson, 9/17/42, Box 20, Unit 208, RWA, BOB.

26. Herbert and Bisio, *Synthetic Rubber,* p. 85.

27. Solo, *Across the High Technology Threshold,* p. vii.

CHAPTER SEVEN. OPM'S LABOR, PURCHASES, AND PRIORITIES DIVISIONS AND SPAB

1. Paul A. C. Koistinen, *The Hammer and the Sword: Labor, the Military, and Industrial Mobilization, 1920–1945* (New York: Arno, 1979); Paul A. C. Koistinen, "Mobilizing the World War II Economy: Labor and the Industrial-Military Alliance,"

Pacific Historical Review 62 (November 1973): 443–78; Civilian Production Administration, *Minutes of the Advisory Commission to the Council of National Defense, June 12, 1940, to October 22, 1941* (Washington, DC: Civilian Production Administration, 1946); Civilian Production Administration, *Minutes of the Council of the Office of Production Management, December 21, 1940, to January 14, 1942,* (hereafter *OMP Minutes*) (Washington, DC: Civilian Production Administration, 1946); and Civilian Production Administration, *Minutes of the Supply Priorities and Allocations Board, September 2, 1941, to January 15, 1942* (hereafter *SPAB Minutes*) (Washington, DC: Civilian Production Administration, 1946). See also Emmerich to Bock, 1/11/56, U.S. Industrial Mobilization; Office for Emergency Management, 1940–1956, Box 30, Emmerich Papers; and James B. Carey, "Proposed Reorganization of OPM," 7/9/41, file 015.715R, and Production Planning Board, Verbatim Minutes, 3/10/41, file 015.715M, Box 30, and AFL, "Memorandum for the Production Planning Board," 4/9/41, file 221, Box 984, Policy Documentation File, WPB.

A few of the more important secondary sources include Richard J. Purcell, *Labor Policies of the National Defense Advisory Commission and the Office of Production Management, May 1940 to April 1942* (Washington, DC: Civilian Production Administration, 1946); R. Burr Smith, "Labor and Manpower Administration in War Production, May 1940 to March 1943," Special Study No. 1, 1943, R. Burr Smith, "The Training-within-Industry Program, July 1940 To December 1943," Brief Survey No. 6, 1944, and J. Carlyle Sitterson, "Industry and Labor Advisory Committees, May 1940 to April 1944," Brief Survey No. 10, 1944, pp. 1–18, Policy Documentation File, WPB; William J. Breen, "Social Science and State Policy in World War II: Human Relations, Pedagogy, and Industrial Training, 1940–1945," *Business History Review* 76 (Summer 2002): 233–66; Edythe W. First, *Industry and Labor Advisory Committees in the National Defense Advisory Commission and the Office of Production Management, May 1940 to January 1942* (Washington, DC: Civilian Production Administration, 1946), pp. 169–229; Ernest C. Mossner, "An Administrative History of the Office of Production Management, 1941," 1943, pp. 64–67, Box 19, Unit 204, RWA, BOB; Civilian Production Administration, *Industrial Mobilization for War: History of the War Production Board and Predecessor Agencies, 1940–1945* (Washington, DC: Civilian Production Administration, 1947), pp. 81–85, 163–69; and Bureau of the Budget, *The United States at War: Development and Administration of the War Program by the Federal Government* (Washington, DC: Bureau of the Budget, 1946), pp. 173–84.

2. On labor and the automobile industry, see chap. 6 at n. 7.

3. Trade union representatives in and outside the Labor Division also clashed at times with the Office of Price Administration and Civilian Supply and the Division of Civilian Supply.

4. The following analysis of the Purchases Division is based on *OPM Minutes,* pp. 1, 2, 3, 8, 28, 36, 58–59, 66; Curtis W. Garrison, "Procurement Policies of the National Defense Advisory Commission and Office of Production Management, May 1940 to December 1941," Special Study No. 39, 1947, pp. 219–69, George W. Mowry, "The Procurement of Quartermaster Supplies, May 1940 to April 1944," Brief Survey No. 7, 1944, pp. 5–6, 12–15, and James W. Fesler, "Relations between the Armed Services and the Advisory Commission to the Council of National Defense, May to December 1940," Special Study No. 3, 1943, pp. 24–33, Policy Documenta-

tion File, WPB; Mossner, "Administrative History of OPM," pp. 42–50, Box 19, Unit 204, RWA, BOB; and CPA, *Industrial Mobilization for War,* pp. 94, 97, 141–45.

5. Garrison, "Procurement Policies of the NDAC and OPM," p. 229.

6. The following analysis of plant sites is based on Gladieux Notes, "OPM-Civil-Military Relations," 12/18/41, Box 19, Unit 200, and Mossner, "Administrative History of OPM," pp. 185–93, Box 19, Unit 204, RWA, BOB; *OPM Minutes,* pp. 10, 22, 36, 37, 73, 84; Garrison, "Procurement Policies of the NDAC and OPM," pp. 92–95; Reginald C. McGrane, *The Facilities and Construction Program of the War Production Board and Predecessor Agencies, May 1940 to May 1945* (Washington, DC: War Production Board, 1945), pp. 40–42, 56–62; and CPA, *Industrial Mobilization for War,* pp. 61–63.

7. The following analysis of small business's role in economic mobilization is based on Rowe to Roosevelt, 4/28/41, PSF: Dollar-a-Year Men, and Odlum to President, 12/19/41, OF: Army and Navy Munitions Board, FDR Papers; French to Wacker, 2/6/46, Box 9, Unit 113, and "Notes on Interview with Stephen E. Fitzgerald," 12/23/41, Box 12, Unit 138, RWA, BOB; Odlum to Rosenman, ca. 1941, Office of Price Administration and Civilian Supply—Office of Production Management, and a long series of letters and documents from Odlum to Rosenman, Knudsen, Hopkins, Roosevelt, and others, Office of Production Management, Box 13, Rosenman Papers; deChazeau to Henderson w/ enc., 10/27/41, deChazeau Memos, WPB Papers, Box 32, Henderson Papers; *OPM Minutes,* pp. 4, 19, 20, 46–47, 49, 50–52, 53, 57, 60, 72; *SPAB Minutes,* pp. 29–30, 37, 42–43, 50; Mossner, "Administrative History of OPM," pp. 160–75, Box 19, Unit 204, RWA, BOB; Garrison, "Procurement Policies of the NDAC and OPM," pp. 271–353; Maryclaire McCauley, "The Conversion of the Consumer Durable Goods Industry to War Production, May 1940 to December 1944," Special Study No. 33, 1947, pp. 201–6, Policy Documentation File, WPB; McGrane, *Facilities and Construction Program,* pp. 51–56; Maryclaire McCauley, *Concentration of Civilian Production by the War Production Board, September 1941 to April 1943* (Washington, DC: War Production Board, 1944), pp. 1–15; Drummond Jones, *Role of the Office of Civilian Requirements in the Office of Production Management and War Production Board, January 1941 to November 1945* (Washington, DC: Civilian Production Administration, 1946), pp. 1–56; and CPA, *Industrial Mobilization for War,* pp. 145–50. See also Jim F. Heath, "American War Mobilization and the Use of Small Manufactures, 1939–1943," *Business History Review* 46 (Autumn 1972): 295–319 (the author cites many of the important publications on small business). More recent publications are also helpful in terms of subject matter and bibliography: Richard H. Keehn and Gene Smiley, "Small Business Reactions to World War II Government Controls," in *Survival of Corporatism during the New Deal Era, 1933–1945,* ed. Robert F. Himmelberg (New York: Garland, 1994), pp. 303–16; Stuart W. Bruchey, ed., *Small Business in American Life* (New York: Columbia University Press, 1980); and Harold G. Vatter, *The U.S. Economy in World War II* (New York: Columbia University Press, 1985), pp. 55–66. U.S. Congress, Senate, *Economic Concentration and World War II: Report of the Smaller War Plants Corporation to the Special Committee to Study Problems of American Small Business,* 79th Cong., 2d sess., S. Doc. 206, 1946, is a treasure trove of information on wartime economics, including the impact of the war on small business. Other congressional sources and citations involv-

ing the armed services will be given below. NDAC activities involving small business are discussed briefly in chap. 3 above.

8. Truman Committee, *Report Concerning Priorities and the Utilization of Existing Manufacturing Facilities,* 77th Cong., 1st sess., 1941, S. Rept. 480, pt. 3, pp. 1–9, and *First Annual Report,* 77th Cong., 2d sess., 1942, S. Rept. 480, pt. 5, pp. 7–14, 39–42; U.S. Congress, Senate, Special Committee to Study and Survey Problems of American Small Business Enterprises, *Additional Report,* 77th Cong., 2d sess., 1942, S. Rept. 479, pt. 2, pp. 1–26, *Additional Report,* 78th Cong., 1st sess., 1943, S. Rept. 12, pt. 1, pp. 1–22, and *Additional Report,* 78th Cong., 1st sess., 1943, S. Rept. 12, pt. 3, pp. 1–7; U.S. Congress, House, Select Committee Investigating National Defense Migration, *First Interim Report,* 77th Cong., 1st sess., 1941, S. Rept. 1286, pp. 1–111, *Second Interim Report,* 77th Cong., 1st sess., 1941, S. Rept. 1553, pp. 1–143, and *Third Interim Report,* 77th Cong., 2d sess., 1942, S. Rept. 1879, pp. 1–109. See also Donald E. Spritzer, *Senator James E. Murray and the Limits of Post-War Liberalism* (New York: Garland, 1985), pp. 69–100.

9. Wheeler quoted in Garrison, "Procurement Policies of the NDAC and OPM," pp. 352–53.

10. The military's procurement and economic mobilization planning is covered in great detail in Koistinen, *Planning War, Pursuing Peace,* pp. 1–207. See also chaps. 2 and 5 above.

11. R. Elberton Smith, *The Army and Economic Mobilization* (Washington, DC: Office of the Chief of Military History, 1959), pp. 59–61, 225, 227–28, 233, 237, 241n, 248–56, 264, 266, 275, 340, 413–34; Erna Risch, *The Quartermaster Corps: Organization, Supply, and Services,* vol. 1 (Washington, DC: Office of the Chief of Military History, 1953), pp. 265–67; and Harry C. Thompson and Lida Mayo, *The Ordnance Department: Procurement and Supply* (Washington, DC: Office of the Chief of Military History, 1960), pp. 40–42.

12. Robert H. Connery, *The Navy and the Industrial Mobilization in World War II* (Princeton, NJ: Princeton University Press, 1951), pp. 115–24; and Julius A. Furer, *Administration of the Navy Department in World War II* (Washington, DC: Naval History Division, 1959), pp. 844, 846–50, 865–67.

13. Garrison, "Procurement Policies of the NDAC and OPM," pp. 346–48.

14. The following analysis of priorities is based on "Hearings on the 1941 Budget Estimates of the Division of Industrial Materials of the Advisory Commission to the Council of National Defense, November 14, 1940," ". . . Office for Coordination of National Defense Purchases . . . , November 15, 1940," and other hearings, Box 13, Unit 147, and Mossner to Herring, "Interview with Mr. Herbert Emmerich," 10/6/43, Box 19, Unit 202, RWA, BOB; Smith to President, 8/12/41, and numerous other correspondence and documents (an excellent summary of the priorities situation between May 1940 and June 1941 is provided by Ginsburg to Rosenman, 8/8/41), Supply Priorities and Allocations Board, Box 16, Rosenman Papers; Coy to President, 5/9/41, OF: Army and Navy Munitions Board, FDR Papers; Entry, 12/28/40, Henderson, Leon: Diary, July 1938–December 1940, WPB Papers, Box 36, Henderson Papers; Wiltse to Fesler (on Hill interview), 1/17/46, 1–4/1946, Box 2, Fesler Papers; Baruch to Roosevelt, 5/7/41, and numerous other related documents, Selected Correspondence, Baruch Papers; *OPM Minutes,* pp. 1–2, 3, 4, 6, 8,

19, 25, 27, 28, 29, 31, 32, 34, 35, 36, 39, 41, 42, 45, 46, 47–48, 49, 53, 54, 55, 60, 62–63, 68, 75, 80; Mossner, "Administrative History of OPM," pp. 52–59, 84–128, 145–59, Box 19, Unit 204, RWA, BOB; Gilbert Convers, "Priorities and Allocations Systems under the National Defense Advisory Commission, Office of Production Management, and War Production Board, May 1940 to November 1942," Special Study No. 36, 1947, Policy Documentation File, WPB; Jones, *Office of Civilian Requirements,* pp. 1–56; CPA, *Industrial Mobilization for War,* pp. 96–97, 171–84; Bureau of the Budget, *United States at War,* pp. 60–63, 73–79; David Novick, Melvin Anshen, and W. C. Truppner, *Wartime Production Controls* (New York: Columbia University Press, 1949), pp. 1–104; Smith, *Army and Economic Mobilization,* pp. 505–55; and Connery, *Navy and Industrial Mobilization,* 92–95 and 102–3.

15. Smith quoted in Convers, "Priorities and Allocations Systems," p. 142. See also Ginsburg to Rosenman, 8/8/41, and Coy to Rosenman, 8/8/41, Supply Priorities and Allocations Board, Box 16, Rosenman Papers.

16. The following analysis of the SPAB is based on Henderson to Roosevelt, 8/16/41, and numerous other correspondence and documents, Office of Price Administration and Civilian Supply—Office of Production Management, Box 13, Smith to Roosevelt, 7/18/41, and numerous other correspondence and documents, Supply Priorities and Allocations Board, Box 16, and Rowe to Rosenman, 8/29/41, Rowe, James, Jr., Box 4, Rosenman Papers; "Notes on Interview with Stephen E. Fitzgerald," 12/23/41, and "Notes on Interview with Don Riley," 10/30/41, Box 12, Unit 138, Gladieux Notes, "Meeting of Smith and Coy with Nelson," 11/26/41, memorandum "Army and Navy Munitions Board vs Office of Production Management," 1/13/42, and other documents, Box 19, Unit 200, and Mossner to Herring, "Interview with Mr. Herbert Emmerich," 10/6/43, Box 19, Unit 202, RWA, BOB; Stimson and Knox to Roosevelt, 11/18/41, and Wallace to Roosevelt, 11/19/41, OF: Supply Priority and Allocations Board, FDR Papers; White House Memoranda, Smith to Roosevelt, 12/13/41, Smith Papers; Gladieux to President, 8/12/41, Alphabetical File, Box 13, Roosevelt, Franklin D.—Conferences with Director and Assistant Director, and President to Coy, 8/2/41, Roosevelt, Franklin D., Box 13, Coy Papers; Ginsburg to Rosenman, 8/8/41, Supply Priorities and Allocations Board: Formation, Etc., Entry, 7/29/41, Henderson, Leon: Diary Notes and Memos to Himself, and Henderson to President, 8/4/41, Henderson, Leon: Memos to the White House, WPB Papers, Box 36, Henderson Papers; George Address to PARB, WPB, 4/13/45, 4–6/1945, and Nathan Address to PARB, WPB, 8/4/45, 7–8/1945, Box 2, Fesler Papers; Production Planning Board, Minutes, 3/13/41–7/9/41, file 015.715M, and Fuller to Biggers, 3/13/41, and numerous other documents, file 015.715R, Box 30, and Doherty to Biggers, 5/29/41, and other documents, file 221, Box 984, Policy Documentation File, WPB; Chambers to Baruch, OPM, w/ enc. (Chambers to Kuznets, 11/3/42), 11/14/42, Washington File, 1942–1945, Box 35, Sec. 2—Government Agencies: War Production Board, Baruch Papers; *OPM Minutes,* pp. 83, 87; *SPAB Minutes,* pp. 4, 19, 21, 24, 30–31, 33–34, 37, 38, 40, 47, 48–50, 50–51, 54, 59, 62, 66, 69–70 (all of the *Minutes* are essential for a better understanding of SPAB operations); Nathan D. Grundstein, "Programming of Defense Production by the National Defense Advisory Commission and Office of Production Management, May 1940 to December 1941," Special Study No. 31, 1947, pp. 270–303, Policy Documentation File, WPB; McCauley, "Consumer Durable Goods Indus-

try," pp. 110–216; Mossner, "Administrative History of OPM," pp. 117–28, 141–44, Box 19, Unit 204, RWA, BOB; Jones, *Office of Civilian Requirements,* pp. 1–56; Bureau of the Budget, *United States at War,* pp. 73–89; and CPA, *Industrial Mobilization for War,* pp. 109–14, 121–40, 189–97.

17. Conference with the President, 4/11/41, 5/29/41, Smith Papers; Roosevelt to Secretary of the Navy, 12/8/41, and Hopkins to Tully, 12/9/41, OF: Strategic Munitions Board, and Roosevelt to Nelson, 2/11/42, OF: Machine Tools, FDR Papers; memorandum Milton to Herring, 1/13/43, Box 12, Unit 188, and Gladieux Notes, "Lend-Lease," 3/4/42, Box 19, Unit 200, RWA, BOB; *OPM Minutes,* pp. 4, 5, 15–16, 29, 37, 45, 47, 52, 61, 70, 79; *SPAB Minutes,* pp. 2, 3, 5–6, 15–16, 34, 37, 38, 40, 43, 49–50, 51, 53, 58, 61; John Morton Blum, *From the Morgenthau Diaries: Years of Urgency, 1938–1941* (Boston: Houghton Mifflin, 1965), pp. 319–43; CPA, *Industrial Mobilization for War,* pp. 71–74, 121–33; and Bureau of the Budget, *United States at War,* pp. 84–89.

CHAPTER EIGHT. WPB: ORGANIZATION AND STAFFING

1. Most of what is outlined below will be fully analyzed in chapters that follow. I will cite here only sources for subjects not subsequently developed and documented.

2. The last figure on WPB executives' positions in their industrial firms includes without-compensation personnel as well as dollar-a-year men and, hence, is slightly different from some other figures cited in the paragraph. A list of all dollar-a-year employees in WPB on March 14, 1942, including their present or previous private affiliations, is available in Dollar-a-Year-Men, War Production Board, WPB Papers, Box 32, Henderson Papers. James A. McAleer, "Policies and Procedures on Dollar-a-Year and without-Compensation Employees of the War Production Board and Predecessor Agencies, May 1940 to March 1944," Brief Survey No. 8, 1944, Policy Documentation File, WPB, includes two invaluable exhibits: exhibit A, "Dollar-a-Year Employees and Temporary Dollar-a-Year Appointments Pending Investigations"; and exhibit B, "Consultants and Technical Advisors Serving on a without Other Compensation Basis." Both exhibits indicate an individual's business connections and positions within the mobilization agencies. (Not all copies of Brief Survey No. 8 include these exhibits.) By far the most thorough and comprehensive summary of vital statistics and data on dollar-a-year men is a 192-massively-oversize-page report prepared for Donald M. Nelson at the request of his assistant, Edwin A. Locke, Jr.: "Dollar-a-Year Personnel on the War Production Board and Predecessor Agencies, May, 1940–September 30, 1944," Box 13, Unit VIII, No. 1, Nelson Papers.

For WPB staffing in general, see Truman Committee, *First Annual Report,* 77th Cong., 2d sess., 1942, S. Rept. 480, pt. 5, pp. 7–10; James A. McAleer, *Dollar-a-Year and Without Compensation Personnel Policies of the War Production Board and Predecessor Agencies, August 1939 to November 1945* (Washington, DC: Civilian Production Administration, 1947); and Civilian Production Administration, *Industrial Mobilization for War: History of the War Production Board and Predecessor Agencies, 1940–1945* (Washington, DC: Civilian Production Administration, 1947), pp. 231–34. For the use of dollar-a-year men in the NDAC and OPM, see chaps. 1 and 4 above.

3. J. Carlyle Sitterson, "Industry and Labor Advisory Committees, May 1940 to

April 1944," Brief Survey No. 10, 1944, and William J. Schuck, "Industry and Labor Advisory Committees in the War Production Board, January 1942 to November 1945," Special Study No. 34, 1947, Policy Documentation File, WPB.

4. The most unequivocal defense of Nelson is presented in Bruce Catton, *The War Lords of Washington* (New York: Harcourt, Brace, 1948); the most recent indictment of the WPB chair is offered in Keith E. Eiler, *Mobilizing America: Robert P. Patterson and the War Effort, 1940–1945* (Ithaca, NY: Cornell University Press, 1997); and a carefully balanced interpretation appears in CPA, *Industrial Mobilization for War.* There is only one biography of Nelson, Terry R. Warth's "Donald Marr Nelson— Archetypical Businessman-Bureaucrat: A Study of the Growing Interdependency between Private Enterprise and the American Government" (Ph.D. diss., University of Southern California, 1984). The literature on World War II economic mobilization is analyzed at length in Paul A. C. Koistinen, "Warfare and Power Relations in America: Mobilizing the World War II Economy," in *The Home Front and War in the Twentieth Century: The American Experience in Comparative Perspective,* ed. James Titus (Colorado Springs, CO: United States Air Force Academy, 1984), pp. 231–43.

Work in primary sources is essential for understanding and assessing Nelson's leadership of WPB. Particularly important are interviews by and presentations to the WPB's Policy Analysis and Records Branch (PARB) by current and past board officials. The Fesler Papers has the richest collection of these documents, which deal, not only with Nelson, but also with many high-level board officials. Three interviews (all marked "Confidential—Not to be Cited") are the most candid, hard-hitting statements in wartime records: Fesler interviews with Milton Katz, 7/13/46, John Lord O'Brian, 7/15/46, and Wayne Coy, 7/17/46, 7–8/1946, Box 2. Also important are Fesler interview with Roe, 3/6/44, 1–8/1942, "Comments on Political and Personal Aspects of War Production Board," 10/27/43, 9–12/1943, memorandum First to Fesler on Gregg address to PARB, WPB, 10/21/44, 10/1944, memorandum Sitterson to Fesler on Gladieux interview, 11/15/44, 11–12/1944, Box 1, memorandum on Gulick address to PARB, WPB, 1/5/45, and memorandum on Gladieux address to PARB, WPB, 3/9/45, 1–3/1945, memorandum on Martin address to PARB, WPB, 6/7/45, 4–6/1945, memorandum on Hill address to PARB, WPB, 7/27/45, and memorandum on Nathan address to PARB, WPB, 8/4/45, 1–8/1945, memorandum Fesler and Jones on Hill interview, 9/10/45, 9–12/1945, and memorandum Wiltse to Fesler on Hill interview, 1/17/46, 1–4/1946, Box 2. Additional interviews and presentations from WPB, Bureau of the Budget, and other records will be cited in chapters that follow. Of invaluable significance along those lines is Gladieux Reminiscences, pp. 300–652.

5. Memorandum on Gulick address to PARB, WPB, 1/5/45, 1–3/1945, Fesler Papers.

CHAPTER NINE. THE ARMED SERVICES' MATERIAL ORGANIZATION FOR WORLD WAR II

1. Chapters 2 and 5 above cover in considerable detail the armed services' organization, policies, and interaction with civilian mobilization agencies between 1940 and 1941. I will not repeat in this chapter all the citations of secondary sources included in those chapters.

2. John D. Millett, *The Organization and Role of the Army Service Forces* (Washington, DC: Office of the Chief of Military History, 1954); and John Kennedy Ohl, *Supplying the Troops: General Somervell and American Logistics in WWII* (DeKalb: Northern Illinois University Press, 1994). With a background in public administration, Millett served in uniform as historian for the ASF. Millett's and Ohl's books complement one another, with Ohl's updating the relevant bibliography. See also *Annual Report of the Services of Supply for the Fiscal Year Ending June 20, 1942, Annual Report of the Army Service Forces for the Fiscal Year 1943, Annual Report of the Army Service Forces for the Fiscal Year 1944*, and *Annual Report of the Army Service Forces for the Fiscal Year 1945*, and *Logistics in World War II: Final Report of the Army Service Forces: A Report to the Under Secretary of War and the Chief of Staff by the Director of the Service, Supply, and Procurement Division, War Department General Staff*, 1947; Keith E. Eiler, *Mobilizing America: Robert P. Patterson and the War Effort, 1940–1945* (Ithaca, NY: Cornell University Press, 1997); Russell F. Weigley, *History of the United States Army*, enlarged ed. (Bloomington: Indiana University Press, 1984), pp. 440–50; Mark S. Watson, *Chief of Staff: Prewar Plans and Preparations* (Washington, DC: Department of the Army, 1950); R. Elberton Smith, *The Army and Economic Mobilization* (Washington, DC: Office of the Chief of Military History, 1959); and the volumes on the various technical services cited in chaps. 2 and 5 above.

Other volumes are helpful: James E. Hewes, Jr., *From Root to McNamara: Army Organization and Administration, 1900–1963* (Washington, DC: U.S. Army Center of Military History, 1975), pp. 57–128; James A. Huston, *The Sinews of War: Army Logistics, 1775–1953* (Washington, DC: Office of the Chief of Military History, 1966), pp. 403–571; Otto L. Nelson, Jr., *National Security and the General Staff* (Washington, DC: Infantry Journal Press, 1946), pp. 314–568; Marvin A. Kreidberg and Merton G. Henry, *History of Military Mobilization in the United States Army, 1775–1945* (Washington, DC: Department of the Army, 1955), pp. 541–694; Forrest C. Pogue, *George C. Marshall: Ordeal and Hope, 1939–1942* (New York: Viking, 1966), pp. 289–301; Forrest C. Pogue, *George C. Marshall: Organizer of Victory* (New York: Viking, 1973), pp. 263–78; Henry L. Stimson and McGeorge Bundy, *On Active Service in Peace and War* (New York: Harper and Bros., 1947), pp. 323–669; Elting E. Morison, *Turmoil and Tradition: A Study of the Life and Times of Henry L. Stimson* (Boston: Houghton Mifflin, 1960), pp. 477–654; Godfrey Hodgson, *The Colonel: The Life and Wars of Henry Stimson, 1867–1950* (New York: Alfred A. Knopf, 1990), pp. 213–390; David F. Schmitz, *Henry L. Stimson: The First Wise Man* (Wilmington, DE: Scholarly Resources, 2001); Jean E. Smith, *Lucius D. Clay: An American Life* (New York: Henry Holt, 1990), pp. 103–220; Eric Larrabee, *Commander in Chief: Franklin Delano Roosevelt, His Lieutenants, and Their War* (New York: Harper and Row, 1987), pp. 96–152; Thomas Parrish, *Roosevelt and Marshall: Partners in Politics and War* (New York: William Morrow, 1989), pp. 343–417; Mark A. Stoler, *George C. Marshall: Soldier-Statesman of the American Century* (Boston: Twayne, 1989), pp. 92–93, 102–8; Mark A. Stoler, *Allies and Adversaries: The Joint Chiefs of Staff, the Grand Alliance and U.S. Strategy in World War II* (Chapel Hill: University of North Carolina Press, 2000); Warren F. Kimball, *Forged in War: Roosevelt, Churchill, and the Second World War* (New York: William Morrow, 1997); Ed Gray, *General of the Army: George C. Marshall, Soldier and Statesman* (New York: W. W. Norton, 1990), pp. 278–80; D. Clayton James, *A Time for Giants: Politics of the American High Command in*

World War II (New York: Franklin Watts, 1987), pp. 210–11; David Eisenhower, *Eisenhower: At War, 1943–1945* (New York: Random House, 1986), pp. 5, 42–46; and John C. Binkley, "The Role of the Joint Chiefs of Staff in National Security Policy Making: Professionalism and Self-Perception, 1942–1961" (Ph.D. diss., Loyola University of Chicago, 1985), pp. 1–117. I cite a host of works on the army that cover or relate to World War II in Paul A. C. Koistinen, *Mobilizing for Modern War: The Political Economy of American Warfare, 1865–1919* (Lawrence: University Press of Kansas, 1997), chap. 4, n. 1, pp. 310–13. In chap. 12, n. 10, below, I cite other sources pertaining to civil-military relations; and, in chap. 16, I deal further with the pricing and profits of military supply. See also Civilian Production Administration (CPA), *Industrial Mobilization for War: History of the War Production Board and Predecessor Agencies, 1940–1945* (Washington, DC: Civilian Production Administration, 1947), pp. 521–27; and Donald M. Nelson, *Arsenal of Democracy: The Story of American War Production* (New York: Harcourt, Brace, 1946), pp. 368–90.

3. These agencies are analyzed in the next chapter.

4. Smith, *Army and Economic Mobilization*, pp. 4–7; Erna Risch and Charles L. Kieffer, *The Quartermaster Corps: Organization, Supply, and Services*, vol. 2 (Washington, DC: Office of the Chief of Military History, 1955), p. 121; and Irving Brinton Holley, Jr., *Buying Aircraft: Materiel Procurement for the Army Air Forces* (Washington, DC: Office of the Chief of Military History, 1964), pp. 557–58. Figures on budgets and spending vary considerably among sources. I use those appearing to be the most accurate.

5. Stimson and Bundy, *On Active Service*, pp. 449–52 (quotation p. 551).

6. Holley, *Buying Aircraft;* and Wesley F. Craven and James L. Cate, eds., *Men and Planes*, vol. 6 of *The Army Air Forces in World War II* (Chicago: University of Chicago Press, 1955), chap. 8. For the vast literature on aircraft, see Paul A. C. Koistinen, *Planning War, Pursuing Peace: The Political Economy of American Warfare, 1920–1939* (Lawrence: University Press of Kansas, 1998), chap. 10, nn. 9–20, pp. 371–74.

7. War Department circular quoted in Millett, *Army Service Forces*, p. 124.

8. Ray S. Cline, *Washington Command Post: The Operations Division* (Washington, DC: Office of the Chief of Military History, 1951); Richard M. Leighton and Robert W. Coakley, *Global Logistics and Strategy, 1940–1943* (Washington, DC: Office of the Chief of Military History, 1955); Richard M. Leighton and Robert W. Coakley, *Global Logistics and Strategy, 1943–1945* (Washington, DC: Office of the Chief of Military History, 1968); Kevin Smith, "British and American Logistics," in *World War II in Europe, Africa, and the Americas, with General Sources: A Handbook of Literature and Research*, ed. Loyd E. Lee (Westport, CT: Greenwood, 1997), pp. 234–50 (which contains a valuable bibliography); Charles R. Shrader, *U.S. Logistics, 1607–1991: A Research Guide* (Westport, CT: Greenwood, 1992); and various essays in Allan R. Millett and Williamson Murray, eds., *Military Effectiveness*, vol. 3, *The Second World War* (Boston: Allen and Unwin, 1988).

9. War Department circular quoted in Ohl, *Supplying the Troops*, p. 146.

10. Ibid., p. 145.

11. Marshall quoted in Pogue, *Marshall: Ordeal and Hope*, pp. 297–98.

12. Robert E. Sherwood, *Roosevelt and Hopkins: An Intimate History* (New York: Harper and Bros., 1948), pp. 160–61, 278–89, 575–77; George McJimsey, *Harry Hopkins: Ally of the Poor and Defender of Democracy* (Cambridge, MA: Harvard University Press, 1987), pp. 152–55, 189, 204–7, 228–29, 234, 261–62, 292–93; Smith,

Army and Economic Mobilization, pp. 126–39; Watson, *Chief of Staff* (consult the index); Constance M. Green, Harry C. Thomson, and Peter C. Roots, *The Ordnance Department: Planning Munitions for War* (Washington, DC: Office of the Chief of Military History, 1955), p. 95; Harry C. Thomson and Lida Mayo, *The Ordnance Department: Procurement and Supply* (Washington, DC: Office of the Chief of Military History, 1960), pp. 12, 33–34, 465; Ohl, *Supplying the Troops,* p. 66; and CPA, *Industrial Mobilization for War,* pp. 51, 100, 130–31.

13. Robert H. Connery, *The Navy and the Industrial Mobilization in World War II* (Princeton, NJ: Princeton University Press, 1951); Robert G. Albion and Robert H. Connery, *Forrestal and the Navy* (New York: Columbia University Press, 1962); Robert G. Albion, *Makers of Naval Policy, 1798–1947,* ed. Rowena Reed (Annapolis, MD: Naval Institute Press, 1980), pp. 347–591; and Julius A. Furer, *Administration of the Navy Department in World War II* (Washington, DC: Naval History Division, 1959). In Koistinen, *Mobilizing for Modern War,* chap. 3, nn. 1–7, pp. 306–10, I cite literature on the navy relevant to World War II.

14. Smith, *Army and Economic Mobilization,* pp. 4–6.

15. Koistinen, *Planning War, Pursuing Peace,* p. 49.

16. For an insightful essay on Roosevelt as commander-in-chief that cites much of the important literature, see Warren F. Kimball, "Franklin Roosevelt: 'Dr. Win-the-War,' " in *Commanders in Chief: Presidential Leadership in Modern Wars,* ed. Joseph G. Dawson III (Lawrence: University Press of Kansas, 1993), pp. 87–105, 198–206. See also Warren F. Kimball, *The Juggler: Franklin Roosevelt as Wartime Statesman* (Princeton, NJ: Princeton University Press, 1991); and Michael D. Pearlman, *Warmaking and American Democracy: The Struggle over Military Strategy, 1700 to Present* (Lawrence: University Press of Kansas, 1999), chap. 7.

CHAPTER TEN. NATIONAL AND INTERNATIONAL MOBILIZATION AGENCIES

1. Milton to Herring, 9/2/42, Box 12, Unit 144, Milton to Herring, 3/11/43, Box 12, Unit 143, B. L. G., "Division of Farm Products," 11/19/40, Box 13, Unit 147, and Milton to Herring, 11/10/42, and other memoranda and documents, Box 19, Unit 203, RWA, BOB; Roosevelt to Byrnes, 10/22/42, and other correspondence, PSF: Executive Office of the President—James F. Byrnes, and Vinson to President, 5/31/44, and other correspondence, PSF: Office of Economic Stabilization, FDR Papers; Baruch to Byrnes, 12/10/43, and other correspondence and documents, Washington File, 1942–1945, Box 32, Sec. 2—Government Agencies: Food Administration–Joint Contract Termination Board, Lubell to Baruch, 11/29/43, and other correspondence and documents, Washington File, 1942–1945, Box 36, Sec. 3—Special Subjects: Agriculture, Patterson to Baruch, 7/26/43, and other correspondence and documents, Washington File, 1942–1945, Box 38, Sec. 3—Special Subjects: Food, Baruch Papers.

There are a number of good secondary sources on agriculture during World War II. The most comprehensive and critical coverage is provided by Bela Gold, *Wartime Economic Planning in Agriculture: A Study in the Allocation of Resources* (New York: Columbia University Press, 1949). Walter W. Wilcox, *The Farmer in the Second World*

War (Ames: Iowa State College Press, 1947), is more generous toward farmers' accomplishments. Writing under the sponsorship of the Committee for Economic Development, Theodore W. Schultz, *Agriculture in an Unstable Economy* (New York: McGraw-Hill, 1945), treats agriculture from a broad perspective. Bureau of the Budget, *The United States at War: Development and Administration of the War Program by the Federal Government* (Washington, DC: Bureau of the Budget, 1946), pp. 321–69, presents the best analysis of the system set up to mobilize agriculture. Harold G. Vatter, *The U.S. Economy in World War II* (New York: Columbia University Press, 1985), pp. 48–55, considers food within the larger patterns of the wartime economy. A number of texts are helpful for understanding the farmer during World War II: Chester W. Wright, *Economic History of the United States* (New York: McGraw-Hill, 1949), pp. 810–14; Harold F. Williamson, ed., *The Growth of the American Economy*, 2d ed. (Englewood Cliffs, NJ: Prentice-Hall, 1951), pp. 690–98; Sidney Ratner, James H. Soltow, and Richard Sylla, *The Evolution of the American Economy: Growth, Welfare, and Decision Making* (New York: Basic, 1979), pp. 427–29; and Stanley Lebergott, *The Americans: An Economic Record* (New York: W. W. Norton, 1984), pp. 467–69.

2. See chap. 1 above.

3. See chap. 1 above.

4. Conference with the President, 5/29/41, and White House Memoranda, Smith to President, 7/18/41, Smith Papers.

There is no comprehensive study of ODT. Information on the office must be pieced together from a number of sources varying in quality: Andrew Stevenson, "Transportation Equipment Policies of the War Production Board and Predecessor Agencies, May 1940 to December 1943," Special Study No. 41, 1947, and Civilian Production Administration (CPA), "Industrial Mobilization for War: History of the War Production Board and Predecessor Agencies, 1940–1945," vol. 2, "Materials and Products," pt. 3, chap. 17, and pt. 4, chaps. 28, 36, Policy Documentation File, WPB; Walter L. McMurtry, "Wartime Problems of American Railroads, 1939–1945," 3 vols. (Ph.D. diss., University of New Mexico, 1983); Bureau of the Budget, *United States at War*, pp. 40, 106, 151, 155–72, 285–86, 492; Civilian Production Administration (CPA), *Industrial Mobilization for War: History of the War Production Board and Predecessor Agencies, 1940–1945* (Washington, DC: Civilian Production Administration, 1947), pp. 560–62; Claude M. Fuess, *Joseph B. Eastman: Servant of the People* (New York: Columbia University Press, 1952); Chester Wardlow, *The Transportation Corps: Responsibilities, Organization, and Operations* (Washington, DC: Office of the Chief of Military History, 1951), pp. 62–68, 308–405; Chester Wardlow, *The Transportation Corps: Movements, Training, and Supply* (Washington, DC: Office of the Chief of Military History, 1956), pp. 11–83, 167–326; John D. Millett, *The Organization and Role of the Army Service Forces* (Washington, DC: Office of the Chief of Military History, 1954), pp. 262–65; and Robert D. Cuff, "United States Mobilization and Railroad Transportation: Lessons in Coordination and Control, 1917–1945," *Journal of Military History* 53 (January 1989): 33–50. McMurtry cites most of the important literature on the railroads in the interwar and war years.

5. Browning Address to PARB, WPB, 4/20/45, 4–6/1945, Box 2, Fesler Papers; Leahy to Wilson, 8/9/43, and other correspondence and documents, Washington File, 1942–1945, Box 33, Sec. 2—Government Agencies: Maritime Department, and Nel-

son to Leahy, 12/1/42, and other correspondence, Washington File, 1942–1945, Box 45, Sec. 3—Special Subjects: Vickery-Gibbs Ship Building Program, Baruch Papers.

Surprisingly, no full-scale study of WSA exists. However, the literature on it is both larger and better than that on ODT: Frederic C. Lane, *Ships for Victory: A History of Shipbuilding under the U.S. Maritime Commission in World War II* (Baltimore: Johns Hopkins University Press, 1951) (chap. 23 discusses at length the relation between and interaction of the Maritime Commission and WSA); George E. Mowry, "The Naval and Maritime Shipbuilding Programs, May 1940 to June 1944," Brief Survey No. 13, 1944, Policy Documentation File, WPB; Charles H. Coleman, *Shipbuilding Activities of the National Defense Advisory Commission and Office of Production Management, July 1940 to December 1941* (Washington, DC: War Production Board, 1945); Bureau of the Budget, *United States at War*, pp. 135–54; William Chaikin and Charles H. Coleman, *Shipbuilding Policies of the War Production Board, January 1942–November 1945* (Washington, DC: Civilian Production Administration, 1947); S. McKee Rosen, *The Combined Boards of the Second World War: An Experiment in International Administration* (New York: Columbia University Press, 1951), pp. 71–130; Wardlow, *Transportation Corps: Responsibilities*, pp. 135–307, Wardlow, *Transportation Corps: Movements*, pp. 84–240, 327–418; Joseph Bykofsky and Harold Larson, *The Transportation Corps: Operations Overseas* (Washington, DC: Office of the Chief of Military History, 1957); Millett, *Army Service Forces*, 254–62; Richard M. Leighton and Robert W. Coakley, *Global Logistics and Strategy, 1940–1943* (Washington, DC: Office of the Chief of Military History, 1955); Robert M. Leighton and Robert W. Coakley, *Global Logistics and Strategy, 1943–1945* (Washington, DC: Office of the Chief of Military History, 1968) (consult indexes); Paul A. C. Koistinen, *The Hammer and the Sword: Labor, the Military, and Industrial Mobilization, 1920–1945* (New York: Arno, 1979), pp. 225–47; Robert P. Browder and Thomas G. Smith, *Independent: A Biography of Lewis W. Douglas* (New York: Alfred A. Knopf, 1986), pp. 163–215; Mark S. Foster, *Henry J. Kaiser: Builder of the Modern American West* (Austin: University of Texas Press, 1989), 68–111; Rene De La Pedraja, *The Rise and Decline of the U.S. Merchant Shipping in the Twentieth Century* (New York: Twayne, 1992), pp. 110–47; John K. Ohl, *Supplying the Troops: General Somervell and American Logistics in WWII* (DeKalb: Northern Illinois University Press, 1994), pp. 98–116; and Stephen B. Adams, *Mr. Kaiser Goes to Washington: The Rise of a Government Entrepreneur* (Chapel Hill: University of North Carolina Press, 1997). See also chap. 3 above.

6. Leiserson to Herring, 1/18/43, and other correspondence and documents, Box 20, Unit 206, RWA, BOB; Baruch to Ickes, 7/7/42, and Ickes to Baruch, 7/14/42, 7/29/42, Selected Correspondence, and Patterson to Ickes, 4/17/43, and other correspondence and documents, Washington File, 1942–1945, Box 33, Sec. 2— Government Agencies: Petroleum Administration for War, Baruch Papers.

The most detailed secondary source is John W. Frey and H. Chandler Ide, eds., *A History of the Petroleum Administration for War, 1941–1945* (Washington, DC: Petroleum Administration for War, 1946). Harole L. Ickes's *The Secret Diary of Harold L. Ickes*, vol. 1, *The First Thousand Days, 1933–1936*, vol. 2, *The Inside Struggle, 1936–1939*, and vol. 3, *The Lowering Clouds, 1939–1941* (New York: Simon and Schuster, 1954–1955), and *Fighin' Oil* (New York: Alfred A. Knopf, 1943), provide much information of varying quality. The latest biographies on Ickes are disappointing in terms of quality and coverage: Graham White and John Maze, *Harold Ickes of the New*

Deal: His Private Life and Public Career (Cambridge, MA: Harvard University Press, 1985); and T. H. Watkins, *Righteous Pilgrim: The Life and Times of Harold L. Ickes, 1874–1952* (New York: Henry Holt, 1990). The organization and structure of OPC/PAW are covered reasonably well in Bureau of the Budget, *United States at War,* pp. 282–92; and CPA, *Industrial Mobilization for War,* pp. 558–60. A host of volumes on the petroleum industry deal with the defense and war years with varying degrees of sophistication and detail: Harvey O'Connor, *The Empire of Oil* (New York: Monthly Review Press, 1962), pp. 66–67, 280–84, 333–34; Harold F. Williamson et al., *The American Petroleum Industry: The Age of Energy, 1899–1959* (Evanston, IL: Northwestern University Press, 1963), pp. 747–94; Gerald D. Nash, *United States Oil Policy, 1890–1964: Business and Government in Twentieth Century America* (Pittsburgh, PA: University of Pittsburgh Press, 1968), pp. 128–79; Anthony Sampson, *The Seven Sisters: The Great Oil Companies and the World They Made* (New York: Viking, 1975), pp. 94–105, 269; Michael B. Stoff, *Oil, War, and American Security: The Search for a National Policy on Foreign Oil, 1941–1947* (New Haven, CT: Yale University Press, 1980); and David S. Painter, *Oil and the American Century: The Political Economy of U.S. Foreign Oil Policy, 1941–1954* (Baltimore: Johns Hopkins University Press, 1986), pp. 1–127. See also CPA, "Industrial Mobilization for War," vol. 2, pt. 4, chap. 27; and Virginia Turrell, "High-Octane Aviation Gasoline Program, 1940–44," Brief Survey No. 12, 1944, Policy Documentation File, WPB. The *Minerals Yearbooks* for the years 1940–1945, cited fully in n. 9 below, also contain some valuable information on oil (consult the tables of contents and the indexes).

7. Paul A. C. Koistinen, *Mobilizing for Modern War: The Political Economy of American Warfare, 1865–1919* (Lawrence: University Press of Kansas, 1997), pp. 255–56; and Paul A. C. Koistinen, *Planning War, Pursuing Peace: The Political Economy of American Warfare, 1920–1939* (Lawrence: University Press of Kansas, 1998), pp. 129–33, 360–61.

8. Petroleum, synthetic rubber, and gasoline rationing are covered in chap. 6 above.

9. There are virtually no secondary sources on the SFAW and predecessor agencies. There are two sets of valuable—actually indispensable—published documents treating coal, lignite, and coke: The first is Bureau of Mines, *Minerals Yearbook Review* (Washington, DC: Department of the Interior, various years); see, e.g., pt. 1 in its entirety and the sections in pt. 3 on bituminous coal, Pennsylvania anthracite, and coke and by-products of *Review, 1940* (1941) and appropriate parts and sections of *Review, 1941* (1942), *Review 1942* (1943), *Review, 1943* (1944), *Review, 1944* (1945), and *Review 1945* (1946). The second is the *Annual Report of the Secretary of the Interior* (Washington, DC: Department of the Interior, various years); see, e.g., pp. 7–10, 19, 23–24, and 451–68 of *Annual Report, 1940* (1940) and appropriate pages (consult the tables of contents and the indexes) for *Annual Report, 1941* (1941), *Annual Report, 1942* (1942), *Annual Report, 1943* (1943), *Annual Report, 1944* (1944), *Annual Report, 1945* (1945), and *Annual Report, 1946* (1946). See also CPA, *Industrial Mobilization for War,* pp. 568–70.

Solid, comprehensive studies of the coal industry are also remarkably few in number. Some of the better ones include Waldo E. Fisher and Charles M. James, *Minimum Price Fixing in the Bituminous Coal Industry* (Princeton, NJ: Princeton University Press, 1955); James B. Hendry, "The Bituminous Coal Industry," in *The*

Structure of American Industry, ed. Walter Adams (New York: Macmillan, 1961), pp. 74–112; James P. Johnson, *The Politics of Soft Coal: The Bituminous Industry from World War I through the New Deal* (Urbana: University of Illinois Press, 1979), which contains the best and most thorough bibliography on coal for the years it covers; and John R. Bowman, *Capitalist Collective Action: Competition, Cooperation, and Conflict in the Coal Industry* (New York: Cambridge University Press, 1989), which is also helpful in terms of bibliography. See also Edward L. Allen, *Economics of American Manufacturing* (New York: Henry Holt, 1952), chap. 9; Hubert E. Risser, *The Economics of the Coal Industry* (Lawrence: School of Business, University of Kansas, 1958); Sam H. Schurr and Bruce C. Netschert, *Energy in the American Economy, 1850–1975: An Economic Study of Its History and Prospects* (Baltimore: Johns Hopkins University Press, 1960) (consult the table of contents); Williamson, ed., *Growth of the American Economy,* pp. 462–65, 710–11, 735–37; and Koistinen, *Planning War, Pursuing Peace,* pp. 163–66 (p. 369 for the citation of additional sources).

There are numerous, high-quality volumes on organized labor in the coal industry, particularly the United Mine Workers of America. They are cited in chap. 15, n. 1, below, and the chapter covers UAW wartime strikes as well.

10. I have briefly dealt with foreign economic policy in chaps. 3, 5, and 7 above. There is remarkably little secondary work on the nation's defense and wartime foreign economic policy. Bureau of the Budget, *United States at War,* pp. 31–35, 44–50, 63–69, 84–89, 403–28, provides the fullest, although still spotty, account. A reasonably full and accurate picture of agencies dealing with wartime economics abroad requires work in document collections, other primary sources, and unpublished studies, as cited below.

11. Conference with the President, 4/11/41, Smith Papers. Lend-Lease and policies and agencies that preceded it are covered in Bureau of the Budget, *United States at War.* Other secondary sources are limited in number, quality, and coverage: Edward R. Stettinius, Jr., *Lend-Lease: Weapon for Victory* (New York: Macmillan, 1944); Warren F. Kimball, *The Most Unsordid Act: Lend-Lease, 1939–1941* (Baltimore: Johns Hopkins University Press, 1969); Alan P. Dobson, *US Wartime Aid to Britain, 1940–1946* (New York: St. Martin's, 1986); Leighton and Coakley, *Global Logistics and Strategy, 1940–1943,* pp. 30–45, 76–116, 247–69, 492–524; Alan S. Milward, *War, Economy and Society, 1939–1945* (Berkeley: University of California Press, 1977), pp. 50–53, 71–74, 272–74, 351–53; Peter B. Kenen, *Giant among Nations: Problems in United States Foreign Policy* (New York: Harcourt, Brace, 1960), pp. 148–52; and Chester P. Kindleberger, *International Economics,* rev. ed. (Homewood, IL: Richard D. Irwin, 1958), pp. 445–50. The two studies of Hopkins provide rich, although scattered, material about and insights concerning Lend-Lease: Robert E. Sherwood, *Roosevelt and Hopkins: An Intimate History* (New York: Harper and Bros., 1948) (consult index); and George McJimsey, *Harry Hopkins: Ally of the Poor and Defender of Democracy* (Cambridge, MA: Harvard University Press, 1987) (consult index).

12. The following analysis of the BEW and its predecessors and successors is based on Lillian L. Buller, "Chronological History of the Economic Defense Board," Box 18, Unit 184, "Administrative History of the Board of Economic Warfare in the Field of International Economic Relations," pts. 1–3, and L. L. B., "Suggested Outline for an Administrative History of International Economic Relations," Box 18, Unit 183, Lillian L. Buller, "Synopsis of New Activities in the Field of International Economic

Consolidation," 6/3/43, Box 18, Unit 186, L. L. B., "The Enemy Branch of the Board of Economic Warfare: A Study in the Relationship of Research to Operations," Box 18, Unit 185, Lillian L. Buller, "Export Control," 6/30/44, Box 18, Unit 187, Milton to Herring, 7/28/42, Box 12, Unit 144, Milton to Herring, 1/13/43, Box 12, Unit 188, H. Venneman, "Interview with S. D. Strauss, Metals Reserve Corporation," 1/21/42, Box 12, Unit 211, Milton to Herring, 10/5/42, and numerous other memoranda, Box 18, Unit 180, Gladieux Notes (on BEW and related subjects), 10/29/41–5/1/42, Box 18, Unit 181, Butler to Gladieux, 6/21/43, and numerous other documents, Box 18, Unit 182, and Gladieux Notes, "International Raw Materials Board," 1/31/42, Box 19, Unit 197, RWA, BOB; Conference with the President, 5/29/41, 6/19/41, 2/7/42, 3/7/42, 12/18/42, 7/15/43, White House Memoranda, Smith to President, 2/6/43, and Daily Record, 1/8/42, Smith Papers; Coy to Hopkins, 6/19/43, Alphabetical File, Box 8, Hopkins, Harry L.— Administrative Assistant, and Conference of the Director and Assistant Director with the President, 12/18/42, Box 13, Roosevelt, Franklin D.—1942, Coy Papers; and Glancy to Baruch, 8/5/41, Perkins to Baruch, 12/3/41, 12/27/41, Baruch to Perkins, 12/5/41, 12/19/41, Perkins to Baruch, 9/1/42 (w/ enc. [article on Wallace and BEW]), 12/9/42, Perkins to Jeffers, 10/15/42, Perkins to Baruch, 1/12/43, Wallace to President, 1/25/43, and Baruch to President, 7/16/43, Selected Correspondence, Baruch Papers. See also Bureau of the Budget, *United States at War;* and CPA, *Industrial Mobilization for War,* pp. 71–73.

13. President to Nelson, 2/11/42, OF: Machine Tools, and memorandum "Munitions Assignments Board," 10/4/43, and other documents and correspondence, OF: Munitions Assignments Board, Smith to Watson, 4/21/42, and other correspondence and documents, PSF: Combined Chiefs of Staff, and Roosevelt to Leahy, 7/16/43, and other correspondence and documents, PSF: Joint Chiefs of Staff, FDR Papers; Milton to Herring, 7/23/42, Box 12, Unit 150, and Milton to Herring, 9/16/42, and other correspondence and documents, Box 19, Unit 197, RWA, BOB; Garry D. Ryan, "Preliminary Inventory of the Records of the United States Joint Chiefs of Staff (Record Group 218)," 1964, pp. iii, 1–4, Modern Military Records, National Archives, College Park, MD; General Services Administration, National Archives and Records Services, National Archives, *Federal Records of World War II,* vol. 2, *Military Agencies* (Washington, DC: National Archives, 1951), pp. 6–8; and "General Administrative Records of the Office of the Executive, 1942–45," and other records, Munitions Assignments Board, RG 333, National Archives, College Park, MD.

The most detailed secondary account of MAB is in Leighton and Coakley, *Global Logistics,* pp. 247–94. Ohl, *Somervell,* pp. 127–42, along with valuable bibliographic data, provides a good, brief analysis of MAB within the larger context of American assistance to its allies and the various agencies for carrying it out. Studies involving Hopkins present helpful insights on MAB's origins. See Sherwood, *Roosevelt and Hopkins,* pp. 469–73; and McJimsey, *Harry Hopkins,* pp. 217–22, 233–39, 252. See also Millett, *Army Service Forces,* 49–53, 180–81, 195–98, 266–67; Ray C. Cline, *Washington Command Post: The Operations Division* (Washington, DC: Office of the Chief of Military History, 1951), pp. 98–104, 176–77; Russell F. Weigley, *History of the United States Army,* enlarged ed. (Bloomington: Indiana University Press, 1984), pp. 447–48, 456–57; and Herman M. Somers, *Presidential Agency, OWMR: The Office of War Mobilization and Reconversion* (Cambridge, MA: Harvard University Press, 1950), p. 73.

14. Milton to Smith, 3/6/43, and numerous other correspondence and documents, Box 19, Unit 197, and S. McKee Rosen, "Some Tentative Generalizations concerning the Combined Boards," 12/16/43, Box 19, Unit 198, RWA, BOB; Batt Address to PARB, WPB, 5/11/45, 4–6/1945, Box 2, Fesler Papers. Not much secondary work has been done on the combined boards in general. The one volume on the subject is Rosen, *Combined Boards.* Since he was on the staff of the Bureau of the Budget during World War II, Rosen had the opportunity to assess firsthand the formation and operation of the combined boards. Most of *Combined Boards* appears to have been written while Rosen served with the bureau. Those parts of the manuscript that appear in the Bureau of the Budget files will be cited in relevant notes below.

15. Coy to President, 8/21/42, and other documents, Box 19, Combined Production and Resources Board, General Records of the Director, 1939–1946, B of B; Milton to Herring, 7/23/42, Box 12, Unit 150, and Milton to Herring, 11/16/42, and other correspondence, and Coy to President, 8/21/42, Box 19, Unit 197, RWA, BOB; and Roosevelt to Nelson, 8/19/42, and numerous correspondence, documents, and reports, PSF: Combined Production and Resources Board, and Roosevelt to Nelson, 6/9/42, and other correspondence and documents, OF: Combined Production and Resources Board, FDR Papers; and Sarah D. Powell, Richard G. Wood, and John E. Taylor, Jr., "Preliminary Inventory of the Textual Records of the Combined Raw Materials Board and the Combined Production and Resources Board (Record Group 179)," 1967, pp. iii–iv, 1–38, Civilian Records, National Archives, College Park, MD (this includes a helpful introduction). National Archives, *Federal Records of World War II,* vol. 1, *Civilian Agencies* (Washington, DC: National Archives, 1950), pp. 1032–34, provides a brief summary of the CPRB and the location of its records. I have researched "Letters Sent by the Board and Committees ('Chronological File'), 1942–45," and the "Security-Classified General Correspondence, 1942–45," Combined Production and Resources Board, 1942–45, both in WPB, with only meager returns. Much more helpful are War Production Board, "History of the Combined Production and Resources Board, June 9, 1942–November 1945," file 083.108R, WPB; George E. Mowry, "The Combined Production and Resources Board and Combined Raw Materials Board, August 1940 to January 1944," Brief Survey No. 5, 1944, Policy Documentation File, WPB; Rosen, *Combined Boards,* pp. 131–89; CPA, *Industrial Mobilization for War,* pp. 224–26, 252–55, 441–43, 570–72, 625–28; and Bureau of the Budget, *United States at War,* pp. 131, 408. National Archives, *Federal Records of World War II,* vol. 1, pp. 1027–48, lists and discusses combined committees and subcommittees, some of which are mentioned above and some not, in addition to various U.S.-Canadian agencies that have not been considered.

16. The movement for a supreme war production council is analyzed in chap. 12 below.

17. S. McKee Rosen, "The Combined Raw Materials Board," 12/23/43, Box 19, Unit 199, RWA, BOB (the manuscript is part of Rosen's volume on the joint boards cited above and discussed in n. 14); Batt to President, 3/18/42, and other correspondence, documents, and reports, OF: Combined Raw Materials Board, FDR Papers; Powell, Wood, and Taylor, "Combined Raw Materials Board and the Combined Production and Resources Board," pp. iii–iv, 1–38; National Archives, *Federal Records of World War II,* vol. 1, pp. 1028–30; "Secret General Correspondence, 1942–45," and "Confidential General Correspondence, 1942–43," Combined Raw Materials Board,

1942–46, and War Production Board, "History of the Combined Raw Materials Board (January 26, 1942 to December 31, 1945)," with cover letters, Whiting to Barton, 10/9/46, and Batt to Belsley, 8/23/46, file 083.208R, WPB; Mowry, "Combined Production and Resources Board and Combined Raw Materials Board"; Rosen, *Combined Boards,* pp. 1–70; CPA, *Industrial Mobilization for War,* pp. 222–24, 570–72, 628–29; and Bureau of the Budget, *United States at War,* pp. 131, 408.

18. S. McGee Rosen, "The Combined Shipping Adjustment Board: The Setting" (w/ evaluations of the manuscript), 1/45, Box 22, Unit 222, RWA, BOB (see n. 14 above); Land to Early, 2/20/42, OF: Combined Shipping Adjustment Board, and Roosevelt to Secretary of War, 12/8/41, and Hopkins to Roosevelt, 1/19/42, OF: Strategic Shipping Board, FDR Papers; National Archives, *Federal Records of World War II,* vol. 1, pp. 1023–24; Rosen, *Combined Boards,* pp. 71–130; and Bureau of the Budget, *United States at War,* pp. 131, 151. See also the text and citations above on the WSA.

19. National Archives, *Federal Records of World War II,* vol. 1, pp. 1026–27; Rosen, *Combined Boards,* pp. 191–256; and Bureau of the Budget, *United States at War,* pp. 131, 339, 408. See also the text and citations above on the WFA.

CHAPTER ELEVEN. CONVERTING AND EXPANDING INDUSTRY, 1942

1. Civilian Production Administration, *Minutes of the War Production Boards, January 20, 1942 to October 9, 1945* (hereafter *WPB Minutes*) (Washington, DC: Civilian Production Administration, 1946), pp. 7, 10, 25–26; *War Production in 1944: Report of the Chairman of the War Production Board* (Washington, DC: War Production Board, 1945), p. 134 (copy in Policy Documentation File, WPB); Civilian Production Administration (CPA), *Industrial Mobilization for War: History of the War Production Board and Predecessor Agencies, 1940–1945* (Washington, DC: Civilian Production Administration, 1947), pp. 273–78; and R. Elberton Smith, *The Army and Economic Mobilization* (Washington, DC: Office of the Chief of Military History, 1959), pp. 6–7. See chap. 7 above on SPAB.

2. The best, albeit brief, analysis of WPB industry branches, later divisions, is in pt. 1, chap. 3, pp. 35–50, of Civilian Production Administration, "Industrial Mobilization for War: History of the War Production Board and Predecessor Agencies, 1940–1945," vol. 2, "Materials and Products," 1947, Policy Documentation File, WPB. See also J. Carlyle Sitterson, "Industry and Labor Advisory Committees, May 1940 to April 1944," Brief Survey No. 10, 1944, and William J. Schuck, "Industry and Labor Advisory Committees in the War Production Board, January 1942 to November 1945," Special Study No. 34, 1947, Policy Documentatiaon File, WPB; and CPA, *Industrial Mobilization for War,* pp. 243–45. For an analysis and documentation of the industry branches/divisions as they evolved from the National Defense Advisory Commission and the OPM through the WPB, see chaps. 1, 4, and 8 above. The figure of forty-two industry branches includes material branches like steel, designated at times separately.

3. On conversion, see "Notes on Budget Hearing, Planning Committee WPB," 5/11/42, Box 12, Unit 211, and Gladieux Notes, "WPB," 7/6/42, Box 19, Unit 200, RWA, BOB; "Transcript of Subcommittee of the Management-Labor Automo-

bile Committee," 1/21/42, and numerous other documents and correspondence, file 631.0423, "Automobile Industry-Plant Conversion," WPB; Murray to President, 12/29/41, OF: War Production Board, FDR Papers; Nathan to Nelson, "Report of the Planning Committee for the Period February 20 to April 4, 1942," and other correspondence and documents, file 072.11, Policy Documentation File, WPB; Patterson to Rosenman w/ enc., 3/26/42, Patterson, Robert, Box 3, and Amberg to Patterson, 4/1/42, and numerous other correspondence and documents, Stimson, Henry, Box 4, Rosenman Papers; Amberg to Patterson, 7/25/42, War Production Board— 1942–43, Amberg Collection; "Brief Biographical Sketches of Key Men in WPB," 1/21/42, file 334/117.6, Office of the Assistant Secretary of War, OSW; Gladieux Reminiscences, pp. 69–444; Baruch to Krock, 6/4/41, Baruch to Batcheller, 12/8/42, Batcheller to Eberstadt, 12/3/42, Carroll to Baruch, 3/26/42, Baruch to Carroll, 4/3/42, and other correspondence, Baruch to Knowlson, 3/15/42, and other correspondence, Baruch to Nelson, 5/7/42, and numerous other correspondence, Replogle to Patterson, 2/4/42, and other correspondence, Willard to Baruch, 1/20/42, and other correspondence, and Baruch to Wood, 2/2/42, and other correspondence, Selected Correspondence, Baruch Papers; *WPB Minutes,* pp. 1, 29–30, 34–35, 37–38, 42–43, 47–48, 64–65, 68–69, 79–81, 84–86; John E. Brigante, "The Planning Committee of the War Production Board: A Chapter in American Planning Experience" (Ph.D. diss., Princeton University, 1948), pp. 115–23; Maryclaire McCauley, "The Conversion of the Consumer Durable Goods Industry to War Production, May 1940 to December 1944," Special Study No. 33, 1947, Policy Documentation File, WPB; CPA, *Industrial Mobilization for War,* pp. 307–24; James A. McAleer, *Dollar-a-Year and without Compensation Personnel Policies of the War Production Board and Predecessor Agencies, August 1939 to November 1945* (Washington, DC: Civilian Production Administration, 1947), pp. 41–55; Keith E. Eiler, *Mobilizing America: Robert P. Patterson and the War Effort, 1940–1945* (Ithaca, NY: Cornell University Press, 1997), pp. 326–45; and Thomas J. Graves, "The Enforcement of Priorities, Conservation and Limitation Orders of the War Production Board, 1942–1944" (Ph.D. diss., Princeton University, 1946) (copy in Box 28, Unit 274, RWA, BOB).

4. Truman Committee, *Hearings, Conversion Program, War Production Board,* 77th Cong., 2d sess., 1942, pt. 12, pp. 4957–5102, 5283–5353; Truman Committee, *Additional Report,* 77th Cong., 2d sess., 1942, S. Rept. No. 480, pt. 8, pp. 1–32; Truman Committee, *Additional Report,* 77th Cong., 2d sess., 1942, S. Rept. No. 480, pt. 9, pp. 1–4; Truman Committee, *First Annual Report,* 77th Cong., 2d sess., 1942, S. Rept. No. 480, pt. 5. See also Donald H. Riddle, *The Truman Committee: A Study in Congressional Responsibility* (New Brunswick, NJ: Rutgers University Press, 1964), pp. 72–73; and Donald M. Nelson, *Arsenal of Democracy: The Story of American War Production* (New York: Harcourt, Brace, 1946), pp. 335–40.

5. U.S. Congress, Senate, *Economic Concentration and World War II: Report of the Smaller War Plants Corporation to the Special Committee to Study Problems of American Small Business* (hereafter *SWPC Report*), 79th Cong., 2d Sess., S. Doc. 206, 1946, pp. 21–53; Civilian Production Administration, *Minutes of the Planning Committee of the War Production Board, February 20, 1942 to April 1, 1943* (hereafter *Planning Committee Minutes*) (Washington, DC: Civilian Production Administration, 1946), pp. 62, 66–68, 69–70, 112–13, 141–44; *WPB Minutes,* pp. 45–46, 87, 100–02, 191–92, 218–19; and CPA, *Industrial Mobilization for War,* pp. 320–22.

6. OPACS and the Division of Civilian Supply in OPM and WPB are covered in chaps. 6–8. For OPACS operations, see Office of Price Administration and Civilian Supply: Executive Orders and Staff Meetings, WPB Papers, Box 34, and Henderson, Leon: Notes and Memos to Himself, WPB Papers, Box 36, Henderson Papers. Differing positions on conversion are presented briefly in Truman Committee, *Hearings, Conversion Program, War Production Board,* 77th Cong., 2d sess., 1942, pp. 4957–5102; Truman Committee, *Additional Report,* 77th Cong., 2d sess., 1942, S. Rept. No. 480, pt. 8, pp. 1–21.

7. For OCS, see Drummond Jones, *The Role of the Office of Civilian Requirements in the Office of Production Management and War Production Board, January 1941 to November 1945* (Washington, DC: Civilian Production Administration, 1946), pp. 57–211; WPB, Requirements Committee Minutes, vol. 1, 3/30/42, 4/1/42, 4/8/42, 6/1/42, 6/26/42, 7/10/42, 7/13/42, and vol. 2, 7/27/42, 7/31/42, 8/5/42, 8/21/42, 8/24/42, 9/16/42, 10/3/42, 10/9/42, 10/16/42, 10/30/42, 11/6/42, 11/11/42, 11/17/42, 11/20/42, 11/30/42, 12/7/42, 12/15/42, 12/18/42, Policy Documentation File, WPB; *WPB Minutes,* pp. 98–99, 143, 188–89; *Planning Committee Minutes,* pp. 18–20, 38–40, 43–44, 104–6, 109–10, 121–23; Brigante, "Planning Committee," pp. 27, 74–77, 115–46; and CPA, *Industrial Mobilization for War,* pp. 331–38.

8. Quoted in Jones, *Office of Civilian Requirements,* p. 67.

9. Hill quoted in ibid., pp. 76–77.

10. For efforts to concentrate curtailed industries, see Jesse Burkhead, "The Concentration Program," ca. 1944, and Harold F. Gosnell and William E. S. Flory, "Comments on *The Concentration Program,*" 7/10/44, Box 19, Unit 195, RWA, BOB; Nelson to President, Second Bi-Monthly Report of the Chairman of the War Production Board, 10/11/42, pp. 10–11, OF: War Production Board, FDR Papers; Strauss to Weiner, 1/3/41, and other correspondence and documents, Concentration of Production, WPB Papers, Box 32, Henderson Papers; Eberstadt to Nelson, 12/5/42, Washington File, 1942–1945, Box 33–Sec. II—Govt. Agencies: Donald M. Nelson, Baruch Papers; *WPB Minutes,* pp. 43, 50, 53–54, 67–68, 100–102, 167–68, 191–92; Planning Committee, *Minutes,* pp. 66–68, 72–73, 122–24, 146–48; Schuck, "Industry and Labor Advisory Committees," pp. 219–25; Maryclaire McCauley, *Concentration of Civilian Production by the War Production Board, September 1941 to April 1943* (Washington, DC: War Production Board, 1944); Jones, *Office of Civilian Requirements,* pp. 89–96, 147–49; and CPA, *Industrial Mobilization for War,* pp. 324–31.

11. The transition from the OCS to the Office of Civilian Requirements is based on Stone to Cohen, 1/28/43, and Swanson to Files, "Notes on OCS," 7/27/42, Box 95, War Production Board, General Records of the Director, 1939–1946, BofB; Gladieux Notes, "War Production Board," 7/15/42, Box 19, Unit 200, RWA, BOB; Cook, "WPB, Office of Civilian Requirements, No. 99A," 1/5/44, Daily Record, 1943, Smith Papers; Key to Stein, 2/24/43, Alphabetical File, Box 2, Bureau of the Budget: Misc. Reports, Coy to Nelson, 9/16/41, Box 12, Office of Production Management, and Conference with the President, 3/25/43, Box 13, Roosevelt, Franklin D.—1943, Coy Papers; deChazeau to Henderson, 10/22/41, and other correspondence, deChazeau Memos, WPB Papers, Box 32, Henderson Papers; Fesler Memorandum (on interview with Fowler), 1/12/44, 1–9/1944, Box 1, Memorandum (on Gordon address to PARB, WPB), 6/29/45, 4–6/1945, Jones to Fesler (on

Hill interview), 8/29/45, 7–8/1945, and Fesler and Jones Memorandum (on Hill interview), 9/11/45, 9–12/1945, Box 2, Fesler Papers; Amberg to Patterson, 3/30/43, and numerous other correspondence, (43–45) War Mobilization, Office of March 16, 1943 to August 31, 1943, USW/OSW; Lester to Brown, 5/28/43, file 300.37, Dorr Collection; Ewing to Byrnes, 4/30/43, PSF: War Production Board, FDR Papers; Carroll to Baruch, 10/5/42, Baruch to Carroll, 10/9/42, Baruch to Nelson, 7/6/42, 12/31/42, Somervell to Baruch w/encs., 5/9/42, and Baruch to Shaw, 3/1/43, Selected Correspondence, Baruch to Byrnes, 1/7/43, Washington File, 1942–1945, Box 28, Sec. 1—Baruch Memo, Carroll to Baruch w/ enc., 2/4/43, Washington File, 1942–1945, Box 29, Sec.—Correspondence: Personal, and Weiner to Baruch w/ encs., 2/4/43, Washington File, 1942–1945, Box 35, Sec. 2—Government Agencies: War Production Board, Baruch Papers; *WPB Minutes,* pp. 136–37, 188–89, 210–11, 223, 228–30, 262–64, 304–5, 312–14, 335–36, 351–54, 361–63, 371–74, 395–98, 424–25; WPB, Requirements Committee Minutes, vol. 3, 1/1/43, 1/13/43, 1/21/43, 2/2/43, 2/12/43, 3/5/43, 4/2/43, 4/16/43, 4/30/43, and vol. 4, 12/3/43, 12/10/43, 12/23/43, 2/10/44, 2/19/44, 5/15/44, 7/11/44, 8/14/44, 9/29–30/44, 11/16/44, 11/24/44, 12/1/44, 12/15/44, 1/17/45, 1/19/45, 2/9/45, 2/17–19/45, 4/18/45, 5/11–12/45, 5/25/45, 6/19/45, 6/22/45, 7/5/45, 8/3/45, 8/10/45, Policy Documentation File, WPB; *Planning Committee Minutes,* 119–21, 123, 170–71; Jones, *Office of Civilian Requirements,* pp. 150–335; and CPA, *Industrial Mobilization for War,* pp. 492, 588–89, 613–23, 750–51, 763–66, 875–87, 961–66. For some interesting background on William Y. Elliott, see Emmerich to Brownlow, 7/30/40, U.S. Industrial Mobilization; Office for Emergency Management, 1940–1956, Box 30, Emmerich Papers; and Milton to Herring, 10/28/42, Box 12, Unit 139, RWA, BOB.

12. WPB budget document quoted in Jones, *Office of Civilian Requirements,* p. 221.

13. CPA, *Industrial Mobilization for War,* pp. 961–66. See also chap. 16 below.

14. The best and most thorough secondary volume on wartime plant is Reginald C. McGrane, *The Facilities and Construction Program of the War Production Board and Predecessor Agencies, May 1940 to May 1945* (Washington, DC: War Production Board, 1945).

15. Ibid., pp. 22, 50, 159, 194, 221. See also Smith, *Army and Economic Mobilization,* pp. 6–7. Total facilities figures involve all construction, including that for agriculture, mining, highways, and military installations in the United States and abroad. Whenever possible, manufacturing plant, which includes machinery and equipment, will be clearly indicated.

16. Gerald T. White, *Billions for Defense: Government Financing by the Defense Plant Corporation during World War II* (University: University of Alabama Press, 1980), pp. 4, 154, n. 9; and *SWPC Report,* pp. 37–50.

17. McGrane, *Facilities and Construction Program,* pp. 22, 50, 159, 194, 221.

18. Construction and facilities programs are analyzed in chaps. 3 and 6 above.

19. CPA, *Industrial Mobilization for War,* pp. 160–63.

20. For the facilities and construction program in 1942, see Smith to President, 6/6/42, President to Nelson, 6/6/42, Nelson to President, 7/1/42, and Carey to Hannum, 11/11/42, Box 95, War Production Board, BofB; President to Nelson, 5/1/42, 5/4/42, Nelson to President, 5/22/42, and other correspondence, and President to Nelson, 5/4/43, and other correspondence, PSF: War Production Board,

and Holmes to Forster, 5/4/42, and President to Nelson, 5/21/42, OF: Army and
Navy Munitions Board, FDR Papers; Milton to Herring, 10/13/42, Box 12, Unit
144, RWA, BOB; Memorandum (on Nathan address to the PARB, WPB), 8/4/45,
7–8/1945, Box 2, Fesler Papers; Patterson to President, 7/27/42, Production—
Confidential, USW/OSW; Forrestal to Baruch w/ enc., 2/6/42, and other correspondence, Land to President, 5/16/42, and Somervell to Baruch w/ encs., 5/9/42,
Selected Correspondence, and Campbell to Baruch, 10/6/43, Washington File,
1942–1945, Box 31, Sec. 2—Government Agencies: Gen. Campbell, Chief of Ordnance, Baruch Papers; *WPB Minutes,* pp. 4–5, 10, 25–26, 29–30, 47–48, 71, 84–86,
98–99, 103–4, 122, 158–60, 180–81, 185–87, 208–10, 215–17, 221–24, 228–30,
280–81, 294–97, 299–301, 351–54, 361–63, 376, 395, 400, 403–4, 407; *Planning
Committee Minutes,* pp. 7, 11, 13, 18–22, 29, 31–32, 36–38, 44–45, 47–51, 55–56,
58, 79–80, 82, 105, 107–8; WPB, Requirements Committee Minutes, vol. 1,
6/24/42, vol. 2, 10/9/42, vol. 3, 1/27/43, and vol. 4, 5/15/44, 7/11/44,
8/14/44, 11/16/44, 2/17–19/45, 5/11–12/45, 8/3/45, Policy Documentation
File, WPB; Brigante, "Planning Committee," pp. 99–114; Truman Committee, *Priorities and the Utilization of Existing Manufacturing Facilities,* 77th Cong., 1st sess.,
1941, S. Rept. No. 480, pt. 3; Truman Committee, *Additional Report,* 77th Cong.,
2d sess., 1942, S. Rept. No. 480, pt. 9; *SWPC Report,* pp. 37–50, 340–49; McGrane,
Facilities and Construction Program, pp. 71–230; Ethan P. Allen, *Policies Governing
Private Financing of Emergency Facilities, May 1940 to June 1942* (Washington, DC:
War Production Board, 1944); Smith, *Army and Economic Mobilization,* 437–502;
Robert H. Connery, *The Navy and the Industrial Mobilization in World War II*
(Princeton, NJ: Princeton University Press, 1951), pp. 344–88; Julius A. Furer,
Administration of the Navy Department in World War II (Washington, DC: Naval His-
tory Division, 1959), pp. 37–38, 64, 218, 237–38, 419–28, 854–61 (see the table of
contents and index for other entries); Wesley F. Craven and James L. Cate, eds., *Men
and Planes,* vol. 6 of *The Army Air Forces in World War II* (Chicago: University of
Chicago Press, 1955), pp. 119–424; Robert R. Russell, "Expansion of Industrial Facilities under Army Air Forces Auspices, 1940–1945," Army Air Forces Historical Studies No. 40, 1947, Wright-Patterson Air Force Base, OH; Frederic C. Lane, *Ships for
Victory: A History of Shipbuilding under the U.S. Maritime Commission in World War
II* (Baltimore: Johns Hopkins University Press, 1951); White, *Billions for Defense;* Gerald T. White, "Financing Industrial Expansion for War: The Origin of the Defense
Plant Corporation Leases," *Journal of Economic History* 9 (November 1949): 156–83;
and CPA, *Industrial Mobilization for War,* pp. 39–44, 212–13, 385–409, 652–62. See
also the numerous other primary and secondary sources cited in chap. 3, n. 7, and
chap. 6, nn. 5, 8, 11, 14, 15, above; and Paul A. C. Koistinen, *The Hammer and the
Sword: Labor, the Military, and Industrial Mobilization, 1920–1945* (New York: Arno,
1979), pp. 644–47.

21. Quoted in McGrane, *Facilities and Construction Program,* p. 78.

22. Philips and Sickle quoted in ibid., pp. 88–89.

23. Roosevelt's May 1, 1942, correspondence to Nelson dealt more with priorities
than facilities, as discussed in chap. 12 below.

24. The feasibility dispute is analyzed in chap. 12 below.

25. Contract modification and cancellation and reconstruction are treated in chap. 17
below.

26. In the following analysis of facilities expansion and construction, I am using the figures from *SWPC Report,* pp. 37–50, 340–49, for purposes of consistency. Other sources cited above at times differ somewhat from those given in the *SWPC Report.*

27. Ibid., pp. 37–50, 340–49.

28. White, *Billions for Defense,* pp. 90, 4, 154 n. 9.

29. *SWPC Report,* pp. 27–37.

30. White, *Billions for Defense,* pp. 8–9, 129–32, uses the figure $6.5 billion for tax-amortized facilities, with 50 percent of the total amount going to 89 corporations and the remainder going to smaller plants or additions to existing facilities.

31. *SWPC Report,* p. 48.

32. White, *Billions for Defense,* pp. 106–9, 123; and Mark S. Foster, *Henry J. Kaiser: Builder in the Modern American West* (Austin: University of Texas Press, 1989), pp. 196–210. For the crash synthetic rubber program, see chap. 6 above; for pipelines, see chap. 10 above. See also Paul A. C. Koistinen, *Planning War, Pursuing Peace: The Political Economy of American Warfare, 1920–1939* (Lawrence: University Press of Kansas, 1998), chaps. 6–7.

33. McGrane, *Facilities and Construction Program,* p. 56.

34. Ibid., pp. 160–61.

35. *Planning Committee Minutes,* pp. 8, 10, 21, 24, 31, 55, 59, 98–99, 117, 124; and Brigante, "Planning Committee," pp. 186–98.

36. Bureau of the Budget, *The United States at War: Development and Administration of the War Program by the Federal Government* (Washington, DC: Bureau of the Budget, 1946), pp. 130–31; and Brigante, "Planning Committee," pp. 52–53, 76–77. The Planning Committee–led feasibility dispute is analyzed in chap. 12 below.

37. Truman Committee, *Third Annual Report,* 78th Cong., 2d sess., 1944, S. Rept. No. 10, pt. 16, pp. 27–28, 178–84; and Koistinen, *Hammer and Sword,* 644–47.

38. Smith, *Army and Economic Mobilization,* p. 499.

39. McGrane, *Facilities and Construction Program,* pp. 195–97; and White, *Billions for Defense,* pp. 125–29. See also Paul Studenski and Herman E. Krooss, *Financial History of the United States: Fiscal, Monetary, Banking, and Tariff, Including Financial Administration and State and Local Finance* (New York: McGraw-Hill, 1952), pp. 455–58.

An enlightening scholarly debate is taking place among historians and economists over the impact of World War II on the West, particularly California. Gary D. Nash argues that wartime spending transformed the West from a largely underdeveloped, extractive economy to one characterized by manufacturing, scientific research, technological development, and service. See his *The American West in the Twentieth Century: A Short History of an Urban Oasis* (Englewood Cliffs, NJ: Prentice-Hall, 1973), *The American West Transformed: The Impact of the Second World War* (Bloomington: Indiana University Press, 1985), and *World War II and the West: Reshaping the Economy* (Lincoln: University of Nebraska Press, 1990). While recognizing that World War II had a major economic effect on California and the West, Roger W. Lotchin, Paul Rhode, and others insist that Western economies, especially that of California, were well advanced by 1939. Wartime spending, therefore, accelerated existing trends rather than creating new ones. See Roger W. Lotchin, *Fortress California, 1910–1961* (New York: Oxford University Press, 1992); Roger W. Lotchin, ed., *Fortress California at War: San Francisco, Los Angeles, Oakland, and San Diego, 1941–1945,* special issue of

Pacific Historical Review 63 (August 1994): 277–420; Paul Rhode, "The Nash Thesis Revisited: An Economic Historian's View," in *Fortress California at War,* ed. Lotchin, pp. 363–92; and Paul Rhode, "California in the Second World War: An Analysis of Defense Spending," in *The Way We Really Were: The Golden State in the Second Great War,* ed. Roger W. Lotchin (Urbana: University of Illinois Press, 2000), pp. 93–119. *Fortress California at War* contains other essays and comments about the war's economic impact, as does Roger W. Lotchin, ed., *The Martial Metropolis: U.S. Cities in War and Peace* (New York: Praeger, 1984). See also Marilynn S. Johnson, *The Second Gold Rush: Oakland and the East Bay in World War II* (Berkeley and Los Angeles: University of California Press, 1993).

40. For the disposal of surplus property, see Baruch to Childs, 3/9/44, Baruch to Clayton, 3/15/44, and numerous other correspondence and documents, Elliott to Baruch, 11/3/44, Forrestal and Patterson to Baruch, 11/1/44, Gillette to Baruch, 3/22/45, and Baruch to Gillette, 4/16/45, and numerous other correspondence, Selected Correspondence, Clayton to Baruch w/ encs., 4/29/44, Washington File, 1942–1945, Box 34, Sec. 2—Government Agencies: Surplus War Property Administration, "Meeting, October 14, 1943, to Consider Contract Termination and Disposition of Government Plants and Stocks" and numerous other correspondence and documents, Washington File, 1942–1945, Box 38, Sec. 3—Special Subjects: Contract Termination, and Searls to Hancock, 7/28/43, and Hancock to Byrnes, 8/9/43, Washington File, 1942–1945, Box 38, Sec. 3—Special Subjects: Fertilizer and Explosives Program, Baruch Papers; French to Hechler, 3/21/46, and numerous other correspondence and documents, Box 13, Unit 69, RWA, BOB; White House Memoranda, Smith to Byrnes, 11/5/43, Smith Papers; Byrnes to President, 9/26/44, and numerous other correspondence and documents, OF: Surplus Property Board Endorsements, and White House News Release, 7/14/44, OF: Office of Contract Settlement, FDR Papers; Truman Committee, *Additional Report,* 78th Cong., 2d sess., 1944, S. Rept. No. 10, pt. 20; Truman Committee, *Additional Report,* 79th Cong., 1st sess., 1945, S. Rept. No. 110, pt. 1; A. D. H. Kaplan, *The Liquidation of War Production: Cancellation of War Contracts and Disposal of Government-Owned Plants and Surpluses* (New York: McGraw-Hill, 1944); James A. Cook, *The Marketing of Surplus War Property* (Washington, DC: Public Affairs Press, 1948); White, *Billions for Defense,* pp. 88–132; Harold G. Vatter, *The U.S. Economy in World War II* (New York: Columbia University Press, 1985), pp. 64–66; Jonathan J. Bean, "Beyond the Broker State: A History of the Federal Government's Policies toward Small Business, 1936–1961" (Ph.D. diss., Ohio State University, 1994), pp. 208–9; and Herman M. Somers, *Presidential Agency, OWMR: The Office of War Mobilization and Reconversion* (Cambridge, MA: Harvard University Press, 1950), pp. 174–81. Two reports in 1945 and 1946 summarize well the state of the economy at war's end and the prospects and achievements of peace, directly or indirectly including the disposal of surplus property: *Wartime Production Achievements and the Reconversion Outlook: Report of the Chairman, War Production Board* (Washington, DC: War Production Board, October 9, 1945) (an unpublished version is available in Policy Documentation File, WPB); and *From War to Peace: Civilian Production Achievements in Transition: Report to the President by John D. Small* (Washington, DC: Civilian Production Administration, 1946).

41. I am continuing to use *SWPC Report,* p. 38, figures. On government-titled

plant, White, *Billions for Defense,* pp. 89–90, says that it is approximately $16 billion; Kaplan, *Liquidation of War Production,* p. 14, puts the amount at $15.5 billion; Cook, *Surplus Property,* p. 15, is closest to the SWPC, with $17 billion; and McGrane, *Facilities and Construction Program,* pp. 22, 50, 159, 194, 221, agrees with White, with a calculation of $15.9 billion. Figures vary in part because some authors stop in 1944 while others continue into 1945.

42. White, *Billions for Defense,* pp. 122–23.

43. Ibid., pp. 90, 129, uses the figures of $7 billion for DPC and $6.5 billion for private investments. I continue to rely on figures from *SWPC Report,* pp. 38, 48.

44. White, *Billions for Defense,* pp. 7–9, 129–32; CPA, *Industrial Mobilization for War,* pp. 656–57; and Smith, *Army and Economic Mobilization,* 456–75. Tax amortization for defense and wartime facilities is analyzed in chap. 3 above.

CHAPTER TWELVE. REFINING WPB ECONOMIC CONTROLS, 1942

1. See chaps. 1 and 4 above.

2. For basic information on the Planning Committee, see files 072.11, 072.101, 072.1011, 072.1012, 072.1013, 072.1014, 072.1015, WPB. See also Memorandum (on Nathan address to the PARB, WPB), 8/4/45, 7–8/1945, Box 2, and Fesler to Brigante, 7/19/48, War Production Board, Box 6, September 1978 Addition, Fesler Papers; Civilian Production Administration, *Minutes of the Planning Committee of the War Production Board, February 20, 1942, to April 1, 1943* (hereafter *Planning Committee Minutes*) (Washington, DC: Civilian Production Administration, 1946); and John E. Brigante, "The Planning Committee of the War Production Board: A Chapter in American Planning Experience" (Ph.D. diss., Princeton University, 1948).

3. See chaps. 1, 3–4, 6–7, 11 above.

4. See chap. 7 above.

5. Civilian Production Administration (CPA), *Industrial Mobilization for War: History of the War Production Board and Predecessor Agencies, 1940–1945* (Washington, DC: Civilian Production Administration, 1947), pp. 273–84.

6. Ibid.; and John E. Brigante, *The Feasibility Dispute: Determination of War Production Objectives for 1942 and 1943* (Washington, DC: Committee on Public Administration Cases, 1950), pp. 32–33. See also Robert H. Connery, *The Navy and the Industrial Mobilization in World War II* (Princeton, NJ: Princeton University Press, 1951), pp. 179–99, 293–315, 409–32; John D. Millett, *The Organization and Role of the Army Service Forces* (Washington, DC: Office of the Chief of Military History, 1954), pp. 45–92, 111–37; Richard M. Leighton and Robert M. Coakley, *Global Logistics and Strategy, 1940–1943* (Washington, DC: Office of the Chief of Military History, 1955); Wesley F. Craven and John L. Cate, eds., *Men and Planes,* vol. 6 of *The Army Air Forces in World War II* (Chicago: University of Chicago Press, 1955), pp. 171–424; R. Elberton Smith, *The Army and Economic Mobilization* (Washington, DC: Office of the Chief of Military History, 1959), pp. 119–212; Julius A. Furer, *Administration of the Navy Department in World War II* (Washington, DC: Naval History Division, 1959), pp. 124–38, 691–736; Duncan S. Ballantine, *U.S. Naval Logistics in the Second World War* (Princeton, NJ: Princeton University Press, 1949); James A. Huston, *The Sinews of War: Army Logistics, 1775–1953* (Washington, DC: Office

of the Chief of Military History, 1966), pp. 410–40; John K. Ohl, *Supplying the Troops: General Somervell and American Logistics in WWII* (DeKalb: Northern Illinois University Press, 1994), pp. 143–60, 181–251; Keith E. Eiler, *Mobilizing America: Robert P. Patterson and the War Effort, 1940–1945* (Ithaca, NY: Cornell University Press, 1997); and Charles R. Shrader, *U.S. Military Logistics, 1607–1991: A Research Guide* (Westport, CT: Greenwood, 1992). For a balanced analysis of World War II mobilization and logistics, see Alan L. Gropman, *Mobilizing U.S. Industry in World War II: Myth and Reality* (Washington, DC: Institute for National Strategic Studies, National Defense University, 1996); and Alan L. Gropman, ed., *The Big "L": American Logistics in World War II* (Washington, DC: National Defense University Press, 1997).

7. The feasibility dispute is based on Smith to President, 10/20/42, War Production Board, General Records of Director, 1939–1946, BofB; Venneman, "Notes on Budget Hearing, Planning Committee, WPB," 5/11/42, Box 12, Unit 211, "Questions Which Might Be Discussed with Mr. Nelson," 7/16/45, Box 4, Unit 32, Key to Files, "Interview with Mr. Donald Nelson," 6/25/45, Box 11, Unit 131, Stone to Director, 11/13/42, and numerous other correspondence and documents, Box 12, Unit 139, Milton to Herring, 8/25/42, and other documents, Box 12, Unit 150, Milton to Herring, 9/16/42, 10/20/42, and numerous other documents, Box 19, Unit 197, and Venneman to Stone, 9/29/42, and other documents, Box 19, Unit 202, RWA, BOB; Nelson to President, 8/42, Roosevelt to Nelson, 10/1/42, Roosevelt to Joint Chiefs of Staff, 10/1/42, Hopkins to President, 10/1/42, Roosevelt to Nelson, 10/30/42, and other documents, PSF: War Production Board, and Baruch to Roosevelt, 3/8/42, PSF: General Correspondence, FDR Papers; Daily Record, "Memorandum Covering the Director's Telephone Conversation with General George C. Marshall, Chief of Staff, concerning Current Army Estimates," 6/11/42, Smith Papers; May to Nelson, 12/4/41, and other documents, file 072.1015, WPB; Matthiessen to Knowlson, 4/4/42, 1–8/1942, Box 1, Marshall to Nelson, 10/6/42, Nelson to Joint Chiefs of Staff, 10/19/42, and Joint Chiefs of Staff to Nelson, 11/26/42, 10–12/1942, Box 1, and Memorandum (on Katz address to PARB, WPB), 8/31/45, 7–8/1945, Box 2, Fesler Papers; Holden to Henderson w/ enc., 10/16/42, and other correspondence, Feasibility of War Production Program, WPB Papers, Box 32, Henderson Papers; Searls to Eberstadt, 10/9/42, Box 163, WPB, 1941–1942, Eberstadt Papers; Amberg to Patterson, 11/23/42, War Production Board—1942–43, Amberg Collection; Boland to O'Connell, 11/21/42, and other documents, War Mobilization, Greenbaum Collection; Baruch to Roosevelt, 12/8/42, Rosenman to Baruch, 12/1/42, and other correspondence, Baruch to Watson w/ enc., 3/9/42, and other correspondence, and Wood to Baruch w/ enc., 1/28/42, and other correspondence, Selected Correspondence, Nathan to Nelson, 9/16/42, Washington File, 1942–1945, Box 29, Sec.—Correspondence: Personal, Baruch to Somervell, 12/24/42, and other documents, Washington File, 1942–1945, Box 34, Sec. 3—Government Agencies: Somervell, Gen. Brehon, ASF, and Chambers to Baruch w/ encs., 11/14/42, Washington File, 1942–1945, Box 35, Sec. 2—Government Agencies: War Production Board, Baruch Papers; *Planning Committee Minutes*, pp. 6–7, 10–11, 13–14, 17–22, 28, 30–34, 36, 40–41, 45, 64–65, 76, 88, 90, 92–96, 127–28, 155–57, 162–63; Civilian Production Administration, *Minutes of the War Production Board, January 20, 1942, to October 9, 1945* (hereafter *WPB Minutes*)

(Washington, DC: Civilian Production Administration, 1946), pp. 7, 26, 41, 44–45, 59, 139–45; Brigante, *Feasibility Dispute;* Brigante, "Planning Committee," pp. 15–55; CPA, *Industrial Mobilization for War,* pp. 273–92; Bureau of the Budget, *The United States at War: Development and Administration of the War Program by the Federal Government* (Washington, DC: Bureau of the Budget, 1946), pp. 298–304; David Novick, Melvin Anshen, and W. C. Truppner, *Wartime Production Controls* (New York: Columbia University Press, 1949); David Novick and George A. Steiner, *Wartime Industrial Statistics* (Urbana: University of Illinois Press, 1949); Simon Kuznets, *National Product in Wartime* (New York: National Bureau of Economic Research, 1945); Donald M. Nelson, *Arsenal of Democracy: The Story of American War Production* (New York: Harcourt, Brace, 1946), pp. 204–5, 376–81; Millett, *Army Service Forces,* pp. 213–20; Smith, *Army and Economic Mobilization,* pp. 154–58; Ohl, *Supplying the Troops,* pp. 56–60, 76–83; and Eiler, *Mobilizing America,* pp. 345–56.

8. Planning Committee Recommendation No. 3, 3/17/42, *Planning Committee Minutes,* pp. 127–28.

9. See chap. 11 above.

10. Stimson insisted that NDAC could not do much involving economic mobilization: "The statutory responsibility is on us and we have got to stand up to it. . . . All that outsiders can do under the present statutes is to help us along in working with the industry of the country." See Stimson Diary, 10/11/40. In arguing against proposed legislation for a civilian agency taking over military procurement, Julius H. Amberg, a principal civilian aide to Patterson, insisted: "It is the responsibility of the War and Navy Departments to win the war. The whole object of civilian agencies is to aid the Army and Navy in this mission." See Julius H. Amberg, "Outline for Preparation of Brief in Opposition to S287 & HR7742 Creating an Office of War Mobilization," 11/17/42, S. 607—OWM—Misc Papers, Amberg Collection. At the conclusion of the Arcadia Conference in Washington, DC, January 1942, Marshall said that he would have to resign as chief of staff if Roosevelt proceeded with the proposal to have the Munitions Assignment Board (MAB) made directly responsible to Roosevelt and Winston Churchill instead of the Combined Chiefs of Staff. Military organizations, he insisted, had to have control of supplies essential to carrying out their operations. Roosevelt acceded to Marshall's argument when the chief of staff was backed by Harry L. Hopkins. See Robert E. Sherwood, *Roosevelt and Hopkins: An Intimate History* (New York: Harper and Bros., 1948), pp. 470–73; Leighton and Coakley, *Global Logistics,* pp. 247–55; and Forrest C. Pogue, *George C. Marshall: Ordeal and Hope, 1939–1942* (New York: Viking, 1965), pp. 283–88. Bureau of the Budget Director Smith reported that Admiral King believed that civilian agencies like WPB had no right to question military requirements. See Smith to Roosevelt, 7/16/43, PSF: Joint Chiefs of Staff, FDR Papers. Bernard L. Gladieux, who directed the Bureau of the Budget's War Organization Section and then joined WPB as administrative assistant to the chair for administration and general operations, explained after the war: "The Army and Navy tolerated the WPB. They realized that it had some uses, but what they primarily wanted was for WPB simply to curtail civilian requirements on the one hand and to give the defense establishments whatever priority actions they wanted on the other hand. Beyond this simple negative function they could not see that WPB had any significantly useful role. In brief, the military thought of WPB as a

service agency to get what was required for military operations without any questions asked and without any disturbance to existing procurement procedures and channels." See Gladieux Reminiscences, pp. 469–70.

For other sources on Roosevelt's relations with Marshall and the Joint Chiefs of Staff, see Otto L. Nelson, *National Security and the General Staff* (Washington, DC: Infantry Journal Press, 1946); Leslie A. Rose, *The Long Shadow: Reflections on the Second World War Era* (Westport, CT: Greenwood, 1978); Glen C. H. Perry, *"Dear Bart": Washington Views of World War II* (Westport, CT: Greenwood, 1982); Henry H. Adams, *Witness to Power: The Life of Fleet Admiral William D. Leahy* (Annapolis, MD: Naval Institute Press, 1985); John C. Binkley, "The Role of the Joint Chiefs of Staff in National Security Policy Making: Professionalism and Self-Deceptions, 1942–1961" (Ph.D. diss., Loyola University of Chicago, 1985); David Eisenhower, *Eisenhower: At War, 1943–1945* (New York: Random House, 1986); D. Clayton James, *A Time for Giants: Politics of the American High Command in World War II* (New York: Franklin Watts, 1987); Eric Larrabee, *Commander in Chief: Franklin Delano Roosevelt, His Lieutenants, and Their War* (New York: Harper and Row, 1987); various articles in Allan R. Millett and Williamson Murray, eds., *Military Effectiveness,* vol. 3, *Second World War* (Boston: Allen and Unwin, 1988); Thomas Parish, *Roosevelt and Marshall: Partners in Politics and War* (New York: William Morrow, 1989); and Ed Cray, *General of the Army: George C. Marshall, Soldier and Statesman* (New York: W. W. Norton, 1990). See also the secondary sources cited in chap. 9 above.

11. See chaps. 1, 3, and 6 above.

12. Brigante, *Feasibility Dispute,* p. 53; and *WPB Minutes,* pp. 131–33, 139–42.

13. Roosevelt to Nelson, 5/1/42, 5/4/42, and Nelson to President, 5/22/42, PSF: War Production Board, FDR Papers; and Brigante, *Feasibility Dispute,* pp. 57–58, 108–9.

14. I am purposefully keeping estimated and purposed production figures as simple as possible. If adjusted carryovers from 1942 were included, demand for 1943 could reach as high as $97 billion, much higher if nonmunition expenditures were totaled in. Few authors come up with the same figures since they tend to include different categories without clearly explaining what they are.

15. See chap. 1 above.

16. See chap. 11 above.

17. Planning Committee Recommendation No. 15, 9/4/42 (*Planning Committee Minutes,* pp. 155–57), w/ attached Simon Kuznets memorandum "Analysis of the Production Program, 1942–1943," Box 10, Unit IV, No. 1, Nelson Papers; Somervell's response to Nathan is reproduced in Brigante, *Feasibility Dispute,* pp. 82–83.

18. Kuznets's response to Somervell is reproduced in large part in Brigante, *Feasibility Dispute,* pp. 84–86. Somervell's earlier effort in behalf of coordinating production and strategy, to which Kuznets referred, involved a complicated proposal in which control over raw materials would be placed largely under military control. See Somervell to Nelson w/ enc., 5/15/42, file 020.2, WPB Doc. No. 91, Policy Documentation File, WPB; Nelson to Somervell, 5/21/42, PSF: War Production Board, FDR Papers; and Drummond Jones, "The Controlled Materials Plan of the War Production Board, November 1942 to November 1945," Special Study No. 37, 1947, pp. 21–28, Policy Documentation File, WPB.

19. Brigante, *Feasibility Dispute,* pp. 94–95. Brigante's study is authoritative but undocumented.

20. Bureau of the Budget, *United States at War,* p. 303, says that Roosevelt backed Nelson's communication with the JCS.

21. See chaps. 3–4, 7–8 above.

22. The transition from a priorities to an allocation system is based on McCandless and Graham to Martin and Stone, 6/24/43, and Graham to Director, 5/3/44, and other documents, War Production Board, General Records of Director, BofB; Reeve to Graham and Key, 2/14/45, Box 11, Unit 131, memorandum "Army and Navy Munitions Board vs Office of Production Management," 1/13/42, and numerous other documents, Box 19, Unit 200, Milton to Herring, 10/20/42, Box 19, Unit 197, and Milton to Herring, 10/12/42, Box 19, Unit 201, RWA, BOB; Nathan to Nelson, 1/12/43, and other documents, file 072.11, WPB; Auxier, Memorandum on Interview with Ferdinand Eberstadt on Origin of CMP, 10/9/46, Jones to Auxier, Memorandum on Interview with William Remington on Origins of the Controlled Materials Plan, 12/9/46, Eberstadt to Auxier w/ encs., 11/8/46, Auxier to Eberstadt, 12/16/46, Eberstadt to Auxier 12/18/46, and Auxier, Memorandum on Comments of John H. Martin on Priorities and Allocations System and CMP, 4/29/47, Controlled Materials Plan (1942–1945), Garrison to Auxier, interview with A. C. C. Hill, Jr., 1/22/47, and Hill to Auxier, 1/15/47, Data on Special Study Drafts, Box 6, War Production Board, Historical Records Section-Administration, WPB; Gladieux Reminiscences, pp. 317–18, 382–85, 425–26; Roosevelt to Nelson, 2/11/42, 5/1/42, 5/21/42, Roosevelt to Joint Chiefs of Staff, 5/1/42, Holmes to Foster, 5/4/42, and Nelson to President, 5/22/42, OF: Army and Navy Munitions Board, FDR Papers; Knowlson to Nelson, 8/10/42, and numerous other correspondence and documents, 1–8/1942, Eberstadt and Kanzler to Chiefs of All Bureaus, Divisions . . . , 10/13/42, 10–12/1942, Boeschenstein to WPB, ca. 7/43, 1–8/1943, Memorandum (on Skuce address to PARB, WPB), 5/11/44, 1–9/1944, First to Fesler (on Gregg address to PARB, WPB), 10/21/44, 10/1944, and First to Fesler (on Novick address to PARB, WPB), 11/13/44, 11–12/1944, Box 1, Memorandum (on George address to PARB, WPB), 4/13/45, Memorandum (on Batt address to PARB, WPB), 5/4/45, Memorandum (on Martin address to PARB, WPB), 6/7/45, 4–6/1945, Memorandum (on Hill address to PARB, WPB), 7/27/45, 7–8/1945, and Wiltse to Fesler (on Hill interview), 1/17/46, 1–4/1946, Box 2, Fesler Papers; Strauss to Eberstadt, 1/21/43, WPB—Controlled Materials Plan, Eberstadt, "Report to War Production Board on the Controlled Materials Plan," 2/9/43, WPB, Controlled Materials Plan—Eberstadt, Eberstadt to Batt, 3/21/42, and other correspondence, WPB, Controlled Materials Plan—1942, and Auxier to Eberstadt, 10/3/46, and other correspondence, WPB—Advisory Council, Box 162, and Wilson to Eberstadt, 10/16/42, and other documents, WPB, 1941–1942, Box 163, Eberstadt Papers; Gilbert to Henderson w/ enc., 10/21/42, and other correspondence, Feasibility of War Production Program, WPB Papers, Box 32, Henderson Papers; Stimson Diary, 5/12/42, 7/19/42, 7/22/42, 8/8/42; Amberg to Patterson, 11/23/42, War Production Board—1942–43, Amberg Collection; Ohly, "Conversation with Julius Amberg, April 19 and 21, 1945," undated, Box 2, Misc., Ohly Papers (the papers were in Ohly's possession when I researched them; they may now be reorganized); Batcheller to Eberstadt, 12/3/42, Brown to Baruch w/ enc., 9/30/42, Eberstadt to Baruch, 5/28/42,

Eberstadt to Baruch, 9/12/42, Grace to Baruch, 11/23/42, Baruch to Hirsch, 9/23/42, and other correspondence and documents, Baruch to Knowlson, 7/20/42, and other correspondence, Baruch to Land, 9/23/42, Baruch to McLennan, 6/27/42, Baruch to Nelson, 3/8/42, and other correspondence, Nelson to Somervell, 5/21/42, Baruch to Nelson, 7/6/42, and Baruch to Weinberg, 2/22/42, and other correspondence, Selected Correspondence, Carroll to Baruch w/ enc., 2/4/43, Washington File, 1942–1945, Box 29, Sec.—Correspondence: Personal, Baruch to Nelson, 12/31/42, Washington File, 1942–1945, Box 33, Sec. 2—Government Agencies: Donald M. Nelson, Eberstadt to Davis and Armstrong, 9/27/42, and McMillan to Baruch w/ enc., 10/24/42, Washington File, 1942–1945, Box 35, Sec. 2—Government Agencies: War Production Board, Baruch Papers; WPB, Requirements Committee Minutes, vols. 1–4, 2/13/42–9/21/45, Policy Documentation File, WPB (these are central to the board's priorities, allocations, and related controls); *WPB Minutes,* pp. 15, 27–28, 31, 38, 42–43, 60–61, 71–72, 93–94, 108–9, 114, 116–17, 131–33, 147, 178–79, 193–94, 208–10, 211, 213–14, 217–18, 221–34, 246–48, 252–54, 265–66, 308–10, 318–20, 351–54, 357–58, 370–74, 402–4; *Planning Committee Minutes,* pp. 20, 44, 49, 50–51, 58–59, 60, 62, 66–68, 69, 72–73, 81, 82, 86–87, 89, 91, 96–97, 101, 107–8, 109–10, 117, 119, 138–140, 158–62; Jones, "Controlled Materials Plan"; Drummond Jones, *The Role of the Office of Civilian Requirements in the Office of Production Management and War Production Board, January 1941 to November 1945* (Washington, DC: Civilian Production Administration, 1946), pp. 57–335; Novick, Anshen, and Truppner, *Wartime Production Controls;* Brigante, "Planning Committee," pp. 70–84; CPA, *Industrial Mobilization for War,* pp. 171–84, 212–22, 261–63, 293–305, 355–95, 429–504; Bureau of the Budget, *United States at War,* pp. 279–320; Calvin L. Christman, "Ferdinand Eberstadt and Economic Mobilization for War, 1941–1943" (Ph.D. diss., Ohio State University, 1971), pp. 59–250; Robert C. Perez and Edward F. Willett, *The Will to Win: A Biography of Ferdinand Eberstadt* (Westport, CT: Greenwood, 1989); Jeffrey M. Dorwart, *Eberstadt and Forrestal: A National Security Partnership, 1909–1949* (College Station: Texas A&M University Press, 1991), pp. 30–68; Smith, *Army and Economic Mobilization,* pp. 505–96; Connery, *Navy and Industrial Mobilization,* pp. 170–78; Millett, *Army Service Forces,* pp. 201–12; Ohl, *Supplying the Troops,* pp. 83–85; Eiler, *Mobilizing America,* pp. 335–45; Robert Cuff, "Organization Capabilities and U.S. War Production: The Controlled Materials Plan of World War II," *Business and Economic History* 19 (1990): 103–12; and Robert Cuff, "From the Controlled Materials Plan to the Defense Materials System, 1942–1953," *Military Affairs* 51 (January 1987): 1–6.

23. WPB, Requirements Committee Minutes, vol. 2, 10/3/42, Policy Documentation File, WPB; and CPA, *Industrial Mobilization for War,* pp. 298–99.

24. See chap. 5 above.

25. Knowlson quoted in CPA, *Industrial Mobilization for War,* p. 471. Unlike with CMP, there is only limited information available on the origins of PRP. John F. Martin claimed that Blackwell Smith was the brains behind OPM's Priorities Division, continued that role in WPB's Priorities Bureau, and principally authored PRP. See Auxier, Comments of John H. Martin on Priorities and Allocation System and CMP, 4/29/47, Controlled Materials Plan (1942–1945), Box 6, War Production Board, Historical Records Section—Administration, WPB. See also "The Reminiscences of

Blackwell Smith," 1989, Oral History Research Office, Columbia University, New York City (interviews conducted by Dorothy Hartman on 12/9/86, 6/24/87, and 12/2/87, edited and corrected by Smith but never put into final form; the interviews are rather disjointed, with critical material left undeveloped and unexplored).

26. Novick, Anshen, and Truppner, *Wartime Production Controls,* p. 5. See also Eberstadt to Batt, 3/21/42, Controlled Materials Plan (1942–1945), Box 6, War Production Board, Historical Records Section—Administration, WPB.

27. Paul A. C. Koistinen, *Planning War, Pursuing Peace: The Political Economy of American Warfare, 1920–1939* (Lawrence: University Press of Kansas, 1998), p. 18.

28. Civilian Production Administration, "Industrial Mobilization for War: History of the War Production Board and Predecessor Agencies, 1940–1945," vol. 2, "Materials and Products," pt. 1, chap. 3, pp. 35–50, Policy Documentation File, WPB; CPA, *Industrial Mobilization for War,* pp. 493–94; and Novick, Anshen, and Truppner, *Wartime Production Controls,* pp. 168–69.

29. For the industry affiliations of WPB officials, see Jones, "Controlled Materials Plan"; and Civilian Production Administration, "Executive Personnel Directory of the War Production Board and Predecessor Agencies, May 1940 to November 1945," Miscellaneous Publication No. 2, 1946, Policy Documentation File, WPB. Much more complete information is available in chap. 8, n. 2, above.

30. Production scheduling is based on PEC, Minutes, Meetings 5–127, 10/28/42–8/27/45 (in some instances, verbatim versions are available), and PEC Documents 1–132, 10/20/44–8/10/45, file 041.05, WPB; *WPB Minutes,* pp. 158–60, 162–63, 165–67, 172–76, 194, 196–97, 215–17, 252–54, 264, 268–71, 341–44, 364–69, 375–80, 395–98; Knowlson to Nelson, 9/21/42, Box 252, 041—Production Executive Committee, WPB, and Nelson to Eberstadt, 9/28/42, Box 252, 041.02—Production Executive Committee, WPB, Personnel, WPB; *Planning Committee Minutes,* pp. 6–7, 64–65, 92–93, 95–98, 101, 104, 108–9, 162–66; Nathan to Nelson, 1/12/43, and other documents, Box 550, 072.11—Planning Committee, WPB; Roosevelt to Byrnes, 3/9/42, and related correspondence, PSF: Executive Office of the President, FDR Papers; Conference with the President, 1/6/43 (with further notes for 2/15/43 and 2/16/43), and White House Memoranda, 2/19/43, Smith Papers; Smith to President, 2/8/43, War Production Board, General Records of the Director, BofB; Milton to Herring, 2/20/43, Box 12, Unit 144, and Milton to Herring, 10/12/42, Box 19, Unit 201, RWA, BOB; Gladieux Reminiscences pp. 444–57, 460–515; Nelson to Stimson, 11/26/42, and other correspondence, 10–12/1942, and Fesler for Files, 12/4/44, 11–12/1944, Box 1, and Fesler to Krug, 9/24/45, 9–12/1945, Box 2, Fesler Papers; memorandum "Production Scheduling," 11/23/42, and other correspondence and documents, Feasibility of War Production, WPB Papers, Box 32, Henderson Papers; Stimson Diary, 1942–1943 (numerous entries); Baruch to Johnson, 3/9/42, Baruch to Lawrence w/ enc., 7/16/42, Lubell to Baruch, 12/16/42, Baruch to McLennan, 6/27/42, and other correspondence, Baruch to Nelson, 3/8/42, Patterson, Knox, and Nelson to Van Nuys w/ enc., 4/14/42, Patterson to Baruch w/ encs., 10/8/42, Baruch to Patterson, 1/6/42, Baruch to Patterson, 12/24/42, Baruch to Somervell, 12/24/42, "Nelson Statement," ca. January 1943, Roosevelt to Baruch, 2/5/43, and Baruch to Shaw, 3/1/43, Selected Correspondence, Nelson to Byrnes, 1/7/43, Washington File, 1942–1945, Box 28, Sec. 1—Baruch Memo., Bell to Baruch, 11/2/42, Baruch to Bell, 11/5/42,

Nathan to Baruch, 11/19/43, Baruch to Nathan, 11/24/43, and Hancock to Shaw, 12/31/42, Washington File, 1942–1945, Box 29, Sec.—Correspondence: Personal, Somervell to Baruch, 12/7/42, and Baruch to Somervell, 12/24/42, Washington File, 1942–1945, Box 34, Sec. 2—Government Agencies: Somervell, Brehon, ASF, and Eberstadt to Wilson w/ enc., 11/12/42, and Chambers to Baruch w/ enc., 2/18/43, Washington File, 1942–1945, Box 35, Sec. 2—Government Agencies: War Production Board, Baruch Papers. See also the citation of primary documents in chap. 8, n. 8, above and n. 58 below. For secondary sources, see Nelson, *Arsenal of Democracy,* pp. 368–90; James F. Byrnes, *All in One Lifetime* (New York: Harper and Bros., 1958), pp. 171–74; William D. Leahy, *I Was There* (New York: McGraw-Hill, 1950), pp. 127, 130–31; Sherwood, *Roosevelt and Hopkins,* pp. 699–700; Brigante, "Planning Committee," pp. 84–98B; Novick, Anshen, and Truppner, *Wartime Production Controls,* pp. 268–86; CPA, *Industrial Mobilization for War,* pp. 505–19, 577–88; Bureau of the Budget, *United States at War,* pp. 298–320; Christman, "Ferdinand Eberstadt," pp. 251–312; Calvin L. Christman, "Donald Nelson and the Army: Personality as a Factor in Civil-Military Relations during World War II," *Military Affairs* 37 (October 1973): 81–83; Millett, *Army Service Forces,* pp. 220–27; Irving B. Holley, Jr., *Buying Aircraft: Materiel Procurement for the Army Air Forces* (Washington, DC: Office of the Chief of Military History, 1964), pp. 247–73; Craven and Cate, eds., *Men and Planes,* pp. 287–98; Ohl, *Supplying the Troops,* pp. 85–90; Smith, *Army and Economic Mobilization,* pp. 597–99; Eiler, *Mobilizing America,* pp. 358–63; Connery, *Navy and Industrial Mobilization,* pp. 191–93; Furer, *Administration of the Navy Department,* pp. 834–46; Dorwart, *Eberstadt and Forrestal,* pp. 51–62; Jordan A. Schwarz, *The Speculator: Bernard M. Baruch in Washington, 1917–1965* (Chapel Hill: University of North Carolina Press, 1981), pp. 415–447; and Paul A. C. Koistinen, *The Hammer and the Sword: Labor, the Military, and Industrial Mobilization, 1920–1945* (New York: Arno, 1979), pp. 656–62.

31. *WPB Minutes,* pp. 68–70, 84–86, 98–99, 117–19, 131–33, 149–50, 158–60, 162–63, 165–67; and CPA, *Industrial Mobilization for War,* pp. 505–7.

32. Truman Committee, *Second Annual Report,* 78th Cong., 1st sess., 1943, S. Rept. 10, pt. 4, pp. 1–13.

33. Planning Committee Recommendation No. 20, 11/6/42, *Planning Committee Minutes,* pp. 163–66.

34. PEC, Minutes Meeting 7, 11/11/42, file 041.05, WPB; quotation from Brigante, "Planning Committee," p. 89.

35. Nelson, *Arsenal of Democracy,* p. 383.

36. Amberg to Patterson, 11/23/42, and other documents, War Production Board, 1942–43, Amberg, "Proposed General Administrative Order of the Chairman of the WPB on Production," undated, and Somervell to Patterson w/ five encs., 11/24/42, and other documents, War Production Board—Miscellaneous, Amberg Collection; Fesler for Files, 9/17/45, and Fesler to Krug, 9/24/45, 041.01—PEC—WPB—Establishment, WPB; and *WPB Minutes,* pp. 161–68.

37. Stimson Diary, 7/22/42, 8/8/42, 8/27/42, 9/1/42, 9/10/42, 9/11/42, 9/17/42, 9/18/42, 9/23/42, 11/25/42, 11/26/42, 11/27/42; and Henry L. Stimson and McGeorge Bundy, *On Active Service in Peace and War* (New York: Harper and Bros., 1948), pp. 491–96.

The Navy Department may have played a critical role in resolving the production-scheduling battle. It reluctantly went along with the War Department to provide a united front. Behind the scenes, Forrestal on November 25, 1942, suggested that WPB schedule production for ships, aircraft, and radar to demonstrate what was involved. The army could not object because it had no control over ships and naval aircraft and radar production was in such a drastic state that WPB assistance was necessary. See Fesler to Krug, 9/24/45, file 041.01, WPB. Actually, civilian mobilization agencies, including NDAC, OPM, and WPB, had been scheduling aircraft production in collaboration with what became the AAF and the navy through an intricate bureaucratic structure. See chap. 3 above; Craven and Cate, eds., *Men and Planes,* pp. 287–98; Holley, *Buying Aircraft,* pp. 247–73; and Millett, *Army Service Forces,* 225–26.

38. Stimson quoted in CPA, *Industrial Mobilization for War,* p. 515.

39. Ibid., pp. 514–17.

40. Novick, Anshen, and Truppner, *Wartime Production Controls,* p. 275.

41. Nearly all the volumes cited in n. 30 above deal in one way or another with the Eberstadt-Wilson controversy and its consequences. The most complete and fully documented account is Christman, "Ferdinand Eberstadt," pp. 251–312. The Eberstadt Papers include a rich collection of documents on the episode. See Entries, 5/6/43, 5/13/43, 5/26/43, 6/15/43, 7/21/43, Box 172, Diaries, 1926–1948; Eberstadt, "Memorandum of Conversation with Mr. Nelson This Morning," 2/16/43, and other memoranda and reproduced news articles and clippings, Box 167, WPB—1942–1943: Charles E. Wilson; Remarks of Eberstadt to the Policy Analysis and Records Branch, 10/5/45, Box 162, WPB—Advisory Council; and Draft Memorandum, 6/28/43, and other memoranda, Box 164, WPB—1943–1944; 1947. See also the primary documents cited in chap. 8, n. 4 above.

42. Stimson Diary, 10/19/42, 10/20/42, 10/21/42, 1/9/43, 2/6/43, 2/15/43, 2/18/43, 2/19/43, 2/22/43, 3/28/43; and Elting E. Morison, *Turmoil and Tradition: A Study of the Life and Times of Henry L. Stimson* (Boston: Houghton Mifflin, 1960), pp. 552–53. Although he does not deal with the homefront, Godfrey Hodgson, *The Colonel: The Life and Wars of Henry Stimson, 1867–1950* (New York: Alfred A. Knopf, 1990), provides astute analysis of his subject. See also Richard N. Current, *Secretary Stimson: A Study in Statecraft* (New Brunswick, NJ: Rutgers University Press, 1954), pp. 202–10; and David F. Schmitz, *Henry L. Stimson: The First Wise Man* (Wilmington, DE: Scholarly Resources, 2001).

43. Gladieux Reminiscences, pp. 491–516; memorandum "Discussion with Mr. Sidney J. Weinberg," 5/21/42, Box 150, 032—Assistants to the Chairman, WPB, General Administrative Order No. 2-79, 2/16/43, and other documents, Box 252, 040—Executive Vice Chairman, WPB, Gulick to Batt, 9/5/42, and other documents, Box 252, 040.6—Ex. Vice Chairman, Functions, Nelson, "Organization and Functions of the Office of Production Vice Chairman," 2/4/43, and other documents and correspondence, Box 252, 040.7—Executive Vice Chairman's Office—Reorganization, WPB.

44. Gladieux Reminiscences, pp. 505–6.

45. The same is true of many authors dealing with economic mobilization for World War II. See, e.g., Millett, *Army Service Forces;* Christman, "Ferdinand Eberstadt"; Eiler, *Mobilizing America;* and this author in earlier publications, particularly Paul A. C. Koistinen, "Warfare and Power Relations in America: Mobilizing the World War II Economy," in *The Home Front and War in the Twentieth Century,* ed. James Titus

(Colorado Springs, CO: United States Air Force Academy, 1984), pp. 91–110, 231–43. Gladieux relates that, when he joined WPB in 1943, his uncertain to negative assessment of Nelson changed to one of appreciation and loyalty. See Gladieux Reminiscences, pp. 491–515, 528–29, 543–45, 553–54, 567–70, 572–73. See also Fesler for Files (on Katz interview), 7/13/46, 7–8/1946, and memorandum "Comments on Political and Personal Aspects of War Production Organization," 10/27/43, 9–12/1943, Box 1, Fesler Papers. For additional and important citation of primary documents on Nelson and WPB, see chap. 8, n. 4, above.

CHAPTER THIRTEEN. THE WPB AT FLOOD TIDE, 1943–1944

1. For the above figures, see Civilian Production Administration, *Industrial Mobilization for War: History of the War Production Board and Predecessor Agencies, 1940–1945* (Washington, DC: Civilian Production Administration, 1947), pp. 533–42, 961–66; R. Elberton Smith, *The Army and Economic Mobilization* (Washington, DC: Office of the Chief of Military History, 1959), pp. 3–31; and U.S. Bureau of the Census, *Historical Statistics of the United States, Colonial Times to 1970* (Washington, DC: U.S. Government Printing Office, 1975), pt. 1, pp. 226–30. The WPB and the CPA provide excellent information on wartime output in forms from the most general to the exceptionally detailed: *War Production in 1944: Report of the Chairman of the War Production Board, June 1945* (Washington, DC: War Production Board, 1945); *Wartime Production Achievements and the Reconversion Outlook: Report of the Chairman, War Production Board, October 9, 1945* (Washington, DC: War Production Board, 1945); *From War to Peace, Civilian Production Achievements in Transition: Report to the President by John D. Small, December 6, 1946* (Washington, DC: Civilian Production Administration, 1946); and Civilian Production Administration, *Official Munitions Production of the United States, by Months, July 1, 1940–August 31, 1945* (Washington, DC: Civilian Production Administration, 1947). On civilian wartime consumption, see also chap. 16 below.

2. Civilian Production Administration, *Minutes of the War Production Board, January 20, 1942 to October 9, 1945* (hereafter *WPB Minutes*) (Washington, DC: Civilian Production Administration, 1946), pp. 5, 7, 47, 52, 79–80, 120–21, 132, 166, 175, 207, 209–10, 217, 221, 246, 264, 281, 284, 319–20, 344, 345, 352, 370, 376, 381–82, 393, 398, 406; Truman Committee, *Third Annual Report*, 78th Cong., 2d sess., 1944, S. Rept. No. 10, pt. 16, pp. 65–73; Maryclaire McCauley, "Evolution of Metals and Minerals Policy of the War Production Board, September 1939 to August 1943," Special Study No. 2, 1943, and Civilian Production Administration (CPA), "Industrial Mobilization for War: History of the War Production Board and Predecessor Agencies, 1940–1945," vol. 2, "Materials and Products," 1947, pt. 2, chap. 4, pp. 145–94, Policy Documentation File, WPB; Charles M. Wiltse, *Aluminum Policies of the War Production Board and Predecessor Agencies, May 1940 to November 1945* (Washington, DC: Civilian Production Administration, 1946), pp. 121–348; and CPA, *Industrial Mobilization for War*, pp. 639–41, 778. See also chap. 6 above.

3. *WPB Minutes*, pp. 5–6, 18, 19, 23–24, 28, 33–34, 47, 49–50, 80–81, 88, 96, 107–8, 129–30, 133–34, 150, 166, 169, 175–76, 183, 209, 217, 224–26, 246–49, 281, 284, 301, 318–19, 328–29, 365, 370, 383–84, 388, 393–94, 407, 419;

McCauley, "Metals and Minerals Policy"; CPA, "Industrial Mobilization for War," vol. 2, pt. 2, chap. 4, pp. 38–64; Truman Committee, *Interim Report on Steel,* 78th Cong., 1st sess., 1943, S. Rept. No. 10, pt. 3; Truman Committee, *Third Annual Report,* 78th Cong., 2d sess., 1944, S. Rept. No. 10, pt. 16, pp. 91–96; and CPA, *Industrial Mobilization for War,* pp. 641–42, 779. See also chap. 6 above.

4. *WPB Minutes,* 5, 8, 24, 31, 35, 47, 80, 102–3, 122, 123–24, 143, 150, 166, 181–82, 183, 210, 217, 244, 271, 281, 284, 352, 370, 380–81, 406; Truman Committee, *Third Annual Report,* 78th Cong., 2d sess., 1944, S. Rept. No. 10, pt. 16, pp. 74–75; McCauley, "Metals and Minerals Policy"; CPA, "Industrial Mobilization for War," vol. 2, pt. 2, chap. 4, pp. 240–338; George R. Kinzie, *Copper Policies of the War Production Board and Predecessor Agencies, May 1940 to November 1945* (Washington, DC: Civilian Production Agency, 1947), pp. 45–198; Charles M. Wiltse, *Evolution of Premium Price Policy for Copper, Lead and Zinc, January 1940 to November 1943* (Washington, DC: War Production Board, 1943), pp. 1–56; Maryclaire McCauley, *The Closing of the Gold Mines, August 1941 to March 1944* (Washington, DC: War Production Board, 1944); and CPA, *Industrial Mobilization for War,* pp. 642–44. See also chap. 6 above.

5. Truman Committee, *Third Annual Report,* 78th Cong., 2d sess., 1944, S. Rept. No. 10, pt. 16, pp. 75–77; CPA, "Industrial Mobilization for War," vol. 2, pt. 2, chap. 4, pp. 48–64, 93–108, 196–218, 369–87; Edythe W. First, "Tin Smelting in the National Defense Program, April 1939 to August 1944," Brief Survey No. 15, 1944, Policy Documentation File, WPB; Charles M. Wiltse, *Lead and Zinc Policies of the War Production Board and Predecessor Agencies, May 1940 to March 1944* (Washington, DC: War Production Board, 1944); David Horton, *Import Policies and Programs of the War Production Board and Predecessor Agencies, May 1940 to November 1945* (Washington, DC: Civilian Production Agency, 1947); and CPA, *Industrial Mobilization for War,* p. 644.

6. *WPB Minutes,* pp. 183, 284, 354, 397–98, 402, 407, 409; Truman Committee, *Interim Report on Lumber and Forest Products,* 77th Cong., 2d sess., 1942, S. Rept. No. 480, pt. 14; Truman Committee, *Third Annual Report,* 78th Cong., 2d sess., 1944, S. Rept. No. 10, pt. 16, pp. 78–83; CPA, "Industrial Mobilization for War," vol. 2, pt. 2, chap. 9, pp. 366–468; and CPA, *Industrial Mobilization for War,* pp. 644–46, 833–34.

7. *WPB Minutes,* pp. 301, 402, 407; CPA, "Industrial Mobilization for War," vol. 2, pt. 2, chap. 6, pp. 116–80; Ethan P. Allen, *Hide and Leather Policies of the War Production Board and Predecessor Agencies, May 1940 to December 1943* (Washington, DC: War Production Board, 1944); and CPA, *Industrial Mobilization for War,* pp. 650, 758–59.

8. *WPB Minutes,* pp. 234–36, 264, 301, 309, 335–36, 406, 416, 420; Marian D. Tolles, "Cotton Textiles Policies of the War Production Board and Predecessor Agencies, May 1940 to November 1945," Special Study No. 38, 1947, Policy Documentation File, WPB; CPA, "Industrial Mobilization for War," vol. 2, pt. 2, chap. 8, pp. 283–359; and CPA, *Industrial Mobilization for War,* pp. 828–30.

9. CPA, *Industrial Mobilization for War,* pp. 630–34, 694–98, 779–80, 826–34; and Maryclaire McCauley, *Pulp and Paper Policies of the War Production Board and Predecessor Agencies, May 1940 to January 1944* (Washington, DC: War Production Board, 1944). See also nn. 6–8 above.

10. For the "must" programs, see Jeffers to President, 12/1/43, Roosevelt to Jeffers, 12/16/42, Leahy to President, 12/16/42, McIntyre to President w/ enc., 12/17/42, Leahy to President, 1/8/43, and Roosevelt to Byrnes, 2/4/43, PSF: Joint Chiefs of Staff, and Roosevelt to Nelson, 10/30/42, and numerous other correspondence and documents, Nelson to Leahy, 12/1/42, Nelson to President, 12/24/42, Roosevelt to Nelson w/ enc., 5/4/43, Nelson to President w/ enc., 5/13/43, and Nelson to President, 5/14/43, PSF: War Production Board, FDR Papers; Eberstadt, memorandum, ca. 6/43, WPB, 1943–1944; 1947, and Eberstadt to Patterson, 4/27/43, and other memoranda, WPB, Patterson-Jeffers Controversy, Box 164, Eberstadt Papers; Nelson to Baruch w/ enc., 6/17/43, Washington File, 1942–45, Box 29, Sec.—Correspondence: Personal, Baruch to Watson w/ enc. (to President), 3/19/43, Baruch to Nelson, 12/31/42, Baruch to Patterson, 12/24/42, and Patterson to Baruch, 12/28/42, Selected Correspondence, Baruch Papers; Truman Committee, *Second Annual Report*, 78th Cong., 1st sess., 1943, S. Rept. No. 10, pt. 4, pp. 4 and 9–11; Truman Committee, *Shipbuilding and Shipping*, 78th Cong., 1st sess., 1943, S. Rept. No. 10, pt. 8; Truman Committee, *Concerning Conflicting War Programs*, 78th Cong., 1st sess., 1943, S. Rept. No. 10, pt. 9; Truman Committee, *Aircraft*, 78th Cong., 1st sess., 1943, S. Rept. No. 10, pt. 10; Truman Committee, *Third Annual Report*, 78th Cong., 2d sess., 1944, S. Rept. No. 10, pt. 16, pp. 7–111, 133–68; CPA, "Industrial Mobilization for War," vol. 2, pt, 6, chaps. 40–45, pp. 5–297, and pt. 7, chaps. 46–49, pp. 3–353; J. Carlyle Sitterson, "The Automobile Industry in War Production, May 1940 to December 1943," Brief Survey No. 1, 1944, Charles M. Wiltse, "Aircraft Production under the War Production Board and Predecessor Agencies, May 1940 to April 1944," Brief Survey No. 2, 1944, Virginia Turrell, "Radio and Radar Activities of the War Production Board, January 1942 to April 1944," Brief Survey No. 3, 1944, William B. Fitzgerald, "The Ordnance Program under the War Production Board and Predecessor Agencies, May 1940 to April 1944," Brief Survey No. 4, 1944, George E. Mowry, "The Procurement of Quartermaster Supplies, May 1940 to April 1944," Brief Survey No. 7, 1944, Virginia Turrell, "Rubber Policies of the War Production Board and Predecessor Agencies, May 1940 to March 1944," Brief Survey No. 11, 1944, and Virginia Turrell, "High-Octane Aviation Gasoline Program, 1940–44," Brief Survey No. 12, 1944, Policy Documentation File, WPB; George E. Mowry, *Landing Craft and the War Production Board, April 1942 to May 1944* (Washington, DC: Civilian Production Administration, 1946); George W. Auxier, *Truck Production and Distribution Policies of the War Production Board and Predecessor Agencies, July 1940 to December 1944* (Washington, DC: Civilian Production Administration, 1946); and CPA, *Industrial Mobilization for War*, pp. 550–52, 609–11, 753–58, 769–77. See also chaps. 3, 6, 10, and 12 above.

11. See chap. 12 above.

12. PEC is discussed below.

13. See also chap. 14 below.

14. For civilian requirements, see Kuznets to Nathan w/ enc. (report prepared under Kuznets's supervision: Planning Branch, WPB, "Civilian Consumption and Output in the United States: Review of 1942 and Prospects for 1943," 2/43), 3/25/43, Box 11, Unit IV, No. 8, and Office of Civilian Requirements, "Third Survey of Consumer Requirements—Household Articles, Equipment and Appliances—Conducted April 17–22, 1944," Box 12, Unit VI, No. 3, Nelson Papers; Smith to Byrnes,

6/18/42, and other correspondence and documents, and Swanson for Files, 7/27/43, War Production Board, and Smith to Byrnes, 8/12/43, and other correspondence, War Mobilization Office, General Records of the Director, 1939–1946, BofB; Ewing to Byrnes, 4/30/43, PSF: War Production Board, FDR Papers; Cook, "WPB, Office of Civilian Requirements, No. 99A," 1/5/44, Daily Record, 1943, Smith Papers; "Summary of Minutes of the Meeting of the Staff," 4/26/45, *Staff Minutes*, Box 274, OWMR; First to Fesler (on Gregg address to PARB, WPB), 10/21/44, 10/1944, Box 1, and Fesler and Jones Memorandum (on Hill interview), 9/11/45, 9–12/1945, Box 2, Fesler Papers; Baruch to Byrnes, 1/7/43, Washington File, 1942–45, Box 28, Sec. 1—Baruch Memo., Hancock, Memorandum on Meeting with Nelson and Wilson, 6/30/43, Washington File, 1942–45, Box 31, Sec. 2—Government Agencies: James F. Byrnes, Chambers to Kuznets, 11/3/42, and Weiner to Baruch w/ enc., 2/4/43, Washington File, 1942–45, Box 35, Sec. 3—Government Agencies: War Production Board, Nelson to Baruch, 6/10/44, Washington File, 1942–45, Box 35, Sec. 2—Government Agencies: War Production Board Reports, Hancock, "Staff Meeting, War Mobilization Committee," 8/3/43, Washington File, 1942–45, Box 38, Sec. 3—Special Subjects: Conspectus, "Memorandum on Maloney Bill," 4/6/43, Washington File, 1942–45, Box 37, Sec. 3—Special Subjects: Senate, Baruch to President, 9/16/43, and other documents, Washington File, 1942–45, Box 39, Sec. 3—Special Subjects: Clothing, Shoes, Etc., and Baruch to Nelson, 12/31/42, "Nelson Statement," ca. 12/42, and Baruch to Krug, 2/13/45, Selected Correspondence, Baruch Papers; *WPB Minutes*, pp. 14, 76, 99, 100–2, 105–7, 135–36, 143, 188–89, 210–11, 223, 229, 262–64, 295–96, 304–5, 312–14, 323–24, 335–36, 351–54, 361–63, 372, 397–98, 421–25; Civilian Production Administration, *Minutes of the Planning Committee of the War Production Board, February 20, 1942, to April 1, 1943* (Washington, DC: Civilian Production Administration, 1946), pp. 20, 38–40, 43–44, 104–5, 106, 109–10, 119, 120–21, 122–23, 170–71; Gladieux Reminiscences, pp. 473, 506–8, 518–30, 533, 536, 543, 561, 574, 617; Truman Committee, *Interim Report on Farm Machinery and Equipment*, 78th Cong., 1st sess., 1943, S. Rept. No. 10, pt. 2; Truman Committee, *Second Annual Report*, 78th Cong., 1st sess., 1943, S. Rept. no. 10, pt. 4, pp. 4–5, 13–14; Truman Committee, *Transportation*, 78th Cong., 1st sess., 1943, S. Rept. No. 10, pt. 13; Truman Committee, *Third Annual Report*, 78th Cong., 2d sess., 1944, S. Rept. No. 10, pt. 16, pp. 9–14, 20–22, 112–20; CPA, "Industrial Mobilization for War," vol. 2, pt. 3, chaps. 13–21, pp. 6–721, and pt. 4, chaps. 22–39, pp. 6–408; Andrew Stevenson, "Transportation Equipment Policies of the War Production Board and Predecessor Agencies, May 1940 to December 1943," Special Study No. 41, 1947, J. Carlyle Sitterson, "Reconversion Activities of the War Production Board, January 1943 to June 1944," Brief Survey No. 9, 1944, and Reginald C. McGrane, "Defense and War Housing Policies of the War Production Board and Its Predecessor Agencies, May 1940 to July 1944," Brief Survey No. 14, 1944, Policy Documentation File, WPB; Drummond Jones, *The Role of the Office of Civilian Requirements in the Office of Production Management and War Production Board, January 1941 to November 1945* (Washington, DC: Civilian Production Administration, 1946), pp. 57–351; Maryclair McCauley, *Concentration of Civilian Production by the War Production Board, September 1941 to April 1943* (Washington, DC: Civilian Production Administration, 1946); J. Carlyle Sitterson, *Development of the Reconversion Policies of the War Production Board, April 1943 to January*

1945 (Washington, DC: Civilian Production Administration, 1946); James A. McAleer, *Farm Machinery and Equipment Policies of the War Production Board and Predecessor Agencies, May 1940 to September 1944* (Washington, DC: War Production Board, 1944); John E. Brigante, "The Planning Committee of the War Production Board: A Chapter in American Planning Experience" (Ph.D. diss., Princeton University, 1948); and CPA, *Industrial Mobilization for War,* pp. 552–54, 698–700, 750–51, 613–23, 765–66. See also chaps. 7–8, and 11 above.

15. Reconversion is analyzed in chap. 17 below.

16. For small business, see Murray to President, 7/2/42, Patman to Rayburn, "A Preliminary Report of the Committee on Small Business of the House to the Speaker of the House of Representatives," 12/17/42, and other correspondence, OF: Smaller War Plants Corporation, Roosevelt to Byrnes, 12/29/42, and other correspondence, PSF: War Production Board, and Nelson to President (second report of WPB), 10/11/42, OF: War Production Board, FDR Papers; Gulick and Fish, "Discussion with Mr. Sidney J. Weinberg," 5/21/42, and other correspondence, file 032, Wilson to Davis w/ enc., 3/4/43, file 040.8, Wilson to Pauley, 3/44, file 041.02, and Fesler to Nathan, 9/9/42, file 072.11, WPB; Tiller to Schaub w/ enc., 7/25/44, Smaller War Plants Corporation, General Records of the Director, BofB; Memorandum (on Robison address to the PARB), 2/3/45, 1–3/1945, Box 2, Fesler Papers; Fowler to Henderson w/ enc., ca. 5/42, Small Business, WPB Papers, Box 35, Henderson Papers; Johnson to Baruch, 6/20/42, Baruch to Johnson, 7/7/42, Baruch to Krug, 7/18/45, and Krug to Baruch, 8/9/45, Selected Correspondence, Maverick to Krug, 4/17/44, and other correspondence, Washington File, 1942–45, Box 34, Sec. 2— Government Agencies: Smaller War Plants Corporation, and Lubell to Baruch, 1/18/44, and other documents, Washington File, 1942–45, Box 44, Sec. 3—Special Subjects: Small Business, Baruch Papers; Maverick to Snyder, 8/17/45, and other documents, Box 273, VJ Day Plans—Smaller War Plants Corporation, OWMR; French to Wacker, 2/8/46, and other documents, Box 9, Unit 13, RWA, BOB; *WPB Minutes,* pp. 45–46, 54, 87, 100–2, 191–92, 218–19; U.S. Congress, Senate, *Economic Concentration and World War II: Report of the Smaller War Plants Corporation to the Special Committee to Study Problems of American Small Business,* 79th Cong., 2d sess., S. Doc. 206, 1946; Robert W. Johnson, *"But, General Johnson—": Episodes in a War Effort* (Princeton, NJ: Princeton University Press, 1944); Jean Christie, *Morris Lewellyn Cooke: Progressive Engineer* (New York: Garland, 1983); Jim F. Heath, "American War Mobilization and the Use of Small Manufacturers, 1939–1943," *Business History Review* 66 (Autumn 1972): 295–319; Jonathan J. Bean, "World War II and the 'Crisis' of Small Business: The Smaller War Plants Corporation, 1942–1946," *Journal of Policy History* 6 (1994): 215–43; Jonathan J. Bean, "Beyond the Broker State: A History of the Federal Government's Policies toward Small Business, 1936–1961" (Ph.D. diss., Ohio State University, 1994), pp. 170–223 (for a published version of this study, see Jonathan J. Bean, *Beyond the Broker State: Federal Policies toward Small Business, 1936–1961* [Chapel Hill: University of North Carolina Press, 1996]); Donald A. Spritzer, "New Dealer from Montana: The Senate Career of James E. Murray" (Ph.D. diss., University of Montana, 1980); Donald A. Spritzer, *Senator James E. Murray and the Limits of Post-War Liberalism* (New York: Garland, 1985); Nancy B. Young, *Wright Patman: Populism, Liberalism, and the American Dream* (Dallas: Southern Methodist University Press, 2000); James H. Soltow, "Structure and Strategy: The Small Man-

ufacturing Enterprise in the Modern Industrial Economy," in *Business and Its Environment: Essays for Thomas C. Cochran,* ed. Harold I. Sharlin (Westport, CT: Greenwood, 1983), pp. 81–99; Harold G. Vatter, *The U.S. Economy in World War II* (New York: Columbia University Press, 1985), pp. 51–66; McCauley, *Concentration of Civilian Production;* CPA, *Industrial Mobilization for War,* pp. 61–63, 145–50, 271–72, 527–32, 572–73, 596–97, 930; Bureau of the Budget, *The United States at War: Development and Administration of the War Program by the Federal Government* (Washington, DC: Bureau of the Budget, 1946), pp. 83–84, 500; Smith, *Army and Economic Mobilization,* pp. 413–34; Harry B. Yoshpe, *The Small Business Man and Quartermaster Contracts, 1940–1942* (Washington, DC: Office of the Quartermaster General, 1943); and Robert H. Connery, *The Navy and the Industrial Mobilization in World War II* (Princeton, NJ: Princeton University Press, 1951), pp. 115–24, 333–38. For hearings and reports of the Senate Special Committee to Study and Survey Problems of American Small Business, the House Select Committee on Small Business, and other congressional committees, see the bibliographies in Spritzer and Bean works cited above. See also chap. 7 above; Harmon Zeigler, *The Politics of Small Business* (Washington, DC: Public Affairs Press, 1961); Stuart W. Bruchey, ed., *Small Business in American Life* (New York: Columbia University Press, 1980); Mansel G. Blackford, *A History of Small Business in America* (New York: Twayne, 1991); Mansel G. Blackford, "Small Business in America: A Historiographic Survey," *Business History Review* 65 (Spring 1991): 1–26; Philip Scranton, *Endless Novelty: Specialty Production and American Industrialization, 1865–1925* (Princeton, NJ: Princeton University Press, 1997); and Sandra M. Anglund, *Small Business Policy and the American Creed* (Westport, CT: Praeger, 2000).

17. Committee names changed over time. I have used the simpler versions.

18. The number of small manufacturers varies among sources depending on dates, definitions, statistics, and the like.

19. See chap. 11 above.

20. Johnson, *"But, General Johnson—,"* p. 55.

21. See chap. 11 above.

22. Carroll K. Shaw, *Field Organization and Administration of the War Production Board and Predecessor Agencies, May 1940 to November 1945* (Washington, DC: Civilian Production Administration, 1947); and CPA, *Industrial Mobilization for War,* pp. 266–72, 592–95, 742–43, 785. See also Shaw to Auxier, 5/10/46, and other correspondence, 5–6/1946, Box 2, and War Production Board, Minutes of Staff Meeting, 12/3/42, and other correspondence and documents, War Production Board, Accession 87-M-46, Box 1, Fesler Papers; and Baruch to Knowlson w/ enc., 3/15/42, and Baruch to Nelson, 2/21/42, Selected Correspondence, Baruch Papers.

23. Gulick to Eberstadt, 7/17/42, and numerous other correspondence and documents, Box 163, WPB, 1941–1942, Eberstadt Papers; Kanzler to Eberstadt, 10/5/42, and other correspondence, 10–12/1942, Box 1, Fesler Papers; Leahy to President w/ enc. (ANMB to Secretaries of War and Navy), 7/27/43, PSF: Army and Navy Munitions Board, and Gulick to McIntyre, 6/25/42, and numerous other correspondence and documents, OF: Army and Navy Munitions Board, FDR Papers; Milton to Herring, 10/20/42, Box 19, Unit 197, and memorandum "Army and Navy Munitions Board vs Office of Production Management," 1/13/42, Box 19, Unit 200, RWA, BOB; John D. Millett, *The Organization and Role of the Army Service Forces*

(Washington, DC: Office of the Chief of Military Service, 1954), pp. 201–2, 210–11, 269–70, 290–92; Smith, *Army and Economic Mobilization,* pp. 144–45; Connery, *Navy and Industrial Mobilization,* pp. 112, 150–178, 352–54; Keith E. Eiler, *Mobilizing America: Robert P. Patterson and the War Effort, 1940–1945* (Ithaca, NY: Cornell University Press, 1997), pp. 187–88, 234, 345; Bureau of the Budget, *United States at War,* pp. 81–82, 126–27, 280–81; and CPA, *Industrial Mobilization for War,* pp. 216–22. See also chap. 5 above.

24. For PEC, see PEC, Minutes, Meeting 5–127, 10/28/42–8/27/45, PEC, Documents 1–132, 10/20/44–8/10/45, and PEC, Meetings and Memos, file 041.05, and Fesler for Files, 9/17/45, and Fesler to Krug, 9/24/45, file 041.01, WPB; McCandless and Graham to Martin and Stone, 6/24/43, and Key to Graham w/ enc., 3/10/44, War Production Board, General Records of the Director, BofB; Conference with the President, 7/13/44, and Daily Record, 11/9/43, 10/3/44, 10/10/44, Smith Papers; Patterson and Forrestal to President, 12/31/43, Roosevelt to Wilson, 1/4/44 (two entries), Roosevelt to Nelson, 8/18/44, and other documents, Memorandum for Conference with Nelson, 8/24/44, Byrnes to President, 9/21/44, and other correspondence, and Hopkins to President, 9/27/44, PSF: War Production Board, FDR Papers; Fesler to Krug, 9/24/45, 9–12/1945, Box 2, Fesler Papers; Stein and Graham to Director, 3/5/44, Meetings 1943, Box 3, OWMR; Hancock to Shaw, 12/31/42, Baruch to Henderson, 11/30/43, Nathan to Baruch, 11/19/43, and Baruch to Nathan, 11/24/43, Washington File, 1942–45, Box 29, Sec.—Correspondence: Personal, Hancock, Memorandum (on talk with Nelson and Wilson), 6/30/43, Washington File, 1942–45, Box 31, Sec. 2—Government Agencies: James F. Byrnes, Chambers to Baruch, 2/18/43, Washington File, 1942–45, Box 35, Sec. 2—Government Agencies: War Production Board, Hancock to Sherwood, 9/30/43, and other correspondence, Washington File, 1942–45, Box 39, Sec. 3—Special Subjects: Industry Advisory Committees, and Baruch to Nelson, 6/13/43, and other documents, 11/16/43 (two entries), Peek to Baruch, 6/23/43, and other correspondence, Wilson to Pinci, 3/16/43, Pinci to Baruch, 3/29/43, Baruch to Childs, 6/27/44, and Baruch to Roosevelt, 1/4/44, 11/15/44, Selected Correspondence, Baruch Papers; *WPB Minutes,* pp. 174, 375, 395; CPA, *Industrial Mobilization for War,* pp. 507–9, 549–50, 580–82, 622–23, 731–51, 791; and Gladieux Reminiscences, pp. 460–652.

25. Wilson is discussed in chap. 12 above. On the leadership qualities of Wilson vis-à-vis Nelson, see Key to Graham w/ enc., 3/10/44, War Production Board, General Records of the Director, BofB; primary sources cited in chap. 8, n. 4, above; and Hancock to Baruch, 3/29/43, Wilson to Baruch, 12/7/44, Arnold to Wilson, 11/22/44, and Baruch to Wilson, 12/13/44, Selected Correspondence, Baruch Papers. There is no biography of Wilson, only a privately printed fifty-page publicity piece by Kent Sagendorph, *Charles Edward Wilson: American Industrialist* (1949). See also Ronald W. Schatz, *The Electrical Workers: A History of Labor at General Electric and Westinghouse, 1923–60* (Urbana: University of Illinois Press, 1983), pp. 10, 59, 167–86, 234, 236; and Jacob Vander Meulen, "Wilson, Charles Edward," in *American National Biography,* ed. John A. Garraty and Mark C. Carnes (New York: Oxford University Press, 1999), 23:557–59.

26. For the Business Advisory Council and the IAB, see Kim McQuaid, "The Business Advisory Council of the Department of Commerce, 1933–1961: A Study in Cor-

porate/Government Relations," in *Research in Economic History: An Annual Compilation of Research*, ed. Paul Uselding (Greenwich, CT: JAI, 1976), pp. 171–97; and Kim McQuaid, *Big Business and Presidential Power: From FDR to Reagan* (New York: William Morrow, 1982), pp. 11–121. WPB-NRA-BAC membership can be traced through McQuaid's studies and in Philip H. Burch, Jr., *Elites in American History: The New Deal to the Carter Administration* (New York: Holmes and Meier, 1980), vol. 3. See also Richard E. Holl, "The Corporate Liberals and the Roosevelt Administration Preparedness Program, 1939–1941" (Ph.D. diss., University of Kentucky, 1996).

27. Gladieux Reminiscences, pp. 501–2.

28. There is surprisingly little quality secondary information on Byrnes. His memoirs—*Speaking Frankly* (New York: Harper and Bros., 1947) and *All in One Lifetime* (New York: Harper and Bros., 1958)—are notable for what they do not say. The OWM years benefit from two studies: Herman M. Somers, *Presidential Agency: OWMR, The Office of War Mobilization and Reconversion* (Cambridge, MA: Harvard University Press, 1950) (a slightly modified version of Herman M. Somers, "Coordinating the Federal Executive" [Ph.D. diss., Harvard University, 1947]); and John W. Partin, "'Assistant President' for the Home Front: James F. Byrnes and World War II" (Ph.D. diss., University of Florida, 1977) (Partin cites other unpublished studies of Byrnes). Somers's study is valuable but must be treated with caution. It is actually an official history researched and written while Somers was a paid employee of OWMR during 1946 and 1947. He had served as a lieutenant colonel in the Industrial Personnel Division, Army Service Forces, throughout most of the war and joined OWMR to write its history. See Hechler to Somers, 6/16/47, Hechler for Files, 5/6/46, 4/29/46, 4/11/46, and Key to Russell, 4/5/45, Box 11, Unit 129, RWA, BOB. Somers's study can be characterized as post–Donald Nelson WPB "establishment," reflecting the views of William Y. Elliott and Lincoln Gordon (both of whom were members of Somers's dissertation committee) and others. Somers exaggerates the accomplishments of OWMR and presents Nelson and his supporters in a negative light and the armed services in a positive one. By comparison, Partin's study is less sophisticated, more a narrative about Byrnes and OWMR than an analysis of them. Nonetheless, careful attention to Partin's work highlights the serious limitations of Somers's book.

Although not dealing with the homefront, Robert L. Messer, *The End of an Alliance: James F. Byrnes, Roosevelt, Truman, and the Origins of the Cold War* (Chapel Hill: University of North Carolina Press, 1982), is valuable. Jordan A. Schwarz, *The Speculator: Bernard M. Baruch in Washington, 1917–1965* (Chapel Hill: University of North Carolina Press, 1981), examines the complicated Baruch-Byrnes relationship. Those writing from the perspective of capital insiders are strangely reticent about Byrnes. See the publications cited elsewhere of Robert E. Sherwood, George McJimsey, Samuel I. Rosenman, Samuel B. Hand, Donald M. Nelson, William D. Leahy, and Henry L. Stimson and McGeorge Bundy. The one major exception is John M. Blum, *From the Morgenthau Diaries: Years of War, 1941–1945* (Boston: Houghton Mifflin, 1967).

Other volumes are helpful: James M. Burns, *Roosevelt: The Soldier of Freedom* (New York: Harcourt Brace Jovanovich, 1970), pp. 262, 339, 343–55, 432, 447, 451–53; Frank Freidel, *Franklin D. Roosevelt: A Rendezvous with Destiny* (Boston: Little, Brown, 1990), pp. 439–40, 494, 499; Alan Brinkley, *The End of Reform: New Deal Liberalism in Recession and War* (New York: Alfred A. Knopf, 1995), pp. 141–43, 152–54, 194–98, 237–45; CPA, *Industrial Mobilization for War*, pp. 338, 415,

554–56, 581–82, 590, 608, 615, 643, 656, 708–9, 719, 721–24, 732, 738–40, 743, 759–61, 770, 783, 787, 789, 801, 806, 808–9, 811, 837, 844, 852–53, 863, 866, 877, 908–10, 912, 974; Bureau of the Budget, *United States at War,* 271–73, 358–69, 371–74, 391–401, 425–28, 439–444, 452–55; John K. Ohl, *Supplying the Troops: General Somervell and American Logistics in WWII* (DeKalb: Northern Illinois University Press, 1994), pp. 89–97, 160–80; Jean E. Smith, *Lucius D. Clay: An American Life* (New York: Henry Holt, 1990), pp. 103–200; and Richard D. Current, *Secretary Stimson: A Study in Statecraft* (New Brunswick, NJ: Rutgers University Press, 1954), pp. 202–7.

See also primary sources: Byrnes to President, 2/43, Roosevelt to Byrnes, 3/9/43, Byrnes to President, 5/14/43, Byrnes to President, 9/15/43, 9/16/43, Roosevelt to Byrnes, 9/28/43, Roosevelt to Byrnes w/ encs., 6/10/44, Byrnes to President, 1/1/45, Byrnes to President, 3/24/45, 3/27/45, and Roosevelt to Byrnes, 3/25/45, PSF: Executive Office of the President—James F. Byrnes, Appleby to President w/ enc., 8/25/44, Rosenman to President, 8/30/44, Byrnes to President, 9/7/44, Byrnes to Krug, Patterson, Forrestal, Land, and McNutt, 11/16/44, and Leahy to President, 11/28/44, OF: Office of War Mobilization and Reconversion, Byrnes to President w/ enc., 11/29/44, OF: Office of Economic Stabilization, and Smith to President, 7/16/43, and Roosevelt to Leahy, 9/6/43, and other correspondence, PSF: Joint Chiefs of Staff, FDR Papers; Conference with the President, 5/9/44, 11/16/44, 3/23/45, 4/18/45, 6/5/45, 8/10/45, 9/13/45, 9/14/45, 9/19/45, White House Memoranda, Smith to President, 9/13/44, 11/9/44, 9/11/45, 11/30/45, 12/6/45, and Smith to Byrnes, 11/8/43, and Daily Record, 11/3/43, 11/9/43, 12/11/43, 2/26/45, 7/3/45, Smith Papers; "Monthly Munitions Report—March 1945," Munitions Reports—Monthly, Box 274, Economic Stabilization Board, Minutes, 10/16/42, Office of Economic Stabilization, Minutes of Board Meetings, Board of Economic Stabilization, Box 606, and "Summary of the Minutes of the Meeting of the Staff," 7/25/45, Staff Minutes, Box 274, and Stein and Graham to Director, 3/6/44, Meetings 1943, Box 3, OWMR; Stone to Smith, 11/13/42, and numerous other correspondence, documents, and reports on executive war organization, Box 12, Unit 139, Milton to Herring, 8/4/42, and other documents, Box 12, Unit 143, Venneman to Stone, 9/29/42, Box 19, Unit 202, and Milton to Herring, 1/13/43, and other memoranda and documents, Box 17, Unit 173, RWA, BOB; Coy to President, ca. 9/42, and other correspondence, Alphabetical File, Box 2, Bureau of the Budget: Repts re Administration of Misc. Agencies, Coy to Rosenman, 8/19/42, and numerous other correspondence and documents, Box 4, Economic Stabilization Authority, Hopkins to Coy, 3/19/41, Box 8, Hopkins, Harry L.—Administrative Assistant, Coy to President, 9/12/41, and other correspondence, Box 13, Roosevelt, Franklin D.—1941, Coy to President, 10/13/42, Box 13, Franklin D. Roosevelt—1943, and Herring to Stone, 9/25/42, and other correspondence and documents, Box 17, War Mobilization—Reports, Coy Papers; Coy to Byrnes, 6/10/43, and Graham to Smith, 9/18/43, War Mobilization Office, General Records of Director, BofB; Hancock, Memorandum (on talk with Nelson and Wilson), 6/30/43, and Hancock to Baruch, 7/22/43, Washington File, 1942–45, Box 31, Sec. 2—Government Agencies: James F. Byrnes, and Hancock, "Staff Meeting, War Mobilization Committee," 8/3/43, Washington File, 1942–45, Box 38, Sec. 3—Special Subjects: Conspectus, Baruch Papers.

29. Somers, *OWMR*, p. 72.

30. Ibid., pp. 35–38; and Paul A. C. Koistinen, *The Hammer and the Sword: Labor, the Military, and Industrial Mobilization, 1920–1945* (New York: Arno, 1979), pp. 464–66, 691–99.

31. Searls quoted in Somers, *OWMR*, p. 62.

32. White House Memoranda, Smith to President, 8/31/44, and Roosevelt to Smith, 9/18/44, Smith Papers. See also Conference with the President, 8/31/44, Smith Papers; and "Meeting in Mr. Baruch's Office," 11/23/43, Washington File, 1942–45, Box 36, Sec. 3—Special Subjects: Agriculture, Baruch Papers.

33. CPA, *Industrial Mobilization for War*, p. 902. See also Baruch to Krug, 2/13/45, Selected Correspondence, Baruch Papers; and Fisher to Clay, 3/26/45, and other correspondence and documents, Clay, Lucius Memos, Box 271, OWMR.

CHAPTER FOURTEEN. ORGANIZED LABOR IN A MOBILIZED ECONOMY, 1940–1945: LABOR SUPPLY

1. The following analysis of labor supply is more fully documented in Paul A. C. Koistinen, *The Hammer and the Sword: Labor, the Military, and Industrial Mobilization, 1920–1945* (New York: Arno, 1979), chaps. 5–6.

2. U.S. Bureau of the Census, *Historical Statistics of the United States, Colonial Times to 1970* (Washington, DC: U.S. Government Printing Office, 1975), p. 126; and Bureau of the Budget, *The United States at War: Development and Administration of the War Program by the Federal Government* (Washington, DC: Bureau of the Budget, 1946), pp. 173–74.

3. See chaps. 1, 3–4, and 7 above. See also Richard J. Purcell, *Labor Policies of the National Defense Advisory Commission and the Office of Production Management, May 1940 to April 1942* (Washington, DC: Civilian Production Administration, 1946); Richard J. Purcell, "Labor Policies of the War Production Board, April 1942 to November 1945," Special Study No. 32, 1946, vol. 1, Policy Documentation File, WPB (this five-volume manuscript is in an extremely disordered state and can be cited only by volume); Koistinen, *Hammer and Sword*, pp. 88–89, 91–93, 144–47, 351–58; and Steven Fraser, *Labor Will Rule: Sidney Hillman and the Rise of American Labor* (New York: Free Press, 1991). Matthew Josephson, *Sidney Hillman: Statesman of American Labor* (Garden City, NY: Doubleday, 1952), still remains valuable.

4. Conference with the President, 2/7/42, 4/16/42, Smith Papers; Coy to President, 2/6/42, and other documents, OF: Cabinet Committee on Mobilization of Manpower, FDR Papers; Rosenman to President, 4/11/42, and other documents, Manpower I, and Lubin to Rosenman, 4/14/42, Manpower II, Rosenman Papers; Gladieux Notes (on manpower administration), 1/31/42, and numerous other correspondence, Box 12, Unit 211, RWA, BOB; Entries, 4/21/42, 4/28/42, Alphabetical File, Box 3, Telephone Transcripts—April 1942, and Coy to President, 2/2/42, and Entry, 12/18/42, Conference of the Director and Assistant Director with the President, Box 13, Franklin D. Roosevelt—1942, Coy Papers; and Bureau of the Budget, *United States at War*, pp. 182–84.

5. Harper to Rosenman w/ enc., 11/3/42, and numerous other correspondence and documents, Manpower II, Rosenman Papers; Conference with the President,

12/4/42, and White House Memoranda, Smith to President, 11/23/42, Smith Papers; Baruch to President, 11/7/42, and Roosevelt to Baruch, Byrnes, and Rosenman, 11/11/42, Selected Correspondence, Baruch Papers; Milton to Herring, 10/8/42, and numerous other correspondence, Box 12, Unit 211, and Milton to Herring, 9/28/42, and other correspondence, Box 12, Unit 143, RWA, BOB; Koistinen, *Hammer and Sword*, pp. 358–72; Bureau of the Budget, *United States at War*, pp. 184–89; and George Q. Flynn, *The Mess in Washington: Manpower Mobilization in World War II* (Westport, CT: Greenwood, 1979), pp. 24–35.

6. Management-Labor Policy Committee (MLPC), Verbatim Minutes, MLPC, Summary Minutes, and War Manpower Commission (WMC), Minutes, Box 20-146, and Management-Labor Policy Committee, Interim Report of the Chairman of the War Manpower Commission, 10/31/42, Interim Report . . . MLPC, Box 5-122, WMC; Lubin to Rosenman w/ enc., 11/21/42, Manpower I, and Mitchell to Gerber, 10/30/42, Manpower II, Rosenman Papers; Milton to Herring, 12/19/42, Box 12, Unit 211, RWA, BOB; Ellen S. Parks, "Management-Labor Policy Committee: A Case Study of Organized Group Participation in Administration," BofB; and Flynn, *Mess in Washington*, pp. 112–18.

7. Herman M. Somers, *Presidential Agency: OWMR, the Office of War Mobilization and Reconversion* (Cambridge, MA: Harvard University Press, 1950), p. 141 n. 5.

8. For the size of the armed forces, see Conference with the President, 6/13/42, and Daily Record, Smith Memorandum on Telephone Conversation with Chief of Staff, 6/11/42, Smith Papers; Rosenman et al., Memorandum to the President, various drafts, 3/43, and numerous other correspondence and documents, Manpower II, and memorandum "Considerations on the Size of the Army," 12/11/42, Army, Rosenman Papers; Rosenman et al. to President, 3/14/43, PSF: War Manpower Commission, and McNutt to Deane, 9/16/42, OF: War Manpower Commission, FDR Papers; Rosenman to Leahy et al. w/ enc., 3/18/43, and numerous other correspondence and documents, Washington File, 1942–45, Box 40, Sec. 3—Special Subjects: Manpower–White House Special Committee, Baruch Papers; Milton to Herring, 11/9/42, Box 12, Unit 144, and Milton to Herring, 9/3/42, and other documents, Box 12, Unit 150, RWA, BOB; Stimson Diary, 9/17/42, 11/6–7/42, 5/11/44 (w/ enc.), 5/10/44, 6/9/44, 1/4/45, 1/9/45; Dorr to Stimson, 9/24/42, and other correspondence, Manpower, and Eustis to Stimson, 5/25/44, and other correspondence and documents, Clark to Patterson, 1/27/43, and Clark to Stimson, 5/26/44, National Service—Official File, OSW; Dorr to Stimson w/ enc., 1/1/45, and other correspondence, Size of the Army, Dorr Collection; Amberg to Patterson, 3/21/44, War Production Board—1944, Amberg Collection; Dorr to Clark, 3/23/44, and Clark to Dorr, 5/25/44, Box 3, Correspondence: Dorr, G. H., Clark to Stimson, 6/13/44, and other correspondence, Box 3, Correspondence: Eustis, Warner, and Williston to Clark w/ encs., 6/14/44, Box 10, Correspondence: Williston, Arthur—1944, Clark Papers; Truman Committee, *Preliminary Report on Manpower*, 77th Cong., 2d sess., 1942, S. Rept. No. 480, pt. 11; U.S. Congress, House, Select Committee Investigating National Defense Migration, *Sixth Interim Report*, 77th Cong., 2d sess., 1942, H. Rept. No. 2589; Samuel I. Rosenman, *Working with Roosevelt* (New York: Harper and Bros., 1952), p. 421; Byron Fairchild and Jonathan Grossman, *The Army and Industrial Manpower* (Washington, D.C.: Office of the Chief of Military History, 1959), pp. 45–56; Civilian Production Administration, *Industrial*

Mobilization for War: History of the War Production Board and Predecessor Agencies, 1940–1945 (Washington, DC: Civilian Production Administration, 1947), pp. 414–16; and Albert A. Blum, *Drafted or Deferred: Practices Past and Present* (Ann Arbor, MI: University of Michigan, 1967), pp. 33–55.

9. Henry L. Stimson and McGeorge Bundy, *On Active Service in Peace and War* (New York: Harper and Bros., 1947), pp. 473–80 (quotation p. 480).

10. Dorr to Stimson, 4/11/44, Manpower, OSW.

11. Koistinen, *Hammer and Sword*, pp. 367, 420.

12. For the SSS, see Haber to McNutt, 3/8/44, and other correspondence, Manpower I, Lubin to Rosenman, 11/12/42, 2/20/43 (w/ enc.), and Stimson to President, 11/5/42, Manpower II, and Roosevelt to Rosenman w/ enc., 3/14/44, and other correspondence, War Department, Rosenman Papers; WMC, Minutes, 10/28/42, 11/4/42, 11/28/42, 1/6/43, and MLPC, Summary Minutes, 10/10/42, 8/10/43, 9/28/43, 4/27/44, 5/31/44, 6/27/44, 2/6/45, 3/27/45 (see also the corresponding Verbatim Minutes), WMC; Conference with the President, 12/4/42, and White House Memoranda, Smith to President, 10/14/42, 11/18/42, Smith Papers; Stimson Diary, 10/19–22/42, 10/30/42, 11/4–5/42, 11/7/42, 2/18/44, 3/10/44, 3/13/44, 3/15–18/44, 3/22–23/44, 3/27/44, 4/3–4/44, 4/7/44, 12/20/44, 12/27–28/44, 4/30/45, 5/1/45; Lovett to Stimson, 10/14/43, and other documents, Manpower, and Roosevelt to Knox and Stimson, 3/11/44, and other documents, Selective Service—Deferment, OSW; Memorandum No. W600-16-42 (on deferments), 9/24/42, and other documents, Adjutant General's Office, file 049.12/175, Planning Branch (PB), USW/OSW; Dorr to Stimson, 10/31/42, and other documents, Selective Service System—National Service Act, McNutt to President, ca. 10/42, Mobilization Resources, Director of, and Patterson to Hancock, 10/19/43, and other documents, Master Plan—West Coast Aircraft Labor Shortage Plan, Dorr Collection; Kapp to Hertz, 10/14/43, West Coast Aircraft, Ohly Papers; Hertz to Patterson, 9/30/43, Final Report, Hertz Collection; Hancock to Patterson, 10/1/43, and Baruch to Byrd w/ encs., 10/2/43, Selected Correspondence, and Patterson to Hancock, 8/7/43, Washington File, 1942–45, Box 38, Sec. 3—Special Subjects: Father Draft, Baruch Papers; Herman M. Somers and John H. Ohly, "War Department Organization for the Handling of Labor Problems in World War II," War Department Monograph No. 2, 1945, U.S. Army Center of Military History, Washington, DC; Leonard J. Wechsler, "War Department Role in the Deferment of Selective Service Inductions," War Department Monograph No. 13a, U.S. Army Center of Military History, Washington, DC; Civilian Production Administration, *Minutes of the War Production Board, January 20, 1942 to October 9, 1945* (hereafter *WPB Minutes*) (Washington, DC: Civilian Production Administration, 1946), pp. 270–71, 324–25; Blum, *Drafted or Deferred;* Fairchild and Grossman, *Army and Industrial Manpower,* pp. 174–76, 197–203, 224–25; George Q. Flynn, *Lewis B. Hershey, Mr. Selective Service* (Chapel Hill: University of North Carolina Press, 1985), pp. 62–134; Flynn, *Mess in Washington,* pp. 47–49, 131–44, 191–216; Bureau of the Budget, *United States at War,* pp. 186–89, 444–50; Civilian Production Administration, *Industrial Mobilization for War,* pp. 749, 845–47; Somers, *Presidential Agency,* pp. 158–70; and Koistinen, *Hammer and Sword,* pp. 346–51, 367–72, 418–29.

13. Stimson Diary, 10/15/42.

14. Constance Kiehl, "U.S. War Manpower Commission: History of the Mobilization of Labor for War Production during World War II," chaps. 2, 4, BofB; Edmond

Kanwit, "War Department Facilities Allocation, Contract Placement, and Cutback Distribution from the Standpoint of Labor Supply and Labor Relations, June 1940 to May 1945," War Department Monograph No. 11, U.S. Army Center of Military History, Washington, DC; Purcell, "Labor Policies of WPB," vol. 2; Robert R. Russell, "Expansion of Industrial Facilities under Army Air Forces Auspices, 1940–1945," Army Air Forces Historical Studies No. 40, 1947, Wright-Patterson Air Force Base, OH; Reginald C. McGrane, *The Facilities and Construction Program of the War Production Board and Predecessor Agencies, May 1940 to May 1945* (Washington, DC: War Production Board, 1945), chaps. 3–5; Fairchild and Grossman, *Army and Industrial Manpower,* chap. 6; and CPA, *Industrial Mobilization for War,* pp. 422–23. See also chap. 11 n. 39.

15. Dorr to Somervell, 7/4/42, and other documents, file 300.05, Dorr Collection; Amberg to Patterson, 1/9/43, and numerous other correspondence and documents, War Manpower Commission, Amberg Collection; Maloney and Ohly to Mitchell, 7/20/42, Labor Supply—Misc. Problems, Mitchell to Somervell, 5/27/43, Placement of Contracts with Regard to Labor Supply, and "Conversation with Julius Amberg," 4/19/45, Misc., Ohly Papers; Boland and O'Connell, memorandum "Procurement Policy—Labor Supply," 11/21/42, Greenbaum Collection; James Doran, "Methods of Handling Labor Supply Problems in Critical Industries and Areas," War Department Monograph No. 9, 1945, U.S. Army Center of Military History, Washington, DC; Purcell, "Labor Policies of WPB," vol. 2; and Koistinen, *Hammer and Sword,* pp. 361–66.

16. Truman Committee, *Preliminary Report on Manpower,* 77th Cong., 2d sess., 1942, S. Rept. No. 480, pt. 11; Purcell, "Labor Policies of WPB," vol. 2; CPA, *Industrial Mobilization for War,* pp. 422–23, 710–11; Bureau of the Budget, *United States at War,* pp. 433–35; and Somers, *Presidential Agency,* 155–57. See also chap. 11 above.

17. For contracting data, see Lubin to Hopkins, 3/3/43, Manpower I, and Stephen to Peck, 3/5/43, and other documents, Manpower II, Rosenman Papers; Memorandum (on Gladieux address to PARB, WPB), 3/9/45, 1–3/1945, and Memorandum (on Nathan address), 8/4/45, and Memorandum (on Hetzel address to PARB, WPB), 8/24/45, 7–8/1945, Box 2, Fesler Papers; "Agenda for the First Meeting of the WPB Manpower Priorities Committee," 9/2/42, and other documents and correspondence, file 700.01-09, and Harrison to Dorr, Mitchell, and West, 12/28/42, file 300.10, Dorr Collection; Green and Murray to Byrnes et al. w/ enc., 3/23/43, and Hancock to Baruch, 2/26/43, Selected Correspondence, Baruch Papers; Earl Latham, "First Narrative on the 'Coordination of War Manpower Commission's Relations with the War Production Board,'" BofB; R. Burr Smith, "Labor and Manpower Administration in War Production, May 1940 to March 1943," Special Study No. 1, 1943, Policy Documentation File, WPB; Purcell, "Labor Policies of WPB," vol. 2; MLPC, Summary Minutes, 9/18/42 (see also corresponding Verbatim Minutes), WMC; *WPB Minutes,* pp. 21, 55–56, 137, 212–13, 237–38; CPA, *Industrial Mobilization for War,* pp. 245–48, 566–67, 589–90; Bureau of the Budget, *United States at War,* pp. 432 n. 5, 435–38; Somers, *Presidential Agency,* pp. 137–43; and Koistinen, *Hammer and Sword,* pp. 361–67, 373–77.

18. Ohly for Files, 4/16/43, and other documents, Labor Utilization—General, Ohly Papers; WMC, "West Coast Manpower Program," 8/19/43, and numerous

other documents and correspondence, Master Plan—West Coast Aircraft Shortage Plan, WMC, Directive No. XIX, 11/18/43, and other documents, Directive No. IXX (i.e., XIX), Dorr to Styer, Clay, and Mitchell, 8/24/43, Labor Requirements Committee—WPB, Patterson to McNutt, 7/3/43, file 200.09-49, Rosenberg to Mitchell, 7/21/43, file 300.36, Dorr to Clay, 12/1/43, and other documents, file 300.53, and "Agreement between the WPB and the WMC . . . ," 9/3/43, and other documents, file 200.02-25, Dorr Collection; Wilson to Patterson and Forrestal, 11/15/43, and numerous other documents and correspondence, file 004.06, USW/OSW; Hancock to Patterson, 8/4/43, War Manpower Commission, Hertz Collection; Anthony to Packard Motor Car Co., 12/4/43, and other documents, Senate Investigation—Manpower, Amberg Collection; Green and Murray to Byrnes et al. w/ enc., 3/23/43, Hancock to Baruch, 2/26/43, and Baruch to Amberg, 1/25/45, Selected Correspondence, Baruch Papers; Minutes of the Advisory Board of the Office of War Mobilization and Reconversion, 2/19–20/45, OWMR; *WPB Minutes,* pp. 270–71; War Manpower Commission, "History of the Bureau of Manpower Utilization in the War Manpower Commission," and Labor Department, "Short History of the War Manpower Commission," 1948, WMC; Army Air Forces, "A History of AAF Activities during World War II in the Field of Industrial Manpower," Wright-Patterson Air Force Base, OH; Russell, "Expansion of Industrial Facilities under AAF"; Arthur Krim and Seymour Peyser, "The Special Project Techniques in the Handling of Critical Plant Area, and Industrial Manpower Problems," U.S. Army Center of Military History, Washington, DC; Bureau of the Budget, *United States at War,* 441–42; Somers, *Presidential Agency,* pp. 154–58; and Flynn, *Mess in Washington,* p. 50.

19. Appley, Executive Director, WMC, "Employment Stabilization Programs," 2/1/43, and "The Program of the War Manpower Commission," 2/8/43, Manpower II, Rosenman Papers; memorandum "Reduction in Production of Non-Ferrous Metals," 2/43, PSF: War Manpower Commission, FDR Papers; WMC, Minutes, 5/6/42, 9/9/42, 10/7/42, 10/28/42, 11/4/42, and MLPC, Summary Minutes, 12/30/42, 2/6/43 (see also corresponding Verbatim Minutes), WMC; Appley to McNutt, WMC Annual Report, 4/20/44, Washington File, 1942–45, Box 35, Sec. 2—Government Agencies: War Manpower Commission, and Lubin to Baruch w/ enc., 9/21/1943, Washington File, 1942–45, Box 40, Sec. 3—Specific Subjects: Manpower—Buffalo Plan, Baruch Papers; Smith to Maloney, 6/5/42, file 049.12/175, and Unsigned Memorandum to Secretary of War, 6/8/43, file 040, USW/OSW; Lund to Nelson, 12/11/42, and other documents, file 300.05a, Dorr Collection; Kiehl, "War Manpower Commission"; Edmond Kanwit, "The Employment Stabilization Plan in the Western Non-Ferrous Metals and Lumbering Industries," 1946, in Kiehl, "War Manpower Commission"; Labor Department, "Short History of WMC"; Purcell, "Labor Policies of WPB," vol. 2; Parks, "Management-Labor Policy Committee"; Bureau of the Budget, *United States at War,* pp. 435–38; Somers, *Presidential Agency,* pp. 143–44; and Flynn, *Mess in Washington,* pp. 111, 119–20, 230. See also chaps. 6 and 13 above.

20. "Report and Recommendations of the Subcommittee of the Senate Military Affairs Committee," ca. 3–9/43, Senator Downey Investigations of West Coast Labor Conditions. See also "West Coast Manpower Program," 8/18/43 (WMC), and "West Coast Manpower Program," 9/4/43 (Byrnes), Master Plan—West Coast Aircraft

Labor Shortage Plan, Dorr Collection; Joel Seidman, *American Labor from Defense to Reconstruction* (Chicago: University of Chicago Press, 1953), p. 161; Koistinen, *Hammer and Sword,* pp. 404–5; and chap. 16 below.

21. Byrnes to McNutt (draft), 8/27/43, and numerous other correspondence and documents, Washington File, 1942–45, Box 40, Sec. 3—Special Subjects: Manpower—West Coast Correspondence, Hancock for Files, 8/11/43, and numerous other correspondence and documents, Washington File, 1942–45, Box 40, Sec. 3—Special Subjects: Manpower, West Coast Reports, Hancock to Baruch, 7/22/43, Washington File, 1942–45, Box 31, Sec. 2—Government Agencies: James F. Byrnes, Hancock to Patterson, 10/29/43, and other correspondence, Washington File, 1942–45, Box 33, Sec. 2—Government Agencies: Robert P. Patterson, Baruch to Wilson, 11/9/43, Washington File, 1942–45, Box 35, Sec. 2—Government Agencies: War Production Board, Patterson Memorandum (on aircraft production), 8/11/43, and other documents, Washington File, 1942–45, Box 36, Sec. 3—Special Subjects: Aviation, and Coblentz to Baruch, 9/9/43, and other correspondence, Selected Correspondence, Baruch Papers; Russell to Knox w/ enc., 8/25/43, War Mobilization Committee Meetings 1943, Box 3, OWMR; Haber to Rosenman, 7/18/44, Manpower I, and Aircraft War Production Council, Inc., "Absenteeism in Aircraft Plants," 3/15/43, Manpower II, Rosenman Papers; MLPC, Summary and Verbatim Minutes, 9/7/43, WMC; *WPB Minutes,* pp. 257–58, 270–71, 275, 281, 293, 324–25; Mitchell to Patterson, 6/26/43, and other correspondence, War Manpower Commission, Amberg Collection; John D. Hertz et al., "Manpower Problems in the West Coast Aircraft Industry," 8/11/43, and other documents, Final Report, Hertz Collection (see also correspondence and documents in the Hertz Collection files Memoranda to Patterson, Hancock, Etc., War Manpower Commission, Manpower Problems, War Manpower Commission—Seattle, and Baruch Report); O'Gara to Dorr, 8/28/43, Aircraft Industry, Problems of, Dorr to McCloy, 8/28/43, Papers Used at Conf. . . . , and Byrnes, "West Coast Manpower Program," 9/4/43, and numerous other documents and correspondence, Master Plan—West Coast Aircraft Shortage Plan, Dorr Collection; AFL, *Annual Proceedings,* 1943, pp. 450, 529–30, 552–53; CIO, *Annual Proceedings,* 1943, pp. 39–41; Mitchell to Somervell, ca. 1942, and other documents and correspondence, Labor–War Department Functions, and Mitchell to Patterson, 2/16/43, and other documents, Labor Supply—Misc. and Misc. Problems, Ohly Papers; Styer to Mitchell, 9/31/43, and Gow and Brennan to Patterson, 11/27/44, file 004.06, USW/OSW; Lovett to Stimson, 10/14/43, and other documents, Manpower, OSW (see also related documents cited in n. 18 above); Purcell, "Labor Policies of WPB," vols. 3–4; Labor Department, "Short History of WMC"; Somers and Ohly, "War Department Organization for Handling Labor Problems"; Army Air Forces, "AAF Activities in Field of Industrial Manpower"; Bureau of the Budget, *United States at War,* pp. 439–44; CPA, *Industrial Mobilization for War,* pp. 707–10, 748–50; Somers, *Presidential Agency,* pp. 144–58; Flynn, *Mess in Washington,* pp. 66–75; Fairchild and Grossman, *Army and Industrial Manpower,* pp. 116–21, 131–54; Blum, *Drafted or Deferred,* pp. 111–23; and Harry B. Yoshpe, *Labor Problems in Quartermaster Procurement, 1939–1944* (Washington, DC: Office of the Quartermaster General, 1945).

22. Baruch and Hancock to Byrnes, 8/19/43, Washington File, 1942–45, Box 40, Sec. 3—Special Subjects: Manpower—West Coast Reports, Baruch Papers. A printed

version of the Baruch-Hancock Report is available in *Cong. Rec.*, 78th Cong., 1st sess., 1943, 89, pt. 6:7589–96.

23. Somers and Ohly, "War Department Organization for Handling Labor Problems," pt. 4, pp. 49–51 (quotation p. 51).

24. MLPC, Summary and Verbatim Minutes, 3/16/45, WMC; Koistinen, *Hammer and Sword,* pp. 524–26; and Flynn, *Mess in Washington,* pp. 121–25.

25. Mitchell to Brown, 5/25/43, and numerous other documents, Labor Supply—Special Projects, Ohly Papers; Patterson, Report to the Secretary of War, 2/1/45–2/14/45, 7/1/45–7/31/45, Under Secretary of War, Office of, Amberg Collection; William McFadden, "The Release of Key Personnel from the Armed Forces during World War II," War Department Monograph No. 13b, U.S. Army Center of Military History, Washington, DC; Fairchild and Grossman, *Army and Industrial Manpower,* pp. 180–89; and Blum, *Drafted or Deferred,* pp. 161–81. See also chap. 6 above.

26. Patterson, Report to the Secretary of War, 1/15/45–1/31/45, 2/15/45–2/28/45, Under Secretary of War, Office of, Amberg Collection; Fairchild and Grossman, *Army and Industrial Manpower,* pp. 177–80, 189–96; and Koistinen, *Hammer and Sword,* pp. 433, 532–33.

27. Krim and Peyser, "The Special Project Techniques"; and Fairchild and Grossman, *Army and Industrial Manpower,* pp. 131–39, 149–54.

28. Conference on Manpower, 1/3/45, and other documents, Labor Branch—IPD (Reports to CG, ASF), Ohly Papers; Gow to Somervell, 1/1/45, and other documents, Reports on ASF Conferences on Manpower, Conference in Somervell's Office, 12/5/44, and other documents, Available Labor Supply—Memos and Figures from IPD-ASF, and Patterson, Reports to Secretary of War, 3/15/45–6/30/45, Under Secretary's Biweekly Reports to Secretary of War, Dorr Collection; Patterson, Reports to Secretary of War, 12/23/44–1/13/45, and other documents, Memos to Judge Patterson, USW, and WMC and Labor Department, "Manpower Outlook First Half of 1945," 1/29/45, and numerous other correspondence and documents, file 004.06, USW/OSW; O'Donnell to McGrady et al., 12/4/44, Labor Relations—General, McGrady Collection; and Koistinen, *Hammer and Sword,* pp. 432–33.

29. Bureau of the Budget, *United States at War,* pp. 173–75, 431–36, 445; Flynn, *Mess in Washington,* pp. 166–67, 172; and Hugh Rockoff, "The United States: From Ploughshare to Swords," in *The Economics of World War II: Six Great Powers in International Comparison,* ed. Mark Harrison (Cambridge: Cambridge University Press, 1998), pp. 98–104. I have adjusted Rockoff's statistics in a few instances.

30. I cited a number of titles on women and the war in Paul A. C. Koistinen, "Warfare and Power Relations in America: Mobilizing the World War II Economy," in *The Home Front and War in the Twentieth Century,* ed. James Titus (Colorado Springs, CO: United States Army Air Force Academy, 1984), p. 235 n. 5. See also William H. Chafe, *The American Woman: Her Changing Social, Economic, and Political Roles, 1920–1970* (New York: Oxford University Press, 1972), revised as William H. Chafe, *The Paradox of Change: American Women in the 20th Century* (New York: Oxford University Press, 1991); William H. Chafe, *Women and Equality: Changing Patterns in American Culture* (New York: Oxford University Press, 1977); Karen T. Anderson, *Wartime Women: Sex Roles, Family Relations, and the Status of Women during World War II* (Westport, CT: Greenwood, 1981); Susan M. Hartmann, *The Home Front and Beyond: American Women in the 1940s* (Boston: Twayne, 1982); D'Ann Campbell, *Women at War with*

America: Private Lives in a Patriotic Era (Cambridge, MA: Harvard University Press, 1984); various chapters and segments in Mark J. Harris, Franklin D. Mitchell, and Steven J. Schechter, *The Homefront: America during World War II* (New York: G. P. Putnam's Sons, 1984); Maureen Honey, *Creating Rosie the Riveter: Class, Gender, and Propaganda during World War II* (Amherst: University of Massachusetts Press, 1984); Maureen Honey, ed., *Bitter Fruit: African American Women in World War II* (Columbia: University of Missouri Press, 1999); John Constello, *Virtue under Fire: How World War II Changed Our Social and Sexual Attitudes* (Boston: Little, Brown, 1985); Sherna B. Gluck, *Rosie the Riveter Revisited: Women, the War, and Social Change* (Boston: Twayne, 1987); Ruth Milkman, *Gender at Work: The Dynamics of Job Segregation by Sex during World War II* (Urbana: University of Illinois Press, 1987); Claudia Goldin, *Understanding the Gender Gap: An Economic History of American Women* (New York: Oxford University Press, 1990); various essays in Kenneth P. O'Brien and Lynn H. Parsons, eds., *The Home-Front War: World War II and American Society* (Westport, CT: Greenwood, 1995); Judy B. Litoff and David C. Smith, *American Women in a World at War: Contemporary Accounts from World War II* (Wilmington, DE: Scholarly Resources, 1997); and Amy Bentley, *Eating for Victory: Food Rationing and the Politics of Domesticity* (Urbana: University of Illinois Press, 1998).

31. Koistinen, *Hammer and Sword,* pp. 490–503; Fairchild and Grossman, *Army and Industrial Manpower,* pp. 156–68; Ulysses Lee, *The Employment of Negro Troops* (Washington, DC: Office of the Chief of Military History, 1966); Richard Polenberg, *War and Society: The United States, 1941–1945* (Philadelphia: J. B. Lippincott, 1972), chap. 4; Flynn, *Mess in Washington,* chap. 7; John M. Blum, *V Was for Victory: Politics and American Culture during World War II* (New York: Harcourt Brace Jovanovich, 1976), chap. 6; Harold G. Vatter, *The U.S. Economy in World War II* (New York: Columbia University Press, 1985), pp. 127–35; Ross Gregory, *America 1941: A Nation at the Crossroads* (New York: Free Press, 1989), chap. 8; Neil A. Wynn, *The Afro-American and the Second World War,* rev. ed. (New York: Holmes and Meier, 1993); and Daniel Kryder, *Divided Arsenal: Race and the American State during World War II* (New York: Cambridge University Press, 2000).

32. Paul A. C. Koistinen, *Mobilizing for Modern War: The Political Economy of American Warfare, 1865–1919* (Lawrence: University Press of Kansas, 1997), pp. 108–13 and n. 7; and J. Garry Clifford and Samuel R. Spencer, Jr., *The First Peacetime Draft* (Lawrence: University Press of Kansas, 1986).

33. Gerald T. Dunne, *Grenville Clark: Public Citizen* (New York: Farrar, Straus, Giroux, 1986) is a workaday account. Much richer is Norman Cousins and J. Garry Clifford, eds., *Memoirs of a Man: Grenville Clark* (New York: W. W. Norton, 1975).

34. The first full analysis of national service is Fairchild and Grossman, *Army and Industrial Manpower,* chap. 11. Others followed: Koistinen, *Hammer and Sword,* chap. 6; George T. Mazuzan, "The National War Service Controversy, 1942–1945," *Mid-America* 57 (October 1975): 246–58; and Flynn, *Mess in Washington,* chap. 4. See also Richard Danzig and Peter Szanton, *National Service: What Would It Mean* (Lexington, MA: D. C. Heath, 1986); Charles C. Moskos, *A Call to Civic Service: National Service for Country and Community* (New York: Free Press, 1988); and Eric B. Gorham, *National Service, Citizenship, and Political Education* (Albany: State University of New York Press, 1992).

35. Distribution of Membership as of April 15, 1944, Box 11, Correspondence,

4/25/44 Executive Board Meeting, and National Council Membership (Men and Women), 7/11/44, Box 11, Correspondence—NWSA—Org—National Council Lists, Clark Papers. In the final report, cited in n. 39 below, National Council numbers are given as 1,050.

36. Degge to Clark w/ enc. (financial statement for the period 12/22/42–12/31/44), 1/4/45, Box 12, Correspondence: NWSA—Finances—George Degg Statement, Clark Papers. The final report sets total revenue for around January 1943–June 1945 at $43,000.

37. Wadsworth to Clark, 3/26/42, Box 10, Correspondence: Wadsworth, James W., Clark Papers. Correspondence among Clark, Wadsworth, Stimson, Patterson, and others is also in the Wadsworth Papers. Included in Box 21 as National Service Series 3C, these papers include ten chronological folders on the Austin-Wadsworth Bill. See also Martin L. Fausold, *James W. Wadsworth, Jr.: The Gentleman from New York* (Syracuse, NY: Syracuse University Press, 1975).

38. "Coddling" appears in Stimson to Roosevelt, 12/30/43, and is included in Stimson Diary, 12/30/43.

39. Grenville Clark and Arthur L. Williston, *The Effort for a National Service Law in World War II, 1942–1945: Report to the National Council of the Citizens Committee for a National War Service Act* (privately printed, 1947), pp. 18, 24, 44, Box 15, Correspondence: Citizens Committee for a NWSA, Clark Papers. The tone of the report may reflect more Arthur Williston, the Citizens Committee secretary, than Clark. The writing of the report is documented in Box 12, Correspondence: National War Service Act, Williston, Arthur L., 1945–49, Clark Papers. Williston's zeal had created problems for Clark and the Citizens Committee in 1944, as explained in Koistinen, *Hammer and Sword*, pp. 488–89.

40. PEC, Minutes, Meeting 40, 8/11/43, file 041.05, WPB.

41. DuPont to Dall, 6/5, 8/44, Box 3, Correspondence: DuPont, Irenee, Duryee to Clark, 2/3/44, Box 3, Correspondence: Duryee, Samuel S., and Eliot to Clark, 2/9/43, Box 4, Correspondence: Eliot, George Fielding, Clark Papers. These three individuals are not representative. The Clark Papers are rich and voluminous. Those on national service are roughly organized as follows: boxes 1–2 contain specialized correspondence of those closely associated with the effort to enact national service legislation; boxes 3–10 contain general correspondence; and boxes 11–16 contain records of the Citizens Committee.

42. See the discussion of the size of the armed services in the text above and nn. 8 and 10 above. See also Dorr to Clark, 3/23/44, 5/15/44, and Clark to Dorr, 5/25/44, Box 3, Correspondence: Dorr, G. H., Clark Papers; and Koistinen, *Hammer and Sword*, pp. 417–18, 487–89.

43. Stimson Diary, 1/15/45.

44. Sanders to Clark (w/ Petersen's handwritten comments on the back), 4/11/42, and other correspondence, Box 8, Correspondence: Sanders, Lewis, and Clark to Nelson w/ enc., 1/27/42, and other documents, Box 6, Correspondence: Nelson, Donald M., Clark Papers; Clark to Nelson, 1/27/42, and Clark, "Memorandum as to the Mobilization of the Manpower of the United States for the Prosecution of the War," 2/11/42, Manpower, Patterson to Stimson, 3/28/42, Under Secretary of War, and Clark to McNutt, 4/20/42, National Service—Official File, OSW; and Flynn, *Lewis B. Hershey*, pp. 84–87.

45. Clark to Roosevelt, 3/21/42, and Roosevelt to Clark, 3/31/42, and other documents and correspondence, Manpower, OSW; "Preliminary Report of the Committee of the War Manpower Commission to the Chairman of a Proposed National War Service Act," ca. 7/42, and other documents, National Service, and Haber, Gavitt, and Tate to McNutt, 8/4/42, and other documents, National Service—Misc., Dorr Collection; and Stimson Diary, 7/10/42.

46. WMC records on national service are extensive. See specifically, WMC, Minutes, and MLPC, Verbatim and Summary Minutes; "Progress Report of the Management-Labor Sub-Committee on National War Service Legislation," 9/4/42, Box 5-124, National Service Legislation—Complete Folder, and MLPC, "National Service Legislation (Voluntarism versus Compulsion)," ca. 3/45, Box 20-216, National Service Legislation; "Interim Report of the Chairman of the War Manpower Commission, Submitted by the Management-Labor Policy Committee," 10/31/42, Box 5-122, Interim Report to WMC from MLPC, 10/31/42, and "Preliminary Report on Part II of Study of National Service Legislation," 9/28/43, Box 20-207, file 5-1. See also the following WMC files: Box 20-207, National War Service Legislation, and file 5-1, Manpower Legislation, D. National Service Thru—1942; Box 5-125, Views on Planning, 5/6/44, and Views on Cutbacks Etc., 5/1/44; Box 5-128, McNutt to OWMR Director Vinson re: V-E Day and the WMC Program; Box 2-56, Work or Fight Legislation; Box 6-152, National War Service Legislation; Box 6-146, National Service; Box 5-113, National War Service Legislation; Box 20-401, Tolan Committee on Migration; Box 7-376 (Information Service), National Service Legislation; and Box 20-216, National Service Legislation—Luce. WPB records on national service are limited but useful: files 833.01, Selective Service Act; 240.2, Labor Administration, 1943; and 240.4, Labor Laws. See also "Recommendations of the Management-Labor Policy Committee in the War Manpower Commission and Declaration by the Representatives of Labor, Agriculture and Management," 11/6/43, National Service—Correspondence, January '43–January '44, Dorr Collection.

47. Nearly every important figure dealing with a labor draft was in contact with the White House. See the files OF 1413-F: National Service Legislation, 1939–1945 (the principal file), OF 1413–1945, OF 4905: War Manpower Commission, PSF: National War Service Law, PSF: Navy, OF 25, OF 407-B, OF 4675, President's Personal File (PPF): 88, 482, and 1958, and Master Speech File 1509: National Service Legislation, FDR Papers. The Rosenman Papers are also rich on White House activity, particularly the files National Service, National Service—Background, State of Union, Manpower I, and Manpower II. See also in the OSW files National Service—Official File, National Service—Safe File, White House Correspondence, Manpower, and Stimson: National Service Testimony, 1/1944; as well as Stimson Diary, 1942–1945; Selected Correspondence, various authors, 1942–1945, and Washington File, 1942–45, Box 41, Sec. 3—Special Subjects: National Service, Baruch Papers; and Conference with the President, 1/7/44, White House Memoranda, 1/9/44, and Daily Record, 1/8–9/44, Smith Papers. The WMC collection and the Clark and Wadsworth Papers are also valuable.

48. Digest of National Service Bills Introduced in Congress during 1942, ca. 11/42, Box 5-113, National War Service Legislation, WMC.

49. The drafting and revising of the Austin-Wadsworth Bill can be traced in the following files of the Clark Papers: Box 3, Correspondence: Dorr, G. H., Box 6, McNutt, Paul V., Box 7, Correspondence: Petersen, Howard C.—1942, Box 8, Correspon-

dence: Sanders, Lewis, Box 9, Correspondence: Sullivan, Francis M., Boxes 9 and 10, Correspondence: Wadsworth, James W., Box 1, Correspondence: Arant, Douglas—1942, 1943, 1944, and 1945, Correspondence: Austin, Warren R., and Correspondence: Bell, Ernest L. Jr., Box 13, Correspondence: National War Service Act—Legislation—the Universal War Service Bill, First Draft (five folders), Box 14, Correspondence: National War Service Act—Legislation, Second Draft (seven folders), Correspondence: National War Service Act—Legislation, Third Draft (eleven folders), and Correspondence: National War Service Act—Legislation, 1/7/43 Revision, 1/12/43 Revision, 2/3/43 Revision, 4/14/44 Revision, and 5/1/44 Revision. A copy of the Austin-Wadsworth Bill as introduced in February 1943 is available in Box 14, Correspondence: National War Service Act—Legislation—Final Draft 2/3/43; a copy of the revised bill introduced in January 1944 and changed in minor ways thereafter is available in Box 14, Correspondence: National War Service Act—Legislation—4/14/44 Draft of Bill (E. L. Bell, Jr.). See also Box 21, Austin-Wadsworth Bill, 4-4-42–3-4/45 (nine folders), Wadsworth Papers.

50. Rosenman's informal group was the same one advising the president on the size of the armed services. See the analysis earlier in the text and n. 8 above, documenting it.

51. U.S. Congress, Senate, Committee on Military Affairs, *Hearings on Manpower (National War Service Bill),* 78th Cong., 1st sess., 1943; and U.S. Congress, House, Committee on Military Affairs, *Hearings on Full Utilization of Manpower,* 78th Cong., 1st sess., 1943. For the Tolan-Kilgore-Pepper Bill, see S. Doc. 607, 78th Cong., lst sess., 2/1/43.

52. Walter Galenson, "Wartime Manpower Practices in Great Britain and Germany," 12/42, Labor Supply—General #1, Ohly to Bishop w/ encs., 1/27/44, and other documents, National Service—#1, Ohly for Files, 2/12/43, Absenteeism, Ohly for Files, 4/9/42, and other documents, Legislation—Dead Bills—(Senate and House of Reps), Ohly Memorandum, 5/18/42, 77th Cong., Mitchell to Brown, 5/25/43, and other documents, Labor Supply—Special Projects, O'Gara Memorandum, 3/15/43, and other documents, Austin-Wadsworth Bill, Barron for Files, 10/5/43, and other correspondence, Labor—Legislation, and "Material Worked Up for National Service," unsigned and undated, National Service—#2, Ohly Collection; Dorr to Stimson, 9/13/43, file 032.1, USW/OSW; memorandum "National Service Legislation in Great Britain, Canada, Australia and New Zealand," 1/18/44, National Service—Misc., and Lester Memorandum, 7/2/43, and other documents, National Service Correspondence—Jan. 43 to Jan. 44, Dorr Collection. See also the ASF files National Service Act, National Service Act, Working File #1, National Service, Working Files—Current Projects, National Service, The Case for National Service—General, National Service, The Case for National Service and Manpower Problems (as a Means of Preventing Draft of Civilian Work) 2, National Service, The Case for National Service and Manpower Problems (Specific Instances of the Effects of Manpower Shortages on Production), National Service, National Service and Manpower Problems—1, General Manpower Picture, National Service, The Case for National Service—National Service and Manpower Problems (Turnover)—2, National Service, The Case for National Service—National Service and Strikes—2, National Service, Statements on National Service—American Legion (Radio Forum), National Service, Statements on National Service—Grenville Clark and Citizens' Committee, National Service, Argument against National Service—General—4, National Service, Views of Various Groups—Other Government Agencies—6, National

Service, View of Various Groups—Labor, National Service, National Service Bill—S. 666—(Commentaries and Critiques), and Prevention of Profiteering—"Conscription of Industry"—Source Material, Boxes 713–14, ASF.

53. Stimson Diary, 12/30/43 (w/ enc. [Stimson to President, 12/30/43]). See also Clark to Stimson, 12/8, 9/43, National Service—Official File, and Stimson et al. to President, 12/28/43, White House Correspondence, OSW; and Stimson Diary, 12/23/43, 12/25/43, 12/27/43, 12/28/43, 12/29/43.

54. Koistinen, *Hammer and Sword,* pp. 475–78. See also National Service—Background State of Union, Rosenman Papers; Rosenman, *Working with Roosevelt,* pp. 421–25; and James F. Byrnes, *All in One Lifetime* (New York: Harper and Bros., 1958), pp. 198–207.

55. U.S. Congress, Senate, Committee on Military Affairs, *Hearings on S. 666,* 78th Cong., 2d sess., 1944.

56. "Recommendations of the Management-Labor Policy Committee in the War Manpower Commission and Declaration by the Representatives of Labor, Agriculture and Management," 11/6/43, National Service—Correspondence, Jan. 43–Jan. 44, Dorr Collection. See also MLPC, "National Service Legislation (Voluntarism versus Compulsion)," ca. 3/45, Box 20-216, National Service Legislation, and other files, WMC.

57. "Meeting on National Service Legislation," 4/20/44, Office of the Secretary of the Navy, 42-3-42, Secretary of Navy Frank Knox, Correspondence Files, 1940–44, General Records of the Department of the Navy, RG 80, National Archives, College Park, MD.

58. American Federation of Labor, *Weekly News Service,* 3/28/44. See also AFL, *Annual Proceedings,* 1940–1945; CIO, *Annual Proceedings,* 1940–1946; American Federation of Labor, Executive Council Minutes of Meetings, 1940–1945, George Meany Memorial Archives, Silver Spring, MD; and Congress of Industrial Organizations, Minutes of the Meetings of the International Executive Board, 1940–1945, Headquarters, International Union of Electrical, Radio and Machine Workers, Washington, DC. In *Hammer and Sword,* I provide full citations on the labor federations' meetings.

59. Truman Committee, *Third Annual Report,* 78th Cong., 2d sess., 1944, Senate Report No. 10, pt. 16, pp. 3–5, 28–32.

60. Stimson Diary, 5/17/44. See also Stimson Diary, 5/24/44; Clark to Stimson, 5/19/44, Stimson to Clark, 5/24/44, Clark to Stimson, 5/26/44, and Clark to Forrestal, 5/10/44, National Service—Official File, OSW.

61. Brennan to Gow, 1/20/45, Manpower—Justice Byrnes Work or Fight Directive, Dorr Collection; Brennan to Gow, 3/22/45, file 004.06, USW/OSW; Dorr to Stimson, 2/18/45, National Service—Official File, OSW; Koistinen, "Mobilizing the World War II Economy," pp. 459–60; Koistinen, *Hammer and Sword,* pp. 521–23; Fairchild and Grossman, *Army and Industrial Manpower,* pp. 200–3; Blum, *Drafted or Deferred,* pp. 192–96; and Somers, *Presidential Agency,* pp. 167–69.

62. Stimson and Forrestal to President, 1/3/43, Patterson to President, 1/5/45, and other documents, file 032.1, USW/OSW; Marshall and King to President, 1/16/45, and President to May, 1/17/45, and other correspondence and documents, National Service—Official File, OSW; Stimson Diary, 12/22/44, 12/24/44, 1/2/45, 1/11/45, 1/12/45, 1/13/45; and *New York Times,* 1/7/45.

63. Maneuvering in and out of Congress over national service between January and April 1945 became exceptionally heated, complex, and confused. Relating all the details at this point would be time-consuming and tedious. The most complete coverage of what took place is presented in Koistinen, *Hammer and Sword*, pp. 528–41; Flynn, *Mess in Washington*, pp. 88–102; and Herman M. Somers, "Coordinating the Federal Executive" (Ph.D. diss., Harvard University, 1947), pp. 367–76.

64. Koistinen, *Hammer and Sword*, pp. 519–21; and Blum, *Drafted or Deferred*, pp. 189–91.

65. U.S. Congress, House, Committee on Military Affairs, *Hearings on Mobilization of Civilian Manpower*, 79th Cong., 1st sess., 1945; and U.S. Congress, Senate, Committee on Military Affairs, *Hearings on Mobilization of Civilian Manpower*, 79th Cong., 1st sess., 1945.

66. MLPC, "National Service Legislation (Voluntarism versus Compulsion)," ca. 3/45, Box 20-216, National Service Legislation, WMC; Minutes of the Advisory Board of the Office of War Mobilization and Reconversion, 1/9–10/45, 1/22–23/45, 2/5–6/45, 2/19–20/45, OWMR; and Koistinen, *Hammer and Sword*, pp. 532–33.

67. MLPC, "National Service Legislation (Voluntarism versus Compulsion)," ca. 3/45, Box 20-216, National Service Legislation, WMC; and Koistinen, *Hammer and Sword*, pp. 536–37.

68. Clark and Williston, *Effort for a National Service Law in World War II*, pp. 57–71. A latter-day version of the Clark-Williston judgment is reached in Keith E. Eiler, *Mobilizing America: Robert P. Patterson and the War Effort, 1940–1945* (Ithaca, NY: Cornell University Press, 1997), pp. 466–71.

CHAPTER FIFTEEN. ORGANIZED LABOR IN A MOBILIZED ECONOMY, 1940–1945: LABOR RELATIONS

1. For a fuller account of and documentation regarding labor relations during World War II, see Paul A. C. Koistinen, *The Hammer and the Sword: Labor, the Military, and Industrial Mobilization, 1920–1945* (New York: Arno, 1979). See also Fred Witney, *Wartime Experiences of the National Labor Relations Board* (Urbana: University of Illinois Press, 1949); James A. Gross, *The Making of the National Labor Relations Board: A Study in Economics, Politics, and the Law*, vol. 1, *1933–1937* (Albany: State University of New York Press, 1974); and James H. Gross, *The Reshaping of the National Labor Relations Board: National Labor Policy in Transition*, vol. 2, *1937–1947* (Albany: State University of New York Press, 1981); Melvyn Dubofsky and Warren Van Tine, *John L. Lewis: A Biography* (New York: Quadrangle, 1977); Melvyn Dubofsky, ed., *Technological Change and Workers' Movements* (Beverly Hills, CA: Sage, 1985); Melvyn Dubofsky and Warren Van Tine, eds., *Labor Leaders in America* (Urbana: University of Illinois Press, 1987); Melvyn Dubofsky, *The State and Labor in Modern America* (Chapel Hill: University of North Carolina Press, 1994); Melvyn Dubofsky, *Hard Work: Making of Labor History* (Urbana: University of Illinois Press, 2000); David Brody, *Workers in Industrial America: Essays on the Twentieth Century Struggle* (New York: Oxford University Press, 1980); John H. Harris, *The Right to Manage: Industrial Relations Policies of American Business in the 1940s* (Madison: University of Wisconsin Press, 1982); Maurice Isserman, *Which Side Were You On? The*

American Communist Party during the Second World War (Middletown, CT: Wesleyan University Press, 1982); Maurice Isserman, *If I Had a Hammer. . . : The Death of the Old Left and the Birth of the New Left* (New York: Basic, 1987); Nelson Lichtenstein, *Labor's War at Home: The CIO in World War II* (New York: Cambridge University Press, 1982); Nelson Lichtenstein, *The Most Dangerous Man in Detroit: Walter Reuther and the Fate of American Labor* (New York: Basic, 1995); John Bernard, *Walter Reuther and the Rise of the Auto Workers* (Boston: Little, Brown, 1983); Francis X. Gannon, *Joseph D. Keenan, Labor's Ambassador in War and Peace: A Portrait of a Man and His Times* (Lanham, MD: University Press of America, 1984); Timothy A. Willard, "Labor and the National War Labor Board, 1942–1945: An Experiment in Corporatist Wage Stabilization" (Ph.D. diss., University of Toledo, 1984); Robert H. Zieger, *American Workers, American Unions, 1920–1985* (Baltimore: Johns Hopkins University Press, 1986); Robert H. Zieger, *John L. Lewis: Labor Leader* (Boston: Twayne, 1988); Robert H. Zieger, *The CIO, 1935–1955* (Chapel Hill: University of North Carolina Press, 1995); Paul F. Clark, Peter Gottlieb, and Donald Kennedy, eds., *Forging a Union of Steel: Philip Murray, SWOC, and the United Steelworkers* (Ithaca, NY: ILR Press, 1987); Michael Goldfield, *The Decline of Organized Labor in the United States* (Chicago: University of Chicago Press, 1987); Stanley Vittoz, *New Deal Labor Policy and the American Industrial Economy* (Chapel Hill: University of North Carolina Press, 1987); Bruce Nelson, *Workers on the Waterfront: Seamen, Longshoremen, and Unionism in the 1930s* (Urbana: University of Illinois Press, 1988); J. Carroll Moody and Alice Kessler-Harris, *Perspectives on American Labor History: The Problems of Synthesis* (DeKalb: Northern Illinois University Press, 1989); Steven Fraser, *Labor Will Rule: Sidney Hillman and the Rise of American Labor* (New York: Free Press, 1991); Stephen Amberg, *The Union Inspiration in American Politics: The Autoworkers and the Making of a Liberal Industrial Order* (Philadelphia: Temple University Press, 1994); Colin Gordon, *New Deals: Business, Labor, and Politics in America, 1920–1935* (New York: Cambridge University Press, 1994); Kevin Boyle, *The UAW and the Heyday of American Liberalism, 1945–1968* (Ithaca, NY: Cornell University Press, 1995); Jeffrey Haydu, *Making American Industry Safe for Democracy: Comparative Perspectives on the State and Employee Representation in the Era of World War II* (Champaign: University of Illinois Press, 1997); James B. Atleson, *Labor and the Wartime State: Labor Relations and the Law during World War II* (Urbana: University of Illinois Press, 1998); and David B. Robertson, *Capital, Labor and the State: The Battle for American Labor Markets from the Civil War to the New Deal* (Lanham, MD: Rowman and Littlefield, 2000).

2. Aaron Levenstein, *Labor, Today and Tomorrow* (New York: Alfred A. Knopf, 1945), p. 157.

3. AFL, *Annual Proceedings,* 1942, pp. 52–61, 182–84; American Federation of Labor, Executive Council Minutes of Meetings, 1/12–17/42, 5/13–22/42, 1/18–27/43, 5/17–27/43, 8/9–16/43, 1/17–27/44, 5/1–9/44, 8/21–29/44, 2/5–15/45, 1/21–31/46, George Meany Memorial Archives, Silver Spring, MD; relevant correspondence in World War II Labor Policy 1941–1942, Special Executive Council Meeting, Roosevelt to Green and Murray, 1/22/42, and other correspondence and documents, Correspondence—World War II Policy, 1941, Green to Duffy, 1/31/42, and numerous other correspondence and documents, Correspondence—

World War II Policy—Labor's Victory Board, 1942, and documents in Convention File 1940 to 1943, Green Papers; and Congress of Industrial Organizations, Minutes of the Meetings of the International Executive Board, 1/24–26/42, 6/3–5/42, 2/5–7/43, Headquarters, International Union of Electrical, Radio and Machine Workers, Washington, DC; Ohly for Files, 12/11/41, Labor Laws, Ohly Papers; Roosevelt to Gentlemen of the Conference, 12/23/41, in John H. Ohly, "History of Plant Seizures during World War II," 3 vols., 1946, app. L-3, U.S. Army Center of Military History, Washington, DC (for a published, edited version, see John H. Ohly, *Industrialists in Olive Drab: The Emergency Operation of Private Industries during World War II,* ed. Clayton D. Lurie [Washington, DC: U.S. Army Center of Military History, 1999]); and Koistinen, *Hammer and Sword,* pp. 148–58.

4. Koistinen, *Hammer and Sword,* pp. 88–93, 128–96, 351–58, 554–620, 672–87; Fraser, *Labor Will Rule,* chap. 16; and Memoranda (on Brooks addresses to the PARB, WPB), 6/15/45, 6/22/45, 4–6/1945, Box 2, Fesler Papers.

5. Roosevelt quoted in Richard J. Purcell, *Labor Policies of the National Defense Advisory Commission and the Office of Production Management, May 1940 to April 1942* (Washington, DC: Civilian Production Administration, 1946), p. 1.

6. Pressman quoted in Dubofsky and Van Tine, *John L. Lewis,* p. 349.

7. Eaton to Knudsen, 12/20/40, and other documents, Labor—1941–42 (1) and (2), and Pettit to Lewis, 12/17/40, Policies, Labor, Amberg Collection; Patterson to Hillman, 9/27/40, and other documents, Labor—Award of Contracts—Policy and General, "Conversations with Julius Amberg," 4/19/45, Misc., and President to Patterson, 11/14/40, Labor—Labor Factors in Award of Contracts—Particular Contracts, Ohly Papers; Ohly Interview with Blackwell Smith, 12/23/40, and other documents, Labor, Petersen Collection; Ohly to McGrady, 2/22/41, file 230.1404, and Procurement Circular No. 43 and other documents, file 160, USW/OSW; *Verbatim Record of Proceedings of the House Committee Investigating Labor Boards and Wagner Act,* vol. 4, no. 9, 10/8/40 (copy in Ohly Papers); Coy for Files, 7/17/41, and other correspondence, Alphabetical File, Box 13, Roosevelt, Franklin D.—1941, Coy Papers; and Byron Fairchild and Jonathan Grossman, *The Army and Industrial Manpower* (Washington, DC: Office of the Chief of Military History, 1959), pp. 35–45.

8. Civilian Production Administration, *Industrial Mobilization for War: History of the War Production Administration and Predecessor Agencies, 1940–1945* (Washington, DC: Civilian Production Administration, 1947), pp. 83–84; Purcell, *Labor Policies of the NDAC and OPM,* pp. 168–89; and Joel Seidman, *American Labor from Defense to Reconversion* (Chicago: University of Chicago Press, 1953), pp. 41–73.

9. Koistinen, *Hammer and Sword,* pp. 99–106.

10. Stimson to Hillman, undated, and other correspondence, Labor—Strike Statistics—General, Ohly Papers; Amberg to Patterson, 6/5/41, and other documents, Misc. and Subject—Strikes, USW/OSW; Ohly to Bundy, 7/17/41, and numerous other documents, Labor 1941–41 (2), Amberg Collection; Stimson Diary, 11/11–12/40, 3/7/41, 3/14/41, 8/19/41; Henry L. Stimson and McGeorge Bundy, *On Active Service in Peace and War* (New York: Harper and Bros., 1947), p. 381; AFL, *Annual Proceedings,* 1940, p. 528; Herman M. Somers and John H. Ohly, "War Department Organization for the Handling of Labor Problems in World War II," War Department Monograph No. 2, 1945, U.S. Army Center of Military History, Wash-

ington, DC; Purcell, *Labor Policies of NDAC and OPM,* pp. 177–80; and Seidman, *American Labor from Defense to Reconstruction,* 44–45.

11. Stimson Diary, 11/26/40, 5/1/41, 5/23/41, 5/26/41, 5/27/41, 5/28/41, 6/11–13/41; Stimson and Knox to President, 5/29/41, and other correspondence in Ohly, "History of Plant Seizures," apps. G-1–G-8, and pp. 11–12; Stimson Memorandum, 6/12/41, and other correspondence, Labor, Strikes, Etc., OSW; Battley to Hines, 9/9/41, file 049.12/175, Patterson to Miles, 5/15/41, Strikes—Confidential, Misc. and Subject, and Patterson to Amberg, 6/9/41, and other correspondence, Misc. and Subject, Strikes, USW/OSW; Perkins to Stimson w/ enc. 6/12/41, Memorandum to Perkins, Amberg Collection; and Koistinen, *Hammer and Sword,* pp. 108–10.

12. Koistinen, *Hammer and Sword,* pp. 111–13.

13. For the North American seizure, see "Military Activity Log, Inglewood Seizure," and other documents, in Ohly, "History of Plant Seizures," apps. H-1–H-4, H-11, and pp. 14–34; Perkins to President, 6/6/41, and other correspondence, Labor, Strikes, Etc., OSW; Hershey to All State Selective Service Directors, 6/13/41, Strikes—Confidential, Misc. and Subject, USW/OSW; Stimson Diary, 6/6–13/41; CIO, *Annual Proceedings,* 1941, pp. 108–10; and Seidman, *American Labor from Defense to Reconstruction,* pp. 48–49.

14. Stimson Diary, 6/6/41.

15. For the coal strikes, see Stimson Diary, 11/7/41, 11/11/41, 11/13/41, 11/14/41; Amberg to Patterson, 11/7/41, and other correspondence, file 463.3, USW/OSW; unsigned memorandum "The Coal Strike," 11/12/41, and other documents, Captive Coal Mines, Amberg Collection; Ohly, "History of Plant Seizures," apps. K-1–K-9, and pp. 75–78; CIO, *Annual Proceedings,* 1941, pp. 9–13, 16–17; Walter Galenson, *The CIO Challenge to the AFL: A History of the American Labor Movement, 1935–1941* (Cambridge, MA: Harvard University Press, 1960), pp. 225–33; Seidman, *American Labor from Defense to Reconstruction,* pp. 64–67; Dubofsky and Van Tine, *John L. Lewis,* pp. 395–404; and Koistinen, *Hammer and Sword,* pp. 116–22.

16. Stimson Diary, 11/13/41.

17. McGrady to Patterson, 11/14/41, in Ohly, "History of Plant Seizures," app. K-4.

18. Stimson Diary, 11/14/41.

19. Elting E. Morison, *Turmoil and Tradition: A Study of the Life and Times of Henry L. Stimson* (Boston: Houghton Mifflin, 1960), p. 515.

20. WDLB is a composite. Labor offices changed quite often.

21. Author's interview with John H. Ohly, 8/1/62.

22. Wesson to Patterson, 10/25/41, file 230.1405, USW/OSW; and Saltonstall to Ohly, 1/30/42, and other documents, Labor—GOPO's—Background and Development of Labor Policy, Ohly Papers.

23. McGrady to Patterson, 10/27/41, and other documents, Labor—GOPO's—Background and Development of Labor Policy, Ohly for Files, 7/14/42, and other documents, Labor—GOPO's—Interpretation and Application of Labor Policy, and Wesson to Patterson, 2/21/42, and other documents, Leg.—Dead Bills (HofR), Ohly Papers; Wesson to Patterson, 11/22/41, and other documents, Labor, Petersen Collection; Patterson to Wesson, 2/28/42, and other documents, file 049.12/175, USW/OSW; and Pressman to McGrady, 5/29/42, and other documents, Plant Protection and Subversive Activity, McGrady Collection.

24. Battley to McGrady, 8/11/41, and other documents, Longshore up to March, 1943, Labor Relations Branch, ASF; and Ohly for Files, 2/18/42, and other documents, Longshore Work on the Eastern and Gulf Coasts, and Bishop for Files, 7/16/42, and other documents, Labor—Unions—Longshoremen, AFL-CIO, Ohly Papers.

25. Ohly for Files, 8/27/42, and other documents, Labor-Maritime Labor Problems (including ATS), Ohly Papers; and Brown to Bishop, 10/29/42, and other documents, Longshore Up to March, 1943, Labor Relations Branch, ASF.

26. Brown Reports, pts. 1 and 2, Pacific and East Coast Longshore Reports (Brown), Labor Relations Branch, ASF: and author's interview with Brown, 6/42. See also numerous reports and correspondence among Brown, his staff, and the army, Douglass V. Brown Papers (in Brown's possession).

27. Volandt Memorandum, 12/8/41, unlabeled folder, Ohly Papers.

28. Koistinen, *Hammer and Sword,* pp. 108–10, 214–25.

29. Ibid., 164–96.

30. Ibid., pp. 99–124, 249–51, 285–332.

31. Stimson Diary, 6/16–17/43; Stimson and Knox to Smith, 6/17/43, file 004.07, USW/OSW; and Ohly, "History of Plant Seizures," pp. 137–43.

32. Seidman, *American Labor from Defense to Reconversion,* pp. 189–90; and Coy to President, 6/19/43, and other correspondence, Alphabetical File, Box 13, Roosevelt, Franklin D.—1943, Coy Papers.

33. Congress of Industrial Organizations, Minutes of the Meetings of the International Executive Board, 7/13–14/45, Headquarters, International Union of Electrical, Radio and Machine Workers, Washington, DC.

34. John T. Dunlop, "The Decontrol of Wages and Prices," in *Labor in Postwar America,* ed. Colston E. Warne et al. (Brooklyn, NY: Ramsen, 1949), pp. 4–5.

35. Lenore A. Epstein and Eleanor M. Snyder, "Urban Price Trends," in *Labor in Postwar America,* ed. Warne, p. 143; and Lenore A. Epstein and Eleanor M. Snyder, "Changes in the Cost of Living during 1943," *Yearbook of American Labor,* ed. Colston E. Warne et al. (New York: Philosophical Library, 1945), pp. 51–68.

36. Richard J. Purcell, "Labor Policies of the War Production Board, April 1942 to November 1945," Special Study No. 32, 1946, vol. 5, Policy Documentation File, WPB. Labor stressed effective price controls: see Executive Offices—Labor Office, Labor Policy Committee Records, Correspondence, Minutes of Meetings, Records of the Office of Price Administration, RG 188, National Archives, College Park, MD.

37. Koistinen, *Hammer and Sword,* 747–73; and Murray to Nelson and Byrnes, 3/7/44, unlabeled folder, Box 3, Murray Papers.

38. Koistinen, *Hammer and the Sword,* pp. 599–618, 672–87; Edythe W. First, *Industry and Labor Advisory Committees in the National Defense Advisory Commission and Office of Production Management, May 1940 to January 1942* (Washington, DC: Civilian Production Administration, 1946); William J. Schuck, "Industry and Labor Advisory Committees in the War Production Board, January 1942 to November 1945," Special Study No. 34, 1946, Policy Documentation File, WPB; Merton W. Ertell, "The C.I.O. Industry Council Plan—Its Background and Implications" (Ph.D. diss., University of Chicago, 1955); and Lichtenstein, *Most Dangerous Man in Detroit,* chap. 8.

39. The labor spokesman is quoted in Purcell, "Labor Policies of WPB," vol. 2.

CHAPTER SIXTEEN. ECONOMIC STABILIZATION

1. For prices, wages, and rationing, see John Kenneth Galbraith, "A Letter to the Historian of the OPA from J. K. Galbraith, Sometime Assistant and Deputy Administrator for Price of the OPA," 7/27/43, and related correspondence, Box 27, Unit 273, RWA, BOB; the three "Miscellaneous Publications" and fifteen "General Publications" of the Office of Price Administration (OPA), including William J. Wilson, John A. Hart, and George R. Taylor's *The Beginnings of OPA* (General Publication No. 1 [Washington, DC: OPA, 1947]), Imogene H. Putnam's *Volunteers in OPA* (General Publication No. 14 [Washington, DC: OPA, 1947]); and Harvey C. Mansfield's *A Short History of OPA* (General Publication No. 15 [Washington, DC: OPA, 1947]) (the latter lists all publications); Drummond Jones, *The Role of the Office of Civilian Requirements in the Office of Production Management and War Production Board, January 1941 to November 1945* (Washington, DC: Civilian Production Administration, 1946); Bureau of the Budget, *The United States at War: Development and Administration of the War Program by the Federal Government* (Washington, DC: Bureau of the Budget, 1946), pp. 235–73, 290–91, 328–29, 353–54, 359–63, 382–401, 492–97; John R. Craf, *A Survey of the American Economy, 1940–1946* (New York: North River, 1947), chaps. 4, 8; Victor A. Thompson, *The Regulatory Process in OPA Rationing* (New York: Columbia University Press, 1950); Lester V. Chandler and Donald H. Wallace, eds., *Economic Mobilization and Stabilization: Selected Materials on the Economics of War and Defense* (New York: Henry Holt, 1951), pts. 3–4; John Kenneth Galbraith, *A Theory of Price Control* (Cambridge, MA: Harvard University Press, 1952); Thomas G. Manning, *The Office of Price Administration: A World War II Agency of Control* (New York: Henry Holt, 1960); Geofrey T. Mills, "The Economics of Price Controls: The OPA Experience, 1941–1946" (Ph.D. diss., University of Illinois at Urbana-Champaign, 1979); Andrew H. Bartels, "The Politics of Price Control: The Office of Price Administration and the Dilemmas of Economic Stabilization, 1940–1946" (Ph.D. diss., Johns Hopkins University, 1980); Hugh Rockoff, *Drastic Measures: A History of Wage and Price Controls in the United States* (New York: Cambridge University Press, 1984), chaps. 4–5; Harold G. Vatter, *The U.S. Economy in World War II* (New York: Columbia University Press, 1985), chap. 5; Hugh Rockoff, "The Response of the Giant Corporations to Wage and Price Controls in World War II," in *The New Deal and Corporate Power: Antitrust and Regulatory Policies during the Thirties and World War II*, ed. Robert F. Himmelberg (New York: Garland, 1994), pp. 297–302; and Hugh Rockoff, "The United States: From Ploughshares to Swords," in *The Economics of World War II: Six Great Powers in International Comparison*, ed. Mark Harrison (Cambridge: Cambridge University Press, 1998), pp. 81–121.

2. H. M. Douty, "Problems and Policies of Dispute Settlement and Wage Stabilization during World War II," in *Economic Mobilization and Stabilization*, ed. Chandler and Wallace, p. 331.

3. Rockoff, *Drastic Measures*, p. 93.

4. Ibid., p. 96.

5. For wage control, see Douty, "Dispute Settlement and Wage Stabilization," pp. 315–50; and Paul A. C. Koistinen, *The Hammer and the Sword: Labor, the Military, and Industrial Mobilization, 1920–1945* (New York: Arno, 1979).

6. The executive order is quoted in Douty, "Dispute Settlement and Wage Stabilization," p. 349.

7. For the anti-inflation program, see Jesse Burkhead, "The Budget Bureau's Integrated Anti-Inflation Program, March–April, 1942," undated, Box 19, Unit 196, RWA, BOB; Bureau of the Budget, *United States at War,* pp. 250–54; John Morton Blum, *From the Morgenthau Diaries,* vol. 3, *Years of War, 1941–1945* (Boston: Houghton Mifflin, 1967), pp. 33–78; Conference with the President, 3/4/42, 3/25/42, 4/1/42, 4/4/42, 4/8/42, 4/10/42, 4/16/42, White House Memoranda, 3/16/42, and Daily Record, 3/25/42, 4/24/42 (two entries), Smith Papers; Smith to President, 7/23/41, OF: Office of Price Administration, FDR Papers; Bell to Byrnes, 11/27/42, Board Member File: Secretary Morgenthau, Office of Economic Stabilization, Box 607, OWMR; and Baruch to Henderson, 4/3/42, and other correspondence, Baruch to Lubin, 2/21/42, and other correspondence, and Baruch to Roosevelt, 9/23/42, and other correspondence, Selected Correspondence, Baruch to Henderson, 7/6/42, and other documents, Washington File 1942–45, Box 39, Sec. 3—Special Subjects: Inflation-Price Control, and Lubell to Baruch, 6/21/42, Washington File 1942–45, Box 39, Sec. 3—Special Subjects: Inflation—Subsidies, Baruch Papers.

8. Burkhead, "Budget Bureau's Integrated Anti-Inflation Program," p. 17, Box 19, Unit 196, RWA, BOB.

9. There is no published study of OES. For efforts to write an official history, see lengthy correspondence and documents, 1943–1947, Box 13, Unit 72, RWA, BOB; and "P. H. C." or Coombs, series of essays, 3/12/47–4/16/47, OES History Project, Office of Economic Stabilization, Box 435, OWMR. See also Weldon to Smith w/ enc., 8/3/42, Board Member File: Harold Smith, Budget, Office of Economic Stabilization, Box 607. OWMR; and Lubin to Rosenman, 8/6/42, and other documents, Alphabetical File, Box 5, Economic Stabilization Authority, Coy Papers.

10. Bureau of the Budget, *United States at War,* p. 386.

11. For the Hold-the-Line Order, see Bartels, "Politics of Price Control," pp. 216–35; Mills, "Economics of Price Control," pp. 80–88; Smith to Byrnes, 3/25/43, Board Member File: Harold Smith, Budget, Murray to International Unions et al., 4/13/43, and other correspondence, Board Member File: Philip Murray, and Green to Roosevelt, 4/14/43, Board Member File: William Green, Office of Economic Stabilization, Box 607, OWMR; Conference with the President, 12/18/42, 6/3/43, 1/7/44, and White House Memoranda, 6/3/43, Smith Papers; Byrnes to President, 5/14/43, PSF: Executive Office of the President—James F. Byrnes, and Vinson to President, ca. 3/44, OF: Office of Economic Stabilization, FDR Papers; and Baruch to Byrnes, 6/13/43, Selected Correspondence, Baruch Papers.

12. Douty, "Dispute Settlement and Wage Stabilization," p. 353.

13. Ibid.

14. Ibid.

15. Rockoff, *Drastic Measures,* p. 109; and Rockoff, "United States," p. 86.

16. Colston E. Warne et al., eds., *Yearbook of American Labor,* vol. 1, *War Labor Policies* (New York: Philosophical Library, 1945), pp. 51–68; and Waldman to Morgenthau, 4/17/43, Board Member File: Secretary Morgenthau, Office of Economic Stabilization, Box 607, OWMR.

17. Warne et al., eds., *Yearbook of American Labor,* app. D, "Excerpts from the Report of the Technical Committee Appointed by the Chairman of the President's Committee on the Cost of Living," pp. 637–39.

18. Rockoff, *Drastic Measures,* pp. 167–71; and Geofrey Mills and Hugh Rockoff, "Compliance with Price Controls in the United States and the United Kingdom during World War II," *Journal of Economic History* 47 (March 1987): 197–213, esp. 203.

19. Robert Higgs, "Wartime Prosperity? A Reassessment of the U.S. Economy in the 1940s," *Journal of Economic History* 52 (March 1992): 41–60. See also Robert Higgs, *Crisis and Leviathan: Critical Episodes in the Growth of American Government* (New York: Oxford University Press, 1987), chap. 9. A sound critique of Higgs's revisionist "Wartime Prosperity?" is presented in Rockoff, "United States," pp. 84–94.

20. Rockoff, "United States," p. 91, table 3.6, col. 4. Assertions in Civilian Production Administration (CPA) *Industrial Mobilization for War: History of the War Production Board and Predecessor Agencies, 1940–1945* (Washington, DC: Civilian Production Administration, 1947), p. 964, that consumer purchases in 1944 were 12 percent above those in 1939 were usually accepted with little question. See also Harold Vatter, "The Material Status of the U.S. Civilian Consumer in World War II: The Question of Guns or Butter," in *The Sinews of War: Essays on the Economic History of World War II,* ed. Geofrey T. Mills and Hugh Rockoff (Ames: Iowa State University Press, 1993), pp. 219–42.

21. Executive Offices—Labor Office, Labor Policy Committee Records, Correspondence, Minutes of Meetings, Records of the Office of Price Administration, RG 188, National Archives, College Park, MD; Minutes of Meeting, Board of Economic Stabilization, Office of Economic Stabilization, Box 606, and Minutes of the Advisory Board of the Office of War Mobilization and Reconversion, Boxes 391–96, OWMR.

22. Koistinen, *Hammer and Sword,* pp. 273–82.

23. For military relations with OPA, see John P. Miller, *Pricing of Military Procurements* (New Haven, CT: Yale University Press, 1949); Robert H. Connery, *The Navy and the Industrial Mobilization in World War II* (Princeton, NJ: Princeton University Press, 1951), pp. 225–92; R. Elberton Smith, *The Army and Economic Mobilization* (Washington, DC: Office of the Chief of Military History, 1959), pp. 226–34, 276–79, 397–412; and Bartholomew H. Sparrow, *From the Outside In: World War II and the American State* (Princeton, NJ: Princeton University Press, 1996), pp. 161–257.

24. For World War II financing, see Simon Kuznets, *National Product in Wartime* (New York: National Bureau of Economic Research, 1945); Henry C. Murphy, *The National Debt in War and Transition* (New York: McGraw-Hill, 1950); Paul Studenski and Herman E. Krooss, *Financial History of the United States* (New York: McGraw-Hill, 1952), pp. 436–58; Lewis H. Kimmel, *Federal Budget and Fiscal Policy, 1789–1958* (Washington, DC: Brookings Institution, 1959), pp. 229–32; John W. Kendrick, *Productivity Trends in the United States* (Princeton, NJ: Princeton University Press, 1961); Milton Friedman and Anna Jacobson Schwartz, *A Monetary History of the United States, 1867–1960* (Princeton, NJ: Princeton University Press, 1963), pp. 546–91; Mark H. Leff, *The Limits of Symbolic Reform: The New Deal and Taxation, 1933–1939* (New York: Cambridge University Press, 1984); Vatter, *U.S. Economy in World War II,* pp. 102–12; John F. Witte, *The Politics and Development of the Federal Income Tax* (Madison: University of Wisconsin Press, 1985), pp. 110–30; Peter Fearon, *War, Prosperity and Depression: The U.S. Economy, 1917–45* (Lawrence: University Press of Kansas, 1987), pp. 280–86; Benjamin J. Klebaner, *American Commercial Banking: A History* (Boston: Twayne, 1990), pp. 165–72; W. Elliot Brownlee, ed., *Funding the Modern American State, 1941–1995: The Rise and Fall of Easy Finance* (Cambridge:

Cambridge University Press, 1996); Sparrow, *From Outside In*, pp. 97–160; and Rockoff, "United States," pp. 107–11.

25. Rockoff, "United States," p. 108.

26. U.S. Bureau of the Census, *Historical Statistics of the United States, Colonial Times to 1970* (Washington, DC: U.S. Bureau of the Census, 1975), pp. 343–51, 353–373, 1105–7.

27. Studenski and Krooss, *Financial History of the United States*, pp. 445–51; and Sparrow, *From Outside In*, pp. 102–9.

28. U.S. Bureau of the Census, *Historical Statistics*, pp. 393–401, 402–11, 1110; Witte, *Federal Income Tax*, p. 125; and Conference of the Director and Assistant Director with the President, 12/18/42, Alphabetical File, Box 13, Roosevelt, Franklin D.—1942, Coy Papers.

29. U.S. Bureau of the Census, *Historical Statistics*, pp. 381–92, 1109; and Studenski and Krooss, *Financial History of the United States*, pp. 448–51.

30. Studenski and Krooss, *Financial History of the United States*, p. 451.

31. Ibid., pp. 451–56; Rockoff, "United States," pp. 107–11; and Sparrow, *From Outside In*, pp. 109–25. See also Milton to Herring, 3/10/43, Box 12, Unit 143, and Milton to Herring, 3/11/43, Box 12, Unit 188, RWA, BOB.

32. Charles Gilbert, *American Financing of World War I* (Westport, CT: Greenwood, 1970), pp. 214, 230; Douty, "Dispute Settlement and Wage Stabilization," p. 353; and Paul A. C. Koistinen, *The Military-Industrial Complex: A Historical Perspective* (New York: Praeger, 1980), p. 108. Most aspects of World War I economic policies are covered at least briefly in Paul A. C. Koistinen, *Mobilizing for Modern War: The Political Economy of American Warfare, 1865–1919* (Lawrence: University Press of Kansas, 1997).

33. Rockoff, "United States," pp. 115–18.

34. Richards C. Osborne, *The Renegotiation of War Profits* (Urbana: University of Illinois Press, 1948), pp. 48–54; and Koistinen, *Mobilizing for Modern War*, pp. 262–64.

35. Paul A. C. Koistinen, *Planning War, Pursuing Peace: The Political Economy of American Warfare, 1920–1939* (Lawrence: University Press of Kansas, 1998).

36. See Osborne, *Renegotiation*, pp. 9–12; and chap. 3 above.

37. Osborne, *Renegotiation*, pp. 12–25.

38. Miller, *Pricing Military Procurements;* Connery, *Navy and Industrial Mobilization*, pp. 225–92; Smith, *Army and Economic Mobilization*, pp. 351–412; and Sparrow, *From Outside In*, pp. 161–257.

39. Osborne, *Renegotiation*, pp. 66–105.

40. Ibid., p. 101.

41. Ibid., p. 94.

42. Smith, *Army and Economic Mobilization*, pp. 411–12.

43. Osborne, *Renegotiation*, pp. 58–63; and Koistinen, *Hammer and Sword*, pp. 283–85.

44. Osborne, *Renegotiation*, pp. 52–58, 67–79. See also Office of Price Administration, *Corporate Profits, 1936–1944*, pt. 3, *First Half 1944: Industry Stabilized at Wartime Peak: 1120 Leading Industrial Corporations* (Washington, DC: Office of Price Administration, 1945); Representative Wright Patman, "Small Business Fares Very Well Under Renegotiation Act—Report of Chairman of War Contracts Price Adjust-

ment Board to House Small Business Committee Answers Criticisms Made on Behalf of Small Firms," *Cong. Rec.*, 79th Cong., 1st sess., 1945, 91, pt. 5:6145–48; and Carl Campbell, *Economic Growth, Capital Gains, and Income Distribution, 1897–1956* (New York: Arno, 1977).

45. See chap. 10, n. 1, above; Fearon, *War, Prosperity and Depression*, pp. 266–72; and Harry P. Jeffrey, Jr., "The Republican Party as a Minority Party in Congress in Wartime, 1943–44" (Ph.D. diss., Columbia University, 1974), pp. 149–63.

46. U.S. Bureau of the Census, *Historical Statistics*, pp. 169, 299–301; and Joel Seidman, *American Labor from Defense to Reconstruction* (Chicago: University of Chicago Press, 1953), pp. 270–71. Estimates vary according to criteria used.

47. Robert R. R. Brooks, "Price Control and Rationing," in *Yearbook of American Labor*, ed. Warne et al., p. 216.

48. Herman P. Miller, *Rich Man, Poor Man* (New York: Thomas Y. Crowell, 1964); and James T. Patterson, *America's Struggle against Poverty, 1900–1985* (Cambridge, MA: Harvard University Press, 1986).

49. See the sources cited in Paul A. C. Koistinen, "Warfare and Power Relations in America: Mobilizing the World War II Economy," in *The Home Front and War in the Twentieth Century*, ed. James Titus (Colorado Springs, CO: United States Air Force Academy, 1984), pp. 232–35, n. 4.

50. Robert J. Lampman, *The Share of the Top Wealth-Holders in National Wealth, 1922–1945* (Princeton, NJ: Princeton University Press, 1962).

51. Koistinen, "Warfare and Power Relations"; Stanley Lebergott, *The American Economy: Income, Wealth, and Want* (Princeton, NJ: Princeton University Press, 1976); Christopher Jencks et al., *Who Gets Ahead? The Determinants of Economic Success in America* (New York: Basic, 1979); U.S. Congress, Joint Economic Committee, *Measuring the Nation's Wealth*, 88th Cong., 2d sess., Joint Committee Print, 1964 (reproduced and distributed for the National Bureau of Economic Research by the Columbia University Press as vol. 29 of the series Studies in Income and Wealth); and Lee Soltow, ed., *Six Papers on the Size Distribution of Wealth and Income* (New York: Columbia University Press, 1969).

52. James MacGregor Burns, *Roosevelt: The Soldier of Freedom* (New York: Harcourt Brace Jovanovich, 1970), pp. vii, 497, 529.

53. For wartime congresses, see Roland Young, *Congressional Politics in the Second World War* (New York: Columbia University Press, 1956); Robert E. Ficken, "The Democratic Party and Domestic Politics during World War II" (Ph.D. diss., University of Washington, 1973); Robert A. Garson, *The Democratic Party and the Politics of Sectionalism, 1941–1948* (Baton Rouge: Louisiana State University Press, 1974); Jeffrey, "The Republican Party as a Minority Party"; David L. Porter, *The Seventy-sixth Congress and World War II, 1939–1940* (Columbia: University of Missouri Press, 1979); Richard N. Chapman, *Contours of Public Policy, 1939–1945* (New York: Garland, 1981); Alan Ware, *The Breakdown of Democratic Party Organization, 1940–1980* (New York: Oxford University Press, 1985); D. B. Hardeman and Donald C. Bacon, *Rayburn: A Biography* (Austin: Texas Monthly Press, 1987); and Thomas P. Wolf, William D. Pederson, and Byron W. Daynes, eds., *Franklin D. Roosevelt and Congress: The New Deal and Its Aftermath* (Armonk, NY: M. E. Sharpe, 2001). See also Richard Polenberg, *War and Society: The United States, 1941–1945* (Philadelphia: J. B. Lippincott, 1972); John Morton Blum, *V Was for Victory: Politics and American Culture during World*

War II (New York: Harcourt Brace Jovanovich, 1976); Ted Morgan, *FDR: A Biography* (New York: Simon and Schuster, 1985), pp. 502–774; Frank Freidel, *Franklin D. Roosevelt: A Rendezvous with Destiny* (Boston: Little, Brown, 1990), pp. 289–607; Patrick J. Maney, *The Roosevelt Presence: The Life and Legacy of FDR* (Berkeley and Los Angeles: University of California Press, 1992), pp. 153–54, 172–77; Kenneth S. Davis, *FDR: Into the Storm, 1937–1940: A History* (New York: Random House, 1993), pp. 395–696; Kenneth S. Davis, *FDR: The War President, 1940–1943: A History* (New York: Random House, 2000); Alan Brinkley, *The End of Reform: New Deal Liberalism in Recession and War* (New York: Alfred A. Knopf, 1995), pp. 175–271; Alan Brinkley, *Liberalism and Its Discontents* (Cambridge, MA: Harvard University Press, 1998); John W. Jeffries, *Wartime America: The World War II Home Front* (Chicago: Ivan R. Dee, 1986); David M. Kennedy, *Freedom from Fear: The American People in Depression and War, 1929–1945* (New York: Oxford University Press, 1999), pp. 381–858; George McJimsey, *The Presidency of Franklin Delano Roosevelt* (Lawrence: University Press of Kansas, 2000), pp. 185–297; Allan W. Winkler, *Home Front U.S.A.: America During World War II*, 2d ed., rev. (Wheeling, IL: Harlan Davidson, 2000); Thomas Fleming, *The New Dealers' War: Franklin D. Roosevelt and the War within World War II* (New York: Basic, 2001); Brian Waddell, *The War against the New Deal: World War II and American Democracy* (DeKalb: Northern Illinois University Press, 2001); I. F. Stone, *Business as Usual: The First Year of Defense* (New York: Modern Age, 1941); I. F. Stone, *The War Years, 1939–1945* (Boston: Little, Brown, 1988); and David Brinkley, *Washington Goes to War* (New York: Alfred A. Knopf, 1988).

54. Allan W. Winkler, *The Politics of Propaganda: The Office of War Information, 1942–1945* (New Haven, CT: Yale University Press, 1978).

55. Philip W. Warken, *A History of the National Resources Planning Board* (New York: Garland, 1979); Marion Clawson, *New Deal Planning: The National Resources Planning Board* (Baltimore: Johns Hopkins University Press, 1981); and Patrick D. Reagan, *Designing a New America: The Origins of New Deal Planning, 1890–1943* (Amherst: University of Massachusetts Press, 1999). See also Conference of Director and Assistant Director with the President, 4/9/43, Alphabetical File, Box 13, Roosevelt, Franklin D.—1943, Coy Papers.

56. U.S. Congress, House, Select Committee Investigating National Defense Migration, *First Interim Report*, 77th Cong., 1st sess., 1941, H. Rept. No. 1286, pp. 63–92, and *Second Interim Report*, 1941, H. Rept. No. 1553, pp. 1–8. There are thirty-four parts to the committee hearings. The Select Committee to Investigate the Interstate Migration of Destitute Citizens conducted the first ten parts between July and November 1940; thereafter, the committee changed its name and held hearings between March 1941 and September 1942, recorded in pts. 11–34.

57. For social services to accommodate the migrating population, see Truman Committee, *First Annual Report*, 77th Cong., 2d sess., 1942, S. Rept. 480, pt. 5, pp. 97–124; Civilian Production Administration, *Minutes of the Advisory Commission to the Council of National Defense, June 12, 1940, to October 22, 1941* (Washington, DC: Civilian Production Administration, 1946), pp. 5, 14, 21, 26, 28, 29–30, 33, 36, 42–43, 49–50, 59, 62–63, 66, 73, 76, 80, 112, 116, 118, 127, 130–31, 159, 160; Civilian Production Administration, *Minutes of the Council of the Office of Production Management, December 21, 1940, to January 14, 1942* (Washington, DC: Civilian Production Administration, 1946), pp. 2, 47–48, 49, 52, 54; Civilian Production Admin-

istration, *Minutes of the War Production Board, January 20, 1942, to October 9, 1945* (Washington, DC: Civilian Production Administration, 1946), pp. 15, 21–22, 27–28, 45, 48–49, 213–14, 230; Bureau of the Budget, *United States at War,* pp. 24, 30–31, 40, 44, 59, 106, 213–14, 393, 497–98; CPA, *Industrial Mobilization for War,* pp. 20, 29, 34–36, 80–81, 102, 153–54, 162–63, 563–64; Reginald C. McGrane, "Defense and War Housing Policies of the War Production Board and Its Predecessor Agencies, May 1940 to July 1944," Brief Survey No. 14, 1944, Policy Documentation File, WPB; Philip J. Funigiello, *The Challenge of Urban Liberalism: Federal-City Relations during World War II* (Knoxville: University of Tennessee Press, 1978), pp. 3–162; Laurence E. Radway, "The Advisory Commission to the Council of National Defense: An Administrative History," 1943, pp. 175–86, 207–15, Box 13, Unit 145, RWA, BOB; Alan Clive, *State of War: Michigan in World War II* (Ann Arbor: University of Michigan Press, 1979); John W. Jeffries, *Testing the Roosevelt Coalition: Connecticut Society and Politics in the Era of World War II* (Knoxville: University of Tennessee Press, 1979); Michael C. C. Adams, *The Best War Ever: America and World War II* (Baltimore: Johns Hopkins University Press, 1994), chap. 6; Edwin Amenta and Theda Skocpol, "Redefining the New Deal: World War II and the Development of Social Provision in the United States," in *The Politics of Social Policy in the United States,* ed. Margaret Weir, Ann Shola Orloff, and Theda Skocpol (Princeton, NJ: Princeton University Press, 1988), pp. 81–122, and other essays in that volume; John Braeman, Robert H. Bremner, and David Brody, *The New Deal: The State and Local Levels* (Columbus: Ohio State University Press, 1975), vol. 2; Kenneth Finegold and Theda Skocpol, *State and Party in America's New Deal* (Madison: University of Wisconsin Press, 1995); and Conference of Director and Assistant Director with the President, 4/9/43, Alphabetical File, Box 13, Coy Papers.

58. Michael Wreszin, "The Dies Committee, 1938," in *Congress Investigates, 1792–1974,* ed. Arthur M. Schlesinger, Jr., and Robert Burns (New York: Chelsea, 1975), pp. 285–323.

59. James T. Patterson, *Congressional Conservatism and the New Deal: The Growth of the Conservative Coalition in Congress, 1933–1939* (Lexington: University of Kentucky Press, 1967).

60. On war and the state, see Arthur A. Stein, *The Nation at War* (Baltimore: Johns Hopkins University Press, 1978); Gregory Hooks, *Forging the Military-Industrial Complex: World War II's Battle of the Potomac* (Urbana: University of Illinois Press, 1991); Bruce D. Porter, *War and the Rise of the State: The Military Foundations of Modern Politics* (New York: Free Press, 1994); and Waddell, *The War against the New Deal.* See also James Gilbert, *Designing the Industrial State: The Intellectual Pursuit of Collectivism in America, 1880–1940* (Chicago: Quadrangle, 1972); Otis L. Graham, Jr., *Toward a Planned Society: From Roosevelt to Nixon* (New York: Oxford University Press, 1976); Otis H. Graham, Jr., *Losing Time: The Industrial Policy Debate* (Cambridge, MA: Harvard University Press, 1992); Barry D. Karl, *The Uneasy State: The United States from 1915 to 1945* (Chicago: University of Chicago Press, 1983); Fred Block, *Revising State Theory: Essays in Politics and Postindustrialism* (Philadelphia: Temple University Press, 1987); Anthony S. Campagna, *U.S. National Economic Policy, 1917–1985* (Westport, CT: Praeger, 1987); and Jerold E. Brown and Patrick D. Reagan, eds., *Voluntarism, Planning, and the State: The American Planning Experience, 1914–1946* (Westport, CT: Greenwood, 1988).

CHAPTER SEVENTEEN. RECONVERSION

1. For basic secondary sources on reconversion, see J. Carlyle Sitterson, *Development of the Reconversion Policies of the War Production Board, April 1943 to January 1945* (Washington, DC: War Production Board, 1945); Drummond Jones and Maryclaire McCauley, *Resumption of Production of Domestic Electric Flat Irons, April 1943 to August 1944* (Washington, DC: War Production Board, 1944); Civilian Production Administration (CPA), *Industrial Mobilization for War: History of the War Production Board and Predecessor Agencies, 1940–1945* (Washington, DC: Civilian Production Administration, 1947), pp. 731–66, 783–822, 857–959; Jack Peltason, *The Reconversion Controversy* (Washington, DC: Committee on Public Administration Cases, 1950); Civilian Production Administration (CPA), "Industrial Reconversion and Civilian Production: History of the Civilian Production Administration, 1945–47," vol. 3, 1946, Policy Documentation File, WPB; and Civilian Production Administration (CPA), "Industrial Mobilization for War: History of the War Production Board and Predecessor Agencies, 1940–1945," vol. 2, "Material and Products," 1947, Policy Documentation File, WPB. See also Herman M. Somers, *Presidential Agency: OWMR, the Office of War Mobilization and Reconversion* (Cambridge, MA: Harvard University Press, 1950); Bureau of the Budget, *United States at War: Development and Administration of the War Program by the Federal Government* (Washington, DC: Bureau of the Budget, 1946), chap. 15; Drummond Jones, *The Role of the Office of Civilian Requirements in the Office of Production Management and War Production Board, January 1941 to November 1945* (Washington, DC: Civilian Production Administration, 1946); Donald M. Nelson, *Arsenal of Democracy: The Story of the War Production Board* (New York: Harcourt, Brace, 1946), chap. 20; Bruce Catton, *The War Lords of Washington* (New York: Harcourt, Brace, 1948), pp. 211–303; Keith E. Eiler, *Mobilizing America: Robert P. Patterson and the War Effort, 1940–1945* (Ithaca, NY: Cornell University Press, 1997), pp. 309–440; R. Elberton Smith, *The Army and Economic Mobilization* (Washington, DC: Office of the Chief of Military History, 1959); Robert H. Connery, *The Navy and the Industrial Mobilization in World War II* (Princeton, NJ: Princeton University Press, 1951); and Paul A. C. Koistinen, *The Hammer and the Sword: Labor, the Military, and Industrial Mobilization, 1920–1945* (New York: Arno, 1979).

2. Kanzler had married Henry Ford's wife's sister. He and Nelson were close, and one scholar (Bernstein) holds him partly responsible for holding up the conversion of the automobile industry early in 1942. See Gladieux Reminiscences, pp. 531–33; and Barton J. Bernstein, "The Automobile Industry and the Coming of the Second World War," *Southwestern Social Science Quarterly* 47 (June 1966): 22–33.

3. Ernest Kanzler, Report to Donald M. Nelson, "Economic Demobilization and Reconversion: The Problems and Some Recommendations," 6/1943, Washington File, 1942–45, Box 40, Sec. 3—Special Subjects: Kanzler Report, Baruch Papers; and Kanzler to Nelson, 6/26/43, 7/3/43, 8/2/43 (w/ enc.), and Unsigned Memorandum, 8/16/43, Box 2357, file 965, and Kanzler to May et al., 4/20/43, Box 2356, file 964, WPB.

4. Novick to Falck, Gordon, and Deutch, 9/24/43, Kuznets, "Post-War Planning within the War Production Board," ca. 9/43, and other documents, Box 2356, file 964, Batcheller to Nelson, 11/17/43, Box 2357, file 965, and Nelson to

Batcheller, 9/20/43, Stevenson to Boulware, 1/15/44, and other documents, Box 2358, file 965R, WPB; memorandum "WPB Documents from Operations Vice Chairman's Office," undated, Stevenson to Batcheller, 10/16/43, 10/18/43, Kohlhepp to Krug, 10/19/43, "WPB Documents from the Program Vice Chairman's Office," ca. 12/1/43, Requirements Committee Document No. 2021, "Statement of Requirements Committee Policy on Manufacture of Controlled, Limited, or Prohibited Items," 11/43, Blaisdell to Nelson, 11/24/43, and Requirements Committee Document No. 2021-A w/ enc., 11/15/43, Washington File 1942–45, Box 42, Sec. 3—Special Subjects: Reconversion, Baruch Papers; Peltason, *Reconversion*, pp. 30–31; CPA, *Industrial Mobilization for War*, p. 622; and Sitterson, *Reconversion*, pp. 14–18.

5. Henderson to Nelson, 7/19/43, Box 2357, file 965, WPB.

6. Batt to Nelson, 8/30/43, Box 2357, file 965, WPB.

7. Johnson quoted in, Peltason, *Reconversion*, p. 81.

8. Kanzler to Nelson, 6/26/43, Box 2357, file 965, WPB.

9. Roland Young, *Congressional Politics in the Second World War* (New York: Columbia University Press, 1956), pp. 197–217; and Eccles to Byrnes, 9/16/43, and other documents, Box 2355, file 961, WPB.

10. Conference with the President, 8/31/43, 10/20/43, 11/2/43 (with Rosenman), 11/4/43, 1/7/44, 2/16/44, 8/31/44, White House Memoranda, Smith to President, 3/14/45, and Daily Record, 8/28/43, 11/16/43, 2/16/44, 2/23/44, 8/29/44, 9/19/44, Smith Papers. See also Bowman to Gladieux and Craine ca. 2/44, Box 2356, file 964, and Krug to Smith, 9/23/44, and documents, Box 2357, file 965, WPB.

11. Minutes, War Mobilization Committee, 10/14/43, Meetings-3-1943-Office of War Mobilization, Box 3, OWMR; and Peltason, *Reconversion*, pp. 30–31 (quotation p. 31).

12. Bureau of the Budget, *United States at War*, pp. 466–67; and John W. Partin, "'Assistant President' for the Home Front: James F. Byrnes and World War II" (Ph.D. diss., University of Florida, 1977), chap. 12.

13. Civilian Production Administration, *Minutes of the War Production Board, January 20, 1942, to October 9, 1945* (hereafter *WPB Minutes*) (Washington, DC: Civilian Production Administration, 1946), pp. 291–93.

14. "Nelson's Statement before Senator George's Committee on November 5, 1943," and Baruch to Henderson w/ enc., 11/30/43, Washington File, 1942–45, Box 29, Sec.—Correspondence: Personal, Baruch Papers; and Peltason, *Reconversion*, p. 31.

15. Baruch to Nelson, 12/14/43, Washington File, 1942–45, Box 29, Sec.—Correspondence: Personal, and Hancock, "Notes on Talk with Nelson and Wilson, Wednesday, December 22, 1943," Washington File, 1942–45, Box 33, Sec. 2—Government Agencies: Donald M. Nelson, Baruch Papers; and J. Carlyle Sitterson, "Reconversion Activities of the War Production Board, January 1943 to June 1944," Brief Survey No. 9, 1944, Policy Documentation File, WPB.

16. Baruch to Nelson, 12/14/43, 1/7/44, and Nelson to Baruch, 12/29/43, Washington File, 1942–45, Box 33, Sec. 2—Government Agencies: Donald M. Nelson, Baruch Papers.

17. Stimson Diary, 1/3/44; Baruch to President, 1/4/44, Selected Correspondence, Baruch Papers; and Henry L. Stimson and McGeorge Bundy, *On Active Service In Peace and War* (New York: Harper and Bros., 1947), pp. 492–95.

18. Correspondence with Patterson, Forrestal, Stimson, Marshall, and others, 1940–1945, and Drew Pearson, "The Washington Merry-Go-Round," 8/26/44, Selected Correspondence, and Pearson, untitled piece, 8/26/44, Washington File, 1942–45, Box 29, Sec.—Correspondence: Personal, Baruch Papers; and Paul A. C. Koistinen, *Mobilizing for Modern War: The Political Economy of American Warfare, 1865–1919* (Lawrence: University Press of Kansas, 1997) (consult indices); and Paul A. C. Koistinen, *Planning War, Pursuing Peace: The Political Economy of American Warfare, 1920–1939* (Lawrence: University Press of Kansas, 1998) (consult indices and p. 204).

19. Stimson Diary, 6/15/43. Jordan A. Schwarz, *The Speculator: Bernard M. Baruch in Washington, 1917–1945* (Chapel Hill: University of North Carolina Press, 1981), is the best secondary source on the Baruch-Byrnes relationship.

20. U.S. Congress, Senate, Bernard M. Baruch and John M. Hancock, *Report on War and Post-War Adjustment Policies,* 78th Cong., 2d sess., 1944, S. Doc. 154. See also Milton to Director, 2/15/43, and other correspondence, Box 22, Unit 231, RWA, BOB; Baruch to Byrnes, 11/4/43, Byrnes to Baruch, 11/5/43, and other documents, Baruch to Ginsburg, 11/22/43, Baruch to Peek, 11/21/43, and other correspondence, Baruch and Hancock to Byrnes, 5/12/44, Baruch to Coblentz, 6/5/44, Hancock Memorandum, 4/28/44, and other documents, Hancock to Byrnes, 9/8/44, Hirsch to Baruch, 7/26/44, Baruch to Hirsch, 9/13/44, May to Recipients of the Planning Division Document #14 w/ enc., 2/3/44, Maverick to Baruch, 2/24/44, Murray to George, 2/19/44, Baruch to Murray, 7/17/44, and Murray to Baruch, w/ encs., 3/14/44, Selected Correspondence, Eberstadt to Baruch w/ enc., 11/6/43, Washington File, 1942–45, Box 29, Sec.—Correspondence: Personal, and Baruch to Byrnes, 11/4/43, and Baruch and Hancock to Byrnes, 5/12/44, Washington File, 1942–45, Box 45, Sec. 3—Special Subjects: War and Post-War Adjustment Unit Records—First Run, Baruch Papers. Samuel Lubell, on Baruch's payroll at the time, did much of the day-to-day work for and wrote drafts of the report. See Carroll to Lubell, 5/22/44, Washington File, 1942–45, Box 29, Sec.—Correspondence: Personal, Lubell, "Demobilization and Post-War Problems," 10/22/[43], and other documents, Washington File, 1942–45, Box 38, Sec. 3—Special Subjects: Demobilization, and Lubell to Baruch, 12/11/43, and numerous other documents, Washington File, 1942–45, Boxes 41–42, Sec. 3—Special Subjects: Reconversion, Baruch Papers. Benjamin V. Cohen also assisted Baruch and Hancock: see Daily Record, 11/16/43, 2/16/44, Smith Papers.

21. Patton to President, 3/1/44, Smith to President, 2/24/44, and Hines to President, 3/3/44, OF: Retraining and Reemployment Administration Container, FDR Papers; Byrnes, News Conference, 2/21/44, Selected Correspondence, Baruch Papers; and Bureau of the Budget, *United States at War,* pp. 466–67, 470, 477.

22. "Immediate [News] Release," 7/14/44, OF: Office of Contract Settlement, G. G. T. to Byrnes w/ enc., 1/10/44, Rosenman to President, 8/25/44, Byrnes to President, 8/28/44, and Byrnes, First Annual Report as Director of War Mobilization and Reconversion, 1/1/45, PSF: Executive Office of the President—James F. Byrnes, FDR Papers; Hancock to Baruch, 5/2/44, 5/3/44, Selected Correspondence, and Baruch to Nelson, 12/14/43, Hancock to Nelson, 1/1/44, 1/3/44, and Byrnes to Nelson, 3/31/44, Washington File, 1942–45, Box 29, Sec.—Correspondence: Personal, Baruch Papers; CPA, *Industrial Mobilization for War,* pp. 655–56;

Bureau of the Budget, *United States at War,* pp. 474–75; Sitterson, *Reconversion,* pp. 8–12; Somers, *Presidential Agency,* pp. 179–80; Smith, *Army and Economic Mobilization,* pp. 618–28; and Schwarz, *The Speculator,* pp. 461–62.

23. Hancock to Baruch, 8/10/44, Selected Correspondence, U.S. Senate, *Report of Proceedings,* Hearings Held before the Committee on Post-War Policy and Planning, Executive Session, 1/7/44, Washington File, 1942–45, Box 37, Sec. 3—Special Subjects: Senate, Baruch Papers; Byrnes to President, 9/26/44, and other documents, OF: Surplus Property Board Endorsements, FDR Papers; and Baxter to Belsley, 6/10/44, and other documents, Box 2356, file 964, WPB. See also chap. 11 above.

24. Bureau of Planning and Statistics, Planning Division, WPB, "War Production and Civilian Output after Victory in Europe, Preliminary Report," Document No. 14, 1/24/44, and May to Recipients of Document #14, 2/3/44, Selected Correspondence, Baruch Papers; Minutes of Meeting of WPB Vice Chairmen re Reconversion Problems, 12/23/43, Homan to Kohlhepp w/ enc. ("WPB Organization to Facilitate Transfer of Productive Resources to Non-War Uses," 12/24/43), 12/27/43, and Livermore to George, 3/25/44, and other documents, Box 2356, file 964, and Minutes of Meeting of WPB Chairmen re Reconversion Problems, 12/30/43, Box 2357, file 965, WPB; Sitterson, *Reconversion,* pp. 14–18, 22–27; CPA, *Industrial Mobilization for War,* pp. 622–23; and Peltason, *Reconversion,* pp. 30–31.

25. War Production Board, Program Adjustment Committee, Meeting 169, 7/28/44, and other correspondence, Box 2356, file 964, "Steps in *Programmed Production* under Proposed Control System for the Transitional Period," 3/1/44, and Stevenson to Boulware, 3/4/44, 5/27/44, Box 2358, file 965R, WPB; Sitterson, *Reconversion,* pp. 39–48; and Catton, *War Lords,* pp. 250–56.

26. Gladieux Reminiscences, pp. 577–617; Homan to Gordon, 4/22/44, 5/16/44 (w/ enc.), and George to Homan, 4/18/44, Box 2357, file 965, WPB; Sitterson to Fesler (on Gladieux interview), 11/15/44, 11–12/1944, Box 1, and Jones to Fesler (on Hill address to PARB, WPB), 8/29/45, 7–8/1945, Box 2, Fesler Papers; Sitterson, *Reconversion,* pp. 70–73; and CPA, *Industrial Mobilization for War,* pp. 733–34.

27. PEC, Minutes, Meeting 55, 57, and 59, 12/23/43, 1/5/44, and 1/19/44, file 041.05, P. T. Homan, "Synopsis of Proposed Improvements in WPB Organization to Regulate Resumption of Non-Military Production," 4/12/44, and other correspondence, Box 252, file 041.11, and Childress to Skuce, 3/28/44, and other documents, Box 2356, file 964, WPB; Sitterson, *Reconversion,* pp. 73–76; CPA, *Industrial Mobilization for War,* pp. 734–36; and Peltason, *Reconversion,* pp. 34–38, 47–56.

28. Byrnes to Nelson, 3/31/44, Washington File, 1942–45, Box 29, Sec—Correspondence: Personal, and Baruch to Nelson, 6/1/44, Nelson to Baruch, 5/25/44, and General Administrative Order No. 2-157, 5/25/44, Washington File, 1942–45, Box 33, Sec. 2—Government Agencies: Donald M. Nelson, Baruch Papers; Gladieux Reminiscences, pp. 587–88, 615; Press Conference of Donald Nelson, 4/14/44, Box 2357, file 965, WPB; and Sitterson, *Reconversion,* pp. 75–76.

29. Byrnes to Wilson, 6/5/44, and PEC, Minutes, Meeting 76, 6/7/44, file 041.05, WPB; CPA, *Industrial Mobilization for War,* pp. 737–39; Sitterson, *Reconversion,* pp. 77–79; and Peltason, *Reconversion,* pp. 57–59.

30. Biographical details on Wilson's reorganization can be traced through CPA, "Executive Personnel Directory of the War Production Board and Predecessor Agen-

cies, May 1940 to November 1945," Miscellaneous Publication No. 2, 1946, Policy Documentation File, and Belsley, Staff Circular, 3/20/43, Box 252, file 040, WPB; *The Army Almanac* (Harrisburg, PA: Stackpole, 1959); Gladieux Reminiscences, pp. 496–99, 536; and Barton J. Bernstein, "The Debate on Industrial Reconversion: The Protection of Oligopoly and Military Control of the Economy," *American Journal of Economics and Sociology* 26 (April 1967): 160–61. See also Wilson to Vice Chairs, w/ enc., 6/5/44, Box 252, file 040.5, and Elliott to Wilson and Bunker, 7/25/44 (two memoranda), Blaisdell to Bunker, 8/3/44, and Homan to Gordon, 5/29/44, and other documents, Box 2357, file 965, WPB.

31. Bernstein, "Debate on Industrial Mobilization," pp. 160–61; and John K. Ohl, *Supplying the Troops: General Somervell and American Logistics in WWII* (DeKalb: Northern Illinois University Press, 1994), chap. 13. By comparison, Nelson was all but exiled from the large corporate scene. When selected to chair WPB, he preferred remaining with Sears, Roebuck and Co., but Board Chair Robert E. Wood forced him to resign. After leaving the board and retiring from government, Nelson turned to employment in Hollywood and peripheral enterprises. See Gladieux Reminiscences, p. 306; Entry, 12/28/40, Henderson, Leon: Diary Notes and Memos to Himself, WPB Papers, Box 36, Henderson Papers; Terry R. Warth, "Donald Marr Nelson— Archetypical Businessman-Bureaucrat: A Study of the Growing Interdependence between Private Enterprise and the American Government" (Ph.D. diss., University of Southern California, 1984), chap. 10; and James C. Worthy, *Shaping an American Institution: Robert E. Wood and Sears, Roebuck* (Urbana: University of Illinois Press, 1984), chap. 3.

32. Nathan to Nelson, 3/15/43, and other documents, Box 2355, file 962.1, Newcomb to Stenett, 4/26/43, and other documents, Box 2355, file 963, and Stevenson to French et al., 5/29/44, and Boulware to Wilson, 6/7/44, 6/10/44, Box 2358, file 965R, WPB; Sitterson, *Reconversion,* pp. 26, 50–53, 89–92, 110–27; Peltason, *Reconversion,* pp. 60–64; CPA, *Industrial Mobilization for War,* 801–2, 867; and Catton, *War Lords,* pp. 250–55.

33. The military and commission officials' response to reconversion can be traced through *WPB Minutes;* PEC, Minutes, file 041.05, WPB; and numerous document collections and secondary sources cited in this and earlier chapters. Clay appears more reasonable in Jean Edward Smith, *Lucius D. Clay: An American Life* (New York: Henry Holt, 1990), than in World War II records.

34. *WPB Minutes,* pp. 293–302; WPB Press Release, Donald M. Nelson, 1/17/44, Box 2358, file 965R, May to Lubell, 1/31/44, and other documents, Box 2355, file 963, and Nelson to WPB Staff and Claimant Agencies, 1/28/44, Wilson to WPB Staff and Claimant Agencies, 1/26/44, Boyd to Chairman of the Program Adjustment Committee, 1/10/44, and Robinson to Wilson, 3/8/44, and other documents, Box 2356, file 964, WPB; Sitterson, *Reconversion,* pp. 37–39; and Peltason, *Reconversion,* pp. 38–42.

35. Koistinen, *Hammer and Sword,* pp. 504–7.

36. Patterson quoted in Sitterson, *Reconversion,* p. 43.

37. Krug quoted in ibid., p. 40.

38. PEC, Minutes, Meeting 84, 8/2/44, file 041.05, and Elliott to Wilson and Bunker, 6/14/44, and Anderson to Wilson, 6/9/44, and other documents, Box 2357, file 965, WPB; and Sitterson, *Reconversion,* pp. 62–65.

39. PEC, Minutes, Meeting 63 and 65, 2/23/44 and 3/15/44, file 041.05, WPB; *WPB Minutes,* pp. 307–14; CPA, *Industrial Mobilization for War,* pp. 794–95; and Sitterson, *Reconversion,* p. 44.

40. PEC, Minutes, Meeting 68–69, 4/5/44–4/12/44, file 041.05, and Wilson to Boulware, 4/28/44, Boulware to Wilson, 4/28/44, and Elliott to Wilson, 5/9/44, and other correspondence, Box 2356, file 964, WPB; CPA, *Industrial Mobilization for War,* pp. 799–801; and Sitterson, *Reconversion,* pp. 46–48.

41. George E. Comer, "Memorandum of Interview with Mr. Donald Nelson," 9/8/43, Washington File, 1942–45, Box 42, Sec. 3—Special Subjects: Reconversion, and Hancock, "Notes on Talk with Nelson and Wilson, Wednesday, December 22, 1943," Washington File, 1942–45, Box 33, Sec. 2—Government Agencies: Donald M. Nelson, Baruch Papers; Ozias to Boulware, 7/29/44, and other documents, Box 2356, file 964, Statement of Donald Nelson before an Executive Session of the Senate Special Committee on Post-War Economic Policy and Planning (two versions), 11/5/43, Nelson to George, 1/2/44, and Nelson to Members of WPB, 3/3/44, Box 2357, file 965, and Stevenson to Bunker, 8/23/44, Box 2358, file 965R, WPB; *WPB Minutes,* 11/43–8/44; Nelson, *Arsenal of Democracy,* chap. 20; Catton, *War Lords,* chaps. 17–21; and Peltason, *Reconversion,* pp. 20–24.

42. Nelson to Maloney, 3/7/44 (copied as Press Release, 3/9/44), Box 2358, file 965R, and *Journal of Commerce,* 3/9–10/44, and other documents, Box 2355, file 963, WPB. See also Stokes to O'Brian, 4/20/44, and other documents, Box 2356, file 964, and Nelson to Maloney, ca. 2/43, Box 2357, file 965, WPB; Nelson, *Arsenal of Democracy,* pp. 396–400; and Sitterson, *Reconversion,* pp. 32–37.

43. *WPB Minutes,* pp. 336–41, 345–46; Peltason, *Reconversion,* pp. 77–78, 94–95; Sitterson, *Reconversion,* pp. 90–91, 102–27; and Catton, *War Lords,* pp. 254–56.

44. Carroll to Baruch, 11/29/43, and other correspondence, Washington File, 1942–45, Box 29, Sec.—Correspondence: Personal, Baruch Papers; Jones and McCauley, *Domestic Electric Flat Irons;* *WPB Minutes,* pp. 307–14; and Sitterson, *Reconversion,* pp. 55–62.

45. U.S. Congress, Senate, *Economic Concentration and World War II: Report of the Smaller War Plants Corporation to the Special Committee to Study Problems of American Small Business, United States Senate,* 79th Cong., 2d sess., S. Doc. No. 206, 1946; Catton, *War Lords,* pp. 196–288; *New York Times,* 7/9/44; Truman Committee, *Third Annual Report,* 78th Cong., 2d sess., 1944, S. Rept. No. 10, pt. 16, pp. 5–22; U.S. Congress, Senate, Special Committee to Investigate the National Defense Program (now the Mead Committee, after its new chair, Senator James M. Mead [D-NY]), *Fourth Annual Report,* 79th Cong., 1st sess., 1945, S. Rept. No. 110, pt. 4, pp. 1–32. Donald R. Riddle, *The Truman Committee: A Study in Congressional Responsibility* (New Brunswick, NJ: Rutgers University Press, 1964), apps. 5–6, pp. 188–94, itemizes in detail the public and executive hearings on which these reports are in large part based.

46. TCB, "Criteria for Release of Plants during the Reconversion Period," 10/23/44, and other documents, Box 2355, file 963, Stevenson to Boulware, ca. 2/44, Homan to Elliott w/ encs., 5/25/44, Stevenson to Belsley w/enc., 5/19/44, Stevenson to Boulware, 5/13/44, 5/15/44, Livermore to Watkins, 6/12/44, and Stevenson, "Statement on War Production Controls," 8/23/44, and other documents, Box 2356, file 964, Teele and Gregg to Nelson, 8/15/43, 8/16/43 (two entries),

8/17/43 (two entries), Box 2357, file 965, and Office of the Operations Vice Chairman, "Policy Guidance in Event of Substantial Downward Revision in War Production Programs, Preliminary Report," 3/4/44, Box 2358, file 965R, WPB; Navy Department, "Weekly Roundup," 12/11/43, and other periodic reports, Washington File, 1942–45, Box 32, Sec. 2—Government Agencies: James Forrestal, Secretary of Navy, Baruch Papers; Sitterson, *Reconversion;* Jones and McCauley, *Domestic Electric Flat Irons;* CPA, "Industrial Mobilization for War," vol. 2; and CPA, "Industrial Reconversion," vol. 3.

47. Robert Griffith, "The Selling of America: The Advertising Council and American Politics, 1942–1960," *Business History Review* 57 (Autumn 1983): 388–412; Mark H. Leff, "The Politics of Sacrifice on the American Home Front in World War II," *Journal of American History* 77 (March 1991): 1296–1318; Roland Marchand, *Advertising the American Dream: Making Way for Modernity, 1920–1940* (Berkeley and Los Angeles: University of California Press, 1985); Roland Marchand, *Creating the Corporate Soul: The Rise of Public Relations and Corporate Imagery in American Big Business* (Berkeley and Los Angeles: University of California Press, 1998); Elizabeth A. Fones-Wolf, *Selling Free Enterprise: The Business Assault on Labor and Liberalism, 1945–60* (Urbana: University of Illinois Press, 1994); Andrew A. Workman, "Manufacturing Power: The Organizational Revival of the National Association of Manufacturers, 1941–1945," *Business History Review* 72 (Summer 1998): 279–317; and William L. Bird, Jr., *"Better Living": Advertising, Media, and the New Vocabulary of Business Leadership, 1935–1955* (Evanston, IL: Northwestern University Press, 1999).

48. Kanzler quoted in Jones and McCauley, *Domestic Electric Flat Irons,* p. 36. See also Stevenson to Belsley, w/enc., 5/19/44, and Stevenson to Boulware, 5/13/44, 5/19/44, 5/15/44, Box 2356, file 964, WPB.

49. Sitterson, *Reconversion,* pp. 49–50.

50. Baruch to Nelson, 12/14/43, Nelson to Baruch, 3/7/44, and Drew Pearson, "Washington Merry-Go-Round," 9/24/44, Washington File, 1942–45, Box 29, Sec.—Correspondence: Personal, and Biddle to Lubell, 1/8/44, Washington File, 1942–45, Box 31, Sec. 2—Government Agencies: Attorney General, Baruch Papers; O'Brian to Nelson, 6/21/44, and other documents, Box 2357, file 965, WPB; Sitterson, *Reconversion,* pp. 22, 53–54; and CPA, *Industrial Mobilization for War,* pp. 686–87, 710–11, 851–53, 913.

51. Andrew Stevenson, a key WPB executive for reconversion, observed late in 1943 that industry "was distrustful of governmental controls and was determined that the process of reconversion was not going to be guided by 'professors and planners,' and on the contrary was determined to 'do it its own way' irrespective of WPB programs" (Sitterson, *Reconversion,* p. 134 [quoting Stevenson]).

52. Office of the Operations Vice Chairman, "Policy Guidance in the Event of Substantial Downward Revisions in War Production Programs: Preliminary Report," 3/4/44, and Stevenson to Boulware, 5/27/44, and other documents, Box 2358, file 965R, WPB; and Sitterson, *Reconversion,* pp. 22, 49–50.

53. Hill to Senator Stewart, 5/31/44, Box 2357, file 965, Schwartz to Wilson, 7/29/44, Winton to May, 7/8/44, Homan to Elliott w/ encs., 5/25/44, and other documents, Box 2356, file 964, Novick to Krug, 12/4/43, and other correspondence, Box 2355, file 963, and Whiteside to Bunker w/ enc., 1/11/44, and other documents, Box 2356, file 963R, WPB; *WPB Minutes,* pp. 336–41; CPA, *Industrial Mobi-*

lization for War, pp. 956–57; Jones and McCauley, *Domestic Electric Flat Irons;* Sitterson, *Reconversion,* pp. 53–62; and CPA, "Industrial Mobilization for War," vol. 2.

54. Henry, Office Memorandum, 7/14/44, Box 2356, file 964, WPB; Stephen K. Bailey, *Congress Makes a Law: The Story behind the Employment Act of 1946* (New York: Columbia University Press, 1950); Karl Schriftgiesser, *Business Comes of Age: The Story of the Committee for Economic Development and Its Impact upon the Economic Policies of the United States, 1942–1960* (New York: Harper and Bros., 1960), pp. 1–134; William S. Hill, Jr., "The Business Community and National Defense: Corporate Leaders and the Military, 1943–1950" (Ph.D. diss., Stanford University, 1979); Robert M. Collins, *The Business Response to Keynes, 1929–1964* (New York: Columbia University Press, 1981), pp. 77–172; Kim McQuaid, *Big Business and Presidential Power: From FDR to Reagan* (New York: William Morrow, 1982), pp. 62–149; Kim McQuaid, "A Response to Industrialism: Liberal Businessman and the Evolving Spectrum of Capitalist Reform, 1886–1960" (Ph.D. diss., Northwestern University, 1975), pp. 189–287; and Alan R. Raucher, *Paul G. Hoffman: Architect of Foreign Aid* (Lexington: University Press of Kentucky, 1985).

55. *WPB Minutes,* p. 293. See also Wilson to Byrnes, 11/4/43, Washington File, 1942–45, Box 42, Sec. 3—Special Subjects: Reconversion, Baruch Papers.

56. PEC, Minutes, Meeting 54, 12/15/43, file 041.05, WPB.

57. Conference with the President, 8/31/44, 10/30/44, Smith Papers; "Excerpt from Broadcast by Leon Henderson, WJZ, New York, 1:00 P.M., August 25, 1944," "From Drew Pearson's Script of August 20," and Pearson, "The Washington Merry-Go-Round," 8/26/44, Selected Correspondence, Baruch Papers; and Frank Freidel, *Franklin D. Roosevelt: A Rendezvous with Destiny* (Boston: Little, Brown, 1990), pp. 494–504.

58. *WPB Minutes,* pp. 336–41; and Boulware to Wilson, 6/10/44, and other correspondence, Box 2355, file 963, and "Reconversion Activities of the War Production Board," 6/10/44, Box 2356, file 964, WPB.

59. *WPB Minutes,* p. 340.

60. WPB Press Release, Donald M. Nelson, 6/18/44, Box 2358, file 965R, Golden to Davis, 10/10/43, and other documents, Box 2356, file 964, and Golden to Bunker, 8/4/44, and other documents, Box 2357, file 965, WPB; Peltason, *Reconversion,* pp. 62–64; and Catton, *War Lords,* pp. 256–58.

61. McCarthy to Baruch w/ enc. (editorial), ca. 7/7/44, Selected Correspondence, Baruch Papers.

62. Gladieux Reminiscences, pp. 589–91, 631–41; "Excerpt from Broadcast by Leon Henderson, WJZ, New York, 1:00 P.M., August 25, 1944," Selected Correspondence, Baruch Papers; and Catton, *War Lords,* pp. 250–58.

63. Patterson quoted in Sitterson, *Reconversion,* pp. 92–93.

64. As quoted in Peltason, *Reconversion,* p. 66. See also Baruch to Marshall, 7/3/44, and Marshall to Baruch, 7/7/44, and other correspondence, Selected Correspondence, Baruch Papers.

65. Leahy to Nelson, 7/7/44, and Baruch to Leahy, 7/10/44, Selected Correspondence, Baruch Papers. Marshall wrote Baruch that he was grateful for his support in opposing "this vicious business of turning to peacetime activities before we have won our victory." Marshall to Baruch, 7/7/44, Selected Correspondence, Baruch Papers. See also Koistinen, *Hammer and Sword,* pp. 313–15, 325–26.

66. PEC, Minutes, Meeting 79, 6/28/44, file 041.05, WPB.

67. *WPB Minutes,* pp. 341–44.

68. Nelson quoted in Peltason, *Reconversion,* p. 76.

69. Ibid., pp. 70–76 (quotation p. 71); and Patterson to Baruch w/ encs., 1/14/45, Selected Correspondence, Baruch Papers.

70. Johnson quoted in Sitterson, *Reconversion,* p. 43.

71. Memorandum "Dear Boss" w/ enc. ("Memorandum to All Vice-Chairmen of the War Production Board on 'Initial Steps in the Approach to Reconversion' "), 7/5/44, Box 12, Unit VII, No. 6, and "Memorandum to All Vice-Chairmen . . . ," 7/7/44, Box 14, Unit E I, No. 127, Nelson Papers; Gladieux Reminiscences, pp. 600–630; Nelson, *Arsenal of Democracy,* p. 211; and Bernstein, "Debate on Industrial Reconversion," pp. 164–70.

72. Shea to Anderson, 7/20/44, and other documents, Box 2355, file 962.1, WPB; *WPB Minutes,* pp. 345–46; and Peltason, *Reconversion,* pp. 76–79.

73. Gladieux Reminiscences, pp. 629–30 (w/ enc. [B. L. G., "Staff Meeting in Mr. Nelson's Office, July 26, 1944 (9:30 A.M. to 1:30 P.M.)," 7/26/44, pp. 631–41]). Gladieux notes that all participants were sworn to secrecy. Peltason *Reconversion,* obviously had access to the memorandum since he briefly summarizes it. See Peltason, *Reconversion,* pp. 81–83. See also unsigned memorandum "Discussion with Mr. Sidney Weinberg," 5/21/42, Box 150, file 032, WPB.

74. Gladieux Reminiscences, pp. 642–52; Peltason, *Reconversion,* pp. 95–104; and Catton, *War Lords,* pp. 274–84.

75. Most World War II mobilization studies present Krug in a neutral to positive way. Unlike Nelson, Krug paid attention to and maintained the support of Baruch. See Krug to Baruch, 9/29/44, and other correspondence, and Baruch to Krug, 1/8/45, and other correspondence, Selected Correspondence, and Krug to Baruch w/ enc., 3/10/45, and other documents, Washington File, 1942–45, Box 29, Sec.— Correspondence: Personal, Baruch Papers. Baruch also began to appear at WPB meetings, something he never did when the WPB was under Nelson. Gladieux had a balanced yet negative view of Krug as a talented opportunist who gratuitously turned against Nelson. See Gladieux Reminiscences, pp. 563, 577–88, 650–52.

76. CPA, *Industrial Mobilization for War,* pp. 742–43.

77. Elliott to Anderson, 6/24/44, Anderson to Wilson and Bunker, 6/21/44, and Middlekamp to Boulware, 6/23/44, and other documents, Box 2356, file 964, and Stevenson to Boulware, 7/27/44, Boulware to Bunker, 8/1/44, Stevenson for Files, 8/5/44, Stevenson to Bunker, 8/15/44, Stevenson for Files, 8/19/44, Stevenson to Bunker, 8/23/44, and Skillman to Stevenson, 8/25/44, Box 2358, file 965R, WPB; and CPA, *Industrial Mobilization for War,* pp. 814–17.

78. Deutch to Krug, w/ enc. (WPB, "Policy Problems in the Expansion of Civilian Production after Victory in Europe, Fourth Draft," 9/2/44), 9/5/44, and other documents, Box 2356, file 964, WPB Press Release, J. A. Krug, 9/5/44, 9/8/44, Box 2358, file 965R, Stevenson, "Statement on War Production Board Controls," 8/23/44, and Ozer to Hetzel, 8/31/44, and other documents, Box 2356, file 964, and Krug to Smith, 10/2/44, and other documents, Box 2357, file 965, WPB; *WPB Minutes,* pp. 350–54, 356–59; and CPA, *Industrial Mobilization for War,* pp. 817–21.

79. Deutch to Krug, 8/28/44, Box 2356, file 964, WPB; and *WPB Minutes,* pp. 350–54.

80. Elliott to Bunker, 8/29/44, and Hetzel to Bunker, 8/15/44, and other documents, Box 2356, file 964, and Whiteside to Bunker w/ enc., 1/13/44, Box 2356, file 963R, WPB; and CPA, *Industrial Mobilization for War*, pp. 817, 821–22.

81. Production Executive Committee Staff, Minutes, Meetings 1–75, 6/2/44–11/29/44, Boxes 266–67, file 041.45/041.45M, Grundstein to Central Records, 7/18/44, and other correspondence, Box 252, file 041.02, and Anderson to Bunker, 8/22/44, Box 252, file 041.04, WPB; Krug to Byrnes w/ enc., 2/19/45, Box 274, Production Executive Committee—Procedure On, OWMR; and CPA, *Industrial Mobilization for War*, pp. 746–47, 783–87, 887–90, 904–6.

82. Nelson quotation from Nelson, *Arsenal of Democracy*, p. 409; Marshall to Baruch, 7/7/44, Selected Correspondence, Baruch Papers; White House Memoranda, Smith to President w/ enc., 8/26/43, Smith Papers; and Peltason, *Reconversion*, pp. 83–94, 107 (Mead Committee quotation pp. 93–94).

83. Bunker to Hancock, 8/15/44, and other correspondence and documents, Box 2356, file 964, WPB; and Peltason, *Reconversion*, pp. 85–87.

84. WPB, Requirements Committee Minutes, vol. 4, 8/14/44, Policy Documentation File, WPB; Bernstein, "Debate on Industrial Reconversion," pp. 165, 169; Sitterson, *Reconversion*, pp. 122–24; and Peltason, *Reconversion*, pp. 94–95, 108–9.

85. Elliott to Krug, 8/30/44, and other documents, Box 2355, file 963, Gregg to Bunker, 8/23/44, and Strachan to Folger, 9/25/44, Box 2356, file 964, and Saposs to Keenan, 9/1/44, Box 2357, file 965, WPB; Bowles to Baruch, 9/12/44, Baruch to Bowles, 9/13/44, and Patterson to Baruch, w/ enc., 11/14/44, and other correspondence, Selected Correspondence, Baruch Papers; and Peltason, *Reconversion*, pp. 107–14.

86. *WPB Minutes*, pp. 363–69; and Peltason, *Reconversion*, pp. 114–17.

87. Patterson to Byrnes, 11/18/44, 11/26/44, Draft Memorandum of Krug, McNutt, Forrestal, and Patterson, 11/24/44, and Patterson to Baruch, 11/14/44, 11/18/44, 11/24/44, 11/26/44, and other documents, Selected Correspondence, Baruch Papers; *WPB Minutes*, pp. 363–69; and Peltason, *Reconversion*, pp. 117–125.

88. Patterson to Baruch w/ enc., 11/4/44, and Baruch to Marshall, 9/6/44, and other correspondence, Selected Correspondence, Baruch Papers; *WPB Minutes*, pp. 363–69; and Peltason, *Reconversion*, pp. 125–28.

89. Byrnes to President, 1/1/45, PSF: Executive Office of the President—James F. Byrnes, FDR Papers; Smith, *Lucius D. Clay*, pp. 188–200; Somers, *OWMR*, pp. 82–84, 104, 117n; and Peltason, *Reconversion*, pp. 128–35.

90. Peltason, *Reconversion*, pp. 136–39.

91. CPA, *Industrial Mobilization for War*, pp. 758–63, 901–3.

92. *WPB Minutes*, pp. 418–20; CPA, *Industrial Mobilization for War*, pp. 753, 857–58; and Bureau of the Budget, *United States at War*, pp. 490–91, 490 n. 41.

93. CPA, *Industrial Mobilization for War*, pp. 904–8, 956–59 (quotation p. 957); and Boulware to Bunker, 8/26/44, Box 2357, file 965, WPB.

94. Stimson Diary, 2/19/45.

95. PEC, Minutes, Meeting 78, 6/21/44, file 041.05, WPB.

96. PEC, Minutes, Meeting 56, 12/29/43, file 041.05, WPB.

97. PEC, Minutes, Meetings 96 and 104, 12/18/44 and 2/19/45, file 041.05, and deChazeau to Bunker, 9/7/44, Box 2356, file 964, WPB; and CPA, *Industrial Mobilization for War*, pp. 762–63.

98. Baruch to Batcheller w/ enc., 12/14/44, and Batcheller to Baruch w/ encs., 12/16/44, Selected Correspondence, Baruch Papers; "OCR Recommendations on Basic Policy Decisions on Reconversion," 7/25/44, and other documents, Box 2357, file 965, WPB; Lawrence to Hyde, 6/29/45, Box 272, Reconversion, OWMR; and CPA, *Industrial Mobilization for War,* pp. 896–900.

99. Peltason, *Reconversion,* p. 121; and CPA, *Industrial Mobilization for War,* pp. 813–14.

100. Krug to Byrnes, 3/10/45, and "Interim Proposal for War Production Action at V-E Day," 3/1/45, Box 2357, file 965, WPB; Peltason, *Reconversion,* p. 136; and CPA, *Industrial Mobilization for War,* pp. 908–13.

101. Regional Directors' Meeting, 9/20/44, and other documents, Box 2355, file 963, S. W. Anderson Address to New York Chamber of Commerce, 10/23/44, and Blaisdell to Krug, 12/1/44, and other documents, Box 2357, file 965, and Byrnes to Krug, 2/1/45, and Stevenson to Batcheller, 1/30/45, 2/2/45, 2/5/45, 2/12/45, 2/16/45, Box 2358, file 965R, WPB; and CPA, *Industrial Mobilization for War,* pp. 901–3, 908–13.

102. Belsley to Elliott w/ enc., 9/7/44, and other documents, Box 2355, file 963, and "Notes on Conversation with Mr. John B. McTigue, Deputy Director, Facilities Bureau," 5/18/44, and Skuce to Small w/ encs., 4/17/45, and other documents, Box 2356, file 964, WPB; and CPA, *Industrial Mobilization for War,* pp. 913–35.

103. Krug to Vinson, 7/4/45, Box 2357, file 965, WPB; and CPA, *Industrial Mobilization for War,* pp. 869–70, 935–59.

104. Small to Nathan, 6/26/45, and other documents, Box 2355, file 963, WPB; and Somers, *Presidential Agency,* pp. 84–90.

105. Wallace to Baruch w/ enc., 6/27/45, and other correspondence, Selected Correspondence, Baruch Papers; Maverick to Snyder, 8/17/45, and other correspondence, file VJ Day Plans—Smaller War Plants Corporation, Box 273, OWMR; Barton J. Bernstein, "The Removal of War Production Board Controls on Business, 1944–1946," *Business History Review* 39 (Summer 1965): 243–60; CPA, *Industrial Mobilization for War,* pp. 950–56; and Darrel R. Cady, "The Truman Administration's Reconversion Policies, 1945–1947" (Ph.D. diss., University of Kansas, 1974).

106. Byrnes to President, 8/17/44, OF: Demobilization, FDR Papers; and Bailey, *Congress Makes a Law,* pp. 30–36.

107. Bureau of the Budget, *United States at War,* p. 471; and Lois MacDonald, "Social Security, 1944 to 1947," in *Labor in Postwar America,* ed. Colston E. Warne et al. (Brooklyn, NY: Remsen, 1949), pp. 257–60.

108. White House Memoranda, Smith to President, 3/14/45 (w/ enc.), 10/16/45, Smith Papers; Bailey, *Congress Makes a Law;* and Frank C. Pierson, "The Employment Act of 1946," in *Labor in Postwar America,* ed. Warne et al., pp. 283–99.

109. David R. B. Ross, *Preparing for Ulysses: Politics and Veterans during World War II* (New York: Columbia University Press, 1969); and Jack S. Ballard, *The Shock of Peace: Military and Economic Demobilization after World War II* (Washington, DC: University Press of America, 1983).

110. John T. Dunlop, "The Decontrol of Wages and Prices," in *Labor in Postwar America,* ed. Warne et al., p. 24.

111. For the postwar breakdown of stabilization policies, see White House Memoranda, Smith to President w/ enc., 8/18/45, Smith Papers; Office of War Mobi-

lization and Reconversion, "Facts Relating to Wage-Price Policy," 10/45, Box 26, Research Department, Murray Papers; Murray to Green, 12/5/46, Green to Murray, 12/6/46, and related correspondence, 12/8/46–3/28/47, Series C—Convention File, 1944–48, Green Papers; AFL, *Annual Proceedings,* 1943–1945; American Federation of Labor, Executive Council Minutes of Meetings, 1943–1946, George Meany Memorial Archives, Silver Spring, MD (for specific entries on the *Proceedings* and Meetings, see Koistinen, *Hammer and Sword,* pp. 747–93); CIO, *Annual Proceedings,* 1943–1944. 1946; Congress of Industrial Organizations, Minutes of the Meetings of the International Executive Board, 1943–1946, Headquarters, International Union of Electrical, Radio and Machine Workers, Washington, DC (for specific entries on the *Proceedings* and Meetings, see Koistinen, *Hammer and Sword,* pp. 747–93); Executive Offices—Labor Office, Labor Policy Committee Records, Correspondence, Minutes of Meetings, 1943–1946, Records of the Office of Price Administration, RG 188, National Archives, College Park, MD; Minutes of the Advisory Board of the Office of War Mobilization and Reconversion, 1–6/45, OWMR; Bureau of the Budget, *United States at War,* pp. 492–97; various articles in *Labor in Postwar America,* ed. Warne et al., including Dunlop, "Decontrol of Wages and Prices," pp. 3–24, Clark Kerr, "Employer Policies in Industrial Relations, 1945 to 1947," pp. 43–76, and H. M. Douty, "Review of Basic American Labor Conditions," pp. 109–36; Melvyn Dubofsky and Warren Van Tine, *John L. Lewis: A Biography* (New York: Quadrangle/New York Times Book Co., 1977), pp. 445–68; Melvyn Dubofsky and Foster R. Dulles, *Labor in America: A History,* 6th ed. (Wheeling, IL: Harlan Davidson, 1999), pp. 326–34; and James T. Patterson, *Grand Expectations: The United States, 1945–1974* (New York: Oxford University Press, 1996), pp. 39–60.

CHAPTER EIGHTEEN.
MOBILIZING THE WORLD WAR II ECONOMY

1. Civilian Production Administration, *Industrial Mobilization for War: History of the War Production Board and Predecessor Agencies, 1940–1945* (Washington, DC: Civilian Production Administration, 1947), pp. 961–66; and Bureau of the Budget, *The United States at War: Development and Administration of the War Program by the Federal Government* (Washington, DC: Bureau of the Budget, 1946), p. 507.

2. Paul A. C. Koistinen, "Warfare and Power Relations in America: Mobilizing the World War II Economy," in *The Home Front and War in the Twentieth Century: The American Experience in Comparative Perspective,* ed. James Titus (Colorado Springs, CO: United States Air Force Academy, 1984), p. 236, n. 9.

3. Raymond W. Goldsmith, "The Power of Victory: Munitions Output in World War II," *Military Affairs* 10 (1946): 79.

4. Ibid., pp. 79–80 (quotation p. 79). I differ with Goldsmith on a labor draft and reducing further consumer expenditures.

A comparative analysis of economic mobilization is very valuable. Sources using that approach are cited in Koistinen, "Warfare and Power Relations in America," p. 236 n. 10. For a number of recent volumes, see Cristann L. Gibson, "Patterns of Demobilization: The US and USSR after World War Two" (Ph.D. diss., University of Denver, 1983); Arthur Marwick, ed., *Total War and Social Change* (New York: St.

Martin's, 1988); John R. Gillis, ed., *The Militarization of the Western World* (New Brunswick, NJ: Rutgers University Press, 1989); Patrick M. Regan, "Organizing Societies for War: Domestic Pressures for and Foreign Policy Consequences of Militarization in the United States and Britain" (Ph.D. diss., University of Michigan, 1992); Geofrey T. Mills and Hugh Rockoff, eds., *The Sinews of War: Essays on the Economic History of World War II* (Ames: Iowa State University Press, 1993); and Mark Harrison, ed., *The Economics of World War II: Six Great Powers in International Comparison* (Cambridge: Cambridge University Press, 1998).

5. G. William Domhoff, *Who Rules America?* (Englewood Cliffs, NJ: Prentice-Hall, 1967), chap. 5, argues along these lines. Barton J. Bernstein, "The Debate on Industrial Reconversion: The Protection of Oligopoly and Military Control of the Economy," *American Journal of Economics and Sociology* 26 (April 1967): 159–72, and Brian Waddell, *The War against the New Deal: World War II and American Democracy* (DeKalb: Northern Illinois University Press, 2001), view the military as more autonomous. Gregory Hooks, *Forging the Military-Industrial Complex: World War II's Battle of the Potomac* (Urbana: University of Illinois Press, 1991), sees the armed forces dominating the wartime economy.

BIBLIOGRAPHICAL ESSAY

Primary sources on mobilizing the World War II economy are nearly unequaled in terms of quantity, quality, and guides for usage. To an unusual degree, furthermore, most of the secondary literature on the subject draws on two seminal volumes: U.S. Bureau of the Budget, *The United States at War: Development and Administration of the War Program by the Federal Government* (Washington, DC: Bureau of the Budget, 1946); and U.S. Civilian Production Administration, *Industrial Mobilization for War: History of the War Production Board and Predecessor Agencies, 1940–1945* (Washington, DC: Civilian Production Administration, 1947). These publications resulted from developments within the Bureau of the Budget, which, in turn, were shaped by the New Deal.

Under the Reorganization Act of April 1939, the President's Committee on Administrative Management ensured that the Budget Bureau served as the president's general staff. In that capacity, the bureau was central to the Franklin D. Roosevelt administration's effort to mobilize the economy. When the National Defense Advisory Commission (NDAC) was set up in May 1940, the bureau selected Bernard L. Gladieux to act as liaison to the commission. Gladieux ultimately emerged as the mobilization specialist, acting through a Defense (later War) Organization Section. Seeking guidance from the past, Gladieux arranged a formal survey of World War I methods. Completed in September 1941, the study concluded that record keeping for and analysis of harnessing the World War I economy were all but useless.

Determined to avoid such an outcome in the current conflict, the Bureau of the Budget late in September 1941 recruited Professor Pendleton Herring, Graduate School of Public Administration, Harvard University, to assist it in records management. Herring was a prominent scholar, noted for publications on the political economy of warfare and civilian-military relations. He ultimately initiated a massive program for collecting, organizing, and supplementing with interviews the records of all economic mobilization offices. Once under way, records management would be followed by narrative accounts of agency operations. These projects, Herring argued, would allow wartime leaders from the president to the field officer better to grasp what had occurred and what needed to be done. Moreover, they would provide current and future individuals and groups complete records and preliminary written accounts of the noncombat aspects of war.

After Pearl Harbor, Herring led in the Budget Bureau arranging for the president's approval of his program. In March 1942, the bureau created a Committee on Records of War Administration (CRWA), with Herring serving as executive secretary. It had members from leading academic associations, the archivist of the United States, the librarian of Congress, and other public administration specialists and academics. CRWA was an advisory body to the War Records Section (WRS) of the bureau that Herring directed and included scholars such as V. O. Key, Jr., a Johns Hopkins University political scientist. With Roosevelt's endorsement, followed by that of Harry S. Truman, and the prominence of CRWA members, WRS had sufficient clout to carry out its charges.

WRS assigned staff members to specialize in mobilization areas such as production, procurement, finance, and manpower and cover all departments and agencies involved. Staff turbulence, however, limited what the section could do. Herring, who served part-time, resigned from WRS in September 1943, although he continued with CRWA. Thereafter, a number of acting, part-time, and full-time chiefs replaced him. WRS staff fluctuated along with its leadership, seldom exceeding ten, but rising as high as thirteen and dropping as low as five. The section was liquidated on June 30, 1946.

Despite problems, WRS accomplished a great deal. During 1942 and 1943, it collected and organized mobilization agency documents and conducted interviews with agency executives. WRS then began writing "first narratives" on the NDAC, the Office of Production Management (OPM), the Board of Economic Warfare, and numerous other administrations. Realizing that it could not handle records management for all, even most, offices, WRS by mid-1942 began encouraging agencies to set up their own programs and expand them to include written accounts. To the degree possible, the section assisted units in getting projects started. In 1945, WRS estimated a 50 percent success rate, with nearly forty agencies pursuing historical programs and others doing so after VJ Day. Beginning late in 1944, the WRS concentrated most of its attention on preparing and publishing *The United States at War.*

Although largely promotional, CRWA had some influence on the Bureau of the Budget's historical efforts. It met on an average of twice a year, reviewed WRS activities, advised it on policies, and read and criticized *United States at War* drafts. With WRS encouragement, CRWA attempted to go beyond an advisory role. Late in 1942, the committee considered a government-sponsored National War History Commission for encouraging and sponsoring historical projects among scholars unaffiliated with government. Something approximating that end took place in October 1943 when CRWA joined the Committee on War Studies (established in September 1943) of the Social Science Research Council (SSRC) to constitute the Advisory Council on War History. This vaguely defined combination of organizations outlined a host of historical studies for suggested authors to undertake, along with proposals for archival assistance and financing. Nothing ever came of these somewhat grandiose plans.

CRWA/WRS in a meaningful way stemmed from the New Deal. The hectic activity and proliferating agencies of the Roosevelt administration created numerous opportunities for administrative management specialists. Most in the field knew one another, worked together, and belonged to the same organizations. The President's Committee on Administrative Management illustrates well the point. Its three members were among the nation's leading figures in public administration: Louis Brownlow founded in Chicago and headed the Public Administration Clearing House; Charles E. Merriam specialized in political theory at the University of Chicago and organized the SSRC; and Luther Gulick, a Columbia University–trained political scientist, directed the Institute of Public Administration in New York. The committee and its twenty-seven-member research staff read like a who's who of the field, included six presidents of the American Political Science Association, and involved numerous individuals ultimately serving wartime government. Brownlow recommended Harold D. Smith to Roosevelt for the directorship of the reorganized Bureau of the Budget. Gulick and Brownlow were members of CRWA/WRS, and they continued to advise the president and his administration throughout the war years. Some of the techniques and aims that Pendleton Herring proposed for WRS in 1942 had been used earlier by the Committee on Public Administration of SSRC in analyzing New Deal agencies, such as the Works Progress Administration, the Tennessee Valley Authority, and the Social Security Board.

CRWA and WRS made themselves most visible with the publication of *The United States at War*. For over a year, both agonized over officially handling the volume. Should it be a report of the Budget Bureau director to the president, a report from the president to Congress, or a report without official sanction? Director Smith and Assistant Director for Administrative Management Donald C. Stone joined CRWA/WRS in finessing the sensitive issue. Truman wrote the foreword to the volume "sent" to him by Smith, who received it from Herring as CRWA chair. Both the president and the bureau director explained the volume's origins and importance without formally endorsing it.

After over a half century, the volume remains the best available introduction to and brief analysis of wartime economic mobilization. *The United States at War* went from preliminary outline late in November 1944 to final draft in July 1946. With V. O. Key acting as general editor and author, eight seasoned WRS members wrote the volume under intense pressure. In so doing, they depended principally on WRS's rich document collection and staff members' unpublished manuscripts. WRS, CRWA, Bureau of the Budget members, and other specialists constantly reviewed the manuscript's progress.

The speed of composition, the fact of multiple authors, and the decision to forgo documentation from WRS records bothered a number of those involved in the project, some of whom were recognized scholars. Key stood out in that regard. Only after extended negotiations and arm-twisting did he agree to be included as an author. To placate him, WRS inserted the next to the last paragraph of the preface (pp. xi–xii), which explains that the book constitutes "an experiment in a new type of public reporting."

Key and others had reasons for their doubts. The volume has serious limitations. Although WRS had access to excellent documentation, it did very little with NDAC and OPM, and it would not share information and unpublished studies with the historical office of the War Production Board (WPB). And the book's chronological-topical organization picks up and drops topics in an often confusing and incomplete way. Additionally, subjects like labor are neglected, while those involving public information and international economics receive full coverage. Intended for the general public, the volume is a far cry from popular history. Unwilling to sacrifice complexity for comprehension, and writing generally and briefly about challenging subjects, the authors ended up with a study largely graspable only by specialists.

All that said, the volume's positives far outweigh its negatives. Besides its enduring value, *The United States at War* is remarkable in another way. It was published under the federal government's auspices without the Bureau of the Budget director or the White House under two presidents ever asking or suggesting that an often hard-hitting, analytic study be modified. Indeed, calls for greater discretion came from CRWA. During its October 20, 1945, meeting, the committee noted: "There was general agreement that in the revision of the manuscript it would be necessary to tone down the references to particular groups and to eliminate "explosive" passages in the document. Members of the Committee pointed to the inadvisability of name calling in a document of this sort" (CRWA, Minutes of session, 10/25/45, p. 5, Unit 12, Box 2, RWA, BOB). Of particular concern was the volume's strident response to the military. Nonetheless, CRWA purposefully kept the writing of *The United States at War* as confidential as possible so as to preclude interference with WRS completing the volume as it saw fit. Perhaps a reason for excluding references to WRS-held documents was that they contain information exceptionally critical of mobilization officials, agencies, and groups.

A principal reason for CRWA/WRS's wide latitude was Director Harold D. Smith. Every inch the professional, Smith recruited a staff reflecting his views and insisted on serving the president in an unbiased way. Smith and Assistant Director Stone supported all reasonable requests of CRWA and WRS. Trusted without question by both Roosevelt and Truman, the Budget Bureau provided scholars and professionals a practically unique safe harbor in the treacherous political seas of the nation's wartime capital.

Outside the Bureau of the Budget, WRS realized its greatest success with WPB. Carryover in personnel from CRWA/WRS to WPB accounts in part for this outcome. WPB and its successor agency, the Civilian Production Administration (CPA), wrote *Industrial Mobilization for War* and authored, edited, or handled a host of other studies.

Donald M. Nelson's pluralism was important to the success of WPB's historical program. With the creation of the board in January 1942, Herbert Emmerich, a Louis Brownlow protégé and associate, continued to serve as secretary or executive secretary, as he had in predecessor agencies. He organized his office as a secretariat with staff members assigned to major policymaking subdivisions. In that way, the Office of the Executive Secretary, serving directly under the chair, emerged as WPB's center for recording, disseminating, and coordinating board policies. In doing so, the office established an effective records-management system. When Emmerich left WPB in March 1942, he was replaced by G. Lyle Belsley, who held a Brookings Institution Ph.D. and who had been a member of the research team for the President's Committee on Administrative Management.

WPB advanced from efficient records management to historical functions in July 1943. Speaking for CRWA, Luther Gulick, head of the Office of Organization Planning, advised Nelson in October 1942 that the Office of the Executive Secretary should adhere more closely to the standards and aims of WRS. On the basis of a Nelson directive and months of preparation, Belsley in July 1943 created within his office the Policy Analysis and Records Branch (PARB). James W. Fesler took over as chief. Fesler was a Harvard-trained political scientist who had been on the research staff of the President's Committee on Administrative Management and served in WPB and its predecessor. He headed PARB until August 1946, concurrently designated as the WPB historian during 1945–1946.

PARB wrote *Industrial Mobilization for War* and two other unpublished volumes, totaling around three thousand pages of typescript. In addition, Fesler's unit prepared and published minutes of major mobilization agencies, oversaw the writing of around seventy-five WPB subdivision histories, and authored, edited, or compiled a host of "Special," "Brief," "Miscellaneous," and other studies.

In carrying out its duties, PARB recruited a large number of professionally trained historians and social scientists. At the outset, the branch had a staff of around fifteen; by 1946, it had grown to ninety-five. An exceptionally conscientious, able administrator and scholar, Fesler carefully supervised all his branch's activities. He and Belsley worked well together. Fesler deserves high praise for the branch's sound and prolific scholarship.

PARB began preparing to write *Industrial Mobilization for War* practically with its origins. The branch's lesser studies helped train it for the larger task, as did organizing WPB's Policy Documentation File: records selected by operating divisions as essential for understanding the origins, evolution, and implementation of board policies.

In October 1945, Fesler and his staff agreed on an outline for *Industrial Mobilization for War,* with parts and chapters divided among eleven authors. Fesler rewrote chapter 12 and wrote the introduction and conclusion. Unlike the Bureau of the Budget volume, and contrary to initial intent, *Industrial Mobilization for War* is footnoted from unpublished primary sources. Before closing down the WPB and turning its responsibilities over to CPA, Julius A. Krug appointed a nearly fifty-person Advisory Council consisting of WPB officials and those from previous agencies. The council, according to Fesler, neither bothered nor assisted PARB. Nonetheless, authors had to be more cautious and circumspect than did their Bureau of the Budget counterparts since WPB was dominated by conservative forces. Fesler left CPA on August 20, 1946, returning to the Political Science Department, University of North Carolina. George W. Auxier, a staff member, took over as PARB chief and WPB historian. While Auxier took responsibility for the prospective volume 2 and other studies, Fesler continued to edit *Industrial Mobilization for War* from Chapel Hill until the manuscript went to the Government Printing Office in January 1947 and was published later in the year.

The major strength of *Industrial Mobilization for War* is in part 3 and portions of part 4, which deal with the critical period from January 1942 through mid-1943. Parts 1 and 2 on NDAC and OPM fail to analyze those agencies adequately. The latter portions of part 3 take on a workaday quality, and parts 4 and 5 are both diffuse and excessively detailed.

The volume is demanding. Over a thousand pages in length, *Industrial Mobilization for War* cannot serve as an introduction to mobilizing the economy. The most sophisticated reader is quickly overwhelmed by challenging concepts and numbing detail. The book is more an analytic encyclopedia than a graspable explication of harnessing the economy. Its density is compounded by a chronological-topical organization that interrupts continuous analysis and frequently duplicates material. All these weaknesses are made worse by an execrable index.

Limitations notwithstanding, *Industrial Mobilization for War,* more than fifty years later, still stands as the most complete and authoritative account of the principal mobilization agencies from NDAC through WPB. No significant scholarship on the subject can afford to overlook the volume and PARB's related work. The volume's breadth and detail have not been duplicated because of daunting prospects.

Together, then, *The United States at War* and *Industrial Mobilization for War* provide a remarkably sound and comprehensive account of World War II mobilization. Appreciating fully the value of the two volumes, ironically, requires a great deal of work in other secondary as well as primary sources. Readers can get from these books only what they bring to them.

Without the encouragement and assistance of CRWA and WRS, WPB and other agencies may not have undertaken historical programs. WRS also played a significant role in keeping World War II economic mobilization records intact and in the right hands. At the end of hostilities, the Army-Navy Munitions Board and the Army Industrial College appeared to be angling for possession of WPB records. War Industries Board documents ended up in the Office of the Assistant Secretary of War after World War I. Numerous permanent government departments were anxious to acquire portions of WPB and other emergency offices' collections. WRS and WPB insisted that all such records be kept together and deposited in the National Archives at the appropriate time. Only then would they be fully available to government agencies, scholars, and the public.

My analysis of CRWA and WRS is based almost entirely on primary sources: Units 1–55 and 232–72, Boxes 1–5 and 22–27, RWA, BOB; and Gladieux Reminiscences, pp. 155–59, 267.

The coverage of PARB also draws mainly from document collections: War History Program, Committee on Records of War Information, and Committee on Records of War Administration, Box 3, Reading File—June (George W. Auxier) and Instructions for Servicing the Policy Documentation File, Box 4, and Data on Special Study Drafts, Box 6, Historical Records Section—Administration, WPB; Units 130–32, Box 11, and frequent reports on the WPB historical program in the files on the CRWA/WRS cited above, RWA, BOB; files 10–12/1942, 1–12/1943, 1–12/1944, Box 1, files 1–12/1945, 1–12/1946, Box 2, files 1947, January 1–24, 1951, Box 3, War Production, Box 4, and Miscellaneous Reports, Box 5, Fesler Papers; and James W. Fesler, unpublished "Memoirs," in Fesler's possession. CPA, *Industrial Mobilization for War*, pp. iii–vi, briefly explains the origins of PARB and lists the authors of the CPA volume along with the Advisory Council. On pp. 987–92, PARB explains the nature of the Policy Documentation File and related holdings and lists all other branch publications and studies.

I have consulted numerous primary document collections. Among the richest is the generally unknown and little used RWA, BOB. The collection has an excellent "Series Inventory," accurately specifying the contents of 290 files in 30 boxes. The fully indexed 744-page Gladieux Interview is crucial.

The WPB's Policy Documentation File and other records (which include those of NDAC, OPM, the Supply Priorities and Allocations Board, and the various combined boards), along with PARB's studies, are indispensable. Nonetheless, WPB official files should be augmented by the invaluable Fesler Papers. At the Franklin D. Roosevelt Library, I have researched with great benefit the FDR, Smith, Rosenman, Henderson, Coy, and McReynolds Papers. The National Archives, College Park, MD, appropriately holds more official records than any other depository. In addition to the WPB and Bureau of the Budget collections, I have gone through the records of the War Manpower Commission, Office of Price Administration, Office of Economic Stabilization, Office of War Mobilization/Office of War Mobilization and Reconversion, Reconstruction Finance Corporation (and subsidiary units), and Munitions Assignment Board. The Baruch Papers are a gold mine, the Eberstadt Papers less so but still significant. Both collections are at Princeton University. The Nelson Papers, in the Huntington Library, include copies of critical documents either not found in other collections or difficult to locate. The Emmerich Papers, at the University of Virginia, are somewhat disappointing but nonetheless useful. The same is true of the Green Papers, Wisconsin State Historical Society, and the Murray Papers, Catholic University. Much more rewarding are the American Federation of Labor, Executive Council Minutes of Meetings, 1940–1945, George Meany Memorial Archives, Silver Spring, MD, and the Congress of Industrial Organizations, Minutes of the Meetings of the International Executive Board, 1940–1945, Headquarters, International Union of Electrical, Radio and Machine Workers, Washington, DC.

Congressional hearings and reports are additionally of great importance to World War II mobilization. I found particularly helpful the hearings and reports of the following committees: in the Senate, the Special Committee to Investigate the National Defense Program, the Special Committee to Study and Survey Problems of American Small Business Enterprises, and the Committee on Military Affairs; in the House of Representatives, the Select Committee Investigating National Defense Migration and the Committee on Military Affairs. I have cited specific hearings and reports in the notes relevant to the subject.

Secondary sources are critical. When I completed my Ph.D. dissertation (Paul A. C. Koistinen, "The Hammer and the Sword: Labor, the Military, and Industrial Mobilization, 1920–1945" [Ph.D. diss., University of California, Berkeley, 1965]) in 1963, scholarship on harnessing the World War II economy was sparse. Nonetheless, I cited in the bibliography all relevant work known to me. A flood of studies became available between 1963 and 1982. In a long essay prepared for a United States Air Force Academy symposium in 1982 (see "Warfare and Power Relations in America: Mobilizing the World War II Economy," in *The Home Front and War in the Twentieth Century: The American Experience in Comparative Perspective*, ed. James Titus [Colorado Springs, CO: United States Air Force Academy, 1984], pp. 91–110, 231–43), I updated my bibliography and evaluated the additions. Since then, a great many published and unpublished sources on the political economy of World War II have become available. In the notes to this volume, I include all previously uncited scholarship relevant to this volume. Readers can locate these citations by consulting the index and establishing where in the text I take up the subject of interest. The index is both thorough and properly cross-referenced. For a useful guide to primary and some secondary sources, see also General Services Administration, National Archives and Records Services, National Archives, *Federal Records of World War II*, vol. 1, *Civilian Agencies* (Washington, DC: National Archives, 1950).

I have done less research in military fields, partly because the armed services had some of the best wartime historical offices. In that regard, the War Department outshone the Navy Department. Several reasons explain the military's high level of performance. Both the army and the navy had existing history offices: the Navy Department's reached back to the late nineteenth century, that of the War Department to the early post–World War I years. Interwar war procurement and industrial mobilization planning, carried out principally by the army but also involving the navy, furthered the military's historical interest in noncombat areas. Probably most significant, World War II made the armed services among the largest, most powerful executive departments and mobilization agencies in the Roosevelt administration. To understand and learn from hostilities, answer to the president, Congress, and the public, highlight accomplishments, and protect their image, the armed services had every reason to ensure that wartime operations were properly recorded. On a lesser but still significant plane, recruits and draftees provided the army and navy with ample personnel for carrying out historical programs, and generous appropriations supplied the funds. Most other offices had difficulties acquiring and holding qualified people and acquiring adequate budgets. Furthermore, with hostilities ended, nearly all emergency agencies and some permanent ones faced the need to cut back or cut off uncompleted projects.

The army's program officially began on July 15, 1942, when the secretary of war directed the commanding generals of the Army Ground Forces, the Army Air Forces (AAF), and the Army Service Forces to set up what were in effect history offices. The Historical Section of the Army War College, dating back to around 1920, supervised all War Department and army history activity between 1939 and 1943. This responsibility was transferred, first, in August 1943 to a newly created Historical Branch in G-2 of the General Staff and, then, in November 1945 to a staff Historical Division. In 1946, the army authorized the massive *United States Army in World War II* series, ultimately carried out by a Special Staff agency, the Office of the Chief of Military History and its successor, the current U.S. Army Center of Military History, located in and about the nation's capital.

The AAF took a different route. At the end of hostilities, it elected to have the seven-volume *Army Air Forces in World War II* written under the direction and editorship of civilian historians who had served during the war in the AAF's historical offices: Wesley Frank Craven of New York University and James Lea Cate of the University of Chicago. By prearranged agreement, the University of Chicago Press published the series between 1948 and 1958.

For WRS reports on military documents and history programs, see Units 1, 6, 8, Box 1, Unit 13, Box 2, Unit 103, Box 8, and Units 124–26, Boxes 10–11, RWA, BOB. Much more thorough is General Services Administration, National Archives and Records Service, National Archives, *Federal Records of World War II,* vol. 2, *Military Agencies* (Washington, DC: National Archives, 1951), pp. 105–6, 150, 158–59, for the War Department and AAF. *United States Army in World War II: Reader's Guide,* ed. and comp. Richard D. Adamczyk and Morris J. MacGregor (Washington, DC: U.S. Army Center of Military History, 1992), provides a convenient and useful summary and other information about the seventy-eight volumes in the series, broken down by subseries. Regrettably, the pamphlet is silent on the project's origins and writing. Some insight along those lines is provided by the first general editor of the series, Kent Robert Greenfield, in *The Historian and the Army* (New Brunswick, NJ: Rutgers University Press, 1954). Much more information is available on the AAF series. In the foreword to vol. 1, *Plans and Early Operations,* of *The Army Air Forces in World War II* (Chicago: University of Chicago Press, 1948), Craven and Cate explain how the series was conceived and executed. In the foreword to a new imprint (Washington, DC: Office of Air Force History, 1983), Richard H. Kohn, chief, Office of Air Force History, provides even further data.

The Navy Department both accomplished a great deal in its historical program and encountered some serious difficulties. Through a curious set of circumstances, large parts of its wartime history ended up being written by civilians and published by commercial houses.

From 1939 into 1944, the small, inadequately staffed Office of Naval Records and Library, created in 1882, managed Navy Department records and performed some historical duties. Samuel Eliot Morison, professor of history, Harvard University, volunteered his services to President Roosevelt early in 1942 to write a combat history of the wartime navy. Whether Secretary of the Navy Frank Knox had any say in the matter is unclear, but he did accept Morison's offer. Morison began his study in June 1942 as a naval reserve officer. Between 1947 and 1962, Little, Brown published the rear admiral's fifteen-volume *History of United States Naval Operations in World War II*. Secretary of the Navy James V. Forrestal in his foreword to vol. 1 (*The Battle of the Atlantic, September 1939–May 1943* [reprint, 1961]) emphatically iterates that Morison's work is not an official history, and the author less forcefully confirms the assertion in his preface to vol. 14 (*Victory in the Pacific, 1945* [reprint, 1961]). Yet, at every step of the way during twenty years of research and writing, the navy assisted Morison with staff, space, and other services.

The outcome for noncombat history was even less happy. In February 1943, Assistant Secretary of the Navy Ralph A. Bard ordered into effect a program of administrative history under the supervision of Robert G. Albion, professor of history, Princeton University, later Harvard University. Albion was hired as a part-time civilian on per diem pay. From 1943 into 1950, he and a staff guided and oversaw the writing of hundreds of often lengthy monographs by various navy subdivisions. The final outcome of all this effort was to be a multivolume administrative history of the wartime navy written by Albion.

With its records and historical program expanding rapidly, the Navy Department in July 1944 organized an Office of Naval History. In 1949, the Office of Naval Records and Library and the Office of Naval History combined to form the Division of Naval History.

Shortly after the division's organization, a crisis developed in Albion's relationship with it. As a result, the navy ended Albion's services, and no administrative history per se was published under his name. In 1951, the Naval History Division secured the services of Rear Admiral Julius Augustus Furer, who had extensive experience in naval administration and historical activities, to complete the study that Albion had started. In 1959, the Naval History Division published under Furer's name *Administration of the Navy Department in World War II*. Nearly 1,050 pages in length, the volume basically summarizes, and in the chapter bibliographies cites, hundreds of administrative histories written during Albion's years of service. More an encyclopedia than a historical account, Furer's work is still a very valuable research source.

Other administrative or institutional history about the navy was published outside the Naval History Division. Of particular importance is Robert H. Connery, *The Navy and the Industrial Mobilization in World War II* (Princeton, NJ: Princeton University Press, 1951). Connery served under Albion during and after World War II. In the volume's foreword, the author explains that Forrestal suggested that he write the book and followed it through to completion. Another volume followed: Robert G. Albion and Robert H. Connery, *Forrestal and the Navy* (New York: Columbia University Press, 1962). And then a final one appeared: Robert G. Albion, *Makers of Naval Policy, 1798–1947*, ed. Rowena Reed (Annapolis, MD: Naval Institute Press, 1980). Reed claims that, at Forrestal's encouragement, Albion gave precedence to this study of larger and greater importance than the one dealing with administrative history. Except for obscure conflict over the *Makers of Naval Policy*, Albion and Connery appear to have had full access to Navy Department records and the cooperation of the department's staff.

Whatever the case, Navy Department history for World War II did get written, although not always in the straight line followed by the War Department or even the more circuitous one of the AAF. Most of the information related above is based on the front matter of the Albion and Connery volumes; the RWA, BOB files on military history; National Archives, *Federal Records of World War II,* vol. 2, *Military Agencies,* pp. 548–49, 578–79; William R. McClintock, "Clio Mobilizes: Naval Reserve Historians during the Second World War," *Public Historian* 13 (Winter 1991): 25–46; and William E. Heimdahl and Edward J. Marolda, comps., *Guide to United States Naval Administrative Histories of World War II* (Washington, DC: Naval History Division, 1976).

The armed services' series and studies are as important to military roles in economic mobilization as are *The United States at War* and *Industrial Mobilization for War* to civilization functions. Any serious study of war mobilization must include these massive scholarly endeavors. Nonetheless, primary documentation about the armed services is essential, particularly for the War Department. My research at the National Archives, College Park, MD, involves Records of the Secretary of War, Assistant Secretary of War, and Under Secretary of War. Included in the Secretary of War Records are collections for the civilian assistants to the secretary and assistant and under secretary: Julius H. Amberg; Goldthwaite H. Dorr; Edwin S. Greenbaum; John D. Hertz; Edward F. McGrady; Howard C. Petersen; and Harry K. Rutherford. Also at the National Archives, College Park, are Records of the Army Service Forces, the Joint Chiefs of Staff, the joint army and navy boards and committees, and the Department of the Navy. The Stimson Papers are at Yale University. At the Library of Congress, Washington, DC, are the Wadsworth Papers; and at the Harry S. Truman Library, Independence, MO, are the Ohly Papers (these papers were in Ohly's possession when I went through them; the library's cataloging may differ from my citations). The Clark Papers are at Dartmouth College. Finally, the Douglass V. Brown Papers were in the author's possession in Cambridge, MA, when I researched them.

Many of the numerous secondary sources on which I have relied, especially the vast number of unpublished studies, are cited in chapter notes. The reader can, as discussed above, rely on the index for locating secondary sources.

INDEX

635

285, 294, 302, 320, 321, 322, 323,
324–326, 330, 331, 345, 357, 505
Conversion. *See* Industrial conversion
Coordinating Area Production Urgency
Committee (WPB), 387
Coordinator of Inter-American Affairs,
186–187
Copper, 22, 63, 87, 90, 126, 129, 136,
144–148, 179, 322, 32, 345
for automobiles, 130
imports, 343
labor shortage, 146, 147
mining, 146, 147
oligopoly, 144
prices, 146
production, 144, 145, 158, 243
prohibited in consumer goods, 184
shortages, 146, 148
as strategic material, 144
use, 144
Corcoran, Thomas G., 108
Cordiner, Ralph J., 334, 335
Corporations, 3, 4, 8, 9, 10, 13, 493–494,
515
and DPC, 58
and military officer retirees, 456, 507
and New Deal, 495–496
and OPM, 75, 92
profits, 433, 434, 437, 508
reconversion, 464, 465, 467, 471, 480,
617(n51)
and strikes, 492
and taxes, 429–430, 433
and wartime economy, 16, 21, 30, 31, 52,
64, 66, 126, 192, 214, 217, 219, 279,
281, 282–283, 320, 336, 337, 353,
354, 355, 402, 415, 438, 502, 507,
508
See also Industrialists; *corporate names*
Corps of Engineers, 34, 36, 227, 231
Cost of living, 414, 432
Cost-plus-fixed-fee (CPFF), 428
Cotton, 249, 344, 345
Council of Economic Advisers, 491
Council of National Defense, 78(fig.). *See
also* National Defense Advisory
Commission, reestablished
Coy, Wayne, 95(fig.), 197(fig.), 312, 360
CPFF. *See* Cost-plus-fixed-fee
CPRB. *See* Combined Production and
Resources Board
Cranes, 179
CRMB. *See* Combined Raw Materials Board
Crowell, Benedict, 221
Crowley, Leo T., 268
CSAB. *See* Combined Shipping Adjustment
Board

CSP. *See* Components Scheduling Plan
Curfews, 485
Curtailment of civilian industries, 184
Curtiss-Wright Corporation, 52, 58, 296
CWS. *See* Chemical Warfare Service

Daily Operations Committee, 256
Dall, Charles Whitney, 392
Davies, Ralph K., 260, 262, 263
Davis, Chester C.
and NDAC, 18, 19(fig.), 21, 25, 31, 51,
52, 54, 64, 248
Davis, William H., 427
DCD. *See* Division of Contract Distribution
DCS. *See* Defense Contract Service
DeChazeau, Marvin G., 140
Defense Constract Service (DCS), 169–170,
173. *See also* Division of Contract
Distribution
Defense Department
secretary (*see* Forrestal, James V.)
Defense Housing Coordinator (OEM), 58
Defense Plant Corporation (DPC), 54, 55,
56–58, 59, 60, 118, 138, 145, 146,
158, 261, 289, 295, 296–297, 300,
503
loan average, 58
Defense plants, 34–35, 47, 171, 308
accelerated depreciation, 55, 300
construction or conversion, 55–56, 275,
308, 379
disposal, 354
efficiency, 297–298
expansion, 53–64, 87, 135, 167, 288–289,
292, 295, 301, 379
expansion costs, 53, 54–56, 60, 275,
288–289, 293, 295, 298
financing, 289, 295, 296
government-owned, privately-operated
(GOPO), 60–61, 298, 411–412, 428
housing, 167
and labor, 379, 482
locations, 25, 31, 51–53, 60, 61, 63
private financing, 57
projected costs, 308
surplus property disposal, 299–301
See also Amortization
Defense Supplies Corporation (RFC), 56,
262
Defense Supplies Rating Plan (OPM), 180
Demobilization, 445, 465, 467, 485, 486,
487, 488, 494, 506. *See also*
Reconversion; *under* Military services
Detmer, Charles F., Jr., 108–109, 112, 129
Dewey, Thomas E., 17
Dies, Martin, 442
Dingell, John D., 490

War Manpower Commission, *continued*
   and USES, 373, 382
   See also Management-Labor Policy
      Committee
War Mobilization and Reconversion Act
   (1944), 448, 490
War Munitions Program, 120, 235, 276,
   290, 305, 306, 307
War Plans Division (General Staff), 233
War Powers Act, Second (1942), 434
War Production Board (WPB), 7, 8, 9, 10,
   79, 93, 113, 114, 123, 148, 167, 174,
   190, 336–339, 425, 450–451, 494,
   496, 501, 503–504, 530–531(n13)
   and AAF, 230, 232
   allocations and priorities, 119, 123,
      206–207, 209, 215, 216, 302–303,
      314–326, 342, 346, 358, 505, 506
   and aluminum, 343
   and ANMB, 122
   Bureau of Field Operations, 355
   Bureau of Planning and Statistics, 335
   chairman (*see* Krug, Julius A.; Nelson,
      Donald M.; Wilson, Charles E.)
   Chemicals Branch, 155
   and civilian needs, 280, 285, 286, 302,
      314, 316, 340, 347–350, 368,
      452–453, 455, 457, 460–461, 479
   Committee on Concentration, 282 (*see
      also* Concentration program)
   as conservative, 359
   and construction, 289–298
   and conversion, 201, 275–284
   and copper, 146–147, 318, 322
   and CRMB, 271
   depreciation rates, 300
   divisions and bureaus, 196, 197(fig.), 198,
      205, 208–209, 210, 211, 212(fig.),
      214, 276–279, 282, 289–290, 304,
      307, 338, 350, 368, 372, 452–453,
      468
   divisions as industry operating units,
      332–333, 337, 347
   executives and BAC, 359
   feasibility issue, 303–314, 319, 342, 358,
      370, 375
   field offices, 355–356
   industry branches, 276–277, 278, 284,
      290
   and inventories, 302
   and JCS, 310, 312, 313, 314–315,
      323–324
   and labor, 142, 163, 164, 370, 372, 380,
      387, 401, 416, 417
   and mobilization agencies, 247
   and OCR, 286, 340, 347–350
   and OCS, 279, 284

   and ODT, 251
   and OPA, 346
   and OP&M, 242
   and OPC, 260
   and OPM and SPAB, 96, 189–190
   organization, 197(fig.), 198–199
   and OWM/OWMR, 363, 368–369
   and PAW, 262
   and peace, 415
   Planning Committee, 191, 192, 210, 211,
      215, 216, 294, 297, 303–305, 306,
      308–309, 310, 311, 313, 316, 321,
      326, 329, 334–335, 338, 346, 347,
      374, 500
   procurement, 166, 283, 295
   Production Executive Committee (PEC),
      192, 206, 208, 209, 210, 307, 328,
      329, 330, 331, 341, 346, 349, 356,
      361, 385, 386, 576–577(n37)
   Production Executive Committee Staff
      (PECS), 455–456
   production scheduling, 326–335, 337, 342,
      358, 458, 359, 361, 369, 378
   PRP, 181
   and rationing, 421
   reconversion, 446, 453–457, 461,
      453–460, 474, 480–481 (*see also under*
      Krug, Julius A.; Nelson, Donald M.)
   and regulation suspension, 446
   reorganization, 204–213, 323–324, 334,
      359
   and rubber, 149, 154, 156, 345
   and SFAW, 265
   and small businesses, 340–341, 350–355
   Smaller War Plants Division (SWPD),
      351–352
   Special Rating Commission, 346
   staff, 195, 196(fig.), 204
   and steel, 143, 318, 322
   and supply and demand, 302, 345, 346,
      370, 372, 380–381, 384
   terminated operations (1945), 446
   and WFA, 248
   and WLB, 344, 346
   and WSA, 256
   See also Civilian Production
      Administration; *under* Industrialists;
      Joint Chiefs of Staff; Military services;
      Priorities
War production council, 504–505
War Production Drive program (1942), 417
War production goal (1943), 188–189
War profits, 433–437
Warrant plan, 321
War Resources Board (WRB), 16, 17, 62, 84,
   100. *See also* Production Planning
   Board